LAW AND CONTROL
IN
SOCIETY

LAW AND CONTROL
IN
SOCIETY

Edited by

RONALD L. AKERS
The University of Iowa

RICHARD HAWKINS
Southern Methodist University

PRENTICE-HALL, INC., ENGLEWOOD CLIFFS, NEW JERSEY

Library of Congress Cataloging in Publication Data

AKERS, RONALD L. COMP.
  Law and control in society.

  (Prentice-Hall sociology series)
  Includes bibliographical references.
  1. Sociological jurisprudence—Addresses, essays,
lectures. I. Hawkins, Richard, joint comp.
II. Title.
Law   340.1'15   74-22213
ISBN 0-13-526095-7

© 1975 by Prentice-Hall, Inc., Englewood Cliffs, New Jersey.

Prentice-Hall Sociology Series
NEIL J. SMELSER, *Editor*

PRINTED IN THE UNITED STATES OF AMERICA

10 9 8 7 6 5 4 3 2 1

Prentice-Hall International, Inc., *London*
Prentice-Hall of Australia, Pty., Ltd., *Sydney*
Prentice-Hall of Canada, Ltd., *Toronto*
Prentice-Hall of India Private Limited, *New Delhi*
Prentice-Hall of Japan, Inc., *Tokyo*

To my wife, Caroline

R. L. A.

To my parents

R. H.

CONTENTS

part three   **ORGANIZATION AND PROCESS IN THE
ADMINISTRATION OF LAW AND CONTROL OF
DEVIANCE**

PREFACE

This book is intended primarily for use in graduate and advanced undergraduate courses in the sociology of law and related courses such as those on the criminal justice system. The assumption is that readers will have some familiarity with basic sociological concepts and methods, recognize leading names in sociology, and be able to read and understand journal articles that are not highly technical, but will not be familiar with the issues and content of the sociology of law or how particular articles fit into the context of the field. Therefore, in addition to including materials of high quality which are directly relevant to the main problems and concerns in the study of law and society, we have tried to select previously published materials and to write materials expressly for this volume with this audience in mind.

The overall conceptualization and plan of the book are indicated in the Introduction. Suffice it here to say that there are four main parts, each of which presents theoretical and empirical discussions of a key issue in the sociology of law: the concept of law, the impact of social variables on the formation and implementation of law, the administration of law, and the impact of law in society. As the title suggests, we emphasize law as a form of control and, particularly in Part Three, tend to focus on the control of deviance through the criminal law and criminal justice system in the United

States. This is not an exclusive concern, however, and we have covered other types of law and issues of interest to sociologists of law. We feel the result is a reasonably balanced coverage, although there is no pretense that we have attended to every part of the field.

At the beginning of each section of readings we have contributed an original substantive essay which attempts to do more than introduce the reprinted readings in the section. Rather, the essays are meant to provide coherence and continuity to the readings by defining the issues in the study of law relative to the topic of the particular section and placing the readings in proper perspective and in the context of the other relevant literature. It is our hope that the organization of the volume and the discussions in the essays complementing and integrating the reading selections make this more valuable for class use than simply a collection of readings.

RONALD L. AKERS
Iowa City, Iowa

RICHARD HAWKINS
Dallas, Texas

LAW AND CONTROL
IN
SOCIETY

INTRODUCTION

This volume is a collection of reprinted and original writings in the sociology of law, which may be defined generally as the study of social variables in the law and of law in society. The sociology of law, as Schur (1968:4) notes, goes beyond simply a concern with the "legal aspects in selected areas of social life" to the "analysis and understanding of this legal system *as such*." The areas of theory and research which revolve around this central concern have been characterized in a number of ways (see Angel, 1968; Schur, 1968:10–14; Timasheff, 1968; Quinney, 1969:5–20; and Mayhew, 1968), but the listing of research areas by Rose (1962) serves as a concise portrayal of the issues in the sociology of law: the formation of law (legislation, lobbying, activities of interest groups, etc.); the implementation of law (courts, police, regulatory agencies, correctional agencies); the impact of law in society; law and the social structure (law as an independent, dependent, and intervening variable vis-à-vis society); and the legal profession. Except for the last, all of these issues are dealt with explicitly here.

While fully aware of the fact that law relates to other institutions in an interdependent way, we make a conceptual distinction between law as a *dependent variable* and law as an *independent variable* in society. What are the social forces which shape or are reflected in the formation and operation of the law (law as *dependent*)? What impact does the existence and operation of law have on society and individuals and groups in society (law as *indepen-*

dent)? The organization of the book reflects the distinction between and concern with these two fundamental questions about the role of law in society.

In order to address these questions adequately, of course, the question of "What is law?" must be answered. Therefore, the materials in Part One are focused on the concept of law. Law is a system of social control—it is a set of substantive and procedural norms and organized roles for the application of sanctions directed toward insuring compliance with the norms. But it is not coterminous with all social control in society, and the purpose of the first part is to indicate the major dimensions which distinguish law from other forms of social norms and control. Then the second part is addressed to the consideration of law as a dependent variable in society. The aim is to show how law is shaped by both broad historical changes in the social structure and the activities of particular groups and collectivities in society.

In Part Three the readings are aimed at the description and analysis of organization and process in the administration of law. The effects of social change and the influence of social variables are felt not only in the making of law but also in its implementation; and in turn it is through the actual administration of law that it has an impact on society. While the general issues of control, dispute settlement, and conflict resolution in the legal system are presented, the emphasis is on the delineation of the variables involved in the control and processing of deviants by agencies of the law.

Law as an independent variable is considered in Part Four. Here the intent is to show the kind and degree of effects the existence and administration of the law has on attitudes, norms, and values as well as groups, organizations, and individuals in society. The focus is on the law as an instrument of social change and the extent to which compliance with legal norms is obtained by the threat of legal sanctions and the socializing influence of law.

We conceive of social control as the central function of law; hence the title, *Law and Control in Society.* This control is not limited to the criminal law. It is also exercised by legislation, administrative policy, and court rulings in race relations, family life, education, the economy, the ecology, and other institutional sectors of society. Delinquency, mental illness, alcoholism, addiction, and other forms of deviance are often controlled by "civil" proceedings and administrative regulation outside of the usual criminal law enforcement and court structure. Violations of antitrust and other legislation regulating professional and business practices are most often dealt with through regulatory boards issuing "cease and desist" orders or taking civil action to collect damage payments. All of these are part of the control structure for dealing with "public" wrongs in which the political state takes the initiative and pursues litigation against offenders. But the orderly settlement of "private" disputes through civil law litigation, in which the primary impetus for pursuing the case lies with the aggrieved private party, is also a mechanism of social control.

In modern society the criminal law, including the substantive law and the enforcement process, is the primary locus of formal societal control, and is, therefore, a prime object of the sociological analysis of law. Thus, the issues of the administration of law and law as independent and dependent variables in society are presented here most often within the context of the criminal law and the legal control of deviance. The political process is the same, and the importance of social and organizational variables remains in the formulation and implementation of all law. But the study of the criminal justice system is just one part of the sociology of law. Therefore, we have attempted to balance the main focus by including readings and discussing literature in the essays which deal with a range of sociology of laws topics other than specifically criminal law.

REFERENCES

ANGELL, ROBERT C., 1968. "The Value of Sociology to Law," pp. 65–78, in Rita James Simon, ed., *The Sociology of Law*. San Francisco: Chandler Publishing Company (originally published, 1933).

MAYHEW, LEON, 1968. "The Sociology of Law," pp. 171–83, in Talcott Parsons, ed., *American Sociology: Perspectives, Problems, and Methods*. New York: Basic Books.

QUINNEY, RICHARD (ED.), 1969. *Crime and Justice in Society*. Boston: Little, Brown.

ROSE, ARNOLD, 1962. "Some Suggestions for Research in the Sociology of Law," *Social Problems*, **9** (Winter): 281–83.

SCHUR, EDWIN M., 1968. *Law and Society*. New York: Random House.

TIMASHEFF, NICHOLAS, 1968. "What is 'Sociology of Law'," pp. 56–64, in Rita James Simon, ed., *The Sociology of Law*. San Francisco: Chandler Publishing Company (originally published 1937).

part one

THE CONCEPT
OF LAW

So unresolved has the meaning of law appeared at times that it is common for one who offers a definition of law to begin with a statement similar to these:

> . . . what is law? This is a question upon which whole libraries have been written, and written, as their very existence shows without definite results being attained [Kantorowicz, 1958:1].

> "Law" and "the legal system" float in a conceptual limbo. Much ink has been spilled seeking answers but the question has frequently been an unanswerable question of essence: "What is law?" [Barkun, 1968:2].

Certainly, defining law has occupied the attention of social, legal, and political scholars for a long time apparently without a resolution on which there is complete consensus. But the enterprise has not been such a conceptual morass as the above statements would lead one to believe. Actually, there is considerable agreement at various points on what constitutes law; these points of agreement should become apparent (and we shall return to them) after reviewing some of the major conceptions of law found in the literature.

Definitions of and theorizing about law can be found at least as early as in the thoughts of Aristotle and were part of the discourse of the great social and political philosophers of the Western world: Hobbes, Locke, Bentham, and others. The pioneering sociologists also, Comte and Spencer and later

Durkheim, Weber, Ward, Sumner, Ross, and others, paid considerable attention to law in society. In the first part of this century there emerged among American legal scholars a concern with what they labeled "sociological jurisprudence"—the study of the interplay between law and society and the application of sociological knowledge and methods to law problems and decisions. The major figures in sociological jurisprudence, such as Holmes, Brandeis, and Cardozo, likewise pondered the meaning of law, as both a specifically juristic and a social phenomenon. The purpose here, however, is not to present a comprehensive review of the place definitions and theories of law have occupied in the history of jurisprudence and sociology of law.[1] Rather, the purpose of this essay is to introduce some of the classic and recent formulations of law as a way of getting a perspective on and presenting important issues in the concept of law.

THE DOMINANT CONCEPT: LAW AS SOCIAL CONTROL THROUGH LEGITIMIZED COERCION

In her orienting essay to a collection of anthropological studies of law, Nader (1965) objects to the nearly universal assumption in anthropology that law has but two functions—social control and settlement of conflict. She argues that there are also latent "extra-legal" functions, e.g., status gaining, therapy, and continuation of conflict. Her critique is a bit misplaced since using social control as a defining characteristic (dispute settlement can be subsumed under social control) does not necessitate neglect of other functions of legal institutions, but she is right in asserting that there is widespread agreement that law is part of society's control system. Anthropologists, sociologists, political scientists, legal scholars and

> . . . almost all authors of treatises dealing with law agree upon one basic characteristic of the phenomena that should belong to this conceptual category [of law], namely, that they should be a form of institutionalized social control [Pospisil, 1968:211].

There is also consensus that the legal system is not coterminous with the whole system of social control, although there are some who tend to conceive of law in such a way that it is equated with the entire normative system of usage, custom, and convention.[2] Most would agree with Davis in the first selection reprinted here that law is just one *type* of social control. The law is a normative system, a system of rules about the way people should behave and the attendant sanctions. There is less agreement on just how to differentiate the law type from other forms

---

[1] There are a number of places where this is done. See, for instance, Davis *et al.* (1962:3–37); Schafer (1969:19–55); Pound (1945); Gurvich (1945).

[2] See the conceptions of law held by Malinowski and Driberry cited in the second selection reprinted here and Meggitt's (1962) conception of law as the totality of "explicit social rules."

of norms and sanctions. However, the dominant theme running through attempts to do this is that legal norms are backed by some form of legitimized or authoritative coercion or force.

LAW AS A SYSTEM OF RULES MADE AND ENFORCED BY THE SOVEREIGN POLITICAL COMMUNITY

The form which this legitimized force takes in definitions of law is most commonly that of the political community in the sense of a governmental unit exercising control over a territory and recognizing no higher secular sovereignty. Such conceptions contain elements which go back to ideas in Roman laws and certainly were adumbrated in European and English political philosophies up through the eighteenth century. But they can most directly be traced to the nineteenth century philosophy of jurisprudence of John Austin (1873). Austinian "philosophy of positive law" views law as the authoritative "command of the sovereign." The "sovereign" obviously can include the sovereign state and its organs, democratic or dictatorial, as well as the "sovereign" in the older sense of a monarch; and it is this broader conception of sovereign which is utilized in neo-Austinian formulation.

E. A. Ross (1901), the first to offer a systematic sociological analysis of social control and law, held an essentially Austinian conception of law: norms of the state backed by coercive force. To Ross, a "natural order" might come about in the absence of social control, but it would be "crude and imperfect" compared to the "artificial order" erected through law and the other "means" of social control (public opinion, belief, social suggestion, social religion, and others). Of these, law is the "most highly specialized and highly finished engine of control employed by society," "the most progressive department of control," and "the cornerstone of the edifice of order." Ross shared with his contemporary William G. Sumner (1906) the belief that law grows out of the "folkways and mores," to use Sumner's phrase or the "immemorial notions and customs of the folk," to use Ross's phrase. But he saw the rules of morality as the expressions of the "will of the public," as distinct from the rules of law which are the "will of the state" (Ross, 1901:56–75, 106–25).

> The characteristic which marks off legal sanctions from all others employed by society, is that they are positive, violent, and to a large extent corporal . . . [Ross, 1901:106].

Roscoe Pound acknowledges Ross's influence in moving from Austinian "analytic jurisprudence" to "sociological jurisprudence." The influence of both can be seen in Pound's (1945:300) definition of law as "social control through the systematic application of the force of politically organized society." Pound notes that to one who enacts the law it is a command; to the individual the law may be seen as a threat or rule of conduct; to the judge the law furnishes rules for decision; to the lawyer law serves as the basis for advising his client on what the courts' or officials' decisions are likely to be. These represent the three parts of the control system which is called *law:* (a) the "legal order," (b) the "authoritative grounds" or guides for determinations and decisions, and (c) the judicial and administrative process (Pound, 1945:300, 312).

The definition of law offered by Davis (1962) in the first selection reprinted here is a latter day representative of the concept of law as the norms made and enforced by the political state and is explicitly based on Pound. For Davis,

> . . . law is defined as the formal means of social control that involves the use of rules that are interpreted, and are enforceable by the courts of a political community" [Davis, 1962:41].

Davis claims that this would include not just the rules themselves but also the agencies (in addition to courts as such) and procedures by which they are enacted, applied, and enforced.

Harvey (1966) also uses this type of definition in examining social changes involving legal functions and roles in tribal, colonial, and independent Ghana. The sanctioning force of the government which is central to both criminal and civil law may not always be used and does not necessarily account for obedience, but it is the defining characteristic of law.

> For the purpose of this study, law has been taken to mean a technique of social ordering deriving its essential characteristic from its ultimate reliance on the reserved monopoly of systematically threatened or applied force in politically organized society [Harvey, 1966:343].

Chambliss and Seidman (1971) offer a recent statement which includes this same sort of definition. Although, they claim that it is not possible to locate the "essence" of law, that the law has many functions, and that no state can rule entirely on the basis of coercion, their idea of law is precisely that of a normative system backed by the power of a political state.

> The touchstone by which we . . . distinguish the normative system in a centralized State and its associated processes, which we comprehend under the term "law," from other norms and processes is that what we call "laws" are those in which the State has a finger, whether as creator of the norms, adjudicator of conflict, or sanctioning agent. . . .
>
> Every normative system induces or coerces activity. The normative system we have defined as "law" uses State power to this end [Chambliss and Seidman, 1971:8–10].

LAW AS THE ASSUMED BASIS FOR, OR PREDICTIONS OF, AUTHORITATIVE DECISIONS

The emphasis in "legal realism" or "sociological jurisprudence" is on the law in action; the law as it is actually carried out and enforced rather than law as a series of rules contained in statutes. We have already seen Pound's version of this emphasis in his notion of the application of force in political society. But his inclusion in legal phenomena of the grounds for decisions and the judicial process come from the acknowledged founder of this school of jurisprudential thought, Oliver Wendell Holmes, as well as from another leading figure in this area, Benjamin Cardozo.

Holmes (1897:461) declared that "the prophecies of what the courts will do in fact, and nothing more pretentious, are what I mean by the law." He was reacting to the concept that decisions of law are arrived at by rigorous deductions from statutory and legal premises.

> The life of the law has not been logic; it has been experience. The felt necessities of the time, the prevalent moral and political theories, intuitions of public policy, avowed or unconscious, even the prejudices which judges share with their fellow-men, have had a good deal more to do than the syllogism in determining the rules by which men should be governed [Holmes, 1881:5].

Cardozo likewise emphasized the law as the prediction of rules which courts will with reasonable certainty act on, but he saw the basis for that prediction coming not only from the intuitions and prejudices of judges but from a known body of principles; this is the law.

> We shall unite in viewing as law that body of principle and dogma which with a reasonable measure of probability may be predicted as the basis for judgement in pending or in future controversies.

> A principle or rule of conduct so established as to justify a prediction with reasonable certainty that it will be enforced by the courts if its authority is challenged, is, then for the purposes of our study, a principle or rule of law [Cardozo, 1924:43–44, 52].

Neither Holmes nor Cardozo was particularly interested in a concept of law which clearly distinguished it from custom or other nonlegal control, as indicated by their pragmatic approach to law as simply that revealed by court-rendered decisions. Not "What is law?" but "What is the law at this time?" was what interested them. However, the focus on the established courts shows that both recognized law to be that which is backed by authoritative force of the political state since the courts are organs of the state.

This same principle of looking to the bases for, or predictions of, authoritative decisions as the law has more recently been used by some anthropologists. For instance, Schapera regards law, as distinct from custom, among the Tswana as "any rule of conduct likely to be enforced by the [native] courts. . . ." (Schapera, 1955:38)

Pospisil broadens the concepts to include decisions by any authority.

> . . . law (ius) manifests itself in the form of a decision passed by a legal authority (council, chief, headman, judge, and the like), by which a dispute is solved, or a party is advised before any legally relevant behavior takes place, or by which approval is given to a previous solution of a dispute made by the participants before it was brought to the attention of authority.

Thus, the field of law consists of principles abstracted from the decisions of authorities [Pospisil, 1968:221–22].

COERCIVE DEFINITIONS AND THE PROBLEM
OF STATELESS SOCIETIES AND INTERNATIONAL RELATIONS

Barkun (1968:60) takes exception to any definition which "distinguishes law from other modes of social control by its ability to use or threaten to use centralized and legitimate physical coercion to secure obedience" (Barkun, 1968:60). Such a conception may apply to the "vertical" structure of centralized political societies but does not apply to the multicentric, "horizontal" structure of segmentary societies (which are most likely to be stateless societies) and the international community (Barkun, 1958:14–35). Barkun believes that primitive societies and the world community represent cases of legal order "without sanctions," but he does not offer a conception of order through law (beyond calling law a "system of manipulable symbols") which would allow distinguishing it from any other order.

However, Barkun does remind us that the conceptions of law just reviewed which place emphasis on social order backed ultimately by the coercive force of the politically organized society (such as Pound's or Davis's) or the behavior of courts and other agencies in the political state (such as Holmes and Cardozo) exclude as law both social control in societies which are not specifically organized as political states and international relations in the absence of a worldwide sovereign state. Barkun interprets the exclusion of these as residing in the definition's element of coercive sanction. However, it should be clear that primitive societies and the international community do not lack the means of coercion; rather they lack the ultimate monopolization of authorized force by a political entity. If the conceptual requirement be dropped that the use of legitimized force in support of norms be in the hands of a political state, then a definition of law can be devised which does in fact include many stateless societies and perhaps the norms of international relationships. Such definitions have been devised.

The best known of these is that of E. Adamson Hoebel. Hoebel was much influenced by Karl Llewellyn, another notable figure in sociological jurisprudence, with whom he collaborated on an analysis of the "law-ways" in traditional Cheyenne society (Llewellyn and Hoebel, 1941). To Llewellyn, the defining characteristic of law is not just force, but force applied in a regular way and authorized within social order, political state, or otherwise. Hoebel (1954) built upon this collaboration by extending his analysis to other stateless societies (such as the Eskimo) and presented this definition:

> A social norm is legal if its neglect or infraction is regularly met, in threat or in fact, by the application of physical force by an individual or group possessing the socially recognized privilege of so acting [Hoebel, 1954:28].

Hoebel intended his conception to apply as well to norms governing the relationships among nations and indeed saw international law as quite analogous to law in primitive societies.

Hoebel's conception is certainly global enough (as is Diamond's, 1971:195) to encompass as legal the social control mechanisms in many societies with no centralized state or formalized political officials, without making the mistake, for which Pospisil (1968:202) takes other anthropologists to task, of "dissolving law into the mass of omnipotent custom." But in so doing Hoebel ignores the feature which epitomizes the "socially authorized agent" who uses the force in reaction to breach of the norms, namely that the authorized individual or group is neither the offended party nor either party to a dispute. This is the major point which is made by Akers (1965) in the second selection reprinted here. Social authorization to punish the offender was clearly given within the social order of the society examined (Kalinga) only in cases where the punishment was meted out by someone other than the offended or his kin. Akers argues that not only was the chance of approved retaliation very low in instances where a neutral party made the punishing decision, but that a defining characteristic of law is that it is not a self-help enterprise in retaliation, vengeance, or retribution; rather law involves a decision by an agent apart from (though not necessarily above) the disputants. For this reason, he proposes modifying Hoebel's conception by the addition of a "socially authorized third person."

In modifying Hoebel's definition in this way Akers has moved the conception back toward that utilized by Max Weber (1954) in his classic sociological analysis of law in economy and society. It is not as restrictive as Weber's, however, for his requires a special "coercive apparatus" for law to exist (Weber, 1954:13). Although he recognized that the political state in the modern world monopolizes the ultimate right to apply violence to secure conformity, he was adamant in insisting that there is "extra-state" law, for ". . . we categorically deny that 'law' exists only where legal coercion is guaranteed by the political authority" (Weber, 1954:17). Thus, Weber's definition also does not rely upon the existence of a political state, retains coercion as an essential ingredient, and allows for a distinction between convention and law. While convention is a form of custom which is externally validated by others responding to deviation from it by disapproval,

> An order will be called *law* if it is externally guaranteed by the probability that coercion (physical or psychological), to bring about conformity or avenge violation, will be applied by a *staff* of people holding themselves specially ready for that purpose [Weber, 1954:5, italics in original].

Gibbs (1966a) conceives of law in terms which are very similar to Weber's, for he distinguishes law from other normative phenomena by saying that ". . . whereas there is a high probability that someone in a special status will attempt to avenge violation of or secure conformity to a law by means including the use of force with a low probability of retaliation, by definition there is no corresponding reaction to violations of extralegal norms" (Gibbs, 1966a:322).

NONCOERCION DEFINITIONS:
LAW AS AUTHORITATIVE DECISION AND PROCEDURE

While law as the authorized use or threat of force is the dominant concept, some writers reject legitimized coercion, whether or not backed by the political state, as a defining characteristic of law. But as Gibbs (1966b) shows, some of the objections (mainly those raised by Hart and Fuller) are based on the confusion of definitions with empirically testable propositions. Coercive definitions ordinarily restrict law to only that legitimized coercion which is applied in a regular and systematic way. But some alternative definitions which reject the criterion of ultimate reliance on force retain and elaborate on the criterion of authorization and proper procedure. Thus they tend to stress not the *content* of the sanctions enforcing conformity or settlement of disputes but rather the *way* in which rules are made and applied.

Kantorowicz (1958) drops the idea that laws involve "state origin" or "state compulsion" and maintains that law cannot be differentiated from social custom either by content or enforceability. Rather law is "A body of rules prescribing external conduct and considered justiciable." (Kantorowicz, 1958:21) To be considered "justiciable" the rules (primary) which prescribe the conduct must be accompanied by rules (secondary) which entitle certain "judicial organs" (not necessarily courts of law as such) to inflict sanctions according to a definite procedure. Apparently it is the procedure which is the crucial defining characteristic, for:

> Wherever we find rules of external conduct applied by judicial organs we find them applied with some more or less "definite" procedure, or without such procedure. In the first case we are faced with what we propose to call law, in the second case, social custom [Kantorowicz, 1958:73–74].

Hart (1961) further elaborates upon the distinction between primary and secondary norms and makes this the centerpiece of his concept of law.

> Under rules of the one type, which may well be considered the basic or primary type, human beings are required to do or abstain from certain actions, whether they wish to or not. [Secondary rules] provide that human beings may by doing or saying certain things introduce new rules of the primary type, extinguish or modify old ones, or in various ways determine their incidence or control their operation [Hart, 1961:78–79].

Law is the "union of primary and secondary rules" and an especially important type of secondary rule is the "rule of recognition." Rules of recognition seem to be crucial, for they acknowledge what is the authoritative source and proper way of determining what the primary rules of law are. They may be as simple as public announcement and recognition or inscription on a monument or as complicated as modern legal systems (Hart, 1961:77–96).

Although he does not recognize the use of force as a "distinguishing mark" of law, Fuller does not present a concise alternative criterion beyond stating that "law is the enterprise of subjecting human conduct to the governance of rules" (Fuller, 1964:106). Rather, Fuller's concern is with the "internal morality" of law, the internal principles (not the content) of a system of rules which constitute the basic requirements for law. Actually Fuller relates the "morality that makes law possible" in a negative way by spelling out eight ways in which it is possible to fail in the creation and maintenance of law. These are: (1) having no rules at all so that only ad hoc decisions reign; (2) making rules unknown or unavailable to those who are expected to obey them; (3) creating retroactive rules; (4) failing to have rules which can be understood; (5) having contradictory rules; (6) having rules which the affected persons are incapable of following; (7) making such frequent changes in the rules that the persons subject to them cannot properly orient their conduct with regard to them; (8) lacking congruence between the rules as announced and the same rules as they are administered or enforced. Here the distinctiveness of a legal system lies in the regularity, internal consistency, and reasonableness with which they are made and applied. A system which does not fail in these is law; one which does is not (Fuller, 1964:39).

Law in Private Groups and Associations. While none dwells on the point, Kantorowicz, Hart, and Fuller do not locate systems which fit their criteria of law exclusively in the political state. Selznick (1969) views law in much the same way as they do, but goes on to include as law, specifically, the normative system of certain forms of nongovernmental social organizations even within politically organized states. His concern with seeing law as a generic element in the structure of many different groups in society, not just the political structure of the state, was foreshadowed by Ehrlich (1936) and Timasheff (1939). To Ehrlich the state is just one type of social association with law; other associations also possess law. Moreover, the legal order of these other associations, religions, corporations, classes, professions, and families, ". . . is not only the original, but also . . . the basic form of law" (Ehrlich, 1936:37). Conformity grows out of living as members of associations, and

> In this respect, the legal norm does not differ from other norms. The state is not the only association that exercises coercion; there is an untold number of associations in society that exercise it much more forcibly than the state [Ehrlich, 1936:63–64].

Timasheff (1939) also located legal order in any group in society which has a body of norms backed by the authority of that group. The state is one such type and differs from the others simply by virtue of being the highest and most powerful. Hence, "state law" is the upper layer of rules made or recognized by the state. The laws of the groups at the lower levels of power are "social law."

Neither Timasheff nor Ehrlich maintains that the internal social orders of all groups and associations in society constitute legal orders, but neither provides a precise definition which allows a distinction between those that do and those that do not. Therefore, they tend to make any social control synonymous with law. This is precisely what Selznick (1969) attempts to avoid. He wants to provide a concept which will be broad enough "to embrace legal experience within 'private' associations, but not so general as to make law . . . equivalent to social control" (Selznick, 1969:4). In developing his concept, Selznick is in agreement with Fuller and Hart.

> In the authoritative use of coercion, whether by private or public agencies, the legal element is not the coercion itself but the invocation of authority.

> We should see law as endemic in all institutions *that rely for social control on formal authority and rule-making* [Selznick, 1969:7, italics in original].

The distinguishing element in law, according to Selznick, then, is the authoritative decision making and rule finding, whether or not the authority is that of the political state. The normative structures of some private organizations, such as universities, churches, formal associations, and industrial bureaucracies, can be said to be law; others such as friendship groups, families, and clubs exercise social, but not legal, control.

All of the definitions of law reviewed here agree that law is a form of social control; laws are social norms, legitimized rules or principles of conduct which guide how persons ought or ought not to behave and for which there is the probability that sanctions will be applied for compliance or noncompliance. None denies that a system of norms enacted and enforced ultimately by the coercive power of the modern political state constitutes a clear-cut instance of law. All of the conceptions of law agree that law can be clearly distinguished in this way from other normative systems in sovereign nations with developed political institutions and specialized law-making and law-enforcing agencies.

There is some disagreement about just how law differs from other parts of the social control system in "stateless" societies and from other phenomena which are similar to law in may respects, such as mediation of disputes, resolution of conflict, internal order of "private" organizations, and the norms of international relations. However, the dominant theme in making this distinction is that the key elements in law are identified as the use or threat of coercion in a regularized way by authorized persons, whether or not these be agents of the political state. In taking exception to this, the tendency has been to identify law in the authoritative or procedural principles by which decisions about norms, and adherence to them, are made. This turns out not to be a great difference in conception, however, for all are willing to include coercive sanctions; it is only that some also want to include authorized decisions even when coercion is not potentially involved as a sanction.

Although Hart (1961) tends to develop the distinction more fully and make more elaborate use of it, all those who reject coercion as a criterion of law and place exclusive emphasis on authoritative decisions distinguish between "primary" and "secondary" norms. Basically, the idea is that some norms relate directly to the conduct of persons in a "primary" way, in the sense that they prescribe how they should and how they should not behave. "Secondary" norms specify the way persons who are authorized to react to instances of violation or conformity to primary norms should behave; they establish rules governing the actions of the reactors and the proper sanctions to be applied and the regular procedure and authoritative source for making decisions about the content and applicability of the primary norms. The recognition of the difference between the existence and substance of the two norms is not unique to noncoercive definitions, however. Indeed, although not always explicit, the distinction is a common theme running through nearly all conceptions of law.

We have noted that most coercive definitions include the requirement that sanctions be applied for norm violation (or to enforce a dispute settlement) in a systematic or socially approved, i.e., normative, way and by socially approved agents. It is not just that force is actually or potentially used, but, to use Gibbs' (1966b) terms, social approval is given to this as a reaction and to certain persons as the reactors. Thus, coercive definitions identify the primary norms which qualify as law by the requirement that their breach be met (or decisions about them be made) in a way and by persons who are authorized, by secondary norms, to do so. This is contained not only in the noncoercive definitions such as those of Hart, Fuller, Selznick, but also in the definitions of Pound, Holmes, Cardozo, and others who locate law in the political state and in the broader coercive definitions of Weber, Hoebel, Akers, and others. Whatever the conception of law, then, one must recognize that both types of norms are involved. In no concept has the defining characteristic of law been located in the content of the primary norms of law; all refer to the secondary norms or the agents and actions governed by them.

The conception of law which best fits the phenomena examined in this volume is one which identifies law as social control exercised by the political community and ultimately backed by coercive sanctions. We are concerned more specifically with law in American society and the whole set of institutions and organizations, the lawmakers, police, courts, and correctional agencies, to whom secondary norms in our society accord authorization to make decisions about and enforce primary legal norms. One should be ever aware that just as primary norms may be violated, secondary norms stipulating proper legal procedure may be violated. By presenting some of what is known about how these organizations in fact operate, one is able to make a judgment as to how closely they conform to the norms of legality.

REFERENCES

AKERS, RONALD L., 1965. "Toward a Comparative Definition of Law," *Journal of Criminal Law, Criminology, and Police Science*, **56** (Sept.):301–6.

AUSTIN, JOHN, 1890. *Lectures on Jurisprudence, or The Philosophy of Positive Law,* 4th ed. London: John Murray (1873).

BARKUN, MICHAEL, 1968. *Law without Sanctions: Order in Primitive Societies and the World Community.* New Haven: Yale University Press.

CARDOZO, BENJAMIN N., 1924. *The Growth of the Law.* New Haven: Yale University Press.

CHAMBLISS, WILLIAM J. and ROBERT B. SEIDMAN, 1971. *Law, Order, and Power.* Reading, Mass.: Addison-Wesley.

DAVIS, F. JAMES, 1962. "The Sociological Study of Law," pp. 3–37 in Davis, et al., *Society and the Law.* New York: Free Press of Glencoe.

DIAMOND, A. S., 1971. *Primitive Law.* London: Methuen and Co.

EHRLICH, EUGENE, 1936. *Fundamental Principles of the Sociology of Law.* Trans. by Walter L. Moll. Cambridge: Harvard University Press.

FULLER, LON, 1964. *The Morality of Law.* New Haven: Yale University Press.

GIBBS, JACK P., 1966a, "The Sociology of Law and Normative Phenomena," *American Sociological Review,* **31** (June):315–25; 1966b, "Sanctions," *Social Problems,* **14** (Fall): 147–59; 1968, "Definitions of Law and Empirical Questions," *Law and Society Review,* **2** (May):429–46.

GURVITCH, GEORGES, 1945. "Social Control," in George Gurvitch and Wilbert Moore, eds., *Twentieth Century Sociology.* New York: Philosophical Library.

HART, H. L. A., 1961. *The Concept of Law.* London: Oxford at the Clarendon Press.

HARVEY, WILLIAM B., 1966. *Law and Social Change in Ghana.* Princeton: Princeton University Press.

HOEBEL, E. ADAMSON, 1954. *The Law of Primitive Man.* Cambridge: Harvard University Press.

HOLMES, OLIVER WENDELL, 1881. *The Common Law.* Cambridge: Harvard University Press (1963), edited by Mark D. Howe; first published 1881 by Little, Brown; 1897, "The Path of the Law," *Harvard Law Review* **10**:457–78.

KANTOROWICZ, HERMANN, 1958. *The Definition of Law.* Cambridge: University Press, edited by A. H. Campbell.

LLEWELLYN, KARL and E. ADAMSON HOEBEL, 1941. *The Cheyenne Way.* Norman: University of Oklahoma Press.

MEGGITT, M. J., 1962. *Desert People: A Study of the Walbiri Aborigines of Central Australia.* Sydney: Angus and Robertson.

NADER, LAURA, 1965. "The Anthropological Study of Law," *American Anthropologist* **67**:3–32.

POSPISIL, LEOPOLD, 1968. "Law and Order" in James A. Clifton, ed., *Introduction to Cultural Anthropology.* New York: Houghton-Mifflin.

POUND, ROSCOE, 1945. "Sociology of Law," in Georges Gurvitch and Wilbert Moore, eds., *Twentieth Century Sociology.* New York: Philosophical Library.

ROSS, EDWARD ALSWORTH, 1901. *Social Control.* New York: Macmillan Co.

SCHAFER, STEPHEN, 1969. *Theories in Criminology: Past and Present Philosophies of the Crime Problem.* New York: Random House.

SCHAPERA, ISAAC, 1955. *A Handbook of Tswana Law and Custom,* 2nd edition. London: Oxford University Press.

SELZNICK, PHILIP, 1969. *Law, Society, and Industrial Justice.* New York: Russell Sage Foundation.

SUMNER, WILLIAM GRAHAM, 1906. *Folkways.* Boston: Ginn and Co.

TIMASHEFF, N. S., 1939. *An Introduction to the Sociology of Law.* Cambridge: Harvard University Press.

WEBER, MAX, 1954. *Max Weber on Law in Economy and Society.* Cambridge: Harvard University Press, edited by Max Rheinstein; trans. by Edward Shils and Max Rheinstein.

LAW AS A TYPE OF SOCIAL CONTROL

F. James Davis
with some collaboration by
E. Eugene Davis and Henry H. Foster, Jr.

At the present as well as at any other time the center of gravity
of legal development lies not in legislation, nor in juristic science,
nor in judicial decision, but in society itself.—EUGEN EHRLICH,
pioneer in the sociology of law [1]

THE PROCESS OF SOCIAL CONTROL

Social control *is the process by which subgroups and persons are influenced to conduct themselves in conformity to group expectations.*[2] A group is any number of persons among whom social interaction (meaningful mutual influence) occurs.[3] The expected behavior in a smaller group, such as a delinquent gang, may be antisocial from the standpoint of a larger group of which it is a part. In this event, both the pressures exerted by the deviant group to get its members to follow its ways and the influences the larger group uses to bring the subgroup into conformity with the dominant expectations are social controls as defined here.

Reprinted from F. James Davis, Henry H. Foster, Jr., C. Ray Jeffery and E. Eugene Davis, *Society and the Law: New Meanings for An Old Profession.* New York: Free Press of Glencoe, 1962, pp. 39–61, by permission of the author and the publisher.

1 Eugen Ehrlich, *Fundamental Principles of the Sociology of Law,* Harvard Univ. Press, Cambridge, 1936, Foreword. A correct understanding of this quotation requires study of Ehrlich's reasoning about the "living law."
2 This is very close to the definition, in H. P. Fairchild, *Dictionary of Sociology,* Philosophical Library, New York, 1944, p. 279. For similar definitions, see: F. E. Lumley, *Principles of Sociology,* McGraw-Hill, New York, 1928, p. 487; J. L. Gillin and J. P. Gillin, *Cultural Sociology,* The Macmillan Co., New York, 1948, pp. 693–694.
3 In Fairchild, *op. cit.,* p. 279, the social control exerted by that large and relatively permanent group we call society is given the name "societal control."

The character of the process varies with the type and size of the group, and controls may be classified from several points of view. Social control may be exerted unconsciously or deliberately, and the controlled person(s) may or may not be conscious of the process.[4] All actions that influence conduct toward conformity may be treated as the means of social control. Specific means of control may be classified as to whether they are formal or informal; examples of the latter are flattery, gossip, ridicule, and praise. From another standpoint, the particular means of control may be classed as to whether they are suggestive, persuasive, or coercive. Suggestion and persuasion are usually accomplished by verbal symbols; coercion may involve language symbols or physical force. The use of physical force, even when unaccompanied by words, is social control when the effect is to support group patterns of conduct.

Those means of social control that involve a reward or penalty are often referred to, respectively, as *positive* and *negative sanctions.* Some discussions of sanctions indicate that all social controls involve some kind of reward or penalty.[5] It may be noted that diffuse sanctions

4 The influence is not necessarily social in the usual sociological sense—that is, of involving language or other symbolic (consciously meaningful) acts.
5 A. R. Radcliffe-Brown, "Social Sanctions," *Encyclopedia of the Social Sciences,* 1933, pp. 531–534; J. W. Bennett and M. M. Tumin, *Social Life,* Alfred A. Knopf, New York, 1948, p. 515; R. M.

(those brought into play by anyone in the group) are informal means of control, and that organized sanctions (those employed only by designated officials) are formal means of control. Other classifications of the social control process [6] will be mentioned in subsequent contexts.

To the degree that men act in conformity to group expectations, others can predict what they will do in given situations. When such predictability is not possible, for whatever reasons, orderly group life is impossible. Shared understandings about what people will do under given conditions are indispensable if the group is to retain its unity and ultimately its very existence. Social control thus facilitates social order and group unity. [7]

Social Control and the Person

Since the maintenance of orderly group life involves encouraging the person and placing restraints upon him, social controls influence personality development. The person may develop a relatively permanent set of habits and attitudes that conform to group expectations, but he does not automatically do so. There may be no lasting, measurable influence of particular controls, and under certain conditions the person may develop antipathies towards group expectations. However,

whenever orderly group life is maintained, the attitudes and habits of group members generally coincide with the values and expectations of the group. A group expectation is but the agreement of a number of persons as to what conduct is right and what is wrong for persons playing roles in a given situation. Such a consensus may become established in the personality structure of the individual, may become a part of what is called conscience, and may operate as a motive. [8] When this occurs we may say that the pressure of those external stimuli we call social controls has resulted in conformist self-control. [9]

As soon as he begins to understand language symbols the small child encounters social controls, at first chiefly in the form of parental ordering and forbidding. [10] Social controls continue to influence conduct and personality development throughout life. Social control and socialization are thus intimately related but different; the former refers to pressures on the person to conform and the latter to the effects of these pressures on the personality. The one involves learning stimuli, the other the actual learning of expected ways or the unlearning of contrary ones. [11] The

MacIver, *Society*, Holt, Rinehart and Winston, New York, 1947, p. 329. Some writers relate this point to Jeremy Bentham's ideas about the effects of pain and pleasure.

[6] For example, see L. L. Bernard, *Social Control in Its Sociological Aspects*, The Macmillan Co., New York, 1939, Chap. 19, pp. 7–9; H. C. Brearley, "The Nature of Social Control," Chap. 1 in *Social Control*, ed. by Jos. S. Roucek, D. Van Nostrand Co., New York, 1947, pp. 9–10; Edwin M. Lemert, "The Grand Jury as an Agency of Social Control," 10 *American Sociological Review* (Dec., 1945), 751–752; Julius Stone, *The Province and Function of Law*, Harvard Univ. Press, Cambridge, 1950, p. 758. Also see the discussion of the concept of social control in Chapter 1.

[7] E. T. Hiller, *Social Relations and Social Structures*, Harper, New York, 1947, p. 658.

[8] Kimball Young, *Sociology*, American Book Co., 1949, pp. 546–557; F. E. Merrill and H. W. Eldredge, *Culture and Society*, Prentice-Hall, Englewood Cliffs, N.J.: 1952, pp. 29–30; Bennett and Tumin, *op. cit.*, p. 53; Radcliffe-Brown, *op. cit.*, p. 205; Kingsley Davis, *Human Society*, The Macmillan Co., New York, 1948, p. 55.

[9] Brearley, *op. cit.*, p. 4.

[10] Paul H. Landis, *Man in Environment*, Thos. Y. Crowell Co., New York, 1949, p. 478.

[11] Chas. W. Coulter, "Social Control and Conditioning of Personality," Chap. 3 in Roucek, *op. cit.*, pp. 31–47. See Talcott Parsons, *The Social System*, The Free Press of Glencoe, New York, 1951, pp. 208, 297–298, for the view that socialization involves learning while social control involves unlearning. This follows from the definition of social control as the process of counteracting "deviation tendencies," and is similar to the position of LaPiere that social control corrects for "errors in socialization." See Richard T. LaPiere, *A Theory of Social Control*, McGraw-Hill, New York, 1954, pp. 25–30. The present definition in-

pressures are brought to bear on persons as they play particular social roles. When people conform, their conduct indicates that they have learned the attitudes and habits the group expects them to adopt in playing given roles.

DEFINITION OF LAW

In this book *law* is defined as *the formal means of social control that involves the use of rules that are interpreted, and are enforceable, by the courts of a political community.* This is intended to be consistent with Pound's definition of law as "the systematic and orderly application of force by the appointed agents" of politically organized society.[12] Pound has noted that law has been used to mean three different things: (1) the legal order, or "the regime of adjusting relations and ordering conduct by politically organized society," (2) the authoritative materials (including rules) that guide administrative and judicial decisions, and (3) the judicial process.[13] It appears that Pound has identified law as the first of these and that when law is so defined it includes the other two. Rules and other authoritative materials (such as annotations and historical interpretations) are tools that constitute an important part of the legal order, and the judicial process refers to the operations of an essential part, the court and law-enforcement machinery.

MacIver's approach to law is in many respects similar to the one adopted here, although he limits his definition to legal rules,[14] a practice frequently followed also by the political scientist.[15] In this book the term "laws" will often be used synonymously with legal rules, and "a law" will mean a particular rule. "Law" will include legal rules but will encompass the various agencies and procedures by which the rules are made, applied, and enforced, including that "law" which is at the end of a policeman's nightstick.

This definition of law is inconsistent with the much broader usages discussed in Chapter 1 only in the sense that it delineates a smaller segment of social control. To take one example, law as defined here is but a limited part of Timasheff's "ethico-imperative coordination."[16] The reasons for restricting the definition of law to the political community are that it is the dominant usage among American legal scholars, political scientists, and sociologists, and that the authors wish to center attention on the Anglo-American legal system. As subsequent discussion will show, the use of this definition is not intended to support the idea that the expressed will of the state is absolutely sovereign. Neither is it intended to preclude the use of materials about preliterate or other systems of social control that do not have courts or other requisites of law as defined above. The line must be drawn somewhere for analysis and communication, yet the greatest amount of understanding of law will come when it is related to total knowledge in the field of social control.

Law as Formal Social Control

Formal social control is characterized by (1) explicit rules of conduct, (2) planned

---

cludes any influences toward conformity, whether directed against a deviant act or not. Thus praise and the setting of an example, even if done unconsciously, are social controls.

[12] Roscoe Pound, *Social Control through Law,* Yale Univ. Press, New Haven, 1942, pp. 25, 49–53; see also, Roscoe Pound, "Sociology of Law," Chap. 11 in *Twentieth Century Sociology* by G. Gurvitch and W. E. Moore, Philosophical Library, New York, 1945, p. 300. "Court" is used here to mean all government tribunals for deciding contested matters, and thus includes many administrative agencies.

[13] Pound, *Social Control through Law,* p. 40.

[14] MacIver, *op. cit.,* p. 328.

[15] Evron M. Kirkpatrick, "Elements of Political Science," Chap. 9 in Emerson P. Schmidt, *Man and Society,* Prentice-Hall, Englewood Cliffs, N.J., 1937, p. 393.

[16] N. S. Timasheff, *An Introduction to the Sociol-*

use of sanctions to support the rules, and (3) designated officials to interpret and enforce the rules, and often to make them. Informal controls, spontaneously employed by any member of a group, are powerful supporters of expectations in small, homogeneous groups. But as life becomes more complex and anonymous these controls become increasingly inadequate for many purposes, and the group establishes formal controls to maintain conformity to its expectations. Law is often said to be at the extreme formal end of the continuum of social control.[17]

Many methods of social control, both formal and informal, are used in multigroup societies. Law and other formal controls become increasingly important as social organization grows more complex; but ostracism, shaming, gossip, and other informal controls continue to influence conduct toward conformity.[18] The conditions under which the two types of control reinforce each other, and under which they are opposed, are not yet clearly understood. In this connection it should be noted that despite their relative impersonality, formal organizations characteristically contain informal group structures that influence their operation.[19] Even law, then,

may be expected to be closely related to certain informal controls, and should be viewed as an approximation to the ideal type of formal social control.

Legal Rules

Informal social controls operate largely with reference to implied rules of conduct; formal social controls involve clearly expressed rules. It has been maintained that handwriting is essential to formal control because of the need for keeping records.[20] Accounts of legal rules, rule interpretations, and rule enforcement must somehow be kept. The fact that the members of such groups as the Icelanders and the Ifugao of the Philippines [21] have memorized a great number of precise regulations suggests that writing and printing are not essential to express rules, but they do greatly facilitate explicitness. It is difficult to conceive of modern legal systems apart from the masses of printed materials.

Legal rules specify proper conduct for the citizen, but they are also guides to the conduct of the various officials charged with enforcing the rules. Many rules or parts of rules are directed specifically toward legal officials. This is true of statements of sanctions. A negative sanction, such as the punishment specified by a criminal law, directs the appropriate officials to impose certain penalties when a given rule of conduct is not heeded. Positive legal sanctions, such as laws providing for rewards for informants or pensions for public servants, also are sets of directions for certain officials. Rules of procedure are also guides for rule-makers, rule-interpreters, advocates of the parties to a dispute,

ogy of Law, Harvard Univ. Committee on Research in the Social Sciences, Cambridge, 1939, pp. 12–17, 248.

17 Bennett and Tumin, *op. cit.,* p. 525. See Richard R. Korn and Lloyd W. McCorkle, *Criminology and Penology,* Holt, Rinehart and Winston, New York, 1959, pp. 75–83 for a discussion of law as a response to the breakdown of other social controls.

18 Gillin and Gillin, *op. cit.,* pp. 704–719. See Richard D. Schwartz, "Social Factors in the Development of Legal Control: A Case Study of Two Israeli Settlements," 63 *Yale Law Journal,* No. 4 (Feb., 1954), 471–491, for an interesting account of a study showing that law developed in a planned community in which informal controls were inadequate to deal with disturbing behavior, and did not develop nearly so much in a somewhat similar community where informal controls were more effective.

19 Robin Williams, *American Society,* Alfred A. Knopf, New York, 1951, pp. 456–459. See Robert

Dubin, *Human Relations in Administration,* Prentice-Hall, Englewood Cliffs, N.J., 1951, pp. 47–78, for an excellent collection of materials on informal groups in large-scale organizations.

20 Young, *op. cit.,* p. 549; Davis, *op. cit.,* pp. 66–67.

21 R. F. Barton, "Ifugao Law," *University of California Publications in American Archaeology and Ethnology,* Vol. 15, No. 1, 1–186.

enforcement officers, or occupants of other legal roles.

In specifying proper conduct, social rules are guides for the behavior of persons playing different roles in the same situation. The rights of one are the duties of the other. If the role rights and duties are clearly understood by all parties, predictability and social orderliness are possible; but otherwise there may be confusion.[22] Particularly in heterogeneous, dynamic societies, social rules are often formulated explicitly to clarify role expectations. Legal rules clarify role rights and duties, and also provide sanctions to support them. A law that grants a right to Person or Group A imposes a legal duty on Person or Group B. The same legal rule that confers a legal privilege on A withholds from B the right to make the corresponding demand. This analysis is refined considerably more in the works of Austin and Hohfeld than is necessary in the present book.[23] Sorokin stresses role rights and duties; but his concept of "law-norms" applies to any formal control and is thus synonymous with explicit social rules in general rather than with legal rules in particular.[24]

Law and the Courts

In all formal agencies of control, provisions are made for designated persons to play specialized roles, and law has many and varied specialists. Unless there are official agencies to decide disputes by interpreting and applying legal rules to given situations—that is, unless there are courts—there is no law as defined here. Unless there is at least one specialist whose function it is to preside over formal sessions and adjudicate contested cases, there is no court. There must be judges, and their decisions must be justified by reference to rules rather than to caprice, or there is no law. Weber's approach sounds like an insistence upon formal control when he writes that law is a regulatory order that requires an enforcement staff; but he includes even the clan under the concept of staff and does not require the presence of a court.[25] Hoebel insists that there be a court and characterizes it as having responsibility, authority, and method. However, his examples indicate a broad conception of the court, one that does not necessarily include specialists, not even the judge.[26] The role of the judge is a key one, even when most disputes do not get to court. The ways in which judges discharge their responsibilities are the subject of much of the legal writing of recent times.

LAW AND THE POLITICAL COMMUNITY

Law as defined above is a means of control employed by a political community. A political community involves "forcible maintenance of orderly dominion over a territory and its inhabitants."[27] How much power do political communities have, and what are the implications for the legal system? This question will be discussed primarily with reference to the state. One political community may contain lesser ones, and in each there is law if the unit can use force to get its inhabi-

[22] Bennett and Tumin, *op. cit.*, pp. 96–101; James M. Reinhardt, Paul Meadows, and John M. Gillette, *Social Problems and Social Policy*, American Book Co., New York, 1952, p. 49.

[23] See E. Adamson Hoebel, *The Law of Primitive Man*, Harvard Univ. Press, Cambridge, 1954, pp. 47–63, for an extended discussion of the idea that all legal relations are between persons, in terms of a modified Hohfeld schema. See also Max Radin, "A Restatement of Hohfeld," 51 *Harvard Law Review* (1938), 1141–1164. . . .

[24] Pitirim A. Sorokin, *Society, Culture and Personality: Their Structure and Dynamics*, Harper, New York, 1947, pp. 70–72.

[25] Max Weber, *Law in Economy and Society*, ed. by Max Rheinstein, Harvard Univ. Press, Cambridge, 1954, p. 6.

[26] Hoebel, *op. cit.*, pp. 22–28. For example, he says such structures as the Cheyenne military council are primitive courts.

[27] Weber, *op. cit.*, p. 338.

tants to obey its rules. The state is the supreme political community, privileged to use force to maintain order in the entire territory. The following quotation clarifies the relationships of government, the nation, and the laws to the state:

The state involves a territory, a government and a people. If the people are unified culturally by common folkways and traditions, they are also called a *nation.* . . . The *government* includes those official agencies and functionaries by means of which the state achieves its ends. The *laws* are rules of the state, codified, enacted, or decreed, and enforced through machinery of government.[28]

Limitations on the Power of the State

The state is not absolutely sovereign. One important reason why its power is limited is that to be effective the system of coercion must be approved of by the members of society. Even the most despotic of governments cannot maintain its power indefinitely without the consent of the governed. The state that bases right on might finds that it must do an enormous amount of policing and that political power is never safe unless the people believe social order is being maintained and other desired services are being rendered.[29] The enforcement of the law of the political community is most sensitive to group convictions in democracies.[30] Constitutions not only outline the essential procedures, but also limit the power of the state to those matters the people consent to place in official hands.

In approving of or resisting the exercise

of governmental power, people often act as members of organized groups that have power. As the modern state arose it was accompanied by the development of powerful voluntary associations, especially in democracies. Political parties, labor unions, trade and manufacturing associations, cooperatives, professional associations, religious organizations, and a host of others wield power in competition with government,[31] and also by influencing legislation and in other ways obtaining political power.[32] This view . . . is called political pluralism.

One means of obtaining approval of governmental coercion is to provide that certain checks and balances will operate to prevent any one person or branch of government from monopolizing power. Besides holding the powers of taxation and appropriation, the state and national legislatures in the United States can create new administrative agencies and prescribe their general policies and can investigate the other branches of government. The executive branch at both the state and national levels can urge particular legislation, veto congressional action, and appoint judges. Our state and federal courts interpret legislation and pass on its constitutionality, and also pass on the methods by which executive powers are used. In turn, the legislative bodies exercise some surveillance over procedural rules for the courts, and legislative action influences the jurisdiction of courts. Often the decisions of courts are not effective unless they receive the support of executive agencies that are necessary for enforcement.[33]

A second major limitation on the power of the state is the fact that, when there are rules of law, power is limited and objec-

28 R. L. Sutherland, J. L. Woodward, and M. A. Maxwell, *Introductory Sociology,* J. B. Lippincott Co., New York, 1952, p. 370.
29 Karl N. Llewellyn and E. Adamson Hoebel, *The Cheyenne Way,* Univ. of Oklahoma Press, Norman, 1941, p. 285; Hoebel, *op. cit.,* pp. 26–27; Ehrlich, *op. cit.,* p. 373; Ehrlich suggests on pp. 71–75 that state power is effective in enforcing laws only in certain areas, notably those concerning taxation and the military.
30 Weber, *op. cit.,* p. 9.

31 Stone, *op. cit.,* pp. 730–735; Stone criticizes Timasheff's view that law requires hierarchical arrangements of power groups, suggesting that power may be integrated in a "federal" manner; see Timasheff, *op. cit.,* pp. 301–302.
32 Floyd A. Cave, "State, Law and Government," Chap. 6 in Roucek, *op. cit.,* pp. 79–90.
33 Williams, *op. cit.,* pp. 218–226.

tive because the ruler is bound by the rules.[34] The provision for a punishment means that certain officials are bound not to exceed it and that their discretion to withhold it is limited. The official who attempts to escape this obligation places his position in jeopardy, and if this is done generally or by persons in high office the legitimacy of the whole power structure of the state is threatened.

It is difficult for the citizenry to have detailed knowledge of the laws, and this imposes a practical limitation on state power. Also, in practice, parties to a dispute may fail to initiate legal action for one reason or another.[35] More knowledge about why people conform to law is needed in order to determine the extent of the power of the state in practice. It has frequently been maintained that conformity is based more on other considerations, such as habits of obedience and the sentiments of one's immediate groups, than on force.[36] Timasheff's view is that men are law-abiding because they know the force is there, but he does not consider the fear of force to be the usual motive for obedience.[37]

The State's Near Monopoly of Power

The force of the state is limited for the many reasons discussed above, but nevertheless it does have a great deal of power. Perhaps recent technological developments have made existing power structures more secure; opponents have great diffi-

culty overbalancing the state's virtual monopoly on the instruments of force.[38] To the extent that it can get the necessary effective power, the state has legal control over all persons and associations within its territory. Within the limits of law it is privileged to use force against all its persons and associations. The amount of effective power varies considerably, but the view that in general the state has a near monopoly of power seems justified.[39]

. . . [T]he broad definitions of law in European legal sociology have been related to the rejection of the concept of absolute state sovereignty. A frequent theme is that law and courts existed prior to the political community and do not depend on it.[40] In some of these treatments the state is explicitly contrasted with society, as though governmental agencies were not institutions of society. Ehrlich, for example, writes that, "Courts do not come into being as organs of the state, but of society," and that the society still has courts of its own.[41] The ideas that government originated in conquest, exploitation, or accident also often lead to the anarchistic view that the state intervenes in society and is not necessary to it.[42]

A sounder view is that government is one phase of formal social control in society. As social organization has become more specialized, and as informal controls have become inadequate in many areas of life, political institutions have emerged to meet certain needs that otherwise could probably not be met. The political community is entrusted with the near monop-

[34] Kurt H. Wolff (trans. and ed.), *The Sociology of Georg Simmel,* The Free Press of Glencoe, New York, 1950, p. 262; Karl Olivecrona, *Law as Fact,* Humphrey Milford, London, 1939, p. 176; Timasheff, *op. cit.,* p. 267.

[35] Ehrlich, *op. cit.,* pp. 367–368.

[36] Rheinstein, *op. cit.,* pp. 12–16; Korn and McCorkle, *op. cit.,* p. 74; Yehezkel Dror, "Values and the Law," *The Antioch Review,* Winter, 1957–58, p. 446; Richard D. Schwartz, "The Effectiveness of Legal Sanctions," a paper presented at the Sept., 1959, meeting of the American Sociological Society.

[37] Timasheff, *op. cit.,* pp. 140–161.

[38] Timasheff, *op. cit.,* p. 240.

[39] Kirkpatrick, *op. cit.,* pp. 390–391.

[40] For example, see Georges Gurvitch, *Sociology of Law,* Philosophical Library, New York, 1942, pp. 250-254, where it is said that it is an historical accident that the state enjoyed "jural primacy" at the same time it was developing political sovereignty.

[41] Ehrlich, *op. cit.,* p. 121.

[42] Robert M. MacIver, *The Web of Government,* The Macmillan Co., New York, 1947, p. 31.

oly of force, but it generally attempts to coordinate activity in much the same ways as other large organizations do.[43] Does force itself not perform useful functions in the society? Perhaps coercion must be used if a social system is to survive, if only to restrain those who would use force against others for their own ends. In the words of MacIver,

There are certain fundamental forms of order and of security which can be maintained only under laws which all must obey. The real service of force is as a safeguard of this order. Force alone cannot protect this order, but without this force as an ally of its other safeguards it could never be secure.[44]

The conclusion that "an antisocial residuum must be coerced" if there is to be social order has also been reached by Pound.[45] Without direct reference to force, an important function of government has been identified as follows:

Be the society simple or complex, there must exist in its framework of institutions one vested with final authority which by its decision ends all disputes. This is government.[46]

And, although they are checked by other governmental agencies, the courts of the political community provide the machinery for final settlements of disputes.

International Law

At present there is no international law, in the full sense as defined here, because there is no international political community. There is no world police force. There are some rules, and there are precedents that carry some weight; but these rules are lacking in uniformity and are not backed up by the sanction of force. There is no

organized force to support the rules, and states must resort to self-help to protect their rights and those of their subjects or submit to unenforceable arbitration. It would seem that the League of Nations contradicted itself when it outlawed force and substituted "rule of law," and then provided for negative sanctions. How can there be effective sanctions if there is no supernational monopoly of force? [47]

The courts of arbitration provided by the Hague conferences of 1899 and 1907 were panels to which states might refer a dispute if they wished. The Permanent Court of International Justice was established at the Hague after World War I to deal only with treaty interpretation and breaches of specific international duties; and many countries, including the United States, did not accept its jurisdiction. National sovereignty did not budge when the League of Nations was created; it gave very little when the United Nations Organization was established, and the "Big Five" nation-states retained unrestricted sovereign power. The International Court of Justice was included in the program of the United Nations, and it has been handling large numbers of private international disputes successfully. Since the Security Council acts like a court in disputes that threaten the peace, following procedural precedents, the International Court of Justice cannot be expected to develop a body of public international law.[48]

43 Sutherland, Woodward, and Maxwell, *op. cit.*, p. 370.

44 MacIver, *Society*, p. 343.

45 Pound, *Social Control through Law*, p. 33.

46 Paul H. Landis, *Man in Environment*, Thos. Y. Crowell Co., New York, 1941, p. 316.

47 Olivecrona, *op. cit.*, pp. 193–210. Compare W. Friedman, "Some Impacts of Social Organization on International Law," 50 *American Journal of International Law* (July, 1956) , 475–513; E. N. Van Kleffens, "The Place of Law in International Relations," *United Nations Review*, Jan., 1955, p. 20.

48 MacIver, *The Web of Government*, pp. 389–400. MacIver suggests that the Security Council be made an administrative organ, subordinate to the General Assembly, and that the adjudication of issues between nations be transferred to the International Court of Justice. See also Charles de Visscher, *Theory and Reality in Public International Law*, Princeton Univ. Press, Princeton, N.J., 1957; and F. Honig, "Diminishing Role of

Nation-states are free to adopt what they wish of international law, and they may withdraw their support of particular rules at any time. Yet, because of the interdependence of interests and considerable agreement as to proper international relations, nation-states limit themselves a good deal.[49] Perhaps this area of comity can be increased much more within the present framework of national sovereignty. Perhaps it can be enlarged to the point of providing as much security against conflict as an international political community could. The discussion of which approach is the more feasible is a matter of whether international cooperation can best be achieved within or outside of the framework of law in the full sense. The United Nations Educational and Scientific Organization (UNESCO), and similar instrumentalities, receive support on both grounds. The conditions of success for agencies that have all the elements of law except the support of political force are not yet clear.

Labor Law

To a large extent, labor law is another area where the parties to dispute may resort to limited self-help, at least so long as the so-called "right" to strike is preserved and courts are not given jurisdiction to resolve such controversies. At the present stage of development, most labor disputes are a matter for private settlement and the government's usual role is that of conciliator, although "unfair" employer or union practices may be enjoined or penalized and strikes by utility workers or government employees may be outlawed. To date there is no national labor "court" or arbitration commission that has authority to enforce a mandatory settlement.

KINDS OF LAW

Law defies exact classification and is often called a "seamless web." Yet the vastness and complexity of the subject require that some attempt at subdivision be made. Classifications from three different standpoints will be considered here: (1) the content of law, (2) the origin of law, and (3) the degree of rationality in the legal system. In the first two instances attention is focused on legal rules, but these categories also refer to the agencies and procedures by which the rules are made, interpreted, and enforced.

Kinds of Law: Content

The content of law may be classed as *substantive* or *procedural*. The former consists of rules concerning rights, powers, duties, and other legal relations that courts are established to administer. Procedural law, often called *adjective law* and sometimes *remedial law*, has to do with the administration of the substantive law; it provides means for maintaining legal rights or for obtaining redress when they are invaded.[50]

---

the World Court," 34 *International Affairs* (April, 1958), 184–194.

49 Timasheff, *op. cit.*, pp. 260–262; Olivecrona, *op. cit.*, p. 200; E. Fletcher, "International Law and International Ethos," 8 *Ecumenical Review* (July, 1956), 393–395.

50 Noel T. Dowling, Edwin W. Patterson, and Richard R. Powell, *Materials for Legal Method*, The Foundation Press, Inc., Chicago, 1946, p. 31. This distinction took on tremendous practical significance when the U.S. Supreme Court ruled, in *Erie R. Co.* v. *Tompkins*, 304 U.S. 64 (1938), that federal courts must apply the *substantive law* of the various states in which they sit in cases coming to the federal courts by reason of diversity of citizenship of the parties. In *procedural* matters, however, all federal district courts must follow the Federal Rules of Civil Procedure, likewise promulgated in 1938. The distinction, though important, is not always easy to make. See e.g., *Guaranty Trust Co.* v. *York* 326 U.S. 99 (1945), especially dissent of Mr. Justice Rutledge; *Cohen* v. *Beneficial Loan Corp.* 337 U.S. 541 (1949), 2 *Moore's Federal Practice*, 2d Ed. 1948, Par. 1.04(4); Tunks, "Categorization and Federalism: Substance and Procedure after *Erie Railroad* v. *Tompkins*," (1939) 34 *Ill. L. Rev.* 271, 274–276.

Although it is difficult to maintain a clearcut distinction,[51] a division is sometimes made between *public* law and *private* law. The former has to do with the structure of government, the duties and powers of officials, and the relationship between the individual and the state. It includes such subjects as constitutional law, administrative law, regulation of public utilities, criminal law and procedure, and law relating to the proprietary powers of the state and its political subdivisions.[52] Private law, on the other hand, refers to the rules, both substantive and procedural, governing relationships between individuals, such as the law of torts, contracts, and property.[53]

A distinction more familiar to the practitioner is that between *civil* and *criminal* law. Criminal law has to do with the definition of crimes and the prosecution and penal treatment of offenders. Civil law, as used in this context, means all law other than criminal law,[54] and would thus encompass private law, as defined above, and a large portion of public law.

Classifications based on content are indispensable to the practicing lawyer. The key number digest system of the West Publishing Company, for example, is built around the seven major subject matter categories emphasized in the following statement:

Law is the effort of society to protect PERSONS in their rights and relations, to guard them in their PROPERTY, enforce their CONTRACTS, hold them to liabilities for their TORTS, punish their CRIMES, by means of REMEDIES administered by GOVERNMENT.

These seven categories are broken down into 34 divisions, which are subdivided into 415 titles, according to subject matter.[55] Comparable subdivisions based on content provide the framework for the various other digests, encyclopedias, and annotated report systems used by lawyers.

Kinds of Law: Origin

Law is sometimes classified on the basis of its origin, which is often suggested by the form of the rule under examination. The basic distinction here is between (1) *legislation,* that is, rules of general application, enacted by a law-making body in politically organized society, and (2) *case law,* which is a by-product of decisions in particular controversies and is expressed with considerable literary freedom by judges in opinions explaining their decisions.[56]

Included in *legislation,* so defined, are constitutions, treaties, statutes, ordinances, administrative regulations, and court rules.[57] Statutes have been further subdivided in many ways. In one scheme, statutes are classed as to whether they are enabling, remedial, or penal. Enabling statutes confer new powers; remedial statutes correct abuses or some other undesirable situation; and penal statutes provide negative sanctions.[58]

The term *common law* is sometimes used as a synonym for "judge-made" law or "case law," as distinguished from legislation, or "enacted law." [59] Much of An-

51 Weber, *op. cit.,* pp. 43–56.

52 Dowling, Patterson, and Powell, *op. cit.,* pp. 30–31; Henry C. Black, *Black's Law Dictionary,* 3d ed., West Publishing Co., St. Paul, Minn., 1933, p. 1461.

53 Dowling, Patterson, and Powell, *op. cit.,* pp. 30–31; Black, *op. cit.,* p. 1419.

54 Dowling, Patterson, and Powell, *op. cit.,* p. 32.

55 Manual, West Publishing Co., 1944, reprinted in part in Dowling, Patterson, and Powell, *op. cit.,* pp. 236–237.

56 Dowling, Patterson, and Powell, *op. cit.,* pp. 14–15.

57 *Ibid.,* pp. 21–28.

58 Black, *op. cit.,* p. 1075.

59 Dowling, Patterson, and Powell, *op. cit.,* pp. 17–20; Thomas E. Atkinson and James H. Chadbourn, *Cases and Other Materials on Civil Procedure,* The Foundation Press, Inc., Brooklyn, 1948, p. 1; 11 *American Jurisprudence,* Common Law, SS 2, 3.

glo-American common law is thought to have been derived from the customs of long ago.[60] Customs, whether local or general, become law when officially adopted by the courts or lawmaking agencies of a political community. If the body of rules resulting from judicial decisions is of general application within the realm, whether it originated in custom or not, it is *common law.* The distinctive feature of Anglo-American common law has been its emphasis on logical development, with decisions in particular cases resting for the most part on precedents found in earlier cases.[61] This is not to say that the growth of the common law has been entirely logical, for old principles have been discarded and new rules formulated to follow changes in prevailing thought as to what is appropriate for the community; but this development is slow and to a large extent unconscious on the part of the courts.[62] This system is to be contrasted with the *civil law* of Europe, which historically has consisted primarily of enacted law, with little regard for judicial precedents.[63]

For this contrast, and for some other purposes, equity law and the rules of other special courts are often included as common law. Originally, however, our common law developed by judicial decision in the so-called "law courts," as distinguished from equity, ecclesiastical, and other special courts. The court of equity, or English High Court of Chancery, was established to facilitate the administration of justice at a time when the law courts had become rigidly bound to a system of writs. The equity court acquired jurisdiction in those areas where the writ system left "no adequate remedy at law." Based on fairness, it met with a popular response. At first the proceedings in equity were very informal and, as there were no binding precedents, results in a particular case were unpredictable and depended on what the chancellor (who was more often a churchman than a lawyer) considered fair; hence the saying that justice in equity courts was meted out "according to the length of the chancellor's foot." [64] Ultimately, binding precedents were developed in equity, and there has since been much fusion of law and equity, particularly on the procedural side; [65] however, the discretion of the equity judge still obtains to some extent.[66]

Classification of rules as to origin often leads to multiple sources, as, for example, when a court passes on the constitutionality of a statute. Again, many common law rules have been codified into statutes.

Kinds of Law: Degree of Rationality

Of the many carefully conceived systems of classification in Weber's work on law, probably the most useful is the one that concerns the extent to which legal systems are rational. The reference is primarily to the type of legal thought involved in the administration of justice. Weber distinguishes between formal rationality and substantive rationality. The former in-

---

[60] O. W. Holmes, Jr., *The Common Law*, Little, Brown, and Co., Boston, 1881, pp. 1–38; Davis, *op. cit.*, p. 66.

[61] Holmes, *op. cit.*, p. 35; Atkinson and Chadbourn, *op. cit.*, p. 1; Dowling, Patterson, and Powell, *op. cit.*, pp. 15–16; K. N. Llewellyn, "Case Law," 3 *Encyclopedia of the Social Sciences*, New York, 1930, 249.

[62] Holmes, *op. cit.*, pp. 35–37. "The truth is, that the law is always approaching, and never reaching, consistency. It is forever adopting new principles from life at one end, and it always retains old ones from history at the other, which have not yet been absorbed or sloughed off" (*Ibid.* at 36).

[63] Atkinson and Chadbourn, *op. cit.*, p. 1; Dowling, Patterson, and Powell, *op. cit.*, pp. 32–33.

[64] Atkinson and Chadbourn, *op. cit.*, pp. 584–585; Roscoe Pound, *An Introduction to the Philosophy of Law*, Yale University Press, New Haven, 1946, pp. 130–131; 19 *American Jurisprudence*, Equity, SS 3, 4.

[65] Many states and the Federal Rules of Civil Procedure (Rule 2) now prescribe that there shall be "one form of action." Atkinson and Chadbourn, *op. cit.*, pp. 107 *et seq.*

[66] Atkinson and Chadbourn, *op. cit.*, pp. 585–586; Pound, *op. cit.*, pp. 131–133.

volves the use of legal procedures that can be controlled by the intellect; formal irrationality exists in law when oracles or substitutes for them are relied on rather than objective means. Substantive rationality in law involves the use of general rules; substantive irrationality exists when a case is decided on some unique ethical, emotional, or political basis instead of by general rules.[67] Apparently referring both to formal and substantive rationality, Weber identifies three types of administration of justice: (1) Khadi justice, (2) empirical justice, and (3) rational justice. The first is the type of justice dispensed by the judge of the Islamic *sharia* court. It is based on religious precepts and so lacking in procedural rules as to seem almost completely arbitrary. This type of justice can also be oriented towards ethical, political, or other practical values. Empirical justice, the deciding of cases by drawing on analogies and by relying on and interpreting precedents, is more rational than Khadi justice but considerably short of complete rationality. Weber refers to the law of the Roman Republic as including elements of all three of these types and to the law of the Roman Empire as highly rational. The Anglo-American system appears to Weber to be largely empirical, with many elements of Khadi justice. He attempts with historical evidence to support the thesis that bureaucratic administration leads to rational justice, while demands for popular justice, individualization of justice, and for taking traditions into account work against legal rationality.[68]

LAW AS A PART OF CULTURE

Law: A Set of Social Institutions

As a part of society's system of social control, law is an aspect of the social organization of the political community. It is a part of the culture—the habits, attitudes, and ideas that are transmitted from one generation to another. Specifically, it is an aspect of the institutionalized part of the culture. Social institutions are organized, and their expectations are stated, as explicit rules that are obligatory and that are supported by specialists. According to Llewellyn,

All you have to do is to borrow a concept from sociology: *Institution,* and to make explicit that you include therein the relevant going practices and the relevant specialists and the relevant physical equipment and the manner of organization of the whole; and Pound's picture of law—the *institution* of law—becomes forthwith a something which any social scientist can look at, understand, make friends with, learn from, and comfortably contribute to. The central aspect of an institution is organized activity, activity organized around the cleaning up of some job.[69]

It is Llewellyn's conviction that the institutional approach can illuminate law as a part of society far more than can the study of legal rules alone. He suggests that firmly rooted but informal legal practices must be taken into account. It may be further suggested that extralegal institutions, such as the political party and the bar association, greatly influence the operation of official legal agencies.

Social institutions, including legal ones, are interrelated. Nobody has put forth the proposition that law completely determines the culture; but many writers have contended that law is completely determined by other social factors, especially economic forces. Law cannot exist independently, of course; all legal acts concern economic, family, educational, or other areas of life. But this does not mean that law is not itself an element of culture, and that it has no influence on the areas of life it seeks to control. Law is

[67] Weber, *op. cit.,* p. 63.
[68] *Ibid.,* pp. 206–223, 349–356; H. H. Gerth and C. Wright Mills, *From Max Weber: Essays in Sociology,* Oxford Univ. Press, New York, 1946, pp. 216–221.

[69] K. N. Llewellyn, "Law and the Social Sciences —Especially Sociology," 14 *American Sociological Review,* 453.

instrumental in making choices and in organizing value systems. Searches for immutable connections between legal institutions and other cultural elements have not been successful, but the evidence at least seems capable of supporting the conclusion that *law and other cultural elements influence each other.*[70] Historically, according to Weber, economic institutions have had chiefly an indirect effect on law, and they have certainly not been its sole determiners. Political organization has been important, and also voluntary associations, legal education, war and military organization.[71]

The values supported by other social institutions perhaps determine the limits within which legal controls operate. Certain values are considered essential and others are subordinate or secondary. What matters most at a given time and place ordinarily will be reflected in law. Where there is ambivalence or disagreement as to the priority of values, legal decisions and the law's enforcement will likely be uncertain and equivocal. For example, we expect law in our time and place to support monogamy but not prostitution and concubinage.[72] Yet prostitution and concubinage may thrive if the policy favoring monogamy takes the form of withholding divorce for whatever cause or limiting it to the grounds of adultery, or if marriages are matters of "convenience." Systems of law have grown out of particular cultural systems, those that are already institutionalized to a considerable degree; but at the same time law helps in the process of value integration. Just how much agreement there must be on values and how much these must already be involved in the functioning of social

institutions before a legal system can be reasonably effective is a difficult question, and one of crucial significance for the future of international law.[73]

Law as an Index of Values and Social Solidarity

Some sociologists have maintained that law is so intimately connected with other institutions that it can serve as an index of at least the most cherished values. One view is that law indicates those forms of conduct believed to be most dangerous to the welfare of the political community. In the discussion of European legal sociology in Chapter 1, it was noted that Ehrlich considered the legal document to be a mirror of group norms. One interesting analysis relates the idea of legal rights, and the use in law of words indicating rightness and uprightness, to similar usages in the Bible and other indicators of our cultural traditions.[74] It has been suggested that a good deal of the present confusion in divorce laws is an index of the current conflicts of values in the marriage and family area.[75] An analysis of the role of voluntary associations in France was based on court decisions and other legal materials. The investigator's interpretation is to the effect that the legal restrictions reflect certain aspects of French cultural history, and that they have played an important part in keeping the role of voluntary associations limited.[76]

---

[70] Timasheff, *op. cit.*, 327–343; see Hoebel, *op. cit.*, Chap. 1, for a discussion of the "theory of imperative selection."

[71] Weber, *op. cit.*, pp. 11–40, 65–97.

[72] LaPiere, *op. cit.*, pp. 31–33. Watson Smith and John M. Roberts, *Zuni Laws, a Field of Values*, Papers of the Peabody Museum of American Archaeology and Ethnology, Vol. 34, No. 1, Harvard Univ., Cambridge, Mass., 1954.

[73] Quincy Wright, *Contemporary Internnational Law: A Balance Sheet*, Doubleday Short Studies in Political Science, Doubleday and Co., Garden City, N.Y., 1955, pp. 7–8. J. L. Kunz, "Pluralism of Legal and Value Systems and International Law," 4 *American Journal of International Law* (July, 1955), 370.

[74] Max M. Laserson, "Rights, Righthandedness and Uprightness," 4 *American Sociological Review* (Aug., 1939), 534–542.

[75] John F. Cuber, *Sociology*, Appleton-Century-Crofts, New York, 1951, p. 444.

[76] Arnold Rose, "Voluntary Associations in France," Chap. 4 in *Theory and Method in the Social Sciences*, Univ. of Minnesota Press, Minneapolis, 1954, pp. 72–115.

The idea that law is a measure of the type of solidarity or unity in a society was stated by Durkheim. He observed that the division of labor was rapidly increasing and that the basis for social cohesion was changing apace. In homogeneous societies, Durkheim reasoned, the basis for group unity is similarity in habits, attitudes and ideas. He called this mechanical solidarity. Early law, he maintained, was repressive, and this penal law was invoked in support of nearly unanimously supported rules of conduct—those reflecting mechanical solidarity. Later, in societies with much division of labor, the basis for group unity came to be the interdependence of widely different persons and groups performing a great variety of functions. Durkeim characterized this as organic solidarity, and contended that a new kind of law—restitutive law—was developing to help cement the new type of society together. Stated concisely, his proposition is that penal law reflects mechanical solidarity, while restitutive law is an index of organic solidarity.[77]

Frank E. Hartung, equating criminal law with Durkheim's repressive penal law and civil law with restitutive law, attempted a test of this thesis by obtaining responses to statements about civil and criminal violations of Office of Price Administration meat regulations. He interviewed a sample of meat wholesalers and the general public. Most of the results lend support to the thesis. The public disapproved of civil violations significantly more than did the meat dealers, though both strongly disapproved of criminal violations. This was interpreted to mean that civil law is an index of social differentiation, while criminal law reflects generally accepted values or social similarity.[78]

In Durkheim's work the idea is at least implicit that some societies are characterized entirely by mechanical solidarity and others entirely by the organic type. Interestingly, Hartung assumed that our society has some of both types, and that criminal law and civil law reflect the two. His study merits repetition with reference to other categories of criminal and civil law, and suggests such further questions as these: (1) can law and law-breaking in some way provide an index of the *amount* of solidarity as well as the type? (2) what are the various forms of social solidarity in our present society? (3) what is the relation of the proportion of mechanical and organic solidarity to the effectiveness of civil law and criminal law? Admittedly, these are extremely general questions, especially at the present stage of demonstrated knowledge in this area.

Korn and McCorkle reach a conclusion that seems contradictory to Durkheim's. Primitive peoples, they say, rely on the individual to enforce social norms upon himself and try to keep him within the influence of the group, unless the ultimate sanction of physical expulsion becomes necessary. Modern political communities have penal controls that psychologically expel the person from the group although physically he remains within it.[79] The type of group unity is not made explicit, but this would seem to mean that societies with organic solidarity are the ones that develop penal law. Any successful attempt to resolve these apparently conflicting views must recognize more than two types of social solidarity; the problem is to learn what kinds of law are produced by various types of social organization. . . . Korn and McCorkle's first category, for example, seems to be limited to the kin-organized society.

Law and Ethics

A number of explanations of the relationship between law and ethics have been

[77] E. Durkheim, *On the Division of Labor in Society,* The Macmillan Co., New York, 1933, Chaps. 1–3; Stone, *op. cit.,* pp. 471–484; also see the brief discussion of Durkheim in Chapter 1.
[78] Frank E. Hartung, "Common and Discrete Group Values," 28 *Journal of Social Psychology* (1953), 3–22.
[79] Korn and McCorkle, *op. cit.,* pp. 76–83.

put forth. For the purpose of discussing this matter, ethics and morals will be used as synonyms and will mean any principles of right conduct. Except for Timasheff,[80] there seems to be general agreement that law and ethics are different. Though there is an overlap, many rules of law are unrelated to rules of morality. If acts that are considered immoral do not directly harm other people, the law may ignore them; conversely, the law may proscribe acts that threaten society even though they are not considered immoral. Legal rules are frequently adopted merely for the sake of expediency, as means to reach certain ends.[81]

It has been argued that it is not the function of law to impose a moral code, that law prescribes rules for overt behavior to be followed regardless of one's thoughts and feelings, while moral codes are to be followed out of personal conviction. Furthermore, the argument runs, laws should be scrupulously kept out of the moral area in our multigroup society with its variety of moral codes; no moral code should be controlled by law unless its practice infringes upon the practice by other groups of theirs.[82] Perhaps no one would contend that law should be strictly separated from those moral rules that are *generally* accepted in the political community, however, such as "Thou shalt not kill." If the view that lawmaking and law-interpreting involve value integration is sound . . . much of law cannot be far removed from the realm of ethics.

Some of law reflects the adoption of particular moral precepts, and the concern for justice shows the general influence of ideas about right and wrong.

Ethical considerations are involved to a considerable degree in laws regarding social welfare and the rehabilitation of persons.[83] Law has been referred to as the "ethical minimum." [84] Perhaps ethics are most involved in the area of criminal law, which is invoked on behalf of the general welfare. Some of criminal law, notably that concerning the personal vices such as homosexuality, reflects legislative adoption of moral standards for situations that do not directly harm other people. Whether it is a question of criminal or civil law, according to Dror in the following statement, law enforcement rests on moral consensus:

In general it seems that, other things being equal, legal norms which are in accord with extralegal norms are more realized in actual behavior than legal norms which are neutral from the point of view of ethical and religious norms, and legal norms which are neutral from the point of view of ethical and religious norms are more realized in actual behavior than legal norms which contradict ethical and religious norms.[85]

Legal Specialists

The specialized roles that are defined in a formal organization constitute a major part of its structure, and the ways these roles are played are crucial in its operation. Legal specialists have been called craftsmen by Llewellyn, who suggests that they are culture-carriers, and that the concepts of craft and craftsmen should be major tools in the institutional analysis of law. He calls for study of the skills, traditions, ideals, organization, morale, and recruiting practices of these crafts.[86] The key legal specialists [are] the members of the legal profession. . . .

80 Timasheff, *op. cit.,* pp. 68–77, 135–154. He treats customs, laws, and morals as the three types of ethics; law is included because it involves rules of conduct, and such rules imply oughtness. This usage of ethics makes it synonymous with all group-supported rules of conduct.
81 E. A. Ross, *Social Control: A Survey of the Foundations of Order,* The Macmillan Co., New York, 1901, pp. 74, 411; Weber, *op. cit.,* p. 7.
82 MacIver, *The Web of Government,* pp. 325–326.

83 Bernard, *op. cit.,* pp. 566–570.
84 Wolff, *op. cit.,* pp. 27-28; C. A. Ellwood, *The Psychology of Human Society,* Appleton-Century-Crofts, New York, 1925, pp. 396–401.
85 Dror, *op. cit.,* p. 447.
86 Llewellyn, *op. cit.,* p. 458.

SUMMARY

Law is one means of accomplishing the process of social control—that is, influencing subgroups and persons to conform to group expectations. Law is defined in this book as the formal means of social control that involves the use of rules that are interpreted, and are enforceable, by the courts of a political community. This definition includes legal rules but also encompasses the agencies and procedures by which the rules are created, applied, and enforced. Law is formal social control because it utilizes explicit rules of conduct, planned sanctions, and designated specialists. Both formal and informal controls are used in modern, multigroup societies, but the former become increasingly important as the social structure grows more complex.

A political community exists when order is maintained among the inhabitants of a territory by the use or threat of force, the state being the supreme political community. The state's power is limited, but it does have a near monopoly of power, and this force stands behind the operations of the courts of law. Since there is no international political community, international law is not law in the full sense as defined here. There are many ways of classifying law, three of which have been discussed in this chapter.

Legal instrumentalities are social institutions and thus are part of the social organization, and of culture. Legal agencies influence other institutions and are influenced by them. Attempts have been made, with some success, to demonstrate that law is an index of values and of the type of social solidarity. Some of law shows the influence of ethics, but much of it seems unrelated to moral precepts. The roles of legal specialists are of central importance in the institutional analysis of law.

TOWARD A COMPARATIVE
DEFINITION OF LAW

Ronald L. Akers

Although American criminology has produced few cross-cultural studies, some criminologists have seen the potential value of comparative analysis to the development of universally valid generalizations about the nature of crime.[1] In the sociology of law also, there is need for comparative work to answer theoretical and practical questions about the growth of legal institutions and the place of law in society. Before the diversity of legal forms can be treated comparatively, however, it is necessary to define law in terms that are applicable to all or most societies. This paper begins the task by applying one possible minimum definition of law to a primitive tribe of the Philippines, the Kalingas, and then suggesting a modification of the definition on the basis of actual cases in that society.

DEFINITION, CLASSIFICATION, AND THE COMPARATIVE METHOD

Criminologists can learn much from social anthropology about the comparative method, which was the cornerstone of Radcliffe-Brown's "natural science of

society."[2] The comparison of many societies reveals the underlying patterns in the diverse and complex variations in human behavior. Ethnographic materials are the basis of comparison, but comparative studies do not proceed directly from ethnographic descriptions. For the perception of patterns and fruitful comparison, there must be classification of the various aspects of whole systems.[3]

Law is the aspect under consideration here; and it is part of the larger system of pressures toward conformity and attempts to prevent deviation from social norms that are termed "social control."[4] The questions that must be answered as a prelude to adequate comparative studies are: (1) What part of the system of social control is law and what part custom; and (2) What is a legal norm and sanction as distinct from other norms and sanctions? For comparative purposes, law must be separated from other kinds of social control.

The classification must start with a search for the essential elements of law among the diverse legal procedures and other forms of social control in many societies. A minimum definition incorporating these elements would then be a first step toward understanding underlying uniformities in law and law-violation and toward meaningful comparisons of legal institutions among primitive, folk, and modern peoples. The difficulty of studying law cross-culturally has been precisely this lack of clarity about the class of behavior or the part of the whole meant by the term "law."

Reprinted by the permission of the *Journal of Criminal Law, Criminology, and Police Science* (published by Northwestern University School of Law), **56** (September, 1965), pp. 301–306, © 1965.

This is a revision of a paper prepared for a seminar in Social Anthropology under the direction of Dr. Marion Pearsall. Grateful acknowledgement is made to Dr. Pearsall for her invaluable criticisms, suggestions and editing of the paper in various stages of preparation, especially the final stage. Any shortcomings of course remain my responsibility.

[1] Clinard, *Criminological Research,* in Merton (Editor), *Sociology Today* 509–535 (1958).

[2] Radcliffe-Brown, *Preface* to Fortes & Evans-Pritchard (Editors) *African Political Systems* xiii (1950).

[3] *Ibid.,* vii.

[4] Davis, *Society and the Law* 39–61 (1962).

With greater clarity about the class of phenomena to be considered under law, important theoretical questions can be asked. For instance, we may hypothesize that law becomes more important as a social control as technological development increases, but only if we know what is meant by law. If the definition includes all sanctioning and enforcing devices, the statement is doubtful and too diffuse to test readily. On the other hand, if the definition includes only the kind of legal machinery found in advanced societies, the hypothesis is a tautology.

Or we may ask other questions. Is there a linear relation between law and technological development, or do some pastoral societies perhaps have more complex legal systems than some of the relatively advanced agricultural societies? How are size and density of population and other demographic factors related to law? What is the relation between law and other substructures of society, and what variations are there from one society to another? Is law more systematically organized with tightly-knit kinship systems or with loosely-knit ones? Does law vary with the relative importance of kinship and territory as bases for social structure? What is the relation between supernatural sanctions and legal sanctions? How do the range of legal norms and rates of offenses vary in different societies? And many more.

These are comparative questions of theoretical importance to comparative law. The answers depend upon the definition of law; and the purpose of this paper is to develop a widely applicable, theoretically sound classifying definition. It is recognized that no concept dealing with the vagaries of human behavior can have completely neat, exact, mutually exclusive categories. Nevertheless, there is need for a definition that minimizes confusion and borderline cases while allowing for a sufficiently wide range of behavior to include all or most societies. Too narrow a concept would exclude too many societies while too broad a concept would not permit clear delineation of a class of behavior in any society; either would limit the extent to which meaningful comparisons could be made.

The plea made here for a precise definition of law should not obscure the fact that for some purposes such a definition is unnecessary, irrelevant, or even an impediment. If the interest is in social control in general, the distinction between legal and other norms is not necessary. Similarly, where law is studied as part of political structure, the distinction between law and custom may be unnecessary or of only secondary concern. Nor is the sort of minimum definition proposed here necessarily relevant for the study of law and law violation in a single society or between societies with very similar, perhaps historically related, legal institutions. It is at the point of asking comparative questions about law in a whole range of varied societies that a minimum yet precise definition of legal behavior is essential.

We can begin defining law by saying that it differs from many other social controls in being *external, formal,* and *negative.*

Social controls are both internal and external. Observance of the law by most members of a society may be largely a matter of controls internalized in the course of socialization. However, no social control system depends entirely on internal controls. There are always imperfect or incomplete internalizations, and external controls are invoked both directly and indirectly.[5] One characteristic of law is that its enforcement is predicated primarily upon the external application of sanctions.

Some norms are informally understood customs carrying customary, informal, or diffuse sanctions. Others are formal, ex-

[5] Nye, *Family Relationships and Delinquent Behavior* 5–8 (1958).

plicitly stated, and often written; they carry regular, organized, and specifically applied sanctions. Legal norms and sanctions are of the latter, formal type.[6]

Lastly, in the sense that legal sanctions include punishment for delict rather than reward for right behavior, they are negative. In law no provision is made to reward the obedient; there is only negative reaction to lawbreakers.

These characteristics are not sufficient for distinguishing legal behavior. External controls serve other institutions also. Many norms are formal, and many negative sanctions occur outside the law. The definition must be further refined.

In modern civilized societies it is possible to define norms as laws if sanctions are applied for their violation by a legally constituted court set up by the political state.[7] Similar formulations are possible for those non-literate societies with formal systems of social control and readily recognizable courts,—many of the African tribal societies, for example. But such definitions are of no use in distinguishing between custom and law in societies which are not "states" or "political communities" and which have no easily recognized courts. For comparative purposes, a definition is needed that satisfactorily classifies law and custom in primitive societies while remaining applicable to Western society.

Several students of primitive society have attempted such definitions. Malinowski, for example, states that, "The rules of law stand out from the rest in that they are left and regarded as the obligations of one person and the rightful claim of another."[8] Driberry suggests that, ". . . law comprises all those rules of conduct which regulate the behavior of indi-

viduals and communities."[9] Their definitions are certainly too broad. Are not table manners also rules of conduct that regulate behavior? What is the difference between the informal mutual obligations and claims of brothers, spouses, or business partners and those required by law?

Hoebel has more recently proposed a concept that seems broad enough to apply to many societies but narrow enough to distinguish between law and other kinds of norms and sanctions.[10] He identifies *privileged force, official authority,* and *regularity* as the common elements; and of these, the *sine qua non* of law is, "the legitimate use of physical coercion by a socially authorized agent."[11] The force may be actual or implied but must be for legitimate cause. Physical coercion otherwise is feud, vendetta, abuse, gangsterism, or something else—not law.

Hoebel's emphasis on force resembles Weber's "coercive apparatus" in readiness for norm enforcement.[12] The coercion need not be applied, but the probability of its application must be recognized. Also, the enforcing agency need not be the judicial bodies familiar to the West.[13] In Hoebel's terms, *no special* agency is needed; the coercive agent may change with the offense. Moreover, the authority to exercise legal sanctions may be allocated to the offended person or his kin group. Indeed, he maintains that this is a principal characteristic of law in primitive societies.

The present study starts with Hoebel's concept, examines it with reference to one primitive society, and suggests modifications in the light of that examination. The approach is the simple one of trying to classify as law or custom, according to

[9] A definition by J. H. Driberry quoted in Hoebel, *The Law of Primitive Man* (1954).
[10] *Ibid.,* 26.
[11] *Ibid.,* 28.
[12] Weber, *Law in Economy and Society* (Translated by Shils and Rheinstein) 13 (1954).
[13] Weber, *Basic Concepts in Sociology* (Translated by Secher) 77 (1962).

[6] Radcliffe-Brown, *Structure and Function in Primitive Society* 206–208 (1959).
[7] Davis, *op. cit., supra* note 4, at 41.
[8] Malinowski, *Crime and Custom in Savage Society* 55 (1959).

Hoebel's definition, the cases reported in Barton's *The Kalingas*.[14] If the definition is useful for comparative purposes, it should differentiate between law and custom in the society with a minimum of confusion. If it does not, its utility may be questioned. If it does, its applicability may be tentatively accepted pending further testing in different societies.

KALINGA CUSTOM AND LAW

Hoebel's definition affirms that norms are identified as law at the point of their breach. If the breach is met with force, in threat or in fact, by a socially recognized agent, the norm is a law. Thus, use of his definition requires identification of socially authorized coercion. It is necessary to ascertain the sanctioning agents and determine whether their exercise of coercive sanctions is socially approved; that is, is the agent's right to apply such sanctions recognized by members of the societal group, including the offender?

In the case of the Kalingas, offenses are liable to retaliation by the offended person or his kinsmen even when a third person intervenes as discussed below. Also, the principle of collective responsibility may extend the application of sanctions to relatives of the offender up to third cousins. In theory and often in practice, the whole kin group is the unit of legal action and responsibility; but there is a tendency to center responsibility on the actual offender or his closest relatives. In addition to the kin group, three types of "third persons", or special agents of norm enforcement, figure prominently in the cases: the *pangat;* the *mangi-ugud;* and the "pact-holder."

The *pangat* are community leaders who

14 Barton, *The Kalingas: Their Institutions and Custom Law* (1949). All information about the Kalingas presented in this paper is taken from this book. Reference is to the native system which at the time the field work was done (1930's) was still functioning as a separate entity alongside the American system.

have emerged through a long process of proving their worth. Their authority is far from absolute; but they perform important functions, especially peace making and mediation. They are called on to discover the culprit in cases of theft, property damage, wounding, and the like as well as to settle both major and minor disputes. The *pangat's* services may be requested by the offended person or his kinsmen; but usually it is the offender's kin who, fearing retaliation, request one or two *pangat* to make peace proposals for them. In some instances, the offender himself calls the *pangat*. In disputes of various sorts, either side may call the *pangat;* or he may be called by persons other than the disputants who wish a peaceful settlement of the disturbance.

In the most serious rivalries, a formal truce is declared and the *pangat* in the case appoint *mangi-ugud,* or go-betweens for each side. In woundings and killings, there are usually two go-betweens appointed for each side; but in adultery cases there is usually only one, who is sent by the offender. The *mangi-ugud* is usually also a *pangat,* though this is not an essential requirement. However, he should possess the leadership qualities of a *pangat*.

If a truce is broken while negotiations are in progress, the *mangi-ugud* has both the right and the duty to kill or wound the violator. According to the Hoebel definition, truce breaking is clearly a law-violation. There is full social approval for the physical coercion exercised by the go-between in such cases. The sanction may exist more as a threat than an actuality, however, as Barton was unable to find actual instances of this use of legal force.

Although the go-between is the only agent with the unqualified right of execution in intratribal disputes, his role on the whole is less important than that of the *pangat* since go-betweens are rarely used. On the other hand, the *pangat* has a relatively permanent position and is consulted in many matters. Moreover, the *pangat* is backed by real legal sanctions; it takes a brave soul to question his decisions in regard to the paying of fines or other forms of retribution. His decisions are supported by public opinion and by the considerable power that resides in the *pangat* and his whole extended kin group. The decreed punishment is further backed by the potential force of the offended party.

There is some doubt about the legality of retaliation by a kin group on its own. Following Hoebel, the sanctioning agent must have social approval. The *pangat* and the *mangi-ugud* have that approval; and in their roles there is at least an incipient tendency to establish a class of personnel with a public mandate to intervene and to adjudicate—thus approaching Weber's conception of law. But the same cannot be said when a kin group acts to avenge a wrong done to one of its members.

If there is some uncertainty about law and law enforcement within a given tribal region, there is little doubt that law and legal machinery occur at the inter-regional level. There are peace pacts between several regions, and each region has several "pact-holders." Indeed, most of Barton's cases are cases of pact violation. However, kinship and intratribal structure remain important in inter-regional contacts; and most pact-holders are *pangat* or nearly so in their own region. In fact, possessing one or more pacts is a means to becoming a *pangat*. In addition to general acceptance, the pact-holder must have the approval of the *pangat* in both communities involved in the pact. The *pangat* thus have veto powers over pact-holders.

The pact-holder supervises relations between his home region and the other pact region and is expected to enforce the terms of the pact. He must investigate offenses by members of his group against anyone in the other region and mete out punishment to offenders or their rela-

tives. Failure in this duty leads to disgrace for himself and his family and may result in a broken peace pact. Punishment usually takes the form of indemnification. If the offense is that of killing or wounding, however, the pact-holder must either (1) kill or wound the offender or one of his kin, or (2) collect fines both for the relatives of the offended person and for himself (as a pact-holder he stands in a fictitious kinship relation to the corresponding pact-holder in the other region).

When the pact-holder exercises his right of execution he often, though not always, pays "wergild" to the victim's kin, which casts some doubt on the degree to which his authority to exact punishment is publicly acknowledged. Yet the pact-holder has a clearer mandate than the go-between, who never pays for his executions. The pact-holder is selected publicly while the go-between is simply appointed by the *pangat* for a particular case. Barton maintains that both have the right of legal execution since "both are agents of the regional unit, of the police power of a budding state." [15] In Hoebel's terms also, their authorization by society to apply such sanctions makes both legal executioners.

Having identified the sanctioning agents and their degree of social approval, we turn now to the problem of classifying Kalinga norms as law or custom.

Some of Barton's cases are clearly custom rather than law; that is, they do not involve real or implied physical sanctions as a rule. Relations between men and their mistresses, for example, follow custom. Neither the mistress nor her children can legally enforce demands on the man, and she is free to accept or reject *his* demands. By custom a man should take care of his mistress, provide for her in illness, avenge her injuries, and leave a little something to their children. But

15 *Ibid.*, 199.

no legal sanctions compel him in these matters; no threat of force is involved, and he is subject only to the informal pressures of their kin groups to do what is "right." (See Barton, Case 17).[16]

Custom also governs broken engagement contracts. When either family breaks such a contract, the other family is usually reimbursed for expenses incurred during the engagement. But there is no threat or use of force; the reimbursement is simply the "genteel" way to soothe the injured pride of the jilted party. Other customary norms are invoked in cases of parental forcing of a marriage, divorce, parent-child relations in various conflicts, certain boundary regulations, and many other situations.

A number of the cases illustrate norms that seem to lie on the border between custom and law according to our definition. In childless marriages, for instance, the norm is for husband and wife to retain separate rights to the property each brought to the marriage; and neither may use the other's propetry without permission. (Case 7) In breaches of this norm, the offended party may call on his (or her) kin to punish the offender. But his threat or use of force does not go unchallenged since the offender may in turn call on relatives to fight back. Community recognition of the right to enforce the norm is thus not complete. At the same time, the norm borders on law since the offense is recognized as a theft; and the offender usually offers indemnity, thus acknowledging, however grudgingly, the other party's right to exact retribution. The theft of small objects from non-relatives is also a border-line example. Such thefts are often settled informally by simple restitution; but at other times, *pangat* and even go-betweens are called and indemnity exacted.

16 The case of law and custom among the Kalingas listed by Barton are numbered consecutively. References to cases here are by number and appear in parentheses in the text.

Rape cases also involve norms which, using the present definition, it is difficult to assign certainly to law or custom. (Cases 102, 103, 104) The Kalingas consider rape impossible since they believe the cooperation of the woman is necessary to achieve penetration. Yet they recognize that a woman can be terrorized into submitting, in which case she and her kin group may retaliate or demand indemnity. Their right of coercive punishment is not fully acknowledged, however. Not only may no indemnity be forthcoming, but they in turn may face retaliation.

Even in serious cases of wounding and killing, the definition does not permit clearcut classification in all instances. The offending party may offer "wergild." If this were accepted without further action or if retaliation on the offending group ended the affair, we might say law was involved. Unfortunately, acceptance of wergild does not insure an end to hostilities. Retaliation may still be resorted to, leading to more retaliation from the other group and eventually to a full-fledged blood feud. (Case 79) Other cases also illustrate the tenuousness of the right to exact regularized and fully accepted punishment. (Cases 3, 20, 22, 30, 31, 63, 88, *et passim*) Thefts, failure to pay debts, wounding and killing, rape, and other acts are breaches of accepted norms; but they do not confer on the injured party an unequivocal right to apply physical force in punishment. Hence we cannot say without reservation that the norms involved are laws by our definition. They may be on the way to becoming laws since wergild frequently is accepted as ample payment and no further retaliation occurs, but at present their status is uncertain.

A more clearly legal norm states that one must not violate *apa,* a temporary injunction against using an unowned place within the region where a relative has died. An *apa* on a location applies to all until it is lifted, and the right to declare a place *apa* is sanctioned by public opinion. In practice, only men with sufficient power to enforce it ever invoke *apa;* but the fact that they are privileged to use force for this purpose suggests that a legal norm is involved. (Cases 22, 23, 24, 25, 27)

Adultery seems to be a special type of law-violation. Adultery is a crime of unfaithful wives only, and a husband may divorce such a wife. For her part, the wife has no claim to her husband's fidelity; and so long as he philanders with unmarried women, no point of law is involved. An aggrieved husband, however, may kill the adulterer on the spot if caught *in flagrante;* or he may accept indemnity from the man. In neither punishment is he ordinarily aided by his kin, which makes adultery something of a special and private case. But public opinion supports the husband as the punishing agent.

Truce breaking during negotiations is clearly illegal by our definition since the go-between has the socially approved power to execute the violator. Another class of truly legal norms surround the peace pacts since pact-holders are authorized to enforce the provisions of the pact which may include boundary definitions, guarantees of neutrality, guarantees of services and safety to visitors in the territory, and other general and specific items. The pacts also charge the pact-holder to recover lost or stolen goods, facilitate the collection of debts, and procure indemnities and revenge where members of his own region have offended persons in the other region.

Many of the offenses which are ambiguous in nature at the regional, or tribal level are clearly offenses against legal norms when the parties involved come from different regions united by peace pacts. The socially authorized agent is the pact-holder who has the ultimate power of physical force in enforcing the provisions of the pact. (Cases 49, 51, 57, 58, 59, 82, *et passim*)

DISCUSSION AND CONCLUSION

The foregoing attempt to apply Hoebel's definition of law to the classification of norms in a particular primitive society indicates some need for modification. Difficulties and confusion arose especially in cases where the "socially authorized agent" of coercion was the offended person himself or his kin group. A definition that allows the real or implied physical force to be exercised by the injured party seems too broad to be useful. At least for the Kalinga data, it becomes ambiguous where kin groups have some sanction for punishing offenders against their members but not enough to protect them from retaliation by the original offender's kin group. Another formulation seems in order; namely:

A social norm is law if its breach is met by physical force or the threat of physical force in a socially approved and regular way by a socially authorized third person.

"Third person" is a generic term for persons or agencies other than the offender and offended or their relatives—unless the kinship role is transcended by an "official" role as is the case with the *pangat,* go-betweens, and pact-holders among the Kalingas. Furthermore, the third person need not apply the force directly himself. He may use others, including the offended and his kin group to exact punishment; but when they apply such sanctions, it must be at the direction of the third person. Lastly, the authorized agent need not stand in constant readiness to enforce norms, as Weber would have it; he may be simply a person who is sometimes called on to settle disputes or adjudicate other cases. At the same time, he must be more than a mediator; his decisions should be respected and considered binding by both parties. Socially sanctioned physical coercion is still the essential ingredient, but it must be authorized by someone other than the offended person or group.

Following the proposed definition would lead to the conclusion that some societies have no law. These societies would have no place in comparative law, but their number is probably not great. The gain in clarity far offsets the loss of range in social forms. Radcliffe-Brown would limit the definition even more:

> . . . the field of law will therefore be regarded as coterminous with that of organized legal sanctions. The obligations imposed on individuals in societies where there are no legal sanctions will be regarded as matters of custom and convention but not of law; in this sense some simple societies have no law, although all customs are supported by sanctions.[17]

One further point may be made. The definition suggested here opens the way to systematic study of linkages between legal and political systems, which are often considered together.[18] The third person may well also be an administrator of political, economic, military, legislative, ritual, and other public affairs; or the third person may be an agent or agency of the political organization assigned specifically to judicial duties. Whatever the relation, attention to it opens up other theoretical problems. For instance, more detailed study of the enforcing roles of *pangat,* go-between, and pact-holder among the Kalingas might show that their interrelations form an incipient political structure based on both kinship and territory.

---

[17] Radcliffe-Brown, *Structure and Function in Primitive Society, op. cit., supra* note 6, at p. 212.

[18] Peristiany, "Law" in *The Institutions of Primitive Society* 39 (1956).

part two

SOCIAL AND POLITICAL FORCES ON THE LAW: LAW AS DEPENDENT

The central theoretical issue in the study of law and society is the nature of interrelationships between law and other institutions and normative systems in society. The question "What is the relationship between law and social order?" as Gibbs (1966:315) notes, is part of the "grand tradition" in the sociology of law (see also Schur, 1968:10–11). Do the values embodied in the law always flow from the prevailing moral sentiments and values of society (i.e., extralegal normative systems), or can it induce changes in them? Is law shaped by the past and current nature of economic, political, educational, familial, and other social institutions, or does the law penetrate these institutions and create changes in them? Is law simply a function of the past prevailing power relationship and the outcome of the political conflict of vying groups in society, or does the law and its instrumentalities determine the nature of those group relationships and oversee the conflict moving it toward just conclusions and compromises? Do people comply with the law because a norm has become incorporated into it and legal sanctions are applied to enforce or does normative compliance proceed entirely on the basis of extralegal contingencies? The sensible answer to these and similar questions is, of course, that law is both an *independent* and *dependent* variable in society; it is *interdependent* with other systems in society. Law is both shaped by and has an independent impact on society; it grows out of and is consistent with extant normative structures and can also influence them to change in one direction or another.

However, it is possible to separate the two questions and examine the social determinants of the formation and implementation of law on the one hand and delineate the impact of law on society on the other hand. Part Two presents some major theoretical and empirical issues in analyzing law as the dependent variable. In this part we shall be concerned mainly with the emergence, change, and operation of law in general. The social influences on the actual behavior of the actors in the formal organizations set up to enforce the law is considered in Part Three which is directed toward presenting the dynamics of the organizations and roles of the law in action. In Part Four we return to the question of law as the independent variable.

There are two general questions in the study of how the formation and enforcement of the law is shaped by other societal forces. First, there is the general question of how law comes to exist as a separate and increasingly specialized institution of social control in society. Second, there is the problem of explaining how law comes to have the normative content it does, is implemented in the way it is, and how these things change.

THE EMERGENCE AND FORM OF LAW IN SOCIETY

There seems to be general agreement in the literature that law emerges when the social structure of a society becomes complex enough that social control and dispute settlement cannot be based entirely on the informal mechanisms of custom and private settlement. Formal control develops when informal control alone is not effective (Schwartz, 1954). As the unifying organization of society moves from that based on kinship and tribe to territorially based political organization, as the economy becomes more diversified and industrialized, and other social institutions become more stratified and specialized, the content of the laws and the structure of the legal system become more complex (see Davis, 1962; Jeffery, 1962; Chambliss and Seidman, 1971).

Law as defined here, as formal social control exercised by and reliant ultimately on the coercive power of the political state, obviously does not exist except in those societies sufficiently complex that there are differentiated political institutions. But the generalization linking legal forms and societal complexity seems to hold even when a broader conception of law such as that given by Akers (1965) in Part One is used. The proposition that the more complex the society the more differentiated the "third party" legal roles are is supported by Schwartz and Miller (1964) in the first article reprinted in this part. Although they do not attempt to locate the level of societal complexity at which distinctive legal norms as such emerge, Schwartz and Miller do find that the system of legal roles is more specialized in the more complex societies.

Durkheim (1964) proposed that the form of legal control is a function of the level of societal diversity or complexity. His thesis is that in societies with "mechanical solidarity" (the less complex societies whose members are integrated through their cultural and functional sameness), the sanctions for crimes are "repressive" or especially punitive. When social integration is achieved through "organic solidarity" (the most socially diverse societies which are integrated through functional interdependence), the legal sanctions are aimed at restitution. Schwartz and Miller (1964) note that in so far as the presence of police roles indicates "repressive" sanctions, their findings do not support Durkheim's theory. Chambliss and Seidman also disagree with Durkheim's contentions. They propose that the legal system in more complex and stratified societies develops out of dispute settlement in which the principle is "winner take all"; hence the control comes to emphasize rule-enforcement and is more punitive than the system in less complex societies which develops out of dispute settlement guided by the principle of "give a little, take a little" and is directed toward reconciliation (Chambliss and Seidman, 1971:33–35). It should be noted in support of Durkheim, however, that the trend in the increasingly complex industrialized societies has been away from harsh punitive enforcement of the law and toward the rehabilitation of and restitution by the offender to society.

Weber (1954) saw an increasing rationality in the "legal thought" of the economically advanced and complex Western societies. In various historical and traditionalist societies the form of legal justice dispensed is based predominantly on irrational grounds (trial by ordeal, divine revelation, etc., or entirely on the individual case). Lawmaking and lawfinding in modern societies are characterized by "substantive" rationality (decisions made which seem just from the point of view of some extralegal belief system or ideology) or "formal" rationality. Formal rationality can be based on adherence to "external characteristics" (observable concrete features) of the facts of the case; but Weber perceived that Western law with its specialized professional roles of judges and lawyers is nearly unique in that it is also reliant on the "logical analysis of meaning" of abstract legal concepts and rules.

LAW IN THE POLITICAL STATE: CONFLICT AND CONSENSUS

Given the existence of a diversified, complex, and politically organized society with a clearly distinct legal system operated through specialized legal roles (which is the focus of this volume), the question of at what level of societal complexity does law emerge and take on certain characteristics is not the key question. Rather the problem of accounting for the actual content and operation of the law becomes paramount.

A number of writers have discerned that there are two major models or theoretical approaches to answering this question. The first of these views the law as growing out of normative *consensus* in society and serving the broad interests and functions of society as a whole. The other views law as formed out of the *conflict* of values and actions of various groups in society and reflecting the more narrow interests of groups and aggregates in society which successfully wield economic, social, and political power.

Chambliss refers to the two "as the 'value-expression' and the 'interest-group' hypotheses" (1969:8). Elsewhere he names the two models of society and law "value-consensus" and "value-antagonism" (Chambliss and Seidman, 1971:17, 40–52).

> The one [value-consensus model] assumes that at the bottom there is a funda-
> mental value-consensus in society which is reflected in the law-making, law-
> applying, and adjudicating machinery of the State. The other [value-antagonism
> model] proposes that control of the State and its awesome machinery of com-
> pulsion is itself the prize for which antagonistic interests struggle [Chambliss
> and Seidman, 1971:17].

Similarly, Quinney contrasts the "consensus" and "conflict" models (1969: 20–25; 1970:8–13), and Hills says that:

> The *value-consensus* position basically asserts that criminal laws reflect those
> societal values which transcend the immediate, narrow interests of various indi-
> viduals and groups, expressing the social consciousness of the whole society. The
> legal norms embodied in the criminal codes emerge through social change in
> response to the needs and requirements essential for the well-being of the entire
> society. . . . In sharp contrast, the exponents of the *interest-group* approach
> . . . [emphasize] the ability of particular groups to shape the legal system to
> serve their needs and safeguard their particular interests. . . . Power, coercion,
> and constraint, rather than the sharing of common values, are the basic or-
> ganizing principles of society in the interest-group perspective [Hills, 1971:3–4,
> italics in original].

The classic statement of the consensus explanation of law as a reflection of widely and deeply held societal norms is found in Sumner (1906). To Sumner the content of law is formed primarily by the incorporation of pre-vailing "folkways and mores"—unformed intuitive standards of right and wrong, crescively developed through time. While not immutable, the folk-ways and mores are persistent and slow to change; laws are made out of and support the extant mores but legislation cannot make new mores.[1] The views of Durkheim (1964), Ross (1901), Pound (1942), Ehrlich (1936), and Friedman (1959) are also representative of the consensus model.

The consensus model was more dominant in the early part of this century than it is now. Although there are those who attribute the existence of certain regulations to the functions they serve in the interest of society as a whole (e.g., Davis, 1966), current sociological thought is more closely attuned to the

---

[1] As Ball et al. (1962), remind us, however, Sumner should not be interpreted as proposing that all law comes from the mores or that law is entirely a dependent variable in society without any independent impact on social change; he felt only that law could not change the mores quickly or easily. Moreover, Sumner was aware of the conflict among the "antagonistic" mores of subgroups in society and that special interest of powerful groups become part of the law. (See Sumner, 1906; especially 39, 55, 109, 169, and 209)

conflict approach as represented by Chambliss (1969) and Quinney (1970), part of whose work is reprinted here as the third selection. (See also Vold, 1958; Quinney, 1969; Chambliss and Seidman, 1971; and Turk, 1969.)

Characterizing the two models in such an unqualified fashion is somewhat misleading, however, for the difference is mainly one of emphasis. The earlier theorists who stressed the law as the formal enactment of widely held norms and aimed toward overall societal purposes also recognized that it is often the enactment of only the norms and interests of specific groups in society. Similarly, those who take basically a conflict approach may also note that some laws are based on general consensual norms. This is understandable since it is clearly the case that law as it is now and will be in modern society results from both; it derives from both the norms for which there is widespread support and consensus and the norms supported primarily by certain social, political, and economic groups in society. Therefore, the question becomes the empirical one of the extent to which a particular law or public policy is in fact constructed or enforced in the service of society-wide or special interests.

Historical research such as that represented by Hall's (1952) study of theft law and Chambliss's (1964) study of vagrancy laws, reprinted here as the second selection, indicates that changes in some laws reflect changes in which *social class* is dominant in society or changes in the interests of that class. The existence of the whole range of "crimes without victims" (Schur, 1965) such as prohibition against drugs, prostitution, homosexuality, gambling, and alcohol can be interpreted as the legislation of the morality of a particular segment of the society, namely the dominant middle class. The original enactment of such laws was influenced by the political activity of groups acting on behalf of the values of the middle class. For example, Gusfield (1963) analyzes the temperance movement's political pressure in support of alcohol prohibition as "status politics." Similarly, the legislation constructing the juvenile court system and legally designating delinquency as specific juvenile status offenses also seems to have resulted from the political action of those who perceived their middle-class values threatened by the life styles of the foreign immigrants and lower-class families (Platt, 1969).

Whether or not these laws, in fact, produce behavioral compliance to the middle-class morality by everyone appears to be secondary. Rather they have the "symbolic function" of the public affirmation of middle-class morality (Gusfield, 1967, 1968; Duster, 1970; Hills, 1971). Thus, even though it is recognized that they are widely violated and regularly go unenforced, the repeal of these laws is vehemently resisted. There is some indication, however, that middle-class support of the moral sentiments expressed in legal prohibition of victimless behavior is weakening and as a result the enforcement of the laws is changing and the laws are being revised. For instance, a study among a middle-class population in the mid-sixties found that there was considerable support for liberalization of abortion policies; although there were still strong negative stereotypes of homosexuals, there was still majority support for easing the laws on homosexual behavior; there was not much support for liberalizing drug policies (Rooney and Gibbons, 1966). The years since have seen liberal reform of the abortion laws in many states and reform of the sodomy laws in some states. The drug policies are now beginning to be revised toward a less punitive policy. Punishment for marihuana offenses has been mitigated (Grupp and Lucas, 1970), and a National Commission (1972) has recommended that legal penalties be removed from the possession of marihuana for use. It may be that there has been a change in the attitudes of middle-class persons toward marihuana, although the 1972 Gallup Poll found that around four out of five of the general population still oppose legalization of marihuana.

Becker (1963) characterizes those who seek out legal support for their version of what is decent and right behavior as "moral entrepreneurs" and presents evidence that in the case of the Marihuana Tax Act the moral entrepreneur was a *governmental agency* itself, the Federal Bureau of Narcotics. Lindesmith (1967) traces the political activity of this same agency in the support of a punitive interpretation of the extant drug laws and the passage of new restrictive drug legislation. However, Dickson (1968) offers an alternative to Becker's interpretation of the FBN's crusade against marihuana, although he does not dispute the bureau's role as a political pressure group. Dickson argues that the narcotics bureau pursued the banning of marihuana as part of its effort to survive as a bureaucratic entity (in addition to whatever moral commitment to the cause individual members of the bureau may have felt).

Research in political science has provided sufficient evidence that in addition to class interests and the wishes of governmental bureaucracies, legislation and administration of the law are shaped by specific *organized pressure groups* representing business, labor, farm, religious, professional, and other groups (Truman, 1962; Zeigler, 1964). Not only the FBN was involved in the passage of the Marihuana Tax Act; the bill was modified before enactment into law to take into account the interests of the medical and pharmaceutical professions, hempseed oil manufacturers, and the birdseed industry (Becker, 1963). Similarly, Roby's (1969) study of the New York law on prostitution, which is reprinted here as the fifth selection in this part, found that in addition to various governmental agencies, the police, prosecutor, mayor's office, a number of other special interest groups such as segments of the business community, the hotel association, and the ACLU were involved in the political maneuverings surrounding the legislation and its enforcement. Akers' study (1968), reprinted here as the fourth selection, makes it clear that the legal regulation of professions are almost entirely an embodiment of the special interests of those professions.

Finally, the conflict may be among large *regions* of the country. The civil rights legislation represented not only the victory of scattered groups of integrationists but also to some extent reflect the greater political power of other regions over the South. Similarly, various trade and tariff laws reflect the economic interests not just of certain groups but also of regions.

All of this adds up to a preponderance of evidence in support of the conflict model as the one which comes closer to the realities of the making and enforcing of laws in modern society. Special interests and values are incorporated into the law not only by the direct political pressure of members of dominant social classes, regions, specific pressure groups, and agencies of the government itself, but also through the indirect incorporation of their values into decisions by actors in the legal system for whom these various groups serve as reference groups. Thus, it can almost be taken for granted that the law supports the norms of groups who have been politically successful. The unresolved issue then is not whether the law is most often the outcome of group conflict; rather it is whether the nature of that conflict is better described as the overwhelming and enduring dominance of a "power elite" or as the "pluralistic" conflict of many different groups with varying amounts of power, which are successful on certain issues and not influential on others, and none of which is all-powerful.

Rose (1967) concludes that the model which best fits empirical reality is one which depicts the American power structure in flux with a variety of power centers making shifting compromises and accommodations but not coalescing at the top into a monolithic all-powerful elite. Similarly, the third selection in this section is a reprint of Quinney's (1970) conflict perspective on group interests and power in the formulation, interpretation, and administration of law which is essentially a "pluralistic" model. Quinney's (1974a, 1974b) latest writings, however, have abandoned this view, and his theory is now clearly a Marxian model of class domination. While recognizing the significance of earlier pluralistic thinking, Quinney argues that critical thinking must go beyond this to

> . . . identify, following research on the power elite, a ruling class that imposes interests on the society in spite of some diversity of interests among groups. . . . Law is the tool of the ruling class. Criminal law, in particular is a device made and used by the ruling class to preserve the existing order. In the United States, the state—and its legal system—exists to secure and perpetuate the interests of the ruling class [1974b:10].

Thus, the conflict among many groups vying for influence on and control of the state and its legal machinery is just surface appearance; the conflict is at best innocuous competition among members of the ruling class who have already achieved complete control of the law and who operate it only to their own interests. The real conflict is between the ruling class and everybody else.

> It is according to the interests of the ruling class that American society is governed. Although pluralists may suggest that there are diverse and conflicting interests among groups in the upper class, what is ignored is that members of the ruling class work within a common framework in the formulation of public policy. Superficially, groups within the ruling class may differ on some issues. But in general they have common interests, and they can exclude members of the other classes from the political process entirely. . . . In contrast to pluralist

theory, radical theory notes that the basic interests, in spite of concrete differences, place the elite in a distinct ruling class.

> The primary interest of the ruling class is to preserve the existing capitalist order. In so doing, this class can protect its existential and material base. This is accomplished ultimately by means of the legal system. Any threats to the established order can be dealt with by invoking the final weapon of the ruling class, its legal system [1974b:20].

Much of Quinney's argument is ideological and philosophical. It offers a critique of American society and sociological theory of the law primarily from a Marxian-based view of what society should be. But the basic notion that it is one overwhelming more or less cohesive elite, which is synonymous with the ruling class with no other interest above the continuance of its own capitalist existence, which entirely determines the content and operation of the law may be considered a viable theory capable of empirical comparison with other theories.

Neither the more pluralistic nor the power elite conceptions deny the importance of power, domination, and conflict. And it is clear that whichever of the two models or some integration of them becomes the major sociological perspective it will fit reality more closely than a model which sees most or all laws coming from and operating in the interest of a broad normative consensus in society. To admit to the primary importance of power and conflict, however, does not deny any place to consensus and the broad public interest in the admixture of influences on the law. This position is recognized even by some conflict theorists:

> It would be a mistake to interpret the foregoing remarks [expounding a conflict interpretation of law] as meaning that all laws represent the interests of persons in power at the expense of persons less influential. In many cases there is no conflict whatsoever between those in power and those not. For most crimes against the person, such as murder, assault, and rape, there is consensus throughout society as to the desirability of imposing legal sanctions for persons who commit these acts. It is also true that *laws are passed which reflect the interests of the general population and which are antithetical to the interests of those in power* [Chambliss, 1969:10, italics added].

There can be little doubt that the core of the criminal law is designed to protect the life and property of everyone, although it may be differentially enforced against the less powerful groups in society. That core does represent a broad consensus in modern society on the undesirability of personal violence, theft, and destruction of property, fraud and other forms of predatory crimes against unwilling victims. As Sellin and Wolfgang (1964) show, there is agreement among diverse groups on what constitutes serious crime and this is congruent with what the law considers serious crime. Even in the areas of the criminal law which specify victimless, morals offenses, it is not certain that the legislated morality is adhered to only by those in the middle class. Similarly there is little normative conflict in the legal regulation of the flow of traffic on public roads, commerce, public health and safety, and so on. The laws designed to protect the environment, control pollution, solve the problems of depletion of natural resources, and deal with other ecological problems clearly accrue to the benefit of the whole society and reflect wide agreement on the necessity of doing so (although there remains disagreement over the most effective and proper means of handling the problem and over such specific issues as population control).

In any of these areas the actual passage and enforcement of the law may be pressed forward by specific groups, but they may claim to be acting, and in fact may be acting, on behalf of the "public interest." The type of collectivity included as an interest group in conflict theory, as we have seen, varies all the way from specified, well organized, and identified pressure groups to large, and ill-defined segments of the population. The values which they support may be those of a minority or of the majority. When the values given formal expression in the law are those of collectivities so diffuse that they become virtually synonymous with the values of the majority or the whole population of the society, it is not accurate to describe the process as one of interest groups winning out in a conflict of norms.

The studies reprinted in Part Two rightly emphasize the activities of interest groups as the main force in the changes in the law. However, a comprehensive explanation of the law must partake of both the consensus and conflict models. The politically powerful subunits of society at any given time can see to it that the law enhances their interests to a great extent, but the law also reflects the past, current, and changing functions and values of the whole society.

BIBLIOGRAPHY

AKERS, RONALD L., 1965. "Toward a Comparative Definition of Law," *Journal of Criminal Law, Criminology, and Police Science,* 56 (Sept.):301–6; 1968, "The Professional Association and the Legal Regulation of Practice," *Law and Society Review,* 3 (May):463–82.

BALL, HARRY V., and GEORGE O. SIMPSON, 1962. "Law and Social Change: Sumner Reconsidered," *American Journal of Sociology,* 67 (March):532–40.

BECKER, HOWARD S., 1963. *Outsiders.* New York: Free Press of Glencoe.

CHAMBLISS, WILLIAM J., 1964. "A Sociological Analysis of the Law of Vagrancy." *Social Problems,* 12 (Summer):67–77.

CHAMBLISS, WILLIAM J. (ed.), 1969. *Crime and the Legal Process.* New York: Mc-Graw-Hill.

CHAMBLISS, WILLIAM J. and ROBERT B. SEIDMAN, 1971. *Law, Order, and Power.* Reading, Mass.: Addison-Wesley.

DAVIS, F. JAMES, 1962. "Law in Operation," in F. James Davis, Harry H. Foster, C. Ray Jeffery, and E. Eugene Davis, *Society and the Law.* New York: Free Press of Glencoe.

DAVIS, KINGSLEY, 1966. "Sexual Behavior," in Robert K. Merton and Robert A. Nisbet, eds., *Contemporary Social Problems,* 2nd ed. New York: Harcourt, Brace, and World.

DICKSON, DONALD T., 1968. "Bureaucracy and Morality: an Organizational Perspective on a Moral Crusade," *Social Problems,* 16 (Fall):143:56.

DURKHEIM, EMILE, 1964. *The Division of Labor in Society.* Trans. by George Simpson, New York: Free Press.

DUSTER, TROY, 1970. *The Legislation of Morality: Law, Drugs, and Moral Judgment.* New York: Free Press.

EHRLICH, EUGENE, 1936. *Fundamental Principles of the Sociology of Law.* Trans. by Walter L. Moll, Cambridge: Harvard University Press.

FRIEDMANN, W., 1959. *Law in a Changing Society.* London: Stevens and Sons.

GIBBS, JACK P., 1966. "The Sociology of Law and Normative Phenomena," *American Sociological Review,* 31 (June):315–25.

GRUPP, STANLEY and WARREN C. LUCAS, 1970. "The 'Marijuana Muddle' as Reflected in California Arrest Statistics and Dispositions," *Law and Society Review,* 5 (November):251–70.

GUSFIELD, JOSEPH R., 1963. *Symbolic Crusade: Status Politics and the American Temperance Movement.* Urbana: University of Illinois Press; 1967, "Moral Passage: The Symbolic Process in Public Designation of Deviance," *Social Problems,* 15 (Fall):175–88; 1968, "On Legislating Morals: The Symbolic Process of Designating Deviance," *California Law Review,* 56:54–73.

HALL, JEROME, 1952. *Theft, Law and Society,* rev. ed. Indianapolis: Bobbs-Merrill.

HILLS, STUART L., 1971. *Crime, Power, and Morality: The Criminal-Law Process in the United States.* Scranton: Chandler Publishing Company.

JEFFERY, C. RAY, 1962. "Criminal Justice and Social Change," in F. James Davis, Harry H. Foster, C. Ray Jeffery, and E. Eugene Davis, *Society and the Law.* New York: Free Press of Glencoe.

LINDESMITH, ALFRED R., 1967. *The Addict and the Law.* New York: Vintage Books.

NATIONAL COMMISSION ON MARIHUANA AND DRUG ABUSE, 1972. *Marihuana: A Signal of Misunderstanding.* New York: New American Library.

PLATT, ANTHONY, 1969. *The Child Savers.* Chicago: University of Chicago Press.

POUND, ROSCOE, 1942. *Social Control through Law.* New Haven: Yale University Press.

QUINNEY, RICHARD (ed.), 1969. *Crime and Justice in Society.* Boston: Little, Brown; 1970, *The Social Reality of Crime.* Boston: Little, Brown; 1974a, *Critique of Legal Order: Crime Control in Capitalist Society.* Boston: Little, Brown; 1974b (ed.), *Criminal Justice in America: A Critical Understanding.* Boston: Little, Brown.

ROBY, PAMELA A., 1969. "Politics and Criminal Law: Revision of the New York State Penal Law on Prostitution," *Social Problems,* 17 (Summer):83–109.

ROONEY, ELIZABETH and DON C. GIBBONS, 1966. "Social Reactions to 'Crimes without Victims,'" *Social Problems,* 13 (Spring):400–410.

ROSE, ARNOLD, 1967. *The Power Structure: Political Process in American Society.* New York: Oxford University Press.

ROSS, EDWARD ALSWORTH, 1901. *Social Control.* New York: Macmillan Company.

SCHUR, EDWIN M., 1965. *Crimes without Victims.* Englewood Cliffs, N.J.: Prentice-Hall; 1968, *Law and Society: A Sociological View.* New York: Random House.

SCHWARTZ, RICHARD D., 1954. "Social Factors in the Development of Legal Control: A Case Study of Two Israeli Settlements," *Yale Law Journal,* 63 (February):471–91.

SCHWARTZ, RICHARD D. and JAMES C. MILLER, 1964. "Legal Evolution and Societal Complexity," *American Journal of Sociology,* 70 (September):159–69.

SELLIN, THORSTEN and MARVIN WOLFGANG, 1964. *The Measurement of Delinquency.* New York: JOHN Wiley & Sons.

SUMNER, WILLIAM GRAHAM, 1906. *Folkways: A Study of the Sociological Importance of Usages, Manners, Custom, Mores, and Morals.* Boston: Ginn and Company.

TRUMAN, DAVID, 1962. *The Governmental Process,* 8th ed. New York: Alfred A. Knopf.

TURK, AUSTIN T., 1969. *Criminality and Legal Order.* Chicago: Rand-McNally.

VOLD, GEORGE, 1958. *Theoretical Criminology.* New York: Oxford University Press.

WEBER, MAX, 1954. *Max Weber on Law in Economy and Society.* Edited by Max Rheinstein. Trans. by Edward Shils and Max Rheinstein. Cambridge: Harvard University Press.

ZEIGLER, HARMON, 1964. *Interest Groups in American Society.* Englewood Cliffs, N.J.: Prentice-Hall.

LEGAL EVOLUTION AND SOCIETAL COMPLEXITY

Richard D. Schwartz and James C. Miller [1]

The study of legal evolution has traditionally commended itself to scholars in a variety of fields. To mention only a few, it has been a concern in sociology of Weber [2] and Durkheim; [3] in jurisprudence of Dicey, [4] Holmes, [5] Pound, [6] and Llewellyn; [7] in anthropology of Maine [8] and Hoebel; [9] in legal history of Savigny [10] and Vinogradoff. [11]

There are theoretical and practical reasons for this interest. Legal evolution [12] provides an opportunity to investigate the relations between law and other major aspects and institutions of society. Thus Maine explained the rise of contract in terms of the declining role of kinship as an exclusive basis of social organization. Durkheim saw restitutive sanctions replacing repressive ones as a result of the growth of the division of labor and the corresponding shift from mechanical to organic solidarity. Dicey traced the growth of statutory law-making in terms of the increasing articulateness and power of public

Reprinted from *American Journal of Sociology,* **70** (September, 1964), 159–69, by permission of the authors and the University of Chicago Press.

[1] The authors are indebted to Arnold S. Feldman, Raoul Naroll, Terrence Tatje, and Robert F. Winch for their helpful comments on this paper. A grant from the Graduate School of Northwestern University aided in the completion of the work.

[2] Max Weber, *Law in Economy and Society,* ed. Max Rheinstein (Cambridge, Mass.: Harvard University Press, 1954). For a discussion and development of Weber's thinking on legal evolution, see Talcott Parsons, "Evolutionary Universals in Society," *American Sociological Review,* XXIX (June, 1964), 350–53.

[3] Émile Durkheim, *The Division of Labor in Society,* trans. George Simpson (Glencoe, Ill.: Free Press, 1947).

[4] A. V. Dicey, *Lectures on the Relation between Law and Public Opinion in England during the Nineteenth Century* (London: Macmillan Co., 1905).

[5] Oliver Wendell Holmes, Jr., *The Common Law* (Boston: Little, Brown & Co., 1881). Holmes's discussion of the place and limitations of historical analysis provides an appropriate background for the present study. "The law embodies the story of a nation's development through many centuries, and it cannot be dealt with as if it contained only the axioms and corollaries of a book of mathematics. In order to know what it is, we must know what it has been, and what it tends to become. But the most difficult labor will be to understand the combination of the two into new products at every stage. The substance of the law at any given time pretty nearly corresponds, so far as it goes, with what is then understood to be convenient; but its form and machinery, and the degree to which it is able to work out desired results depend very much on its past" (pp. 1–2). In stressing history as providing an explanation for procedure rather than substance, Holmes points to those aspects of legal development that—in the present

study at least—appear to follow highly uniform sequences of change.

[6] Roscoe Pound, "Limits of Effective Legal Action," *International Journal of Ethics,* XXVII (1917), 150–65; and *Outlines of Lectures on Jurisprudence* (5th ed.; Cambridge, Mass.: Harvard University Press, 1943). See also his *Interpretations of Legal History* (London: Macmillan Co., 1930).

[7] Karl N. Llewellyn, *The Common Law Tradition: Deciding Appeals* (Boston: Little, Brown & Co., 1960).

[8] Sir Henry Maine, *Ancient Law* (London: J. M. Dent, 1917).

[9] E. Adamson Hoebel, *The Law of Primitive Man* (Cambridge, Mass.: Harvard University Press, 1954).

[10] Frederick von Savigny, *Of the Vocation of Our Age for Legislation and Jurisprudence,* trans. Abraham Hayward (London: Littlewood & Co., 1831).

[11] Paul Vinogradoff, *Outlines of Historical Jurisprudence,* Vols. I and II (London: Oxford University Press, 1020–22).

[12] The term "evolution" is used here in the minimal sense of a regular sequence of change over time in a given type of unit, in this case, societies. This usage neither implies nor precludes causal links among the items in the sequence. For a discussion of diverse uses of, and reactions to, the term "evolution," see Sol Tax (ed.), *Issues in Evolution* (Chicago: University of Chicago Press, 1960).

opinion. Weber viewed the development of formal legal rationality as an expression of, and precondition for, the growth of modern capitalism.

For the most part, these writers were interested in the development of legal norms and not in the evolution of legal organization. The latter subject warrants attention for several reasons. As the mechanism through which substantive law is formulated, invoked, and administered, legal organization is of primary importance for understanding the process by which legal norms are evolved and implemented. Moreover, legal organization seems to develop with a degree of regularity that in itself invites attention and explanation. The present study suggests that elements of legal organization emerge in a sequence, such that each constitutes a necessary condition for the next. A second type of regularity appears in the relationship between changes in legal organization and other aspects of social organization, notably the division of labor.

By exploring such regularities intensively, it may be possible to learn more about the dynamics of institutional differentiation. Legal organization is a particularly promising subject from this point of view. It tends toward a unified, easily identifiable structure in any given society. Its form and procedures are likely to be explicitly stated. Its central function, legitimation, promotes crossculturally recurrent instances of conflict with, and adaptation to, other institutional systems such as religion, polity, economy, and family. Before these relationships can be adequately explored, however, certain gross regularities of development should be noted and it is with these that the present paper is primarily concerned.

This article reports preliminary findings from cross-cultural research that show a rather startling consistency in the pattern of legal evolution. In a sample of fifty-one societies, compensatory damages and mediation of disputes were found in every so-

ciety having specialized legal counsel. In addition, a large majority (85 per cent) of societies that develop specialized police also employ damages and mediation. These findings suggest a variety of explanations. It may be necessary, for instance, for a society to accept the principles of mediation and compensation before formalized agencies of adjudication and control can be evolved. Alternatively or concurrently, non-legal changes may explain the results. A formalized means of exchange, some degree of specialization, and writing appear almost universally to follow certain of these legal developments and to precede others. If such sequences are inevitable, they suggest theoretically interesting causative relationships and provide a possible basis for assigning priorities in stimulating the evolution of complex legal institutions in the contemporary world.

METHOD

This research employed a method used by Freeman and Winch in their analysis of societal complexity.[13] Studying a sample of forty-eight societies, they noted a Guttman-scale relationship among six items associated with the folk-urban continuum. The following items were found to fall in a single dimension ranging, the authors suggest, from simple to complex: a symbolic medium of exchange; punishment of crimes through government action; religious, educational, and government specialization; and writing.[14]

13 Linton C. Freeman and Robert F. Winch, "Societal Complexity: An Empirical Test of a Typology of Societies," *American Journal of Sociology*, LXII (March, 1957), 461–66.
14 This ordering has not been reproduced in other studies that followed similar procedures. Freeman repeated the study on another sample and included four of the six items used in the first study. They scaled in a markedly different order, from simple to complex: government specialization, religious specialization, symbolic medium of exchange, writing. The marked change in position of the first

To permit the location of legal characteristics on the Freeman-Winch scale, substantially the same sample was used in this study. Three societies were dropped because of uncertainty as to date and source of description [15] or because of inadequate material on legal characteristics.[16] Six societies were added, three to cover the legally developed societies more adequately [17] and

three to permit the inclusion of certain well-described control systems.[18]

Several characteristics of a fully developed legal system were isolated for purposes of study. These included counsel, mediation, and police. These three characteristics, which will constitute the focus of the present paper,[19] are defined as follows:

counsel: regular use of specialized non-kin advocates in the settlement of disputes

mediation: regular use of non-kin third party intervention in dispute settlement

police: specialized armed force used partially or wholly for norm enforcement.

These three items, all referring to specialized roles relevant to dispute resolution, were found to fall in a near-perfect Guttman scale. Before the central findings are described and discussed, several methodological limitations should be noted.

First, despite efforts by Murdock [20] and

---

and third items appears attributable to changes in definition for these terms (Linton C. Freeman, "An Empirical Test of Folk-Urbanism," [unpublished Ph.D. dissertation, Northwestern University, 1957], pp. 45, 49–50, 80–83). Young and Young studied all six items in a cross-cultural sample of communities, changing only the definition of punishment. Their ordering is somewhat closer to, but not identical with, that found by Freeman and Winch (*op. cit.*). From simple to complex, the items were ordered as follows: punishment, symbolic medium of exchange, governmental specialization, religious specialization, writing, educational specialization (Frank W. and Ruth C. Young, "The Sequence and Direction of Community Growth: A Cross-Cultural Generalization," *Rural Sociology*, XXVII [December, 1962], 374–86, esp. 378–79).

In the present study, we will rely on the Freeman-Winch ratings and orderings, since the samples overlap so heavily. The reader should bear in mind, however, that the order is tentative and contingent upon the specific definitions used in that study.

15 Southeastern American Negroes and ancient Hebrews.

16 Sanpoil.

17 Three societies—Cambodian, Indonesian, and Syrian—were selected from the Human Relations Area Files to increase the number of societies with counsel. The procedure for selection consisted of a random ordering of the societies in the Human Relations Area Files until three with counsel were located in geographically separate regions. These were then examined to determine the presence or absence of other legal characteristics. The random search eliminated the possibility of a bias in favor of societies conforming to the scale type.

The three societies were quota sampled by region to represent a randomly determined three of the following six regions: Asia, Africa, the Middle East, North America, South America, and Oceania. Purposely omitted from the sample were Europe and Russia because they were already represented in the "counsel" type in the Freeman-Winch sample. Selection from different regions was designed to avoid the problem, first noted by Francis Galton, that cross-cultural regularities might be

due to diffusion rather than to functional interrelationships. For a discussion of the problem and evidence of the importance of geographical separateness in sampling, see Raoul Naroll, "Two Solutions to Galton's Problem," *Philosophy of Science*, XXVIII (1961), 15–39; Raoul Naroll and Roy G. D'Andrade, "Two Further Solutions to Galton's Problem," *American Anthropologist*, LXV (October, 1963), 1053–67; and Raoul Naroll, "A Fifth Solution to Galton's Problem," *American Anthropoligst*, Vol. LXVI (forthcoming).

18 These three—Cheyenne, Comanche, and Trobrianders—were selected by James C. Miller before the hypothesis was known to him. Selection of both the Comanche and Cheyenne is subject to some criticism on the grounds that they were prone to diffusion, but this hardly seems a serious difficulty in view of the difference in their scale positions. At all events, the coefficients of reproducibility and scalability would not be seriously lowered by eliminating one of the two.

19 The original study also included damages, imprisonment, and execution. These were dropped from the present analysis, even though this unfortunately limited the scale to three items, to permit focus on statuses rather than sanction. Data on damages will be introduced, however, where relevant to the discussion of restitution.

20 George Peter Murdock, "World Ethnographic Sample," *American Anthropologist*, LIX (August, 1957), 664–87.

others, no wholly satisfactory method has been devised for obtaining a representative sample of the world's societies. Since the universe of separate societies has not been adequately defined, much less enumerated, the representativeness of the sample cannot be ascertained. Nevertheless, an effort has been made to include societies drawn from the major culture areas and from diverse stages of technological development.

Second, societies have been selected in terms of the availability of adequate ethnographic reports. As a result, a bias may have entered the sample through the selection of societies that were particularly accessible—and hospitable—to anthropological observers. Such societies may differ in their patterns of development from societies that have been less well studied.

Third, despite the selection of relatively well-studied societies, the quality of reports varies widely. Like the preceding limitations, this problem is common to all cross-cultural comparisons. The difficulty is mitigated, however, by the fact that the results of this study are positive. The effect of poor reporting should generally be to randomize the apparent occurrence of the variables studied. Where systematic patterns of relationship emerge, as they do in the present research, it would seem to indicate considerable accuracy in the original reports.[21]

Fourth, this study deals with characteristics whose presence or absence can be determined with relative accuracy. In so doing, it may neglect elements of fundamental importance to the basic inquiry. Thus no effort is made to observe the presence of such important phenomena as respect for law, the use of generalized norms, and the pervasiveness of deviance-induced disturbance. Although all of these should be included in a comprehensive theory of legal evolution, they are omitted here in the interest of observational reliability.[22]

[21] On this point see Donald T. Campbell, "The Mutual Methodological Relevance of Anthropology and Psychology," in Francis L. K. Hsu (ed.), *Psychological Anthropology* (Homewood, Ill.: Dorsey Press, 1961), p. 347. This inference should be treated with caution, however, in light of Raoul Naroll's observation that systematic observer bias can lead to spurious correlations (*Data Quality Control: A New Research Technique* [New York: Free Press of Glencoe, 1962]).

[22] Determination of the presence of a characteristic was made after a detailed search by Miller of the materials on each society in the Human Relations Area Files. His search began with a thorough reading for all societies of the material filed under category 18, "total culture." (All categories used are described in detail in George P. Murdock *et al., Outline of Cultural Materials* [4th rev. ed.; New Haven, Conn.: Human Relations Area Files, 1961].) This was followed by a search of the annotated bibliography (category 111) to locate any works specifically dealing with legal or dispute settling processes. When found, works of this kind were examined in detail. In addition, materials filed under the following categories were read: community structure (621), headmen (622), councils (623), police (625), informal in-group justice (627), intercommunity relation (628), territorial hierarchy (631), legal norms (671), liability (672), offenses and sanctions (68), litigation (691), judicial authority (692), legal and judicial personnel (693), initiation of judicial proceedings (694), trial procedure (695), execution of justice (696), prisons and jails (697), and special courts (698). If this search did not reveal the presence of the practice or status under investigation, it was assumed absent. The principal sources relied on for these determinations are given in a mimeographed bibliography which will be supplied by the authors on request.

A reliability check on Miller's judgments was provided by Robert C. Scholl, to whom the writers are indebted. Working independently and without knowledge of the hypotheses, Scholl examined a randomly selected third of the total sample. His judgments agreed with those of Miller 88 per cent, disagreed 4 per cent, and he was unable to reach conclusions on 8 per cent of the items. If the inconclusive judgments are excluded, the reliability reaches the remarkable level of 96 per cent.

The use of a single person to check reliability falls short of the desired standard. In a more detailed and extensive projected study of the relationships reported here, we plan to use a set of three independent naïve judges. For discussion of the problems involved in judging cross-cultural materials see John W. M. Whiting and Irvin L. Child, *Child Training and Personality* (New Haven, Conn.: Yale University Press, 1953), pp. 39–62; and Guy E. Swanson, *The Birth of the*

Fifth, the Guttman scale is here pressed into service beyond that for which it was developed. Originally conceived as a technique for the isolation of uni-dimensional attitudes, it has also been used as a means of studying the interrelationship of behavior patterns. It should be particularly valuable, however, in testing hypotheses concerning developmental sequences, whether in individuals or in societies.[23] Thus, if we hypothesize that A must precede B, supporting data should show three scale types: neither A nor B, A but not B, and A and B. All instances of B occur-

---

Gods (Ann Arbor: Michigan University Press, 1960), pp. 32–54.

[23] The use of the Guttman scale is extensively treated by Robert L. Carneiro in "Scale Analysis as an Instrument for the Study of Cultural Evolution," *Southwestern Journal of Anthropology*, XVIII (1962), 149–69. In a sophisticated critique of the Carneiro paper, Ward L. Goodenough suggests that quasi-scales may be needed for charting general evolutionary trends and for treating the traits that develop and then fail to persist because they are superseded by functional equivalents ("Some Applications of Guttman Scale Analysis to Ethnography and Culture Theory," *Southwestern Journal of Anthropology*, XIX [Autumn, 1963], 235–50). While the quasi-scale is a desirable instrument for analyzing supersedence, Goodenough appears unduly pessimistic about the possible occurrence of approximately perfect scales, see p. 246. Studies that obtained such scales, in addition to the one reported here, include Freeman and Winch, *op cit.*; Stanley H. Udy, " 'Bureaucratic' Elements in Organizations: Some Research Findings," *American Sociological Review*, XXII (1958), 415–18; Frank W. and Ruth C. Young, "Social Integration and Change in Twenty-four Mexican Villages," *Economic Development and Cultural Change*, VIII (July, 1960), 366–77; and Robert L. Carneiro and Stephen L. Tobias, "The Application of Scale Analysis to the Study of Cultural Evolution," *Transactions of the New York Academy of Sciences*, Series II, XXVI (1963), 196–207.

The suggestion that Guttman scales could be used for discovering and testing temporal sequences was made earlier by Norman G. Hawkins and Joan K. Jackson in "Scale Analysis and the Prediction of Life Processes," *American Sociological Review*, XXII (1957), 579–81. Their proposal referred, however, to individuals rather than societies.

ring without A represent errors which lower the reproducibility of the scale and, by the same token, throw doubt in measurable degree on the developmental hypothesis.[24] Although the occurrence of developmental sequences ultimately requires verification by the observation of historic changes in given units, substantiating evidence can be derived from the comparative study of units at varying stages of development. The Guttman scale seems an appropriate quantitative instrument for this purpose.

FINDINGS

In the fifty-one societies studied, as indicated in Table 1, four scale types emerged. Eleven societies showed none of the three characteristics; eighteen had only mediation; eleven had only mediation and police; and seven had mediation, police, and specialized counsel. Two societies departed from these patterns: the Crow and the Thonga had police, but showed no evidence of mediation. While these deviant cases merit detailed study, they reduce the reproducibility of the scale by less than 2 per cent, leaving the coefficient at the extraordinarily high level of better than .98.[25] Each characteristic of

---

[24] The developmental inference does not preclude the possibility of reversal of the usual sequence. It merely indicates which item will be added if any is acquired. Cf. S. N. Eisenstadt, "Social Change, Differentiation and Evolution," *American Sociological Review*, XXIX (June, 1964), 378–81. The finding of a scale also does not rule out the possibility that two items may sometimes occur simultaneously, although the existence of all possible scale types indicates that no two items invariably occur simultaneously and that when they occur separately one regularly precedes the other.

[25] This coefficient of reproducibility far exceeds the .90 level suggested by Guttman as an "efficient approximation . . . of perfect scales" (Samuel Stouffer [ed.], *Measurement and Prediction* [Princeton, N.J.: Princeton University Press, 1950]). The coefficient of scalability, designed by Menzel to take account of extremeness in the distribution of items and individuals, far exceeds the .65 level that he generated from a scalability analysis of

Table 1 Scale of Legal Characteristics

Society	Counsel	Police	Mediation	Errors	Legal Scale Type	Freeman-Winch Scale Type
Cambodians	x	x	x	—	3	*
Czechs	x	x	x	—	3	6
Elizabethan English	x	x	x	—	3	6
Imperial Romans	x	x	x	—	3	6
Indonesians	x	x	x	—	3	*
Syrians	x	x	x	—	3	*
Ukrainians	x	x	x	—	3	6
Ashanti	—	x	x	—	2	5
Cheyenne	—	x	x	—	2	*
Creek	—	x	x	—	2	5
Cuna	—	x	x	—	2	4
Crow	—	x	—	1	2	0
Hopi	—	x	x	—	2	5
Iranians	—	x	x	—	2	6
Koreans	—	x	x	—	2	6
Lapps	—	x	x	—	2	6
Maori	—	x	x	—	2	4
Riffians	—	x	x	—	2	6
Thonga	—	x	—	1	2	2
Vietnamese	—	x	x	—	2	6
Andamanese	—	—	x	—	1	0
Azande	—	—	x	—	1	0
Balinese	—	—	x	—	1	4
Cayapa	—	—	x	—	1	2
Chagga	—	—	x	—	1	4
Formosan aborigines	—	—	x	—	1	0
Hottentot	—	—	x	—	1	0
Ifugao	—	—	x	—	1	0
Lakher	—	—	x	—	1	2
Lepcha	—	—	x	—	1	3
Menomini	—	—	x	—	1	0
Mbundu	—	—	x	—	1	3
Navaho	—	—	x	—	1	5
Ossett	—	—	x	—	1	1
Siwans	—	—	x	—	1	1
Trobrianders	—	—	x	—	1	*
Tupinamba	—	—	x	—	1	0
Venda	—	—	x	—	1	5
Woleaians	—	—	x	—	1	0
Yakut	—	—	x	—	1	1
Aranda	—	—	—	—	0	0
Buka	—	—	—	—	0	0
Chukchee	—	—	—	—	0	0
Comanche	—	—	—	—	0	*
Copper Eskimo	—	—	—	—	0	0
Jivaro	—	—	—	—	0	0
Kababish	—	—	—	—	0	1
Kazak	—	—	—	—	0	0
Siriono	—	—	—	—	0	0
Yaruro	—	—	—	—	0	0
Yurok	—	—	—	—	0	1

*Not included in Freeman-Winch sample.

Coefficient of reproducibility = 1 − 2/153 = .987; coefficient of scalability = 1 − 2/153−120 = .94; Kendall's tau = + .68.

legal organization may now be discussed in terms of the sociolegal conditions in which it is found.

MEDIATION

Societies that lack mediation, constituting less than a third of the entire sample, appear to be the simplest societies. None of them has writing or any substantial degree of specialization.[26] Only three of the thirteen (Yurok, Kababish, and Thonga) use money, whereas almost three-fourths of the societies with mediation have a symbolic means of exchange. We can only speculate at present on the reasons why mediation is absent in these societies. Data on size, using Naroll's definition of the social unit,[27] indicate that the maximum community size of societies without mediation is substantially smaller than that of societies with mediation.[28] Because of their small size, mediationless societies may have

Guttman's American Soldier data. Herbert A. Menzel, "A New Coefficient for Scalogram Analysis," *Public Opinion Quarterly*, XVII (Summer, 1953), 268–80, esp. 276. The problem of determining goodness of fit for the Guttman scale has still not been satisfactorily resolved (see W. S. Torgerson, *Theory and Methods of Scaling* [New York: John Wiley & Sons, 1958], esp. p. 324). A method utilizing χ^2 to test the hypothesis that observed scale frequencies deviate from a rectangular distribution no more than would be expected by chance is suggested by Karl F. Schuessler, "A Note on Statistical Significance of Scalogram," *Sociometry*, XXIV (September, 1961), 312–18. Applied to these data, Schuessler's Test II permits the rejection of the chance hypothesis at the .001 level. $\chi^2 = 60.985$ *(7df)*.

26 Statements of this type are based on the ratings in the Freeman-Winch study, as noted in n. 14 above. For societies that did not appear in their sample, we have made our own ratings on the basis of their definitions.

27 Raoul Naroll, "A Preliminary Index of Social Development," *American Anthropoloist*, LVIII (August, 1956), 687–720.

28 Data were obtained for thirty-nine of the fifty-one societies in the sample on the size of their largest settlement. Societies with mediation have a median largest settlement size of 1,000, while those without mediation have a median of 346. Even eliminating the societies with developed

fewer disputes and thus have less opportunity to evolve regularized patterns of dispute settlement. Moreover, smaller societies may be better able to develop mores and informal controls which tend to prevent the occurrence of disputes. Also, the usually desperate struggle for existence of such societies may strengthen the common goal of survival and thus produce a lessening of intragroup hostility.

The lack of money and substantial property may also help to explain the absence of mediation in these societies. There is much evidence to support the hypothesis that property provides something to quarrel about. In addition, it seems to provide something to mediate with as well. Where private property is extremely limited, one would be less likely to find a concept of damages, that is, property payments in lieu of other sanctions. The development of a concept of damages should greatly increase the range of alternative settlements. This in turn might be expected to create a place for the mediator as a person charged with locating a settlement point satisfactory to the parties and the society.

This hypothesis derives support from the data in Table 2. The concept of damages occurs in all but four of the thirty-eight societies that have mediation and thus appears to be virtually a precondition for mediation. It should be noted, however, that damages are also found in several (seven of thirteen) of the societies that lack mediation. The relationship that emerges is one of damages as a necessary but not sufficient condition for mediation. At present it is impossible to ascertain whether the absence of mediation in societies having the damage concept results from a simple time lag or whether some other factor, not considered in this study, distinguishes these societies from those that have developed mediation.

cities, the median largest settlement size remains above 500 for societies with mediation.

Table 2 Damages in Relation to Legal Functionaries

	No Mediation	Mediation Only	Mediation and Police	Mediation, Police, and Counsel	Total
Damages	7	17	10	7	41
No damages	6*	3	1	0	10
Total	13	20	11	7	51

*Includes Thonga, who have neither mediation nor damages, but have police.

POLICE

Twenty societies in the sample had police—that is, a specialized armed force available for norm enforcement. As noted, all of these but the Crow and Thonga had the concept of damages and some kind of mediation as well. Nevertheless, the occurrence of twenty societies with mediation but without police makes it clear that mediation is not inevitably accompanied by the systematic enforcement of decisions. The separability of these two characteristics is graphically illustrated in ethnographic reports. A striking instance is found among the Albanian tribesmen whose elaborately developed code for settling disputes, Lek's Kanun, was used for centuries as a basis for mediation. But in the absence of mutual agreements by the disputants, feuds often began immediately after adjudication and continued unhampered by any constituted police.[29]

From the data it is possible to determine some of the characteristics of societies that develop police. Eighteen of the twenty in our sample are economically advanced enough to use money. They also have a substantial degree of specialization, with full-time priests and teachers found in all but three (Cheyenne, Thonga, and Crow), and full-time governmental officials, not mere relatives of the chief, present in all but four (Cuna, Maori, Thonga, and Crow).

Superficially at least, these findings

[29] Margaret Hasluck, *The Unwritten Law in Albania* (Cambridge: Cambridge University Press, 1954).

seem directly contradictory to Durkheim's major thesis in *The Division of Labor in Society*. He hypothesized that penal law—the effort of the organized society to punish offenses against itself—occurs in societies with the simplest division of labor. As indicated, however, our data show that police are found only in association with a substantial degree of division of labor. Even the practice of governmental punishment for wrongs against the society (as noted by Freeman and Winch) does not appear in simpler societies. By contrast, restitutive sanctions—damages and mediation—which Durkheim believed to be associated with an increasing division of labor, are found in many societies that lack even rudimentary specialization. Thus Durkheim's hypothesis seems the reverse of the empirical situation in the range of societies studied here.[30]

[30] A basic difficulty in testing Durkheim's thesis arises from his manner of formulating it. His principal interest, as we understand it, was to show the relationship between division of labor and type of sanction (using type of solidarity as the intervening variable). However, in distinguishing systems of law, he added the criterion of organization. The difficulty is that he was very broad in his criterion of organization required for penal law, but quite narrow in describing the kind of organization needed for non-penal law. For the former, the "assembly of the whole people" sufficed (*op. cit.*, p. 76); for the latter, on the other hand, he suggested the following criteria: "restitutive law creates organs which are more and more specialized: consular tribunals, councils of arbitration, administrative tribunals of every sort. Even in its most general part, that which pertains to civil law, it is exercised only through particular functionaries: magistrates, lawyers, etc., who have become apt in this role because of very special training"

COUNSEL

Seven societies in the sample employ specialized advocates in the settlement of disputes. As noted, all of these societies also use mediation. There are, however, another thirty-one societies that have mediation but do not employ specialized counsel. It is a striking feature of the data that damages and mediation are characteristic of the simplest (as well as the most complex) societies, while legal counsel are found only in the most complex. The societies with counsel also have, without exception, not only damages, mediation, and police but, in addition, all of the complexity characteristics identified by Freeman and Winch.

It is not surprising that mediation is not universally associated with counsel. In many mediation systems the parties are expected to speak for themselves. The mediator tends to perform a variety of functions, questioning disputants as well as deciding on the facts and interpreting the law. Such a system is found even in complex societies, such as Imperial China. There the prefect acted as counsel, judge, and jury, using a whip to wring the truth from the parties who were assumed a priori to be lying.[31] To serve as counsel in that setting would have been painful as well as superfluous. Even where specialized counsel emerge, their role tends to be ambiguous. In ancient Greece, for instance, counsel acted principally as advisors on strategy. Upon appearance in court they sought to conceal the fact that they were specialists in legal matters, presenting themselves merely as friends of the parties or even on occasion assuming the identity of the parties themselves.[32]

At all events, lawyers are here found only in quite urbanized societies, all of which are based upon fully developed agricultural economies. The data suggest at least two possible explanations. First, all of the sample societies with counsel have a substantial division of labor, including priests, teachers, police, and government officials. This implies an economic base strong enough to support a variety of secondary and tertiary occupations as well as an understanding of the advantages of specialization. Eleven societies in the sample, however, have all of these specialized statuses but lack specialized counsel. What distinguishes the societies that develop counsel? Literacy would seem to be an important factor. Only five of the twelve literate societies in the sample do not have counsel. Writing, of course, makes possible the formulation of a legal code with its advantages of forewarning the violator and promoting uniformity in judicial administration. The need to interpret a legal code provides a niche for specialized counsel, especially where a substantial segment of the population is illiterate.[33]

(p. 113). In thus suggesting that restitutive law exists only with highly complex organizational forms, Durkheim virtually insured that his thesis would be proven—that restitutive law would be found only in complex societies.

Such a "proof," however, would miss the major point of his argument. In testing the main hypothesis it would seem preferable, therefore, to specify a common and minimal organizational criterion, such as public support. Then the key question might be phrased: Is there a tendency toward restitutive rather than repressive sanctions which develops as an increasing function of the division of labor? Although our present data are not conclusive, the finding of damages and mediation in societies with minimal division of labor implies a negative answer. This suggests that the restitutive principle is not contingent on social heterogeneity or that heterogeneity is not contingent on the division of labor.

[31] Sybille van der Sprenkel, *Legal Institutions in*

Manchu China (London: Athlone Press, 1962). See also Ch'ü T'ung-tsu, *Law and Society in Traditional China* (Vancouver, B.C.: Institute of Pacific Relations, 1961).

[32] A. H. Chroust, "The Legal Profession in Ancient Athens," *Notre Dame Law Review*, XXIX (Spring, 1954), 339–89.

[33] Throughout the discussion, two sets of explanatory factors have been utilized. The observed pattern could be due to an internal process inherent in legal control systems, or it could be depen-

CONCLUSIONS

These data, taken as a whole, lend support to the belief that an evolutionary sequence occurs in the development of legal institutions. Alternative interpretations are, to be sure, not precluded. The scale analysis might fail to discern short-lived occurrences of items. For instance, counsel might regularly develop as a variation in simple societies even before police, only to drop out rapidly enough so that the sample picks up no such instances. Even though this is a possibility in principle, no cases of this kind have come to the authors' attention.

Another and more realistic possibility is that the sequence noted in this sample

---

dent upon the emergence of urban characteristics. It does seem clear, however, that the legal developments coincide to a considerable extent with increased "urbanism" as measured by Freeman and Winch. Evidence for this assertion is to be found in the correlation between the Freeman-Winch data and the legal scale types discerned. For the forty-five societies appearing in both samples, the rank correlation coefficient (Kendall's tau) between positions on the legal and urbanism scales is + .68. While this coefficient suggests a close relationship between the two processes, it does not justify the assertion that legal evolution is wholly determined by increasing urbanism. A scatter diagram of the interrelationship reveals that legal characteristics tend to straddle the regression line for five of the seven folk-urban scale positions, omitting only scale types 2 (punishment) and 3 (religious specialization). This suggests that some other factor might emerge upon further analysis that would explain why roughly half of the societies at each stage of urbanism appear to have gone on to the next stage of legal evolution while the others lag behind. A promising candidate for such a factor is the one located by Gouldner and Peterson in their cross-cultural factor analysis of Simmons' data and described by them as "Apollonianism" or "Norm-sending" (Alvin W. Gouldner and Richard A. Peterson, *Technology and the Moral Order* [Indianapolis: Bobbs-Merrill Co., 1962], pp. 30–53).

To test whether the legal sequence has a "dynamic of its own," it would seem necessary to examine the growth of legal systems independent of folk-urban changes, as in subsystems or in societies where the process of urbanization has already occurred. The data covered here do not permit such a test.

---

does not occur in societies in a state of rapid transition. Developing societies undergoing intensive cultural contact might provide an economic and social basis for specialized lawyers, even in the absence of police or dispute mediation. Until such societies are included in the sample, these findings must be limited to relatively isolated, slowly changing societies.

The study also raises but does not answer questions concerning the evolution of an international legal order. It would be foolhardy to generalize from the primitive world directly to the international scene and to assume that the same sequences must occur here as there. There is no certainty that subtribal units can be analogized to nations, because the latter tend to be so much more powerful, independent, and relatively deficient in common culture and interests. In other ways, the individual nations are farther along the path of legal development than subtribal units because all of them have their own domestic systems of mediation, police, and counsel. This state of affairs might well provide a basis for short-circuiting an evolutionary tendency operative in primitive societies. Then too, the emergent world order appears to lack the incentive of common interest against a hostile environment that gave primitive societies a motive for legal control. Even though the survival value of a legal system may be fully as great for today's world as for primitive societies, the existence of multiple units in the latter case permitted selection for survival of those societies that had developed the adaptive characteristic. The same principle cannot be expected to operate where the existence of "one world" permits no opportunity for variation and consequent selection.

Nonetheless, it is worth speculating that some of the same forces may operate in both situations.[34] We have seen that

---

[34] For an interesting attempt to develop a general theory of legal control, applicable both to discrete societies and to the international order,

damages and mediation almost always precede police in the primitive world. This sequence could result from the need to build certain cultural foundations in the community before a central regime of control, as reflected in a police force, can develop. Hypothetically, this cultural foundation might include a determination to avoid disputes, an appreciation of the value of third-party intervention, and the development of a set of norms both for preventive purposes and as a basis for al-

---

see Kenneth S. Carlston, *Law and Organization in World Society* (Urbana: University of Illinois Press, 1962).

locating blame and punishment when disputes arise. Compensation by damages and the use of mediators might well contribute to the development of such a cultural foundation, as well as reflecting its growth. If so, their occurrence prior to specialized police would be understandable. This raises the question as to whether the same kind of cultural foundation is not a necessary condition for the establishment of an effective world police force and whether, in the interest of that objective, it might not be appropriate to stress the principles of compensatory damages and mediation as preconditions for the growth of a world rule of law.

A SOCIOLOGICAL ANALYSIS OF THE LAW OF VAGRANCY

William J. Chambliss

With the outstanding exception of Jerome Hall's analysis of theft [1] there has been a severe shortage of sociologically relevant analyses of the relationship particular laws and the social setting in which these laws emerge, are interpreted, and take form. The paucity of such studies is

Reprinted from *Social Problems,* **12** (Summer, 1964), pp. 67–77, by permission of the author and The Society for the Study of Social Problems.

For a more complete listing of most of the statutes dealt with in this report the reader is referred to Burn, *The History of the Poor Laws.* Citations of English statutes should be read as follows: 3 Ed. 1. c. 1. refers to the third act of Edward the first, chapter one, etc.

[1] Hall, J., *Theft, Law and Society,* Bobbs-Merrill, 1939. See also, Alfred R. Lindesmith, "Federal Law and Drug Addiction," *Social Problems* Vol. 7, No. 1, 1959, p. 48.

somewhat surprising in view of widespread agreement that such studies are not only desirable but absolutely essential to the development of a mature sociology of law.[2] A fruitful method of establishing the direction and pattern of this mutual influence is to systematically analyze particular legal categories, to observe the changes which take place in the categories and to explain how these changes are themselves related and to stimulate changes in the society. This paper is an attempt to provide such an analysis of the law of vagrancy in Anglo-American Law.

[2] See, for example, Rose, A., "Some Suggestions for Research in the Sociology of Law," *Social Problems* Vol. 9, No. 3, 1962, pp. 281–283, and Geis, G., "Sociology, Criminology, and Criminal Law," *Social Problems* Vol. 7, No. 1, 1959, pp. 40–47.

LEGAL INNOVATION:
THE EMERGENCE OF THE LAW
OF VAGRANCY IN ENGLAND

There is general agreement among legal scholars that the first full fledged vagrancy statute was passed in England in 1349. As is generally the case with legislative innovations, however, this statute was preceded by earlier laws which established a climate favorable to such change. The most significant forerunner to the 1349 vagrancy statute was in 1274 when it was provided:

Because that abbies and houses of religion have been overcharged and sore grieved, by the resort of great men and other, so that their goods have not been sufficient for themselves, whereby they have been greatly hindered and impoverished, that they cannot maintain themselves, nor such charity as they have been accustomed to do; it is provided, that none shall come to eat or lodge in any house of religion, or any other's foundation than of his own, at the costs of the house, unless he be required by the governor of the house before his coming hither.[3]

Unlike the vagrancy statutes this statute does not intend to curtail the movement of persons from one place to another, but is solely designed to provide the religious houses with some financial relief from the burden of providing food and shelter to travelers.

The philosophy that the religious houses were to give alms to the poor and to the sick and feeble was, however, to undergo drastic change in the next fifty years. The result of this changed attitude was the establishment of the first vagrancy statute in 1349 which made it a crime to give alms to any who were unemployed while being of sound mind and body. To wit:

Because that many valiant beggars, as long as they may live of begging, do refuse to labor,

giving themselves to idleness and vice, and sometimes to theft and other abominations; it is ordained, that none, upon pain of imprisonment shall, under the colour of pity or alms, give anything to such which may labour, or presume to favour them towards their desires, so that thereby they may be compelled to labour for their necessary living.[4]

It was further provided by this statute that:

. . . every man and woman, of what condition he be, free or bond, able in body, and within the age of threescore years, not living in merchandize nor exercising any craft, nor having of his own whereon to live, nor proper land whereon to occupy himself, and not serving any other, if he in convenient service (his estate considered) be required to serve, shall be bounded to serve him which shall him require . . . And if any refuse, he shall on conviction by two true men, . . . be committed to gaol till he find surety to serve.

And if any workman or servant, of what estate or condition he be, retained in any man's service, do depart from the said service without reasonable cause or license, before the term agreed on, he shall have pain of imprisonment.[5]

There was also in this statute the stipulation that the workers should receive a standard wage. In 1351 this statute was strengthened by the stipulation:

An none shall go out of the town where he dwelled in winter, to serve the summer, if he may serve in the same town.[6]

By 34 Ed 3 (1360) the punishment for these acts became imprisonment for fifteen days and if they "do not justify themselves by the end of that time, to be sent to gaol till they do."

A change in official policy so drastic as this did not, of course, occur simply as a matter of whim. The vagrancy stat-

---

[3] 35 Ed. 1. c. 1.

[4] 35 Ed. 1. c. 1.
[5] 23 Ed. 3.
[6] 25 Ed. 3 (1351).

utes emerged as a result of changes in other parts of the social structure. The prime-mover for this legislative innovation was the Black Death which struck England about 1348. Among the many disastrous consequences this had upon the social structure was the fact that it decimated the labor force. It is estimated that by the time the pestilence had run its course at least fifty per cent of the population of England had died from the plague. This decimation of the labor force would necessitate rather drastic innovations in any society but its impact was heightened in England where, at this time, the economy was highly dependent upon a ready supply of cheap labor.

Even before the pestilence, however, the availability of an adequate supply of cheap labor was becoming a problem for the landowners. The crusades and various wars had made money necessary to the lords and, as a result, the lord frequently agreed to sell the serfs their freedom in order to obtain the needed funds. The serfs, for their part, were desirous of obtaining their freedom (by "fair means" or "foul") because the larger towns which were becoming more industrialized during this period could offer the serf greater personal freedom as well as a higher standard of living. This process is nicely summarized by Bradshaw:

By the middle of the 14th century the outward uniformity of the manorial system had become in practice considerably varied . . . for the peasant had begun to drift to the towns and it was unlikely that the old village life in its unpleasant aspects should not be resented. Moreover the constant wars against France and Scotland were fought mainly with mercenaries after Henry III's time and most villages contributed to the new armies. The bolder serfs either joined the armies or fled to the towns, and even in the villages the free men who held by villein tenure were as eager to commute their services as the serfs were to escape. Only the amount of 'free' labor avail-

able enabled the lord to work his demesne in many places.[7]

And he says regarding the effect of the Black Death:

. . . in 1348 the Black Death reached England and the vast mortality that ensued destroyed that reserve of labour which alone had made the manorial system even nominally possible.[8]

The immediate result of these events was of course no surprise: Wages for the "free" man rose considerably and this increased, on the one hand, the landowners problems and, on the other hand, the plight of the unfree tenant. For although wages increased for the personally free laborers, it of course did not necessarily add to the standard of living of the serf, if anything it made his position worse because the landowner would be hard pressed to pay for the personally free labor which he needed and would thus find it more and more difficult to maintain the standard of living for the serf which he had heretofore supplied. Thus the serf had no alternative but flight if he chose to better his position. Furthermore, flight generally meant both freedom and better conditions since the possibility of work in the new weaving industry was great and the chance of being caught small.[9]

It was under these conditions that we find the first vagrancy statutes emerging. There is little question but that these statutes were designed for one express purpose: to force laborers (whether personally free or unfree) to accept employment at a low wage in order to insure the landowner an adequate supply of labor at a price he could afford to pay. Caleb Foote concurs with this interpretation when he notes:

The anti-migratory policy behind vagrancy legislation began as an essential complement

[7] Bradshaw, F., *A Social History of England*, p. 54.
[8] *Ibid.*
[9] *Ibid.*, p. 57.

of the wage stabilization legislation which accompanied the breakup of feudalism and the depopulation caused by the Black Death. By the Statutes of Labourers in 1349-1351, every ablebodied person without other means of support was required to work for wages fixed at the level preceding the Black Death; it was unlawful to accept more, or to refuse an offer to work, or to flee from one county to another to avoid offers of work or to seek higher wages, or to give alms to able-bodied beggars who refused to work.[10]

In short, as Foote says in another place, this was an "attempt to make the vagrancy statutes a substitute for serfdom." [11] This same conclusion is equally apparent from the wording of the statute where it is stated:

Because great part of the people, and especially of workmen and servants, late died in pestilence; many seeing the necessity of masters, and great scarcity of servants, will not serve without excessive wages, and some rather willing to beg in idleness than by labour to get their living: it is ordained, that every man and woman, of what condition he be, free or bond, able in body and within the age of threescore years, not living in merchandize, (etc.) be required to serve . . .

The innovation in the law, then, was a direct result of the afore-mentioned changes which had occurred in the social setting. In this case these changes were located for the most part in the economic institution of the society. The vagrancy laws were designed to alleviate a condition defined by the lawmakers as undesirable. The solution was to attempt to force a reversal, as it were, of a social process which was well underway; that is, to curtail mobility of laborers in such a way that labor would not become a commodity for which the landowners would have to compete.

[10] Foote, C., "Vagrancy Type Law and Its Administration," *Univ. of Pennsylvania Law Review* (104), 1956, p. 615.
[11] *Ibid.*

STATUTORY DORMANCY: A LEGAL VESTIGE. In time, of course, the curtailment of the geographical mobility of laborers was no longer requisite. One might well expect that when the function served by the statute was no longer an important one for the society, the statutes would be eliminated from the law. In fact, this has not occurred. The vagrancy statutes have remained in effect since 1349. Furthermore, as we shall see in some detail later, they were taken over by the colonies and have remained in effect in the United States as well.

The substance of the vagrancy statutes changed very little for some time after the first ones in 1349-1351 although there was a tendency to make punishments more harsh than originally. For example, in 1360 it was provided that violators of the statute should be imprisoned for fifteen days [12] and in 1388 the punishment was to put the offender in the stocks and to keep him there until "he find surety to return to his service." [13] That there was still, at this time the intention of providing the landowner with labor is apparent from the fact that this statute provides:

and he or she which use to labour at the plough and cart, or other labour and service of husbandry, till they be of the age of 12 years, from thenceforth shall abide at the same labour without being put to any mistery or handicraft: and any covenant of apprenticeship to the contrary shall be void.[14]

The next alteration in the statutes occurs in 1495 and is restricted to an increase in punishment. Here it is provided that vagrants shall be "set in stocks, there to remain by the space of three days and three nights, and there to have none other sustenance but bread and water; and after the said three days and nights, to be had

[12] 34 Ed. 3 (1360).
[13] 12 R. 2 (1388).
[14] *Ibid.*

out and set at large, and then to be commanded to avoid the town." [15]

The tendency to increase the severity of punishment during this period seems to be the result of a general tendency to make finer distinctions in the criminal law. During this period the vagrancy statutes appear to have been fairly inconsequential in either their effect as a control mechanism or as a generally enforced statute.[16] The processes of social change in the culture generally and the trend away from serfdom and into a "free" economy obviated the utility of these statutes. The result was not unexpected. The judiciary did not apply the law and the legislators did not take it upon themselves to change the law. In short, we have here a period of dormancy in which the statute is neither applied nor altered significantly.

A SHIFT IN FOCAL CONCERN

Following the squelching of the Peasant's Revolt in 1381, the services of the serfs to the lord ". . . tended to become less and less exacted, although in certain forms they lingered on till the seventeenth century . . . By the sixteenth century few knew that there were any bondmen in England . . . and in 1575 Queen Elizabeth listened to the prayers of almost the last serfs in England . . . and granted them manumission." [17]

In view of this change we would expect corresponding changes in the vagrancy laws. Beginning with the lessening of punishment in the statute of 1503 we find these changes. However, instead of remaining dormant (or becoming more so) or being negated altogether, the vagrancy statutes experienced a shift in focal concern. With this shift the statutes served a

new and equally important function for the social order of England. The first statute which indicates this change was in 1530. In this statute (22 H.8.c. 12 1530) it was stated:

If any person, being whole and mighty in body, and able to labour, be taken in begging, or be vagrant and can give no reckoning how he lawfully gets his living; . . . and all other idle persons going about, some of them using divers and subtil crafty and unlawful games and plays, and some of them feigning themselves to have knowledge of . . . crafty sciences . . . shall be punished as provided.

What is most significant about this statute is the shift from an earlier concern with laborers to a concern with *criminal* activities. To be sure, the stipulation of persons "being whole and mighty in body, and able to labour, be taken in begging, or be vagrant" sounds very much like the concerns of the earlier statutes. Some important differences are apparent however when the rest of the statute includes those who ". . . can give no reckoning how he lawfully gets his living"; "some of them using divers subtil and unlawful games and plays." This is the first statute which specifically focuses upon these kinds of criteria for adjudging someone a vagrant.

It is significant that in this statute the severity of punishment is increased so as to be greater not only than provided by the 1503 statute but the punishment is more severe than that which had been provided by *any* of the pre-1503 statutes as well. For someone who is merely idle and gives no reckoning of how he makes his living the offender shall be:

. . . had to the next market town, or other place where they [the constables] shall think most convenient, and there to be tied to the end of a cart naked, and to be beaten with whips throughout the same market town or other place, till his body be bloody by reason of such whipping.[18]

---

[15] 11 H. & C. 2 (1495).

[16] As evidenced for this note the expectation that ". . . the common gaols of every shire are likely to be greatly pestered with more numbers of prisoners than heretofore . . ." when the statutes were changed by the statute of 14 Ed. c. 5 (1571).

[17] Bradshaw, *op. cit.*, p. 61.

[18] 22 H. 8. c. 12 (1530).

But, for those who use "divers and subtil crafty and unlawful games and plays," etc., the punishment is ". . . whipping at two days together in manner aforesaid." [19]

. . . scourged two days, and the third day to be put upon the pillory from nine of the clock till eleven before noon of the same day and to have one of his ears cut off.[20]

And if he offend the third time ". . . to have like punishment with whipping, standing on the pillory and to have his other ear cut off."

This statute (1) makes a distinction between types of offenders and applies the more severe punishment to those who are clearly engaged in "criminal" activities, (2) mentions a specific concern with categories of "unlawful behavior," and (3) applies a type of punishment (cutting off the ear) which is generally reserved for offenders who are defined as likely to be a fairly serious criminal.

Only five years later we find for the first time that the punishment of death is applied to the crime of vagrancy. We also note a change in terminology in the statute:

and if any ruffians . . . after having been once apprehended . . . shall wander, loiter, or idle use themselves and play the vagabonds . . . shall be eftfoons not only whipped again, but shall have the gristle of his right ear clean cut off. And if he shall again offend, he shall be committed to gaol till the next sessions; and being there convicted upon indictment, he shall have judgment to suffer pains and execution of death, as a felon, as an enemy of the commonwealth.[21]

It is significant that the statute now makes persons who repeat the crime of vagrancy a felon. During this period then, the focal concern of the vagrancy statutes becomes a concern for the control of felons and is no longer primarily concerned with the movement of laborers.

These statutory changes were a direct response to changes taking place in England's social structure during this period. We have already pointed out that feudalism was decaying rapidly. Concomitant with the breakup of feudalism was an increased emphasis upon commerce and industry. The commercial emphasis in England at the turn of the sixteenth century is of particular importance in the development of vagrancy laws. With commercialism came considerable traffic bearing valuable items. Where there were 169 important merchants in the middle of the fourteenth century there were 3,000 merchants engaged in foreign trade alone at the beginning of the sixteenth century.[22] England became highly dependent upon commerce for its economic support. Italians conducted a great deal of the commerce of England during this early period and were held in low repute by the populace. As a result, they were subject to attacks by citizens and, more important, were frequently robbed of their goods while transporting them. "The general insecurity of the times made any transportation hazardous. The special risks to which the alien merchant was subjected gave rise to the royal practice of issuing formally executed covenants of safe conduct through the realm." [23]

Such a situation not only called for the enforcement of existing laws but also called for the creation of new laws which would facilitate the control of persons preying upon merchants transporting goods. The vagrancy statutes were revived in order to fulfill just such a purpose. Persons who had committed no serious felony but who were suspected of being capable of doing so could be apprehended and incapacitated through the application of vagrancy laws once these laws were

19 *Ibid.*
20 *Ibid.*
21 27 H. 8. c. 25 (1535).

22 Hall, *op. cit.,* p. 21.
23 *Ibid.,* p. 23.

refocused so as to include ". . . any ruf-fians . . . [who] shall wander, loiter, or idle use themselves and play the vaga-bonds . . ." [24]

The new focal concern is continued in 1 Ed 6. c. 3 (1547) and in fact is made more general so as to include:

Whoever man or woman, being not lame, im-potent, or so aged or diseased that he or she cannot work, not having whereon to live, shall be lurking in any house, or loitering or idle wandering by the highway side, or in streets, cities, towns, or villages, not applying them-selves to some honest labour, and so continu-ing for three days; or running away from their work; every such person shall be taken for a vagabond. And . . . upon conviction of two witnesses . . . the same loiterer (shall) be marked with a hot iron in the breast with the letter V, and adjudged him to the person bringing him, to be his slave for two years . . .

Should the vagabond run away, upon conviction, he was to be branded by a hot iron with the letter S on the forehead and to be thenceforth declared a slave forever. And in 1571 there is modification of the punishment to be inflicted, whereby the offender is to be "branded on the chest with the letter V" (for vagabond). And, if he is convicted the second time, the brand is to be made on the forehead. It is worth noting here that this method of punishment, which first appeared in 1530 and is repeated here with somewhat more force, is also an indication of a change in the type of person to whom the law is intended to apply. For it is likely that nothing so permanent as branding would be applied to someone who was wander-ing but looking for work, or at worst merely idle and not particularly danger-ous *per se*. On the other hand, it could well be applied to someone who was likely to be engaged in other criminal activities in connection with being "vagrant."

By 1571 in the statue of 14 El. C. 5 the shift in focal concern is fully developed:

All rogues, vagabonds, and sturdy beggars shall . . . be committed to the common gaol . . . he shall be grievously whipped, and burnt thro' the gristle of the right ear with a hot iron of the compass of an inch about; . . . And for the second offense, he shall be ad-judged a felon, unless some person will take him for two years in to his service. And for the third offense, he shall be adjudged guilty of felony without benefit of clergy.

And there is included a long list of per-sons who fall within the statute: "proctors, procurators, idle persons going about us-ing subtil, crafty and unlawful games or plays and some of them feigning them-selves to have knowledge of . . . absurd sciences . . . and all fencers, bearwards, common players in interludes, and min-strels . . . all juglers, pedlars, tinkers, petty chapmen . . . and all counterfeiters of licenses, passports and users of the same." The major signifiance of this statute is that it includes all the previously defined offenders and adds some more. Significantly, those added are more clearly criminal types, counterfeiters, for example. It is also significant that there is the fol-lowing qualification of this statute: "Pro-vided also, that this act shall not extend to cookers, or harvest folks, that travel for harvest work, corn or hay."

That the changes in this statute were seen as significant is indicated by the fol-lowing statement which appears in the statute:

And whereas by reason of this act, the com-mon gaols of every shire are like to be greatly pestered with more number of prisoners than heretofore hath been, for that the said vaga-bonds and other lewd persons before recited shall upon their apprehension be committed to the said gaols; it is enacted . . .[25]

And a provision is made for giving more money for maintaining the gaols. This seems to add credence to the notion that

24 27 H. 8. c. 5 (1535).

25 14 Ed. c. 5. (1571).

this statute was seen as being significantly more general than those previously.

It is also of importance to note that this is the first time the term *rogue* has been used to refer to persons included in the vagrancy statutes. It seems, *a priori,* that a "rogue" is a different social type than is a "vagrant" or a "vagabond"; the latter terms implying something more equivalent to the idea of a "tramp" whereas the former (rogue) seems to imply a more disorderly and potentially dangerous person.

The emphasis upon the criminalistic aspect of vagrants continues in Chapter 17 of the same statute:

Whereas divers *licentious* persons wander up and down in all parts of the realm, to countenance their *wicked behavior;* and do continually assemble themselves armed in the highways, and elsewhere in troops, *to the great terror* of her majesty's true subjects, *the impeachment of her laws,* and the disturbance of the peace and tranquility of the realm; and whereas many outrages are daily committed by these dissolute persons, and more are likely to ensue if speedy remedy be not provided. (Italics added)

With minor variations (*e.g.,* offering a reward for the capture of a vagrant) the statutes remain essentially of this nature until 1743. In 1743 there was once more an expansion of the types of persons included such that "all persons going about as patent gatherers, or gatherers of alms, under pretense of loss by fire or other casualty; or going about as collectors for prisons, gaols, or hospitals; all persons playing of betting at any unlawful games; and all persons who run away and leave their wives or children . . . all persons wandering abroad, and lodging in alehouses, barns, outhouses, or in the open air, not giving good account of themselves," were types of offenders added to those already included.

By 1743 the vagrancy statutes had apparently been sufficiently reconstructed by

the shifts of concern so as to be once more a useful instrument in the creation of social solidarity. This function has apparently continued down to the present day in England and the changes from 1743 to the present have been all in the direction of clarifying or expanding the categories covered but little has been introduced to change either the meaning or the impact of this branch of the law.

We can summarize this shift in focal concern by quoting from Halsbury. He has noted that in the vagrancy statutes:

". . . elaborate provision is made for the relief and incidental control of destitute wayfarers. These latter, however, form but a small portion of the offenders aimed at by what are known as the Vagrancy Laws, . . . many offenders who are in no ordinary sense of the word vagrants, have been brought under the laws relating to vagrancy, and the great number of the offenses coming within the operation of these laws have little or no relation to the subject of poor relief, but are more properly directed towards the prevention of crime, the preservation of good order, and the promotion of social economy." [26]

Before leaving this section it is perhaps pertinent to make a qualifying remark. We have emphasized throughout this section how the vagrancy statutes underwent a shift in focal concern as the social setting changed. The shift in focal concern is not meant to imply that the later focus of the statutes represents a completely new law. It will be recalled that even in the first vagrancy statute there was reference to those who "do refuse labor, giving themselves to idleness and vice and sometimes to theft and other abominations." Thus the possibility of criminal activities resulting from persons who refuse to labor was recognized even in the earliest statute. The fact remains, however, that the major emphasis in this statute and in the statutes

[26] Earl of Halsbury, *The Laws of England,* Butterworth & Co., Bell Yard, Temple Bar, 1912, pp. 606–607.

which followed the first one was always upon the "refusal to labor" or "begging." The "criminalistic" aspect of such persons was relatively unimportant. Later, as we have shown, the criminalistic potential becomes of paramount importance. The thread runs back to the earliest statute but the reason for the statutes' existence as well as the focal concern of the statutes is quite different in 1743 than it was in 1349.

VAGRANCY LAWS IN THE UNITED STATES

In general, the vagrancy laws of England, as they stood in the middle eighteenth century, were simply adopted by the states. There were some exceptions to this general trend. For example, Maryland restricted the application of vagrancy laws to "free" Negroes. In addition, for *all* states the vagrancy laws were even more explicitly concerned with the control of criminals and undesirables than had been the case in England. New York, for example, explicitly defines prostitutes as being a category of vagrants during this period. These exceptions do not, however, change the general picture significantly and it is quite appropriate to consider the U. S. vagrancy laws as following from England's of the middle eighteenth century with relatively minor changes. The control of criminals and undesirables was the *raison d'être* of the vagrancy laws in the U. S. This is as true today as it was in 1750. As Caleb Foote's analysis of the application of vagrancy statutes in the Philadelphia court shows, these laws are presently applied indiscriminately to persons considered a "nuisance." Foote suggests that ". . . the chief significance of this branch of the criminal law lies in its quantitative impact and administrative usefulness." [27] Thus it appears that in America the trend begun in England in the sixteenth, seven-

teenth and eighteenth centuries has been carried to its logical extreme and the laws are now used principally as a mechanism for "clearing the streets" of the derelicts who inhabit the "skid roads" and "Bowerys" of our large urban areas.

Since the 1800's there has been an abundant source of prospects to which the vagrancy laws have been applied. These have been primarily those persons deemed by the police and the courts to be either actively involved in criminal activities or at least peripherally involved. In this context, then, the statutes have changed very little. The functions served by the statutes in England of the late eighteenth century are still being served today in both England and the United States. The locale has changed somewhat and it appears that the present day application of vagrancy statutes is focused upon the arrest and confinement of the "down and outers" who inhabit certain sections of our larger cities but the impact has remained constant. The lack of change in the vagrancy statutes, then, can be seen as a reflection of the society's perception of a continuing need to control some of its "suspicious" or "undesirable" members.[28]

A word of caution is in order lest we leave the impression that this administrative purpose is the sole function of vagrancy laws in the U. S. today. Although it is our contention that this is generally true it is worth remembering that during certain periods of our recent history, and to some extent today, these laws have also been used to control the movement of workers. This was particularly the case during the depression years and California is of course infamous for its use of vagrancy laws to restrict the admission of migrants from other states.[29] The vagrancy

[27] Foote, *op. cit.*, p. 613. Also see in this connection, Irwin Deutscher, "The Petty Offender," *Federal Probation*, XIX, June, 1955.

[28] It is on this point that the vagrancy statutes have been subject to criticism. See for example, Lacey, Forrest W., "Vagrancy and Other Crimes of Personal Condition," *Harvard Law Review* (66), p. 1203.

[29] Edwards *vs* California. 314 S: 160 (1941).

statutes, because of their history, still contain germs within them which make such effects possible. Their main purpose, however, is clearly no longer the control of laborers but rather the control of the undesirable, the criminal and the "nuisance."

DISCUSSION

The foregoing analysis of the vagrancy laws has demonstrated that these laws were a legislative innovation which reflected the socially perceived necessity of providing an abundance of cheap labor to landowners during a period when serfdom was breaking down and when the pool of available labor was depleted. With the eventual breakup of feudalism the need for such laws eventually disappeared and the increased dependence of the economy upon industry and commerce rendered the former use of the vagrancy statutes unnecessary. As a result, for a substantial period the vagrancy statutes were dormant, undergoing only minor changes and, presumably, being applied infrequently. Finally, the vagrancy laws were subjected to considerable alteration through a shift in the focal concern of the statutes. Whereas in their inception the laws focused upon the "idle" and "those refusing to labor" after the turn of the sixteenth century and emphasis came to be upon "rogues," "vagabonds," and others who were suspected of being engaged in criminal activities. During this period the focus was particularly upon "roadmen" who preyed upon citizens who transported goods from one place to another. The increased importance of commerce to England during this period made it necessary that some protection be given persons engaged in this enterprise and the vagrancy statutes provided one source for such protection by re-focusing the acts to be included under these statutes.

Comparing the results of this analysis with the findings of Hall's study of theft

we see a good deal of correspondence. Of major importance is the fact that both analyses demonstrate the truth of Hall's assertion that "The functioning of courts is significantly related to concomitant cultural needs, and this applies to the law of procedure as well as to substantive law." [30]

Our analysis of the vagrancy laws also indicates that when changed social conditions create a perceived need for legal changes that these alterations will be effected through the revision and refocusing of existing statutes. This process was demonstrated in Hall's analysis of theft as well as in our analysis of vagrancy. In the case of vagrancy, the laws were dormant when the focal concern of the laws was shifted so as to provide control over potential criminals. In the case of theft the laws were re-interpreted (interestingly, by the courts and not by the legislature) so as to include persons who were transporting goods for a merchant but who absconded with the contents of the packages transported.

It also seems probable that when the social conditions change and previously useful laws are no longer useful there will be long periods when these laws will remain dormant. It is less likely that they will be officially negated. During this period of dormancy it is the judiciary which has principal responsibility for *not* applying the statutes. It is possible that one finds statutes being negated only when the judiciary stubbornly applies laws which do not have substantial public support. An example of such laws in contemporary times would be the "Blue Laws." Most states still have laws prohibiting the sale of retail goods on Sunday yet these laws are rarely applied. The laws are very likely to remain but to be dormant unless a recalcitrant judge or a vocal minority of the population insist that the laws be applied. When this happens we can an-

[30] Hall, *op. cit.*, p. XII.

ticipate that the statutes will be negated.[31] Should there arise a perceived need to curtail retail selling under some special circumstances, then it is likely that these laws will undergo a shift in focal concern much like the shift which characterized the vagrancy laws. Lacking such application the laws will simply remain dormant except for rare instances where they will be negated.

This analysis of the vagrancy statutes (and Hall's analysis of theft as well) has demonstrated the importance of "vested interest" groups in the emergence and/or alteration of laws. The vagrancy laws emerged in order to provide the powerful landowners with a ready supply of cheap labor. When this was no longer seen as necessary and particularly when the landowners were no longer dependent upon cheap labor nor were they a powerful interest group in the society the laws became dormant. Finally a new interest group emerged and was seen as being of great importance to the society and the

laws were then altered so as to afford some protection to this group. These findings are thus in agreement with Weber's contention that "status groups" determine the content of the law.[32] The findings are inconsistent, on the other hand, with the perception of the law as simply a reflection of "public opinion" as is sometimes found in the literature.[33] We should be cautious in concluding, however, that either of these positions are necessarily correct. The careful analysis of other laws, and especially of laws which do not focus so specifically upon the "criminal," are necessary before this question can be finally answered.

In conclusion, it is hoped that future analyses of changes within the legal structure will be able to benefit from this study by virtue of (1) the data provided and (2) the utilization of a set of concepts (innovation, dormancy, concern and negation) which have proved useful in the analysis of the vagrancy law. Such analyses should provide us with more substantial grounds for rejecting or accepting as generally valid the description of some of the processes which appear to characterize changes in the legal system.

---

[31] Negation, in this instance, is most likely to come about by the repeal of the statute. More generally, however, negation may occur in several ways including the declaration of a statute as unconstitutional. This later mechanism has been used even for laws which have been "on the books" for long periods of time. Repeal is probably the most common, although not the only, procedure by which a law is negated.

[32] M. Rheinstein, *Max Weber on Law in Economy and Society*, Harvard University Press, 1954.
[33] Friedman, N., *Law in a Changing Society*, Berkeley and Los Angeles: University of California Press, 1959.

THE SOCIAL REALITY OF CRIME:
A SOCIOLOGY OF CRIMINAL LAW

Richard Quinney

FROM SOCIOLOGICAL JURISPRUDENCE TO SOCIOLOGY OF CRIMINAL LAW

Law is not merely a complex of rules and procedures; Pound taught us that in calling for the study of "law in action." For some purposes it may be useful to think of law as autonomous within society, developing according to its own logic and proceeding along its own lines. But law also simultaneously reflects society and influences it, so that, in a social sense, it is both social product and social force. In Pound's juristic approach, however, law represents the consciousness of the total society. This *consensus* model of (criminal) law has been described in the following way: "The state of criminal law continues to be—as it should—a decisive reflection of the social consciousness of a society. What kind of conduct an organized community considers, at a given time, sufficiently condemnable to impose official sanctions, impairing the life, liberty, or property of the offender, is a barometer of the moral and social thinking of a community." [11] Similarly, Pound, formulating his theory of interests, felt that law reflects the needs of the well-ordered society. In fact, the law is a form of "social engineering" in a civilized society:

For the purpose of understanding the law of

today, I am content to think of law as a social institution to satisfy social wants—the claims and demands involved in the existence of civilized society—by giving effect to as much as we may with the least sacrifice, so far as such wants may be satisfied or such claims given effect by an ordering of human conduct through politically organized society. For present purposes I am content to see in legal history the record of a continually wider recognizing and satisfying of human wants or claims or desires through social control; a more embracing and more effective securing of social interests; a continually more complete and effective elimination of waste and precluding of friction in human enjoyment of the goods of existence—in short, a continually more efficacious social engineering.[12]

Thus, the interests Pound had in mind would maintain and, ultimately, improve the social order. His was a *teleological* as well as consensus theory of interests: men must fulfill some interests for the good of the whole society; these interests are to be achieved through law. In Pound's theory, only the right law can emerge in a civilized society.

Jurisprudence has generally utilized a *pluralistic* model with respect to law as a social force in society. Accordingly, law regulates social behavior and establishes social organization; it orders human relationships by restraining individual actions and by settling disputes in social relations. In recent juristic language law functions "first, to establish the general framework, the rules of the game so to speak, within and by which individual and group life shall be carried on, and secondly, to adjust the conflicting claims which different individuals and groups of

11 Wolfgang Friedmann, *Law in a Changing Society* (Harmondsworth, England: Penguin Books, 1964), p. 143. A similar statement is found in Jerome Michael and Mortimer J. Adler, *Crime, Law and Social Science* (New York: Harcourt, Brace, 1933), pp. 2–3.

12 Pound, *An Introduction to the Philosophy of Law*, pp. 98–99.

individuals seek to satisfy in society." [13] For Pound, the law adjusts and reconciles conflicting interests:

Looked at functionally, the law is an attempt to satisfy, to reconcile, to harmonize, to adjust these overlapping and often conflicting claims and demands, either through securing them directly and immediately, or through securing certain individual interests, or through delimitations or compromises of individual interests, so as to give effect to the greatest total of interests or to the interests that weigh most in our civilization, with the least sacrifice of the scheme of interests as a whole. [14]

In Pound's theory of interests, law provides the general framework within which individual and group life is carried on, according to the postulates of social order. Moreover, as a legal historian has written, "The law defines the extent to which it will give effect to the interests which it recognizes, in the light of other interests and of the possibilities of effectively securing them through law; it also devises means for securing those that are recognized and prescribes the limits within which those means may be employed." [15] In the interest theory of sociological jurisprudence, then, law is an instrument that controls interests according to the requirements of social order.

Pound's theory of interests included a threefold classification of interests, including the individual, the public, and the social:

Individual interests are claims or demands or

desires involved immediately in the individual life and asserted in the title of that life. Public interests are claims or demands or desires involved in life in a politically organized society and asserted in the title of that organization. They are commonly treated as the claims of a politically organized society thought of as a legal entity. Social interests are claims or demands or desires involved in social life in a civilized society and asserted in the title of that life. It is not uncommon to treat them as the claims of the whole social group as such. [16]

Pound warned that the types are overlapping and interdependent and that most can be placed in all the categories, depending upon one's purpose. He argued, however, that it is often expedient to put claims, demands, and desires in their most general form; that is, into the category of social interests.

Surveying the claims, demands, and desires found in legal proceedings and in legislative proposals, Pound suggested that the most important social interest appears to involve security against actions that threaten the social group. [17] Others are interest in the security of domestic, religious, economic, and political institutions; morals; conservation of social resources; general progress, including the development of human powers and control over nature to satisfy human wants; and individual life, especially the freedom of self-assertion. According to Pound, any legal system depends upon the way in which these interests are incorporated into law.

My theoretical perspective on criminal law departs from the general tradition of

[13] Carl A. Auerbach, "Law and Social Change in the United States," *U.C.L.A. Law Review,* 6 (July, 1959), pp. 516–532. Similarly, see Julius Stone, *The Province and Function of Law* (Cambridge: Harvard University Press, 1950), Part III; Julius Stone, *Social Dimensions of Law and Justice* (Stanford: Stanford University Press, 1966), chaps. 4–8.

[14] Roscoe Pound, "A Survey of Social Interests," *Harvard Law Review,* 57 (October, 1943), p. 39.

[15] George Lee Haskins, *Law and Authority in Early Massachusetts* (New York: Macmillan, 1960), p. 226.

[16] Pound, "A Survey of Social Interests," pp. 1–2.

[17] Pound, "A Survey of Social Interests," pp. 1–39. Other aspects of the theory of interests are discussed by Pound in the following publications: *The Spirit of the Common Law* (Boston: Marshall Jones, 1921), pp. 91–93, 197–203; *An Introduction to the Philosophy of Law,* pp. 90–96; *Interpretations of Legal History* (New York: Macmillan, 1923), pp. 158–164; *Social Control through Law,* pp. 63–80.

the interest theory of sociological jurisprudence in a number of ways. First, my perspective is based on a special conception of society. Society is characterized by diversity, conflict, coercion, and change, rather than by consensus and stability. Second, law is a *result* of the operation of interests, rather than an instrument that functions outside of particular interests. Though law may control interests, it is in the first place *created* by interests. Third, law incorporates the interests of specific persons and groups; it is seldom the product of the whole society. Law is made by men, representing special interests, who have the power to translate their interests into public policy. Unlike the pluralistic conception of politics, law does not represent a compromise of the diverse interests in society, but supports some interests at the expense of others. Fourth, the theoretical perspective of criminal law is devoid of teleological connotations. The social order may require certain functions for its maintenance and survival, but such functions will not be considered as inherent in the interests involved in formulating substantive laws. Fifth, the perspective proposed here includes a conceptual scheme for analyzing interests in the law. Finally, construction of the perspective is based on findings from current social science research.

LAW IN POLITICALLY ORGANIZED SOCIETY

Authority relations are present in all social collectivities: some persons are always at the command of others. As order is established in a society, several systems of control develop to regulate the conduct of various groups of persons. Human behavior is thus subject to restraint by varied agencies, institutions, and social groupings —families, churches, social clubs, political organizations, labor unions, corporations, educational systems, and so forth.

The control systems vary considerably in the forms of conduct they regulate, and most provide means for assuring compliance to their rules. Informal means, spontaneously employed by some persons, such as ridicule, gossip, and censure, may ensure conformity to some rules. Control systems may, in addition, rely upon formal and regularized means of sanction.

The *legal system* is the most explicit form of social control. The law consists of (1) specific rules of conduct, (2) planned use of sanctions to support the rules, and (3) designated officials to interpret and enforce the rules.[18] Furthermore, law becomes more important as a system of control as societies increase in complexity. Pound wrote that "in the modern world law has become the paramount agent of social control. Our main reliance is upon force of a politically organized state."[19]

Law is more than a system of formal social control; it is also a body of specialized rules created and interpreted in a *politically organized society,* or the state, which is a territorial organization with the authorized power to govern the lives and activities of all the inhabitants. Though other types of organized bodies may possess formal rules, only the specialized rule systems of politically organized societies are regarded here as systems of law."[20]

[18] F. James Davis, "Law as a Type of Social Control," in F. James Davis, Henry H. Foster, Jr., C. Ray Jeffery, and E. Eugene Davis, *Society and the Law* (New York: The Free Press of Glencoe, 1962), p. 43.

[19] Pound, *Social Control through Law*, p. 20.

[20] The rule systems of societies other than those which are politically organized may be adequately referred to, for comparative purposes, in any number of quasilegal ways, such as nonstate law, primitive law, or "lawways." Perhaps, even better, such systems of rules could be described simply as "tradition," "normative system," or "custom." The concept of law is expanded to include the control systems of other than politically organized society among such writers as Bronislaw Malinowski, *Crime and Custom in Savage Society* (London: Routledge and Kegan Paul, 1926); E. Adamson Hoebel, *The Law of Primitive Man* (Cambridge: Harvard University Press, 1954); William M. Evan,

Law, as a special kind of institution, again is more than an abstract body of rules. Instead of being autonomous within society and developing according to its own logic, law is an integral part of society, operating as a force in society and as a social product. The law is not only that which is written as statutes and recorded as court opinions and administrative rulings, but is also a method or *process* of doing something.[21] As a process, law is a dynamic force that is continually being *created* and *interpreted*. Thus, law in action involves the making of specialized (legal) decisions by various *authorized agents*. In politically organized society, human actions are regulated by those invested with the authority to make specified decisions in the name of the society.

Furthermore, law in operation is an aspect of politics—it is one of the methods by which public policy is formulated and administered for governing the lives and activities of the state's inhabitants. As an act of politics, law and legal decisions do not represent the interests of all persons in the society. Whenever a law is created or interpreted, the values of some are necessarily assured and the values of others are either ignored or negated.

THE INTEREST STRUCTURE

Modern societies are characterized by an organization of differences. The social differentiation of society, in turn, provides the basis for the state's political life. Government in a politically organized society operates according to the interests that characterize the socially differentiated positions. Because varied interests are distributed among the positions, and because the positions are differently equipped with the ability to command, public policy represents specific interests in the society. Politically organized society, therefore, may be viewed as a differentiated *interest structure*.

Each *segment* of society has its own values, its own norms, and its own ideological orientations. When these are considered to be important for the existence and welfare of the respective segments, they may be defined as *interests*.[22] Further, interests can be categorized according to the ways in which activities are generally pursued in society; that is, according to the *institutional orders* of society. The following may then serve as a definition of interests: *the institutional concerns of the segments of society*. Thus, interests are grounded in the segments of society and represent the institutional concerns of the segments.

The institutional orders within which interests operate may be classified into fairly broad categories.[23] For our use, these may be called: (1) *the political,* which regulates the distribution of power and authority in society; (2) *the economic,* which regulates the production and distribution of goods and services; (3) *the religious,* which regulates the relationship of man to a conception of the supernatural; (4) *the kinship,* which regulates sexual relations, family patterns, and the procreation and rearing of children; (5)

"Public and Private Legal Systems," in William M. Evan (ed.), *Law and Sociology* (New York: The Free Press of Glencoe, 1962), pp. 165–184; Philip Selznick, "Legal Institutions and Social Controls," *Vanderbilt Law Review,* 17 (December, 1963), pp. 79–90.

[21] For this conception of law, as applied to criminal law, see Henry M. Hart, Jr., "The Aims of the Criminal Law," *Law and Contemporary Problems,* 23 (Summer, 1958), pp. 401–441.

[22] The view here that interests are not distributed randomly in society but are related to one's position in society follows Marx's theory of economic production and class conflict. See Ralf Dahrendorf, *Class and Class Conflict in Industrial Society* (Stanford: Stanford University Press, 1959), especially pp. 3–35.

[23] The conception of institutional orders closely follows that of Hans Gerth and C. Wright Mills, *Character and Social Structure* (New York: Harcourt, Brace, 1953), especially pp. 25–26.

the educational, which regulates the formal training of the society's members; and (6) *the public,* which regulates the protection and maintenance of the community and its citizens. Each segment of society has its own orientation to these orders. Some, because of their authority position in the interest structure, are able to have their interests represented in public policy.

The segments of society differ in the extent to which their interests are organized. The segments themselves are broad statistical aggregates containing persons of similar age, sex, class, status, occupation, race, ethnicity, religion, or the like. All these have *formal interests;* those which are advantageous to the segment but which are not consciously held by the incumbents and are not organized for action. *Active interests,* on the other hand, are manifest to persons in the segments and are sufficiently organized to serve as the basis for representation in policy decisions.[24]

Within the segments, groups of persons may become aware of and organize to promote their common interests; these may be called *interest groups.* Public policy, in turn, is the result of the success gained by these groups.

The interest structure is characterized by the unequal distribution of *power* and *conflict* among the segments of society. It is differentiated by diverse interests and by the ability of the segments to translate their interests into public policy. Furthermore, the segments are in continual conflict over their interests. Interests thus are structured according to differences in power and are in conflict.

Power and conflict are linked in this conception of interest structure. Power, as the ability to shape public policy, produces

24 The distinction between formal interests and active interests is similar to the distinction Dahrendorf makes between latent and manifest interests. See Dahrendorf, *Class and Class Conflict in Industrial Society,* pp. 173–179.

conflict among the competing segments, and conflict produces differences in the distribution of power. Coherence in the interest structure is thus ensured by the exercise of force and constraint by the conflicting segments. In the conflict-power model, therefore, politically organized society is held together by conflicting elements and functions according to the coercion of some segments by others.

The conflict-power conception of interest structure implies that public policy results from differential distribution of power and conflict among the segments of society. Diverse segments with specialized interests become so highly organized that they are able to influence the policies that affect all persons in the state. Groups that have the power to gain access to the decision-making process are able to translate their interests into public policy. Thus, the interests represented in the formulation and administration of public policy are those treasured by the dominant segments of the society. Hence, public policy is created because segments with power differentials are in conflict with one another. Public policy itself is a manifestation of an interest structure in politically organized society.

FORMULATION AND ADMINISTRATION OF CRIMINAL LAW

Law is a form of public policy that regulates the behavior and activities of all members of a society. It is *formulated* and *administered* by those segments of society which are able to incorporate their interests into the creation and interpretation of public policy. Rather than representing the institutional concerns of all segments of society, law secures the interests of particular segments, supporting one point of view at the expense of others.

Thus, the content of the law, including the substantive regulations and the procedural rules, represents the interests of the segments of society that have the power to shape public policy. Formulation of law allows some segments of society to protect and perpetuate their own interests. By formulating law, some segments are able to control others to their own advantage.

The interests that the power segments of society attempt to maintain enter into all stages of legal administration. Since legal formulations do not provide specific instructions for interpreting law, administration of law is largely a matter of discretion on the part of *legal agents* (police, prosecutors, judges, juries, prison authorities, parole officers, and others). Though implementation of law is necessarily influenced by such matters as localized conditions and the occupational organization of legal agents, the interest structure of politically organized society is responsible for the general design of the administration of criminal justice.

Finally, the formulation and administration of law in politically organized society are affected by changing social conditions. Emerging interests and increasing concern with the protection of various aspects of social life require new laws or reinterpretations of old laws. Consequently, legal changes take place within the context of the changing interest structure of society.

INTERESTS IN CONTEMPORARY SOCIETY

Interests not only are the principal forces behind the creation and interpretation of law, but they are changing the very nature of government. For centuries the state was the Leviathan, protector, repository of power, main source of the community's economic and social life. The state unified and controlled most of the activities of the society. In recent times, however, it is apparent that some groups and segments of society have taken over many of the state's functions:

The question must be raised in all seriousness

whether the "overmighty subjects" of our time—the giant corporations, both of a commercial and non-commercial character, the labor unions, the trade associations, farmers' organizations, veterans' legions, and some other highly organized groups—have taken over the substance of sovereignty. Has the balance of pressures and counter-pressures between these groups left the legal power of the State as a mere shell? If this is a correct interpretation of the social change of our time, we are witnessing another dialectic process in history: the national sovereign State—having taken over effective legal political power from the social groups of the previous age—surrenders its power to the new massive social groups of the industrial age.[25]

Some analysts of the contemporary scene have optimistically forecasted that checks of "countervailing power" will adequately balance the interests of the well organized groups.[26] This pluralistic conception disregards the fact that interest groups are grossly unequal in power. Groups that are similar in power may well check each others' interests, but groups that have little or no power will not have the opportunity to have their interest represented in public policy. The consequence is government by a few powerful private interest groups.

Furthermore, the politics of private interests tends to take place outside of the arena of the public governmental process. In private politics, interest groups receive their individual claims in return for allowing other groups to press for their interests.[27] Behind public politics a private government operates in a way that not only guarantees rewards to well organized groups but affects the lives of us all.

If there be any check in this contemporary condition, it is in the prospect that

25 Friedmann, *Law in a Changing Society*, pp. 239–240.
26 John Kenneth Galbraith, *Modern Capitalism* (Boston: Houghton Mifflin, 1952).
27 See Theodore Lowi, "The Public Philosophy: Interest-Group Liberalism," *American Political Science Review*, 61 (March, 1967), pp. 5–24.

the "public interest" will take precedence over private interests. Interest groups, if for no other reason than their concern for public relations, may bow to the commonweal. Optimistically, the public interest may become an ideal fulfilled, no matter what the source of private power.

But the fallacy in any expectation of the achievement of the public good through the "public interest" is that the government which could foster such a condition will become again in a new age an oppressive interest in itself. That age, in fact, seems to be upon us. Increasingly, as Reich has argued, "Americans live on government largess—allocated by government on its own terms, and held by recipients subject to conditions which express 'the public interest.' " [28] While the highly organized, scientifically planned society, governed for the social good of its inhabitants, promises the best life that man has ever known, not all of our human values will receive attention, and some may be temporarily or permanently negated.

In raw form we cannot hold optimistically to either government by private interests or public interest by government largess. The future for individual man appears to lie in some form of protection from both forms of government. Decentralized government offers some possibility for the survival of the individual in a collective society. But more immediately, that protection must be sought in procedural law, a law that must necessarily be removed from the control of either the interests of private groups or public government. The challenge for law of the future is that it creates an order providing fulfillment for individual values that are

28 Charles A. Reich, "The New Property," *Yale Law Journal*, 73 (April, 1964), p. 733.

now within our reach, values that paradoxically are imminent because of the existence of interests from which we must now seek protection. A new society is indeed coming: Can a law be created apart from private interests which assures individual fulfillment within a good society?

.   .   .

The perspective on criminal law in politically organized society provides the basis for understanding how particular criminal laws are formulated. Following this perspective, criminal laws—including the enactments of legislatures, court decisions, and administrative rulings—are formulated by those segments of society which have the power to shape public policy. The formulation of criminal law is thus an act of politics: Public policy is established by some for governing the lives and affairs of all inhabitants of a society. Crime, then, is a definition of human conduct that is created in the course of the political life of the community.

Lawmaking, according to this perspective, represents the translation of specific group interests into public policy. For the most part, criminal laws support particular interests to the neglect or negation of other interests, thus representing the concerns of only some members of society. Though some criminal laws may involve a compromise of conflicting interests, more likely than not, criminal laws mark the victory of some groups over others. The notion of a compromise of conflicting interests is a myth perpetuated by a pluralistic model of politics. Some interests never find access to the lawmaking process. Other interests are overwhelmed in it, not compromised. But ultimately some interests succeed in becoming criminal law, and are able to control the conduct of others.

THE PROFESSIONAL ASSOCIATION
AND THE LEGAL REGULATION OF PRACTICE

Ronald L. Akers

The political ideologies, identifications, affiliations, participation, contribution to campaign funds, government employment, seeking and holding office, and other aspects of the political behavior of incumbents of various occupations, professions and strata have been investigated.[1] There are also some discussions of the political power of professions, almost exclusively concerned with the legal and medical groups. But the study of professional associations as political pressure groups and their impact on the formulation and administration of the law has been relatively neglected. Professions are prominent among the many pressure groups actively pressing claims upon and through government,[2] attempting to have a part in shaping any public policy that affects their interest. There is ample suggestion in the literature that major portions of their efforts are directed toward the state licensure and practice laws.[3]

However, there has been little research into the amount and kind of involvement of professional associations in the process of getting practice acts written, passed, and enforced. The purpose of this paper is to describe, on the basis of exploratory research, the role of professional organizations in influencing, and the interprofessional conflict relevant to, public policy

Reprinted from the official publication of the Law and Society Association *Law and Society Review,* **2** (May, 1968), pp. 463–482, by permission of the author and the Law and Society Association.

Author's note: This paper is based on research that was part of a larger study of the political power of professions while the author was on National Science Foundation Fellowship tenure. See R. Akers, *Professional Organization, Political Power, and Occupational Laws,* 1966 (unpublished Ph.D. dissertation, University of Kentucky).

[1] O. Glantz, *Political Identifications of Occupational Strata,* in *Man, Work, and Society* 419–31 (S. Nosow & W. Form eds. 1962); J. Hardman, *The Power Motivation of the American Labor Movement, id.* at 431–36; S. Lipset & M. Schwartz, *The Politics of Professionals,* in *Professionalization* 299–310 (H. Vollmer & D. Mills eds. 1966); H. Hall, *Scientists and Politicians,* id. at 310–21; B. Barber, *Some Problems in the Sociology of the Professions,* 92 *Daedalus* 669–88 (1962); W. Glaser, *Doctors and Politics,* 66 *Am. J. Soc.* 230–45 (1960); R. Lewis, *New Power at the Polls: The Doctors,* in *Politics in the United States* 180–85 (H. Turner ed. 1955); see also the selective bibliographies on ideologies, politics, and occupations in Nosow and Form, *supra* at 587–88.

[2] Nearly every listing, inventory, classification, or comprehensive discussion of pressure groups in American society includes the "big three" of business, labor and agriculture, occupational groups with special emphasis on professionals, and usually some mention of a miscellaneous assortment of veteran, women, reform, motoring, civil rights, religious and other groups. H. Zeigler calls the big three plus the professional groups, the "big four" in *Interest Groups in American Society* 93–232 (1964); V. Key, *Politics, Parties and Pressure Groups* 54–65, 92ff. (1958); D. Truman, *The Governmental Process* 68–108 (1962); R. Williams, *American Society: A Sociological Interpretation* 272–75 (1963).

[3] A. Carr-Saunders & P. Wilson, *The Emergence of Professions* in Nosow and Form, *supra* note 1, at 205; B. Barber, *supra* note 1, at 683–84; W. Goode, *Community Within a Community: The Professions,* 22 *Am. Soc. Rev.* 195 (1957); Goode, *Encroachment, Charlatanism, and the Emerging Professions: Psychology, Sociology, and Medicine,* 25 *Am. Soc. Rev.* 905 (1960); H. Wilensky, *The Professionalization of Everyone,* 70 *Am. J. Soc.* 145–46 (1964); Wilensky, *The Dynamics of Professionalism: The Case of Hospital Administration,* 7 *Hosp. Adm.* 17 (1962); Truman, *supra* note 2, at 93–96; Key, *supra* note 2, at 118, 135–37; H. Gasnell & M. Schmitt, *Professional Associations,* 179 *Annals* 25–33 (1935); B. Zeller, *Pressure Politics in New York* 158–86 (1937); D. McKean, *Pressures on the Legislature of New Jersey* 72 (1938).

regulating professional practice. The study reflects the concrete situation found in one state but also is concerned more generally with the pressure activities of state and national professional organizations.

Varying amounts of data were collected from a total of twenty-three informants representing the chiropractic, dental, medical, optometric, and pharmacy professions in Kentucky. At least one person for each profession was located who had been "in" on the groundwork and had taken an active part in influencing licensing legislation. "Formal" depth interviews lasting up to three hours were held with these informants.[4] All persons cooperating in the study were utilized not as "respondents" but as "informants" in the sense that this latter term has come to acquire in anthropological fieldwork. They were not asked their personal attitudes or opinions (although these undoubtedly influenced their replies), and there was no interest in their personal or social characteristics. Rather they were questioned as persons knowledgeable about a system in which they occupied strategic positions.

In addition, much source material, providing data that would have required many additional interview hours to acquire, was made available to the investigator.[5] Also, published sources relating to each profession were consulted, and questions relevant to occupational laws were included on a questionnaire sent to the national offices of each association.

[4] The interview schedule was constructed on the basis of an exhaustive content analysis of the relevant practice acts. Informants were questioned regarding desirable provisions in the law, the part played by the association in influencing its passage, and the nature of opposition met.

[5] Included in this material were journals, books, pamphlets, booklets, committee reports, minutes of meetings, private correspondence, personal papers, unpublished manuscripts, bulletins and communiques, copies of court decisions, copies of laws from other states, and drafts, suggestions, proposals, and bills considered before introduction to the legislature.

HISTORICAL AND GENERAL PERSPECTIVE

The foundings of state associations were often for the express purpose of promoting occupational legislation, sometimes in a defensive move to prevent other, already established, professions from regulating them. The New Jersey Pharmaceutical Association (1870), for instance, was formed only after steps were undertaken by the "medical society of New Jersey to force legislative measures on 'all dispensers of medicines' in the state." [6] Within a week of the formation of the New York Optical Society (1896), a bill to regulate the practice of refracting opticians (the early denotation of optometrists) was introduced into the New York legislature.[7] Securing passage of a medical practice act was one of the main reasons for the organization of the Virginia medical society.[8] The initial organization of each of the five professions in Kentucky was shortly followed by the enactment of a practice act. (See Table 1.) Since its organization, each association has been the driving force in legislation regulating practice in its own field. "Laws have been enacted, amended, and re-enacted at the suggestion of the association, hoping to secure the police power of the state [for] elimination of the undesirable practitioner." [9]

While the state associations have always been involved and remain in the frontlines of legislative struggle to obtain suitable practice laws, effective nationwide state regulation was achieved only through the combined effort of state and national

[6] G. Sonnedecker, *Kremer's and Urdang's History of Pharmacy* 180 (1963).
[7] M. Cox, *Optometry, The Profession* 35 (1957); E. Arrington, *History of Optometry* 21–22 (1929).
[8] Eds. of the Yale L.J., *The American Medical Association: Power, Purpose, and Politics in Organized Medicine,* in Vollmer & Mills, *supra* note 1, at 321.
[9] R. Sprau & E. Gennett, *History of Kentucky Dentistry* 7, 97–106 (1960).

organizations.[10] Medicine, which was the first of the five professions to organize at the national level, achieved licensing laws in all states first. It was followed by pharmacy and dentistry which organized nationally shortly after medicine. Optometry, nationally organized later, was licensed in all states at a later date, and the last of the five to have a national association, chiropractic, still is not licensed in all states. (See Table 1.)

Although federal legislation has come

maries of major provisions of various acts, results of national surveys, reports, model statutes, legal advice, and forums for discussing common problems, and in general put the weight of national organization behind enactment of state laws.[12]

INITIATION AND SUPPORT OF PENDING LEGISLATION

The state association, in conjunction with the examining board, initiates moves

Table 1   Dates at Which Practice Legislation Enacted and at Which Organizations Founded

Profession	Date First Organized in Kentucky	Nationally	Date by Which Licensed in Kentucky	in All States
Chiropractic	1916	1910	1917	—a
Dentistry	1870	1859	1878	1935
Medicine	1851	1847	1870	1915
Optometry	1916	1897	1920	1939
Pharmacy	1870	1852	1874	1935

Source: Based on data reported in S. Spector and W. Frederick, OCCUPATIONAL LICENSING IN THE STATES 78-88 (1952), on data from interviews, and on the ENCYCLOPEDIA OF ASSOCIATIONS (F. Ruffner, Jr. ed. 1964).

aBy 1952, chiropractors were licensed in 44 states; in 1963 New York passed a chiropractic act, but chiropractic still is not licensed in 3 states.

to assume greater importance for the national associations than it did formerly,[11] the national bodies have not ceased to aid the state associations through the years. Each national association has a legislative committee or council which, as part of its responsibilities, cooperates with state and local societies in legislative matters. The national bodies provide the state societies with copies of state laws, charts and summaries of

for legislation, decides what provisions should be added, deleted, or changed, drafts preliminary and final proposed bills, persuades a legislator to introduce the bill, and works for its passage throughout the time it is being considered. If proposed practice legislation comes from any other direction, the association will oppose it and work for its defeat.

10 S. Spector & W. Frederick, *Occupational Licensing Legislation in the States* 18–21 (1952); C. Stetler & A. Moritz, *Doctor, Patient and the Law* 13 (1962); Sonnedecker, *supra* note 6, at 179; *Remington's Practice of Pharmacy* 14 (E. Martin, *et al.* ed. 1961); Arrington, *supra* note 7, at 197.

11 For instance, the AMA and the ADA give regular reports through their respective journals on federal legislation of interest to the medical and dental professions; *see* 190 J.A.M.A. 313 & 347 (1964); 69 J.A.D.A. 58–87 (1964).

12 R. McCluggage, *A History of the American Dental Association* 368–69 (1959); American Dental Association, *The American Dental Association: Its Structure and Function* 22–23 (1957); 69 J.A.D.A. 607–12 (1964); 67 J.A.D.A. 884–92 (1963); 58 J.A.D.A. 27 (1959); 35 J.A.O.A. 1045 (1964); Martin, *et al.*, *supra* note 10, at 1698–1703; 4 Ja. PhA. Ns. 202 (1964); D. Anderson, *The Present Day Doctor of Chiropractic* 9 (1956); Stetler & Moritz, *supra* note 10, at 16; O. Garceau, *The Political Life of the American Medical Association* 165 (1961); J. Burrow, *AMA: Voice of American Medicine* 54–66 (1963).

Because its members must work with the law continually, the examining board is often the first to become aware of needed changes and inadequacies in the laws. But it is the state association that provides the manpower and organization needed to see the move for legislation through to fruition. The background and drafting of the completely revised Dental Practice Act, which passed the Kentucky legislature in 1964, was accomplished over a two-year period by a joint revision committee made up of two persons from the association's Executive Committee, two from its Legislative Committee, and two from the state board. This revision committee was appointed by the House of Delegates of the Kentucky Dental Association, and after the committee had decided on the changes it wanted and the attorneys had written the amendments in suitable language, the proposed bill was presented to the association's House for its discussion and approval.

This seems to be typical of licensing bills.

The executive secretary and corresponding secretary of the [chiropractic] association were on the committee that drafted the law, and [other] . . . men and women in the association were involved in the legislation.

The board drafted suggestions for changes, then turned them over to the [optometric association's] legislative committee which went over suggestions and then discussed them with the board.

The present medical practice act was written under the guidance of the Commissioner of Health at the time, who was also secretary of the state medical association and the board of health.

The key man in the drafting and support of the bill was [Health Commissioner]. Associational personnel and facilities were involved in the discussions, making of drafts, and so on. A tremendous amount of time and effort went into the law; it went through 15 or 20 drafts before it reached the floor [of the legislature].

The secretary of the state pharmaceutical association and the pharmacy board also was centrally instrumental in the legislative efforts of organized pharmacy in the state. The pharmacy bills through, the years have been associational bills, and the state organization through a Special Legislative Action Committee has instituted vigorous campaigns to gain legislative support for pharmacy proposals.

Once it has been fairly well agreed that new legislation is needed, the committee charged with the leg work holds several meetings to thrash out consensus on exactly what will be asked for and, with legal counsel, how it will be asked. Preliminary steps include consulting model statutes and/or looking at the provisions in the relevant laws of other states.

We wrote to other state boards; looked at the laws of other states, particularly laws of successful states and picked out what we thought to be the better portions . . . used suggestions and clauses from other states. Other state boards and associations were very helpful in sending us their laws and offering suggestions.

None of the organizations in Kentucky made use of nationally prepared model laws, but with one exception, all communicated with and utilized resource materials from national offices. One organization was in continuous communication with the national office during the time the bill was being prepared and when it was pending in the General Assembly. Letters were exchanged with the attorney for the national association, who tendered advice and personal assistance, and indeed wrote a suggested draft of the law.

When the bill is introduced into the legislature, the problem becomes one of mobilizing membership behind the bill, convincing legislators that it is a good law that protects public welfare, and rallying enough votes to get it through both houses.

A number of things may happen to a bill to foil the efforts of its supporters. Mistiming, unforeseen objections to minor provisions, overlong committee consideration, deliberate killing in committee, or passing one house and failing the other are some of the pitfalls that must be avoided. Sometimes the workings of the Assembly seem frustratingly unpredictable and malleable under pressure yet simultaneously unyielding and grossly ineffective in producing "good" legislation.

"That legislature is a funny thing. Any bill that has any merit at all can't get through. You could propose a bill against sin and by the time it got through the legislature, it would be so changed you wouldn't recognize it."

"You ever been to Frankfort? It's something. A bill to inspect boilers was defeated on Friday. Labor groups and others went out on the weekend—there's no way to prove it, but money was passed, favors were done—and on Monday, the bill was called back and passed. We all know this happens, it's the way bills get through the legislature."

None of the informants would admit that such tactics were used by his group, although each knew of instances where they had been used by others. Each presented his group as relying mainly on moral suasion, argumentation, discussion with legislators, and public relations.[13]

One successful professional organization in the state, for example, surveys the state following the elections to find out how well its membership know the elected representatives and senators.

Who is Senator John Doe's dentist? Who is a relative? Who is a good friend? Each contact is given the opportunity to let us know how much influence he can have on what particular [congressmen]. When the Legislature convenes we feel that we know all the members of the General Assembly pretty well. We keep

a cross file of the legislators in the office. This includes the Governor as well as all other elected officials.

When a bill is referred to committee, several influential members of the profession are asked to be prepared to defend the bill in committee. These people are introduced to the committee and the presentation is skillfully and effectively made. "We, with the assistance of our attorney, usually draft a brief and concise statement and have available mimeographed copies for each one present [at the committee hearing]."

The amount of plain hard leg work that the above description implies is an inevitable ingredient in influencing occupational legislation.

I spent six weeks in Frankfort when we were trying to get this thing through. We would talk to a legislator at his home and then be camping on his doorstep when he came back to Frankfort.

(Your tactics were mostly personal contact and persuasion then?)

Yes, you have to talk to these fellows at their homes and then be waiting for them when they come back. They can tell you one thing there and do another in Frankfort.

(Did you attend legislative committee hearings?)

Yes, we had to just talk and present our case. We see them over and over again and talk to them about the bill.

Much work and careful planning can come to nought, however, if the support of powerful government officials and legislators is not forthcoming. By the same token, such support at strategic moments can insure success.

We had no trouble at all. Governor ——— came to the committee meeting and went as far as he could for us. He said that no group should be prevented from upgrading itself. The bill hurt no one and it helped us; it should be passed.

13 J. Dodson, *How to Pass a Bill in Frankfurt*, 27 *Ky. Phar.* 10–12, 24–27 (1964).

THE BOARD AND ASSOCIATION

There is generally a close relationship between the statutorily created boards and the private professional associations. These ties prevail not only in the formulation of the law, but also in its administration.

The enforcement of the law is, of course, the responsibility of an examining board, but a board will quite often—and sometimes routinely—work through the ethics or grievance committee of the corresponding association in disciplining practitioners. If the association cannot bring the recalcitrant practitioner into line, the board proceeds with the more formal and legal sanctions at its command. The association's effort in dealing with unethical and illegal practice sometimes extends to financial subsidization of the board. For instance, the Kentucky Dental Association has been financially supporting the board's investigative and prosecution activities by amounts of $2,500 to $3,000 per year. This is a pattern found all over the United States. One state dental society's monetary assistance for a board's enforcement activities averages $31,000 a year.[14]

Sometimes the board uses part of its revenues from license and renewal fees to subsidize the association. This may even be required by law, as in the case of Kentucky pharmacy; $2 of the renewal fees for each pharmacist's license in the state must be turned over to the association. But the same thing may be accomplished more informally. "The board really helps support the association. The board pays about two-thirds of the administrative director and executive secretary's salary, and he only puts in about one-third of his time for the board."

The optometric board pays for the office space used by the association and for its promotion booth at state fairs. The chiropractic board also has made use of its

funds to ease the financial burden of the association. The pharmacy, optometric, and dental boards and associations all have some type of joint personnel and shared office space, buildings, clerical employees, and other facilities, and the medical profession at one time had much the same kind of arrangement.

When the association gets too big and/or the job of keeping up with all licensed practitioners and law violations become too burdensome, the board and the association are apt to be separated.

Historically the [medical] association and the board have worked together and been very close. Until recently, the commissioner [of Health] was secretary of both the board and association. When ———— came in they were separated; he was recommended to separate the two jobs—just too much for one man to handle . . . [the associational executive secretary] had his office in the same place as the Board of Health office when it was in Louisville, up to about 5 or 6 years ago. There has always been a close relation of the medical profession and public health, and the Board of Health and the KMA still maintain close contact.

Chiropractic has yet another pattern of overlapping personnel. The board of examiners appoints and pays the expenses of inspectors who keep check on practice throughout the state and report to the board. One inspector is appointed for each of the seven administrative districts of the state chiropractic association; he is considered a district officer of the association, however, and serves it as well as the board.

These are, for the most part, informal arrangements whereby the interests of the associations are more closely reflected in the actions of the regulatory boards. More formal control often is acquired through special provisions in the law giving the association control, either directly or indirectly, over appointments to board membership. In Kentucky, only chiropractic does not have a statutory clause requiring

14 *Report of the American Association of Dental Examiners Committee on Legislation* 4 (1962).

Table 2   Associational Control Over Board Appointments in 48 States

	Number of States in Which Board Is Appointed		
Profession	Directly by Association	From Association List	Without Association
Chiropractic	0	10	35
Dentistry	3	26	19
Medicine	3	20	25
Optometry	0	17	31
Pharmacy	0	25	23

Source: Based on data reported in S. Spector & W. Frederick, OCCUPATIONAL LICENSING IN THE STATES 78-88 (1952).

the governor to make board appointments from lists submitted by the state associations. Table 2 shows the extent to which each of the five professions has managed to secure this right in all forty-eight contiguous states.

THE INTERORGANIZATIONAL CONTEXT: OPPOSITION AND ALLIANCE

Successfully influencing public policy depends not only upon the resources and organizational strength of the state and national associations, but also upon the degree of opposition from, and alliance with, other groups. Thus, any analysis of the role of organized professions as pressure groups must include the interorganizational context in which political influence is exercised. Since the kind and degree of opposition met was different for each of the five professions, they will be considered separately. Then a "peak" organization and its membership will be described.

Chiropractic is defined by the AMA as a "cult" or "sectarian" practice [15] and chiropractors perceive their only consistent and significant opposition as coming from organized medicine.

Everything we try to do in Frankfort, the doctors oppose. . . . They tried to put a spite bill in, one that would put chiropractic under

the Department of Health. They were not successful. The legislators know a spite bill when they see it—but it was introduced on the floor.

. . . they just didn't want us to have a law. They didn't detail their opposition. They were just generally opposed to us.

Over the years, this medical opposition has been duplicated in state after state and at the federal level.[16]

By the same token, organized chiropractic is almost routinely in opposition to medically sponsored legislation. At the time the present medical practice act was pending:

Chiropractors talked to ———— . . . Chiropractors are always afraid that medical legislation will chip away their domain. Physicians consider them quacks.

They look suspect [sic] on any medical or health legislation; they look with great suspicion on them.

The medical profession is not, however, the only adversary of chiropractic legislation, and chiropractors sometimes find themselves opposing and opposed by, dentistry and pharmacy.[17] These groups have stood together either in supporting legislation that chiropractic was opposed to or in objecting to bills sponsored by chiropractors. Consequently chiropractors have

[15] American Medical Association, *Opinions and Reports of the Judicial Council* § 3, 11–12 (1964).

[16] T. McClusky, *Your Health and Chiropractic* 147–64 (1957).

[17] KPhA News, Feb. 15, 1962 and Feb. 23, 1962.

come to see themselves as a beleaguered minority fighting powerful foes.[18] The other groups do not assess the chiropractors as underdogs, however; they see organized chiropractic as a strong legislative opponent. A jointly sponsored medical-dental "cancer quackery" bill passed, but ". . . the chiropractors who have quite a lobby in our state had the bill in trouble."

Chiropractors have a pretty good lobby going in Kentucky. There are about 2000 physicians, 1900 dentists, and 1500 pharmacists, but 150 chiropractors can raise more noise than all of us put together.

Optometrists have not been defined by the AMA as cult practitioners, but they are listed as "irregular practitioners." It is, therefore, deemed unethical for a physican to lecture to optometric groups or employ optometrists.[19] Optometrists have met with medical opposition from the very beginning of their attempts to secure practice acts in the various states.[20] This medical-optometric conflict is seen in Kentucky where the major stumbling block to passage of the optometric licensing law was the combined medical-opticianry opposition.

We had to agree to the opticians law to get ours. The KMA said they would fight the optometry law to the last unless optometrists did not oppose a law to license opthalmic dispensers. The AOA attorney advised it would be better to lose the optometry bill then to let the dispenser's bill get through. But we agreed to it anyway. It hasn't made much difference; the opticians do not have a very good law anyway.

The dentists' successful efforts to enact an extensive revision of the dental act met with little difficulty, with the exception of some last-minute attempts by the

Dental Laboratory Guild in the state to amend the bill. The dental technicians were outmaneuvered both behind the scenes and on the floor, and the Dental Act passed with only one dissenting vote. At the same time, the dentists were able to bottle up a bill introduced by the State Dental Laboratory Guild.

Our forces were organized. We placed on call the heads of the Prosthetic Departments of both the Schools of Dentistry . . . we had our key men make personal contacts with members [of the house committee] . . . The Laboratory Guild appeared at the Capital. They sent telegrams to the Legislature and Representative ——— tried to get a public hearing on the Bill.

The bill did not come to the floor, but instead was referred to the Rules Committee where it remained until the end of the session.

Pharmacists have for years tried to secure the enactment of a major revision of the Pharmacy Practice Act, without much success. In one instance a bill was successfully steered through both houses only to have the Governor veto it. "He got mad at the board because we wouldn't license some friend of his . . ." But the problems have come from organized groups, also.

We have had some horticulturists oppose us in the past. This last time we had the Kentucky Hospital Association and the Farm Bureau and Hardware Association against us. Hospital administrators weren't against us in the past. They didn't have a real good organization until now. They didn't before so we didn't get much real opposition from them. Now they have their own attorney and a good organization.

The hospital administrators were opposed to sections prohibiting the dispensing of drugs for in-patients in hospitals by non-pharmacists, and the Farm Bureau and feed dealers were afraid that the bill would place commercial poisons, insec-

---

[18] McClusky, *supra* note 16, at 157; Anderson, *supra* note 12, at 9.
[19] American Medical Association, *supra* note 15, at 13–14.
[20] Arrington, *supra* note 7, at ii–iv, 19–22.

ticides, etc. under control of the Pharmacy Board.

Organized medicine, dentistry, and pharmacy in the state all have representatives, along with nurses and hospital administrators, in a peak organization known as the Council on Allied Medical Services. Each year the member organizations present their respective legislative plans for the consideration of the other members. An effort is then made to settle conflicts and differences of opinion occasioned by any member's proposals. Ordinarily, this means that each member group can present bills to the Assembly, confident that it will have the cooperation of the other members. This is not always the case, however, as evidenced by the conflict between the pharmacists and the hospital administrators. But the Council at least provides a meeting ground for pre-session compromises, so that the members are not faced with unexpected opposition from other member groups during the brief time that the legislature is in session. This alliance of health professions does not include chiropractors and optometrists, who thus do not have the opportunity to meet with other groups under agreement-inducing conditions. In fact, one of the reasons the Council was organized some years ago was specifically to combat chiropractors and optometrists.

". . . we would not want either chiropractors or optometrists on the Council. [We] organized the Council a few years ago. One of our main concerns at the time was that chiropractors and some others would jump in on the Kerr-Mills payments."

The cooperation among the members of the Council seems to extend only slightly beyond agreeing not to oppose one another's plans, but it does sometimes extend to active support of another member's legislation or plans to fight some bill. Thus, if chiropractors and optometrists sponsor legislation which a Council member is against, other member organizations may also oppose it. If there are differences between two members of the Council, the other member groups are likely to refrain from taking sides and to try to smooth out the problems. Whereas, optometrists and chiropractors may meet objections from a coalition of other organizations, the members of the Council are less likely to find such serious opposition.

The general picture of the context of conflict among the five professions in Kentucky can be summarized as follows: Chiropractic and optometry generally do not oppose one another but have not made any apparent efforts to cooperate with and support one another. Medicine, dentistry, and pharmacy in recent times have not actively opposed one another and, in fact, are members of an allied group of health professions. Medicine and chiropractic consistently oppose each other, and sometimes optometry and medicine engage in political combat. Medicine, dentistry and pharmacy occasionally all oppose certain aspects of chiropractic's legislation. Secondarily, they may be politically opposed to optometry. Medicine and dentistry seem to cooperate more closely than any other two groups, and they seldom oppose pharmaceutical legislation, although not always wholeheartedly supporting it. Finally, each profession experiences conflict with additional groups besides the other four health professions.

DISCUSSION

While this exploratory study does not provide systematic answers to theoretical questions, it does fill some descriptive gaps in our knowledge about the operation of professional organizations as pressure groups in the enactment and administration of licensure and practice laws. But whatever empirical studies such as this contribute, their major importance lies in the relevant questions they generate and the establishment of problem parameters for future and more definitive research.

Some of these issues will be discussed in this concluding section.

All of the organized professions in this study were regularly and consistently engaged in influencing the laws and constantly concerned with the way they are enforced by the regulatory boards. The practice acts are written by, introduced to the legislature on behalf of, sponsored by, and enacted largely because of the lobby activities of the state associations backed by the national organizations. One of the aims of the political actions of these groups is the promotion of the "license and mandate" claims of professions.[21] While the laws do regulate practice for the protection of the public, they are not so much legislated *against* as *for* and *by* the professions.

It would be a mistake, however, to assume automatically, perhaps cynically, that the *real* goal of a profession in influencing laws is to benefit itself and that only lip service is paid to benefiting the public. It is suggested that the goals of professional associations include both protection of the profession and protection of the public. The two goals, of course, need not be conflicting and are most often served simultaneously by the same law. They do conflict sometimes, however, and it is true that when both can not be served, professions often promote that which best suits their interests even though this may be contrary to the public good. Many provisions of practice acts are plainly meant to enhance the organized profession's jurisdictional claims, support its concept of what constitutes its area of competence, bring it more influence and prestige, protect it from encroachment, and support its autonomy in a particular area, with little regard to what is best for the public. At the same time, professions just as vigorously have supported provisions which safeguard against

abuses, ill-treatment, fraud, incompetence, and malpractice at the hands of the profession's members or of unqualified quacks and charlatans.

In some cases where parts of a proposed act would clearly benefit the professional organization but which would have unknown or undesirable effects on public interest, the profession may in fact opt for the public by dropping those provisions. For instance, a provision was proposed for an Optometric Practice Act which would have required as a condition for license renewal that all practitioners attend lectures or two-day courses at the annual meetings of the state association for "postgraduate education." Such a provision had been incorporated into an earlier Chiropractic Act, and registration at the annual chiropractic meetings subsequently increased considerably. However, although it was recognized that such a provision would have automatically increased attendance and registration fees at state meetings, and even though no outside opposition was met on the issue, optometrists decided to eliminate the provision from their proposals. The reason given for this action was that attendance at these meetings might be misrepresented to the public by individual practitioners as real post-graduate training, and further even if this did not happen, such a requirement carried no clear benefit to the public. As one informant said: "But you must first work to the good of the public. If [the provision] doesn't do that, then we have no business putting it in; the same is true for any of the [other parts]."

But, on the other hand, less altruistic explanations are obviously possible, and the situation is simply presented as an example of an organized profession's claim to be placing the public interest above its own. The ambiguity of such a situation is clearly apparent. There is great need for systematic data on the relative frequency with which this happens and with which the other goals of the profession are pur-

21 E. Hughes, *Men and Their Work* 77–78 (1958); Hughes, *The Study of Occupations,* in *Sociology Today* 447 (R. Merton, *et al.* ed. 1959).

sued at the expense of the public well-being. This research did not provide such data or furnish guidelines as to what might be done to ensure that such pressure groups do not produce legislative outcomes detrimental to public welfare. This remains a serious policy question deserving further research.

The impact of the private association on the public interest is complicated by the close interrelationship between the association and the public regulatory agency. In the literature there is little recognition of the degree of interrelationship beyond some mention of the association's power in determining board appointments and regulations.[22] However, it appears that their activities, personnel, facilities, and even finances overlap to such an extent that it is not entirely correct to say that the association "influences" the board's administration of public policy in the same sense that it influences the formulation of that policy by the legislature. It is not even influence in the same sense that all "client groups" of governmental agencies come to have an impact on the agencies' decisions.[23] The cooperation between the two sometimes reaches the point of near identity. Again, there is no conclusive evidence that this arrangement necessarily results in regulatory decisions which detract from public welfare. But this is a possibility and one safeguard already in effect in California could be tried elsewhere. In that state, each examining board has a lay member who is supposed to represent the "public."

The point is that we do not know the degree to which public interest is or is not served by the pressure activities of professional groups. Further insights into this would be helped if we knew the outcome not only of the type of law discussed here but also a body of comparable policy which has been formed without the participation of pressure groups. There are no licensure and practice statutes and regulations which have been enacted and promulgated without the direct participation of the regulated profession and other groups with which they are in alliance or conflict. Research into this problem, then, would have to look to other types of public policy around which no pressure groups have formed or on which they have had little impact.

Hopefully, this kind of research would also provide some answers to the related problem of accounting for the presence of direct interest group pressure on some issues and its relative absence on others. Certainly, interest groups may form around any issue in the making and administering of the law. But the question is, when are they likely to do so and when is their influence likely to be decisive? Important as they are, group pressures form only part of the total political process out of which policy grows. It grows not only out of the compromise and victory of group pressures, but also out of a range of influences in the social, economic, and normative structures of society. How influential identifiable group pressures are in the formulation and administration of law is an empirical question which must be answered for given types of issues and policies.

However, it would appear that, in general, the closer policy comes to reflecting widespread moral sentiment or agreed upon values or to attempting to solve issues of widespread concern, the more difficult it is to attribute its existence to the relative influence of specified groups. This does not mean that interest groups will not become involved in such issues and indeed attempt to sway public sentiment. But they are likely to be more circumspect about it, and the known or probable public reaction becomes a more important element in the public decision-maker's actions. Thus, even though pressure groups may be involved in these

---

22 Key, *supra* note 2, at 36; W. Boyer, *Bureaucracy on Trial* 24–26 (1964); Wilensky (1964), *supra* note 3, at 145–46.

23 Zeigler, *supra* note 2, at 277–99.

issues, the public's view of the rightness or wrongness of certain policies may be crucial in determining whether the groups have their way. Interests other than those of the groups directly involved may be reflected in public decisions through the impact of reference groups. A legislator or a public official identifying with the interests and values of his reference groups, needs and probably will get, no direct pressure from them to act in their behalf. Specialized legislation, on the other hand, usually lacks widespread interest, relates to few other reference group values, and therefore is most influenced by direct lobby activity. We may say, then, that the more restricted the population to which the policy refers and the less visible the outcome, the more it is susceptible to and likely to be subjected to direct group pressures.

Professional practice acts fall into this specialized category. Their passage is not very much in the public eye, and popular views have, at best, an indirect and diffuse impact on their contents. Usually, each practice act governs only one profession, and it is not surprising that it will contain just about what that profession wants, unless it infringes upon the claimed prerogatives of other groups. This infringement is upon groups within—not outside of—the same sphere of activity. Opposition may come from other contiguous professional and semi-professional groups but is unlikely to come from a concerned public.

The next problem is to determine the extent to which patterns of influence and conflict found here are repeated for other political issues. For instance, the same professions included in this study also have an interest in a number of federal policies, in workmen's compensation, in publicly supported health insurance and welfare plans, and in public health laws of various kinds. These are issues which do excite wider interest, relate to segments of society well beyond the health professions

to which they refer, and have relatively visible public outcomes. Supposedly, the affected professions play proportionately a much smaller part in shaping these policies than they do in the legal regulation of practice. This suggests an ideal research site for pursuing further the questions of the formation of group pressure, its relative impact on legislation, and its relationship to public interest.

Several other questions could be raised. What is the relative position of professions in the overall political power structure of modern society? What is the power status of one profession relative to others? What is the relative impact of state and national associations on occupational and other laws? And equally important, what is the impact of the laws and their administration on the actual practice and organization of the various professions? What historically has been the role of professions as pressure groups and how has this changed?

The study of political power and the law is part of the larger theoretical issue relating to the place of law as both an independent and dependent variable in society. Obviously, the approach in this study is just one way of accounting for the content of public policy. Empirical research on this question may take the form of either a longitudinal or a current study of some policy in the making or historical reconstruction of the way a policy came into being.[24] Although, as noted above, the study of the law-making process is not entirely the study of pressure politics, in modern society politics and law are intermeshed. The political process in general and pressure politics in partic-

24 J. Hall, *Theft Law and Society* (1952); W. Chambliss, *A Sociological Analysis of the Law of Vagrancy*, 12 *Social Problems* 67–77 (1964); H. Becker, *Outsiders* 135–46 (1963); A. Lindesmith, *Federal Law and Drug Addiction*, 7 *Social Problems* 48–59 (1959); D. Dykstra, *The History of a Legislative Power Struggle*, Wis. L. Rev. 402–29 (Spring 1966).

ular should receive increased attention in the sociology of law.[25]

The bulk of the effort to answer questions about the political process, understandably, has been made by political scientists. However, some of the questions should receive more sociological attention than they customarily are given. Sociologists should be able to make valuable contributions in some of the problem areas traditionally included within the intellectual concerns of political science. For instance, one of the more interesting questions raised by this research is: Given that the professions do operate as pressure groups, what explains the varied success of the five professions in securing desired and blocking unwanted legislation? In more general form, this has remained a central theoretical issue in political science. Why is one group more powerful than another in influencing the law?

What is the group basis of political power? What group properties and other variables make for political success? [26]

It is in the study of such problems that sociologists with their knowledge of group and organizational characteristics and appreciation of society as an interdependent system should be able to make a real contribution. A sociological perspective may not provide any improvement in a comprehensive theory of the political process, but it can enable clearer specification of important aspects of the internal structure of political groups and their interrelationships with groups in the larger sociopolitical context. Pressure politics, not only of professions but other groups as well, and their ability to achieve influence in the law-making process, studied in a variety of contexts and with a variety of methods, is a legitimate and fruitful area for future sociological attention.

---

[25] A. Rose, *Some Suggestions for Research in the Sociology of Law, Social Problems* 281 (1962); C. Auerbach, *Legal Tasks for the Sociologist,* 1 *L. & Soc. Rev.* 98–99 (1966).

[26] Truman, *supra* note 2, at 13; M. Irish & J. Prothro, *The Politics of American Democracy* 336 (1959).

POLITICS AND CRIMINAL LAW:
REVISION OF THE NEW YORK STATE PENAL LAW ON PROSTITUTION

Pamela A. Roby

Persons are not "criminals" unless a law defines their behavior as "crime." The purpose of this paper is to examine the political process through which certain behavior is defined as criminal and other behavior as noncriminal. What groups and persons influence the decisions through which penal laws are created? When groups have conflicting interests, which interests are written into law? Under what conditions are groups or individuals able to shape the law in the manner in which they intend?

Durkheim early in his career stressed the apolitical nature of law, ". . . once we grant that there is a determinate order in social existence, we necessarily reduce the role of the lawgiver. For if social institutions follow from the nature of things, they do not depend upon the will of any citizen or citizens." [1] Marx, on the other hand, maintained that law makers along with the state were the "arm of the bourgeois class" and that although the groups which ruled changed over time, they always belonged to the bourgeoisie. Domestic legislation was for the ruling class and against the proletariat. [2]

Excerpts reprinted from *Social Problems* **17** (Summer, 1969), pp. 83–109, by permission of the author and The Society for the Study of Social Problems. (Footnotes renumbered.)

The writer is grateful to Peter J. McQuillan, Judge Amos Basel, Mrs. Joan Cox and members of the American Civil Liberties Union who assisted her in tracing the history of the law and to Richard Quinney and Dennis Wrong who made many useful suggestions on an earlier draft of the paper.

[1] E. Durkheim, *Montesquieu and Rousseau*, 40 (1965).
[2] K. Marx and F. Engels, *The German Ideology* (1947), pp. 23–46.

More recently, Schur in discussing the relationship between law and the social order has argued that a legal system "represents an institutionalization of conflict, for it provides social means of resolving the specified disputes and in some sense reconciling the more general conflicts of interests and values within a society." [3] In this view, the formulation of law is a political process, i.e., a process in which individuals and groups attempt "to gain, limit, escape, or resist power." [4]

The essence or definition of power has been the source of considerable debate within the social sciences. Gerth and Mills and Blau stress the asymmetry of power relations. [5] Wrong has maintained that power is *not* completely asymmetrical, for intercursive power is characterized by a division of scopes between parties. Thus "one actor controls the other with respect to particular situations or scopes . . . while the other is dominant in other areas of situated activity." [6]

Over the sum of scopes some are "less equal than others," but except in those cases of physical violence when the person is no longer treated as a human being, all exercise some degree of power or reciprocal influence. In the formulation of law, one group may obtain its interests in the

[3] E. Schur, *Law and Society*, 139 (1968). Cf. Quinney, "Crime in political perspective," 8 *Am. Behavioral Scientist* (1964).
[4] D. Wrong, "Some problems in defining social power," 73, *American Journal of Sociology* (1968), pp. 675–6. In this paper we will use Wrong's definition of power, "the production of intended effects by some men upon the behavior of other men."
[5] H. Gerth and C. W. Mills, *Character and Social Structure*, 193 (1953); P. Blau, *Exchange and Power in Social Life*, 118 (1964).
[6] Wrong, *op. cit.*, 673.

writing of a particular article while another may do so with respect to another section of the law. Groups which are unable to shape the enacted law according to their interests may be able to affect the enforcement of the law or to amend the law at a later date.

Given these diverse characterizations of the nature of law and of power, we turned to the Revised Penal Law of New York State in an effort to gain a clearer understanding of the relationship between law and the exercise of power within society. The recent revision of the Penal Law which became effective September 1, 1967 and the efforts of various groups to amend certain of the revised articles provide sociologists with a unique opportunity to study the social processes through which behaviors come to be defined as criminal or noncriminal. The 1965 Penal Law represents a complete reorganization of the 1864 New York State Field Commission Revised Code of Criminal Procedure which became effective in 1881 and was amended in 1909.[7] The recent revision redefined certain previously noncriminal acts as criminal and previously criminal acts as noncriminal, placed related crimes together under logically related titles, transferred many provisions from the 1909 Code of Criminal Procedure and Penal Law to other more appropriate State laws, clarified previously ambiguous definitions and provisions, and prescribed new sentencing schemes.

METHOD

Of the approximately 520 sections in the 1965 New York State Penal Law, we will examine article 230 which represents a "deviant" case. Most articles of the Law were not debated outside of the Penal Law and Criminal Code Revision (PLCCR) Commission either before or after their enactment. Article 230 was one of a small

number of articles debated during the Public Hearings held in November 1964 on the Proposed Revised Penal Law and one of the very few articles which was revised by the Commission in accordance with sentiments expressed in the Public Hearings.[8] The article was not debated by the legislature before its passage, but it was the center of much controversy after it became effective September 1, 1967.[9]

Sections 230.00, 230.05, and 230.10 of the 1965 New York State Penal Law read as follows:

§ 230.00 Prostitution

A person is guilty of prostitution when such person engages or agrees or offers to engage in sexual conduct with another person in return for a fee.

Prostitution is a violation. L. 1965, c. 1030, eff. Sept. 1, 1967.

§ 230.05 Patronizing a prostitute

A person is guilty of patronizing a prostitute when:

1. Pursuant to a prior understanding, he pays a fee to another person as compensation for such person or a third person having engaged in sexual conduct with him; or

2. He pays or agrees to pay a fee to another person pursuant to an understanding that in return therefor such person or a third person will engage in sexual conduct with him; or

3. He solicits or requests another person to

---

7 N. Y. L. 1965, c. 1030, c. 1030.

8 Public Hearings on Proposed New York Penal Law (N.Y. Senate Int. 3918, N.Y. Assembly Int. 5376) (1964).

9 *N. Y. Times,* March 17, 1965: 35: 3. Articles exempting from criminal liability deviant sexual intercourse between consenting adults and eliminating adultery as a crime created the most controversy when the Proposed Revised Penal Law appeared before the State Legislature. After the 1965 Penal Law became effective, the provisions dealing with the authority of policemen to shoot to kill when confronting criminals and suspects, with abortion and with prostitution appeared to have created the most public controversy. Cf. *N. Y. Times,* Dec. 17, 1967, 1: 1.

engage in sexual conduct with him in return for a fee.

Patronizing a prostitute is a violation. L. 1965, c. 1030, eff. September 1, 1967

§ 230.10 Prostitution and patronizing a prostitute; no defense

In any prosecution for prostitution or patronizing a prostitute, the sex of the two parties or prospective parties to the sexual conduct engaged in, contemplated, or solicited is immaterial, and it is no defense that:

1. Such persons were of the same sex; or
2. The person who received, agreed to receive or solicited a fee was a male and the person who paid or agreed or offered to pay such a fee was a female. L. 1965, c. 1030, eff. Sept. 1, 1967.

We chose to study this "deviant," i.e. controversial, article so that we could analyze the political processes which were a part of the formulation of the law.[10] The choice of a controversial article was necessary because secrecy veiled most of the PLCCR Commission debates (except for supporting arguments which were published with the law). Minutes of the Commission meetings were available only to Commission members and Commission staff. The Assistant Counsel to the Commission explained that what went on in the Commission was "confidential so that it wouldn't become political." By analysing an article which was publicly debated, we were able to infer many of the factors influencing the Commission's decisions. In making generalizations from the history of article 230, we must remember, however, that most articles were passed without public notice and that the politics involved in their formulation

were confined to the room of the Penal Law Revision Commission.[11]

Data were collected for the study by means of interviews;[12] summary analyses of the prostitution cases reported in the "Docket Sheets" of the Criminal Court of New York City and of data on arraignments and dispositions of prostitution, disorderly conduct and loitering cases contained in the Statistics Office of the Criminal Court; and examination of the transcript of the Public Hearings held by the PLCCR Commission on the Proposed Penal Law, law review articles and books which suggested means of dealing with prostitution in New York state, and clippings gathered by the Albany New Clipping Service which were contained in the Chief Assistant Counsel of the PLCCR Commission's file on "Prostitution and Article 230."[13]

FINDINGS

The development of article 230 may be divided into five phases: 1) the Penal

[10] For a discussion of "deviant case analysis," see R. Merton, *Social Theory and Social Structure* (1949), pp. 194–5, and Kendall and Wolf, "The Analysis of Deviant Cases in Communications Research," in P. Lazarsfeld and F. Stanton (eds.), *Communications Research 1948–9* (1949), pp. 152–79.

[11] For the purposes of the present study we intentionally selected a section of the Penal Law which had been the focus of much controversy. We believe, however, that if we were to trace the history of less controversial sections of the law back in time, we would find that they too were wrought, at some point in their development, from political struggles among groups who were concerned with what the law should be and who had differing self-interests.

[12] The writer interviewed members of the PLCCR Commission, judges, plainclothes policemen; legal aid lawyers; representatives of the New York City Police Legal Bureau and the Bureau of Public Morals; members of the Mayor's Committee on Criminal Justice and the Mayor's Committee on Prostitution, New York City; the New York City's Mayor's Counsel; the director of and attorneys for the New York Civil Liberties Union; and the Counsel to the State Senate's Committee on Codes.

[13] The last set of clippings are important for they represent the majority of articles read by Peter J. McQuillan and Richard G. Denzer, the staff members who prepared article 230 for the Commission's consideration and wrote the practice commentary on the article in the Penal Law.

Law and Criminal Code Revision Commission's writing of the "Proposed New York Penal Law," article 235 (1962-1964); 2) introduction of the "Proposed Penal Law" as a study bill in the New York State Assembly and Senate (1964), public hearings on the proposed law (November 1964), and the Commission's subsequent rewriting of the law relating to prostitution (retitled article 230); 3) enactment of the 1965 Penal Law by the New York State Senate and Assembly (March 1965); 4) enforcement of and public reactions to the 1965 Penal Law following September 1, 1967, the date it became effective; 5) proposed amendments to article 230, *1965 New York Penal Law*.[14]

The Proposed Penal Law

The 1909 Code of Criminal Procedure which was still in effect in 1961 represented the PLCCR Commission's point of departure for the drafting of the 1965 Penal Law.[15] In the 1909 CCP, prostitution was defined as a form of vagrancy and subject to a penalty of up to three years in a reformatory or one year in jail.

Between 1909 and 1965, the Code of Criminal Procedure was amended piecemeal, and shaped and reshaped by judge-made decisions. Prostitution, as described in the 1909 CCP, § 887 (4), was originally

interpreted as an act which could be committed only by females.[16] This interpretation was later reversed, and in 1960 prostitution was held to include homosexual as well as heterosexual situations.[17]

Section 887.4(f), a 1919 amendment to § 887.4, was also subject to much controversy.[18] It extended the vagrancy provision to include any person "who in any way, aids or abets or participates in the doing of any of the acts" of prostitution. Many lawyers were of the opinion that subdivision (f) extended the vagrancy provision to the customer of the prostitute, but no judge actually ruled that a patron was "guilty."[19] In 1936 Judge Rudich held that the Legislature in enacting the clause "intended to reach . . . the porters, the maids, the many other henchmen, assistants, and lieutenants to procurers, prostitutes, and madames, all aiding, abetting, and participating in the business of prostitution and making their living therefrom . . . and not the male customer of the prostitute."[20]

By 1961 most of the Penal Law and Code of Criminal Procedure, like the section relating to prostitution, had become unwieldy and outdated. Consequently, Governor Nelson Rockefeller recommended that a commission be appointed to study these laws. Of the nine original Commission members, three were appointed by the Governor, three by the Temporary President of the Senate, and three by the Speaker of the Assembly.[21] The Commission was later expanded to include twelve members in addition to the chairman. All of the Commission's

---

14 We followed the development of the Penal Law in relation to prostitution through May 1968 and the conclusion of the 1968 State legislative session. Since many groups remain dissatisfied with article 230, it is likely that new amendments will be filed for the 1969 legislature. Therefore the story of the political processes surrounding article 230 is as yet unfinished. (On March 29, 1969, while this article was in press, the New York State Senate and Assembly amended Section 230.00 to read as follows: "A person is guilty of prostitution when such person engages or agrees or offers to engage in sexual conduct with another person in return for a fee. Prostitution is a *class B Misdemeanor*." This act will take effect September 1, 1969. *Laws of New York 1969*, Chapter 169.)

15 1909, N.Y.S., C.C.P., § 887(4), § 891-a.

16 People v. Gould, 111 N.Y.S.2d 742 (1952).

17 People v. Gould, 111 N.Y.S.2d 742 (1952) reversed on other grounds: 306 NY 352; People v. Hale, 8 NY2d 1962 (1960).

18 N.Y. Laws 1919, c. 502; People v. Edwards, 180 N.Y.S. 631 (1920).

19 D. Clarke, "It Takes Two—But the Customer is Always Guiltless," Public Hearings, *op. cit.*

20 People v. Anonymous, 292 N.Y.S. 282 (1936).

21 *NY Penal Law 1965* x (McKinney, 1965).

members belonged to the New York Bar Association.[22]

The Commission was given no time limit in which to complete its work. Therefore, it was possible for the Commission members, in one of their early meetings, to decide to overhaul rather than to simply amend the outdated and technically unwieldy 1909 Penal Law and the Code of Criminal Procedure.[23]

The actual process of overhauling the law proceeded step by step. The staff first drafted an area of law and presented it at a Commission meeting. Then the Commission discussed it and voted on the draft. Many of the Commission debates were heated. A few articles passed practically without change; most involved several revisions, and some were redrafted twenty or more times. In debates concerning most areas of law, the members considered their own experience with the law; the Model Penal Code and the sociological, psychological and peneological remarks included in its commentary; the recently revised Illinois and Wisconsin Penal Laws; and the advice of persons outside of the Commission whom they considered expert with respect to the practical (i.e. non-legal) or legal implications of a given article (generally the Commission staff sent drafts of articles to and sought the advice of the organizations whom it thought might be interested in the matter contained in the articles); the existing structure of the New York courts; and the advice of the *ex-officio* members, assemblymen and senators on what they

thought the legislature would pass.[24] . . .

After nearly four years of work, the Commission published the *Proposed Penal Law*. This was introduced as a study bill at the 1964 Legislative Session.[25] The bill was not to be voted upon, but was a means of eliciting the Senators' and Assemblymen's as well as the general public's opinions regarding the Commission's proposals. This was the law's first large preview. The only section pertaining directly to the 1965 P.L. §§ 230.00, 230.05, 230.10 read as follows:

§ 235.00 Prostitution

A person is guilty of prostitution when he or she commits or submits to, or offers to commit or to submit to, any sexual act with or upon another person, whether of a different or of the same sex, in return for a fee or compensation.

Prostitution is a violation [26]

The proposed article, unlike the 1959 Model Penal Code and the 1961 Illinois Criminal Code, did not make patrons guilty. According to staff members, the New York PLCCR Commission's first inclination was to leave the law concerning prostitutes' customers unclear. Later the Commission decided it was best to strive for clarity and to follow existing practice

---

[22] One wonders if some of the provisions of the new law might have been different had sociologists, psychologists, or other professionals been included on the Revision Commission. Although in many respects the Commission's membership was representative of many diverse legal groups, District Attorneys' offices appeared to be heavily represented.

[23] A. Hechtman, Assistant Counsel, N.Y. Penal Law and Criminal Code Revision Commission, Oct. 23, 1967.

[24] The legislatures' advice may have been a conservative influence on the Commission's decision-making. On the other hand, the Commission's thinking appeared generally to be ahead of that of the people of New York State and the legislatures' counsel may have shown the Commission the degree to which it had to compromise its ideals so as to prevent the Proposed Penal Law from being rejected in its entirety. A staff member pointed out, "An example of the level of New York thinking is provided by the fact that the deletion of the adultery article did not pass the legislature even though no one had been arrested under it since 1874."

[25] 1964 N.Y. Senate Int. 3918, N.Y. Assembly Int. 5376.

[26] Proposed N.Y. Penal Law § 235.00 (1964).

by excluding any reference to prostitutes' patrons from the Proposed Penal Law.[27]

By stating in the proposed article that "a person is guilty of prostitution when *he or she . . .*" the Commission eliminated any question as to the generality of prostitution. This decision was in keeping with the 1960 decision of *People v. Hale,* discussed above, where prostitution was held to include homosexual as well as heterosexual situations. It was also in accord with the United Nations Declaration on the Rights of Women and expressed the same intent as the terminology used in the Model Penal Code (1959 Draft) and in the statutes of Illinois, New Jersey, and Hawaii.[28]

The proposed article also made prostitution a "violation" rather than a crime, the maximum sentence for a violation being fifteen days rather than a year in jail or three years in a reformatory.

Arnold Hechtman, Assistant Counsel to the Commission, explained the Commission's decision to make prostitution a violation by saying that since there is no health program in New York for prostitutes, the Commission could not write a law to treat prostitutes clinically. Because of sentiment in New York State, the Commission members felt that they had to keep prostitution "on the books." Therefore, they resorted to "the next best action and whittled the punishment for prostitution down as far as they felt they could— down to a 'violation'." Hechtman defended this change as in keeping with existing practice by adding that even under the old law, in New York City prostitutes were generally given only five to thirty days, and the latter only when they were uncooperative.[29] In Upstate New York, however, prostitutes were generally given longer sentences.

27 Cf. People v. Anonymous, 292 NYS 282 (1936).
28 B. George, "Legal, Medical and Psychiatric Considerations in the Control of Prostitution," 60 *Mich. L. Rev.* (1962).
29 A. Hechtman, Interview, Oct. 23, 1967.

Public Hearings and Revision of the Proposed Penal Law

In November 1964 the Commission held public hearings throughout the state on the Proposed Penal Law. What was the purpose of these hearings? One Commission staff member remarked, "Public hearings are hog wash." He explained the meaning of his statement by saying that the public seldom knows what goes on in the legislature. Therefore, only organized interest groups, which have generally already made their wishes known to the Commission at the Commission's closed meetings or by letters, appear at the public hearings. A few of the same groups, such as the societies concerned with humanity to animals, spoke at the public hearings in all four cities. He added that the public hearings are politically useful because they satisfy the public's wish to be heard. If the Commission makes changes following the hearings, he claimed, it is generally not because of the public's statements, but because the Commission is continually rethinking the law. If the Commission rejects groups' opinions, the groups can go to their legislatures, he added. In summary, this staff member believed that interested, organized groups possessing sufficient power would eventually obtain their wishes with or without public hearings and that the general public would remain ignorant of the legal changes.

Article 235 of the Proposed Penal Law was one of the few articles which was rewritten, prior to being presented to the legislature, in accordance with the wishes which groups expressed at the public hearings. In its final form, the article was numbered two-hundred and thirty and the section defining prostitution finally read as given above.

Few changes were made in the definition of prostitution. Only the words "or compensation" were deleted from the clause of the Proposed Penal Law which defined prostitution as sexual conduct "in return for a fee *or compensation.*"[30] The clause defining the generality of the act was placed in a separate section, 230.10, as noted above.

The main issue in the development of the law on prostitution offenses and the main source of controversy after the law's enactment was whether "patronizing a prostitute" should be classified as an "offense." It will be remembered that in the Proposed Penal Law "patronizing a prostitute" was not classified as an offense. . . .

Following the public hearings, the PL-CCR Commission added § 230.05 concerning patrons. The section as passed by the legislature is given above. In its comments on article 230., the Commission termed the addition of the new offense, "Patronizing a Prostitute," the most important change in the article. In explaining the change, the Commission wrote:

Though not presently an offense in New York, such "patronizing" conduct is proscribed in various forms by the penal codes of several other jurisdictions, including the recently revised codes of Illinois and Wisconsin and it is included as an offense in the American Law Institute's Model Penal Code.

At the public hearings held by the Commission with respect to the proposed Penal Law, and in conferences and correspondence with the Commission and its staff, a number of persons and organizations have strongly urged the inclusion of a "patronizing" offense. The reasons most vigorously advanced are: (1) that criminal sanctions against the patron as well as the prostitute should aid in the curtailment of prostitution; and (2) that to penalize the

prostitute and exempt the equally culpable patron is inherently unjust.

After consideration of these contentions, the Commission decided to include the indicated patronizing offense in the new bill as a proper corollary to prostitution.[31]

Enactment and Enforcement of the Law

In 1965, the new sections passed the legislature without comment. The *New York Times* merely noted, "In another revision the commission recommended that the customer of a prostitute, as well as the prostitute herself, be made subject to prosecution. Mr. Bartlett (chairman) said he was 'persuaded that there is no moral or ethical reason to exclude the customer from criminal liability in a sex-for-hire situation.'"[32]

The new law radically changed the legal status of prostitutes' patrons and modified the status of prostitutes. In addition, the law prevented police from using customers as witnesses in prosecutions, and *technically* prohibited plainclothesmen from obtaining solicitations from and subsequently testifying against prostitutes. The one legal basis for arresting prostitutes and patrons was for plainclothesmen to observe a couple while the patron offered and the prostitute accepted a fee for sexual conduct.[33] As the time for the new law to become effective approached, one wondered whether the police would attempt to enforce the legal changes, follow traditional practice, or attempt to amend the law.

In May, 1967, the police ended their practice of having patrolmen who made arrests act as prosecutors in Women's Court.[34] During the early summer months,

---

[30] During the public hearings Dr. Biegel stated that he believed the words, "or compensation," should be deleted from the article because "if a young man takes a girl . . . to a theatre, (and) afterward she allows him liberties, she gives him a compensation." He added, ". . . the whole concept of the male-female relationship in our culture . . . is based on compensation." Evidently the Commission also agreed that the definition of prostitution needed to be made more specific. Biegel, N.Y. Public Hearings, *op. cit.,* 514.

[31] N. Y. Penal Law, Comments § 230.05 (McKinney 1965).
[32] *N. Y. Times,* March 17, 1965, 35: 3.
[33] The latter was Judge Amos Basel's interpretation of the law. Interview, Dec. 8, 1967.
[34] *N. Y. Times,* May 10, 1967, 49: 4. Sept. 15, 1967 Part 9 of the Criminal Court, City Magistrates'

the police relaxed their prostitution pick-ups.[35] This relaxation may have been in anticipation of the Revised Penal Law or a consequence of the Police Department's energies being diverted by racial unrest. Whatever the cause, an alleged influx of prostitutes began to descend upon Manhattan and the Times Square area.[36] Some persons say that a rumor went around among prostitutes that prostitution was legal.[37] According to these sources, prostitutes came to New York from around the nation and around the world; others came out of retirement; and some women entered the business for the first time.

The dimensions of the "invasion," and whether the invasion actually took place, are unknown. The amount of prostitution which exists at any one time cannot, as many sociologists and other writers have pointed out, be measured by arrest rates. Arrest rates, particularly for prostitution, go up and down more as a result of pressures from the political and police system than as a consequence of the actual rate of prostitution.[38] New York politicians, businessmen, and police may have begun to talk about an influx of prostitutes and the need for a "clean-up" because they

were dissatisfied with the law becoming "soft" on prostitutes. Also representatives of the Police Department appeared to speak periodically to newsmen about "increases in prostitution." Only a year before the alleged '67 influx, S. V. Killorin, Commander of the Third Division, had stated, "For some reason, many prostitutes seem to be coming from out of town." [39]

Members of the PLCCR Commission staff who naturally felt some need to protect the new law, questioned whether the actual rate of prostitution had risen at all.[40] Whatever the dimensions of the alleged "influx," in August the police reportedly were pressured by politicians, Midtown businessmen, and City Hall to "clean-up" the Times Square area.[41] The New York Hotel Association complained especially bitterly about the influx.[42]

August 20th, the first day of the Times Square "clean-up," marked the start of a fiery checker-board game between the police and the district attorney's office on the one hand, and the Civil Liberties Union, the Legal Aid Society, and certain judges on the other. . . .

During the rapid changes in prostitution cleanup procedures, how was the new "patron" law being enforced? We observed that the newspapers contained no

---

Court, commonly called the "Women's Court" was discontinued. Thereafter sexual offenses by women were handled in Part 1C.

35 Basel, *op. cit.*

36 *N. Y. Times,* Nov. 9, 1967, 33: 4; *N. Y. News,* May 18, 1967.

37 Judge Basel, *op. cit.* The *N. Y. News* also reported, ". . . the city is suffering an influx of out-of-town prostitutes and their male associates as the joyful word spreads through the V-grapevine that Fun City is becoming Sin City. The invasion was inspired by the recent announcement by Police Commissioner Leary that the police intended to abandon their 57-year old role as prosecutors of the girls." *N.Y. News,* May 18, 1967.

38 Murtagh and Harris document New York City trends in pressures for "cleanups" and subsequent rises in prostitution arrest rates. Murtagh and Harris, *op. cit.* J. Skolnick, *Justice Without Trial* (1966); S. Wheeler, "Criminal Statistics," 58, *J. of Criminal L., Criminology and Police Science* (1967).

39 *N. Y. Times,* Nov. 17, 1966.

40 World-wide rumor transmission among prostitutes that prostitution had been legalized in New York City may be questioned on the basis of previous sociological findings. For instance, Clinard and Quinney note that because prostitution is, by its very nature, competitive, prostitutes seldom develop a high degree of organization within their profession and have a "limited argot or special language." Professional organization or cohesion would be necessary for large-scale rumor transmission. M. Clinard and Quinney, *Criminal Behavior Systems,* 256 (1967). Cf. Mauer, "Prostitutes and criminal argots," 44 *American Journal of Sociology* (1939), pp. 546–550. On the other hand, many and perhaps most prostitutes are tied in with the organized underworld.

41 Zion, "Prostitution: The midtown roundup," *N. Y. Times,* Oct. 1, 1967.

42 Basel, *op. cit.*

reports or stories on arrests of "Johns." [43] Because the papers generally contain monthly or bi-monthly reports on prostitution arrests, and frequently include public interest stories about prostitutes, we asked the Criminal Court Statistics Office to show us their record on the arraignments and dispositions of persons charged with "patronizing prostitutes." Table 1 contains summary statistics of the arraignments and dispositions of cases under §§ 230.00, 230.05 for September 1967 through February 1968. In comparing the figures for "prostitution" and "patronizing a prostitute," we should remember that in addition to the 1,159 prostitution arrests under § 230.00 during the months of September and October, over 2,000 women were arrested for loitering or disorderly conduct.[44]

Of the *new* prostitution and patronizing cases, only six percent were for patronizing a prostitute during the months of September and October. Of the 508 *convicted* dispositions, only 0.8 percent were for patronizing a prostitute.[45] Between November and February an average of 14 patrons were arrested monthly as compared with an average of 35 during September and October; only one of these cases was convicted. The high number of prostitution arrests during October and November (monthly average 738) returned to normal (400-500 a month) between December and February.

Three observations may be made from these statistics. First, since the only legal basis for arresting prostitutes was for plainclothesmen to observe a couple while the patron offered and the prostitute accepted a fee for sexual conduct, the enforcement of the law was not consistent with the provisions of the new law. Second, since 72 persons had been arrested

on patronizing charges during September and October, the newspapers by not reporting on any of the patronizing cases were obviously extending a courtesy to patrons which they do not extend to prostitutes. Third, the decline in the number of prostitution arrests between December and February indicates either that the prostitutes who "swarmed to New York City" during October left quickly after the police clampdown, or that the increase in prostitution arrests was an artifact of political pressures.

Not only patrons but high priced call-girls were ignored by the police during the "clean up" period. The large number of arrests of Times Square "street-walkers" and the small number of arrests of call-girls may be interpreted in two ways: First, in enforcement practices, there may be decreasing moralistic concern with the private actions of individuals. Second, street-walkers and their customers rank lowest in prestige among those who participate in prostitution or patronizing prostitutes. Call-girls serve "upper class," sometimes famous, patrons for high fees. One madame, described as well-known among New York's upper classes, publishes a book on her girls. The "class A" girls frequently accompany corporation customers to dinner and the theatre as well as engage in sexual conduct with them.[46] Because such behavior is generally not regarded as offensive, political groups do not exert pressure upon the police and City Hall to "clean it up."

We have seen that in its enforcement practice, the Police Department reacted initially to § 230.00 and prostitution by unconstitutionally "sweeping" the streets of prostitutes under the cloak of legality provided by the sections on loitering and disorderly conduct. The Department reacted to the new "violation" of patronizing prostitutes by making a small number of token arrests of patrons and by letting

43 Albany News Service and *N. Y. Times Index.*
44 1965 NYS Penal Law § 240.20.
45 In October, 17 of the arrests under 1965 NYS Penal Law § 230.00 were male prostitutes. Docket sheets, Criminal Court, New York City.

46 *N. Y. Times*, Jan. 20, 1960, 71: 1, 2.

Table 1 City Wide Arraignments and Dispositions: §§230.00, and 230.05, Prostitution and Patronizing*

Court Offense and Month:	New Cases	Total Dispos.	Disch.	Unable to Locate	Trans'd other Courts	Convicted Plea Guilty	After Trial	Finded	Fine and Imp.	Str. Sent.	Release Uncond.	Cond.	Prob.
Sept. 1967:													
Patron.	37	17	14	—	—	3	—	—	—	1	2	—	—
Prostitution	413	403	143	40	—	191	29	3	—	183	24	10	—
October 1967:													
Patron.	35	25	22	—	2	1	—	—	—	1	—	—	—
Prostitution	746	467	159	5	9	288	6	3	4	214	50	23	—
November 1967:													
Patron.	27	26	25	—	—	1	—	—	—	1	—	—	—
Prostitution	731	450	187	4	3	241	15	7	—	226	11	11	—
December 1967:													
Patron.	8	12	12	—	—	—	—	—	—	—	—	—	—
Prostitution	412	292	143	2	—	142	5	3	—	117	17	10	—
January 1967:													
Patron.	15	—	19	2	—	—	—	—	—	—	—	—	—
Prostitution	467	490	218	9	2	234	27	2	—	217	21	21	—
February 1967:													
Patron.	5	10	9	—	1	—	—	—	—	—	—	—	—
Prostitution	588	—	312	8	2	237	28	57	—	167	28	—	—
Total September-February:													
Patron.	127	90	101	2	3	5	—	—	—	3	2	—	—
Prostitution	3,357	2,102	1,162	68	16	1,333	110	75	—	1,124	151	85	—

*New York City, Criminal Court Statistics Office, statistical worksheet. These figures do not include prostitutes who were arrested under sections of the law other than prostitution, i.e. loitering or disorderly conduct.

most "Johns" go. In turn, the New York Civil Liberties Union, the Legal Aid Society and certain judges reacted to the police actions by defending the women's rights.

In what other ways did the community react to the new provisions? The Hotel Association and businessmen in the Times Square area vociferously complained to the police and City Hall about the influx of prostitutes. The New York Commission on the United Nations Secretariat allegedly complained about the arrest of businessmen and other visitors from foreign countries who did not realize that "patronizing prostitutes" was an offense. The hotel managers felt that not only did the prostitutes inconvenience persons staying at their hotels but that sex was used as a come-on for many ancillary crimes such as muggings, petty larceny, extortion, and breaking and entering.

In addition to the "clean-up," City Hall reacted to the political pressure exerted by the hotels and businessmen by creating the Mayor's Committee on Prostitution. Mr. Daniel C. Hickey, President of the New York City Hotel Association, was appointed to the fifteen man committee.[47] In November, Mayor Lindsay sat in on the committee's first session and was reported by the press as "deeply concerned" with the problem.[48]

At its first meeting, the Committee set up three sub-committees, which, in effect, represented the various interests in the controversy:

1. Penal Law Revision: Chairman, Judge Amos Basel, Criminal Court.
2. Rehabilitation of Prostitutes in Correction Facilities: Chairman, Mary K. Lindsay, Former Superintendent of the Women's House of Detention.

3. Study Group to Determine Non-Criminal Approaches to the Problem of Prostitution: Chairman, Dr. Alfred Freedman, Department of Psychiatry, New York Medical College.

Queens District Attorney Thomas Mackell was appointed chairman of the overall Committee. In May 1967 Mackell had written to Governor Rockefeller "repeating a suggestion that he said he made 'long ago' that 'prostitution be dealt with by a specially qualified social agency rather than an already overburdened criminal justice machinery.'"[49] Mackell had made similar proposals to Mayor Lindsay and legislative leaders as well as expressing them publicly in the *New York Law Journal.*[50]

Mrs. Joan Cox, an attorney for the Legal Aid Society who worked in the Women's Court for seven years, also served on the Committee. She agreed with Mackell that prostitution should not be punished except as a public nuisance. However, she said she was not opposed to fines, because, "after all, prostitutes pay no income taxes!"[51] The Vera Institute of Justice has also recommended a "halfway house" in which prostitutes would be offered a full battery of services from psychiatrists, psychologists, social workers, and vocational guidance experts.[52]

In a formal statement, Judge Basel, Chairman of the Subcommittee on Penal Law, said he feared that the state penal code would make "Fun City" the vice capital of the world. He added, "I think that until a method is devised for effectively treating them as social problems— and such a method has not yet been found —we should leave the old law on the books."[53] In an interview, Basel said that

---

[47] The New York Hotel Association represents the wealthier hotels; most inexpensive hotels which cater largely to prostitutes and their patrons are not included in its membership.

[48] *N. Y. Times,* Nov. 1, 1967.

[49] *N. Y. L. J.,* May 23, 1967.

[50] Mackell, "Prostitution," *N.Y.L.J.,* Oct. 27, 1967.

[51] Mrs. Joan Cox, Attorney, Legal Aid Society and member, Mayor's Commission on Prostitution, interview, Dec. 12, 1967.

[52] *N. Y. Times,* Editorial, Aug. 15, 1967.

[53] Basel quoted in *Syracuse Post Standard,* Aug. 23, 1967.

he thought it would be very worthwhile for a Foundation to give a group of psychiatrists and other professionals money to devise an experimental demonstration center or clinic for rehabilitating prostitutes. He pointed out, that to his knowledge, no such experiment had been tried.[54]

Proposed Amendments

The Police Department, along with the hotel association, most vigorously opposed the law.[55] In September 1967, the Department prefiled draft amendments to the Penal Law for the 1968 legislature. One amendment, if passed would have extended the loitering section (240.35.3) to include "loitering for the purpose of . . . prostitution. [56] In support of this proposed amendment, the Department wrote:

The inclusion of this provision within the 'loitering' section of the Penal Law would be of great assistance to law enforcement officials in combating prostitution. The actions of these individuals have always had a deterious effect on the business and social life of the community. This proposal should prove instrumental in eradicating or substantially decreasing the problem of street walkers.

Furthermore, it is the opinion that such amendment would result in a decrease in the incidence of venereal disease and in the number of muggings, assaults, and robberies which are often a by-product of this type of activity.[57]

Two other proposed amendments prefiled by the Department would: 1) extend the loitering provisions to include loitering for the purpose of engaging in an offense (rather than only loitering for the purpose of engaging in a crime: § 240.35-(6), and 2) make prostitution a class *B* misdemeanor (a crime) rather than a violation (230.00.).[58] If prostitution were made a class B misdemeanor, prostitutes could be sentenced to a maximum of 91 days, still considerably less than the 3 year maximum reformatory sentence provided under 1909 § 891 (a). In support of the first provision, the Department stated:

This additional authority would be of great assistance to law enforcement officials in combating prostitution as the prostitutes who are observed approaching different people at various intervals would have to give a reasonably credible account of such actions.[59]

The Police Department argued that prostitution should be made a class B misdemeanor on the basis that:

Though other provisions of Article 230 (i.e. those for the promotion of prostitution) of the Revised Penal Law are directed primarily at organized vice and those who knowingly advance or profit from prostitution such activities are impossible in the main without the prostitute and her services. To designate 'prostitution' as a violation with a penalty of a term not to exceed 15 days is highly unrealistic. Such a penalty is tantamount to 'licensing' prostitutes and results in turnstile justice and an increase in such activities.[60]

54 Basel, interview, Oct. 26, 1967.

55 In an interview with Captain Behan, Commanding Officer, Bureau of Public Morals, Police Department, the writer was told that because the Police Department is a semi-military organization, neither the Captain nor the Police Legal Bureau had the authority to speak about or distribute copies of its draft amendments.

56 New York City Police Department, "An Act to Amend the Penal Law, In Relation to Persons Loitering for the Purpose of Committing Prostitution," prefiled for the 1968 N.Y.S. Legislature.

57 New York City Police Dept., Draft of memorandum in support of "An Act to amend the penal law, in relation to persons loitering for the purpose of committing prostitution" (1967).

58 New York City Police Department, "An Act to amend the penal law in relation to persons loitering for the purpose of committing an unlawful act," and "An Act to amend the penal law, in relation to the punishment for engaging in prostitution," prefiled for the 1968 New York State Legislature.

59 N. Y. C. Police Dept., "An Act to amend the penal law in relation to persons loitering for the purpose of committing an unlawful act" (1967).

60 N. Y. C. Police Dept., Draft of Memorandum in Support of "An Act to amend the penal law, in relation to the punishment for engaging in prostitution" (1967).

To the writer's knowledge, the Police Department prefiled no amendment to eliminate the "patronizing" clause from the Penal Law. Perhaps the Department did not do so because it could effectively evade enforcing the law or because it believed it could not defeat the political pressure which was shown to support the "patronizing provision" during the Penal Law public hearings.

The Buffalo area police and legislators were also against the new law's provisions pertaining to prostitution. Assemblyman Albert J. Hausbeck of Buffalo's 114th District said that the new Penal Law was too lenient on convicted prostitutes and that he intended to prefile three amendments to the new State Penal Code.[61] Captain Kenneth Kennedy, commander of the Buffalo Vice Enforcement Bureau, speaking before the Rotary Club asked, "If the legislators want open prostitution, why don't they just say so?" He predicted that disease, broken homes, and involvement of organized crime in prostitution would follow the "condonation" of it under the new law, and he blamed "do-gooders" for the changes in the law saying they have perpetrated "frauds" on legislators and the public to support unfounded theories that prostitution does not harm.[62]

In January the Mayor's Committee on Prostitution recommended that the offense of prostitution be reclassified from a violation to a class A misdemeanor, effective September 1, 1968. The recommendation was submitted to the State Senate in the form of an amendment to the Penal Law.[63] The amendment, if passed, would have increased the maximum penalty for the offense from fifteen days to one year imprisonment.

At the same meeting, the Committee disapproved several pending bills, including that submitted by the Police Department, on prostitution. One would have made prostitution a Class B misdemeanor. It was disapproved on the ground that the three month sentence would not allow sufficient time for rehabilitation. Several bills extending the loitering statutes to include "offenses" (i.e. prostitution under the Revised Penal Law) were disapproved on the grounds of doubtful constitutionality.

In a memo in support of the amendment to make prostitution a Class A misdemeanor, Judge Basel wrote: [64]

The subcommittee felt that the reclassification of prostitution from a violation to a class A misdemeanor would aid rehabilitative efforts and provide more effective law enforcement. This reclassification will put New York law in line with the majority of the other states, where the maximum penalties for prostitution are generally either six months or one year imprisonment. The subcommittee felt that until a social solution to the problem of prostitution was found the penal sanctions should be changed in order to afford effective law enforcement. The fifteen day maximum penalty, it was felt, defeated both rehabilitative and preventive objectives.

The change in the law would allow the courts to place first-time offenders and others on probation for up to three years so that they could be given guidance and an opportunity to restructure their lives. Under the present law, convicted prostitutes cannot be placed on probation since probation is available only for those convicted for misdemeanors and felonies, whereas prostitution is an offense. Moreover, the reclassification would give the courts the opportunity to sentence the offender to a term in a halfway house or a similar institution, should they be established, so that she could receive close supervision and concerted rehabilitative efforts.

The present law has greatly accelerated the turnstile justice associated with the punish-

61 *Buffalo Evening News,* Oct. 9, 1967; *Buffalo Courier Express,* Oct. 9, 1967.
62 *Buffalo Evening News,* Oct. 27, 1967; *Buffalo Courier Express,* Oct. 5, 1967.
63 An Act to Amend the Penal Law, in relation to prostitution, introduced by Mr. Griffin to the Senate (890), State of New York, Jan. 3, 1968.
64 Memo from Judge Basel, Chairman, Subcommittee on the Penal Law to Hon. Thomas Mackell, Chairman, Mayor's Committee on Prostitution.

ment of prostitutes. Since the Penal Law took effect in September 1967, the average sentence for prostitution has been a mere five days.

Streetwalkers in New York City pose a serious problem in that, particularly in the midtown area, they offend public sensibilities as they almost openly ply their trade. This disturbs local businessmen, theatre-goers, tourists and others. The lenient sentence prescribed by the new law has compounded the problem by attracting out-of-town prostitutes to New York. Police reports indicate that since the summer of 1967 there has been a tremendous influx of prostitutes from other states.

Moreover, it should be realized that there is a serious correlation between prostitution and other criminal activity. Police statistics and hotel reports indicate that prostitutes are frequently involved in robberies and larcenies from their prospective clients.

In April the Senate committed the bill to amend the Penal Law to the Committee on Codes. The Committee debated the bill and voted *not* to send it back to the Senate for a vote. This action meant that the sections of the Penal Law concerning prostitution would remain unchanged for at least another year.

Why, when so many seemingly politically influential groups were pressuring for a higher prostitution penalty, did the Committee vote "no"? In an interview, Mr. Martin Schaum, Counsel to the Committee on Codes, gave three reasons for the "no" vote.[65] First, the Committee believed that the Penal Law Commission's decision to make prostitution a violation had been well considered and that the Law had been in effect too short a time for any group to be able to evaluate its effectiveness. Second, the Committee feared that giving prostitutes one year sentences would overcrowd the jails. Third, the senators on the committee did not believe that the act of prostitution warranted a one year jail sentence.

65 M. Schaum, Counsel to the Committee on Codes, N. Y. Senate, June 4, 1968, telephone interview.

Scanning the occupations and affiliations of the committee members, we noted two additional factors which may have influenced the Committee's decision. First, all of the sixteen committee members were lawyers.[66] The New York Bar Association, and lawyers generally, respected and supported the Penal Law Commission (which is also composed entirely of lawyers) and its decisions. Had businessmen or the police, particularly those of New York City or Buffalo, been represented on the committee, the decision might well have been in support of the amendment. At least vigorous opposition would have been expressed toward voting down the amendment. Second, John Dunne, a member of the Committee, was also a member of the PLCCR Commission. Although we cannot be certain of Dunne's position since the Committee did not release minutes of its meetings, we imagine that he supported leaving the Penal Law unchanged.

SUMMARY AND CONCLUSIONS

This study suggests that law-making and law-enforcement cannot be understood as apolitical, technical, value-free processes. Theories of law must include a knowledge of the political processes.[67] Further study will be required to adequately characterize the relationship between law and the exercise of power in society. The findings of this study could provide a framework for such research.

Throughout the development of the New York State Penal Law, Section 230, numerous interest groups and individuals worked diligently in an effort to have the law written or enforced in the manner they desired.[68] The results of their efforts

66 Eighty percent of the N. Y. Senators were also lawyers in 1968.
67 Cf. R. Quinney, *op. cit.,* 19.
68 For discusssions of the techniques and strategies used by other interest groups see Stedman, "Pressure groups and the American tradition," 319 *Annals Am. Acad. Pol. and Social Sci.* (1958), pp.

clearly illustrate the limited comprehensiveness of power suggested by Wrong.[69] During the five stages in the formulation and enforcement of the Penal Law concerning prostitution, power shifted from first one interested group to another. One group frequently exercised power with respect to one section of the law while another did so with respect to another section. In the final stage of the law's history, civil liberties and welfare groups dominated over businessmen and the police with respect to the clause making prostitution a violation subject to a maximum fifteen day sentence while the police and businessmen dominated over the civil liberties and welfare groups with respect to the nonenforcement of the "patron" clause.

Under what conditions were certain individuals or groups able to shape the law in the manner in which they intended? . . . A small number of organizations and individuals, represented by the president of the American Social Health Association and a retired chief probation officer of the N.Y.C. Magistrates Court, were able to insert the "patron" clause into the Law. These groups possessed legal knowledge, were aware of the PLCCR Commission's pending actions and that their own interests would be affected by these actions, and recognized that by acting they could probably affect the law. Because of these factors and because groups with opposing views slept, the groups favoring the patron clause were able to make the clause part of the law. The groups opposing the patron clause, however, appeared to represent a larger proportion of the public

and were able to later resist enforcing the new law.[70] Consequently, the only lasting effect of the "patron clause" was to prohibit the police from using patrons as witnesses against prostitutes.

The formulation and enforcement of the law for arresting and penalizing prostitutes was more complex than that for patrons. Power shifted rapidly from group to group. . . . Largely under the influence of Judge Murtagh who had actively campaigned for reform in moralistic laws and was widely respected, the PLCCR Commission reduced the penalty for prostitution from a maximum of one year to 15 days imprisonment. After this change was enacted into law, it was assailed by hotel owners, businessmen, the police and a few legislators. Their pressure led to a police "clean-up" of prostitution in Manhattan. Civil liberties and welfare groups condemned the "clean-up," and after much controversy the legal bases for many

---

123–9; V. O. Key, Jr., *Politics, Parties, and Pressure Groups* (1958); H. Turner, "How Pressure Groups Operate," 319 *Annals Am. Acad. Pol. and Social Sci.* (1958), pp. 63–72; D. Truman, *The Governmental Process* (1951); L. Rainwater and W. Yancey, *The Moynihan Report and the Politics of Controversy* (1967).

[69] Cf. Wrong, *op. cit.*, 673. The "comprehensiveness" of power refers to the number of scopes in which actors exercise power.

[70] The power of forces opposing the "patron's" penalty was discussed by Flexner in the twenties: "The professional prostitute being a social outcaste may be periodically punished without disturbing the usual course of society. . . . The man, however, is something more than a partner in an immoral act; he discharges important social and business relations, is a father or brother responsible for the maintenance of others, has commercial or industrial duties to meet. He cannot be imprisoned without damaging society (i.e. those with influence in society)." Over thirty years later, Davis wrote, "Although the service is illegitimate, the citizen cannot ordinarily be held guilty, for it is inadvisable to punish a large portion of the populace for a crime . . . that has no political significance. Each such citizen participates in the basic activities of the society, in business, government, the home, the church, etc. To disrupt all of these by throwing him in jail for a mere vice would cause more social disruption and inefficiency than correcting the alleged crime would be worth." In 1968 in New York State, contrary to Davis' expectations, the patron *can* be held guilty, but the theory upon which Davis based his expectations remains true for the law is seldom enforced. A. Flexner, *Prostitution in Europe* (1920), 108; Davis, "Sexual Behavior," in R. Merton and R. Nisbet, *Contemporary Social Problems* (1966), 358. Material in parentheses added by writer.

of the arrests were held to be unconstitutional. Once it was no longer possible to arrest prostitutes in mass, the police and other groups submitted amendments to the New York State legislature to make prostitution a Class A misdemeanor subject to a maximum penalty of one year imprisonment and to extend the loitering section to include "loitering for the purpose of prostitution." Nearly ten months after the 1965 NYS Penal Law became effective, the NYS Senate Committee on Codes killed these amendments leaving the new law concerning prostitution at least temporarily unchanged.

The conditions for groups' power, . . . also varied from stage to stage in the history of the controversy.[71] The primary bases for groups obtaining power appeared to be 1) their awareness of the various actions taken and to be taken in the formulation or enforcement of the law; 2)

[71] For other discussions of conditions or sources of power see R. Bierstedt, "An analysis of social power," 15 *American Sociological Review* (1950); and R. Dahl, *Who Governs?* (1961).

their recognition of the importance of these actions to their interests; 3) their professional (especially legal) knowledge or expertise; 4) their public (scattered and unorganized) support gained through their expertise and conscious appeals to the community; 5) their political and financial support by organized groups; 6) their personal charisma; and 7) their means to informally withhold needed support or cooperation from the significant actor.

In summary, this study suggests that behaviors are not "automatically" defined as criminal. The formulation and enforcement of the 1965 NYS Penal Law on prostitution were *political* processes involving numerous efforts on the part of a relatively small number of interested groups to obtain the means to affect the behavior of other men. During these processes, the groups which exercised power with respect to any particular section of the law changed over time, and at most instances in time different groups exercised power over different sections of the law.

part three

ORGANIZATION AND PROCESS IN THE ADMINISTRATION OF LAW AND CONTROL OF DEVIANCE

A: Selection into Control Agencies: The Police

As noted in Part One, in politically organized society the use of legitimized force in social control is monopolized by the state. In modern industrialized societies the apparatus set up to exercise this control is highly specialized and bureaucratized. This is, of course, part of the general tendency toward more complex division of labor and bureaucratization of all institutions in society. Indeed an organizational response to each new set of perceived social problems is common; witness the proliferation of national, state, and local environmental protection agencies in response to the widespread concern over the ecological balance and pollution of air, water, and land. It is difficult to think of any behavior which could not be brought under the jurisdiction of some type of regulatory bureaucracy whether it be some private system of rules and control or the large and pervasive civil and criminal legal systems. While recognizing that similar organizational processes are operative in any regulatory decision in any bureaucracy, our immediate concern here is not with all types of organizations or even with all agencies in the entire legal system. Rather we focus on that part of the law in operation, as manifested in complex formal organizations, included in the "criminal justice system." Our orienting question is: What organizational, environmental, personal, and other social variables account for the decisions control agents make as to who and what is selected for their intervention? That is, what behavior and which people are identified and processed as deviant?

To what extent does the invocation of the criminal justice process depend on the behavior of the "clients" or on factors in the system itself? We shall look at the criminal justice system as a flow chart with a number of decision points. We want to know what variables are operative in the initial selection into the formal control machinery and at each subsequent point of police, judicial, and correctional decisions.

SELECTION INTO CONTROL AGENCIES

There are basically three ways that deviance comes to the attention of the control agents in the criminal justice system. *Self-referral,* such as "turning yourself in" or otherwise voluntarily submitting to apprehension by law enforcement agents does occur but is not very common. The most common source of referral is by the action of other citizens who act as *complainants* reporting their own victimization or acting as witnesses to illegal behavior. Finally, the enforcement, surveillance, and undercover work of *control agents* themselves may produce the initial referral of supposed offenders into the system.

The vast majority of deviant behavior that is potentially liable to selection into the enforcement machinery is never brought to official attention. Whatever social control is exercised over rule-breaking is most often informal; no official action is called for or taken. Victim surveys indicate that over half of the incidents of criminal behavior are not reported to the police (Biderman et al., 1967; Ennis, 1967; Hawkins, 1973). It has been estimated that nine out of ten minor delinquents acts and eight out of ten major juvenile violations never become known to the police (Erickson and Empey, 1965:140–41). Only a portion of those who could be officially classified as mentally ill become legally adjudicated as mentally incompetent (Spitzer and Denzin, 1968:464).

These data indicate that to understand the selection process by which some people become enmeshed in the criminal justice system we need to be concerned with the questions of how and why citizens decide to initiate formal sanctions. Under what conditions are individuals or groups threatened, embarrassed, victimized, or disturbed enough to deem informal social control ineffective and invoke formal control mechanisms?

To examine the citizen's decision to invoke formal social control it is helpful to differentiate two types of victimization. The first is the traditional form of victimization where one has something stolen or is assaulted by another. Here the offender is likely to be a stranger (with the exception of some crimes against person such as assault and homicide), and the citizen must decide if the police should be informed of the incident. Many things may prompt reporting: it may be a requirement on an insurance policy; the victim may desire personal retribution; the victim may feel it is his duty to call the police;

or others may have observed the incident and the victim feels informal pressure to report (cf. Gibbs, 1966). Other factors could be listed, but what is of interest is the fact that less than half the cases of criminal victimization are reported to the police by the victim. One reason for not initiating formal sanctions may be fear of self-incrimination in cases of crimes without victims and victim-precipitated acts (Schafer, 1968). Victim surveys indicate that the major reasons for not reporting are (1) not wanting to get involved, i.e., wishing to avoid the bother of a police investigation, signing a complaint, appearing in a court, etc.; (2) a feeling that nothing can be done—there was no chance of recovery of items or little perceived chance of catching the offender; and (3) considering the incident a private matter and therefore not wishing to inform the police (Hawkins, 1973). In sum, many victims do not report crimes because they see no payoff in initiating sanctions. The reporting of victimization might be increased if incentives were provided. Although not intended as an incentive, recent legislation in the area of victim compensation may increase the probability of reporting by the victims of criminal acts.

A second type of victimization involves behavior problems or persistent rule violations by a member of one's primary group such as the family. This would include the behavior of the problem drinker, the chronically incorrigible juvenile, the bizarre and inappropriate behavior of the mentally ill, and so on. The usual initial response to this behavior within the primary group is some form of accommodation: normalization, denial, balancing, or attenuation of seriousness. Thus the deviant actions of the group member may remain hidden for years from the view of official control agents. Recourse to formal control systems, then, comes only at the point of some critical incident which breaks the accommodation and convinces the other members of the group that the problem has become so severe that it can no longer be overlooked (Yarrow et al., 1955; Jackson, 1954).

Control agencies, with varying degrees of explicitness, attempt to diffuse information which facilitates citizens' definitions of a problem as deserving formal or professional attention. In this way they seek to recruit clients much as other organizations seek resources for their productive goals (Dohrenwend and Chin-Shong, 1967; Scheff, 1966; Kadushin, 1966; Berger, 1963:62). Much of this diffusion is produced by national advertising campaigns warning of the dangers of drugs, alcohol, etc., and describing the clues to suicide and mental illness. The police often conduct local crime prevention drives, providing a "crime check" telephone number, and otherwise trying to increase reporting. Antidrug campaigns encourage anonymous tips to the police about pushers. Thus, control agents themselves are indirectly involved in producing citizen-initiated control actions. But they also play a much more direct role in the definition and rates of deviance in society. We turn now to a discussion of that more direct role, specifically the structural variables which affect the observability of deviant activities to the police, the first major decision point in the criminal justice system.

VISIBILITY OF CRIMINAL BEHAVIOR TO THE POLICE

A number of factors determine the observability of citizen behavior by control agents. Technological advances make behavior more visible to the police. Crimes become known to the police by electronic and radar detection, television monitoring of expressways, hallways, and parking lots, burglar alarms, and hidden cameras in stores and banks. On-site discovery of crimes is influenced by the patrol patterns of the police, the aggressive surveillance by special squads such as vice and narcotics squads, the degree of police access to an area (e.g., public versus private places), referral from other control agencies, the reputation of an area of the city, the presence of "facilitating hardware" such as burglar tools, car-stripping equipment, or weapons (cf. Lofland, 1969), and various situational factors which help police define suspicious circumstances or probable cause (Sacks, 1972).

Rather than attempt an exhaustive delineation of all variables which effect official observability of behavior in society, we shall illustrate the impact of social structure by focusing on the relationship of surveillance by control agencies to the social class of those observed. Perhaps the most consistent finding of crime and deviance research is that individuals from lower class backgrounds are disproportionately represented in official rates of deviant behavior. Rather than assume as some theorists (Merton, 1938; Cohen, 1955; Cloward and Ohlin, 1960; Miller, 1958) have that this means a disproportionate amount of deviant behavior in the lower class, a case could be made that the rates reflect a greater observability of persons of lower-class status to control agents. While not all the variation in official rates can be explained in this way, surveys of self-reported deviance clearly indicate that the actual rates of deviance are much more evenly distributed across social-class lines than official data would indicate (Erickson and Empey, 1965; Nye et al., 1958; Akers, 1964; Hirschi, 1969). Thus, the very characteristics of lower-class living which have been identified as having etiological significance, for deviance may be seen as a factor which affects official recognition and selection of deviant behavior (Empey and Lubeck, 1971:143–82; Kitsuse and Cicourel, 1963).

Based on the statistical reputation of lower-class areas of the city as high crime and delinquency areas, police patrol patterns provide greater coverage of lower-class areas; the probability of on-site detection increases, and the known crime rate is increased, which justifies the continuation of the intense patrol patterns. Moreover, since the activities of lower-class groups are more likely to be geared to public places, parks, streets, alleyways, vacant lots, bars, etc., which do not require search warrants for police access, as do private places, whatever deviance there is in the lower class is more visible than that in middle- and upper-class groups (Stinchcombe, 1963; Liebow, 1967; Suttles, 1968; Chambliss and Seidman, 1971:331–33).

The policy decisions made by city hall and the police department may force some forms of deviance that could occur anywhere into lower-class areas. For instance, decisions to keep certain undesirable violations, which seem not to yield to enforcement activity, out of sight of respectable citizens lead to official tolerance of prostitution, public intoxication, vagrancy, and homosexual behavior as long as they occur in lower-class areas. Locating these activities in these areas contributes to the incidence of other crimes, e.g., rolling drunks, victimizing clients of prostitutes, assaults on prostitutes and homosexuals, and so on (Hills, 1971:24).

All of this contributes to the conceptions held by law enforcement agents that there is a greater need for crime control among certain areas and groups in the community (Bayley and Mendelsohn, 1969:163). A double standard of law enforcement may develop, perhaps inadvertently, such that more crime is officially handled in lower-class areas. However, this double standard may mean greater attention by the police without a concomitant greater readiness to arrest. For example, Egon Bittner (1967) reports that the police were not likely to enforce the law strictly on skid row. Rather, the police saw their mission as one of maintaining an uneasy peace in the neighborhood. Also, Wilson (1968b:114–17) found that police handling of juveniles in some middle class suburbs was more formal than in some working-class neighborhoods.

The behavior of the lower class may also be more visible to enforcement agencies because of their greater contact with other public agencies for dealing with social problems. Many in the lower class are on welfare, are drawing unemployment compensation, or are seeking work through state employment offices. The overview that these agencies have of the lives of their clients often increases the chances that the deviant behavior of the clients is detected and referred to the police. One study of statutory rape cases in a California city found that a large number of these cases became known to the police through information provided by welfare officials. The agencies also helped to provide willing complainants to the police in these cases by threatening to cut off aid unless the case was prosecuted (Skolnick and Woodworth, 1967:109).

On the other side of the coin, the middle and upper classes enjoy many advantages in avoiding detection and official processing. We have already noted that most of their behavior occurs in private places. Another influence is that the deviant activities of the upper classes may be quite different in type than lower class offenses:

> The considerable involvement of middle- and upper-class persons in low visibility, occupationally linked behavior in violation of important legal norms is much less likely to invoke the criminal process and result in harsh penalties. Much of their illegal behavior in this occupational context officials will process through civil courts, government administrative boards, and quasi-judicial tribunals whose sanctions are likely to be defined as less punitive and "criminal" by both the public and the offenders themselves [Hills, 1971:20].

Thus middle- and upper-class individuals may simply encounter different control agencies, and the lower class thereby becomes overrepresented in the criminal justice system. When upper-class individuals are brought into criminal proceedings, they have more resources and power to fight the case. This power may be known and respected by the police and consequently official action may be less likely when suspects are upstanding citizens (Chambliss, 1969:86). This implies another "entrance" factor: police discretion.

POLICE DISCRETION

The term "discretion" is often used in discussions of the police but it is seldom adequately defined. Discretion in a very general sense means decision on formal versus informal handling of a case. Most discussions of discretion are couched in terms of whether to make an arrest or not (cf. Goldstein, 1963, 1967). However many other elements are involved. Webster defines discretion as (1) the quality of being discrete, (2) ability to make responsible decisions; and (3) a—individual choice or judgment; b—power of free decision or latitude of choice within certain legal bounds. Police work at various times involves each of these elements. To understand when these elements come into play it is necessary to specify two levels of police discretion.

The first level can be termed general or departmental discretion. Reference at this level is to the "ability to make responsible decisions" aspects of the definition. Police departments through their training and departmental directives take responsibility for the placement of patrolmen on the beat, selection of patrol patterns of mobile units, and the degree of area saturation of police observance. Discretion of this type originates with the mayor, police chief, or field supervisor and becomes a department policy matter. These directives may be temporary, as in cases of community or political pressure to crack down on certain offenses, or represent relatively permanent policy.

Departmental discretion may also involve directives to ignore certain law violations. Thus police may be instructed not to arrest homosexuals in known gay bars in certain sections of the city or not to arrest prostitutes because the courts are so lenient that the girls are back on the street the same evening earning next week's bail money. Departments also have directives, usually of a permanent nature, in regard to the handling of drug users or of prostitutes who may be used as informants or in setting up a big drug pinch. Here departmental discretion may involve refusal to prosecute past violations (which will involve the cooperation of the prosecutor's office), or may involve a tacit agreement to ignore future violations (cf. Goldstein, 1960). At times, informants may be given money to purchase drugs, or be allowed free access to personal supplies of drugs.

The second level of discretion may be termed interactional or field discretion. These are decisions made by patrolmen in the field in cases where departmental directives are not applicable. The decisions on whether and how to intervene in an incident involve the "individual choice" and "latitude of choice within legal bounds" aspects of the definition. Field discretion involves two elements. First the decision on whether to intervene in a suspicious incident or to ignore it; second, if intervention is selected, how should the incident be handled—law enforcement or peace keeping? (Wilson, 1968b:7). Police officers are quick to realize that their training does not provide all the answers in field encounter situations. In field situations, the officer is "on his own" and is the first to admit that directives from the department, academy training, and knowledge of procedural and substantive law do not provide much help. The uninitiated patrolmen experience a "reality shock" in patrol work regardless of the extent of their training (Niederhoffer, 1967:51–54). Police manuals do not provide extensive guidelines on police discretion. Legislation on the question in most states has supported the police officer's right to exercise discretion, while "only a few states have declared that police 'shall' arrest when such evidence exists" (LaFave, 1965:80). Wide discretion is specifically prescribed in certain types of cases, e.g., juvenile offenses. Piliavin and Briar (1964) note that this emphasis on individual discretion by officers produces problems for the police. They are expected to justify their juvenile dispositions in terms of the character of the youth, rather than simply providing evidence that a crime had been committed. This requirement, meaning police must make judicial rather than more clear-cut ministerial decisions, increases "the uncertainty and ambiguity for officers in the situation of apprehension because no explicit rules [exist] for determining which disposition different types of youth should receive" (Piliavin and Briar, 1964:209).

Discretion involves a decision as to how a situation should be handled and what role the officer should play. Police roles encompass four areas: law enforcement, peace-keeping (group-level order problems), order maintenance (community order), and public-service functions (Banton, 1964; Bittner, 1967; Cumming et al., 1965; Wilson, 1968b). Many field decisions require a choice between law enforcement and peace-keeping roles. The wrong choice may lead to an order maintenance problem.[1] The Kerner Report concluded that major precipitating incidents in the 1967 riots were police actions, many which involved attempts at law enforcement (Kerner, 1968:6). Recently some police departments have received directives from city officials to stop law enforcement activity in time of civil unrest. In Washington, D.C., and New York City following Martin Luther King's assassination, police were instructed to stand by while looting and vandalism occurred, rather than attempt to enforce the law. Under these conditions, unobtrusive methods of law enforcement such as summons rather than physical arrests, or photographing individuals violating the law are alternatives to arrest.

In addition to the law enforcement–peace-keeping distinction, we can classify field encounters as either citizen-initiated or police-initiated actions. Combining these four possibilities produces the typology illustrated in Table A.

Since peace-keeping situations are much more ambiguous and lack the pro-

---

[1] At times, police prejudge a situation as an order maintenance problem; this often results in a "police riot" where police take advantage of an ambiguous situation and treat it as a civil disorder, thereby justifying the unbridled use of force against undesirables (Walker, 1968; Stark, 1972).

Table A   Four Kinds of Discretionary
Situations

		Basis of Police Response	
		Police-Initiated	Citizen-Initiated
Nature of Situation	Law Enforcement	I	II
	Peace Keeping	III	IV

(Adapted from Wilson, 1968b:85)

cedural and substantive law guidelines found in law enforcement incidents, we expect a greater range of discretion by police in the former type of settings. However it must be pointed out that the situation only partly dictates the role the police officer will play. He has relatively wide discretion to treat law violating incidents as peace keeping (cf. Bittner, 1967), but is more restricted when serious law violations occur. Most officers will not treat an armed robbery in progress as peace-keeping nor other felonies as other than law enforcement situations. An exception is aggravated assaults between family members where these are often treated unofficially as peace keeping, in part because of the lack of willingness of the victim to sign a complaint. This occurs so often that some departments handle these situations through departmental directives (Goldstein, 1960).

The greatest range of potential police discretion is found in police-initiated actions rather than citizen complaints for two reasons. First, the police make the initial decision of whether to intervene or ignore a situation in on-view encounters. When citizens initiate the complaint, the option is largely absent.[2] Second, research (Black, 1970) indicates that the complainant's wishes significantly affect police discretion, a point we shall enlarge upon shortly. For these reasons we would predict that police discretion would be greatest in police-initiated peace keeping situations (Type III). Less discretion would be found in Type IV and Type I situations, with the least discretion being exercised in citizen-initiated law enforcement settings (Type II).

The decision as to which role the officer will play may not be formed ahead of time, but may evolve out of the interaction. Indeed many patrolmen say that options should not be closed off initially by statements such as "you're

---

[2] An exception would be incidents where police do not respond to a citizen's call. Ennis, in a national survey of victims, found that police did not physically respond to citizens' requests for assistance in 23 percent of the cases (Ennis, 1970:94). Ennis does not account for this seemingly high percentage. It may be that police handle many cases on the phone rather than physically visiting the scene. In a victim survey conducted in Seattle, only 1 percent of victims calling police said they did not respond (Hawkins, 1970).

under arrest," since then the peace-keeping option is forgone and the officer cannot choose it without being open to the charge of backing down. This *emergent quality* of discretion points up the difficulty of controlling or reducing decision-making by the officer in the field. Police quickly point out that many lawyers who write articles on strategies of controlling police discretion have apparently never been on the street to witness police–suspect situations.[3]

In addition to interactional variables which affect field discretion, and general discretion flowing from departmental directives, organizational factors in the police department also influence the amount and type of field discretion. In large departments there may be specialized bureaus to handle specific types of offenses, e.g., the juvenile bureau. Where special bureaus are set up, patrolmen in the field may almost automatically arrest and refer suspects to bureau members who make most of the discretionary decisions. This essentially means moving the discretion decision one step from intake to agents who were not at the scene. Consequently, the situational factors which might affect discretion in one city may not affect arrests in cities with juvenile bureaus. It also means that decisions involving criminal intent, potential harm of offense, and mitigating circumstances are now based on written accounts provided by the field officers and in some cases "verbal dossiers" provided by arresting policeman (Cicourel, 1968).

In addition to the effect on the table of organization of the police department, the style of the department will affect decisions to arrest. Wilson (1968a) found that a West Coast police department which he classified as "professional," i.e., legalistic style (high salary scale, high entrance requirements, out of state recruitment), had very high arrest rates for juveniles, suggesting that little field discretion was being exercised. An East Coast department, which he termed "fraternal" (nonprofessional, membership based on ethnic and neighborhood origins) the arrest rate for juveniles was very low. Arrest rates were low in the fraternal department in part because bringing in juveniles was not seen as a "good pinch." More important perhaps was the fact that most of the police officers were products of the neighborhoods they patrolled and they could empathize with juveniles who got into trouble. They may have known the juvenile or the family, or they may have had similar problems when growing up in that area.

---

[3] An interesting sidelight of writings on police discretion is the unquestioned assumption that police discretion is bad, and that it is something which must be controlled and reduced. Granted that most of the writing on the topic is done by lawyers concerned with problems of controlling police power, recent developments in sociology should bring this assumption into question. The extensive literature subsumed under the rubric of "labeling theory" suggests the dysfunctions of official processing of criminal and deviant behavior. Implicit in labeling theory is a call for more community tolerance of behaviors, i.e., more discretion in the handling of deviant behavior such that informal methods of control are exhausted first (cf. Scheff, 1966; Lemert, 1967). An adequate test of the assumption that discretion should be reduced would require a comparison of recidivism in groups of individuals informally handled by police and those arrested and officially processed. Unfortunately such studies remain to be done.

FIELD ENCOUNTERS: THE CITIZEN AND POLICE DISCRETION

In this section we analyze the variables which operate in the social setting of enforcement. What are the situational determinants of police decision making? Given similar situations, why are arrests made in some instances but not in others? The article by Black and Reiss on police encounters with juveniles reprinted as the first selection in this section is an attempt to assess some of the situational aspects of police work. The study suggests that an adequate analysis of police encounters must focus on the roles of the police officer, suspect (if present), complainant, victim, informant, and bystanders. In the following review of research on police encounters we shall attempt to provide an analysis of how the citizen influences law enforcement.

Police encounters with citizens are situations of unequal power (Toch, 1970:80). Police encounters, unlike many in society, are asymmetric and closed to negotiation of identities to some extent. This imbalance inherent in the situation, when combined with perceptions of hostility on both sides, sets the stage for conflict in police–citizen encounters.

The perception of hostility may involve a shared misunderstanding, which then has self-fulfilling consequences. For example, the mass media often give the impression that many citizens have problems with the police and consequently have negative attitudes toward them. Coverage of civil disorders, policing of protest marches, and exposés on police scandals give the public an impression of police which suggests wanton brutality, disregard for civil liberties in all action, and rampant corruption. In spite of these negative images from the mass media, surveys indicate that the vast majority of citizens hold positive attitudes toward the police (Smith and Hawkins, 1973). Studies also indicate that police may perceive citizens as having more hostile attitudes than is in fact the case (McNamara, 1967:221; Wilson, 1968b:28; Bayley and Mendelsohn, 1969; Groves, 1968).

The type of enforcement situation will influence the levels of hostility (Bordua and Tifft, 1971). Generally, peace-keeping activities are more ambiguous for the police and citizens than law enforcement incidents. What constitutes disorderly conduct is much more difficult to define than armed robbery. The policeman enforcing the law shows less uncertainty in his actions and the offender, too, is likely to have a clear idea of how to play the role of "suspect" (Hudson, 1970:181); peace-keeping activity may increase the level of hostility "because its unexpected nature makes [the officer] more apprehensive and partly because he tends to communicate this apprehension to the citizen" (Wilson, 1968b:20). When police officers expect a hostile reception they may take a more authoritarian attitude in initiating the encounter; this stance is taken to insure that police actions will be seen as legitimate and reduce potential challenges to police authority (Skolnick, 1966:62; Werthman and Piliavin, 1967; McNamara, 1967:213; Neiderhoffer, 1967).

The shared misunderstandings held by the police and the public may generate more police brutality, some of which is covered by the mass media, and the cycle continues. The self-fulfilling aspect of shared misunderstandings does not deny the reality of hostility in some segments of society. Youth and minority groups are likely to have strong negative attitudes toward police based in part on their greater contact with police (Smith and Hawkins, 1973). Our point is that perceptions brought to the encounter may at times take precedence over negotiated identities. Indeed there may be no time for negotiation between the parties. McNamara (1967:212) found that almost half of the police officers surveyed felt that "if a patrolman thinks he may have to use force in a situation he should use it right after his entrance into the situation in order to gain the advantage of surprise."

Recognizing that police encounters are initially situations of power imbalance and are often set against a backdrop of hostility (some of which is real, some imagined), what other factors affect police behavior in the field? One major factor in determining arrest is the demeanor of the suspect. A recent study of police processing of delinquents found that blacks were more likely to be arrested than whites (Ferdinand and Luchterhand, 1970). In an attempt to discover the reasons for the apparent harshness in disposition, the researchers conducted a self-reported deliquency study of black and white youths in the neighborhood. They found that whites had higher rates for self-reported offenses than blacks and were also more likely to have antisocial attitudes. Consequently, police action did not reflect the actual level of law violations in these two racial groups. The authors also measured the extent of authority rejection for blacks and whites and found the former group much higher on these indicators. They conclude that blacks were more likely to be arrested because more severe dispositions were given to those whose attitudes were particularly defiant.

More direct evidence of the impact of demeanor on disposition comes from a California study which compared formal disposition to the police officer's perception of the suspect's cooperation. Two-thirds of the cases where youths were classified as uncooperative resulted in arrest, while only 4 percent of the cooperative youths were arrested (Piliavin and Briar, 1964:211). In the Black and Reiss (1970) article reprinted here it is clear that the demeanor–disposition relationship was not linear, but that those who were antagonistic and those who were extremely differential were more likely to be arrested than those who were merely "civil." Extreme politeness was apparently taken as an attempt to con the officer, and consequently arrest was more probable.

Black and Reiss (1970) also indicate that a second situational factor which greatly influences police disposition in the field is the preferences of the complainant (see also Black, 1970). Citizens have a great impact on police discretion and therefore influence the crime rates in two ways: First, rates are affected by citizen decisions to call the police when victimized, or when a crime is observed. Second, they influence the legal definition of events at the scene. Thus "the operational influence of citizens gives crime rates a peculiarly democratic flavor" (Black, 1970:739). One consequence is that racial differences in police arrests (in the Black and Reiss study) were due to citizen preferences rather than police prejudice, since the proportions of arrests in police-initiated actions were nearly equal and black complainants were more likely to demand arrest than were whites (cf. Black and Reiss, 1972).

Black (1970) also found that police were less likely to comply with requests for written reports when offenders were fellow family members or friends; requests for official action were most frequently honored when offenders were felt to be strangers. Demeanor of the complainant also affected police compliance with preferences stated. Antagonistic complainants were less likely to have their preferences translated into action. There was no effect of race of complainant on police compliance with citizen requests for action. Social class was slightly related to police compliance with citizen requests, but only in felony cases where police "were somewhat more likely to comply with white-collar complainants than with those of blue-collar status" (Black, 1970: 746).

In addition to input from suspects and complainants, many other situational factors affect the application of the law in the field. Police seldom invoke their law enforcement prerogative on skid row due to situational definitions of private property, and the goal of keeping things quiet in the area (Bittner, 1967). The form and outcome of police encounters with the public may be determined by the comments and the mood of bystanders to an incident. Police may ignore a violation or make a quick arrest in cases of doubtful evidence, simply to avoid a confrontation which might jeopardize order maintenance. Other situationally determined factors include evidence and probable cause for arrest, availability of a willing complainant to go to court, assessment of the legitimacy of the victimization, and role of the victim in his victimization. (On other factors affecting disposition, see Terry, 1967; Weiner and Willie, 1971.)

PROFESSIONALISM AND POLICE: A METHOD OF CONTROLLING POLICE DISCRETION?

The term "professional" has been liberally applied to discussions of police work in recent years. Many of these discussions have overlooked an important distinction between professional police departments and police work as a profession. A professional police department is characterized by universal rules and judgments, recruitment based on achievement rather than ascriptive criteria, enforcement of laws without respect to who is the object of enforcement, member commitment to general standards and to experts in police science, and authority resting more with the rule and not the incumbent within the organization (Wilson, 1968b:11–12). Professionalization of a department usually means change in the structural form of the organization and the requirements for employment, especially for those at the top of the table of organization—however, the line worker may not become more professional. It is in this sense that "police organization becomes 'professionalized' not their members" (Bordua and Reiss, 1966:73). Such professionalization of the department mitigates against the professionalism of line officers (patrolmen) in a number of ways: First there is an increasing centralization of both command and control in professionalized departments. Decision making is more likely to be from a central command rather than the precinct or street. Second the investigative function of the police has moved to a technical elite, i.e., specialized bureaus—juvenile bureau (Bordua and Reiss, 1967: 289–90). In short, the professionalization of police departments decreases discretion (independent decision making) exercised by patrolmen, the very opposite of what we would expect if police work as an occupation were more of a profession.

Wilensky (1964) in his discussion of the potential professionalization of *everyone,* suggests that professionalization is best conceived as a process, and the various occupations may be differentiated as to their developmental state. Wilensky lists five definitional characteristics of professions which he sees as stages of development: first, securing a definition of territory and showing how it is best qualified to operate in the area; second, the establishment of training schools, ideally attached to established universities; third, the formation of a professional association which aids in maintaining territorial domination; fourth, a political agitation stage in order to win the support and authority of legal recognition for the protection of the job territory and also the provision of a universal code of ethics for members. This fourth stage involves concern with licensing and certification of its own members by a professional association. The final stage involves the application of a formal code of ethics to members' behavior—an elimination of the unqualified and unscrupulous; in short, self-regulation is the major form of control over members' activities. There is also concern with reducing internal competition and protection of clients under service ideals which are developed explicitly at this stage (Wilensky, 1964:142–45).

The police are roughly at stage three and are moving into stage four. They have not moved for licensing or certification control of members, but they have become more politically active (cf. Stark, 1972). Police have not developed an effective universal professional code of ethics, nor has any society been charged with the disciplining of errant officers. To the extent that police professionalization continues, it will probably be achieved first by the technical elites in the department rather than by patrolmen and other low-ranking officers.

The degree of professionalization affects the extent to which occupants are granted authority.

> Any occupation wishing to exercise professional authority must find a technical basis for it, assert an exclusive jurisdiction, link both skill and jurisdiction to standards of training, and convince the public that its services are uniquely trustworthy [Wilensky, 1964:138].

Police have their greatest problem with this latter point. There is great reluctance on the part of society to trust the police due to the inherent range of power they possess. Because of this lack of trust and need for external review, control of the police has been placed in the legal system. This external control is probably the greatest obstacle in the path of the professionalism of police work. It is difficult, if not impossible, to develop a true profession where control is external to the organization. Police are restricted even more than nurses are in the medical profession. Both policemen and nurses are subordinate professions under the dominant professions of law and medicine (Freidson, 1970). This lack of dominance precludes exclusive jurisdiction in the sense of the term which implies an exclusive right to deal completely with a problem.[4] The police have jurisdiction in the area of law enforcement and maintaining public order, but they do not have exclusive rights to adjudicate these problems. (Exceptions might be in juvenile cases where adjudication is partially relegated to officers in the field who are instructed to use maximum discretion.) However, police are not seen as judge and jury, and it will probably never be the case that such decisions will be totally surrendered to the police.

Skolnick (1966) suggests that police have developed a managerial professionalism as opposed to a legal professionalism. This view stresses the conception of police officers as craftsmen rather than legal actors. Craftsmen are seen as having individual initiative to make decisions within bureaucracies such that the decisions contribute to administrative efficiency. Thus the police, in Skolnick's view, are not merely automatons following directives, but are closer to innovators in the application of the law.

The craftsman orientation implies that "bureaucracy can hope to achieve efficiency only by allowing officials to initiate their own means for solving specific problems that interfere with their capacity to achieve productive results." However, to the extent police organizations "operate mainly on grounds of administrative efficiency, the development of the rule of law is frustrated" (Skolnick, 1966:237–38). The administrative efficiency emphasis is hampered by the consideration of civil liberties. The police lose sight of the fact that the main purpose of the law is to make their task more difficult, i.e., to provide procedural safeguards for the citizenry being served. The stress on efficiency produces very unprofessional conduct, such as police brutality (Westley, 1953), violations of procedural law, and other rule adaptations or work crimes which help to get the job done (cf. Blumberg, 1967). In sum,

4 The other aspect of jurisdiction, right of access to a certain problem, has not been a problem for the police. While other occupational groups such as chiropractors and pharmacists must carve out and legally protect their domain (Akers, 1968), this has been done for the police by legislatures. The legislative mandate may be seen as a form of licensure which provides the police with a legal monopoly in their work. However, the police, even with a legal mandate, are in a sense being threatened by rival claims to their domain. The increasing numbers of private enforcement agencies (Scott and McPherson, 1971) and to a less extent the involvement of citizens in law enforcement programs (Campbell et al., 1970:437–54) challenge the uniqueness of the police task.

organizational demands make police control through professionalization problematic, forcing a reliance on other methods.

TRADITIONAL CONTROLS OVER POLICE BEHAVIOR

Responsibility for control of the police resides mainly in the courts and other external agencies. The courts control behavior in a number of ways. First they create much of the procedural law which guides police behavior in the field. The problem of surveillance has traditionally been more of concern to the courts than the creation of procedural safeguards. A major means of control of police is by exclusion of cases brought before the court. The exclusionary rule maintains the bounds of law enforcement, but only to a very limited extent. (See the article by Paulsen et al., included here, which describes the control mechanisms operating on police behavior.) A problem with the exclusionary rule is that it is effective only in those incidents in which the case gets to court. Cases disposed of in other ways such as plea bargaining and plea copping are less visible to the court. The major problem is that only about 10 percent of police work involves law enforcement. Thus even if all these cases go to court (now the proportion going to trial is about 5–10 percent of cases), only a small proportion of police action can be reviewed. The vast majority of police actions go unmonitored by the courts. Another problem is that police may abuse the exclusionary rule with no real penalty (penalty is assumed to be loss of the case). Police may arrest certain persons knowing full well that cases will be thrown out of court, but the arrests are made as a form of harrassment. This is true of police action against gambling and prostitution in some areas (Goldstein, 1960).

In addition to court review of cases, other forms of *ex post facto* controls on police action include citizen-initiated civil or criminal action to regress grievances. Civil actions against the police include false arrest suits, or suits involving defamation of character. Criminal action can be instigated by citizens in cases of brutality and personal injury at the hands of the police. Another control involves court-ordered injunctions to prevent police action against certain groups in society, e.g., black panthers or other political groups (see Paulsen, et al., 1970).

Police may also be controlled from without by civilian review boards or the ombudsmen system—agencies independent of the police department. Police officers have strongly opposed the formation of civilian review boards and recently have been successful in weakening or removing these control structures. The New York City Police Department Patrolman's Benevolent Association recently launched a successful campaign to have voters repeal civilian review boards (Stark, 1972:194–98). Ombudsman systems have been suggested, but few have been implemented, again because of police opposition.

Police actions are also reviewed and controlled by the leaders of city government. Mayors may establish a committee within city government to review citizen complaints. Control of this type is often turned over to the police themselves, and committees are formed and directed by the chief of police who must make necessary changes or implement punishment. These internal review committees are preferred by police, even though they create some morale problems for the chief and the department. Internal review boards are supposed to investigate charges of brutality, violations of due process, and may review disciplinary decisions made by superiors over line officers. Internal review has been largely ineffective for a number of reasons. The first has been alluded to above—the dilemma that faces the chief who is charged with disciplining his men and maintaining morale and trust of the department. A second problem is that police may cover up or fail adequately to investigate incidents that come before the board. The major problem is that regardless of the integrity of the board, the public may perceive it as an unsympathetic control mechanism, and thus over time may stop bringing legitimate complaints against the police.

Given the discretionary aspects of police work and the situational determinants of action in various settings, it is very difficult to predict or to regulate by statute or departmental directive the action of officers in the field. As noted previously, the police officer has first hand knowledge of the incident and can assess the situational elements invoked in the criminal action, the attitudes of the suspects, criminal intent, etc. Details of the case, by the time they are reviewed by the court, are highly selective and stereotyped accounts of the incident. This feeling by police that they had more information than the judge leads to resentment and conflict between the court and the police. These factors, coupled with the relative ineffectiveness of extant control policies for police behavior, have forced reformers to question the basic police role. Professionalism, while not achieving effective control at the present time, may do so if drastic changes in current conceptions of police work are made.

Making police work more professional by professionalizing the men rather than the organization may be a first step. Professionalization leading to increasing the adjudicative power of the police will require higher levels of education and training. Paralegal training may be required such that police will become legal actors. As mentioned earlier, reward systems of police organizations must be changed if this is to be accomplished. The professionalization of police work might entail changes in current practices of recruitment. A dual level of entrance might be instituted similar to that used in the armed services so that individuals with advanced degrees do not start at the bottom (Stark, 1972:227). Lateral entry into police organizations for experienced men would permit the transfer of personnel between agencies without loss of rank.

The role of the police must also be altered—some of the roles could be filled by others. Police could be taken off traffic duty, especially traffic direction and crowd-control work. Many of the social-service functions performed by the police could be taken over by civilian agencies, perhaps private firms operating for profit (Wilson, 1968b). Stark (1972) suggests a separation of patrol and investigative units. Detective and special squads could be placed under the district attorney's office which would improve investigative efficiency and strengthen cases. This separation might benefit patrol officers by increasing prestige within this group. Presently detectives have higher status, while patrol work is less desirable and lower in prestige (Skolnick, 1966). Also the present system tends to move better educated and more experienced officers off the beat and into investigative work. Consequently the least "professional" officers are making the most wide-ranging and important decisions on the application of the law. The change would also remove one step in the processing machinery since transactions would be between patrolmen and the district attorney's office (detectives) rather than current patrolmen–detective–prosecutor's office transactions.

A third requirement in the modification of the police task involves changes in substantive law which would permit more professional police work. It is now well known that the "overcriminalization" of public and private behaviors presents many problems to the police (e.g., Dobrovir, 1970). Crime such as gambling, prostitution, drugs, homosexuality, etc.—a crime without a victim, when prohibited by law, "establishes the economic basis for black market operations or helps to produce situations in which police efficiency is impaired and police corruption encouraged" (Schur, 1965:6; also Packer, 1968). The lack of public consensus on the illegality of these activities, plus the element of willing exchange, makes police enforcement difficult. Since police must act as complainants, extra-legal actions are encouraged. For these and other reasons, the police image and police work would be facilitated by legalization of many of these activities. The overloading of the criminal law with unnecessary controls on behavior only makes the police officer's job more difficult. All the professionalization in the world will not improve the quality of law enforcement unless there are concomitant changes in the substantive law.

REFERENCES

Akers, Ronald L., 1964. "Socio-Economic Status and Delinquent Behavior: A Retest," *Journal of Research in Crime and Delinquency*, 1 (January); 1968, "The Professional Association and the Legal Regulation of Practice," *Law and Society Review*, 2 (May):463–82.

Banton, Michael, 1964. *The Police and the Community*. London: Tavistock.

Bayley, David H. and Harold Mendelsohn, 1969. *Minorities and the Police*. New York: The Free Press.

Berger, Peter L., 1963. *Invitation to Sociology*. New York: Anchor Books.

Biderman, Albert D., Louise A. Johnson, J. McIntyre, and A. W. Weir, 1967. *Report on a Pilot Study in the District of Columbia on Victimization and Attitudes toward Law Enforcement*. Washington, D.C.: U.S. Government Printing Office.

Bittner, Egon, 1967. "The Police on Skid-row: A Study of Peace Keeping," *American Sociological Review*, 32 (October):699–715.

Black, Donald J., 1970. "Production of Crime Rates," *American Sociological Review*, 35 (August):733–48.

BLACK, DONALD J. and ALBERT J. REISS, JR., 1970. "Police Control of Juveniles," *American Sociological Review,* 35 (February):63–77; 1972, "Patterns of Behavior in Police and Citizen Transactions," in Charles E. Reasons and Jack L. Kuykendall, eds., *Race, Crime and Justice.* Pacific Palisades, California: Goodyear Publishing Company.

BLUMBERG, ABRAHAM S., 1967. "The Practice of Law as Confidence Game: Organizational Cooptation of a Profession," *Law and Society Review,* 1 (June):15–39.

BORDUA, DAVID J. and ALBERT J. REISS, JR., 1966. "Command, Control and Charisma: Reflections on Police Bureaucracy," *American Journal of Sociology,* 72 (July): 68–76; 1967, "Law Enforcement," in Paul F. Lazarsfeld, William H. Sewell and Harold L. Wilensky, eds., *The Uses of Sociology.* New York: Basic Books.

BORDUA, DAVID J. and LARRY L. TIFFT, 1971. "Citizen Interviews, Organizational Feedback, and Police-Community Relations Decisions," *Law and Society Review,* 6 (November):155–82.

CAMPBELL, JAMES S., JOSEPH R. SAHID and DAVID P. STANG, 1970. *Law and Order Reconsidered: A Staff Report to the National Commission on the Causes and Prevention of Violence.* New York: Bantam Books.

CHAMBLISS, WILLIAM J., 1969. *Crime and the Legal Process.* New York: McGraw-Hill Book Company.

CHAMBLISS, WILLIAM J. and ROBERT B. SEIDMAN, 1971. *Law, Order, and Power.* Reading, Mass.: Addison-Wesley.

CICOUREL, AARON V., 1968. *The Social Organization of Juvenile Justice.* New York: John Wiley and Sons.

CLOWARD, RICHARD A. and LLOYD E. OHLIN, 1960. *Delinquency and Opportunity.* New York: The Free Press.

COHEN, ALBERT K., 1955. *Delinquent Boys.* New York: The Free Press.

CUMMING, ELAINE, IAN CUMMING, and LAURA EDELL, 1965. "Policeman as Philosopher, Guide and Friend," *Social Problems,* 12 (Winter):276–86.

DOBROVIR, WILLIAM A., 1970. "The Problem of 'Overcriminalization'," in James S. Campbell, Joseph R. Sahid, and David P. Stang, eds., *Law and Order Reconsidered.* New York: Bantam Books.

DOHRENWEND, BRUCE P. and EDWIN CHIN-SHONG, 1967. "Social Status and Attitudes Toward Psychological Disorder: The Problem of Tolerance of Deviance," *American Sociological Review,* 32 (June):417–33.

EMPEY, LAMAR T. and STEVEN G. LUBECK, 1971. *Explaining Delinquency.* Lexington, Mass.: D. C. Heath and Company.

ENNIS, PHILIP H., 1967. *Criminal Victimization in the United States.* Washington, D.C.: U.S. Government Printing Office; 1970, "Crime, Victims and the Police," in Michael Lipsky, ed., *Police Encounters.* Chicago: Aldine Publishing Company.

ERICKSON, MAYNARD L. and LAMAR T. EMPEY, 1965. "Class Position, Peers and Delinquency," *Sociology and Social Research,* 49 (April):268–82.

FERDINAND, THEODORE N. and ELMER G. LUCHTERHAND, 1970. "Inner-City Youth, The Police, the Juvenile Court, and Justice," *Social Problems,* 17 (Spring):510–27.

FREIDSON, ELIOT, 1970. *Profession of Medicine.* New York: Dodd, Mead, and Company.

GIBBS, JACK P., 1966. "Sanctions." *Social Problems,* 14 (Fall):147–59.

GOLDSTEIN, HERMAN, 1963. "Police Discretion: The Ideal versus the Real," *Public Administration Review,* 23 (September):140–48; 1967, "Police Policy Formulation: A Proposal for Improving Police Performance," *Michigan Law Review,* 65 (April):1123–46.

GOLDSTEIN, JOSEPH, 1960. "Police Discretion Not To Invoke the Criminal Process: Low Visibility Decisions in the Administration of Justice," *Yale Law Journal,* 69 (March):543–88.

GROVES, W. EUGENE, 1968. "Police in the Ghetto," in Peter Rossi and James S. Coleman, eds., *Supplemental Studies for the National Advisory Commission on Civil Disorders.* New York: Praeger Publishing Company.

HAWKINS, RICHARD, 1970. *Determinants of Sanctioning Initiations for Criminal Victimization.* Unpublished Ph.D. Dissertation, Department of Sociology, University of Washington; 1973, "Who Called the Cops: Decisions to Report Criminal Victimization," *Law and Society Review,* 7 (Spring):427–43.

HILLS, STUART L., 1971. *Crime, Power, and Morality.* Scranton: Chandler Publishing Company.

HIRSCHI, TRAVIS, 1969. *Causes of Delinquency.* Berkeley: University of California Press.

HUDSON, JAMES R., 1970. "Police-Citizen Encounters that Lead to Citizen Complaints," *Social Problems,* 18 (Fall):179:93.

JACKSON, JOAN K., 1954. "The Adjustment of the Family to the Crisis of Alcoholism," *Quarterly Journal of Studies on Alcohol,* 15 (December):564–86.

KADUSHIN, CHARLES, 1966. "The Friends and Supporters of Psychotherapy: On Social Circles in Urban Life," *American Sociological Review,* 31 (December):786–802.

KERNER, OTTO, 1968. *Report of the National Advisory Commission on Civil Disorders.* New York: Bantam Books.

KITSUSE, JOHN I. and AARON V. CICOUREL, 1963. "A Note on the Uses of Official Statistics," *Social Problems,* 11 (Fall):131–39.

LAFAVE, WAYNE R., 1965. *Arrest: The Decision to Take a Suspect into Custody.* Boston: Little, Brown and Company.

LEMERT, EDWIN M., 1967. *Human Deviance, Social Problems and Social Control.* Englewood Cliffs, N.J.: Prentice-Hall.

LIEBOW, ELLIOT, 1967. *Tally's Corner.* Boston: Little, Brown and Company.

LOFLAND, JOHN, 1969. *Deviance and Identity.* Englewood Cliffs, N.J.: Prentice-Hall.

McNAMARA, JOHN H., 1967. "Uncertainties in Police Work: The Relevance of Police Recruits' Backgrounds and Training," in David J. Bordua, ed., *The Police.* New York: John Wiley and Sons, Inc.

MILLER, WALTER B., 1958. "Lower Class Culture as a Generating Milieu of Gang Delinquency," *Journal of Social Issues,* 14 (1958):5–18.

MERTON, ROBERT K., 1938. "Social Structure and Anomie," *American Sociological Review,* 3 (October):672–82.

NIEDERHOFFER, ARTHUR, 1967. *Behind the Shield.* New York: Anchor Books.

NYE, F. IVAN, JAMES F. SHORT, JR., and V. J. OLSON, 1958. "Socio-Economic Status and Delinquent Behavior," *American Journal of Sociology,* 63 (January): 318–29.

PACKER, HERBERT L., 1968. *The Limits of the Criminal Sanction.* Stanford: Stanford University Press.

PAULSEN, MONRAD G., CHARLES WHITEBREAD, and RICHARD BONNIE, 1970. "Securing Police Compliance with Constitutional Limitations: The Exclusionary Rule and Other Devices," in James S. Campbell, *et al.,* eds., *Law and Order Reconsidered.* New York: Bantam Books.

PILIAVIN, IRVING and SCOTT BRIAR, 1964. "Police Encounters with Juveniles," *American Journal of Sociology,* 70 (September):206–14.

SACKS, HARVEY, 1972. "Notes on Police Assessment of Moral Character," in David Sudnow, ed., *Studies in Social Interaction.* New York: The Free Press.

SCHAFER, STEPHEN, 1968. *The Victim and His Criminal.* New York: Random House.

SCHEFF, THOMAS J., 1966. *Being Mentally Ill.* Chicago: Aldine Publishing Company; 1968, "Negotiating Reality: Notes on Power in the Assessment of Responsibility," *Social Problems,* 16 (Summer):3–17.

SCHUR, EDWIN M., 1965. *Crimes Without Victims.* Englewood Cliffs: Prentice-Hall.

SCOTT, THOMAS M. and MARLYS McPHERSON, 1971. "The Development of the Private

Sector of the Criminal Justice System," *Law and Society Review,* 6 (November): 267–88.

SKOLNICK, JEROME H., 1966. *Justice Without Trial.* New York: John Wiley and Sons, Inc.

SKOLNICK, JEROME H., and J. RICHARD WOODWORTH, 1967. "Bureaucracy, Information and Social Control: A Study of Morals Details," in David J. Bordua, ed., *The Police.* New York: John Wiley and Sons.

SMITH, PAUL E., and RICHARD HAWKINS, 1973. "Victimization, Types of Citizen-Police Contacts, and Attitudes toward the Police," *Law and Society Review,* 8 (1973):135–52.

SPITZER, STEPHAN P. and NORMAN K. DENZIN, 1968. *The Mental Patient.* New York: McGraw-Hill Book Company.

STARK, RODNEY, 1972. *Police Riots.* Belmont, California: Focus Books.

STINCHCOMBE, ARTHUR L., 1963. "Institutions of Privacy in the Determination of Police Administrative Practice," *American Journal of Sociology,* 69 (September):150–60.

SUTTLES, GERALD D., 1968. *The Social Order of the Slum.* Chicago: University of Chicago Press.

TERRY, ROBERT M., 1967. "The Screening of Juvenile Offenders," *Journal of Criminal Law, Criminology and Police Science,* 58 (June):173–81.

TOCH, HANS H., 1970. "Psychological Consequences of the Police Role," in Arthur Niederhoffer and Abraham S. Blumberg, eds., *The Ambivalent Force.* Waltham, Mass.: Ginn and Company.

WALKER, DANIEL, 1968. *Rights in Conflict.* New York: Bantam Books.

WEINER, NORMAN L. and CHARLES V. WILLIE, 1971. "Decisions by Juvenile Officers," *American Journal of Sociology,* 77 (September):199–210.

WERTHMAN, CARL and IRVING PILIAVIN, 1967. "Gang Members and the Police," in David J. Bordua, ed., *The Police.* New York: John Wiley and Sons.

WESTLEY, WILLIAM A., 1953. "Violence and the Police," *American Journal of Sociology,* 59 (July):34–41.

WILSENSKY, HAROLD L., 1964. "The Professionalization of Everyone," *American Journal of Sociology,* 70 (September):137–58.

WILSON, JAMES Q., 1968a. "The Police and the Delinquent in Two Cities," in Stanton Wheeler, ed., *Controlling Delinquents.* New York: John Wiley and Sons, Inc.; 1968b. *Varieties of Police Behavior.* Cambridge: Harvard University Press.

YARROW, MARIAN R., CHARLOTTE G. SCHWARTZ, HARRIET S. MURPHY, and LEILA C. DEASY, 1955. "The Psychological Meaning of Mental Illness in the Family," *Journal of Social Issues,* 11 (1955):12–24.

POLICE CONTROL OF JUVENILES

Donald J. Black and
Albert J. Reiss, Jr.

Current theory on deviant behavior and social control inquires very little into either the organized processes by which deviance is detected or the patterns by which deviance is sanctioned, countenanced, or ignored once it is found out. Despite a ground swell of concern with *social reactions* to deviant behavior—the core of the labeling approach to deviance—the sociology of social control remains a conceptually retarded body of knowledge. One way of drawing detection and sanctioning differentials into the analytical bounds of theory is to define deviance in terms of the probability of a control response. Thus, *individual or group behavior is deviant if it falls within a class of behavior for which there is a probability of negative sanctions subsequent to its detection*.[1]

Reprinted from *American Sociological Review*, 35 (February 1970), pp. 63–77, by permission of the authors and the American Sociological Association.

The research reported in this paper was supported by Grant Award 006, Office of Law Enforcement Assistance, United States Department of Justice, under the Law Enforcement Assistance Act of 1965, as well as by grants from the National Science Foundation and the Russell Sage Foundation. Maureen Mileski, Stanton Wheeler and Abraham S. Goldstein made helpful comments on earlier drafts of the paper.

[1] This conceptualization consciously bears the imprint of Max Weber's work. For example, he defines "power" as "the probability that one actor within a social relationship will be in a position to carry out his own will despite resistance, regardless of the basis on which this probability rests" (Parsons, 1964:152). Weber defines "law" as follows: ". . . An order will be called *law* when conformity with it is upheld by the probability that deviant action will be met by physical or psychic sanctions aimed to compel conformity or to punish disobedience, and applied by a group of men especially empowered to carry out this function" (Parsons, 1964:127). Cf. the translation of this definition in Max Rheinstein (1966:5).

For any form of behavior to be classified as deviant, the probability of negative sanctions must be above zero when the behavior is detected. The greater the probability of sanction, the more appropriate is the classification as deviant.[2] Therefore, whether or not a given form of behavior is deviant and the extent to which it is deviant are empirical questions.

Detection and sanctioning involve separate probabilities. Some forms of deviance, such as those that arise in private places, have extremely low probabilities of detection. Types of deviance that rarely are detected may nonetheless have very high sanction probabilities. In other cases the converse may be true. Furthermore, the particular probabilities of detection and sanctioning may be closely tied to homicide, for example, the probability of detection is high, as is the probability of some form of negative sanction. The probability of official detection of incest surely is low, while the likelihood of sanctioning may be high when incest is detected. Public drunkenness would seem to have a high detection but a low sanctioning probability. Analogous probabilities could be calculated for types of deviance that fall within jurisdictions other than the criminal law.[3]

[2] This does not, of course, preclude a probability of positive sanctions for the behavior. Some forms of deviant behavior are encouraged by subcultures that bestow positive sanctions for behavior which is handled as deviant in the wider community. One interesting but untouched problem in deviant behavior theory is that of the relative effects of joint probabilities of positive and negative sanctions in producing behavior of a given class.

[3] One consequence of following this approach is that a control system can be examined from the standpoint of the deviant who is concerned with calculating his *risks* in the system. Oliver Wendell Holmes (1897) proposed this perspective as an

A control approach, as here propounded, implies three basic types of deviance: (1) undetected deviance, (2) detected, unsanctioned deviance, and (3) sanctioned deviance.[4] These are the three conditions under which empirical instances of deviant behavior appear in relation to control systems. An instance of undetected deviance occurs if an act or a behavior pattern occurs for which there would be a probability of sanction *if it were detected.* Undetected marijuana-smoking is deviant, for example, since there is a probability of negative sanction when an instance of this *class* of behavior is discovered. When a clearly drunken person is encountered on the street by a policeman but is not arrested, an instance of detected, unsanctioned deviance has taken place. The third type, sanctioned deviance, is self-explanatory.

An elaboration of the analytical distinctions necessary in a control approach would exceed the bounds of this discussion. However, two additional elementary distinctions must be noted. A distinction must be made between official, or formal, detection and sanctioning, on the one hand, and informal detection and sanctioning, on the other. Any approach to deviant behavior that does not inquire into the relations between official and informal control systems is incomplete. In other words, the notion of "social control of deviant behavior" should always have an organizational or system reference. Secondly, it is important to distinguish between the detection of deviant acts and the detection of persons who commit these acts. The general conditions under which persons are linked to deviant acts is a problem for investigation. Informal as well as official control systems involve detective work and the pursuit of evidence.

It should not be surmised from the foregoing that a sociology of the deviance-control process consists solely in the analysis of detection and sanctioning processes. Such would be an overly narrow conception of the subject matter, as well as a distorted analytical description of how control systems operate. The foregoing is oriented mainly to the *case-by-case* responses of control systems to deviant behavior. The framework is not geared to the analysis of control responses that bypass the problems of detection and sanctioning altogether. For instance, it ignores totally symbolic social control responses, such as may sometimes be found in the enactment of rules where there is no attempt to detect or sanction violations of those rules (Arnold, 1935; Gusfield, 1963). It also neglects the preventive aspects of social control. For example, control systems sometimes take measures to limit opportunities for deviant behavior by constraining the actions of all members of a social category, a tactic illustrated by curfew ordinances, occupational licensing laws, food stamp requirements for welfare recipients, and preventive detection of felony suspects. Thus, an emphasis upon detection and sanctioning differentials should not deflect interest from other important properties of social control systems.

This paper presents findings on citizen and police detection of juvenile deviance and on the sanctioning of juveniles through arrest in routine police work. It makes problematic situational conditions that increase the probability of sanction subsequent to the detection of violative behavior. Put another way, it makes problematic conditions (besides rule-violative behavior itself) that give rise to differentials in official sanctioning. It is a study of law-in-action. Since all of the data per-

---

approach to the legal system: "If you want to know the law and nothing else, you must look at it as a bad man, who cares only for the material consequences which such knowledge enables him to predict, not as a good one, who finds his reasons for conduct, whether inside the law or outside of it, in the vaguer sanctions of conscience."

[4] The definition of deviance presented above excludes what may appear to be the fourth logical possibility, i.e., undetected, sanctioned deviance.

tain to police encounters with alleged delinquents, the relationship between undetected and detected delinquency is not treated.

THE METHOD

The findings reported here derive from systematic observation of police-citizen transactions conducted during the summer of 1966. Thirty-six observers—persons with law, law enforcement, and social science backgrounds—recorded observations of routine patrol work in Boston, Chicago, and Washington, D.C. The observer training period comprised one week and was identical across the three cities. The daily supervision system also was similar across the cities. The observers rode in scout cars or, less frequently walked with patrolmen on all shifts on all days of the week for seven weeks in each city. To assure the inclusion of a large number of police-citizen encounters, we gave added weight to the times when police activity is comparatively high (evening watches, particularly weekend evenings).

No attempt was made to survey police-citizen encounters in all localities within the three cities. Instead, police precincts in each city were chosen as observation sites. The precincts were selected so as to maximize observation in lower socioeconomic, high crime rate, racially homogeneous residential areas. This was accomplished through the selection of two precincts each in Boston and Chicago and four precincts in Washington, D.C. The findings pertain to the behavior of uniformed patrolmen rather than to that of policemen in specialized divisions such as juvenile bureaus or detective units.[5]

The data were recorded by the observers in "incident booklets," forms much like

interview schedules. One booklet was filled out for every incident that the police were requested to handle or that they themselves noticed while on patrol.[6] A total of 5,713 of these incidents were observed and recorded. This paper concerns only those 281 encounters that include one or more juvenile suspects among the participants.

THE CONTEXT

Although large police departments invariably have specialized divisions for handling incidents that involve juveniles, the great majority of juvenile encounters with policemen occur with general duty, uniformed patrolmen, rather than with "youth officers." Youth officers receive most of their cases on a referral basis from members of the uniformed patrol division.[7] Usually these referrals enter the police system as arrests of juveniles by uniformed patrolmen. It will be seen, however, that uniformed patrolmen arrest only a small fraction of the legally liable juvenile suspects with whom they have encounters in the field. Youth bureau officers, then, determine what proportion of those arrested will be referred to juvenile court. The outputs of the patrol division thus become the inputs for the youth bureau, which in turn forwards its outputs as inputs to the court.[8] By the

[5] Very little research on the police has dealt with the routine work of the uniformed patrol division. For a review of investigations on the police see Bordua and Reiss (1967). A recent exception is James Q. Wilson (1968); his study, however, relies primarily upon official statistics.

[6] These booklets were not filled out in the presence of the policemen. In fact, the officers were told that our research was not concerned with police behavior but, rather, that we were concerned *only* with citizen behavior toward the police and the kinds of problems citizens make for the police. In this sense the study involved systematic deception.

[7] In two of the cities investigated, however, aggressive youth patrols ("gang dicks") are employed in the policing of juveniles. Most youth officers spend much of their time behind their desks dealing with referrals and work relatively little "on the street."

[8] Most research on the control of juveniles begins at stages beyond the police field encounter. (Examples are Goldman, 1963; Terry, 1967; McEachern and Bauzer, 1967; Cicourel, 1968; Wheeler, 1968).

time a juvenile is institutionalized, therefore, he has been judged a delinquent at several stages. Correspondingly, sanctions are levied at several stages; institutionalization is the final stage of a sanctioning *process,* rather than *the* sanction for juvenile deviance.

After the commission of a deviant act by a juvenile, the first stage in the elaborate process by which official rates of delinquency are produced is detection. For the police, as for most well-differentiated systems of social control, detection is largely a matter of organizational mobilization, and mobilization is the process by which incidents come to the initial attention of agents of the police organization. There are two basic types of mobilization of the police: *citizen-initiated,* or "reactive" mobilization, and *police-initiated,* or "proactive" mobilization, depending upon who makes the original decision that police action is appropriate. An example of a citizen-initiated mobilization occurs when a citizen phones the police to report an event and the radio dispatcher sends a patrol car to handle the call. A typical police-initiated mobilization takes place when a policeman observes and acts upon what he regards as a law violation, or as in the case of a "stop-and-frisk," a "suspicious" person or situation.

Popular and even sociological conceptions of the police err through an over-reliance on proactive imagery to characterize police operations. Although some specialized divisions of municipal police departments, such as traffic bureaus and vice units, do depend primarily upon proactive mobilization for their input of cases, in routine patrol work the great majority of incidents come to police attention through the citizen-initiated form of mobilization. The crime detection function is lodged mainly in the citizenry rather than in the police. Moreover, most police work with juveniles also arises through the initiative of citizen complainants. In this sense, the citizen population in good

part draws the boundaries of its own official rate of juvenile delinquency.[9]

DETECTION OF JUVENILE DEVIANCE

Observation of police encounters with citizens netted 281 encounters with suspects under 18 years of age, here treated as juveniles.[10] The great majority of the juveniles were from blue-collar families.[11] Of the 281 police-juvenile encounters, 72% were citizen-initiated (by phone) and 28% were initiated by policemen on patrol. Excluding traffic violations, these proportions become 78% and 22%, respectively. The mobilization of police control of juveniles is then overwhelmingly a reactive rather than a proactive process. Hence it would seem that the moral standards of the citizenry have more to do with the definition of juvenile deviance

[9] Even in proactive police work, police initiative may be in response to citizen initiative. Proactive police units often are highly dependent upon citizen intelligence, though the dependence usually is once removed from the field situation (see Skolnick, 1966). For example, citizens occasionally provide the police with intelligence about *patterned* juvenile behavior, such as complaints provided by businessmen about recurrent vandalism on their block or recurrent rowdiness on their corner. These may lead the police to increase surveillance in an attempt to "clean up" the area.

[10] The relatively rare police encounters with suspects of mixed age status—adults and juveniles together—are excluded from this analysis. Further, it should be emphasized that the unit of analysis here is the encounter rather than the individual juvenile. Many encounters include more than one suspect.

[11] It sometimes is difficult for a field observer to categorize a citizen according to social class status. During the observation period two broad categories were used, blue-collar and white-collar, but observers occasionally were unable to make the judgment. The precincts sampled were mainly populated by lower status citizens; so, not surprisingly, the vast majority of the citizen participants were labeled blue-collar by the observers. This majority was even larger for the suspects involved. Consequently, there are not enough white-collar suspect cases for separate analysis. However, the small number of juveniles of ambiguous social class status are combined with the blue-collar cases in this analysis.

than do the standards of policemen on patrol.[12]

Moreover, the incidents the police handle in citizen-initiated encounters differ somewhat from those in encounters they bring into being on their own initiative. (See Table 1.) This does not mean, however, that the standards of citizens and policemen necessarily differ; the differences between incidents in reactive and proactive police work seem to result in large part from differences in detection opportunities, since the police are limited to the surveillance of public places (Stinchcombe, 1963). For example, non-criminal disputes are more likely to occur in private than in public places; they account for 10% of the police-juvenile contacts in citizen-initiated work but for only 3% of the proactive encounters. On the other hand, the "suspicious person" is nearly always a police-initiated encounter. Traffic violations, too, are almost totally in the police-initiated category; it is simply not effective or feasible for a citizen to call the police about a "moving" traffic violation (and nearly all of these cases were "moving" rather than "standing" violations). In short, there are a number of contingencies that affect the detection of juvenile deviance in routine policing.

Table 1   Percent of Police Encounters with Juvenile Suspects According to Type of Mobilization and Race of Suspect, by Type of Incident

Type of Incident	Type of Mobilization and Race of Suspect						
	Citizen-Initiated		Police-Initiated		All Citizen-Initiated	All Police-Initiated	All Encounters
	Negro	White	Negro	White			
Felony	10	—	10	—	5	5	5
Misdemeanor: Except Rowdiness	18	11	5	14	15	9	13
Misdemeanor: Rowdiness	62	77	40	33	69	37	60
Traffic Violation	1	—	26	28	*	27	8
Suspicious Person	—	1	17	22	*	19	6
Non-Criminal Dispute	8	12	2	3	10	3	8
Total Percent	99	101	100	100	99	100	100
Total Number	(109)	(94)	(42)	(36)	(203)	(78)	(281)

*.5% or less.

A broader pattern in the occasions for police-juvenile transactions is the overwhelming predominance of incidents of minor legal significance. Only 5% of the police encounters with juveniles involve alleged felonies; the remainder are less serious from a legal standpoint. Sixty per cent involve nothing more serious than juvenile rowdiness or mischievous behavior, the juvenile counterpart of "disorderly conduct" or "breach of the peace" by adults. This does not mean that the social significance of juvenile deviance is minor for the citizens who call the police or for the police themselves. It should be noted, moreover, that these incidents do not necessarily represent the larger universe of juvenile deviance, since (1) in many cases the juvenile offender is not apprehended by the police, and (2) an unknown number of delinquent acts go undetected. Nonetheless, these incidents represent the inputs from which uni-

[12] Some police-citizen conflict may be generated when citizens view the police as reluctant to respond to their definitions of deviance. Citizens regard this as "police laxity" or "underenforcement." This complaint has lately been aired by some segments of the Negro community.

formed patrolmen produce juvenile arrests and thus are the relevant base for analyzing the conditions under which juveniles are sanctioned in police encounters.

Another pattern lies in the differences between Negro and white encounters with policemen. In the aggregate, police encounters with Negro juveniles pertain to legally more serious incidents, owing primarily to the differential in felony encounters (see Table 1). None of the encounters with white juveniles involved the allegation of a felony, though this was true of 10% of the transactions with Negro juveniles in both citizen- and police-initiated encounters. Apart from this difference between the races, however, the occasions for encounters with Negro and white juveniles have many similarities.

It might be noted that the data on the occasions for police-juvenile encounters do not in themselves provide evidence of racial discrimination in the selection of juveniles for police attention. Of course, the citizen-initiated encounters cannot speak to the issue of discriminatory *police* selection. On the other hand, if the police tend to stop a disproportionate number of Negroes on the street in minor incident situations, we might infer the presence of discrimination. But the findings in Table 1 do not provide such evidence. Likewise, we might infer police discrimination if a higher proportion of the total Negro encounters is police-initiated than that of the total white encounters. Again the evidence is lacking: police-initiated encounters account for 28% of the total for both Negro and white juveniles. More data would be needed to assess adequately the issue of police selectivity by race.

INCIDENTS AND ARREST

Of the encounters patrol officers have with juvenile suspects, only 15% result in arrest.[13] Hence it is apparent that by a large margin most police-juvenile contacts are concluded in the field settings where they arise.[14] These field contacts, 85% of the total, generally are not included in official police statistics on reported cases of juvenile delinquency, and thus they represent the major invisible portion of the delinquency control process. In other words, if these sample data are reasonably representative, the probability is less than one-in-seven that a policeman confronting a juvenile suspect will exercise his discretion to produce an ófficial case of juvenile delinquency. A high level of selectivity enters into the arrest of juveniles. This and subsequent sections of the paper seek to identify some of the conditions which contribute to that selection process.

A differential in police dispositions that appears at the outset of the analysis is that between Negroes and whites. The overall arrest rate for police-Negro encounters is 21%, while the rate for police-white encounters is only 8%. This difference immediately raises the question of whether or not racial discrimination determines the disposition of juvenile suspects. Moreover, Table 2 shows that the arrest rate for Negroes is also higher within specific incident categories where comparisons are possible. The race difference, therefore, is not merely a consequence of the larger number of legally serious incidents that occasion police-Negro contacts.

Apart from the race difference, Table 2 reveals that patrol officers make proportionately more arrests when the incident is relatively serious from a legal standpoint. The arrest rate for Negro en-

[13] The concept of arrest used here refers only to transportation of a suspect to a police station, not to the formal booking or charging of a suspect with a crime. This usage follows Wayne R. LaFave (1965).

[14] The arrest rate for adult suspects is somewhat higher than that for juvenile suspects. For findings on the policing of adults see Donald J. Black (1968:170–262). The present analysis is similar to that followed in Black's study.

Table 2 Percent of Police Encounters with Juvenile Suspects According to Type of Incident and Race of Suspect, by Field Disposition

Field Disposition	Felony		Mis-demeanor: Ex. Rowdiness		Mis-demeanor: Rowdiness		Traffic Violation		Suspicious Person		Non-Criminal Dispute		All Negro	All White	All Encounters
	N	W	N	W	N	W	N	W	N	W	N	W			
Arrest	73	–	36	20	13	8	8	–	–	(1)	–	–	21	8	15
Release-in-Field	27	–	64	80	87	92	92	100	(7)	(8)	100	100	80	92	85
Total Percent	100	–	100	100	100	100	100	100	–	–	100	100	101	100	100
Total Number	(15)	–	(22)	(15)	(85)	(84)	(12)	(10)	(7)	(9)	(10)	(12)	(151)	(130)	(281)

Type of Incident and Race of Suspect

135

counters is twice as high for felonies as it is for the more serious misdemeanors, and for encounters with both races the arrest rate for serious misdemeanors doubles the rate for juvenile rowdiness. On the other hand, policemen rarely make arrests of either race for traffic violations or for suspicious person situations. Arrest appears even less likely when the incident is a noncriminal dispute. The disposition pattern for juvenile suspects clearly follows the hierarchy of offenses found in the criminal law, the law for adults.

It is quite possible that the legal seriousness of incidents is more important in encounters between *patrol* officers and juveniles than in those between *youth* officers and juveniles. As a rule, the patrol officer's major sanction is arrest, arrest being the major formal product of patrol work. By contrast, the youth officer has the power to refer cases to juvenile court, a prosecutorial discretion with respect to juveniles that patrolmen in large departments usually do not have. Whether he is in the field or in his office, the juvenile officer plays a role different from that of the patrolman in the system of juvenile justice. For this reason alone, the factors relating to the disposition of juveniles may differ between the two. The youth officer may, for example, be more concerned with the juvenile's past record,[15] a kind of information that usually is not accessible to the patrolman in the field setting. Furthermore, past records may have little relevance to a patrol officer who is seeking primarily to order a field situation with as little trouble as possible. His organizational responsibility ends there. For his purposes, the age status of a suspect may even be irrelevant in the field.

Conversely, the youth officer may find that the juvenile court or his supervisor expects him to pay more attention to the juvenile's record than to the legal status of a particular incident. In short, the contingencies that affect the sanctioning of juveniles may vary with the organizational sources of the discretion of sanction.

SITUATIONAL ORGANIZATION AND ARREST

Apart from the substance of police encounters—the kinds of incidents they involve—these encounters have a social structure. One element in this structure is the distribution of situational roles played by the participants in the encounter. Major situational roles that arise in police encounters are those of suspect or offender, complainant, victim, informant, and bystander.[16] None of these roles necessarily occurs in every police encounter.

In police encounters with suspects, which account for only about 50% of all police-citizen contacts,[17] particularly important is the matter of whether or not a citizen complainant participates in the situational action. A complainant in search of justice can make direct demands on a policeman with which he must comply. Likewise a complainant is a witness of the police officer's behavior; thus he has the ability to contest the officer's version of an encounter or even to bring an official complaint against the officer himself. In these respects as well as others, the complainant

---

[15] In a study of youth bureau records, it was found that past record was an important factor in the referral of juveniles to the probation department and to the juvenile court (Terry, 1967). Past record was also found to be an important factor in the sanctioning decisions of youth officers in the field (Piliavin and Briar, 1964).

[16] For a discussion of the pivotal roles of lay persons in the control of mentally ill persons, see Erving Goffman's discussion of the complainant's role in the hospitalization of the offender (1961: 133–146).

[17] Less than 50% of the citizen-initiated encounters involve a suspect. Police-initiated encounters, by contrast, typically do result in police-suspect interaction. However, almost nine-in-ten encounters patrol officers have with citizens are initiated by citizens. In the modal police encounter, the major citizen participant is a complainant (Black, 1968:45, 92, and 156).

injects constraints into police-suspect confrontations. This is not to deny that the complainant often may be an asset to a policeman who enters a pre-existing conflict situation in the field. The complainant can provide what may be otherwise unavailable information to a situationally ignorant patrolman. The patrol officer is a major intelligence arm of modern police systems, but he, like other policemen, must live with a continual dependence upon citizens for the information that it is his allotted responsibility to gather. Furthermore, when a suspect is present in the field situation, the information provided by a complainant, along with his willingness to stand on his word by signing a formal complaint, may be critical to an arrest in the absence of a police witness.

The relationship between arrest and the presence of a complainant in police-juvenile encounters is shown in Table 3. It is

versus 8%. This latter difference is all the more striking since felony situations and traffic and noncriminal dispute situations, which may be regarded as confounding factors, are excluded from the tabulation.

It also should be noted that as far as the major citizen participants are concerned, each of these encounters is racially homogeneous. The comparatively rare, mixed race encounters are excluded from these computations. Thus the citizen complainants who oversee the relatively severe dispositions of Negro juveniles are themselves Negro. The great majority of the police officers are white in the police precincts investigated, yet they seem somewhat more lenient when they confront Negro juveniles alone than when a Negro complainant is involved. Likewise, it will be recalled (Table 3) that the arrest difference between Negro and white juveniles all but disappears when no complainant

Table 3   Percent of Police Encounters with Juvenile Suspects According to Situational Organization and Race of Suspect, by Field Disposition. (Table Excludes Felonies, Traffic Violations, and Non-Criminal Disputes.)

Field Disposition	Situational Organization and Race of Suspect				All Suspect Only	All Complainant and Suspect	All Encounters
	Suspect Only		Complainant and Suspect				
	Negro	White	Negro	White			
Arrest	14	10	21	8	11	16	13
Release-in-Field	86	90	79	92	89	84	87
Total Percent	100	100	100	100	100	100	100
Total Number	(66)	(93)	(48)	(26)	(159)	(74)	(233)

apparent that this relation between situational organization and disposition differs according to the suspect's race. Particularly interesting is the finding that when there is no citizen complainant in the encounter the race difference in arrest rates narrows to the point of being negligible—14% versus 10% for encounters with Negro and white juveniles respectively. By contrast, when a complainant participates, this difference widens considerably to 21%

is involved. These patterns complicate the question of racial discrimination in the production of juvenile arrests, given that a hypothesis of discrimination would predict opposite patterns. Indeed, during the observation period a strong majority of the policemen expressed anti-Negro attitutes in the presence of observers (Black and Reiss, 1967:132–139). It might be expected that if the police were expressing their racial prejudices in discriminatory arrest practices, this would be more notice-able in police-initiated action than in action initiated by citizens. But the op-posite is the case. All of the encounters involving a citizen complainant in this sample were citizen-initiated typically by the complainants themselves. Proactive police operations rarely involve complain-ants. To recapitulate: the police are par-ticularly likely to arrest a Negro juvenile when a citizen enjoins them to handle the incident and participates as a complainant in the situational action, but this is not characteristic of police encounters with white juveniles. Finally, it is noteworthy that Negro juveniles find themselves in encounters that involve a complainant proportionately more than do white ju-veniles. Hence, the pattern discussed above has all the more impact on the overall arrest rate for Negro juveniles. Accord-ingly, the next section examines the role of the complainant in more detail.

THE COMPLAINANT'S PREFERENCE AND ARREST

If the presence of a citizen complainant increases the production of Negro arrests, then the question arises as to whether this pattern occurs as a function of the com-plainant's mere presence, his situational behavior, or something else. In part, this issue can be broached by inquiring into the relationship between the complain-ant's behavioral preference for police action in a particular field situation and the kind of disposition the police in fact make.[18]

Before examining this relationship, however, it should be noted that a rather large proportion of complainants do not

[18] Jerome Hall (1952:317–319) suggests several propositions concerning the probability of criminal prosecution. One of Hall's propositions is particu-larly relevant in the present context: "The rate of prosecution varies directly in proportion to the advantage to be gained from it by the complain-ant or, the rate is in inverse proportion to the disadvantages that will be sustained by him."

express clear preferences for police action such that a field observer can make an ac-curate classification. Moreover, there is a race differential in this respect. Consider-ing only the misdemeanor situations, the Negro complainant's preference for action is unclear in 48% of the police encounters with juveniles, whereas the comparable proportion drops to 27% for the encoun-ters with white complainants and juve-niles. Nevertheless, a slightly larger proportion of the Negro complainants ex-press a preference for arrest of their ju-venile adversaries—21%, versus 15% for whites. Finally, the complainant prefers an informal disposition in 31% of the Negro cases and in 58% of the white cases. Thus white complainants more readily express a preference for police leniency toward juvenile suspects than do Negro complain-ants.

Table 4 suggests that white juveniles benefit from this greater leniency, since the police show a quite dramatic pattern of compliance with the expressed prefer-ences of complainants. This pattern seems clear even though the number of cases necessitates caution in interpretation. In not one instance did the police arrest a juvenile when the complainant lobbied for leniency. When a complainant ex-plicitly expresses a preference for an arrest, however, the tendency of the police to comply is also quite strong. Table 4 in-cludes only the two types of misdemeanor, yet the Negro arrest rate when the com-plainant's preference is arrest (60%) climbs toward the rate of arrest for felonies (73%, Table 2). In no other tabulation does the arrest rate for misdemeanors rise so high. Lastly, it is notable that when the complainant's preference is unclear, the arrest rate falls between the rate for com-plainants who prefer arrest and those who prefer an informal disposition.

These patterns have several implica-tions. First, it is evident that the higher arrest rate for Negro juveniles in encoun-ters with complainants and suspects is

Table 4 Percent of Police Encounters with Juvenile Suspects That Involve a Citizen Complainant According to Race of Suspect and Complainant's Preference, by Field Disposition. (Table Excludes Felonies, Traffic Violations, and Non-Criminal Disputes.)

| | Race of Suspect and Complainant's Preference | | | | | | | | |
| | Negro | | | White | | | | | |
Field Disposition	*Prefers Arrest*	*Prefers Informal Disposition*	*Preference Unclear*	*Prefers Arrest*	*Prefers Informal Disposition*	*Preference Unclear*	*All Negro Encounters*	*All White Encounters*	*All Encounters*
Arrest	60	—	17	(1)	—	(1)	21	8	16
Release-in-Field	40	100	83	(3)	100	(6)	79	92	84
Total Percent	100	100	100	—	100	—	100	100	100
Total Number	(10)	(15)	(23)	(4)	(15)	(7)	(48)	(26)	(74)

largely a consequence of the tendency of the police to comply with the preferences of complainants. This tendency is costly for Negro juveniles, since Negro complainants are relatively severe in their expressed preferences when they are compared to white complainants vis-à-vis white juveniles. Furthermore, it will be remembered that it is in encounters with this situational organization rather than in those with suspects alone that the race differential is most apparent. Given the prominent role of the Negro complainant in the race differential, then, it may be inappropriate to consider this pattern an instance of discrimination on the part of policemen. While police behavior follows the same *patterns* for Negro and white juveniles, differential *outcomes* arise from differences in *citizen* behavior (cf. Werthman and Piliavin, 1967).

Another implication of these findings is more general, namely, that the citizen complainant frequently performs an adjudicatory function in police encounters with juveniles. In an important sense the patrol officer abdicates his discretionary power to the complainant. At least this seems true of the encounters that include an expressive or relatively aggressive complainant among the participants. To say that the complainant often can play the role of judge in police encounters is tanta-

mount to saying that the moral standards of citizens often can affect the fate of juvenile suspects. Assuming that the moral standards of citizens vary across social space, i.e., that there are moral subcultures, then it follows that police dispositions of juvenile suspects in part reflect that moral diversity. To this degree policemen become the unwitting custodians of those moral subcultures and thereby perpetuate moral diversity in the larger community. Assuming the persistence of this pattern of police compliance, then it would seem that police behavior is geared, again unwittingly, to moral change. As the moral interests of the citizenry change, so will the pattern of police control. Earlier it was noted that most police encounters with juveniles come into being at the beckoning of citizens. Now it is seen that even the handling of those encounters often directly serves the moral interests of citizens.[19]

[19] Paul Bohannan (1967) notes that a core function of legal institutions is to *re*institutionalize the normative standards of nonlegal institutions. In other words, the legal process represents an *auxiliary* control resource for *other* normative systems. (Also see Bohannan, 1968.)

The patterned compliance of the police with citizens may be understood partly as an instance of the reinstitutionalization function of the legal process. Police control of juveniles, for example, is partly a matter of reinforcement of the broader

SITUATIONAL EVIDENCE AND ARREST

Another variable that might be expected to affect the probability of arrest is the nature of the evidence that links a juvenile suspect to an incident. In patrol work there are two major means by which suspects are initially connected with the commission of crimes: the observation of the act itself by a policeman and the testimony by a citizen against a suspect. The primary evidence can take other forms, such as a bloodstain on a suspect's clothing or some other kind of physical "clue," but this is very unusual in routine patrol work. In fact, the legally minor incidents that typically occasion police-juvenile contacts seldom provide even the possibility of non-testimonal evidence. If there is neither a policeman who witnesses the incident nor a citizen who gives testimony concerning it, then ordinarily there is no evidence whatever in the field setting. Lastly, it should be emphasized that the concept of evidence as used here refers to "situational evidence" rather than to "legal evidence." Thus it refers to the kind of information that appears relevant to an observer in a field setting rather than to what might be acceptable as evidence in a court of law.

In about 50% of the situations a police officer observes the juvenile offense, excluding felonies and traffic violations. Hence, even though citizens initially detect most juvenile deviance, the police often respond in time to witness the behavior in question. In roughly 25% of the situations the policeman arrives too late to see the offense committed but a citizen gives testimonial evidence. The remaining cases, composed primarily of non-criminal disputes and suspicious person situations, bear no evidence of criminal conduct. In a heavy majority of routine police-juvenile encounters, the juvenile suspect finds himself with incriminating evidence of some sort. The low arrest rate should be understood in this context.

On the other hand, it should not be forgotten that these proportions pertain to misdemeanor situations and that the arrests are all arrests without a formal warrant. The law of criminal procedure requires that the officer witness the offense before he may make a misdemeanor arrest without warrant. If the officer does not observe the offense, he must have a signed complaint from a citizen. Such is the procedural law for adults. The law for juveniles, however, is in flux as far as questions of procedure are concerned.[20] It is not at all clear that an appellate court would decide on a juvenile's behalf if he were to appeal his case on the grounds that he was arrested for a misdemeanor

---

[20] This has been all the more the case since the U.S. Supreme Court decision in 1967, *In re Gault,* 387 U.S. 1. The *Gault* decision is a move toward applying the same formal controls over the processing of juvenile suspects as are applied in the adult criminal process. For an observation study of juvenile court encounters see Norman Lefstein, *et al.* (1969). This study includes a discussion of constitutional issues relating to the processing of juveniles.

It might be added that from a social control standpoint, neither police deviance from procedural law, in the handling of juveniles or adults, nor the low rate of detection and sanctioning of this deviance should be surprising. Rarely can a law of any kind be found without deviance, and equally rare is the detection rate or sanctioning rate for any form of legal deviance near the 100% level. Curiously, however, social scientists seem to take for granted low enforcement of substantive law, while they take low control of deviance by the agents of law, such as policemen, to be an empirical peculiarity. Much might be gained from an approach that would seek to understand both forms of legal deviance and control with the same analytical framework. Moreover, substantive control and procedural control can be profitably analyzed in terms of their inter-relations (cf. Llewellyn, 1962:22). Procedural control of the police—for example, limitations on their power to stop-and-frisk—can decrease detection and sanctioning probabilities for certain forms of substantive deviance, such as "possession of narcotics."

---

institution of authority based upon age status. The police support adult authority; in parent-child conflicts the police tend to support parental authority.

even though the arresting officer neither witnessed the act nor acquired a formal complaint from a citizen. Even so, it might be expected that the rate of arrest would be higher in encounters where the act is witnessed by a policeman, if only because these would seem to be the situations where the juvenile suspect is maximally and unambiguously liable. But this expectation is not supported by the observation data (see Table 5).

linquency vastly underestimates even the delinquent acts that policemen witness while on patrol. In this sense the police keep down the official delinquency rate.[21] One other implication of the low arrest rate should be noted. Because the vast majority of police-juvenile contacts are concluded in field settings, judicial control of police conduct through the exclusion of evidence in juvenile courts is potentially emasculated. Police control of

Table 5 Percent of Police Encounters with Juvenile Suspects According to Major Situational Evidence and Race of Suspect, by Field Disposition. (Table Excludes Felonies and Traffic Violations.)

Field Disposition	Major Situational Evidence and Race of Suspect								All Negro Encounters	All White Encounters	All Encounters
	Police Witness		Citizen Testimony		No Evidence		Not Ascertained				
	N	W	N	W	N	W	N	W			
Arrest	16	10	22	14	—	4	(2)	—	15	9	12
Release-in-Field	84	90	78	86	100	96	(7)	(2)	85	91	88
Total Percent	100	100	100	100	100	100	—	—	100	100	100
Total Number	(57)	(69)	(36)	(21)	(22)	(28)	(9)	(2)	(124)	(120)	(244)

In Table 5 it is shown that in "police witness" situations the arrest rate is no higher but is even slightly, though insignificantly, lower than the rate in "citizen testimony" situations. It is possible that some or all of these arrests where the major situational evidence lies with the testimony of a citizen would be viewed as "false" arrests if they involved adult suspects, though this legal judgment cannot be made with certainty. It is conceivable, for example, that some citizen complainants signed formal complaints at the police station subsequent to the field encounters.

The low arrest rate in "police witness" situations is striking in itself. It documents the enormous extent to which patrolmen use their discretion to release juvenile deviants without official sanction and without making an official report of the incident. Official statistics on juvenile de-

juveniles—like that of adults (Reiss and Black, 1967)—may be less prosecution-oriented than the law assumes. In other words, much about the policing of juveniles follows an informal-processing or harassment model rather than a formal-processing model of control.[22] From a

21 Citizens do not necessarily perceive the "delinquency problem" as a function of official delinquency rates and are probably more concerned with what they know about patterns of *victimization* in their communities or neighborhoods. Many citizens may be inclined more to a folk version of the control approach than a labeling approach to delinquency. Their very concern about "the problem" may be partly a dissatisfaction with the existing detection and sanctioning probabilities they divine about juvenile deviance.

22 Michael Banton (1964:6–7) makes a distinction between "law officers," whose contacts with citizens tend to be of a punitive or inquisitory character, and "peace officers," who operate within the moral consensus of the community and are less concerned with law enforcement for its own sake. He suggests

behavioral standpoint, law enforcement generally is not a legal duty of policemen.

On the other hand, the importance of situational evidence should not be analytically underestimated. Table 5 also shows that the police very rarely arrest juveniles when there is no evidence. In only one case was a juvenile arrested when there was no situational evidence in the observer's judgment; this was a suspicious person situation. In sum, then, even when the police have very persuasive situational evidence, they generally release juveniles in the field; but, when they do arrest juveniles, they almost always have evidence of some kind. When there is strong evidence against a suspect, formal enforcement becomes a privilege of the police officer. This privilege provides an opportunity for discriminatory practices (Davis, 1969:169–176).

THE SUSPECT'S DEFERENCE AND ARREST

A final factor that can be considered in its relation to the situational production of juvenile arrests is the suspect's degree of deference toward the police. Earlier research on police work suggests a strong association between situational outcomes and the degree of respect extended to policemen by suspects, namely, the less respectful the suspect, the harsher the sanction (Piliavin and Briar, 1964; Westley, 1953). In this section it is shown that the observation data on police-juvenile contacts draw a somewhat more complex profile of this relationship than might have been anticipated.

Before the findings on this relationship

are examined, however, it should be noted that the potential impact of the suspect's deference on juvenile dispositions in the aggregate is necessarily limited. Only a small minority of juveniles behave at the extremes of a continuum going from very deferential or very respectful at one end to antagonistic or disrespectful at the other. In most encounters with patrolmen the outward behavior of juvenile suspects falls between these two extremes: the typical juvenile is civil toward police officers, neither strikingly respectful nor disrespectful. The juvenile suspect is civil toward the police in 57% of the encounters, a rather high proportion in view of the fact that the degree of deference was not ascertained in 16% of the 281 cases. The juvenile is very deferential in 11% and antagonistic in 16% of the encounters. Thus if disrespectful juveniles are processed with stronger sanctions, the subpopulation affected is fairly small. The majority of juvenile arrests occur when the suspect is civil toward the police. It remains to be seen, however, how great the differences are in the probability of arrest among juveniles who display varying degrees of deference.

The relationship between a juvenile suspect's deference and his liability to arrest is relatively weak and does not appear to be unidirectional. Considering all of the cases, the arrest rate for encounters where the suspect is civil is 16%. When the suspect behaves antagonistically toward the police, the rate is higher—22%. Although this difference is not wide, it is in the expected direction. What was not anticipated, however, is that the arrest rate for encounters involving very deferential suspects is also 22%, the same as that for the antagonistic group. At the two extremes, then, the arrest rate is somewhat higher.

Table 6 shows the arrest rates of suspects, excluding felony situations, according to their race and degree of deference toward police. The bi-polar pattern appears in the encounters with Negro ju-

---

that patrol officers principally are peace officers, whereas detectives and traffic officers, for example, are more involved in law enforcement as such. Banton's distinction has been elaborated by Bittner (1967) and Wilson (1968). Except when patrolmen handle felony situations involving juveniles, the policing of juveniles is mainly a matter of maintaining peace.

Table 6   Percent of Police Encounters with Juvenile Suspects According to the Suspect's Race and Degree of Deference Toward the Police, by Field Disposition. (Table Excludes Felonies.)

Field Disposition	Race and Suspect's Degree of Deference								
	Negro				White				
	Very Deferential	Civil	Antagonistic	Not Ascertained	Very Deferential	Civil	Antagonistic	Not Ascertained	All Encounters
Arrest	20	15	24	—	10	9	13	12	12
Release-in-Field	80	85	76	100	90	91	87	88	88
Total Percent	100	100	100	100	100	100	100	100	100
Total Number	(20)	(72)	(21)	(23)	(10)	(76)	(23)	(21)	(266)

veniles, though in the encounters with white juveniles it does not. In fact, the number of cases where a white juvenile is extreme at one end or the other, particularly where he is very deferential, is so small as to render the differences insignificant. Likewise there is a case problem with the Negro encounters, but there the differences are a little wider, especially between the encounters where the suspect is civil as against those where the suspect is antagonistic. Overall, again, the differences are not dramatic for either race.

Because of the paucity of cases in the "very deferential" and "antagonistic" categories, the various offenses, with one exception, cannot be held constant. It is possible to examine only the juvenile rowdiness cases separately. In those encounters the arrest rates follow the bipolar pattern: 16% for very deferential juveniles, 11% for civil juveniles, and 17% for the encounters where a juvenile suspect is antagonistic or disrespectful. When felony, serious misdemeanor, and rowdiness cases are combined into one statistical base, the pattern is again bipolar: 26%, 18%, and 29% for the very deferential, civil, and antagonistic cases respectively.

Nothing more than speculation can be offered to account for the unexpectedly high arrest rate for juveniles who make an unusually great effort to behave respectfully toward policemen. First, it might be suggested that this finding does not necessarily conflict with that of Piliavin and Briar (1964), owing to an important difference between the coding systems employed. Piliavin and Briar use only two categories, "cooperative" and "uncooperative," so the "very deferential" and "civil" cases presumably fall into the same category. If this coding system were employed in the present investigation, the bipolar distribution would disappear, since the small number of "very deferential" cases would be absorbed by the larger number of "civil" cases and the combined rate would remain below the rate for the "antagonistic" cases. This, then, is one methodological explanation of the discrepancy in findings between the two investigations.

One substantive interpretation of the pattern itself is that juveniles who are and who know themselves to be particularly liable to arrest may be especially deferential toward the police as a tactic of situational self-defense. After all, the notion that one is well-advised to be polite to policemen if one is in trouble is quite widespread in the community. It is a folk belief. These findings might suggest that this tactic is by no means fool-proof. In any event the data do not provide for a test of this interpretation. It would seem that a good deal more research is needed pertaining to the relations between situational etiquette and sanctioning.

OVERVIEW

This paper examines findings on the official detection and sanctioning of juvenile deviance. It begins with a conception of deviance that emphasizes sanctioning *probabilities,* thereby linking the empirical operation of social control systems to the analytical definition of deviant behavior itself. In the present investigation, the central concern is to specify situational conditions that affect the probability of sanction by arrest subsequent to the mobilization of policemen in field settings. It is a control approach to juvenile deviance. Simultaneously it is a study of interaction between representatives of the legal system and juveniles—a study of law-in-action.

Several major patterns appear in the finding from the observation research. It would seem wise to conclude with a statement of these patterns in propositional form. Observation of police work in natural settings, after all, is hardly beyond an exploratory phase.

  I: Most police encounters with juveniles arise in direct response to citizens who take the initiative to mobilize the police to action.

  II: The great bulk of police encounters with juveniles pertain to matters of minor legal significance.

  III: The probability of sanction by arrest is very low for juveniles who have encounters with the police.

  IV: The probability of arrest increases with the legal seriousness of alleged juvenile offenses, as that legal seriousness is defined in the criminal law for adults.

  V: Police sanctioning of juveniles strongly reflects the manifest preferences of citizen complainants in field encounters.

  VI: The arrest rate for Negro juveniles is higher than that for white juveniles, but evidence that the police behaviorally orient themselves to race as such is absent.

  VII: The presence of situational evidence linking a juvenile to a deviant act is an important factor in the probability of arrest.

  VIII: The probability of arrest is higher for juveniles who are unusually respectful toward the police and for those who are unusually disrespectful.

Collectively the eight propositions, along with the corollary implications suggested in the body of the analysis, provide the beginning of an empirical portrait of the policing of juveniles. At some point, however, a descriptive portrait of this kind informs theory. This paper proceeds from a definition of deviance as any class of behavior for which there is a probability of negative sanction subsequent to its detection. From there it inquires into factors that differentially relate to the detection and particularly the official sanctioning of juveniles. Hence it inquires into properties that generate a control response. This strategy assumes that sanctioning probabilities are contingent upon properties of social situations besides rule-violative behavior. Since deviance is defined here in terms of the probability of sanction, it should now be apparent that the referent of the concept of deviance may include whatever else, besides rule-violative behavior, generates sanctioning. The present analysis suggests that sanctioning is usually contingent upon a configuration of situational properties. Perhaps, then, deviance itself should be treated theoretically as a configuration of properties rather than as a unidimensional behavioral event. A critical aspect of the sociology of deviance and control consists in the discovery of these configurations. More broadly, the aim is to discover the social organization of deviance and control.

The topic at hand embraces a good deal more than police encounters with juveniles. There is a need for information about other contexts of social control, studies of other detection and sanctioning processes. There is a need for comparative analysis. What is the role of the complainant upon comparable occasions? Is a complainant before a policeman analogous to an interest group before a legislature? Little is known about the differences and similarities between legal and nonlegal systems of social control. What is the effect of evidence in non-legal contexts? How is a policeman before a suspect like a psychiatrist before a patient or a pimp before a whore? Are there varieties of procedural control over the sanctioning process in non-legal contexts? To what extent are other legal processes responsive to moral diversity in the citizen population? The intricacies of social control generally are slighted in sociology. Correspondingly the state of the general theory of deviance and control is primitive.

REFERENCES

ARNOLD, THURMAN N., 1935. *The Symbols of Government.* New Haven, Connecticut: Yale University Press.

BANTON, MICHAEL, 1964. *The Policeman in the Community.* London: Tavistock Publications Limited.

BITTNER EGON, 1967. "The police on skid-row: A study of peace-keeping." *American Sociological Review, 32* (1967):699–715.

BLACK, DONALD J., 1968. *Police Encounters and Social Organization: An Observation Study.* Unpublished Ph.D. Dissertation, Department of Sociology, University of Michigan.

BLACK, DONALD J. and ALBERT J. REISS, JR., 1967. "Patterns of behavior in police and citizen transactions," pp. 1–139 in President's Commission on Law Enforcement and Administration of Justice, *Studies in Crime and Law Enforcement in Major Metropolitan Areas,* Field Surveys III, Volume 2. Washington, D.C.: U.S. Government Printing Office.

BOHANNON, PAUL, 1967. "The differing realms of the law," pp. 43–56 in P. Bohannon, ed., *Law and Warfare: Studies in the Anthropology of Conflict.* Garden City, New York: The Natural History Press. 1968. "Law and legal institutions," pp. 73–78 in David L. Sills, ed., *International Encyclopedia of the Social Sciences,* Volume 9. New York: The Macmillan Company and the Free Press.

BORDUA, DAVID J. and ALBERT J. REISS, JR., 1967. "Law enforcement," pp. 275–303 in Paul Lazarsfeld, William Sewell, and Harold Wilensky, eds.,

The Uses of Sociology. New York: Basic Books.

CICOUREL, AARON V., 1968. *The Social Organization of Juvenile Justice.* New York: John Wiley and Sons, Inc.

DAVIS, KENNETH CULP, 1969. *Discretionary Justice: A Preliminary Inquiry.* Baton Rouge, Louisiana: Louisiana State University Press.

GOFFMAN, ERVING, 1961. *Asylums: Essays on the Social Situation of Mental Patients and Other Inmates.* Garden City, New York: Anchor Books.

GOLDMAN, NATHAN, 1963. *The Differential Selection of Juvenile Offenders for Court Appearance.* New York: National Council on Crime and Delinquency.

GUSFIELD, JOSEPH R., 1963. *Symbolic Crusade: Status Politics and the American Temperance Movement.* Urbana, Illinois: University of Illinois Press.

HALL, JEROME, 1952. *Theft, Law and Society.* Indianapolis, Indiana: The Bobbs-Merrill Company. (Second Edition.)

HOLMES, OLIVER WENDELL, 1897. "The path of the law." *Harvard Law Review,* 10 (1897):457–78.

LaFAVE, WAYNE R., 1965. *Arrest: The Decision to Take a Suspect into Custody.* Boston, Massachusetts: Little, Brown and Company.

LEFSTEIN, NORMAN, VAUGHAN STAPLETON, and LEE TEITELBAUM, 1969. "In search of juvenile justice: Gault and its implementation," *Law and Society Review, 3* (1969):491–562.

LLEWELLYN, KARL N., 1962. *Jurisprudence: Realism in Theory and Practice.* Chicago, Illinois: University of Chicago Press.

McEACHERN, A. W. and RIVA BAUZER, 1967. "Factors related to disposition in juvenile police contacts," pp. 148–60 in Malcolm W. Klein, ed., *Juvenile Gangs in Context.* Englewood Cliffs, New Jersey: Prentice-Hall, Inc.

PARSONS, TALCOTT (ed.), 1964. *Max Weber: The Theory of Social and Economic Organization.* New York: The Free Press.

PILIAVIN, IRVING and SCOTT BRIAR, 1964. "Police encounters with juveniles," *American Journal of Sociology, 70* (1964):206–14.

REISS, ALBERT J., JR. and DONALD J. BLACK, 1967. "Interrogation and the criminal process," *The Annals of the American Academy of Political and Social Science, 374* (1967):47–57.

RHEINSTEIN, MAX (ed.), 1966. *Max Weber on Law in Economy and Society.* Cambridge, Massachusetts: Harvard University Press.

SKOLNICK, JEROME H., 1966. *Justice without Trial: Law Enforcement in Democratic Society.* New York: John Wiley and Sons, Inc.

STINCHCOMBE, ARTHUR L., 1963: "Institutions of privacy in the determination of police administrative practice," *American Journal of Sociology*, **69** (1963) :150–60.

TERRY, ROBERT M., 1967. "The screening of juvenile offenders," *Journal of Criminal Law, Criminology and Police Science*, **58** (1967):173–81.

WERTHMAN, CARL and IRVING PILIAVIN, 1967. "Gang members and the police," pp. 56–98 in David J. Bordua, ed., *The Police: Six Sociological Essays*. New York: John Wiley and Sons, Inc.

WESTLEY, WILLIAM A., 1955. "Violence and the police," *American Journal of Sociology*, **59** (1953):34–41.

WHEELER, STANTON (ed.), 1968. *Controlling Delinquents*. New York: John Wiley and Sons, Inc.

WILSON, JAMES Q., 1968. *Varieties of Police Behavior: The Management of Law and Order in Eight Communities*. Cambridge, Massachusetts: Harvard University Press.

VIOLENCE AND THE POLICE

William A. Westley

Brutality and the third degree have been identified with the municipal police of the United States since their inauguration in 1844. These aspects of police activity have been subject to exaggeration, repeated exposure, and virulent criticism. Since they are a breach of the law by the law-enforcement agents, they constitute a serious social, but intriguing sociological, problem. Yet there is little information about or understanding of the process through which such activity arises or of the purposes which it serves.[1]

This paper is concerned with the genesis and function of the illegal use of violence by the police and presents an explanation based on an interpretative understanding of the experience of the police as an occupational group.[2] It shows that (a)

the police accept and morally justify their illegal use of violence; (b) such acceptance and justification arise through their occupational experience; and (c) its use is functionally related to the collective occupational, as well as to the legal, ends of the police.

The analysis which follows offers both an occupational perspective on the use of violence by the police and an explanation of policing as an occupation, from the perspective of the illegal use of violence. Thus the meaning of this use of violence is derived by relating it to the general behavior of policemen as policemen, and occupations in general are illuminated through the delineation of the manner in which a particular occupation handles one aspect of its work.

The technical demands of a man's work tend to specify the kinds of social relationships in which he will be involved and to select the groups with whom these relationships are to be maintained. The social definition of the occupation invests its members with a common prestige position. Thus, a man's occupation is a major determining factor of his conduct and social

Reprinted from the *American Journal of Sociology*, **59** (July, 1953), pp. 34–41, by permission of the author and The University of Chicago Press. Copyright 1953 by the University of Chicago.

[1] This paper presents part of a larger study of the police by the writer. For the complete study see William A. Westley, "The Police: A Sociological Study of Law, Custom, and Morality" (unpublished Ph.D. dissertation, University of Chicago, Department of Sociology, 1951).

[2] Interpretative understanding is here used as defined by Max Weber (see *The Theory of Social and Economic Organization*, trans. Talcott Parsons [New York: Oxford University Press, 1947], pp. 88).

identity. This being so, it involves more than man's work, and one must go beyond the technical in the explanation of work behavior. One must discover the occupationally derived definitions of self and conduct which arise in the involvements of technical demands, social relationships between colleagues and with the public, status, and self-conception. To understand these definitions, one must track them back to the occupational problems in which they have their genesis.[3]

The policeman finds his most pressing problems in his relationships to the public. His is a service occupation but of an incongruous kind, since he must discipline those whom he serves. He is regarded as corrupt and inefficient by, and meets with hostility and criticism from, the public. He regards the public as his enemy, feels his occupation to be in conflict with the community, and regards himself to be a pariah. The experience and the feeling give rise to a collective emphasis on secrecy, an attempt to coerce respect from the public, and a belief that almost any means are legitimate in completing an important arrest. These are for the policeman basic occupational values. They arise from his experience, take precedence over his legal responsibilities, are central to an understanding of his conduct, and form the occupational contexts within which violence gains its meaning. This then is the background for our analysis.[4]

The materials which follow are drawn from a case study of a municipal police department in an industrial city of approximately one hundred and fifty thousand inhabitants. This study included partici-

[3] The ideas are not original. I am indebted for many of them to Everett C. Hughes, although he is in no way responsible for their present formulation (see E. C. Hughes, "Work and the Self" in Rohrer and Sherif, *Social Psychology at the Crossroads* [New York: Harper & Bros., 1951]).
[4] The background material will be developed in subsequent papers which will analyze the occupational experience of the police and give a full description of police norms.

pation in all types of police activities, ranging from walking the beat and cruising with policemen in a squad car to the observations of raids, interrogations, and the police school. It included intensive interviews with over half the men in the department who were representative as to rank, time in service, race, religion, and specific type of police job.

DUTY AND VIOLENCE

In the United States the use of violence by the police is both an occupational prerogative and a necessity. Police powers include the use of violence, for to them, within civil society, has been delegated the monopoly of the legitimate means of violence possessed by the state. Police are obliged by their duties to use violence as the only measure adequate to control and apprehension in the presence of counterviolence.

Violence in the form of the club and the gun is for the police a means of persuasion. Violence from the criminal, the drunk, the quarreling family, and the rioter arises in the course of police duty. The fighting drunk who is damaging property or assailing his fellows and who looks upon the policeman as a malicious intruder justifies for the policeman his use of force in restoring order. The armed criminal who has demonstrated a casual regard for the lives of others and a general hatred of the policeman forces the use of violence by the police in the pursuit of duty. Every policeman has some such experiences, and they proliferate in police lore. They constitute a common-sense and legal justification for the use of violence by the police and for training policemen in the skills of violence. Thus, from experience in the pursuit of their legally prescribed duties, the police develop a justification for the use of violence. They come to see it as good, as useful, and as their own. Furthermore, although legally their use of violence is limited to the requirements of the arrest and the protection of themselves and the community, the contingencies of their occupation lead them to enlarge the area in which violence may be used. Two kinds of experience—that with respect to the conviction of the felon and that with respect to the control of sexual conduct—will illustrate how and why the illegal use of violence arises.

1. THE CONVICTION OF THE FELON

The apprehension and conviction of the felon is, for the policeman, the essence of police work. It is the source of prestige both within and outside police circles, it has career implications, and it is a major source of justification for the existence of the police before a critical and often hostile public. Out of these conditions a legitimation for the illegal use of violence is wrought.

The career and prestige implication of the "good pinch" [5] elevate it to a major end in the conduct of the policeman. It is an end which is justified both legally and through public opinion as one which should be of great concern to the police. Therefore it takes precedence over other duties and tends to justify strong means. Both trickery and violence are such means. The "third degree" has been criticized for many years, and extensive administrative controls have been devised in an effort to eliminate it. Police persistence in the face of that attitude suggests that the illegal use of violence is regarded as functional to their work. It also indicates a tendency to regard the third degree as a legitimate means for obtaining the conviction of the felon. However, to understand the strength of this legitimation, one must include other factors: the competition between

patrolman and detectives and the publicity value of convictions for the police department.

The patrolman has less access to cases that might result in the "good pinch" than the detective. Such cases are assigned to the detective, and for their solution he will reap the credit. Even where the patrolman first detects the crime, or actually apprehends the possible offender, the case is likely to be turned over to the detective. Therefore patrolmen are eager to obtain evidence and make the arrest before the arrival of the detectives. Intimidation and actual violence frequently come into play under these conditions. This is illustrated in the following case recounted by a young patrolman when he was questioned as to the situations in which he felt that the use of force was necessary:

One time Joe and I found three guys in a car, and we found that they had a gun down between the seats. We wanted to find out who owned that gun before the dicks arrived so that we could make a good pinch. They told us.

Patrolmen feel that little credit is forthcoming from a clean beat (a crimeless beat), while a number of good arrests really stands out on the record. To a great extent this is actually the case, since a good arrest results in good newspaper publicity, and the policeman who has made many "good pinches" has prestige among his colleagues.

A further justification for the illegal use of violence arises from the fact that almost every police department is under continuous criticism from the community, which tends to assign its own moral responsibilities to the police. The police are therefore faced with the task of justifying themselves to the public, both as individuals and as a group. They feel that the solution of major criminal cases serves this function. This is illustrated in the following statement:

[5] Policemen, in the case studied, use this term to mean an arrest which (*a*) is politically clear and (*b*) likely to bring them esteem. Generally it refers to felonies, but in the case of a "real" vice drive it may include the arrest and *conviction* of an important bookie.

There is a case I remember of four Negroes who held up a filling station. We got a decription of them and picked them up. Then we took them down to the station and really worked them over. I guess that everybody that came into the station that night had a hand in it, and they were in pretty bad shape. Do you think that sounds cruel? Well, you know what we got out of it? We broke a big case in ————. There was a mob of twenty guys, burglars and stick-up men, and eighteen of them are in the pen now. Sometimes you have to get rough with them, see. The way I figure it is, if you can get a clue that a man is a pro and if he won't cooperate, tell you what you want to know, it is justified to rough him up a little, up to a point. You know how it is. You feel that the end justifies the means.

It is easier for the police to justify themselves to the community through the dramatic solution of big crimes than through orderly and responsible completion of their routine duties. Although they may be criticized for failures in routine areas, the criticism for the failure to solve big crimes is more intense and sets off a criticism of their work in noncriminal areas. The pressure to solve important cases therefore becomes strong. The following statement, made in reference to the use of violence in interrogations, demonstrates the point:

If it's a big case and there is a lot of pressure on you and they tell you you can't go home until the case is finished, then naturally you are going to lose patience.

The policeman's response to this pressure is to extend the use of violence to its illegal utilization in interrogations. The apprehension of the felon or the "good pinch" thus constitutes a basis for justifying the illegal use of violence.

2. CONTROL OF SEXUAL CONDUCT

The police are responsible for the enforcement of laws regulating sexual conduct. This includes the suppression of sexual deviation and the protection of the public from advances and attacks of persons of deviant sexual tendencies. Here the police face a difficult task. The victims of such deviants are notoriously unwilling to co-operate, since popular curiosity and gossip about sexual crimes and the sanctions against the open discussion of sexual activities make it embarrassing for the victim to admit or describe a deviant sexual advance or attack and cause him to feel that he gains a kind of guilt by association from such admissions. Thus the police find that frequently the victims will refuse to identify or testify against the deviant.

These difficulties are intensified by the fact that, once the community becomes aware of sexual depredations, the reports of such activity multiply well beyond reasonable expectations. Since the bulk of these reports will be false, they add to the confusion of the police and consequently to the elusiveness of the offender.

The difficulties of the police are further aggravated by extreme public demand for the apprehension of the offender. The hysteria and alarm generated by reports of a peeping Tom, a rapist, or an exhibitionist result in great public pressure on the police; and, should the activities continue, the public becomes violently critical of police efficiency. The police, who feel insecure in their relationship to the public, are extremely sensitive to this criticism and feel that they must act in response to the demands made by the political and moral leaders of the community.

Thus the police find themselves caught in a dilemma. Apprehension is extremely difficult because of the confusion created by public hysteria and the scarcity of witnesses, but the police are compelled to action by extreme public demands. They dissolve this dilemma through the illegal utilization of violence.

A statement of this "misuse" of police powers is represented in the remarks of a patrolman:

Now in my own case when I catch a guy like

that I just pick him up and take him into the woods and beat him until he can't crawl. I have had seventeen cases like that in the last couple of years. I tell that guy that if I catch him doing that again I will take him out to those woods and I will shoot him. I tell him that I carry a second gun on me just in case I find guys like him and that I will plant it in his hand and say that he tried to kill and that no jury will convict me.

This statement is extreme and is not representative of policemen in general. In many instances the policeman is likely to act in a different fashion. This is illustrated in the following statement of a rookie who described what happened when he and his partner investigated a parked car which had aroused their suspicions:

He [the partner] went up there and pretty soon he called me, and there were a couple of fellows in the car with their pants open. I couldn't understand it. I kept looking around for where the woman would be. They were both pretty plastered. One was a young kid about eighteen years old, and the other was an older man. We decided, with the kid so drunk, that bringing him in would only really ruin his reputation, and we told him to go home. Otherwise we would have pinched them. During the time we were talking to them they offered us twenty-eight dollars, and I was going to pinch them when they showed the money, but my partner said, "Never mind, let them go."

Nevertheless, most policemen would apply no sanctions against a colleague who took the more extreme view of the right to use violence and would openly support some milder form of illegal coercion. This is illustrated in the statement of another rookie:

They feel that its okay to rough a man up in the case of sex crimes. One of the older men advised me that if the courts didn't punish a man we should. He told me about a sex crime, the story about it, and then said that the law says the policeman has the right to use the amount of force necessary to make an arrest

and that in that kind of a crime you can use just a little more force. They feel definitely, for example, in extreme cases like rape, that if a man was guilty he ought to be punished even if you could not get any evidence on him. My feeling is that all the men on the force feel that way, at least from what they have told me.

Furthermore, the police believe, and with some justification it seems, that the community supports their definition of the situation and that they are operating in terms of an implicit directive.

The point of this discussion is that the control of sexual conduct is so difficult and the demand for it so incessant that the police come to sanction the illegal use of violence in obtaining that control. This does not imply that all policemen treat all sex deviants brutally, for, as the above quotations indicate, such is not the case. Rather, it indicates that this use of violence is permitted and condoned by the police and that they come to think of it as a resource more extensive than is included in the legal definition.

LEGITIMATION OF VIOLENCE

The preceding discussion has indicated two ways in which the experience of the police encourages them to use violence as a general resource in the achievement of their occupational ends and thus to sanction its illegal use. The experience, thus, makes violence acceptable to the policeman as a generalized means. We now wish to indicate the particular basis on which this general resource is legitimated. In particular we wish to point out the extent to which the policeman tends to transfer violence from a legal resource to a personal resource, one which he uses to further his own ends.

Seventy-three policemen, drawn from all ranks and constituting approximately 50 per cent of the patrolmen, were asked, "When do you think a policeman is justified in roughing a man up?" The intent of

Table 1   Bases for the Use of Force Named by 73 Policemen[a]

Type of response		Frequency	Percentage
(A)	Disrespect for police	27	37
(B)	When impossible to avoid	17	23
(C)	To obtain information	14	19
(D)	To make an arrest	6	8
(E)	For the hardened criminal	5	7
(F)	When you know man is guilty	2	3
(G)	For sex criminals	2	3
Total		73	100

[a]Many respondents described more than one type of situation which they felt called for the use of violence. The "reason" which was either (a) given most heatedly and at greatest length and/or (b) given first was used to characterize the respondent's answer to the question. However, this table is exhaustive of the types of replies which were given.

the question was to get them to legitimate the use of violence. Their replies are summarized in Table 1.

An inspection of the types and distribution of the responses indicates (1) that violence is legitimated by illegal ends (A, C, E, F, G) in 69 per cent of the cases; (2) that violence is legitimated in terms of purely personal or group ends (A) in 37 per cent of the cases (this is important, since it is the largest single reason for the use of violence given); and (3) that legal ends are the bases for legitimation in 31 per cent of the cases (B and D). However, this probably represents a distortion of the true feelings of some of these men, since both the police chief and the community had been severely critical of the use of violence by the men, and the respondents had a tendency to be very cautious with the interviewer, whom some of them never fully trusted. Furthermore, since all the men were conscious of the chief's policy and of public criticism, it seems likely that those who did justify the use of violence for illegal and personal ends no longer recognized the illegality involved. They probably believed that such ends fully represented a moral legitimation for their use of violence.

The most significant finding is that at least 37 per cent of the men believed that it was legitimate to use violence to coerce

respect. This suggests that policemen use the resource of violence to persuade their audience (the public) to respect their occupational status. In terms of the policeman's definition of the situation, the individual who lacks respect for the police, the "wise guy" who talks back, or any individual who acts or talks in a disrespectful way, deserves brutality. This idea is epitomized in admonitions given to the rookies such as, "You gotta make them respect you" and "You gotta act tough." Examples of some of the responses to the preceding question that fall into the "disrespect for the police" category follow:

Well, there are cases. For example, when you stop a fellow for a routine questioning, say a wise guy, and he starts talking back to you and telling you you are no good and that sort of thing. You know you can take a man in on a disorderly conduct charge, but you can practically never make it stick. So what you do in a case like that is to egg the guy on until he makes a remark where you can justifiably slap him and, then, if he fights back, you can call it resisting arrest.

Well, it varies in different cases. Most of the police use punishment if the fellow gives them any trouble. Usually you can judge a man who will give you trouble though. *If there is any slight resistance,* you can go all out on him. You shouldn't do it in the street though. Wait until you are in the squad car, because, even if you are in the right and a guy takes a poke at you, just when you are hitting back somebody's just likely to come around the corner, and what he will say is that you are beating the guy with your club.

Well, a prisoner' deserves to be hit when he goes to the point where he tries to put you below him.

You gotta get rough when a man's language becomes very bad, when he is trying to make a fool of you in front of everybody else. I think most policemen try to treat people in a nice way, but usually you have to talk pretty rough. That's the only way to set a man down, to make him show a little respect.

If a fellow called a policeman a filthy name, a slap in the mouth would be a good thing, especially if it was out in the public where calling a policeman a bad name would look bad for the police.

There was the incident of a fellow I picked up. I was on the beat, and I was taking him down to the station. There were people following us. He kept saying that I wasn't in the army. Well, he kept going on like that, and I finally had to bust him one. I had to do it. The people would have thought I was afraid otherwise.

These results suggest (1) that the police believe that these private or group ends constitute a moral legitimation for violence which is equal *or superior* to the legitimation derived from the law and (2) that the monopoly of violence delegated to the police, by the state, to enforce the ends of the state has been appropriated by the police as a personal resource to be used for personal and group ends.

THE USE OF VIOLENCE

The sanctions for the use of violence arising from occupational experience and the fact that policemen morally justify even its illegal use may suggest that violence is employed with great frequency and little provocation. Such an impression

would be erroneous, for the actual use of violence is limited by other considerations, such as individual inclinations, the threat of detection, and a sensitivity to public reactions.

Individual policemen vary of course in psychological disposition and past experience. All have been drawn from the larger community which tends to condemn the use of violence and therefore have internalized with varying degrees of intensity this other definition of violence. Their experience as policemen creates a new dimension to their self-conceptions and gives them a new perspective on the use of violence. But individual men vary in the degree to which they assimilate this new conception of self. Therefore, the amount of violence which is used and the frequency with which it is employed will vary among policemen according to their individual propensities. However, policemen cannot and do not employ sanctions against their colleagues for using violence,[6] and individual men who personally condemn the use of violence and avoid it whenever possible [7] refuse openly to condemn acts of violence by other men on the force. Thus, the collective sanction for the use of violence permits those men who are inclined to its use to employ it without fear.

All policemen, however, are conscious of the dangers of the illegal use of violence. If detected, they may be subject to a lawsuit and possibly dismissal from the force. Therefore, they limit its use to what they think they can get away with. Thus, they recognize that, if a man is guilty of a serious crime, it is easy to "cover up" for their brutality by accusing him of resisting arrest, and the extent to which they be-

6 The emphasis on secrecy among the police prevents them from using legal sanctions against their colleagues.
7 Many men who held jobs in the police station rather than on beats indicated to the interviewer that their reason for choosing a desk job was to avoid the use of violence.

lieve a man guilty tends to act as a precondition to the use of violence.[8]

The policeman, in common with members of other occupations, is sensitive to
the evaluation of his occupation by the
public. A man's work is an important aspect of his status, and to the extent that he
is identified with his work (by himself
and/or the community) he finds that his
self-esteem requires the justification and
social elevation of his work. Since policemen are low in the occupational prestige
scale, subject to continuous criticism, and
in constant contact with this criticizing
and evaluating public, they are profoundly
involved in justifying their work and its
tactics to the public and to themselves.
The way in which the police emphasize
the solution of big crimes and their violent
solution to the problem of the control of
sexual conduct illustrate this concern.
However, different portions of the public
have differing definitions of conduct and
are of differential importance to the policeman, and the way in which the police define different portions of the public has
an effect on whether or not they will use
violence.

The police believe that certain groups
of persons will respond only to fear and
rough treatment. In the city studied they
defined both Negroes and slum dwellers
in this category. The following statements,
each by a different man, typify the manner
in which they discriminate the public:

In the good districts you appeal to people's
judgment and explain the law to them. In the
South Side the only way is to appear like you
are the boss.

You can't ask them a question and get an
answer that is not a lie. In the South Side the
only way to walk into a tavern is to walk in
swaggering as if you own the place and if

---

[8] In addition, the policeman is aware that the
courts are highly critical of confessions obtained
by violence and that, if violence is detected, it
will "spoil his case."

somebody is standing in your way give him an
elbow and push him aside.

The colored people understand one thing.
The policeman is the law, and he is going to
treat you rough and that's the way you have
to treat them. Personally, I don't think the
colored are trying to help themselves one bit.
If you don't treat them rough, they will sit
right on top of your head.

Discriminations with respect to the public are largely based on the political power
of the group, the degree to which the police believe that the group is potentially
criminal, and the type of treatment which
the police believe will elicit respect from
it.

Variations in the administration and
community setting of the police will introduce variations in their use of violence.
Thus, a thoroughly corrupt police department will use violence in supporting the
ends of this corruption, while a carefully
administered nonpolitical department can
go a long way toward reducing the illegal
use of violence. However, wherever the
basic conditions here described are present, it will be very difficult to eradicate the
illegal use of violence.

Given these conditions, violence will be
used when necessary to the pursuit of duty
or when basic occupational values are
threatened. Thus a threat to the respect
with which the policeman believes his occupation should be regarded or the opportunity to make a "good pinch" will tend
to evoke its use.

CONCLUSIONS

This paper sets forth an explanation of
the illegal use of violence by the police
based on an interpretative understanding
of their occupational experience. Therefore, it contains a description and analysis
of *their* interpretation of *their* experience.

The policeman uses violence illegally

because such usage is seen as just, acceptable, and, at times, expected by his colleague group and because it constitutes an effective means for solving problems in obtaining status and self-esteem which policemen as policemen have in common. Since the ends for which violence is illegally used are conceived to be both just and important, they function to justify, to the policeman, the illegal use of violence as a general means. Since "brutality" is strongly criticized by the larger community, the policeman must devise a defense of his brutality to himself and the community, and the defense in turn gives a deeper and more lasting justification to the "misuse of violence." This process then results in a transfer in property from the state to the colleague group. The means of violence which were originally a property of the state, in loan to its law-enforcement agent, the police, are in psychological sense confiscated by the police, to be conceived of as a personal property to be used at their discretion. This, then, is the explanation of the illegal use of violence by the police which results from viewing it in terms of the police as an occupational group.

The explanation of the illegal use of violence by the police offers an illuminating perspective on the social nature of their occupation. The analysis of their use of brutality in dealing with sexual deviants and felons shows that it is a result of their desire to defend and improve their social status in the absence of effective legal means. This desire in turn is directly related to and makes sense in terms of the low status of the police in the community, which results in a driving need on the part of policemen to assert and improve their status. Their general legitimation of the use of violence *primarily* in terms of coercing respect and making a "good pinch" clearly points out the existence of occupational goals, which are independent of and take precedence over their legal mandate. The existence of such goals and patterns of conduct indicates that the policeman has made of his occupation a preoccupation and invested in it a large aspect of his self.

SECURING POLICE COMPLIANCE
WITH CONSTITUTIONAL LIMITATIONS:
THE EXCLUSIONARY RULE AND OTHER DEVICES

Monrad G. Paulsen · *Charles Whitebread* · *Richard Bonnie*

The Supreme Court of the United States has evolved rules governing police conduct in making searches and arrests (now eavesdropping and wiretapping as well) from the imprecise words of the Fourth Amendment: "The right of the people to be secure in their persons, houses, papers, and effects, against unreasonable searches and seizures, shall not be violated, and no warrants shall issue, but upon probable cause, supported by oath or affirmation, and particularly describing the place to be searched, and the person or things to be seized." The Court's decisions have set constitutional limits on permissible police conduct, and in recent years these limits have become binding on State as well as federal officers. . . .

THE EXCLUSIONARY RULE

Until 1914 the general view of the nation's courts, state and federal, was that all material and relevant evidence should

Excerpts reprinted from *Law and Order Reconsidered: A Staff Report to the National Commission on the Causes and Prevention of Violence,* prepared by James S. Campbell, Joseph R. Sahid, and David P. Stang. Bantam Books, 1970, pp. 390–436, excerpts. (Footnotes have been renumbered.)

This chapter was prepared by Dean Monrad G. Paulsen, Professor Charles Whitebread, and Assistant Professor Richard Bonnie of the University of Virginia School of Law.

The authors gratefully acknowledge the contribution of Robert W. Olson, whose Note on Grievance Response Mechanisms for Police Misconduct in the June 1969 issue of the *Virginia Law Review* contains views similar to those expressed in this chapter. Finally, we note the valuable research efforts of Craig H. Norville, W. Tracey Shaw and Russell R. French, also students at the School of Law.

be admissible in a criminal case without regard to the manner by which it was obtained. The first important change in judicial opinion is recorded in *Weeks* v. *United States.*[1]

By a motion made prior to trial, the defendant in *Weeks* sought the return of property taken from him by police without a semblance of lawfulness. His house had been entered without a warrant and thoroughly searched in his absence. The trial court ordered the return of all the property taken save that "pertinent" to the charge against him (use of the mails for transporting lottery tickets). The Supreme Court reversed in a unanimous opinion, holding that even the material relating to the offense should have been returned. The Court based its decision on two main points:

(1) "The tendency of those who execute the criminal laws of the country to obtain conviction by means of unlawful seizures and enforced confessions . . . *should find no sanction* in the judgments if the courts which are charged at all times with the support of the Constitution and to which people of all conditions have a right to appeal for the maintenance of such fundamental rights"[2];

(2) "If letters and private documents can thus be seized and held and used in evidence against a citizen accused of an offense, the protection of the Fourth Amendment declaring his right to be secure against such searches and seizures *is of no value,* and, so far as those placed are concerned, *might well be stricken* from the Constitution."[3]

[1] 232 U.S. 383 (1914).
[2] *Id.* at 392 (italics supplied).
[3] *Id.* at 393 (italics supplied).

The first point has been echoed by Justices of impressive authority. Justice Holmes has written, "We have to choose, and for my part I think it a less evil, that some criminal should escape than the Government should play an ignoble part."[4] Mr. Justice Brandeis put the point that the use of illegally obtained evidence, "is denied in order to maintain respect for law; in order to promote confidence in the administration of justice; in order to preserve the judicial process from contamination."[5] Judge Roger Traynor of California observed in *People* v. *Cahan*,[6] "The success of the lawless venture depends entirely on the court's lending its aid by allowing the evidence to be introduced."

The facts of *Cahan* underscore the point. The police conduct there involved two separate trespasses into a private home in order to install a microphone. The action was undertaken after permission had been received from the Los Angeles chief of police. The entire purpose of the illegal conduct was to obtain evidence for use in court. The incident was planned and approval was obtained at the highest level of police authority. It was not the case of a rookie policeman who misjudged the complicated law of search and seizure.

The spectacle of government breaking the law and employing the fruits of illegal conduct seems likely to breed disrespect for both the law and the courts. It does not seem daring to suggest that in such disrespect may lie the seeds of violent conduct.

The second point, that without the exclusionary evidence rule the constitutional guarantees of the Fourth amendment are of "no value," has also proved persuasive in the decisive cases. In *Mapp* v. *Ohio*,[7] which extended the exclusionary evidence rule to the States, Mr. Justice Clark wrote; . . . "[without the rule] the freedom from state invasions of privacy would be so ephemeral . . . as not to merit this Court's high regard as a freedom implicit in the concept of ordered liberty." Mr. Justice Traynor, again in *People* v. *Cahan*,[8] affirmed, "Experience has demonstrated . . . that neither administrative nor civil remedies are effective in suppressing lawless searches and seizures." At another point in that opinion, which embraced the exclusionary rule for the state of California six years before *Mapp*, Justice Traynor explained the action of the California Court: "other remedies have completely failed to secure compliance with the constitutional provisions on the part of police officers."[9]

Whether the exclusionary rule actually does effectively deter the police is a question without a firm answer. No solid research puts the question to rest. The assumption is that the police wish to convict those who commit crimes and that, if we bar the use of evidence illegally obtained, the police will conform to the rules in order to achieve that aim.

We know that the expanded application of the exclusionary rule has been accompanied by many efforts at police education. Courses in police academies, adult education programs for police sponsored by local headquarters, and courses in colleges and universities offered to police on the issues presented by the Fourth Amendment have sprung up nearly everywhere. More and more police leaders affirm the necessity for staying within the rules. More and more police departments have become interested in the formulation of guidelines for the officer on the beat who must make snap judgments. It is difficult not to credit the exclusionary rule for some of these developments.

One criticism of primary reliance on the exclusionary rule to deter police misconduct is that, despite its rationale of

---

[4] *Olmstead* v. *United States*, 277 U.S. 438, 470 (1928). (Dissenting opinion.)
[5] *Id.* at 484. (Dissenting opinion.)
[6] 44 Cal. 2d 434, 445, 282 P. 2d 905, 912 (1955).
[7] 367 U.S. 643 (1961).

[8] *Supra* note 6, at 913.
[9] *Id.* at 911.

deterrence through deprivation of incriminating evidence, it does not deter when police act in situations where prosecution is not contemplated. If officers merely seek to harass a citizen, the exclusionary rule does not influence the officers to cease.[10]

We do see this point not as an argument against the rule, however, but rather as a reason for the creation of other remedies. The need is for supplementation, not abandonment.

Another question is: will reliance on the exclusionary rule breed police violence? If the police are "handcuffed" and are therefore unable to obtain convictions, will they impose extrajudicial punishment? Will they subject dangerous "criminals" (so identified by the police) to beatings and harassments? If so, the need is again for additional remedies—not necessarily abandonment of the rule. It is important to remember, as well, that if the police are "handcuffed" it is because of the *rules of search and seizure* and not because of the rule of exclusion. The rule of exclusion tells nothing of the rules governing the police: the exclusionary rule can operate with strict limitations on police activity as well as with limitations which permit the police a wide latitude in the choice of behavior. . . .

We believe that the exclusionary rule will and ought to endure as a primary device for securing police compliance with the law. Judge Friendly's suggestion in *Soyka,* the limitations on the "fruit of the poisonous tree" doctrine and the "harmless error" rule—each aims to escape the potentially severe implications of the rule in cases where police misconduct was not grave and where the defendant seems clearly guilty of a serious offense. The political forum echoes with the outcry

that public safety is being submerged to a "literal" interpretation of constitutional limitations and that the exclusionary rule is but a sanctuary for the guilty. It is not surprising, therefore, that some judges are groping for ways to tailor the remedy to the outrageousness of the police misconduct and the gravity of the defendant's offense. We are in sympathy with this solicitude for effective law enforcement. We believe, however, the exclusionary evidence rule to be an exceedingly functional instrument for securing police compliance with the law. We should therefore be very cautious in fashioning limitations on the scope of the rule so as not to undercut its deterrent effect.

A final point about the exclusionary rule and its relation to violence: we may guess that urge to destructive behavior is greatest when the actor is moved by a sense of frustration grounded in a feeling of injustice which he is unable to combat. The exclusionary rule, however, provides an outlet within the law for frustration stemming from the belief that the defendant has been treated unjustly by the police. By a motion to suppress the defendant can in effect strike back at authority in the very proceeding which is aimed at convicting him. We now turn to other means, besides the exclusionary rule, of enforcing the substantive rules governing permissible police conduct.

DAMAGE REMEDIES UNDER STATE LAW

In general, a policeman is personally liable under state law for torts arising from his law enforcement activities.[11] Consideration of tort liability must proceed simultaneously on two fronts: effectiveness as a deterrent and utility as a mode of redress. In order to eliminate violent response to alleged police misconduct, our society must

---

[10] Barrett, "Personal Rights, Property Rights and the Fourth Amendment," 1960 *Sup. Ct. Rev.* 46, 54–55. An example of police misconduct not reached by the exclusionary rule is the Plainfield search described in Bean, "Plainfield: A Study in Law and Violence," 6 *Am. Crim. L.Q.* 154 (1968).

[11] Dakin, "Municipal Immunity in Police Torts," 16 *Clev. Mar. L. Rev.* 448 (1967).

achieve both of these objectives. The average citizen must be confident that police misconduct is the deviant rather than the normal behavior and that he can recover for injury suffered due to police improprieties.

Substantive tort law theoretically permits recovery for some egregious acts of police misconduct. Liability for false arrest or false imprisonment may arise from a warrantless arrest lacking "probable cause." An illegal invasion of a person's home or seizure of his property constitutes a trespass to land or chattels. Because of damage limitations, however, plaintiff's victory in a suit for trespass will be only nominal unless the errant policeman has been carelessly destructive or overtly ill-willed. Where the police officer has employed an unreasonable amount of force under certain circumstances, he is liable for assault and battery. Despite the availability of these causes of action, however, the chances of adequate recovery are so slim that there is usually no inducement to sue. . . .

In any event, a majority of states have refused to waive governmental immunity in police tort cases [12] despite repeated urgings by a multitude of legal scholars.[13] And it is unlikely that they will do so at least until the scope of liability is sufficiently limited.

Thus, the most fruitful approach is to abandon delusions of broad deterrence and substantial redress and to concentrate on the grosser forms of abuse where the tort remedy can be useful. Actual injury caused by serious breaches of duty committed in utter disregard of proper standards of police conduct should be redressed by the courts in tort suits. The imperatives of such an approach are utilization of a good faith defense and more extensive governmental assumption of liability.

DAMAGE REMEDIES UNDER FEDERAL LAW

In addition to his state common law tort remedies, a citizen aggrieved by police misconduct may have a cause of action under 42 U.S.C. § 1983 which provides:

Every person who, under color of any statute, ordinance, regulation, custom, or usage, of any State or Territory, subjects, or causes to be subjected, any citizen of the United States, or other person within the jurisdiction thereof to the deprivation of any rights, privileges, or immunities secured by the Constitution and laws, shall be liable to the party injured in an action at law, suit in equity, or other proper proceeding for redress.

---

12 A growing disenchantment for the doctrine has recently led some states and cities to abolish it by statute. E.g., Cal. Gov't Code §§ 815.2, 825, 825.2 (1966); Minn. Stat. Ann. § 466.02 (1963); N.Y. Ct. Cl. Act. § 8 (1963); Wash. Rev. Code of Wash. Ann. § 4.920.090 (1962). Others have abolished the doctrine by judicial fiat. *Hargrove* v. *Cocoa Beach*, 96 So. 2d 130 (Fla. 1957); *Steele* v. *Anchorage*, 385 P. 2d 582 (Alas. 1963); *Stone* v. *Arizona Highways Comm.*, 93 Ariz. 384, 381 P. 2d 107 (1963); *Molitor* v. *Kaneland Community Unit Dist. No. 302*, 18 Ill. 2d 11, 163 N.E. 2d 89 (1959); *Williams* v. *Detroit*, 364 Mich. 231, 111 N.W. 2d 1 (1961); *McAndrew* v. *Mularchuk*, 33 N.J. 172, 162 A. 2d 820 (1960); *Kelso* v. *Tacoma*, 63 Wash. 2d 912, 390 P. 2d 2 (1964); *Holtyz* v. *Milwaukee*, 17 Wis. 2d 26, 115 N.W. 2d 618 (1962). A District of Columbia judge has recently ruled that the government may be sued when its policemen are accused of brutality. *Washington Post*, Jan. 7, 1969, at D1.

Five states have modified sovereign immunity where the municipality has insurance. Idaho Code Ann. § 41-3505 (1961); Mo. Ann. Stat. § 71.185

(Supp. 1969); N.H. Rev. Stat. Ann. § 412.3 (1968); N.D. Cent. Code § 40-43-07 (1968); Ut. Stat. tit. 29, § 1403 (Supp. 1968). Illinois and Connecticut indemnity governmental employees for judgments incurred for torts committed in the course of carrying out their duties. Comm. Gen. Stat. § 7-465 (Supp. 1969); Ill. Rev. Stat., Ch. 24, § 1-4-5 (1962), § 1-4-6 (Supp. 1969).

13 Fuller and Casner, "Municipal Tort Liability in Operation," **54** *Harv. L. Rev.* 437 (1941); Jaffe, "Suits Against Governments and Officers Damage Action," **77** *Harv. L. Rev.* 209 (1963); Lawyer, "Birth and Death of Government Immunity," **15** *Clev. Mar. L. Rev.* 529 (1966); Tooke, "The Extension of Municipal Liability in Tort," **19** *U. Va. L. Rev.* 97 (1932).

The statute in its present form is substantially unchanged from its passage in 1871 as the civil section of what is popularly known as the Ku Klux Act.[14] It is clear that this statute originally was designed to inhibit and give a remedy for the widespread abridgement of Negro rights that characterized the Reconstruction period in the South. Recently, however, the Supreme Court has read the broad statutory language to authorize civil tort suits in federal courts against state law enforcement officers,[15] and a steady stream of such cases now flows through the lower federal courts.[16]

In the landmark case, *Monroe* v. *Pape*,[17] James Monroe alleged that 13 Chicago policemen broke into his home at 5:45 a.m., routed his whole family from bed, ransacked every room in his house, detained him at the police station for 10 hours on "open charges," and finally released him without filing criminal charges against him. The Supreme Court, holding this complaint actionable under Section 1983, adopted the *Screws* and *Classic* definition of "under color of law," and noted that even action wholly contrary to state law is nevertheless action "under color of law" if the policemen are clothed with the indices of authority. Moreover, the *Monroe* majority held that since Section 1983 does not include the word "willfully," a complainant need neither allege nor prove a "specific intent to deprive a person of a federal right."[18] Finally, the Court reasoned that since one of the purposes of Section 1983 was to afford a federal right in federal courts, the federal remedy is supplementary to any existing state remedy and the state remedy need not be exhausted before its invocation.

The major issue that remained after the sweeping *Monroe* decision was whether some degree of bad faith or other fault in the deprivation of the citizen's constitutional rights is an element of the federal cause of action under Section 1983. The court confronted this issue in its 1967 decision in *Pierson* v. *Ray*.[19] In that case petitioners, a group of Negro and white clergymen were arrested for sitting-in at a segregated interstate bus terminal in Mississippi. Subsequent to their arrest and conviction, the statutory provision upon which their arrest had been based was declared unconstitutional and their cases were remanded and later dropped. In their subsequent suit for false arrest and violation of Section 1983, the Supreme Court proclaimed that the defenses of "good faith and probable cause" were available to the policemen-defendants under Section 1983 just as they were under Mississippi law of false arrest. Although the *Pierson* decision established that policemen are not strictly liable for unconstitutional activity, the scope of the defenses which it recognized is not yet clear. On the other hand, the federal defenses could be tied to state law, thereby

---

[14] 17 Stat. 13 § 1 (1871).

[15] *Pierson* v. *Ray*, 386 U.S. 547 (1967); *Monroe* v. *Pape*, 365 U.S. 167 (1961).

[16] The past 8 years have witnessed a marked increase in cases under 42 U.S.C. § 1983. The annual numbers of private civil actions filed in district courts under the Civil Rights Act are in the Annual Report[s] of the Administrative Office of the United States (Table C2)

Year	Number of Cases
1958	220
1959	247
1960	280
1961	270
1962	357
1963	424
1964	645
1965	994
1966	1,154

Not all of these cases alleged police misconduct; many were directed at other state and local officials by citizens claiming to have been unreasonably deprived of economic rights—licenses, contracts and the like.

[17] 365 U.S. 167 (1961).

[18] *Id.* at 187. Further, the Court states: "Section 1979 [now 1983] should be read against the background of tort liability that makes a man responsible for the natural consequences of his actions. *Id.*

[19] 386 U.S. 547 (1967).

attaching only in those states which allow a good faith defense in the subsequent invalidation context, as did Mississippi in *Pierson*. On the other hand, it would appear that the Court contemplated something broader—a federal standard of fault not tied to state law or to any particular factual context, and most observers have so assumed.

Because of the difficulty of segregating "probable cause" from the lawfulness of the conduct itself, and because "good faith" suggests a completely subjective standard, we suggest that these labels are inappropriate tools for defining the proper defense in the present context. The purpose of a defense in a police tort suit, under state law or under Section 1983, should be to immunize conduct illegal only because of an honest mistake in judgment *or* an unforeseeable change in the law. The proper standard, and one which both state and post-*Pierson* lower federal courts in fact have been applying,[20] is

whether the policeman's act was "reasonable" in light of circumstances, both legal and situational, about which he knew or should have known.

An additional question remaining after *Pierson* is the scope of police activity covered by the "rights, privileges, or immunities" clause of Section 1983. It clearly covers illegal searches or seizures and unconstitutional arrests. And there is some evidence that it also covers gross acts of police brutality, conduct which denies due process because it shocks the conscience.[21] In any event, however, Section 1983 cannot be employed to regulate the day-to-day conduct of the policeman on patrol—the seemingly trivial acts of harassment and misunderstanding which in gross, may elicit violence against the police by ghetto residents.[22]

---

20 E.g., *Whirl* v. *Kern,* 407 F.2d 781 (5th Cir. 1969); *Hughes* v. *Smith,* 264 F. Supp. 767 (D.N.J. 1967). In *Whirl,* the Court held that subjective good faith could not exculpate a sheriff from § 1983 liability to a person who had been detained improperly in jail for almost nine months because of a failure to process the papers dismissing the indictment against him. The "good faith and probable cause" talisman just doesn't fit in such circumstances. In finding the requisite fault in *Whirl,* the Court simply held that this police omission was unreasonable despite the absence of bad faith.

Moreover, prior to *Pierson,* many courts applied such a standard: "One essential requirement of an action under this section is that the plaintiff show facts which indicate that the defendant, at the time he acted, knew or as a reasonable man should have known that his acts were ones which would deprive the plaintiff of his constitutional rights or might lead to that result." *Bowens* v. *Knazze,* 237 F. Supp. 826 (N.D. Ill. 1965). See *Cohen* v. *Norris,* 300 F. 2d 24 (9th Cir. 1962) (unforeseeability due to defects in a warrant may be a good defense); *Bargainer* v. *Michal,* 233 F. Supp. 270 (N.D. Ohio, 1964) (police must be protected from "honest misunderstandings of statutory authority and mere errors of judgment."); *Beauregard* v. *Winegard,* 363 F. 2d 901 (9th Cir. 1966) (where probable cause for an arrest exists,

civil rights are not violated even though innocence may subsequently be established—even actual malice in undertaking an investigation will not permit recovery if that investigation produced probable cause).

21 *Bargainer* v. *Michal,* 233 F. Supp. 270 (N.D. Ohio 1964), where the court in diction conceded the difficulty of applying § 1983 to an assault by a policeman unaccompanied by an arrest. See also, *Selico* v. *Jackson,* 201 F. Supp. 475, 478 (S.D. Cal. 1962); "[Where] . . . facts are alleged which indicate not only an illegal and unreasonable arrest and an illegal detention, but also an unprovoked physical violence exerted upon the persons of the plaintiffs . . . It certainly cannot seriously be urged that defendant acted as a result of error or honest misunderstanding." See *Basista* v. *Weir,* 340 F. 2d 74 (3d Cir. 1965); *Hardwick* v. *Hurley* 289 F. 2d 529 (7th Cir. 1961); *Hughes* v. *Smith,* 264 F. Supp. 767 (D.N.J. 1967); *Dodd* v. *Spokane County,* 393 F. 2d 330 (9th Cir. 1968) (assault by prison official actionable); *Jackson* v. *Martin,* 261 F. Supp. 902 (N.D. Miss. 1966) (allegation provocation shot plaintiff states a good cause of action under § 1983).

22 *Lankford* v. *Gelston,* 364 F. 2d 197 (4th Cir. 1966). Here where police officers had on 300 occasions over 19 days, searched third persons' homes, without search warrants and on uninvestigated and anonymous tips, for suspects, the court, in granting petitioners injunctive relief from this practice, said: "There can be little doubt that actions for money damages would not suffice to repair the injury suffered by the victims of police

Nevertheless, Section 1983—like the state tort remedy—is a potentially useful device for compensating the individual citizen substantially injured by unlawful police action. To be sure, an action under Section 1983 is subject to all the intrinsic weakness of any tort remedy—limited personal assets of the police, no provision for payment of damages from municipal or state funds, the expense of maintaining the suit, the difficulty of establishing damages, the disadvantaged position of the usual plaintiff in the community, and the threat such assessments against individual policemen pose to vigorous and efficient law enforcement efforts.[23] Despite these inherent limitations, however, Section 1983's federal remedy for deprivation of constitutional rights does permit compensation of citizens whose person or property is significantly damaged due to clearly unlawful police activity.

Many commentators on Section 1983's use to control police conduct claim its application must be limited to the egregious case so that it does not hamper legitimate law enforcement by penalizing the policeman for mere error in judgment and honest misunderstanding.[24] We agree with this

goal for the federal remedy as well as the state remedies, but argue that the present "probable cause and good faith" defense available to the police under *Pierson* v. *Ray* as applied in subsequent cases and as we have refined it, together with the law of damages under this section, in fact limit the scope of the remedy. Our conclusion, then, must be that, while the federal civil damages remedy cannot be a regulator of everyday police conduct, it can provide a remedy to individuals severely injured by outrageous instances of police illegality.[25] As an important and essential supplement to other devices for controlling police violence, it should be implemented at the federal level by rationalized damage rules and docket priority and at the state level by municipal assumption of liability and cost of suit.

INJUNCTION

The injunction offers the prospect of immediate relief from unconstitutional conduct and a powerful deterrent from engaging in that specific conduct. Simply as a matter of judicial equitable prerogative, such relief is easily justified. The remedies at law for this threatened or continuing deprivation of liberty are at present clearly inadequate except in a

---

searches . . . [T]he wrongs inflicted are not readily measurable in terms of dollars and cents. Indeed the Supreme Court itself has already declared that the prospect of pecuniary redress for the harm suffered is 'worthless and futile.' Moreover, the lesson of experience is that the remote possibility of money damages serves as no deterrent to future police invasions." *Id.* at 202.

23 *Report of the National Advisory Commission on Civil Disorders* (Washington, D.C.: Government Printing Office, 1968), at 159. (Hereinafter cited as *Kerner Report*.):

"Harassment or discourtesy may not be the result of malicious or discriminatory intent of police officers. Many officers simply fail to understand the effects of their actions because of their limited knowledge of the Negro community. . . .

"In assessing the impact of police misconduct, we emphasize that the improper acts of relatively few officers may create severe tensions between the department and the entire Negro community."

24 See Shapo, "Constitutional Tort: *Monroe* v. *Pape* and the Frontiers Beyond," 60 *N.W.U.L.* Rev. 277, 327–29 (1965).

25 A sampling of the cases in which recoveries were made for police violence reveals truly outrageous conduct.

See *McArthur* v. *Pennington*, 253 F. Supp. 420 (E.D. Tenn. 1963) ($5100 total damages proper for wrongful arrest by a city policeman—$1800 out of pocket damage to plaintiff, $1600 lost wages and the rest for humiliation, mental suffering and injury to reputation); *Brooks* v. *Moss*, 242 F. Supp. 531 (W.D.S.C. 1965) ($3,500 actual damages and $500 punitive damages proper where plaintiff received a serious blow to the head and such an attack and the subsequent false criminal prosecution were clearly in violation of his constitutional rights); *Jackson* v. *Duke*, 259 F. 2d 3 (5th Cir. 1958) (Award of $5000 to person who was pistol whipped, knocked down and stomped, kicked in the face, throat and stomach, falsely arrested, falsely accused of drunkenness and unlawfully jailed was not excessive).

limited context, a conclusion emphatically asserted by the Supreme Court in *Mapp* v. *Ohio* [26] and reaffirmed in our discussion above. The injury may surely be irreparable, both to the plaintiff and the community.[27]

But injunctions issued against individual police officers to refrain from future violations, in addition to raising much the same substantive and practical problems noted above in connection with damages, also present an insuperable enforcement problem. The order must cover all types of illegal conduct or it cannot operate fairly; yet if an injunction issued upon proof of any illegality whatever, it would replace internal police disciplinary procedures with inflexible judicial oversight of the conduct of all police officers. Since the court's only sanction is contempt, it would be extremely heavy-handed and even more disruptive of legitimate law enforcement efforts than effective and broad damage remedies. Such a remedy represents the worst of all possible worlds.

Thus, instead of utilizing the remedial force of the injunction in a way destructive of law enforcement, a court must look to those who make the rules which the individual police officers are supposed to obey. The goal of injunctive relief should be to induce the Departments to establish guidelines consistent with constitutional mandates and to use their internal disciplinary procedures to enforce these rules. Whether this goal can be achieved by equitable relief issued by either state or federal courts is the subject of this section.

The various state courts which have faced the question have left no clear statement of the law. In fact, there seem to be two separate lines of authority. Some courts have emphasized the institutional irresponsibility of injunctive interference

with law enforcement activity.[28] Under this view, the plaintiff should be left to whatever civil remedies at law he has available or to his defenses in a criminal prosecution should one be brought. Other courts, perhaps a majority, have felt no institutional hesitations, but have placed heavy burdens on the plaintiff to show clearly lack of a reasonable basis for the allegedly illegal police actions and the presence of malice or bad faith.[29] Thus, even these courts have interfered only where the police are pursuing a clearly illegal course of conduct against an identifiable plaintiff or group of plaintiffs. . . .[30]

In summary, although state cases are ambiguous and federal cases are sparse, it would appear that the injunction at either level is another useful fringe remedy. Where immediate relief from a clearly unconstitutional course of conduct against identifiable persons is prayed for, the injunction should issue. Otherwise the courts should not interfere directly with the enforcement of the criminal law.

CRIMINAL SANCTIONS

Although both state and federal statute books include criminal sanctions for illegal police conduct such as false arrest

---

[26] 367 U.S. 643 (1961); See also *Wolf* v. *Colorado*, 338 U.S. 25, 41–44 (1949) (Murphy, J., dissenting).
[27] *Lankford* v. *Gelston*, 364 F. 2d 197 (4th Cir. 1966), at 202; see *Pierce* v. *Society of Sisters*, 268 U.S. 510, 536 (1925).

[28] E.g., *City of Jacksonville* v. *Wilson*, 157 Fla. 838, 27 So. 2d 108, 112, (1946); *Delaney* v. *Flood*, 183 N.Y. 323, 76 N.E. 209 (1906). See also, Annot., 83 A.L.R. 2d 1007, 1016–17 (1962).
[29] No injunction will issue if the plaintiff fails to move that the police acted without reasonable grounds or probable cause. See *Seaboard N.Y. Corp.* v. *Wallander*, 192 Misc. 227, 80 N.Y.S. 2d 715 (Sup. Ct. 1948); *Monfrino* v. *Gutelius*, 66 Ohio App. 293, 33 N.E. 2d 1003 (1939); *Kalwin Business Men's Ass'n.* v. *McLaughlin*, 216 App. Div. 6, 214 N.Y. Supp. 507 (1926); *Joyner* v. *Hammond*, 199 Iowa 919, 200 N.W. 571 (1924). The police will also be enjoined if they acted maliciously or in bad faith. See *Hague* v. *CIO*, 307 U.S. 496 *aff'g with modifications* 191 F. 2d 774 (3d Cir. 1939); Comment, "Federal Injunctive Relief From Illegal Search," 1967 *Wash. U.L.Q.* 104, 109–110.
[30] See, e.g., *Upton Enterprises* v. *Strand*, 195 Cal. App. 2d 45, 15 Cal. Rptr. 486 (1961).

and trespass, they are rarely employed.[31] It is well established that in criminal prosecutions for false arrest the defendant must have criminal intent and that his good faith is a complete defense.[32] At common law no trespass to property is criminal unless it is accompanied by a breach of the peace.[33] Moreover, most states require criminal intent as an element [34] of the crime, either by statute or by judicial interpolation where the statute itself is silent.[35] Where intent is an element, the defenses of good faith [36] or color of title will lie unless there has been a breach of the peace.[37]

The dearth of case law on the subject indicates the impotency of criminal prosecution of police officers as a remedy for their misconduct. Professor Foote, a leading authority on judicial remedies against the police, could find only four cases—all for false imprisonment—for the period 1940-55.[38] We have been unable to unearth any additional reported cases for the subsequent 13 years. No authoritative explanation has been given for the absence of prosecution for police offenses, but the reasons are not difficult to surmise. Prosecutors are probably reluctant to enforce these dormant criminal sanctions against police offenses because they anticipate, in our view correctly, a detrimental effect on law enforcement which is the goal of both departments, and because they consider the punishment too harsh.

As a supplement to state criminal remedies for police misconduct, 18 U.S.C. § 242 imposes a federal penalty on anyone who, under color of law, willfully deprives a person of his constitutional rights.[39] Because Section 242 is a criminal statute it has been narrowly construed. The Supreme Sourt in *Screws* v. *U. S.*,[40] upholding this statute against an attack that it was void for vagueness, interpreted the statutory requirement of willful violation to mean that the defendant must have had or been motivated by a specific intent to deprive a person of his constitutional rights.[41]

This narrow construction of the statute together with the reticence of prosecutors

---

[31] As of 1960, less than half of the States had any criminal provisions relating directly to unreasonable searches and seizures. The punitive sanctions of the 23 states attempting to control such invasions of the right of privacy are collected in *Mapp* v. *Ohio,* 367 U.S. 643, 652 note 7 (1960).

[32] *Commonwealth* v. *Cheney,* 141 Mass. 102, 6 N.E. 724 (1886) (if an officer makes an arrest and it turns out that no crime has been committed, his good faith in the performance of his official duty is a defense to a criminal prosecution, although it would not be a civil action). See also *Commonwealth* v. *Trunk,* 311 Pa. 555, 167 A. 333 (1933); *Henderson* v. *State,* 95 Ga. App. 830, 99 S.E. 2d 270 (1957).

[33] 52 *Am. Jur.* Trespass Sec. 84 (1944).

[34] *Brown* v. *Martinez,* 68 N.M. 271, 361 P. 2d 152 (1961); *Owens* v. *Town of Atkins,* 163 Ark. 82, 259 S.W. 396 (1924).

[35] *People* v. *Winig,* 7 Misc. 2d 803, 163 N.Y.S. 2d 995 (1957); *People* v. *Barton,* 18 AD 2d 612, 234 N.Y.S. 2d 263 (1962); *Barber* v. *State,* 199 Ind. 146, 155 N.E. 819 (1927).

[36] *State* v. *Faggart,* 170 N.C. 737, 87 S.E. 31 (1915).

[37] *State* v. *Turner,* 60 Conn. 222, 22 A. 542 (1891). *Whittlesey* v. *U.S.* 221 A. 2d (1966).

[38] Foote, "Tort Remedies for Police Violations of Individual Rights," 39 *Minn. L. Rev.* (1955) at 494.

[39] Whoever, under color of any law, statute, ordinance, regulation or custom, willfully subjects any inhabitant of any State, Territory, or District to the deprivation of any rights, privileges or immunities secured or protected by the Constitution or laws of the United States, or to different punishments, pains, or penalties, on account of such inhabitant being an alien, or by reason of his color, or race, than are prescribed for the punishment of citizens, shall be fined not more than $1,000 or imprisoned not more than one year, or both. June 25, 1948, ch. 645, 62 Stat. 696. 18 U.S.C. § 242 (1964).

[40] 325 U.S. 91 (1945).

[41] "But in view of our construction of the word 'willfully,' the jury should have been instructed that it was not sufficient that petitioners had a generally bad purpose. To convict it was necessary for them to find that petitioners had the purpose to deprive the petitioner of a constitutional right . . ." at 107.

Further: "When they act willfully in the sense in which we use the word, they act in open defiance or unreckless disregard of a constitutional requirement which has been made specific and definite."

to bring actions against the police [42] have rendered Section 242 an impotent deterrent to police violence. Although there have been a handful of cases brought under this provision and some convictions,[43] this sanction has been applied only to the most outrageous kinds of police brutality.[44] Because the application of criminal sanctions to police misconduct is justified only when the policeman is clearly acting as a lawless hoodlum,[45] it is totally unrealistic to anticipate that this federal criminal provision will ever be transformed so as to control the conduct of the police.

Unlawful search and seizure, malicious procurement of a warrant and excess of authority under a warrant have been punishable as misdemeanors under federal

---

[42] See Foote, *supra* note 38; but see Caldwell and Brodie, "Enforcement of the Criminal Civil Rights Statute, 18 U.S.C. Section 242. In Prison Brutality Cases," 52 *Geo. L.J.* 706 (1964) which suggests that since the creation of the Civil Rights Division of the Justice Department there has been more action under this statute. The cases he cites have little to do with police conduct outside the prison setting.

[43] In the area of police conduct exclusive of the prison setting there have been only nineteen cases since the *Screws* decision of which thirteen ended in conviction. See especially, *Miller* v. *United States*, 404 F. 2d 611 (5th Cir. 1968) where the court upheld the conviction of two Louisiana police officers for wilfull brutality and infliction of summary punishment by making their police dog bite the suspect in order to coerce a confession from him.

[44] *Williams* v. *United States*, 341 U.S. 97 (1951) (private detective holding special officers cards of city police brutally beat confessions from suspected lumber yard thieves); *Lynch* v. *United States*, 189 F. 2d 476 (5th Cir.), *cert. den.* 342 U.S. 831 (1950) (Officer of laws who, having prisoner in his custody, assaulted and beat him was found guilty under this section). See also, *Apodaca* v. *United States*, 188 F. 2d 932 (10th Cir. 1951); *United States* v. *Jackson*, 235 F. 2d 925 (8th Cir. 1951); *Koehler* v. *United States*, 189 F. 2d 711 (5th Cir. 1951), *cert. den.* 342 U.S. 852, rehearing den., 342 U.S. 889.

[45] See our argument above that any looser standard would gravely and unduly hamper law enforcement efforts.

law for decades.[46] Yet the annotations following these statutory provisions dealing with illegal police activity reveal no decided cases. That these sanctions have been completely ignored for so long graphically underscores the need for remedies other than state and federal criminal statutes to deter and if necessary punish arbitrary police conduct.

As a final part of this synopsis of criminal provisions affecting the police, some mention should be made of the longstanding suggestion that judges use their contempt power to discipline offending officers.[47] The contempt sanction, we have concluded, is much too harsh. Moreover, since judges are probably institutionally incapable of discovering on their own motion instances of police misconduct, this sanction would be applied only when the given facts in an adversary proceeding clearly indicate unlawful police action. Yet we already have better legal remedies for these egregious instances of police violence. Finally, since the proposed "contempt of the Constitution" [48] is an indirect criminal contempt, the accused police officer would probably have a right to a separate jury trial.[49] The prospect of a second trial militates further against

---

[46] 68 Stat. 803, 18 U.S.C. 2236 (1948) (unlawful search and seizure); 62 Stat. 803, 18 U.S.C. 2236 (1948) (malicious procurement of a warrant); 62 Stat., 803, 18 U.S.C. 2234 (1948) (exceeding authority under a warrant).

[47] The first formulation of this proposal is in 8 Wigmore, *Evidence*, Sec. 2184 (3d ed. 1940).

> The natural way to do justice here would be to enforce the healthy principle of the Fourth Amendment directly, i.e., by sending for the high-handed, over-zealous marshal who had searched without a warrant, imposing a thirty-day imprisonment for his contempt of the Constitution, and then proceeding to affirm the sentence of the convicted criminal.

For a recent development of this theme, see Blumrosen, "Contempt of Court and Unlawful Police Action," 11 *Rutgers L. Rev.* 526 (1957).

[48] 8 Wigmore, *Evidence*, Sec. 2184–85 (3d ed. 1940); and *id.* at 526–29.

[49] *Bloom* v. *Illinois*, 391 U.S. 194 (1968).

stretching the contempt power to these frontiers never envisioned for it. . . .

INTERNAL REVIEW

Every major police department has formal machinery for processing citizen complaints. To the extent that such machinery is fairly and effectively invoked, it can discipline misbehaving officers and deter the misconduct of other policemen. But in practice, internal review is largely distrusted by outsiders [50] for a variety of reasons.

For internal review procedures to be meaningful, complaints against the police must not only be readily accepted, but actively encouraged. Yet much criticism of police review has been directed at the hostile response of some departments to civilian complaints. In some instances, complex procedural formalities discourage filing of grievances.[51] Some departments will disregard anonymous telephone complaints and a few require sworn statements from complainants.[52] Allegations of police brutality, in particular, are often regarded as affronts to the integrity of the force which demand vigorous defense.[53] Accordingly, certain departments have in the past charged many complainants with false reports to the police as a matter of course,[54] or have agreed to drop criminal

charges against the aggrieved party if he in turn abandons his complaint.[55] While most departments have abolished such practices, many potential allegations of police misconduct are apparently still withheld because of fear of retaliation.[56]

An impartial acceptance of all complaints against the police is necessary to instill confidence in a police review board. In fact, an increased volume of complaints filed with the police might often indicate that a department is winning rather than losing the trust of a community. To this end, the Police Task Force of the Crime Commission recommended that police departments accept all complaints from whatever source, process complaints even after complainants have dropped their charges, and advertise widely their search for police grievances of all types.[57] Many urban police departments have apparently adopted or already complied with these proposals.[58]

Although nearly all departments investigate all complaints, about half entrust the task exclusively to the local unit to which the accused officer was assigned.[59] The

---

50 *Field Surveys V, A National Survey of Police and Community Relations.* Prepared by the National Center on Police and Community Relations, Michigan State University, for the President's Commission on Law Enforcement and Administration of Justice 193–205 (1967).

51 Crime Commission, *Task Force Report: The Police,* at 195. Citizen apathy is apt not to tolerate the effort and delays incident to a complicated procedure for filing complaints. See Niederhoffer, "Restraint for the Police: A Recurrent Problem," 1 *U. Conn. L. Rev.* 288–296 (1968).

52 Note, "The Administration of Complaints by Civilians Against the Police," 77 *Harv. L. Rev.* 501–502 (1964).

53 See Niederhoffer, *supra* note 51, at 296.

54 In Washington, D.C., in 1962 the Police Department charged 40 percent of all persons who complained of police abuse with filing a false report.

By contrast, only 0.003 percent of those who reported other crimes were similarly charged. Michigan State Survey, *supra* note 50, at 204.

55 Crime Commission, *Task Force Report: The Police,* at 195.

56 See J. Lohman and G. Misner, *The Police and the Community: The Dynamics of Their Relationship in a Changing Society,* II, at 174 (1966). Governor's Select Commission on Civil Disorder, State of New Jersey, *Report for Action* 35 (1968).

57 Crime Commission, *Task Force Report: The Police,* at 195.

58 *Id.*

59 Michigan State Survey, *supra* note 50, at 201–202. The Harvard Study found fewer than 5 percent of responding departments relied exclusively on a special independent unit to investigate complaints. But some, such as the New York City Department, provided for review of line investigations by a specially assigned supervisor. In Los Angeles, an Internal Affairs Division had the discretion to supplement a local investigation with an independent inquiry of its own. Note, "The Administration of Complaints by Civilians Against the Police," *supra* note 52, at 503–05.

central organization usually supervises such investigations in varying degrees, but the relative autonomy of local units in gathering evidence concerning a complaint can both strain objectivity and engender further police misconduct.[60] Since investigative findings determine whether a complaint will be processed further or dismissed as groundless, a local investigating team is offered the opportunity to clear its working comrade. Accordingly, the investigation may at times be designedly haphazard, or the complainant may be harassed into dropping his charges or a potential witness may be browbeaten into not testifying.[61]

Special internal investigative units for complaints of police misconduct are common to many departments, and should be the established norm, particularly for large urban forces. Such internal special units would presumably face less conflict of interest than local units in dealing with the policeman's conduct. An outwardly more objective inquiry might reduce grounds for public suspicion of police investigation of their own misconduct.

A sizable minority of departments do not provide formal adversary hearings for allegations of even the most egregious police misconduct.[62] In such instances, the police chief or commissioner will usually determine from investigative findings whether an officer should be disciplined. In organizations where hearings are conducted before a police review board, the format varies. It has been found that almost half of departments that provide hearings hold them secretly, and one-fifth deny the complainant rights to cross-examine witnesses or bring counsel to the hearings.[63] Such secrecy and lack of procedural safeguards inevitably foster suspicion about the fairness of internal review.[64] Furthermore, the recommendations of the review boards, which usually are implemented by the police chief, are seldom disclosed to either the public or the complainant.[65] Such a practice deprives hearings of their value in promoting community relations. For a full explanation of a dismissed complaint could publicly vindicate the police officer who in fact behaved responsibly, and the news of actual disciplinary action could placate citizen indignation over police misconduct. Thus if hearings are open to the public, quasi-judicial trial procedures are followed, and review board

---

[60] The line investigator, whose views are likely to parallel those of his accused colleague, may not find the alleged violation particularly offensive. J. Lohman & G. Misner, *supra* note 56, II, at 203. His disposition to vigorously investigate may also be dampened by the realization that he may be the subject of a similar investigation in the future by the defending officer. Michigan State Survey, *supra* note 50, at 219. Finally, a sense of organizational loyalty may persuade a local investigator to whitewash the indiscretions of a compatriot in the interests of preserving the department's reputation. Niederhoffer, *supra* note 51, at 296.

[61] Crime Commission, *Task Force Report: The Police,* at 196.

[62] Note, "The Administration of Complaints by Civilians Against the Police," *supra* note 52, at 506.

[63] *Id.* at 507. About 40 percent of trial boards have no jurisdiction over a complaint while a civil or criminal suit is pending against either the accused officer or the complainant. That a hearing should be barred by a civil action or an unrelated criminal prosecution is inexplicable. Furthermore, 25 percent of the review boards are prohibited from hearing a complaint after a related judicial determination has exonerated the policeman or convicted the complainant. Yet the absence of legal liability seems irrelevant to the need to discipline a miscreant officer. *Id.* at 506.

[64] Michigan State Survey, *supra* note 50, at 223. Even when the hearings are open to the public, the complainant is rarely allowed to examine the investigation report for purposes of rebuttal. *Id.* at 203. It has been noted that in police hearings the citizen often appears to be the one on trial, as he is barraged with irrelevant and threatening questioning, J. Lohman and G. Misner, *supra* note 56, II, at 203.

[65] Michigan State Survey, *supra* note 50, at 203. The complainant is typically merely assured that his grievance has been adequately handled, which leaves him feeling ignored as he suspected he would be in the first place. J. Lohman and G. Misner, *supra* note 56, I, at 172, 174.

decisions fully publicized, the popular image of the police could be profitably enhanced.[66]

A major criticism of internal review is that it seldom produces meaningful discipline of persons guilty of police misconduct.[67] Even when an officer is disciplined, the punishment is often so light as to be a token that aggravates rather than satisfies the grievant.[68] By contrast, many departments impose relatively severe penalties for violations of minor internal regulations. Thus tardiness or insubordination may warrant an automatic suspension that is more onerous than the sanction for physical abuse of a citizen.[69] The frequency of rigorous internal discipline for minor departures from departmental regulations magnifies the relative failure of police departments to discipline

an officer for abusive treatment of a citizen. The inference is that internal review is more attuned to enforcing organizational disciplines than redressing citizen grievances.

Internal review is undoubtedly the quickest and most efficient method of regulating the conduct of peace officers.[70] It is perhaps axiomatic that organizational superiors are in the most favorable position to control their subordinates. Similarly, a police chief is probably best qualified to formulate the standards for police conduct. He also can utilize the best available investigative facilities plus his unique expertise in police operations to mete out appropriate disciplinary measures. A punishment decreed by an insider is likely to be accepted by both the miscreant officer and the department as a whole. On the other hand, control imposed from the outside is bound to be more sporadic and hence less effective than persistent self-discipline. Furthermore, constant second-guessing by strangers might undermine police morale and induce the kind of bureaucratic inertia that seems to plague several other governmental agencies sapped of their local autonomy.

Despite the inherent advantages of self-regulation, however, its difficulties in projecting an image of fairness with regard to complaints from the citizenry suggests that it should be supplemented by some form of external review. Whether or not internal review procedures are conducive to objective inquiry, the mechanism is seldom invoked by those minority groups which encounter the police most directly and frequently.[71] Since the police cannot

---

[66] It would seem that the many covert incidents of internal review hurt the police more than help them. Surely all the safeguards against public exposure must lead many people to think the police's wash is dirtier than it really is.

[67] Michigan State Survey, *supra* note 50, at 186. Prior to the establishment of a citizen Police Advisory Board, no Philadelphia officer had ever been disciplined on the basis of a citizen complaint of police abuse. Coxe, "The Philadelphia Police Advisory Board," 2 *L. in Trans. Q.* 179, 185 (1965). Of 30 brutality complaints to the Inspection Officer of the Newark Police Department in 1966–67, none resulted in a policeman being charged. New Jersey Report, *supra* note 94, at 35.

[68] A recent study indicated that in 32 cases of proven brutality in Detroit, the punishment exceeded a written reprimand only twice. See Michigan State Survey, *supra* note 50, at 186. Much criticism was directed at the leniency of a recent ruling by a police chief that an officer accused of brutality be fined $50 and ordered to attend a human relations course at the police academy. See *Washington Post,* Sept. 19, 1968, at B1, Sept. 23. 1968, at A20.

[69] In Philadelphia, "rude or offensive language or conduct offensive to the public" invokes the same five-day suspension as "unexcused tardiness." In fact, the entire Disciplinary Code seems geared to punishing conduct the Department finds offensive to its own tastes, rather than those of the public. See J. Lohman and G. Misner, *supra* note 56, II, at 204.

[70] For a discussion of the advantages and disadvantages of internal review, see Note, "The Administration of Complaints by Civilians Against the Police," *supra* note 52, at 51.

[71] In 1966–67, fewer brutality complaints were brought to the Newark police than to other agencies, such as the Neighborhood Legal Services Project. New Jersey Report, *supra* note 56, at 36. In addition to the citizen apathy and fear of retaliation mentioned at notes 50 and 53, *supra,*

redress an aggrieved citizen with money damages, the conspicuously rare punishment of policemen on the basis of outside complaints can create the popular impression that police review is a sham designed to appease rather than relieve the victims of police violence. Furthermore, this failure to win public approval deprives internal review of its efficacy as a forum for vindicating officers slandered by groundless complaints.[72]

The concept of internal review is also limited by the degree to which a departmental superior can extricate himself from the conflict of interest he faces in judging citizen complaints against the police. To be fair, he must suppress a natural feeling of loyalty toward his subordinates. On the other hand, he faces the possibility that concession to citizen demands will undermine the morale of his organization. Thus even the conscientious police commissioner may encounter difficulty in properly handling complaints. Police departments have a self-interest like any other entity, and if a police department tacitly overlooks misconduct by its patrolmen, then such a department cannot be expected to condemn itself publicly through internal review mechanisms.[73] In such a case, only an ex-

ternal organization can offer consistently impartial and objective review of allegations of police misconduct.

CIVILIAN REVIEW BOARDS

Dissatisfaction with both internal and judicial processing of police misconduct complaints prompted a few cities to experiment with civilian review boards. These boards, sitting independently of the police structure, adjudicated the merits of citizen grievances, either dismissing them as groundless or recommending that departmental superiors discipline the miscreant officer. Such external review was designed to project an appearance of fairness unattainable by internal mechanisms. At the same time, the civilian review boards were able to pass judgment on discourteous or harassing police practices which do not constitute judicially remediable wrongs but which nevertheless infuriate the grievant and intensify community hostility toward the police. Yet the boards did not purport to displace preexisting channels: the ultimate power to discipline remained with the police themselves, and the courts' jurisdiction over complaints was never abridged.

Civilian review boards have operated at one time or another in Philadelphia, New York City, Washington, and Rochester. The Washington board, however, could entertain only complaints referred to it by the police commissioner,[74] and the jurisdiction of the Rochester board was limited to allegations of unnecessary or excessive force.[75] Therefore, the New York and Philadelphia experiences contribute more expansively to an examination of civilian review.

---

other factors may discourage complaints by minority groups. Some persons evidently are disposed never to trust an agency against which they have a grievance. *Kerner Report, supra* note 23, at 310. "If the black community perceives the police force as an enemy of occupation, then they are not going to take the trouble to file their complaints with the enemy," Niederhoffer, *supra* note 51, at 295.

[72] We believe that an internal review board—in which the police department itself receives and acts on complaints—regardless of its efficiency and fairness, can rarely generate the necessary community confidence, or protect the police against unfounded charges." *Kerner Report, supra* note 23, at 162.

[73] "Perhaps the single most potent weapon against unlawful police violence is a police commander who will not tolerate it. The converse is also true: where police leaders assume a permissive attitude toward violence by their men, they are often licensing brutality." United States Commission on

Civil Rights, 1961, *Commission on Civil Rights Report: Justice,* V, at 82.

[74] See *Report of the President's Commission on Crime in the District of Columbia* (Washington, D.C.: Government Printing Office, 1966), at 219–23.

[75] Crime Commission, *Task Force Report: The Police,* at 200.

The New York Civilian Complaint Review Board (CCRB), created by executive order in July 1966 and abolished by popular referendum four months later, consisted of four civilians appointed by the Mayor and three policemen named by the police commissioner.[76] The CCRB was empowered to accept, investigate, and review any citizen complaints of police misconduct involving unnecessary or excessive force, abuse of authority, discourteous or insulting language, or ethnic derogation.[77] Upon receipt of a complaint, the board directed its specially assigned investigative staff of police officers to interview the complainant, the accused policeman, and any witnesses. If the investigation report revealed no serious dispute on the facts, a conciliation officer attempted to negotiate an informal settlement. If the policeman had acted properly under the circumstances, the board explained to the citizen that his grievance stemmed from a misunderstanding of the situation or of police duties. Where the officer had been mistaken or neglectful, or the injury had been minimal, the complainant was assured the misconduct had been amply considered and would not be repeated. Where both parties were at fault or where the citizen was particularly incensed, a joint confrontation of the parties was arranged which would hopefully result in mutual understanding and apologies.[78] If a complaint was conciliated or deemed unsubstantiated, the accused officer was expressly notified that the complaint would not appear on his record.[79]

When the seriousness of the alleged offense or a heated dispute over the facts precluded informal conciliation, the CCRB conducted a formal hearing, at which both complainant and policeman had rights to representation by counsel and cross examination of witnesses.[80] The board made findings of fact, upon which it either dismissed the complaint or recommended "charges" to the police commissioner. No specific disciplinary measures emerged from the CCRB, whose final rulings recommended further departmental consideration of a complaint rather than punishment.[81]

The New York CCRB elicited 440 complaints during its 4-month existence, as compared to the approximate annual average of 200 received by the police-operated Complaint Review Board prior to 1966.[82] Nearly half the grievances alleged unnecessary force, but a substantial number involved discourtesy and abuse of authority.[83] Significantly, many of the complaints emerged not from the criminal context, but from police involvement in private or family disagreements.[84] That only half the complaints were filed by members of minority groups could be attributed to insufficient publicity and the CCRB's short tenure.[85] Of the 146 complaints ultimately processed by the CCRB, 109 were dismissed after investigation, 21 were conciliated, 11 were referred elsewhere, 4 culminated in recommended "charges," and one resulted in a reprimand from the board.[86]

The brevity of the New York experiment defies meaningful evaluation, but the Police Advisory Board (PAB) operated continually in Philadelphia from 1958 through 1967, when its normal activities were enjoined. The PAB closely resembled

---

[76] A. Black, *The People and the Police* 78 (1968). The author, who was Chairman of the New York Civilian Review Board, blamed the referendum results on an extensive publicity campaign against the board speared by the Fraternal Order of the Police and the fact that a "yes" vote at the polls was curiously a vote against the CCRB. *Id.* at 208–15.

[77] *Id.* at 86–87.

[78] *Id.* at 113–15.

[79] *Id.* at 93.

[80] *Id.* at 122–26.

[81] *Id.* at 130.

[82] *Id.* at 94.

[83] *Id.* at Appendix IV.

[84] *Id.* at 101.

[85] *Id.* at 100.

[86] Crime Commission, *Task Force Report: The Police*, at 201.

the CCRB, except that the Philadelphia board had no specially assigned investigative staff, held open hearings, lacked power to subpoena witnesses, and recommended specific disciplinary measures to the commissioner for valid complaints. From 1958 until mid-1966, the PAB received 571 citizen complaints, of which 42 percent alleged brutality, 22 percent harassment, 19 percent illegal entry or search, and 17 percent other misconduct.[87] During this period, the PAB recommended 18 reprimands, 23 suspensions, 2 dismissals, and 3 recommendations of police officers, and 33 expungings of complainants' arrest records.[88] With few exceptions, the police department cooperated by implementing the board's proposals.[89]

The record of the PAB reveals several positive accomplishments. It evidently achieved some degree of support from the minority communities where police presence was most volatile; one-half of all complaints were filed by Negroes in a city that was three-quarters white.[90] Dispositions most frequently emerged from informal settlements.[91] This conciliation process, it is presumed, permitted grievance resolutions acceptable to both citizen and officer with a minimum of the adversary tensions normally incident to an open formal hearing. Furthermore, the complainant would often be uninterested in seeing the policeman disciplined; he may have sought only an apology or eradication of an unjustified arrest record.

The PAB also submitted an annual report to the Mayor, which allowed broader expression of citizen judgment on police policies than would usually flow from the case by case approach. The police department followed the 1962 report's suggestion

that definitive guidelines for the proper use of handcuffs be established.[92] In 1965 the PAB requested that the police rectify apparent patterns of physical mistreatment of apprehended persons in station houses and discourtesy directed at civilian inquiries.[93] The annual report thus enabled the PAB to expose the most persistent sources of citizen irritation in the interest of enabling the police both to improve their services and to enhance their public image. Finally, a prominent Philadelphian has noted he remembers no occasion prior to the board's operation in which the police department had ever diciplined an officer solely on the basis of civilian complaint.[94]

The successes of civilian review have been counterbalanced by marked failures, some of which are probably unique to the Philadelphia experience. Few complaints were filed with the PAB. The number exceeded 100 only in 1964, and the annual rate of complaints received evinces an erratic, rather than an upward trend.[95] The diminutive community response to the board was partly attributable to its lack of publicity. As a result of limited press coverage and a non-existent publicity budget, many citizens knew nothing of the board's operation or even its existence.[96] There is also suspicion that some policemen actively discouraged complaints on infrequent occasions. . . .[97]

Probably the real issue here is that, despite their monopoly on the use of force, policemen fiercely resent being singled out among all other local governmental officials for civilian review. Implicit in the board's very existence seems to be an assumption that policemen are characteristically arbitrary or brutal and have to be

---

87 See table in J. Lohman and G. Misner, *supra* note 56, at 236.
88 See table in *id.* at 245.
89 *Id.* at 259.
90 Coxe, *supra* note 67, at 183–84.
91 See table in J. Lohman and G. Misner, *supra* note 56, at 254–255.

92 *Id.*
93 *Id.* at 255.
94 Coxe, *supra* note 67, at 185.
95 See table in J. Lohman and G. Misner, *supra* note 56, at 236.
96 Coxe, *supra* note 67, at 183–84.
97 J. Lohman and G. Misner, *supra* note 56, at 253.

watched. Since policemen apparently believe that civilian review boards symbolize society's contemptuous discrimination against them, the ill feeling the institution provokes may not be worth the benefits it may confer. Indeed, the high controversy associated with the term "civilian review board" suggests the appellation will not be attached to any future grievance response agencies.

Another source of police antagonism may have been the adversary nature of the PAB's hearing procedures. The adversary process is not only costly and protracted, but when complainant and policeman are pitted against each other in formal opposition, hearings convey the appearance of a battleground.[98] As a consequence, the civilian review board seems in some ways to aggravate, rather than minimize, the frictions between police and community. Yet the object of external review should be improvement of existing police services, not establishment of a rival police department. To the extent that a board departs from ameliorating tensions through informal conciliation and moves toward affixing blame in formal adjudication, it fails to improve police-community relations.

To relate the defects of civilian review boards is not, however, to reject the concept of civilian review itself. Both the Kerner[99] and Crime Commissions[100] recognized the importance of independent nonjudicial review of police conduct, and yet also did not recommend that civilian review boards be established in cities where they did not already exist. Indeed, the qualified achievements of the review

board seem to have flowed more from the merits of external surveillance than the mechanism that seeks to achieve it. If civilian review can be institutionalized so as to placate rather than polarize police-citizen differences, its potential may be realized. The ombudsman has been offered as just such an institution.

THE OMBUDSMAN

The Scandinavian ombudsman system has been adopted by several foreign governments in recent years, and the idea of importing it to America has received much attention.[101] The ombudsman is, most simply, an external critic of administration. In 1807, Sweden appointed the first ombudsman, who was charged with surveillance of all bureaucratic agencies. Finland adopted the institution in 1919, and by 1967 it had spread to ten other countries.[102] In the countries where he exists, the ombudsman is usually a prominent jurist, and is aided by a staff of lawyers. He is appointed by the national legislature, and in some countries has jurisdiction over municipal, as well as national administrative agencies.[103]

The ombudsman's goal is improvement of administration rather than punishment of administrators or redress of individual grievances.[104] Thus, instead of conducting

---

98 This image probably poisoned the other incidents of review board activity as well. Police investigations for the board may have been colored by the temptation to save a fellow officer from persecution at a hearing. Similarly, many a complainant must have decided filing a grievance was not worth incurring the wrath of the police at a formal trial.

99 *Kerner Report, supra* note 23, at 162.

100 Crime Commission, *Challenge of Crime in a Free Society*, at 103.

101 See, e.g., Walter Gellhorn, *Ombudsman and Others* (Cambridge: Harvard University Press, 1966); Gellhorn, *When Americans Complain: Governmental Grievance Procedures* (Cambridge: Harvard University Press, 1966); Donald C. Rowat, ed., *The Ombudsman, Citizen's Defender* (London: Allen and Unwin, 1965); Stanley V. Anderson, ed., *Ombudsman for American Government?* (Englewood Cliffs, N.J.: Prentice Hall, 1968).

102 Rowat, "The Spread of the Ombudsman Idea," in *Ombudsman for American Government?, id.* at 7.

103 See Bexelius, "The Ombudsman for Civil Affairs," in *The Ombudsman, Citizen's Defender, supra* note 101, at 22, 28.

104 The following description of the ombudsman's powers is taken from Gwyn, "Transferring the Ombudsman," in *Ombudsman for American Government?, supra* note 101, at 27, 38–40.

formal hearings associated with adjudication, he relies primarily on his own investigations to collect information. He is authorized to receive all civilian complaints against any administrator or department. But valid complaints do not generally invoke adversary confrontations for purposes of adjudicating the propriety of past conduct by an official. Rather, individual grievances serve to alert the ombudsman to questionable administrative policies that deserve investigation. In accordance with his focus on future practices rather than past grievances, the ombudsman may even initiate investigation at his own discretion in the absence of a citizen complaint. To facilitate his inquiries, he may request explanation from an appropriate official, examine an agency's files, or call witnesses and conduct a hearing. On the basis of his findings, the ombudsman may recommend corrective measures to the agency although he cannot compel an official to do anything. In some countries, he may also prosecute a delinquent official, although this power is rarely exercised. In any case, he takes great pains to explain his conclusions to bureaucrats, complainants, and the general public. Since the ombudsman enjoys almost demi-god status in some countries, administrators are likely to heed his criticisms and citizens are not apt to be disturbed when he finds complaints groundless. Furthermore, administrators evidently feel benefitted not only by the ombudsman's rejection of warrantless accusations, but also by his suggestions of fairer and more efficient policies and procedures. At the same time, citizens can see their grievances being translated into broad policy guidelines.

Professor Gellhorn, an eminent proponent of the ombudsman would avoid the tragic flaw of civilian review boards by accepting complaints about any local public servants, not just policemen.[105]

105 W. Gellhorn, *When Americans Complain: Governmental Grievance Procedures, supra* note 101, at 192.

Furthermore, Gellhorn contends, full processing of each citizen complaint before referral to administrative superiors for further consideration constitutes a cumbersome duplication of effort and an unjustifiable displacement of the police department as primary investigator and arbiter of charges against its members.[106] The thrust of his argument is that meaningful improvement in police administration will emerge not from sporadic disciplinary proceedings but rather from imposing upon departmental superiors absolute accountability for the actions of their subordinates.[107] Therefore, the ombudsman should initiate his inquiries only upon charges that departmental superiors have given inadequate attention to a complaint of police misconduct. The focus of evaluation is then not the guilt of a particular policeman, but the policies and procedures by which police superiors have assessed a citizen's allegation of such guilt.[108] The ombudsman, thus relieved of the adversary adjudications that made civilian review boards so unpopular, could supposedly transcend the individual case to address himself to the broader policies of police administration.

We reject Professor Gellhorn's proposal because it eliminates that conciliatory process which was the primary strength of the civilian review boards. If frustration over police practices is indeed a major cause of urban disorders,[109] and if many of the grievances which engender such frustrations can indeed be alleviated by an apology or police explanation,[110] then informal conciliation of the individual case is a necessary function of complaint channels. Because his ombudsman is in effect a court of appeals bound by the factual findings of the police department,

106 *Id.* at 191.
107 *Id.* at 193.
108 *Id.* at 191.
109 *Kerner Report, supra* note 23, at 284.
110 J. Lohman and G. Misner, *supra* note 56, at 284.

it must be presumed that any informal accommodations Gellhorn envisions must be effected by internal processes. Yet such an arrangement presupposes a preexisting community trust of the police, the lack of which supposedly made external review desirable in the first place. When a police department is unable to project an impartial appearance, informal negotiation of a compromise between citizen and policeman must be attempted by an external agency *before* a complaint is referred to the police department for adversary adjudication. Whereas policy orientation undoubtedly offers creative possibilities for external review, the ombudsman should not divorce himself from the individual case to the degree that Professor Gellhorn recommends.

CONCLUSION AND RECOMMENDATIONS

To recapitulate for a moment, none of the remedies discussed above can successfully control the everyday conduct of the policeman on the beat—the harassment and abuse which yields no actual physical damage and results less from ill will than from poor training. The exclusionary rule can remedy denials of constitutional rights in cases which go to trial and result in convictions. Civil damage actions, state or federal, can redress egregious misconduct resulting in actual damage. Injunctive relief can halt and deter systematic misconduct directed at an identifiable person or group of persons. However, solutions for the basic problems of police-community relations cannot be imposed from the outside: as even the most pessimistic commentators have recognized, primary responsibility for everyday police discipline must rest within the police department.

Nevertheless, since internal review has been uniformly sluggish, some kind of outside pressure must be brought to bear to induce voluntary correction of illegal and otherwise abusive police conduct. Mandatory injunctions issued by federal district courts are too cumbersome for this purpose and are susceptible to complete disruption of the internal review mechanism. The civilian review boards are doomed to futility since they pit the aggrieved citizen against the police department in a formal adversary proceeding; in short, someone always wins and someone is always resentful. The ombudsman, on the other hand, shifts the focus from dispute resolution to evaluation of the department's grievance response mechanism. Yet, since the primary goals of an effective complaint mechanism are to provide an objective forum and encourage its use, individual grievances must remain in the forefront, and their dispositions must be publicized.

What is needed is a hybrid of the ombudsman and the external review agency, whose operation would have the following attributes:

(1) The primary responsibility for police discipline must remain with the police department itself.

(2) Nevertheless, there must be an easily accessible agency external to the police department, which processes citizen complaints in their inception rather than on appeal from the police.

(3) In each case, this agency should:
   (a) make an independent investigation of the complaints;
   (b) publicly exonerate the police if the complaint is groundless;
   (c) in cases of misunderstanding or minor abuse, attempt to resolve the dispute through an informal conciliation meeting;
   (d) if efforts at conciliation should fail or if the police behavior was unacceptable, make recommendations to the Department regarding discipline or ways to relieve tension;
   (e) keep each citizen complainant aware of the disposition of his complaint.

(4) On all matters, the agency should keep the public aware of its actions and the Department's response to its recommendations and should publish periodic reports and conclusions.

(5) So as not to single out the police for special oversight the agency should be responsible for processing citizen complaints not only against the police but also against other basic governmental service agencies, such as those responsible for welfare and employment. (For purposes of this chapter, however, we shall focus only on the relation of such an agency to the police department.)

While we affirm that our proposed agency will possess many of the attributes of the Scandinavian "ombudsman," it nevertheless differs from it in many material respects. For purposes of simplicity, however, we will call our agency "ombudsman." Its functioning we will now describe in somewhat greater detail.

Person with claims of police misconduct shall register them directly with the ombudsman without first seeking internal police review. He and his investigative staff shall first make findings of fact. If, after such an investigation, the complaint is found to be groundless, the ombudsman shall order it dismissed. If, however, his findings indicate police impropriety, the ombudsman has two courses open to him—informal conciliation and, if that fails, recommendation to the police commissioner that disciplinary action be taken.

In the first instance, the ombudsman's most useful function is to act as a conciliation agent between the police department and the aggrieved citizen. Since many of the citizen's grievances stem from seemingly trivial incidents, the ombudsman may be able to satisfy the aggrieved citizen by bringing him together with the offending policeman. Out of such meetings might come an apology by the officer for his indiscretion and a better understanding by the citizen of the tensions of day-to-day police work.

Such conciliation procedures and favorable results may seem at first blush naive; however, experience with ombudsmen in foreign countries indicates that concilia-

tion is their strongest weapon in their efforts to eliminate the rough edges of modern bureaucracy.[111] The citizen will often be quite satisfied with an apology or an explanation. Thus, the cumulation of such simple meetings may do much to offset the hostility and violence which can arise when citizens feel powerless against what they perceive as thoughtless and arrogant uses of governmental power.

When a complaint is found to be meritorious and conciliation attempts have failed or are clearly unsuitable, the ombudsman shall send a recommendation to the police department that a particular officer be disciplined. The ombudsman shall make such recommendation only as the last resort in any given case. On receipt of such recommendation, the responsibility for discipline shall be with the department itself.

What if the police department decides not to act on the ombudsman's recommendation? This knotty problem really presents two separate issues—non-action in a given case and non-action in most cases (indicating a course of conduct by the department not to heed the recommendation of the ombudsman). We feel that the systematic refusal of the department to cooperate with the ombudsman can be overcome by bringing it to public light in the ombudsman's periodic reports. The force of public opinion should push a clearly defiant police department into action. Although many citizens fear undue hampering of police efforts to curb crime, few will sanction police lawlessness. Moreover, refusal to heed the recommendations of the independent ombudsman should engender indignant response even from members of the majority community who have little contact with the police.[112]

Despite our concern for refusal to act on the ombudsman's recommendation as a

111 Rowat, *supra* note 101; and Gellhorn, *Ombudsman and Others, supra* note 101.
112 See also, *Kerner Report, supra* note 23, at 163.

general course of conduct, we emphasize that the department must retain discretion in each case to decide whether there should be disciplinary action and what the punishment should be. Maintenance of police morale and efficient law enforcement require that the department make the final decision. Thus, if in individual instances the police department disagrees with the ombudsman's recommendation, the department's good faith should be accepted.

In sum, then, if the police department systematically refuses to respond to the ombudsman's recommendation with reasonable exercises of internal discipline, the ombudsman should bring this recalcitrance to public attention in his periodic reports and rely on public pressure to activate internal police machinery. On the other hand, should the police generally follow his suggestions but occasionally refuse to act, the ombudsman should seek an explanation and accept such exercises of discretion as good faith determinations that in their opinion no action was justified.

Whatever the outcome of departmental action on the ombudsman's recommendations, his final duty in the processing of citizen complaints will be to publicize the action taken. First, he should inform the complainant directly of the action taken on his complaint. In addition, he should record both his and the Department's dispositions for general information to the public. We suggest that in informing the general public he should not refer by name to the officer disciplined but merely should report that as a result of his recommendation the department fined, suspended, etc., an officer on a given date. The purpose of informing the complainant of the outcome of the case is to give him confidence that his complaint was duly considered and acted upon. The more general record serves to keep the public aware that legitimate grievances

against the police do have an effective, nonviolent outlet.

In addition to processing citizen grievances, the ombudsman should publish periodic reports. We suggest that these public reports be submitted every six months. At the very least, such reports should include statistical accounts of the number and disposition of private complaints coming to his attention. Moreover, because naked statistics are often subject to inconsistent interpretations, the ombudsman should make an assessment of the overall performance of his office and responsiveness of the police to his suggestions. He must reiterate that this assessment is the ombudsman's most potent weapon for marshalling public support and for prodding a recalcitrant police force. Together with an assessment of the ombudsman's work with the police in dealing with private complaints, the report should contain recommendations of a general nature drawn from an overview of the complaints. For example, the ombudsman might recommend that a slight change in present police practice could eliminate a substantial irritant in police community relations.

His recommendations should extend not only to police practice guidelines but also to legislative action he deems necessary to defuse the ghettos or improve law enforcement. For instance, a very common complaint in ghetto communities is that the police do not readily respond to calls for help. If the reason is that the police force is substantially undermanned, the ombudsman could lend the authority of his voice to call for the legislative body to allocate more money for more police services. By making substantive recommendations to the legislature and suggesting guidelines for police practice to minimize citizen complaints the ombudsman's reports could be a truly effective force for vigorous yet benign law enforcement. . . .

B: Disposition of Cases
in Control Agencies

Social control agencies have been classified as service organizations because their raw material is people rather than objects. Service organizations include schools, universities, hospitals, clinics, welfare agencies, unemployment bureaus, juvenile courts, police departments, prisons, and other people-processing institutions. Most service organizations involve voluntary relationships between professionals and clients, while control agencies involve asymmetric, usually involuntary, relationships between agencies and "clients." Further, unlike other service organizations, in control agencies it is difficult to know for whom the services are provided. Control agencies obviously provide social control functions for the community and specific victims of criminal acts. But because they are also assigned rehabilitative as well as punitive goals in providing the control function, they are often seen as providing "services" to those apprehended.

Service organizations, as opposed to economic production organizations, "are generally assumed to be more concerned with social goals and less with profit and loss" (Lefton, 1970:19). Consequently, a service ethic rather than a profit motive is generally assumed to underlie the activities of people-processing agencies. This is not to say that control agencies are not concerned with money. Control bureaucracies must often justify their existence to legislators and others in order to receive continued support for their activities from the public. Control agencies must argue that past funding has produced results and that future support is warranted.

Service organizations process reactive objects. Patients and prisoners talk back, demand their rights, and at times demand part of the action. Service organizations, and even some control organizations have recently provided a larger role for the client within the organization:

> In recent years service organizations of all kinds have "invited" clients to take a more active part in organizational life. The fact that this democratization of bureaucracy has in some cases opened Pandora's Box is hardly surprising: Mental hospitals, for example, through devices such as patient government, family visitation, community advisory groups, and others, have drawn the patient . . . into the organizational system in quite real and sometimes authoritative ways. . . . Welfare agencies—largely through OEO—have taken welfare recipients directly into their membership, thus breaking through the hallowed crust traditionally separating staff from clients. Prisons also have been toying for a long time with ways of engaging inmates in the work of the organization [Rosengren, 1970:119].

The fact that clients can react to and shape the service organization while being processed opens up new and interesting problems for organizational analysis. For example, to what extent do these processes influence their course of passage through the organization? Do the inmates really run the asylum? We would expect the negotiation power of clients to be greater in voluntary service agencies than in control agencies, but even in the latter, the deviants may significantly affect their future. Roth found that patients committed to a TB sanitarium were instrumental in negotiating their medical discharge date (Roth, 1963). Similarly, the prisoner influences his release date by doing good time and impressing the parole board by taking advantage of training programs within the prison.

Lefton and Rosengren (1966) provide an analytic approach to service organizations. They suggest that these organizations can be classified in terms of each agency's concern with the client's past and future biography. Agencies vary in their concern about the time span or longitudinality of their clients. Organizational interest may range from a truncated span of time as in a hospital emergency room or the booking room of a police department to an almost indeterminant time span in cases of prisons and psychiatric hospitals. Organizations also hold varying degrees of interest in the client's biographical space or the "surroundings" of a client. This lateral dimension ranges from no concern about the details of the individual (e.g., emergency room, traffic court) to an extensive concern with the current social situation in which the client lives (e.g., psychiatric outpatient treatment facilities). Given the dimensions of longitudinal and lateral interest of organizations in clients, Lefton and Rosengren outline the four logical combinations. While their examples were drawn mainly from medical service organizations, the classification can be applied to legal control agencies as Table B indicates.

When processing involves a number of agencies, we would expect some overlap of client concerns, especially in organizations of Types II and IV. In terms of interagency relationships, Lefton and Rosengren predict longi-

Table B   Organizational Interest in Clients

Type	Examples	Biographical Interest	
		Lateral (Social Space)	Longitudinal (Social Time)
I	Police Departments Public Defender's Office Adult Criminal Court Small Claims Court Jails Commitment Boards Welfare Agencies (agency-directed)	−	−
II	State and Federal Prisons Reform Schools Psychiatric Hospitals District Attorney's Office Parole Boards	−	+
III	Juvenile Bureau Juvenile Court Court Psychiatric Clinics Welfare Agencies (client-directed)	+	−

IV	Probation Department
	In-Community Treatment and
	    Prevention Programs (e.g.
	    Provo Experiment,
	    Synanon, etc.)
		+	+

Adapted from Lefton and Rosengren, 1966:806.

tudinal organizations will manifest a greater concern with other agency contacts, and that these contacts are likely to be formalized. Litwak (1970:146) suggests three forms of interagency exchanges or linkages. The first is through the transmission of printed matter—records, files, requisitions, etc. A second type of agency linkage is through a superbureaucracy which oversees and coordinates the activities of various agencies.[1] An example would be a community chest organization to coordinate all local fund raising drives. A third type involves informal ties through primary group contacts between members of various agencies.

Conflict between agencies is predicted if the agencies are divergent in their client concerns. This would, of course, be only one of many reasons for interagency conflict. Stoll (1968), in the article reprinted in this section, suggests that agencies differ in attitudes about free will–determinism, which affects their reactive stance toward deviance; a free-will ideology leads to demanding punishment and determinism leads to an emphasis on disinterested rehabilitation. The punishment–treatment ideologies seem a greater focus for conflict

[1] Such a coordinating bureaucracy has been proposed for the criminal justice system by a recent staff report to the Violence Commission (cf. Campbell et al., 1970:274–77).

than lateral–longitudinal discrepancies, although both may be operating in certain situations.[2]

Interagency conflict also may be the result of organizational ethocentrism, variations in perceptions of the esteem of other control agents (Haurek and Clark, 1967), concern with professional territory and jurisdiction, variations in operating philosophies (Miller et al., 1968), misunderstandings of the functions of other agencies, etc. With conflict between agencies being generated from so many sources, it is somewhat surprising that any work gets done. The conflict is overcome in a large part by the interdependency of organizations in the processing of cases. The necessity for coordination in the production of cases sets the stage for the development of rather complex exchange processes between agencies. Coordination is often an uneasy peace maintained by each agency's control over resources required for efficient operation by other agencies.

EXCHANGE PROCESSES IN SOCIAL CONTROL AGENCIES

There are many reasons for suggesting that we have a nonsystem of criminal justice in this country. Responsibility is spread over many agencies with problems of coordination and jurisdiction always topics for negotiation (Campbell et al., 1970). Another equally serious problem with the criminal justice nonsystem is the lack of clear-cut guidelines or goals as to what is to be achieved by societal intervention in social problems.

Problems of coordination and exchange are evident in the juvenile court which is a lateral agency concerned with many aspects of the individual's life and character, as well as specific actions which may have led to a particular arrest. Rosengren (1970:124) sums up the major problems faced by lateral institutions such as the juvenile court:

> A broad lateral orientation normally means that the organization draws support from many different groups in the community. This is potentially a divisive pattern because it leads to competitive processes among supporters, with the organization itself as the target for manipulation and control.

Support for this assertion is found in a study of a large metropolitan juvenile court by Robert Emerson (1969). He documents the importance of the exchange process between the juvenile court and other agencies on which the court relies for its cases. The image Emerson builds is one of a juvenile court judge who is more or less an arbiter of cases, coordinating and placating the demands of other agencies which have an input to the proceedings. The judge,

2 Evidence for the hypothesis that agent's attitudes and perceptions of esteem split along punishment–rehabilitation lines is found in Haurek and Clark's (1967:54, 59) study showing that police held social workers in low esteem and social workers held prosecuting attorneys, court officials, and the police in low regard. Stanton Wheeler et al. (1968:41–45), found police and courts psychiatrists holding very opposite views on delinquency.

in the process of negotiation with and placation of vested interests groups, really loses much of his assumed independence (also Matza, 1964).

While exchange and negotiation permeate all aspects of the criminal justice system—both in and out of court—these processes are perhaps most visible in the juvenile court. The court, historically charged with a concern for the social space (laterality) of juveniles, consequently stresses many extra-legal factors in the deposition of cases (Platt, 1969a). More is required than simply knowledge that a crime was committed; the court systematically inquires into family background, school performance, reputation of parents, past behaviors as officially recorded by school, police department, or probation records. In short, the concern of the court is to establish the moral character of each youth and make dispositions accordingly (Emerson, 1969). Since the range of possible information which may have a bearing on moral character is so large, the court must entertain the suggestions of many community agencies. The potential for conflict is great and it is incumbent upon the juvenile court judge to provide conflict resolution so that cases can be quickly and efficiently processed.

Agency–court relations can be divided into roughly two areas based on traditional orientation to cases: enforcement agencies and treatment agencies. Enforcement agencies which have entree to the court include the police, the prosecutor's office, probation officers, and, to a lesser extent, schools and welfare agencies which can act as direct referral agencies to the court. The exchange process between the court and enforcement agencies can be seen in the case of the police. The conflicts which evolve between these two agencies is due in a large part to the problem of the "visibility of errors" (Wheeler et al., 1968). The police feel the courts are too lenient while the court sees the police as overly punitive; each agency sees only half of the picture. The police fail to realize that the court does not see or review informal dispositions by police officers, and the court is often not aware of the extent of police adjudication. An exception is when very serious cases come to the attention of the court, where records show a long history of informal disposition by police. These exceptions contribute to the conflict. This natural conflict between the court and enforcement agencies is resolved through an exchange of services. Each agency controls certain resources or rewards, and, through negotiation, a reciprocal agreement evolves which facilitates "getting the work done."

The court holds power over the police in disposition of cases and has the right to oversee and control police activities. The court also has the power to support the legitimacy and authority of police actions and the personal integrity of the individual police officers who appear before the courts (Emerson, 1969:51). With these aspects more or less explicit in the interagency relationships, exchanges are made and standardized expectations arise which reduce conflict and facilitate coordination of effort. The court's interaction with the second type of agency—treatment resources—is much more discretionary and negotiated in nature than are the largely unavoidable contacts with enforcement agencies (Emerson, 1969:57–72).

Some observers might suggest that the juvenile court is an atypical criminal justice agency since the court has historically been antilegalistic "in the sense that it derogated civil rights and procedural formalities, while relying heavily on extra-legal techniques" (Platt, 1969b:29). Although originally designed as a welfare rather than a legal approach to deviance, and thus the avoidance of the "trappings" of a criminal court, recent court decisions have brought the child-saving movement full circle. The decisions of *Kent, Gault,* and *Winship* [3] have restored many of the procedural safeguards of adult criminal proceedings, and, therefore, have moved the court closer to the legal model originally rejected by the child-saving movement.

However, the degree of legalism of the agency does not seem to affect the extent of negotiation. Similar exchange processes have been found in adult criminal proceedings such that many observers have commented on the lack of adversary confrontation in the disposal of cases (Skolnick, 1967; Blumberg, 1967, reprinted here). David Sudnow (1965) suggests how lawyers in a public defender's office work hand-in-hand with the police and prosecutor to facilitate dispositions—usually through the agreement to plead guilty for considerations. Around 90 percent of adult criminal cases are handled via guilty pleas. They are necessary in the sense that an increase of only 3 or 4 percent of the number of cases going to trial would stifle an already overloaded court system. A section from the Presidents' Crime Commission, "Disposition Without Trial" (reprinted here), suggests the wide variety of negotiative stances taken to assure a guilty plea in adult criminal cases. Similarly, Blumberg's observations of the cooptation of defense attorneys by the court provides insights into the affect of exchange processes on the lawyer's role in the legal system.

Similar processes of exchange and negotiation are, of course, found in civil actions. A recent study of suits arising from traffic accidents found that more than 95 percent of all bodily injury claims made against insured drivers were settled out of court (Ross, 1970:141). Since the vast majority of both criminal

---

[3] In 1966, the *Kent* decision on the transfer of jurisdiction from juvenile to adult court gave the following safeguards to the juvenile: (1) a full hearing on the issue of transfer to adult court; (2) the assistance of counsel at such a hearing; (3) full access to social records gathered and used by the court to determine whether transfer should be made; and (4) a statement of the reasons of jurisdiction waiver. In the *Gault* case of 1967, the child and his parents must (1) be notified regarding the charges in advance of the hearing so that the defendent has a reasonable opportunity to prepare for it; (2) be informed of the right to be represented by counsel, or be provided with counsel if the defendent cannot afford one; and (3) be informed of the right to refuse to testify for fear of self-incrimination and be granted the right to confront and cross-examine witnesses. Thus *Gault* provided the delinquent with the due process rights which were applicable to adults. The *Winship* case in 1970 said the juvenile court was required, in cases of acts which would be crimes if committed by an adult, to prove guilt beyond a reasonable doubt, replacing the civil dictum of guilt by a preponderance of evidence criterion (Caldwell and Black, 1971: 220–25).

and civil cases are decided by negotiation, the effect of the law is largely indirect. As one observer notes:

> The settlement practices of insurance companies constitute another factor which has a great impact on the actual operation of tort law today. The vast majority of accident claims never get into any stage of litigation; only an in- finitesimal proportion of them ever come to trial. The "law" that directly governs the disposition of most tort claims, then, consists in these practices. The legal rules affect most cases only to the extent that they are reflected in the process of settlement [Fleming James, quoted in Ross, 1970:235].

In summary, we have suggested how and why interagency cooperation and coordination are attained in the network of social control agencies. The orga- nizational demands of efficiency and economy of operations necessitate much of the negotiated exchanges found between control agencies. These exchanges have significantly altered the traditional roles of many control agents (e.g., lawyers, probation officers). These exchanges also point up the fact that while ideological differences may exist between agencies, these are often placed aside in the name of efficiency. Each ideological camp (punishment–rehabilitation) by the nature of the required exchanges must make concessions. It is not sur- prising that the goals and means of the various criminal justice agencies are both nebulous and potentially counterproductive. The bureaucratic demands for efficiency may significantly alter the case disposition criteria used within and between control agencies. We shall now examine analytically the process of creating, adjudicating, and disposing of cases and the resultant criteria used in these processing decisions. The final section attempts to assess the deviant's response to the negotiative aspects and the altered criteria of disposition.

CASE DISPOSITION

Each social control agency develops a particular "clientele" or universe of individuals designated as a control problem. These individuals take on dis- tinctive characteristics because of the selection process involved in referral to, and acceptance by, the agencies. Private agencies have the greatest control over the population they serve since they may refuse to accept certain trouble cases. These cases are often dumped on to public agencies which serve similar func- tions. Public agencies may handle problem cases through referral to other agencies, thereby keeping the most amenable cases for treatment. Each control agency will identify individuals in need of help and develop means of acquir- ing access and jurisdiction for these cases (Scott, 1970). The samples drawn from the potential pool of deviants will be influenced by the source of referral. Mental health clinics are more likely to accept referrals from professionals than from laymen (Teele and Levine, 1968:116). Police may not take the ini- tiative in the handling of mental illness cases for fear that the psychiatric hospital may refuse the case, thereby leaving the officer in a very difficult position (Bittner, 1967). In addition to acceptance policies and referral sources, the clientele of an agency is determined by the definitional breadth of the classification system used to delimit deviance, the diagnostic and prognostic biases of the agency, and the particular professional monopoly which some agencies may enjoy (Freidson, 1966).

In the process of agency identification of deviance, the actions of the agencies indirectly affect the definitions of deviance held by laymen. Consequently, the "recruitment" strategies of control agencies may create deviance where none was *seen* to exist previously.

> In the course of defining and classifying the universe which they claim needs their services, all control agencies in effect become responsible for drawing clearer lines than in fact exist either in everyday life or in the processes by which people were originally led into their services, and agencies may come to define people as deviant who would not ordinarily have been so defined. *Both professionalism and bureaucratization objectify deviance and reify diagnostic categories.* In this sense, while such agencies may not actually create deviant roles, they do by the nature of their activities refine and clarify their boundaries and, by assuming responsibility for their control, add elements to the roles that may not have existed previously, and so encourage pulling new people into them [Freidson, 1966:82–83, emphasis added].

While processing individuals thought to be deviant, control agencies are simultaneously spreading the gospel about their good works, and thus the public receives instructions, inadvertently, as to the particular deviant role in question. In their zeal to root out deviance, the control agency is in a sense making sure that they will continue to have a publicly recognized pool of deviants upon which they can draw.

While the processing agency's work may have implications for the category systems held by laymen, the activities also "objectify deviance and reify diagnostic categories" within the control agency itself. Category systems evolve which provide a structure or pattern to diverse events routinely encountered. These systems may be diagnostic classifications, legal codes, coding guides, etc. The crucial issue is how these category systems provide an answer to the omnipresent question of the control agent: How does the agent objectify "the raw material he observes so that others can arrive at similar inferences"? (Cicourel, 1964:5) The term "processing stereotype" is offered as a solution to the agent's problem of accounting for his decisions to superiors in the organization. Processing stereotypes are consensually held, simplified images used by processing agents to categorize and order their environment. It is intended as an analytic concept subsuming what Sudnow (1965) has termed "normal crimes" and what Scheff (1966) has interchangeably referred to as "normal cases," "diagnostic stereotypes," or "typification."

These simplified images may have as their referent the "moral character" of the processee, the motive imputed to the behavior in question, the background characteristics of the suspect, the *modus operandi* of the act, and other aspects. This typification of the actor and the action can be seen as the removal of unique background characteristics and specific contextual factors of the case so that "essential features of socially recognized 'familiar scenes' may be detected" (Garfinkel, 1967:36). These standardized background expectancies become the basis for the agent's attitudes and behavior vis-à-vis the typified actor or action.

It is assumed that the unstated background expectancies which are substituted for the unique aspects of cases under review help to render the agent's activities meaningful to himself and to other agents. Processing stereotypes are thus used in order to:

> . . . prepare the object for definite evaluation and disposition. The transformation of the object, therefore, is always part of the manipulation of background expectancies in order to make the descriptive accounts of what happened convincing and justifiable vis-à-vis evaluations and dispositions [Cicourel, 1968:16].

A number of factors involved in the socialization of processing agents may influence processing stereotype formation. Scheff has noted that when diagnostic categories are learned in medical school they are often based on extreme cases: ". . . the tendency to use extreme examples for analytic clarity reinforces the popular stereotype of the extremeness of mental illness and serves also to reify behavioral classifications (such as paranoid behavior, depression) into concrete disease entities" (Scheff, 1967:4). Freidson (1966:96) also notes that agents may reify labels by insisting on correct usage. Thus agents seeing laymen using unsophisticated labels such as "nerves" for mental illness may, in an attempt to educate the public, deliberately overemploy stigmatized labels.

While processing stereotypes may evolve through the particular training provided for control agents, it is probably true that these categorization schemes, in the main, develop on the job. It is proposed that processing stereotypes are generated and used as a response to the demands of the bureaucratic organization on its personnel to appear efficient, to process a large volume of cases, to reduce uncertainty and ambiguity in disposition, and to promote the smooth flow of individuals through the system. In short, processing stereotypes can be seen as part of the informal system which supplements the formal norms of control agencies (see Blumberg, 1967, reprinted here). The processing stereotypes, by circumventing the formal norms of the agency, produce case dispositions based on the agent's perception of what is due the offender. The system operates on the assumption that everyone coming before the public defender is guilty. As Scheff makes clear in his article included here, similar assumptions are made in commitment proceedings by psychiatrists; moreover, as Sudnow (1965) shows, the processing stereotypes change the official meaning of many extant legal categories.

The reward structure of most formal control organizations often operates in such a way that processing stereotypes will evolve. The fact that public appointed officials involved in commitment hearings are usually paid a flat fee per case suggests that an informal system of disposition will develop which maximizes the volume of cases processed per day (Scheff, 1964). The typification of like cases permits a smoother operation of the system. Cases can be more easily passed among persons within the same agency or between agencies. As noted earlier, the organizational demands to process a large number of cases in a very short time conflict with many of the legal requirements of "due process."

Typification of cases also permits the interchange of personnel within the organization. Sudnow makes this point with reference to "station-manning" in the public defender's office: "The PD sees defendants only at those places in their paths when they appear in the court he is manning. A given defendant may be 'represented' by one PD at arraignment, another at preliminary hearing, a third at trial and a fourth when sentenced" (Sudnow, 1965:265). Goffman also remarks that interchanging of staff in mental hospitals is common practice (1961:353ff). The same is true of large public hospitals and clinics (Freidson, 1967).

Processing stereotypes also serve to structure the interaction between agent and processee. The typified image stabilizes the role relationship, which increases the efficiency and speed of handling. Commitment hearings present a good example of this; the officials, since they have the records of the case before them, do not have to establish the patient's moral character "from scratch." Similarly, within the court system Sudnow found that the public defender's pretrial questioning of the defendant was terminated "when he had enough information to confirm the case's typicality and construct a typifying portrayal of the present defendant" (Sudnow, 1965:270).

Records and official reports of a case are generated by various control agents in their daily round. The dossiers created may be quite extensive as in social reports prepared for juvenile court hearings where many agencies have an input, or they may be very truncated and superficial as in police field encounter reports or admittance records to a mental hospital. Some understanding of the role of records and forms is required for an adequate understanding of case disposition decisions. Social control may be characterized as processing rather selective case histories of individuals, and the individual involved is seldom called upon to provide information or to make appearances. In adult criminal cases, disposition is informally implemented through the negotiation of the defense attorney and the prosecutors office (Skolnick, 1967). The individual has very little impact since his attorney will usually outline what options are available (if any) and advise him how to plead. The individual is visible only in the brief ceremony in court to plead guilty to the charge. In juvenile court, most of the decisions are made between control agents and the judge before the formal hearing based on the records produced by the various agencies under the court. (This may change with the recent *Winship* decision.) Thus court hearings or commitment proceedings are often mere formalities which take little time and require little fresh input from the accused (Lemert, 1967:94; Scheff, 1964).

IMPACT OF PROCESSING ON DEVIANT'S SENSE OF JUSTICE

In Part Four, we shall be concerned with the broad question of the impact of law on society. A part of that question is the impact of the control agencies on the behavior of the people whom they process. Here we are concerned with some of the unintended consequences for the individual who passes through legal control agencies and is subjected to their processing stereotypes. We have already indicated that stigmatized labels may limit one's ability to move out of deviant roles. This is a central contention in the "labeling" perspective on deviance. To use Lemert's terms, an outcome of being processed by formal agencies is that the individual is moved from "primary" to "secondary" deviance.

> Deviations remain primary deviations or symptomatic and situational as long as they are rationalized or otherwise dealt which as functions of a socially acceptable role. . . . When a person begins to employ his deviant behavior or a role based upon it as a means of defense, attack, or adjustment to the overt and covert problems created by the consequent societal reaction to him, his deviation is secondary [Lemert, 1951:75–76].

When the individual actively begins to react to the categorization provided by the control agency, labeling theorists speak of a new set of independent variables. Regardless of the initial cause of a behavior, societal reaction has now become a major determinant of future deviance.

Scheff (1966) and other labeling theorists have argued that public labeling is likely to have the most affect on future behavior. Garfinkel (1956) has termed the public settings of deviance accusation such as trials, commitment proceedings, and preliminary hearings *status degradation ceremonies,* which function to create social types which will be rejected by conforming individuals.[4] The typing is necessary to give legitimacy to the processing agents and to promote the future conformity of the witnesses, i.e., upstanding citizens who view the event.

Thus, in addition to the typification which takes place in the control network prior to public hearings (see the previous discussion of processing stereotypes), the ceremonies themselves are organized so that social types are created. The unique aspects of the biography and the deviant incident must be glossed so that the criminal nature of the deed and the individual are demonstrated. These public labeling ceremonies and the resultant deviant role applications make passage out of most deviant roles very difficult. Erikson (1964) notes that,

---

[4] These are public ceremonies in two senses. First, some may be held in, and are readily accessible to, witnesses for the public such as newspaper reporters, television journalists, etc. Second, the ceremonies involve public officials, i.e., individuals acting as representatives of the state. A trial may have both aspects of "public" involved, while a juvenile court hearing which is closed to the public, and where care is taken to avoid publicizing the proceedings (e.g., names of suspects not released), is public only in the second sense.

in this society, no formal ceremonies mark passage out of the deviant role. There are no activities parallel to the degradation ceremonies which ascribed the deviant role type. The records and the corresponding stereotyped image of the deviant tend to follow the processee after "release." The fact that stigma attaches to most deviant roles is well known, and the obstacles of a record are difficult to overcome (Schwartz and Skolnick, 1964). Simple knowledge by the public of association with a social control agency, even on a voluntary basis, may produce informal reactions from others (Phillips, 1963).

A major impact of the processing experience is the effect on the processed individual's sense of justice or fairness. We have suggested a number of ways in which the organizational demands for smooth and efficient processing of large numbers of cases produces alterations in the criteria of disposition, in the use of legal categories and charges to insure convictions, and the making of deals so that the officials involved feel the suspect "gets his due." In light of these processes, a sense of justice may be difficult if not impossible to foster in the accused. Also many extralegal factors (i.e., factors not directly related to the law violation) affect probabilities of arrest and prosecution. As mentioned earlier, such factors as wishes of the complainant, police discretion, race, reputation of an area of the city, etc., all influence entrance and continuance in social-control agencies. If the impact of the extraneous factors is perceived by the deviant, we would expect a sense of injustice to develop.

Matza, in a discussion of the sense of justice developed by the juvenile court, delineates five dimensions of fairness: cognizance, consistency, competence, commensurability, and comparison (1964:106). Each component may be used to indict juvenile justice agencies. Matza suggests that the very operations of the juvenile control system, and its attendant ideology, facilitate a neutralization of controls that may result in delinquency. Matza notes that "the ideology of child welfare supports the delinquent's viewpoint in two ways. It confirms his conception of irresponsibility, and it feeds his sense of injustice" (1964:98).

Cognizance refers to the legitimacy of surveillance of activity. One may feel it is unfair if he is being watched more closely than members of other groups in society (Matza, 1964:108). Cognizance is influenced by the processing stereotypes of an agency in that these typified images determine, in part, what the agents will look for and where they will look. The self-fulfilling aspects of surveillance and apprehension may result in vicious cycles of reaction to deviance (Lemert, 1951, 1967; Parsons, 1951; Pittman and Gillespie, 1967). In addition to the sense of injustice that derives from oversurveillance of activities (e.g. parolees, probationers), the deviant may feel that his biography has not been accurately rendered by control agents. This is likely to occur if the deviant realizes that "almost anyone's life course could yield up enough denigrating facts to provide grounds for the record's justification of commitment" (Goffman, 1961:159). In this case cognizance refers to selective attention to background characteristics such that negative aspects are overrepresented, which is likely to produce resentment.

Consistency of actions is often hard to find in many processing agencies. It was suggested above that processing stereotypes are part of an informal system within processing bureaucracies which provide standardized guidelines to action when formal criteria for action are ambiguous or absent. The deviant may sense a high level of inconsistency when he is aware of the formal principles of the agency, yet observes decisions being made on seemingly unrelated criteria. The accused is supposedly in a system which assumes innocence until proven guilty, provides for trial by peers, and prescribes an adequate defense for the indigent. Instead he finds a shuffling of legal categories based on a stereotyped picture of his case, a complex system of assuring guilty pleas, and a public defender more concerned with getting a reduction in charge than raising questions of innocence and how it might be proven in court. One reason that the inconsistencies are so glaring, even to the first-time offender who is likely to suffer at the hands of bargain justice, is that society has perpetuated a due process myth. The mass media cover large trials in part because of the difficulties involved in observing plea bargaining. Radio and television shows give the impression of automatic trials. Even the court itself helps to perpetuate the myth. Newman (1966) notes that the judge always asks the defendant who is entering a guilty plea if there has been any deal made. The accused is told beforehand to say "no" to this question. The judge and the accused, as well as other officials of the court, know a deal has been made but continue in the charade. Since solving and thereby clearing crimes is a valued commodity within the police organization, those suspects who can provide information, or who are willing to admit to a large number of crimes, have the greatest bargaining power. The first-time offender who was unfortunate enough to be arrested after his initial burglary has nothing to bargain with. Thus the ironic situation evolves of the more highly involved and sophisticated criminal coming off better in the control network than the first-time offender who often has the book thrown at him. This is another example of the inconsistent aspects of the criminal justice system which does not go unrecognized by those deviants involved. This form of inconsistency coincides with Matza's component of commensurability. Clearly, when the individual who admits to one hundred burglaries comes out ahead of the individual who commits one, the resultant punishment has not fit the crime (Skolnick, 1966).

The prevalence of processing stereotypes in the large control bureaucracies mitigates against the commensurability component of justice. This is especially true in juvenile court where the doctrine of individualized justice is professed, but also applies to the adult criminal court in terms of *mens rea*, mitigating circumstances, and self-defense. Earlier we suggested how processing stereotypes and the heavy reliance on records rather than testimony tends to reduce and obscure the unique aspects of the case. Also the processing of stereotypes implies that typical cases get typical dispositions in terms of sanctions. Therefore the deviant may conclude that his punishment was not commensurate with his actions, and a sense of injustice is generated.

Another component of injustice—the perception of incompetence of official control agents—is perhaps easiest to understand; police corruption, unenforceable laws, cries of police brutality and police hypocrisy—all operate to undermine the legitimacy of the law and the agents charged with its enforcement. Matza notes that the common complaints of control agents, e.g., low pay, high case loads, lack of autonomy, etc., may indirectly contribute to the sense of incompetency which may be imputed to the agents. The delinquent may feel that if the job is so bad, the individual must be incompetent or he would have sought out a better occupation. Since most people in society feel that incompetence does exist in our control agencies, it is not difficult for the delinquent to generalize these feelings to justify his own violation of the law.

These five components of injustice are seen as growing out of exposure to social-control agencies and their processing procedures.[5] A sense of injustice may arise for other reasons, two of which will be briefly discussed here. First, in civil disputes, the absence of a tribunal, or lack of access to such a forum, may generate feelings of injustice. In Roscoe Pound's words, "it is a denial of justice in small causes to drive litigants to employ lawyers and it is a shame to drive them to legal aid societies to get as charity what the state should give as a right" (Pound, 1913:318). This right was recognized early in this century with the establishment of small claims courts to bring justice to those who could ill afford to take cases to extant civil courts. The article, "Small Claims Court: Reform Revisited," reprinted here, traces the history of these courts and suggests the extent to which they have been successful in bringing justice to the poor.

The small claims court was an attempt to provide legal resolution to minor contract disputes in a setting that did away with the delays of a jury trial and the cumbersome procedural and evidentiary requirements. As such, it parallels Weber's concept of *kadi* justice. This form is found in primitive societies where a wise elder or kadi in the community dispenses justice without apparent procedural controls. Something akin to "individualized justice" may accrue:

> The kadi does not really render his decisions without any reference to rules or norms. He operates with an extremely wide frame of relevance in which, in principle, everything matters. . . . [However], the kadi *seems* to render decisions without reference to rules or norms and is engaged in what *appears to be* a completely free evaluation of the particular merits of each case [Matza, 1964:118–19].

[5] It is an interesting empirical question as to whether injustice is present prior to the accused being brought into the formal control network or whether the processing experiences generate the sense of unfairness. A third possibility is that injustice is not really sensed or developed until the deviant is placed in a total institution charged with rehabilitation. Unfortunately little empirical work has been done on the question. One recent study of boys sentenced to a reformatory by the juvenile court found that the sense of injustice was low. The majority of boys felt that their dispositions were justified (Baum and Wheeler, 1968:171). For an attempt to theoretically link concepts of processing stereotypes and sense of injustice to labeling effects, see Hawkins and Tiedeman, 1975.

In this nonlateral, nonlongitudinal control agency, the mystification which accompanies most court proceedings is reduced, and the processing stereotypes which affect cases where many control agents have an input should also have less impact in case disposition. Consequently, the sense of injustice should be reduced relative to that encountered in other courts, especially criminal courts. This of course assumes that other problems can be resolved, such as the domination of the small claims courts by businesses that use the facilities for collection-agency functions, and the resultant disadvantage of the naïve indigent person, unskilled and inexperienced in the ways of the court, confronting trained, experienced business agents (Carlin et al., 1967:36).

Another sense of injustice derives from laws which are seen as unfair or unjust. One way in which unpopular laws may be countered is through jury nullification. Nullification [6] refers to an acquittal based on rejection of the rule of law, rather than on fact, i.e., facts may clearly show guilt, or the defendant may admit to committing an act, but the jury acquits due to disagreement on the law. This topic is of interest because it highlights questions about the functions of juries in the application of the law, and how the jury might serve as a legitimate and controlled forum where the conflicting value orientations in society are played out. Kadish and Kadish, in an article included here, provide a brief historical review of the status of jury nullification and show how this concept forces a more explicit accounting of the role of jurors in our system of justice.

William Kunstler, a vocal advocate of jury nullification, states that the basic argument involved is deceptively simple

> . . . because the jury is ideally a representative cross section of the community, it ought to be able to acquit a defendant who admits the commission of certain formally illegal acts, the commission of which the community, represented by the jury, approves. The major difficulty with this approach is that jurors, almost without exception, have no idea of the extent of their power in this respect, and under recent case law, they cannot be enlightened as to this power [Kunstler, 1969:71].

In this conception, the jury stands between the law and the defendant, and thus jury review, as well as judicial review of the law, offers some protection against arbitrary or despotic acts of the state (Mirkin, 1973:69). In the words of one observer, "the jury stands between the will of the state and the will of the people as the last bastion in law to avoid the barricades in the street. To a large extent, the jury gives the judicial system a legitimacy it would otherwise not possess" (Scheflin, 1972:182).

As Kunstler points out, its use is problematic because jurors do not know the principle of ruling on the law as well as the facts, and most states prohibit

---

6 Hung juries may result because some members refuse to convict based on a rejection of the law, while all may be in agreement on questions of fact. This outcome might be termed partial nullification since the defendant may be retried. For a discussion of how hung jury outcomes may be classified as partial nullification, see Kadish and Kadish, *supra*.

attorneys from bringing up this point. Indeed only two states, Maryland and Indiana, provide for judicial instructions to the jury which mentions this principle (Scheflin, 1972). Jury nullification, on the whole, has little affect on the law's application since most criminal offenses never get to trial; when it does occur, it is case related, and thus does not directly rectify bad laws. It is through a series of jury nullifications that legislators may rewrite or remove a statute. Thus failure of juries to convict marihuana users in those states with high penalties probably contributed to the lessening of criminal sanctions for using this drug. However, the jury may play a supplementary but increasingly influential role in the interrelationship of law and society.

REFERENCES

BAUM, MARTHA and STANTON WHEELER, 1968. "Becoming an Inmate," in Stanton Wheeler, ed., *Controlling Delinquents*. New York: John Wiley and Sons.

BITTNER, EGON, 1967. "Police Discretion in Emergency Apprehension of Mentally Ill Persons," *Social Problems,* **14** (Winter):278–92.

BLUMBERG, ABRAHAM S., 1967. "The Practice of Law as Confidence Game; Organizational Cooptation of a Profession," *Law and Society Review,* **1** (June):15:39.

CAMPBELL, JAMES S., JOSEPH R. SAHID, and DAVID P. STANG, 1970. *Law and Order Reconsidered: A Staff Report to the National Commission on the Causes and Prevention of Violence*. New York: Bantam Books.

CALDWELL, ROBERT G., and JAMES A. BLACK, 1971. *Juvenile Delinquency*. New York: Ronald Press.

CARLIN, JEROME E., JAN HOWARD, and SHELDON L. MESSINGER, 1967. *Civil Justice and the Poor: Issues for Sociological Research*. New York: Russell Sage Foundation.

CICOUREL, AARON V., 1964. *Method and Measurement*. New York: The Free Press; 1968, *The Social Organization of Juvenile Justice*. New York: John Wiley and Sons.

EMERSON, ROBERT, 1969. *Judging Delinquents*. Chicago: Aldine Publishing Company.

ERIKSON, KAI T., 1964. "Notes on the Sociology of Deviance," in Howard S. Becker, ed., *The Other Side*. New York: The Free Press.

FREIDSON, ELIOT, 1966. "Disability as Social Deviance," in Marvin B. Sussman, ed., *Sociology and Rehabilitation*. Washington, D.C.: American Sociological Association; 1967, "Health Factories, the New Industrial Sociology," *Social Problems,* **14** (Spring):493–500.

GARFINKEL, HAROLD, 1956. "Conditions of Successful Degradation Ceremonies," *American Journal of Sociology,* **61** (March):420–24; 1967, *Studies in Ethnomethodology*. Englewood Cliffs: Prentice-Hall.

GOFFMAN, ERVING, 1961. *Asylums*. New York: Doubleday-Anchor.

HAUREK, EDWIN W. and JOHN P. CLARK, 1967. "Variants of Integration of Social Control Agencies," *Social Problems,* **15** (Summer):46:60.

HAWKINS, RICHARD and GARY TIEDEMAN, 1975. *The Creation of Deviance: Interpersonal and Organizational Determinants*. Columbus, Ohio: Charles E. Merrill Publishing Co.

KADISH, MORTIMER R. and SANFORD H. KADISH, 1971. "The Institutionalization of Conflict: Jury Acquittals," *Journal of Social Issues,* **27**:199–217.

KUNSTLER, WILLIAM M., 1969. "Jury Nullification in Conscience Cases," *Virginia Journal of International Law,* **10** (December):71–84.

LEFTON, MARK, 1970. "Client Characteristics and Structural Outcomes," in William R. Rosengren and Mark Lefton, eds., *Organizations and Clients*. Columbus, Ohio: Merrill Publishing Company.

LEFTON, MARK and WILLIAM R. ROSENGREN, 1966. "Organizations and Clients: Lateral and Longitudinal Dimensions." *American Sociological Review*, 31 (December): 802–10.

LEMERT, EDWIN M., 1951. *Social Pathology*. New York: McGraw-Hill Book Company; 1967, "The Juvenile Court-Quest and Realities," in The President's Commission on Law Enforcement and Administration of Justice, Task Force Report: Juvenile Delinquency and Youth Crime. Washington, D.C.: U.S. Government Printing Office.

LITWAK, EUGENE, 1970. "Towards the Theory and Practice of Coordination between Formal Organizations," in William R. Rosengren and Mark Lefton, eds., *Organizations and Clients*. Columbus, Ohio: Merrill Publishing Company.

MATZA, DAVID, 1964. *Delinquency and Drift*. New York: John Wiley and Sons.

MILLER, WALTER B., R. C. BAUM, and R. McNEIL, 1968. "Delinquency Prevention and Organizational Relations," in Stanton Wheeler, ed., *Controlling Delinquents*. New York: John Wiley and Sons.

MIRKIN, HARRIS G., 1973. "Judicial Review, Jury Review and the Right of Revolution against Despotism," *Polity*, 6 (Fall):36–70.

NEWMAN, DONALD J., 1966. *Conviction: The Determination of Guilt or Innocence without Trial*. Boston: Little, Brown.

PARSONS, TALCOTT, 1951. *The Social System*. New York: The Free Press.

PHILLIPS, DEREK L., 1963. "Rejection: A Possible Consequence of Seeking Help for Mental Disorders," *American Sociological Review*, 28 (December):963–72.

PITTMAN, DAVID J. and DUFF G. GILLESPIE, 1967. "Social Policy and Deviancy Reinforcement: The Case of the Public Intoxication Offender," in David J. Pittman, ed., *Alcoholism*. New York: Harper and Row.

PLATT, ANTHONY, 1969a. *The Child Savers: The Invention of Delinquency*. Chicago: University of Chicago Press; 1969b, "The Rise of the Child-Saving Movement: A Study in Social Policy and Correctional Reform," *Annals*, 381 (January): 21-34.

POUND, ROSCOE, 1913. "The Administration of Justice in the Modern City," *Harvard Law Review*, 26:302–18.

PRESIDENT'S COMMISSION LAW ENFORCEMENT AND ADMINISTRATION OF JUSTICE, 1967. *Task Force Report: The Courts*. "Disposition without Trial." Washington, D.C.: U.S. Government Printing Office, pp. 4–13.

ROSENGREN, WILLIAM R., 1970. "The Careers of Clients and Organizations," in William R. Rosengren and Mark Lefton, eds., *Organizations and Clients*. Columbus, Ohio: Merrill Publishing Company.

ROSS, H. LAWRENCE, 1970. *Settled Out of Court*. Chicago: Aldine Publishing Company.

ROTH, JULIUS A., 1963. *Timetables: Structuring the Passage of Time in Hospital Treatment and Other Careers*. Indianapolis: Bobbs-Merrill Company.

SCHEFF, THOMAS J., 1964. "The Societal Reaction to Deviance: Ascriptive Elements in the Psychiatric Screening of Mental Patients in a Midwestern State," *Social Problems*, 11 (Spring):401–14; 1966, *Being Mentally Ill*. Chicago: Aldine Publishing Company; 1967, *Mental Illness and Social Processes*. New York: Harper and Row, Publishers.

SCHEFLIN, ALAN W., 1972. "Jury Nullification: The Right To Say No," *Southern California Law Review*, 45:168–226.

SCHWARTZ, RICHARD D., and JEROME SKOLNICK, 1964. "Two Studies of Legal Stigma," in Howard S. Becker, ed., *The Other Side*. New York: The Free Press.

SCOTT, ROBERT A., 1970. "The Construction of Conceptions of Stigma by Professional

Experts," in Jack D. Douglas, ed., *Deviance and Respectibility*. New York: Basic Books.

SKOLNICK, JEROME H., 1966. *Justice without Trial*. New York: John Wiley and Sons, Inc.; 1967, "Social Control in the Adversary System," *Journal of Conflict Resolution,* 11 (March):52–70.

STOLL, CLARICE S., 1968. "Images of Man and Social Control," *Social Forces,* 47 (December):119–35.

SUDNOW, DAVID, 1965. "Normal Crimes: Sociological Features of the Penal Code in a Public Defender Office," *Social Problems,* 12 (Winter):255–76.

TEELE, JAMES E. and SOL LEVINE, 1968. "The Acceptance of Emotionally Disturbed Children by Psychiatric Agencies," in Stanton Wheeler, ed., *Controlling Delinquents*. New York: John Wiley and Sons.

WHEELER, STANTON, E. BONACHICH, M. R. CRAMER, and I. K. ZOLA, 1968. "Agents of Delinquency Control," in Stanton Wheeler, ed., *Controlling Delinquents*. New York: John Wiley and Sons.

Clarice S. Stoll

In everyday conversation about others' behavior one hears such statements as "he couldn't help himself" or "he knew what he was doing." The speaker makes reference to another's behavior in terms of the imputed control or self-determination other has over his behavior. The imputation of control relates to the speaker's notions of causality in human behavior. To postulate that one can "help one's self" is to assume that individuals can will their actions.

Furthermore, lay notions of causality serve as one basis for developing an evaluation of others. There is a tendency to connect self-determination with moral responsibility. The delinquent who "knew what he was doing" is judged blameworthy and deserving of punishment. However, the hysteric who "couldn't help himself" is judged guiltless and immune from castigation (though not from all societal intervention). Hence the self-willed deviant is morally reprehensible, while the unintentional wrongdoer is merely unattractive.[1]

Observations that people do judge others partly on the basis of some lay theory of behavior has led several theorists —Mead, Aubert and Messinger, Parsons— to develop hypotheses relevant for understanding the process of social control.[2] The propositions which result lead to a model of social control for the purpose of studying, first, sources of strain in any social control network which are the consequence of discrepancies in the ideologies held by various control agents; second, for identifying critical points in the career of a deviant as he is exposed to both the ideologies and behavior of control agents. Such a model is applicable for both ideal-typical comparison of various social control networks or deviant careers and predictions of change in actual social control processes.

POSTULATES

In his essay on punitive justice Mead describes how hostility is a natural reaction to crime, not because crime is physically damaging, but because it attacks the values society cherishes.[3] Reiterating Durkheim, he states that public hostility passes over into self-assertions which are functional instead of destructive. Punitive attitudes further serve to "crush" the criminal, isolate him from the rest of society, and as a result, paralyze society's good intentions of reform.

Mead's unique contribution is to distinguish that parts of a population are more

Reprinted from *Social Forces,* **47** (December, 1968), pp. 119-27, by permission of the author and the University of North Carolina Press.

Colin J. Williams and Paul McFarlane made important contributions to the preparation of this paper.

1 The distinction between voluntary and involuntary deviance is not the only basis upon which laymen define someone as a particular type of deviant. As Lemert has discussed, such factors as the frequency, visibility, or degree of injury shape the observer's redefinition of the nonconformist. One interesting question is the manner in which these situational variables pattern themselves such that the observer concludes that the deviant is behaving either involuntarily or self-consciously. For example, is there a point beyond which frequent, visible promiscuity leads an observer to decide that the deviant is "neurotic?"

2 George H. Mead, "The Psychology of Punitive Justice," *American Journal of Sociology,* 23 (1918), pp. 577–602; Vilhelm Aubert and Sheldon Messinger, "The Criminal and the Sick," *Inquiry,* 1 (1958), pp. 137–60; and Talcott Parsons, "Definitions of Health and Illness in the Light of American Values and Social Structure," in *Social Culture and Personality* (New York: The Free Press, 1964).

3 Mead, *op. cit.,* p. 581 ff.

punitive than others. He observed that sociology had influenced certain segments of the population to seek to understand criminals as victims of social and psychological conditions beyond their control. Social workers in particular had adopted this perspective and developed a sympathetic view toward the treatment of criminals. Others involved in the legal process, however, affirmed the responsibility of the criminal for his own fate. Mead concludes that an irreconcilable contradiction exists in the structure of controls for treating criminals. "The social worker in the court is the sentimentalist, and the legalist in the social settlement, in spite of his learned doctrine, is the ignoramus." [4]

Thus Mead proposes that an individual's ideology of deviant behavior is one determinant of preferences for controlling the deviant.[5] In his own illustration, Mead shows how individuals' occupations serve to provide images of man or lay theories of behavior.[6] To the social worker the criminal is a patient; to the lawyer, a self-conscious law breaker. The social worker wants to treat the criminal; the lawyer, punish him.

Aubert and Messinger assert similarly that variations in preferences for controlling deviants can be predicted from individuals' assumptions as to the cause of nonconformity.[7] Those who hold deviance to be the result of conscious defiance of rules (the "wickedness" assumption) will

expect deviants to be punished. Those who view the nonconformity as the result of external forces (the "sickness" assumption) will prefer that deviants be assisted in a return to a normal state, but without accompanying chastisement. As with Mead, Aubert and Messinger recognize that there may be conflict within the society as to the nature of a particular form of deviance.

Parsons has proposed that one important dimension for classifying the major forms of deviance is whether society holds the deviant to be responsible for his behavior or not. He has stated that illness is distinguishable from other types of nonconformity in that the sick person is not held responsible for his behavior because he did not will his action. Furthermore, *within* the major types—illness, sin, disloyalty, crime—there may be exceptions to the general definition. For example, there are illnesses in some primitive societies which are held to be the fault of the victim.[8]

Implicit in these theoretical discussions is a set of postulates concerning the style and effectiveness of social control with respect to any chosen type of deviance. The core concept for the analysis is the social control agents' image of man with respect to their belief about the ability of individuals to control their own destiny. Furthermore, Mead observes that occupations related to meeting problems of social control (sometimes known as "people-work") are likely to have a formalized ideology of human behavior which is a basis for the expression of the occupational role requirements. Simply put, theory guides practice. In more specific form the first postulate takes two interpretations: [9]

[4] *Ibid.*, p. 592.

[5] Mead also suggests that social status and punitiveness are inversely related. "The man who has achieved an economic, a legal, or any social triumph does not feel the impulse to physically annihilate his opponent, and ultimately the mere sense of security of his social position may rob the stimulus to attack of all its power." *Ibid.*, p. 581.

[6] For an analysis of conflict among occupational groups derived from the different ideologies of behavior each occupation provides, see Charles Y. Glock and Rodney Stark, "Religion and the Social Sciences: Images of Man in Conflict," in *Religion and Society in Tension* (Chicago: Rand McNally & Co., 1965).

[7] Aubert and Messinger, *op. cit., passim.*

[8] And whereas most sin is treated to be within the responsibility of the individual sinner, original sin is viewed as something inherent in the human condition. Parsons, *op. cit.*, pp. 270–273.

[9] Freidson has added a second dimension to ideologies of deviance: imputed prognosis, whether the deviant is believed to be curable or not.

1A. *To the extent that individuals believe nonconformity to be conscious defiance of rules (or are voluntarists, hold "wickedness" assumptions), then they will prefer to restrict and castigate deviants.*

1B. *To the extent that individuals believe nonconformity to be the result of external forces (or are determinists, hold "sickness" assumptions), then they will prefer to treat or cure deviants without accompanying opprobrium.*

Studies in diverse populations with respect to various types of deviance offer data in support of both interpretations.[10] For example, Nettler found that child care agents who held deterministic theories of human behavior were less punitive toward problem children.[11] Accordingly, in a study of public acceptance of the alcoholic, Mulford and Miller related definitions of the alcoholic as sick (in contrast to morally weak) with faith in medical therapy for alcoholism.[12] Less direct evidence exists in the studies which relate the ideologies of mental hospital staff personnel to custodial modes of role performance.[13] Finally, an investigation of college rule violations found that students with voluntaristic assumptions concerning the nature of adolescent deviance were supportive of university punitive policies toward thieves and cheats. Those students who held positivistic assumptions did not wish any intervention on the part of the university toward rule breakers.[14]

Parenthetically, there are some provocative social-psychological questions tacit in this approach to social behavior. The proposition that causal assumptions will shape social control preferences is part of a more general axiom in sociology that individuals interact with others partly on the basis of expectations as to how people behave.[15] One is led to ask to what extent such expectations or lay theories of behavior are congruent with various scientific stances. Are there individuals who behave on an economic model, as though others are calculating their rewards and costs; or, on a deterministic model, that others' behavior is somehow fated; or, on a psychoanalytic model, that others really mean other than they show on the surface; or, that life is a zero-sum game and all others are competitors?[16] Note that the

---

Curable types of deviance in which the deviant is held to be responsible for his behavior will result in limited punishment, while hopeless cases would bring permanent incarceration, execution, or banishment. In cases where the deviant is not held to be responsible, yet curable, there will be education or therapy; if not responsible, yet hopeless to change, there will be protective custody.

This analysis suggests two more hypotheses in accord with Postulate 1:

1C. *To the extent that a deviant is perceived to be curable, there will be a preference for intense rehabilitative efforts.*

1D. *To the extent that a deviant is perceived to be incapable of change, there will be a preference for permanent isolation of the deviant from society.*

See "Disability as Deviance" in *Sociology and Rehabilitation* (American Sociological Association, n.d.), pp. 71–99.

[10] No statement can be made to the probable size of the relation between ideology of deviance and preference for social control.

[11] Gwynn Nettler, "Cruelty, Dignity, and Determinism," *American Sociological Review*, 24 (1959), pp. 375–384.

[12] Harold A. Mulford and Donald E. Miller, "Public Acceptance of the Alcoholic as Sick," *Quarterly Journal of Alcohol Studies*, 25 (1964), pp. 314–324.

[13] For a discussion of this literature, see Sten Johansson, "Custodialism Among Mental Hospital Personnel," *Acta Sociologica*, 10 (1967), pp. 288–306.

[14] "Thieves, Cheats and Slovens: The Social Psychology of Social Control," unpublished Ph.D. dissertation, Rutgers University, 1966. The relationships held controlling for the respondent's support of the norms being violated. For example, voluntarists were more likely to be punitive toward thieves even if they themselves were thieves.

[15] For example, see Hans Zetterberg, "Compliant Actions," *Acta Sociologica*, 22 (1957), pp. 179–201.

[16] It is noteworthy that we are discussing theories as to how others are perceived to behave, not assumptions as to one's own behavior. It seems unlikely that all but the most extreme positivists do not believe that they have *some* control over their own destiny. One can similarly imagine an

few models mentioned here cannot be distinguished solely on the basis of their causal assumptions. Thus a second problem is to identify the major dimensions of images of man, whether lay or scientific, other than the imputation of causality.

Returning to the topic of social control, the second postulate is implicit in Mead's analysis of social work and legalist attitudes toward the criminal.

2. *To the degree that there are contradictions in ideologies of deviance between agents of control and no institutionalized means for coping with the contradiction, then there will be strains in the social control network.*

Such strains may be points around which social change occurs, either out of the direct confrontation of conflicting agents, or through latent effects of the contradictions upon the participants in the process. The discussion below will detail several ways in which change is likely to take shape.

The third postulate relates to the effects of conflicting ideologies upon the deviant who is exposed to various agents as he travels through the control network.

3. *To the degree that the nonconformist is exposed to discrepant definitions of his deviance, some personal adaptations will result, such adaptations having implications for his apprehension, disposition, and rehabilitation.*

In other words, conflicting ideologies of deviance place the deviant in role strain.[17] The deviant may opt for one set of definitions over another, attempt to satisfy competing demands as well as possible, or develop a wholly idiosyncratic set of ex-

pectations for himself. The particular adaptation will depend upon such circumstances as the legitimacy of competing agents, the availability of deviant peer support, degree of isolation from normals. We shall now examine the way in which role strain may be structured for various deviant career types.

THE SOCIAL CONTROL NETWORK

The utility of the postulates is enhanced by referral to a model of social control networks. This model facilitates comparative analysis of types of deviance and assists in uncovering exceptions to the propositions.

Freidson has suggested that it is not impractically inaccurate to schematize the career of the deviant by reference to the agents he runs afoul of. Such a career may be imagined as a progression through segments of a complicated maze with many entrances and exits, and with a number of different labyrinths. On the paths stand the agents of social control who assume responsibility for holding or sending on the wayfarer.[18]

Starting with Freidson's conceptualization it is possible to build a general model of social control networks by classifying the various agents by function, thus reducing the maze to three segments or labyrinths. First are the agents of *detection and surveillance,* who may be informal, as a victim who reports a crime, or formal, as the policeman who apprehends a criminal suspect. Second are the agents of *diagnosis and disposition,* who judge upon the validity of detection agents' assumptions that a deviant is at hand and who formulate future course of treatment for the individual. Finally, there are agents of *rehabilitation,* who can assume that the individual is deviant and work to return him to a state of performing in society with as much a normal manner as possible. The

---

individual believing that his own life is fated, yet others have freedom to act.

17 The types of adaptations, the conditions under which they will occur, and consequences for deviant rehabilitation are discussed in the writer's "Solutions of Role Strain and the Deviant Career" (mimeo).

18 Freidson, *op. cit.,* p. 90.

custodial as well as therapeutic staff of institutions are included in this category.

If, next, one identifies the control agents as to their ideologies of deviance, it is possible to note at once two types of discrepancies in the control network. *Lateral* discrepancies occur where more than one agent is present in a segment of the maze, with such agents holding different definitions of the deviant. *Longitudinal* discrepancies are present wherever the deviant is exposed to differing definitions of his role as he progresses from one stage to another. A prevalent form of lateral discrepancy is in the total institutional settings where custodial and therapeutic staff typically disagree as to the nature of the deviant under treatment. A longitudinal discrepancy occurs when a mentally-ill person is diagnosed and referred by a doctor to a restrictive state institution.

In comparing the control networks for major types of deviance, several distinguishing characteristics are apparent. First, the number of individuals or roles which meet the three functions can be one or many. Simply in listing the roles or individuals composing the control networks suggests a basis for scaling deviance in terms of the complexity of the deviant careers. By implication, the individual's ability to travel through the network in a manner free from strain of transition will vary. For example, the detection, diagnosis, and rehabilitation in the case of sin will all be met by one's self for members of the most protesting Protestant religions.[19] In the case of crime, there is almost a score of participants. Police, by-standers, victims detect the deviant; lawyers, judges, social workers are involved in the allocation process; guards, occupational counselors, therapists, probation officers and others are sources of rehabilitation. Even given an ideal case where all agents agree as to the definition of the deviant in terms of imputed responsibility, the fact that numerous individual role players and occupational groups participate in the network suggests the presence of strains in the system.

Another distinguishing characteristic of control networks is the degree of consensus as to the definition of deviance. The many agents who detect and diagnose physical ailments are in agreement that the deviant is not responsible for his disabled state, that he is curable, and that he deserves treatment. This agreement would include the doctor diagnosing a tumor, the surgeon removing it, the nurses who handle the patient, and the therapists who assist in rehabilitation.[20] In contrast, the ideologies of agents who control crime contradict one another. The criminal, through access to subculture ideology, denies his responsibility. The police define the crime as deliberate defiance of law; the social worker does not. The police want to punish the criminal; the social worker, treat him. The criminal wants no reaction from control agents at all. Clearly the potential for role strain is less for the nonconformist with a physical ailment than for the criminal.

According to the postulates discussed we should be able to make several deductions utilizing the model of the social control network as described. First, given the ideologies of each of the control agents, we would predict the form of treatment or style of handling a deviant faces at any

---

19 Even when a formal agent is introduced, as a confessor, the very privacy of the confession act, the certain removal of "blemishes" of sin through penance, suggests that sinning is the best of all deviance. This would be true not only in terms of its forbidden rewards, but also for its certain, relatively painless cure. Perhaps this is why the scope of behaviors included as sins is so vast: no one can avoid not being a sinner for a very long period of time.

20 Conflicting definitions of deviance in this instance, if any, would be likely between the family or friends related to the deviant and the therapeutic agents. The discrepancy will be with respect to the degree of curability rather than the degree of responsibility to be attached to the patient for his illness.

stage in his career. Next, by focusing upon discrepancies in ideologies among control agents, we would be able to locate potential sources of change in the system of controls, taking into account the interaction and accommodation of agents with one another. Finally, we are led to ask how a particular patterning of ideologies presents problems for the deviant who is exposed to this sequence of demands, especially with regard to his eventual rehabilitation.

In actual application of the model and postulates, however, certain empirical deviations occur. For example, there are cases where knowledge of an agent's ideology of deviance does not predict well his style of acting toward a deviant. A catalogue of these deviations from our predictions forms a list of specifications of the postulates, or, in other words, defines the scope of the predictions. The remainder of the paper will address two applications of the framework: a catalogue of cases when theory does not predict reality; some conditions under which conflicting ideologies may lead to change in the structure or functioning of controls.

WHEN THEORY DOESN'T GUIDE PRACTICE

To say that control agents' definitions of deviance shape their style of acting toward deviants assumes that occupational groups can in fact be characterized as having a basic ideology with respect to the deviant being treated. But it is not always the case that knowledgeable observers might agree that there is an occupational ideology, say, among judges, toward a certain crime, such as homosexuality. It seems likely that consensus within an occupation would be least for those types of deviance at the margins of the so-called pure types (crime, sin, illness, disloyalty). Included in the marginal types of deviance are mental illness, addictive diseases, sexual abnormalities.

The absence of an ideology raises ques-

tions as to the relationships among occupations of social control. Would the judge passing sentence on the homosexual, lacking an occupational ideology for his decision, refer to other occupational ideologies, or would he use his own personal ideology of homosexuality? If he does refer to another expert ideology, which would hold sway: the psychiatric view that the deviate is sick or the psychological view that homosexuality is a learned response?

A second reason for failing to find consensus as to the nature of deviance within an occupational grouping would be a function of the occupation itself. Especially relevant here are the ancillary therapeutic professions in mental hospitals and prisons: recreational therapists, occupational therapists, work counselors. Training for these occupations centers upon technical skills (e.g., how to recreate) rather than upon the therapeutic effects of the activities. Such therapists will be exposed to conflicting ideologies in the institutions: the restrictive ethic of lower echelon staff and the therapeutic orientation of administration. Given the professional aspirations of these new occupations, along with the status similarity of their members to the administrative staff, it is probable that these occupations will in time develop positivistic, therapeutic orientations toward their clients.

The problem of identifying the ideological position of any occupational group presents, of course, problems only for ideal-typical analysis of social control networks. In the study of a particular jurisdiction, presumably one would be able to measure the attitudes of each of the control agents toward the deviants they treat. Assuming then that agents can be assigned a score on positivism-permissiveness or voluntarism-restrictiveness, why shouldn't we be able to predict fully the control agent's behavior from his theory?

One possibility is that the ideology is purely rhetoric, a device for making an impression.[21] Some observers have questioned whether much that is held to go on in mental hospitals is in fact rhetoric. They suggest that many practices are labeled as therapeutic when in fact they are restrictive and punitive.[22]

Secondly, the ideology may prescribe actions not within the agent's opportunities for implementation. The case of social workers in our largest cities is notable here. Excessive bureaucratic demands obviate the possibility of usefully assisting the client. In some agencies demands force the social worker to treat the client, contrary to his own convictions, in an impersonal manner.

Another possibility is that occupations differ in the degree to which they are (or believe themselves to be) held responsible or accountable for errors in their judgment. As a result of the recent Supreme Court decision concerning the rights of the accused, police may be less likely today to revert to certain illegal, punitive practices in handling some types of criminals, such as sex deviates. In order to let their occupational or personal attitudes toward the deviate be fulfilled, the police must now defer to the other agents of control who are (and have always been) the legitimate agents of diagnosis and disposition.

Furthermore, the occupations are not in segregated, closed systems, notably at the rehabilitation stage. Here the protective and therapeutic agents are often part of a bureacracy, with the occupations form-

ing a status hierarchy. In one case known to the writer, the custodially-oriented head nurse of a diagnostic ward was stymied in expressing her strong convictions by the ward administrator, a psychiatrist. (She later resigned and was replaced by a therapeutively-oriented nurse.)

To summarize, it is proposed that the best theoretical intentions may be led astray in practice whenever the propounded ideology is rhetoric, when opportunities to implement theoretical guidelines are not available, or when accommodations must be made with others who are also managing the deviant.

Discrepancies between stated beliefs and practices can have an insidious effect upon the career of the deviant. If recognized, the deviant may interpret the agent's behavior as hypocrisy. In Matza's analysis of the delinquent career, the delinquent's perception of social workers, police, and judges as hypocrites is shown to nurture a sense of injustice, which further neutralizes delinquent behavior.[23]

IDEOLOGY AND CHANGE

The second postulate states that conflicting ideologies among control agents will produce strains in the social control network. Such strains may be one focus point for social change. The fact that there are *not* conflicting ideologies does not indicate the absence of strains, of course.

As was noted above, there are instances where an ideology is *not* converted into practice. One agent, a judge, may act upon the basis of another's rhetoric, the prison warden's, in deciding how to sentence some type of criminal. The judge may send the man to prison, on the belief that there are special facilities for rehabilitating the criminal. Strains exist in two ways. The deviant moves from court to prison only to learn that special facilities are not

21 The distinction between rhetoric and ideology was brought out by Donald W. Ball, "The conceptual difference between the two is that rhetoric speaks to communication, both style and content, while ideology refers to perception and justification in terms of the ideologue's conception of the relevant portions of the world. It is quite conceivable that individual actors will utilize a rhetoric without any ideological convictions as regards its validity, but with a recognition of its pragmatic efficacy . . . ," footnote 6 in "An Abortion Clinic Ethnography," *Social Problems*, 14 (1967), pp. 293–301.

22 For example, Erving Goffman, *Asylums* (New York: Doubleday & Co., 1961).

23 David Matza, *Delinquency and Drift* (New York: John Wiley & Sons, 1964).

what they were stated to be. In addition, there is a possibility that in acting on the basis of the warden's rhetoric and sending the man to prison, the judge placed the criminal in a less rehabilitative situation than parole would offer.

Another instance where agreement in ideologies may lead to strains is when agents argue over the contribution each should make in handling the deviant. Psychiatric social workers and psychiatrists are of one accord on the definition of mental illness, but the social workers want greater autonomy in their work. In particular they would like to perform tasks such as lead group therapy sessions in hospitals.

If there are differences in ideology among control agents, they seem more likely to appear at the final, most problematic, stage, the rehabilitation stage, of the control process. Discrepancies are probably least likely at the disposition stage, where one agent has authority to make the final decision as to the course of treatment for the deviant. If other agents are present at this stage, they are there to provide diagnostic evidence. The doctor and referee physicians, the judge and court lawyers, the psychiatrists and clinical psychologists, each agree as to the definition of cases to be disposed. (Disagreements will arise not over the nature of deviance, but over whether the individual at hand is a deviant and in need of treatment.)

At the detection stage ideological disagreement may occur between the informal agents who refer a suspected deviant and the formal agents: the bystander to a crime and the police; the family of a mentally-ill woman and the psychiatrist. Lack of agreement has implications for the entry of the deviant into the formal control network. Thus many neighborhoods have their "village idiots," pathologically-behaving people who are felt to be strange, not sick, and thus never receive medical treatment.

At the rehabilitation stage, conflict in ideologies among agents who treat or protect the deviant is a typical characteristic of total institutions and social agencies. Hence one would expect more changes in the rehabilitation than detection and disposition practices. There are several ways in which occupational groups resolve their conflicts, often with implications for the treatment of the deviant.

Sometimes change occurs through the relations and adaptations of professional organizations with one another. The most effective changes occur through legislation supported by professional group lobbies. For example, psychiatric-interest groups have been successful in redefining the definition of the sexual criminal so as to make him available for treatment rather than punitive incarceration.

Within particular institutions a compromise ideology may be sought among conflicting agents. Glaser has described one method of prison reform in which custodial and therapeutic staff are forced to interact frequently over cell block problems. Over time a new ideology develops, one which encompasses both custodial and therapeutic goals.[24]

Another solution is for agents to agree to disagree. In other words, a pluralistic consensus is reached, based upon the division of labor in the organization.[25] The guards control and punish; the psychologist gives weekly therapy sessions. Each agrees not to interfere with the other in order to keep the institution running smoothly.

DISCUSSION

The customary approach to the study of deviance and social control has been to focus upon characteristics of the deviant.

[24] Daniel Glaser, *The Effectiveness of a Prison and Parole System* (Indianapolis: Bobbs-Merrill Co., 1965).
[25] For varieties of consensus, see Thomas J. Scheff, "Toward a Sociological Model of Consensus," *American Sociological Review*, 32 (1967), pp. 32–46.

As one result specialties have formed along the commonsense lines found in society, giving rise to criminology and medical sociology. There has been little formal interchange between these specialties. Except for the approach supplied by Lemert,[26] there is little conceptualization on a level to include both illness and motivated deviance. Goffman's work on total institutions is a rare attempt toward the study of the organization of social controls, be they medical, penal, or religious.[27]

This paper presents another attempt to integrate knowledge of deviance and social control as to crosscut traditional boundaries. The basis of the approach is a model of the social control network as it consists of the sequence of potential agents who manage a deviant. Such a model has several advantages: (1) it is applicable for all types of deviance; (2) it provides a dynamic perspective to problems, (3) it provokes questions not only as to the structure and functioning of controls on the system level, but also as to the effects of system organization upon the individual participants.[28]

In the present paper the model was used to examine the scope of one theory of social control. The theory states that by identifying control agents as to their ideologies of deviance one can predict the style of their behavior toward deviants, locate sources of strain in the control network, and identify points of role strain in a deviant career. Applications of the model led to some qualifications of the propositions.

The illustrations here point to but a few of the applications of the model as accompanied by this particular theory. It might be fruitful to apply model and theory in a similar manner for study of the utilization of medical facilities (by comparing the fit between public and medical ideologies of illnesses); normative change (by examining how ideologies of deviance change as a result of the resolution of conflict between control agents); the stratification relationships of occupational groups (through observing the resolutions of conflict, the attempts of groups to influence one another, and the aspirations of one group to the status of another).

The model of a social control network in itself is a means of scaling the complexity of deviant careers. Furthermore, while the present analysis identifies control agents as to their images of the deviant, conceivably one could identify them on other relevant dimensions. For example, scaling the agents as to degree of professionalism raises questions as to strains in the control network related to work style, social status, and educational background of the agents. And given the status or educational level of the typical deviant, one can investigate the interactions between him and each agent, drawing conclusions as to the probable success of social control. Finally, both the model and the theory relating images of man to social control are applicable for comparative analysis of major forms of deviance, such as illness and crime. Similar attempts to discover conceptualizations at this level of generality will provide more meaning to the mass of empirical findings in criminology and medical sociology.

26 Edwin Lemert, *Human Deviance, Social Problems, and Social Control* (Englewood Cliffs, New Jersey: Prentice-Hall, 1967).

27 *Ibid.*, chap. 1.

28 Haurek and Clark's study of interaction patterns of social control agents implicitly applies the approach presented in this paper with respect to the integration of the social control system. Their study locates malintegration in control networks related to the ideological split between punitive and welfare orientations. The theory presented here would further suggest that the areas of malintegration located by Haurek and Clark may provoke role strain upon the deviant traveling through the system. See Edward W. Haurek and John P. Clark, "Variants of Integration of Social Control Agencies," *Social Problems*, 15 (1967), pp. 46–60.

Much of the basic legal structure of the criminal process rests on the assumption that criminal cases initiated by the police will be decided in a trial by court or by jury. Limited statistical data and a number of studies, including those recently conducted by the American Bar Foundation,[1] by the Commission staff, and by others,[2] indicate that this assumption is not justified.

Most cases are disposed of outside the traditional trial process, either by a decision not to charge a suspect with a criminal offense or by a plea of guilty. In many communities between one-third and one-half of the cases begun by arrest are disposed of by some form of dismissal by police, prosecutor, or judge.[3] When a decision is made to prosecute, it is estimated that in many courts as many as 90 percent

From The President's Commission on Law Enforcement and Administration of Justice, *Task Force Report: The Courts* (Washington, D.C.: U.S. Government Printing Office, 1967), pp. 4–13.

[1] The history of the American Bar Foundation Project, which commenced in 1953, is recounted in LaFave, *Arrest—the Decision to Take a Suspect Into Custody,* ix (1965). The discussion that follows draws heavily on the work of the American Bar Foundation Project, including Professor La-Fave's book and another volume in the series, Newman, *Conviction—the Determination of Guilt or Innocence Without Trial* (1966), as well as manuscripts of several other volumes now in preparation.

[2] Staff Studies, *Administration of Justice in the Municipal Court of Baltimore,* and *Administration of Justice in the Recorders' Court of Detroit,* printed in Appendix B of this [Task Force Report]; Subin, *Criminal Justice in a Metropolitan Court* (1966); President's Comm'n on Crime in the District of Columbia, Rep. 239–40 (1966).

[3] See, *e.g.* 1965 FBI *Uniform Crime Reports* 103 (table 12); Cal. Dep't Justice, *Crime and Delinquency in California* 53 (1965); 1964 *Ill. Sup. Ct. Ann. Rep.* 63; 1964–65 *Administrative Director of the N.J. Courts Ann. Rep.* 13 (table B-8).

of all convictions are obtained by guilty pleas.[4]

Many overburdened courts have come to rely upon these informal procedures to deal with overpowering caseloads, and some cases that are dropped might have been prosecuted had sufficient resources been available. But it would be an oversimplification to tie the use of early disposition solely to the problem of volume, for some courts appear to be able to deal with their workloads without recourse to such procedures. Furthermore, the flexibility and informality of these discretionary procedures makes them more readily adaptable to efforts to individualize the treatment of offenders than the relatively rigid procedures that now typify trial, conviction, and sentence. It would require radical restructuring of the trial to convert sentencing procedures into a comparable opportunity for the prosecution and the defense to discuss dispositional alternatives. Moreover, by placing less emphasis on the issue of culpability, discretionary procedures may enable the prosecutor to give greater attention to what disposition is most likely to fit the needs of those whose cases he considers. The pressures on the prosecutor to insist on a disposition that fits the popular conception of punishment are less before conviction, when the defendant has not officially and publicly been found guilty.

There are many cases in which trial would be clearly inappropriate. Often it becomes evident that the accused is innocent. Often while he appears to be technically guilty, criminal prosecution would serve no legitimate purpose. As Judge Charles Breitel has noted:

If every policeman, every prosecutor, every

[4] See page 9, *infra.*

court and every post-sentence agency performed his or its responsibility in strict accordance with rules of law precisely and narrowly laid down, the criminal law would be ordered but intolerable.[5]

In addition, there are obvious practical advantages to disposing of large numbers of cases without trial. The results are relatively prompt and certain compared to trial dispositions and therefore represent a substantial economy of resources. Even when criminal prosecution is appropriate, charges may be dropped or reduced in exchange for a plea of guilty simply to conserve resources for more important cases.

The main dangers in the present system of nontrial dispositions lie in the fact that it is so informal and invisible that it gives rise to fears that it does not operate fairly or that it does not accurately identify those who should be prosecuted and what disposition should be made in their cases. Often important decisions are made without adequate information, without sound policy guidance or rules, and without basic procedural protections for the defendant, such as counsel or judicial consideration of the issues. Because these dispositions are reached at an early stage, often little factual material is available about the offense, the offender, and the treatment alternatives. No record reveals the participants, their positions, or the reason for or facts underlying the disposition. When the disposition involves dismissal of filed charges or the entry of a guilty plea, it is likely to reach court, but only the end product is visible, and that view often is misleading. There are disturbing opportunities for coercion and over-reaching, as well as for undue leniency. The very informality and flexibility of the procedures are sources both of potential usefulness and of abuse.

It is essential to bring to these disposi-

tions some, although clearly not all, of the attributes of the trial process. First, facts bearing both on the offense and on the character of the offender should be brought out systematically before decisions as to nontrial dispositions are made. Second, these important decisions must be surrounded with some procedural regularity. Finally, provision should be made for fuller judicial consideration of dispositions which involve criminal sanctions or some intrusive, although nonpenal, alternative.

THE DECISION WHETHER
TO BRING CHARGES

Before a formal information or indictment is lodged in court, the prosecution has an opportunity to consider not only which charges to press but also whether to press toward conviction at all. The decision whether to file formal charges is a vitally important stage in the criminal process. It provides an opportunity to screen out cases in which the accused is apparently innocent, and it is at this stage that the prosecutor must decide in cases of apparent guilt whether criminal sanctions are appropriate.

In many instances the defendant presents a serious threat to the security and safety of the community, and invocation of the criminal process is clearly indicated. Community attitudes justifiably demand that the armed robber, the corrupt public official, and the hardened, persistent offender be subjected to the full weight of condemnation. But in many cases effective law enforcement does not require punishment or attachment of criminal status, and community attitudes do not demand it. Not all offenders who are guilty of serious offenses as defined by the penal code are habitual and dangerous criminals. It is not in the interest of the community to treat all offenders as hardened criminals; nor does the law require that the courts do so. It is at the charge stage that the

[5] Breitel, "Controls in Criminal Law Enforcement," 27 *U. Chi. L. Rev.* 427 (1960).

prosecutor should determine whether it is appropriate to refer the offender to non-criminal agencies for treatment or for some degree of supervision without criminal conviction.

The police have a similar decision to make earlier in the process, and they adopt varying responses to criminal conduct.[6] When serious criminal conduct is involved, the police objective will be arrest and full invocation of the criminal process. When less serious violations are involved, the police may ignore the situation (as in some instances of intoxication), or they may attempt on-the-scene conciliation (as in some instances of family disputes). Sometimes offenders are arrested and released (as may be true in the case of fights and brawls), and often referrals to social agencies are deemed appropriate (as in the case of some mentally disordered offenders).

But the police decision whether to arrest must usually be made hastily, without relevant background information, and often under pressure of a pending disturbance. There is ordinarily no opportunity for considered judgment until the time when formal charges must be filed, usually the next stage of the proceedings.

In some places particularly when less serious offenses are involved, the decision to press charges is made by the police or a magistrate rather than by the prosecutor. The better practice is for the prosecutor to make this decision, for the choice involves such factors as the sentencing alternatives available under the various possible charges, the substantiality of the case for prosecution, and limitations on prosecution resources—factors that the policeman often cannot consider and the magistrate

cannot deal with fully while maintaining a judicial role.[7]

The legitimacy and necessity of the prosecutor's discretion in pressing charges have been long recognized.[8] There are many cases in which it would be inappropriate to press charges. In some instances, a street fight, for example, the police may make lawful arrests that are not intended to be carried forward to prosecution. When the immediate situation requiring police intervention has passed, the defendant is discharged without further action. Often it becomes apparent after arrest that there is insufficient evidence to support a conviction or that a necessary witness will not cooperate or is unavailable; an arrest may be made when there is probable cause to believe that the person apprehended committed an offense, while conviction after formal charge requires proof of guilt beyond a reasonable doubt. Finally, subsequent investigation sometimes discloses the innocence of the accused.

When there is sufficient evidence of guilt, tactical considerations and law enforcement needs may make it inadvisable to press charges. Prosecutors may, for example, drop charges in exchange for a potential defendant's cooperation in giving information or testimony against a more

---

6 See, *e.g.,* LaFave, *op. cit. supra* note 1; Skolnick, *Justice Without Trial—Law Enforcement in Democratic Society* (1966); Goldstein, *Police Discretion Not To Invoke the Criminal Process—Low-Visibility Decisions in the Administration of Justice,* 69 YALE L.J. 543 (1960). See also Report of the Police Task Force of this Commission, ch. 2.

7 *Cf.* ALI, Model Code of Pre-arrangement Procedure § 6.02 (Tent. Draft No. 1, 1966).

8 "He [the prosecutor] must appraise the evidence on which an indictment may be demanded and the accused defendant tried, if he be indicted, and in that service must judge of its availability, competency and probative significance. He must on occasion consider the public impact of criminal proceedings, or, again, balance the admonitory value of invariable and inflexible punishment against the greater impulse of 'the quality of mercy.' He must determine what offenses, and whom, to prosecute. . . . Into these and many others of the problems committed to his informed discretion it would be sheer impertinence for a court to intrude. And such intrusion is contrary to the settled judicial tradition." *Howell* v. *Brown,* 85 F. Supp. 537, 540 (D. Neb. 1949). See also *Pugach* v. *Klein,* 193 F. Supp. 630, 635 (S.D.N.Y. 1961); Kaplan, "The Prosecutorial Discretion—A Comment," 60 *Nw. U. L. Rev.* 174 (1965).

serious offender. They may need to conserve their resources for more serious cases.

In some cases invocation of the criminal process against marginal offenders seems to do more harm than good. Labeling a person a criminal may set in motion a course of events which will increase the probability of his becoming or remaining one. The attachment of criminal status itself may be so prejudicial and irreversible as to ruin the future of a person who previously had successfully made his way in the community, and it may foreclose legitimate opportunities for offenders already suffering from social, vocational, and educational disadvantages.[9] Yet a criminal code has no way of describing the difference between a petty thief who is on his way to becoming an armed robber and a petty thief who succumbs once to a momentary impulse. The same criminal conduct may be the deliberate act of a professional criminal or an isolated aberration in the behavior of a normally law abiding person. The criminal conduct describes the existence of a problem, but not its nature or source. The system depends on prosecutors to recognize these distinctions when bringing charges.[10]

Among the types of cases in which thoughtful prosecutors commonly appear disinclined to seek criminal penalties are domestic disturbances; assaults and petty thefts in which victim and offender are in a family or social relationship; statutory rape when both boy and girl are young; first offense car thefts that involve teenagers taking a car for a short joyride; checks that are drawn upon insufficient funds; shoplifting by first offenders, particularly when restitution is made; and criminal acts that involve offenders suffering from emotional disorders short of legal insanity.

In addition, a large proportion of the cases in the criminal courts involve annoying or offensive behavior rather than dangerous crime.[11] Almost half of all arrests are on charges of drunkenness, disorderly conduct, minor assault, petty theft, and vagrancy. Many such offenders are burdened by economic, physical, mental, and educational disadvantages. In many of these cases effective law enforcement does not require prosecution.

The Existing System

A major difficulty in the present system of nontrial dispositions is that when an offender is dropped out of the criminal process by dismissal of charges, he usually does not receive the help or treatment needed to prevent recurrence. A first offender discharged without prosecution in the expectation that his conduct will not be repeated typically is not sent to another agency; in fact, in most communities there are few agencies designed to deal with his problems. Whether mental illness, youth, or alcoholism is the mitigating factor, there rarely is any followup. In the struggle to reduce the number of cases that compete for attention, there is little time to consider the needs of those who are dropped out of the process.

In some places attempts are made to refer offenders in need of treatment to appropriate community agencies. The health, education, and welfare programs to which offenders may be referred range from family service agencies to foster families, from medical treatment to mental health facilities and vocational training, and from shelters to specialized facilities for the alcoholic, the narcotics addict, and the mentally retarded. In a few places the threat of prosecution is used to guarantee that the offender follows through with a proposed program of treatment, submits to supervision, makes

---

[9] See Goldstein, *supra* note 6, at 590 (appendix).
[10] Remington & Rosenblum, "The Criminal Law and the Legislative Process," 1960 *U. Ill. L.F.* 481.

[11] 1965 FBI *Uniform Crime Reports* 110–11 (table 19); Commission's General Report, ch. 2.

restitution, or performs some other condition of his release.

In Washington, D.C., for example, the U.S. Attorney's office generally does not prosecute apparently casual first offense shoplifters, the offender is warned that a second offense will lead to prosecution. In first offender cases involving checks returned for insufficient funds, an informal hearing with representatives of the police and of the store which received the check usually results in dismissal of the charges upon the offender's agreement to make restitution.[12] Many cases involve relatively minor acts of violence stemming from domestic or neighborhood brawls and are initiated largely by citizens' complaints. In these cases the prosecutor holds an informal hearing attended by the complainant and the offender and attempts to resolve the problem which prompted the complaint. "He may warn the person complained against to stay away from the complainant or face prosecution. He may suggest the return of property or the payment of support or refer the parties to a family counseling agency." [13]

In Baltimore this kind of informal adjustment is performed by a magistrate, who holds court in a police precinct station.[14] In Detroit the police, who play an active part in the charge decision, hold informal hearings to deal with bad check and shoplifting cases.[15] The adjustment division, a special unit of the Recorder's Court probation department, also disposes of criminal complaints; it deals with 4,000-5,000 persons monthly, mainly women with complaints of nonsupport and other domestic problems. Warrants of arrest are issued for only about 3 percent of the complaints filed. In Chicago the police

department refers many cases, again primarily family problems, to the Municipal Court's social service department, which sees about 10,000 clients yearly, most of whom receive counseling or are referred to other agencies. In Minneapolis, a somewhat similar procedure is used, although there the probation office performs the screening service under the supervision of the prosecutor's office. New York City has established an independent agency, the Youth Counsel Service, which, upon referral from the prosecutor, investigates cases involving youthful offenders and makes recommendations for noncriminal treatment. The Service may refer the youth to other agencies for care and rehabilitation.

Pre-judicial determination of criminal charges is particularly common in the juvenile courts, and is described in detail in the Task Force Report on Juvenile Delinquency and Youth Crime. In many juvenile courts more than half of all cases are disposed of at the intake stage. Although in some communities these decisions are guided by policies and surrounded by some procedural regularity, ordinarily they are made on an informal, case-by-case basis.

Other, more formal alternatives to prosecution have been developed. For example, the Department of Justice has authorized a procedure for deferred prosecution of juveniles known as the "Brooklyn plan." In general, a juvenile will not be considered a subject for the plan unless his violation of law is not serious, his previous behavior and background are good, and the prospects for future lawful behavior are favorable. After investigation and report by a probation officer and with approval of the parents, the U.S. Attorney may place a juvenile on unofficial probation for a definite period. The conditions to be observed during this period may be similar to those for probation following adjudication. When the juvenile successfully completes this period of unofficial

12 See Subin, *op. cit., supra* note 2, at 31–32.
13 *Id.* at 54.
14 Staff Study, *Administration of Justice in the Municipal Court of Baltimore,* printed in Appendix B of [*Task Force Report: The Courts*].
15 3 American Bar Foundation, The Administration of Criminal Justice in the United States—Pilot Project Rep. 570 (mimeo. 1957).

probation, the case is closed and the juvenile is left without the stigma of a court record. If he violates the conditions, he may then be prosecuted as a juvenile delinquent.

In some jurisdictions a similar disposition is possible even after the case reaches court. For example, in the magistrates' courts of Maryland the defendant may receive the disposition of "probation before conviction." A similar disposition in lower courts in Massachusetts is termed "case continued without finding." In both instances if the individual stays out of further difficulty for a given period of time, usually six months to a year, and follows a recommended course of action, such as outpatient psychotherapy or attendance at Alcoholics Anonymous, the case is closed. Failure to cooperate or a further encounter with the law could lead to conviction and imposition of sentence on the earlier charge.[16] Probation without conviction, provided for by statute in several States,[17] appears to be used widely elsewhere without specific statutory authority.

A number of innovative programs are designed to deal with alcoholics, in part as a response to increasing doubts about the legality of the criminal approach to this problem.[18] The Denver Municipal Court, for example, conducts a group therapy "honor court" program for offenders with drinking problems. Since the court has limited probation services available, this program is manned entirely by the chief judge and members of his administrative staff. A large alcoholism treatment unit in a city hospital provides inpatient and outpatient care for referrals.

Numerous programs have been established to provide services for persons who might otherwise be prosecuted for such crimes as vagrancy, public drunkenness, and disorderly conduct. New York City has a short-term hostel care program for homeless men. Denver has established a "group home" for elderly evacuees from a skid row renewal project. Boston has in operation a center to coordinate community services for homeless alcoholics and other men on skid row.

Although some of these programs are promising, the system for making the charge decision remains generally inadequate. Prosecutors act without the benefit of direction or guidelines from either the legislature or higher levels of administration; their decisions are almost entirely free from judicial supervision. Decisions are to a great extent fortuitous because they are made on inadequate information about the offense, the offender, and the alternatives available. At this stage in the process the prosecutor generally knows only a few bare facts about the offense. He generally knows little about the accused, except perhaps what is revealed by a prior criminal record. In many places little consideration is given to cases where guilt is apparent but criminal sanctions seem inappropriate. Often cases are prosecuted that should not be. Often offenders in need of treatment, supervision, or discipline are set free without being referred to appropriate community agencies or followed up in any way.

In most places there is little liaison between the prosecutor and community agencies which could assist an offender. The prosecutor, frequently overworked, has difficulty searching out noncriminal dispositions, and it is open to question whether he is the appropriate official to perform this searching function. He may have few professional qualifications to decide what treatment alternatives are ap-

---

[16] Examples of similar procedures in the lower courts of Kansas, Wisconsin, and Michigan are given in chapter 11 of Newman, *op. cit. supra* note 1.

[17] *E.g., Fla. Stat. Ann.* § 948.01 (Supp. 1966); *Md. Ann. Code* art. 27 § 641 (Supp. 1966). Probation without conviction is provided for in the *Model Sentencing Act* § 9 (1963).

[18] See *Easter* v. *District of Columbia,* 361 F.2d 50 (D.C. Cir. 1966) ; *Driver* v. *Hinnant,* 356 F.2d 761 (4th Cir. 1966) . This subject is discussed in chapter 9 of the Commission's General Report.

propriate for particular offenders. Consultative services to analyze the offender's medical, psychiatric, and social situation; to consider that situation in light of available community resources; and to make appropriate recommendations are at best limited and in many places are not available. But the basic problem is that in many communities the resources for dealing with offenders and their problems are totally inadequate. The development of such resources is clearly essential; detailed recommendations to this end are made in chapters 3 and 6 of the Commission's General Report.

Improving the Charge Decision

GATHERING AND SHARING INFORMATION. A prosecutor should have several kinds of information if he is to make sound charge decisions. He must evaluate the strength of his case. Police reports usually provide him with some facts about the offense, but often he needs more. Before a prosecutor decides whether to charge or dismiss in any case that is not elementary, he should review the case file to determine whether more evidence and witnesses are available than the police have uncovered. In addition, the prosecutor needs to know enough about the offender to determine whether he should be diverted from the criminal track. Greater involvement of court probation departments and the availability of probation officers for consultation with the prosecutor and defense counsel at this stage of the proceedings are clearly advisable. Often the prosecutor needs to know whether there are facilities in the community for treating such medical or behavioral problems as the offender may have and whether those facilities will accept him.

In cases in which there is an indication that intensive treatment or supervision is needed, the prosecutor and defense counsel should be able to obtain a thorough investigation of the accused's background

and treatment needs. A special division might be created in the prosecutor's office or in the public defender's office to conduct such an investigation. In some places the parties might call upon the probation office for help; in others a representative from a community agency could be designated. Some communities might choose to create a new agency to coordinate community services for offenders, conduct background investigations, and prepare treatment programs for consideration by prosecutor and defense counsel. Where a Youth Services Bureau has been created, as recommended by the Commission in chapter 3 of the General Report, it could conduct the investigation in youthful offender cases. Where neighborhood law offices have been created under programs of the Office of Economic Opportunity, they might be called upon for help.

Chapter 4 of this report discusses ways in which other information relevant to the disposition at this stage can be gathered. Techniques will vary; what is essential is that the relevant information be gathered so that dispositional decisions can be made on a rational basis.

Defense counsel has an important role to play at this stage, and he should be involved wherever an intrusive disposition or significant penalty is likely. Counsel can assist in gathering information and formulating a treatment program; he can help persuade the prosecutor of the appropriateness of a noncriminal disposition.

It is unusual for either attorney to have sufficient information; it is even more unusual for them to share it. But the early accumulation and sharing of information might well lead to early agreements between the prosecution and the defense about how some cases should be disposed of, thus saving time and futile legal maneuvering. The prosecutor should have the benefit of defense counsel's views and suggestions, as well as an idea of how strong the case for the defense is. By the same token, defense counsel should be familiar with the prosecution's case and the prosecutor's views in order to advise his client whether to seek a noncriminal disposition, to plead guilty, or to insist on a trial.

A conflict often exists between the need for a frank exchange of information and defense counsel's obligation to act only in ways favorable to his client. Defense counsel may possess information adverse to his client, or the prosecutor may have erroneous information which defense counsel knows paints an unjustifiably favorable picture of his client. Obviously all exchanges of information must be explicitly authorized by the defendant, and appropriate provision should be made to ensure that a defendant's statements and information disclosed are not used against him in the event of a trial. But subtle and difficult questions of professional responsibility will remain. Experience may offer guides for some of the problems presented; other norms may be provided by efforts such as the American Bar Association's redefinition of the Canons of Professional Ethics or the consideration of the role of counsel by the ABA Special Project on Minimum Standards for Criminal Justice.

THE PRECHARGE CONFERENCE. A conference between the prosecutor and defense counsel before formal charges are filed would provide an opportunity for them to discuss the appropriateness of noncriminal disposition of the case.

Prosecutors should establish guidelines for convening such conferences, indicating those classes of cases in which conferences might be held as a matter of course, for example, when the offense involves conduct characteristic of a recognized disorder, such as alcoholism or mental disease; when the offense is a minor crime against property; or when the age of the defendant, his history of family and employment stability, or the absence of any prior criminal record indicate that he is a good risk. Discussions should of course

be held when there are indications that the evidence of guilt is insufficient for trial or otherwise raises doubts in the prosecutor's mind whether prosecution of the case is warranted. The object of discussion in such cases would be whether the charges should be dismissed outright. The guidelines should also provide that in cases not specifically covered, conferences may be convened at the discretion of the prosecutor and defense counsel may submit appropriate information showing the desirability of a conference.

When there is a factual basis for the charge, the central concern at the precharge conference should turn to the question of what disposition is most appropriate for the offender and whether prosecution or noncriminal methods are the preferable way to attain that disposition. Among the factors that might be weighed in determining whether to adopt a noncriminal disposition are: (1) the seriousness of the crime and the effect upon the public sense of security and justice if the offender were to be treated without criminal conviction; (2) the place of the case in effective law enforcement policy, particularly for such offenses as tax evasion, white collar crimes, and other instances where deterrent factors may loom large; (3) whether the offender has medical, psychiatric, family, or vocational difficulties; (4) whether there are agencies in the community capable of dealing with his problems; (5) whether there is reason to believe that the offender will benefit from and cooperate with a treatment program; and (6) what the impact of criminal charges would be upon the witnesses, the offender, and his family. Even if the case is ultimately prosecuted, the conference will have served many useful purposes, including an increase in the discovery and consideration of the facts on both sides, a narrowing of the trial issues, and formulation of a sounder basis for negotiated guilty plea discussions.

Adoption of the proposed precharge

conference will no doubt entail some added administrative burden for prosecutors, but that burden should not be exaggerated. In many communities, for example, much of the needed offender information may be gathered from existing sources. Moreover, as some cases which might have been sent forward for prosecution are diverted to noncriminal disposition and others are routed out earlier in the process, prosecution resources would be freed for concentration on serious offenders and disputed cases.

NONCRIMINAL ALTERNATIVES. When the prosecutor decides that a case should not be prosecuted criminally, a simple dismissal will often be appropriate: Investigation may reveal that the accused is not guilty of the offense for which he was arrested, or that although he is guilty, the offense is minor and there is no reason to believe he will commit such an offense again. But there are many cases where some followup should be provided: The offender may be an alcoholic or a narcotics addict; he may be mentally ill; he may have been led to crime by his family situation or by his inability to get a job. If he is not helped, he may well return to crime.

There are many cases in which minimal intrusions on the defendant's liberty would be all that seem necessary. Often it will be enough simply to refer the offender to the appropriate agency in the community, and hope that he will take advantage of the help offered. The prosecutor might, for example, be willing to drop charges if the defendant goes to an employment agency and makes a bona fide effort to get a job, or if he consults a family service agency, or if he resumes his education. The prosecutor retains legal power to file a charge until the period of limitations has run, but as a practical matter, unless the offense is repeated, it would be unusual for the initial charge to be revived.

While ideally there should be no intrusion on the defendant's liberty without a judicial finding of guilt and imposition of sanction, it may not be feasible to insist on this protection when the intrusion is so minimal. As noted above, there is a great deal of informal adjustment of cases now. A prosecutor might develop statements of policy with the approval of the court, defining with some precision the kinds of dispositions he proposes to make without seeking court approval. It might be advisable to limit the time during which the prosecutor would be authorized to reinstitute charges, as the Commission recommends in the juvenile area when youths are referred to a Youth Services Bureau. Such a disposition would not require elaborate procedural steps. A simple notation in the prosecutor's files would show that the charges were dismissed and the accused referred to a particular agency. Offenders would know that if they were arrested for the same offense again, full prosecution would be very likely.

But there are some cases where a simple referral may be inadequate: The offender may present too great a danger to the community; he may require longer supervision, or referral may have been tried before unsuccessfully. Yet subjecting the offender to the stigma of a criminal conviction may be undesirable. If the disposition involves significant restrictions on the accused or is of sustained duration, approval by the court should be required to assure that there is a factual basis for the charge, that no undue pressure has been put on the defendant to accept the disposition, and that the disposition is appropriate. Such an agreement might entail the kinds of conditions that would be appropriate for probation following conviction. The agreement might, for example, require supervision of the defendant's activities by a probation officer; it might require that the defendant give up certain associates; it might require that he cooperate with a program of treatment for alcoholism, narcotics addiction, or mental illness; it might require that he reside in a halfway house, or enter a mental institution for some definite period of time.

In such cases a written agreement, executed by the prosecutor, defense counsel, and the accused, should be submitted to the court and become effective only upon court approval. Depending upon local procedure, this agreement could take the form of a consent decree, and the prosecutor would be authorized to initiate prosecution only if the accused violated its terms. A substantial modification of the terms of the disposition should be presented to the court for review as part of an amended decree. Normal time limitations governing the filing of the charges might be suspended. If the prosecutor fears that it might not be feasible to try the charge at a later date, the decree could include an admission by the defendant, a stipulation of facts, or the depositions of witnesses.

There are of course dangers in granting such discretionary power to prosecutors and judges. Ordinarily the state can apply compulsory sanctions, inside prison or out, only after an offense has been proved or a guilty plea has been entered. And the permissible sanctions are limited by a maximum fixed by the legislature. There is a danger that the prosecutor's agreement to dismiss charges may induce the defendant to accept an alternate disposition consisting of onerous, unreasonable, or even illegal conditions. There is an additional danger that an alternate disposition could become a justification for indeterminate commitment. Recently reported instances of judicial attempts to obtain consent to sterilization and of prosecutorial intervention in the family life of the accused illustrate the possibilities of abuse. One safeguard is that the offender must, at any point in the process, have the right to insist on trial and criminal disposition. But there is nevertheless a danger that the prospect of criminal

prosecution would be so dire as to force the offender to accept an unreasonable, although less onerous, alternative. The proposal here that the agreement be recorded and submitted to court for approval would tend to minimize this danger.

An accused might be induced to accept a burdensome, although noncriminal, program of treatment on the basis of a flimsy charge of which he clearly would be found not guilty if he insisted on his right to trial. Obviously the accused is under strong pressure to accept any disposition which does not carry the stigma of a criminal conviction. The problem is very similar to that which arises in the negotiation of a guilty plea. Similar protections, discussed in more detail in the following section, should be provided. The reviewing judge should, in the first place, determine that there is a factual basis for the charge. If the judge determines that there is no basis for the charge, he should inform the accused, who then would be free to pursue or reject the recommended program without the threat of a criminal charge. The judge should also consider the amount of pressure that was put on the accused to agree to a noncriminal alternative and determine whether it constituted an overwhelming inducement to surrender the right to trial. If he is not satisfied, the case should be set for trial. When the agreement includes any factual admissions or depositions prejudicial to the defendant, he should be allowed to withdraw them. When feasible, trial should take place before a different judge, who would not be influenced by involvement in the consent decree decision.

The final safeguard would be the presence of counsel, which should be required wherever an intrusive disposition is under consideration. Counsel would ensure that the other safeguards provided are meaningful. And counsel is necessary for the accused to make an informed decision

Table 1   Rates of Guilty Pleas in Selected States

State (1964 statistics unless otherwise indicated)	Total con- victions	Guilty pleas	
		Number	Percent of total
California (1965)	30,840	22,817	74.0
Connecticut	1,596	1,494	93.9
District of Columbia (year ending June 30, 1964)	1,115	817	73.3
Hawaii	393	360	91.5
Illinois	5,591	4,768	85.2
Kansas	3,025	2,727	90.2
Massachusetts (1963)	7,790	6,642	85.2
Minnesota (1965)	1,567	1,437	91.7
New York	17,249	16,464	95.5
Pennsylvania (1960)	25,632	17,108	66.8
U.S. District Courts	29,170	26,273	90.2
Average [excluding Pennsylvania] [1]			87.0

[1] The Pennsylvania figures have been excluded from the average because they were from an earlier year, and the types of cases included did not appear fully comparable with the others.

whether to agree to a noncriminal disposition requiring burdensome performance on his part.

THE NEGOTIATED PLEA OF GUILTY

The question of guilt or innocence is not contested in the overwhelming majority of criminal cases. A recent estimate is that guilty pleas account for 90 percent of all convictions; and perhaps as high as 95 percent of misdemeanor convictions.[19] But the Commission has found it difficult to calculate with any degree of certainty the percentage of cases disposed of by guilty plea, since reliable statistical information is limited. Clearly it is very high. The following statistics indicate the number and percentage of guilty plea convictions in trial courts of general jurisdiction in States in which such information was available. [See Table 1.]

A substantial percentage of guilty pleas are the product of negotiations between the prosecutor and defense counsel or the

accused, although again precise data are unavailable.[20] Commonly known as "plea bargaining," this is a process very much like the pretrial settlement of civil cases. It involves discussions looking toward an agreement under which the accused will enter a plea of guilty in exchange for a reduced charge or a favorable sentence recommendation by the prosecutor. Even when there have been no explicit negotiations, defendants relying on prevailing practices often act on the justifiable assumption that those who plead guilty will be sentenced more leniently.

Few practices in the system of criminal

[19] ABA Project on Minimum Standards for Criminal Justice, Pleas of Guilty 1 (Tent. Draft 1967); Newman, *op. cit. supra* note 1, at 3 n.l.

[20] The *University of Pennsylvania Law Review* surveyed 205 prosecutors' offices in the most populous counties of 43 States. Roughly 80 responses were received. More than half of the offices in this group reported that 70 percent or more of the defendants pleaded guilty, and of these guilty pleas between 30 and 40 percent resulted from negotiations. Approximately 11 percent of the offices responding indicated that 70 percent or more of guilty pleas were negotiated, while 28 percent indicated that 10 percent or less were negotiated. See Note, "Guilty Plea Bargaining—Compromises by Prosecutors to Secure Guilty Pleas," 112 *U. Pa. L. Rev.* 865, 896–99 (1964); *cf.* Comment. "The Influence of the Defendant's Plea on Judicial Determination of Sentence," 66 *Yale L. J.* 204, (1956).

justice create a greater sense of unease and suspicion than the negotiated plea of guilty.[21] The correctional needs of the offender and legislative policies reflected in the criminal law appear to be sacrificed to the need for tactical accommodations between the prosecutor and defense counsel. The offense for which guilt is acknowledged and for which the sentence is imposed often appears almost incidental to keeping the business of the courts moving.

The system usually operates in an informal, invisible manner. There is ordinarily no formal recognition that the defendant has been offered an inducement to plead guilty. Although the participants and frequently the judge know that negotiation has taken place, the prosecutor and defendant must ordinarily go through a courtroom ritual in which they deny that the guilty plea is the result of any threat or promise.[22] As a result there is no judicial review of the propriety of the bargain—no check on the amount of pressure put on the defendant to plead guilty. The judge, the public, and sometimes the defendant himself cannot know for certain who got what from whom in exchange for what. The process comes to look less rational, more subject to chance factors, to undue pressures, and sometimes to the hint of corruption. Moreover, the defendant may not get the benefit he bargained for. There is no guarantee that the judge will follow the prosecutor's recommendations for lenient sentence. In most instances the defendant does not know what sentence he will receive until he has pleaded guilty and sentence has been imposed. If the defendant is disappointed, he may move to withdraw his plea, but

there is no assurance that the motion will be granted, particularly since at the time he tendered his guilty plea, he probably denied the very negotiations he now alleges.[23]

A more fundamental problem with plea bargaining is the propriety of offering the defendant an inducement to surrender his right to trial. This problem becomes increasingly substantial as the prospective reward increases, because the concessions to the defendant become harder to justify on grounds other than expediency. There is always the danger that a defendant who would be found not guilty if he insisted on his right to trial will be induced to plead guilty. The defendant has an absolute right to put the prosecution to its proof, and if too much pressure is brought to discourage the exercise of this right, the integrity of the system, which the court trial is relied upon to vindicate, will not be demonstrated. When the prosecution is not put to its proof and all the evidence is not brought out in open court, the public is not assured that illegalities in law enforcement are revealed and corrected or that the seriousness of the defendant's crimes are shown and adequate punishment imposed. Prosecutors who are overburdened or are insufficiently energetic may compromise cases that call for severe sanctions.

Despite the serious questions raised by a system of negotiated pleas, there are important arguments for preserving it. Our system of criminal justice has come to depend upon a steady flow of guilty pleas. There are simply not enough judges, prosecutors, or defense counsel to operate a system in which most defendants go to trial. Many of the Commission's proposals, such as the recommendation to expand

---

21 See Comment, "Official Inducement to Plead Guilty—Suggested Morals for a Marketplace," 32 *U. Chi. L. Rev.* 167 (1964).

22 *Cf. Shelton* v. *United States*, 242 F.2d 101 (5th Cir.), *rev'd*, 246 F.2d 571 (5th Cir. 1957) (en banc), *rev'd per curium on confession of error*, 356 U.S. 26 (1958).

23 See, *e.g., United States* v. *Hughes*, 325 F.2d 789 (2d Cir. 1964), *cert. denied*, 377 U.S. 907 (1965); *United States* v. *Lester*, 247 F. 2d 496 (2d Cir. 1957); *cf. Ga. Code Ann.* § 27–1404, allowing withdrawal of a guilty plea as a matter of right at any time before judgment.

appointment of counsel for the indigent, will strain the available resources for many years. If reliance on trial were increased at this time, it would undoubtedly lower the quality of justice throughout the system. Even were the resources available, there is some question whether a just system would require that they be allocated to providing all defendants with a full trial. Trial as we know it is an elaborate mechanism for finding facts. To use this process in cases where the facts are not really in dispute seems wasteful.

The plea agreement, if carried out, eliminates the risk inherent in all adversary litigation. No matter how strong the evidence may appear and how well prepared and conducted a trial may be, each side must realistically consider the possibility of an unfavorable outcome. At its best the trial process is an imperfect method of factfinding; factors such as the attorney's skill, the availability of witnesses, the judge's attitude, jury vagaries, and luck will influence the result. Each side is interested in limiting these inherent litigation risks. In addition, the concessions of a negotiated plea are also commonly used by prosecutors when a defendant cooperates with law enforcement agencies by furnishing information or testimony against other offenders.

Confining trials to cases involving substantial issues may also help to preserve the significance of the presumption of innocence and the requirement of proof beyond a reasonable doubt. If trial were to become routine even in cases in which there is no substantial issue of guilt, the overwhelming statistical probability of guilt might incline judges and jurors to be more skeptical of the defense than at present.

Because of the invisibility of the plea bargaining system, the essential issues involved have generally not received adequate consideration by the courts. Some courts have, however, begun to look at the system for what it is and to focus on

the need to regulate it to assure that neither public nor private interests are sacrificed. As a Federal Court of Appeals noted in a recent case:

> In a sense, it can be said that most guilty pleas are the result of a "bargain" with the prosecutor. But this, standing alone, does not vitiate such pleas. A guilty defendant must always weigh the possibility of his conviction on all counts, and the possibility of his getting the maximum sentence, against the possibility that he can plead to fewer, or lesser, offenses, and perhaps receive a lighter sentence. The latter possibility exists if he pleads guilty . . .
>
> No competent lawyer, discussing a possible guilty plea with a client, could fail to canvass these possible alternatives with him. Nor would he fail to ascertain the willingness of the prosecution to "go along." . . .
>
> The important thing is not that there shall be no "deal" or "bargain," but that the plea shall be a genuine one, by a defendant who is guilty; one who understands his situation, his rights, and the consequences of the plea, and is neither deceived nor coerced.[24]

Some jurisdictions appear to be able to deal with their caseloads without reliance on negotiated guilty pleas. The discussion in this chapter should not be taken as suggesting that plea bargaining should be introduced in courts that have satisfactory alternatives. Particularly in single judge courts it may be feasible to introduce the safeguards that would enable a negotiated plea system to operate fairly and effectively. Indeed this chapter does not resolve the issue whether a negotiated guilty plea system is a desirable method of dealing with cases. Rather the discussion is directed to improving the operation of the plea bargaining system in those jurisdictions where negotiations are ordinary occurrences.

24 *Cortez* v. *United States*, 337 F.2d 699, 701 (9th Cir. 1964).

Forms and Uses of Negotiated Pleas

The plea agreement follows several patterns.[25] In its best known form it is an arrangement between the prosecutor and the defendant or his lawyer whereby the accused pleads guilty to a charge less serious than could be proven at trial. "Less serious" in this context usually means an offense which carries a lower maximum sentence. The defendant's motivation is to confine the upper limits of the judge's sentencing power. Similar results are obtained when the plea is entered in return for the prosecutor's agreement to drop counts in a multicount indictment or not to charge the defendant as a habitual offender. In some situations the benefits obtained by the defendant may be illusory, as when he bargains for a reduction in counts unaware that local judges rarely impose consecutive sentences.

Charge reduction is tied to the exercise of the prosecutor's discretion as to what offenses he will charge originally. Although the charge process is distinct from the plea negotiation, the two are closely related by the prosecutor's expectations at the time of charge as to the likely course bargaining will take, and by the important role bargaining for reduced charges plays in the exercise of the prosecutor's discretion.

Plea negotiations concerning charges provide an opportunity to mitigate the harshness of a criminal code or to rationalize its inconsistencies and to lead to a disposition based on an assessment of the individual factors of each crime. The field over which these negotiations may range is broad; the defendant's conduct on a single occasion may justify separate charges of robbery, larceny, assault with a deadly weapon, assault, or disorderly conduct. Some of these offenses are felonies, while others are misdemeanors, and the maximum sentences may range from 30 years to less than 1 year. Conviction of a felony may involve serious collateral disabilities, including disqualification from engaging in certain licensed occupations or businesses, while conviction of a misdemeanor may not. The prosecutor often has a wide range of penal provisions from which to choose. His choice has enormous correctional implications, and it is through charge bargaining that in many courts he seeks to turn his discretion to his own advantage.

Charge reduction may be used to avoid a mandatory minimum sentence or a restriction on the power to grant probation. In these instances the agreed plea becomes a way of restoring sentencing discretion when it has in part been eliminated from the code. Charge reduction is also used to avoid the community opprobrium that attaches to conviction of certain offenses. Thus to avoid being labeled a child molester or homosexual, the defendant may offer to plead guilty to a charge such as disorderly conduct or assault.

The plea agreement may take forms other than a reduction of charges. A defendant may plead guilty to a charge that accurately describes his conduct in return for the prosecutor's agreement to recommend leniency or for a specific recommendation of probation or of a lesser sentence than would probably be imposed if the defendant insisted upon a trial. Although in theory the judge retains complete discretion as to sentence, in reality the negotiations are conducted by the prosecutor and the defendant or his attorney on the assumption that the recommended sentence will be imposed. The practices of individual judges vary, but they are likely to be known to the parties. Some judges neither request nor accept sentencing recommendations, and others give them differing weight in different cases. But many judges feel obligated to accept such recommendations, because they know that it is essential to the plea negotiation sys-

---

25 See generally Newman, *op. cit. supra* note 1; Enker, *Perspectives in Plea Bargaining*, printed as appendix A in [*Task Force Report: The Courts*].

tem. In some instances the judge may indicate explicitly that he will impose a particular sentence if the defendant pleads guilty. This can lead to the undesirable involvement of the judge as an active participant in negotiations, lending the weight of his power and prestige to inducing the defendant to plead guilty.[26]

Other forms of plea bargaining may involve judge shopping. In places where there are wide sentencing disparities, a plea of guilty may be entered in exchange for the prosecutor's agreement that the defendant will appear before a particular judge for sentencing.

Problems in Current Plea Bagaining Practices

There are many serious problems with the way that the plea bargaining system is administered. In the first place bargaining takes place at a stage when the parties' knowledge of their own and each other's cases is likely to be fragmentary. Presentence reports and other investigations into the background of the offender usually are made after conviction and are unavailable at the plea bargain stage. Thus the prosecutor's decision is usually made without the benefit of information regarding the circumstances of the offense, the background and character of the defendant, and other factors necessary for sound dispositional decisions. In too many places the acceptance of pleas to lesser offenses, which began as a device to individualize treatment, becomes routine, with a standard reduction for certain charges.

The informality and wide variation in practice among prosecutors and trial judges regarding plea bargains often cause bewilderment and a sense of injustice among defendants. Some may be denied the opportunity to participate in the bargaining process and the benefits which

may accrue because they or their counsel are unaware of the customary practices of plea negotiation. Others may come away from a system which invites judge shopping with justifiable feelings that they have been treated improperly.

Too often the result may be excessive leniency for professional and habitual criminals who generally have expert legal advice and are best able to take full advantage of the bargaining opportunity. Marginal offenders, on the other hand, may be dealt with harshly, and left with a deep sense of injustice, having learned too late of the possibilities of manipulation offered by the system.

The most troublesome problem is the possibility that an innocent defendant may plead guilty because of the fear that he will be sentenced more harshly if he is convicted after trial or that he will be subjected to damaging publicity because of a repugnant charge. The danger of convicting the innocent obviously must be reduced to the lowest possible level, but the fact is that neither trial nor plea bargain is a perfectly accurate procedure. In both, the innocent face the risk of conviction. The real question is whether the risks are sufficiently greater in the bargaining process to warrant either abandoning it entirely or modifying it drastically. Such improper practices as deliberate and unwarranted overcharging by the prosecutor to improve his bargaining position, threats of very heavy sentences if the defendant insists on a trial, or threats to prosecute relatives and friends of the defendant unless he pleads guilty may, on occasion, create pressures that can prove too great for even the innocent to resist. The existence of mandatory minimum sentences aggravates this problem since they exert a particularly heavy pressure on defendants to relinquish their chance of an acquittal.[27] Inadequate discovery procedures

---

[26] See *United States* ex rel. *Elksnis* v. *Gilligan*, 256 F. Supp. 244 (S.D.N.Y. 1966); *United States* v. *Tateo*, 214 F. Supp. 560 (S.D.N.Y. 1963).

[27] Studies show a far greater incidence of bargaining in Michigan, where sentences for certain

often impair counsel's ability to appraise the risks of trial. Clearly those courts that continue to use a negotiated plea system must take vigorous steps to reduce these potential abuses.

Restructuring the Plea Bargaining System

The process as presently constituted contains some safeguards to prevent innocent defendants from pleading guilty. Most judges take pains to assure that the defendant is in fact guilty by questioning him or hearing evidence before accepting a plea of guilty. In some jurisdictions the presentence investigation contains a careful evaluation of the facts underlying the charge.

The recommendations which follow are intended to convert the practice of plea bargaining into a visible, forthright, and informed effort to reach sound dispositional decisions; they are meant to assure a measure of judicial control so that dispositions which are against the interests of the public or the defendant can be avoided.

Whenever the defendant faces a significant penalty, he should be represented by counsel, whether the offense is classified as a felony or a misdemeanor. The presence of counsel helps ensure that the plea is reliable, that the risks of litigation have been considered, and that no unfair advantage has been taken of the defendant.

Prosecutors who practice plea bargaining should make the opportunity to negotiate equally available to all defendants. Rather than leaving it to the defendant to seek charge and sentence concessions, the prosecutor should publish procedures and standards, making clear his availability to confer with counsel and listing the factors

deemed relevant. The defendant should be able to include within the disposition all crimes, charged or not, which could be charged within the jurisdiction of the court.

Discussions between prosecutor and defense counsel should deal explicitly with dispositional questions and the development of a correctional program for the offender. A plea negotiation is fundamentally a negotiation about the correctional disposition of a case and is, therefore, a matter of moment to both the defendant and the community. If the offense is a serious one, a plea bargain should be founded on the kind of information available to both parties that is gathered by probation departments for presentence reports. Less complete information may be adequate for less serious cases.

The full and frank exchange of relevant information regarding the offender and the offense, already discussed in connection with the decision whether to charge, is equally essential at this stage of the proceedings. When a precharge conference has been held, the data assembled by both parties may be used in the plea negotiations. In addition procedures should be adopted which would enable the parties to call upon the probation office or some other factfinding agency to obtain what is in effect a presentence investigation for use in the negotiation discussions. In the District of Columbia the defender's office has an experimental project, in many respects resembling a probation service, for evaluating defendants and developing correctional plans for them. Defense counsel should painstakingly explain to the defendant the terms of the proposed agreement and the alternatives open to him.

The negotiations should be freed from their present irregular status so that the participants can frankly acknowledge the negotiations and their agreement can be reviewed by the judge and made a matter

---

crimes are legislatively mandated, than in Wisconsin, where judges have greater discretion in sentencing. See Newman, *op. cit. supra* note 1, at 53–56, 177–84.

of record. Upon the plea of guilty in open court the terms of the agreement should be fully stated on the record and, at least in serious or complicated cases, reduced to writing. If there is a written memorandum, it should contain an agreed statement of the facts of the offense, the opening positions of the parties, the terms of the agreement, background information relevant to the correctional disposition and an explanation of why the negotiated disposition is appropriate. This material should be probed by judicial questioning. Use of a memorandum is preferable to relying entirely upon judicial questioning, because it should encourage more thoughtful negotiations and a more complete consideration of the agreement by the judge. Regardless of which procedure is chosen, the judge's questions at the time of plea should be transcribed and filed.

Judicial supervision is not an effective control when the system of plea bargaining is built on tacit rather than explicit understandings. When there has been explicit discussion of a charge reduction or of a sentencing recommendation, the terms of the discussions will be well defined, and the judge will be in a position to enquire into them. But the judge is in a different position when a defendant pleads guilty to a particular offense in the expectation that a given sentence will be imposed, or when a prosecutor agrees to a reduction in charge or to an adjournment that results in the case coming before a particular judge in the expectation that the defendant will be led thereby to plead guilty. In these cases counsel may in good faith insist that the steps taken were unilateral and not pursuant to an agreement, and the judge's ability to intervene in these decisions will be less.

Inevitably the judge plays a part in the negotiated guilty plea.[28] His role is a deli-

cate one, for it is important that he carefully examine the propriety of the agreement without undermining his judicial role by becoming excessively involved in the negotiations. The judge's function is to ensure the appropriateness of the correctional disposition reached by the parties and to guard against overcharging by the prosecutor or an agreed sentence that is inappropriately light in view of the crime or so lenient as to constitute an irresistible inducement to the defendant to plead guilty. The judge's role is not that of one of the parties to the negotiation, but that of an independent examiner to verify that the defendant's plea is the result of an intelligent and knowing choice. The judge should make every effort to limit his participation to avoid formulating the terms of the bargain. His power to impose a more severe sentence than the one proposed as part of the negotiation presents so great a risk that defendants may feel compelled to accept his proposal.

Before accepting the plea of guilty, the judge, in open court, should determine that the defendant's plea is the result of an intelligent and knowing choice and not based on misapprehension. The judge should make sure that the defendant understands the nature of the charge, his

---

[28] The role for the judge in the guilty plea process suggested in this chapter should be compared with the approach taken by the ABA Project on Minimum Standards for Criminal Justice, *op.*

cit. supra note 25, at 71–77 (§ 3.3). Both recognize that the judge should not become an active participant in the discussions leading to a plea agreement. This chapter places greater emphasis on the importance in the negotiating stage of gathering dispositional information, including even the equivalent of a presentence investigation. If this approach is taken the parties should be able to present to the judge more information concerning the case and the defendant than might otherwise be available. The ABA draft, on the other hand, contemplates that the presentence investigation will occur after plea (p. 74) and, therefore, that the judge would be in a position to give only a preliminary indication of the acceptability of the agreement at the time the plea is tendered. Both approaches recognize the desirability of assuring that the defendant who pleads guilty on the basis of an agreement receives the benefit of his bargain.

right to trial, the consequences of his plea, and the defenses available to him. The judge also should determine that there is a factual basis for the plea, by specific inquiry of the prosecutor, the defendant, his counsel, or witnesses, or by consideration of other evidence.[29] Such inquiry should be more precise and detailed than the brief and perfunctory question-and-answer sequence that has been common in some courts.

The judge should assess the inducements that have been offered to the defendant for his plea. If a written memorandum of the negotiation has been submitted, he should inquire whether the plea has resulted from any inducements not set forth in the memorandum. He must decide whether undue pressure has been put on the defendant to plead guilty. This decision is admittedly an extremely difficult one to make and calls for a careful weighing of the inducements offered and the ability of the defendant to exercise a real choice.

The judge also must decide that the agreed disposition is fair and appropriate in light of all the circumstances. The judge should determine that the disposition is consistent with the sentencing practices of the jurisdiction and that the prosecutor did not agree to an inadequate sentence for a serious offender. The court should be given and apprised of all information and diagnostic reports concerning the offender. If the judge feels that additional investigation is in order, entry of the plea should be postponed pending completion of a presentence investigation. He should weigh the agreed disposition against factors similar to those that would be considered on the imposition of sentence after a trial: the defendant's need for correctional treatment, the circumstances of the case, the defendant's cooperation, and the requirements of law enforcement. If the agreed sentence appears within the reasonable range of an appropriate sentence after trial, it should satisfy the need to deal effectively with the offender yet not be an improper inducement. This standard may provide a somewhat clearer context for judicial consideration of the plea by putting it on the same footing as a sentencing decision, but the inherent difficulty of the sentencing choice is still present.

Only if the judge is satisfied that these criteria have been met should he indicate that the disposition is acceptable to him.[30] Otherwise he should deny entry of the plea. For example, if the judge is not satisfied that there is a factual basis for the plea, he should set the case for trial. If he determines that the plea is not entered knowingly, he should advise the defendant of the relevant issues and allow additional time for him to reconsider the plea. If he decides that a more severe sentence should be imposed, the defendant should be permitted to withdraw his plea. Neither the written memorandum nor any statements made at the judicial inquiry should be received in evidence.

Provision must be made for situations in which the judge finds the agreement unacceptable and in which the case is set for trial. In such instances the judge's function as arbiter at the trial would be complicated by his participation during the plea proceedings and the knowledge thus obtained. Procedures should be established for referral of trial and all further proceedings in the case to another judge, if possible. Application of these procedures in the many single judge courts would, of course, continue to raise vexing issues.

The steps suggested in this section are not proposed as a final answer to the problems presented by plea bargaining. They

---

[29] *Cf. Fed. R. Crim.* p. 11.

[30] Not only will such detailed inquiry result in fairer procedures, but the slight additional time spent in careful questioning will eliminate most collateral attacks on guilty pleas, thus saving judicial time in the long run.

are designed to minimize the dangers of these practices. They do not resolve the central question whether our system of justice should rely to the extent it does on practices that place such heavy pressures on a defendant to plead guilty. But ex-perience with a plea bargaining system in which negotiations are open, visible, and subject to judicial scrutiny should help to identify the risks involved in the system, and indicate the need for and direction of further change.

THE PRACTICE OF LAW AS CONFIDENCE GAME: ORGANIZATIONAL COOPTATION OF A PROFESSION

Abraham S. Blumberg

COURT STRUCTURE DEFINES ROLE OF DEFENSE LAWYER

The overwhelming majority of convictions in criminal cases (usually over 90 per cent) are not the product of a combative, trial-by-jury process at all, but instead merely involve the sentencing of the individual after a negotiated, bargained-for plea of guilty has been entered.[1] Al-though more recently the overzealous role of police and prosecutors in producing pretrial confessions and admissions has achieved a good deal of notoriety, scant attention has been paid to the organizational structure and personnel of the criminal court itself. Indeed, the extremely high conviction rate produced without the features of an adversary trial in our courts would tend to suggest that the "trial" becomes a perfunctory reiteration and validation of the pretrial interrogation and investigation.[2]

The institutional setting of the court defines a role for the defense counsel in

Excerpts reprinted from the official publication of the Law and Society Association, *Law and Society Review,* 1 (June 1967), pp. 15–39, by permission of the author and The Law and Society Association. (Footnotes renumbered.)

[1] F. J. Davis et al., *Society and the Law: New Meanings for an Old Profession* 301 (1962); L. Orfield, *Criminal Procedure from Arrest to Appeal* 297 (1947).

D. J. Newman, "Pleading Guilty for Considerations: A Study of Bargain Justice," 46 *J. Crim. L. C. & P.S.* 780–90 (1954). Newman's data covered only one year, 1954, in a midwestern community, however, it is in general confirmed by my own data drawn from a far more populous area, and from what is one of the major criminal courts in the country, for a period of fifteen years from 1950 to 1964 inclusive. The English experience tends also to confirm American data, see N. Walker, *Crime and Punishment in Britain: An Analysis of the Penal System* (1965). See also D. J. Newman, *Conviction: The Determination of Guilt or Innocence Without Trial* (1966), for a comprehensive legalistic study of the guilty plea sponsored by the American Bar Foundation. The criminal court as a social system, an analysis of "bargaining" and its functions in the criminal court's organizational structure, are examined in my forthcoming book, *The Criminal Court: A Sociological Perspective,* to be published by Quadrangle Books, Chicago.

[2] G. Feifer, *Justice in Moscow* (1965). The Soviet trial has been termed "an appeal from the pretrial investigation" and Feifer notes that the Soviet "trial" is simply a recapitulation of the data collected by the pretrial investigator. The notions of a trial being a "tabula rasa" and presumptions of innocence are wholly alien to Soviet notions of justice. ". . . the closer the investigation resembles the finished script, the better. . . ." *Id.* at 86.

a criminal case radically different from the one traditionally depicted.[3] Sociologists and others have focused their attention on the deprivations and social disabilities of such variables as race, ethnicity, and social class as being the source of an accused person's defeat in a criminal court. Largely overlooked is the variable of the court organization itself, which possesses a thrust, purpose, and direction of its own. It is grounded in pragmatic values, bureaucratic priorities, and administrative instruments. These exalt maximum production and the particularistic career designs of organizational incumbents, whose occupational and career commitments tend to generate a set of priorities. These priorities exert a higher claim than the stated ideological goals of "due process of law," and are often inconsistent with them.

Organizational goals and discipline impose a set of demands and conditions of practice on the respective professions in the criminal court, to which they respond by abandoning their ideological and professional commitments to the accused client, in the service of these higher claims of the court organization. All court personnel, including the accused's own lawyer, tend to be coopted to become agent-mediators [4] who help the accused redefine his situation and restructure his perceptions concomitant with a plea of guilty.

Of all the occupational roles in the court the only private individual who is officially recognized as having a special status and concomitant obligations is the lawyer. His legal status is that of "an

officer of the court" and he is held to a standard of ethical performance and duty to his client as well as to the court. This obligation is thought to be far higher than that expected of ordinary individuals occupying the various occupational statuses in the court community. However, lawyers, whether privately retained or of the legal-aid, public defender variety, have close and continuing relations with the prosecuting office and the court itself through discreet relations with the judges via their law secretaries or "confidential" assistants. Indeed, lines of communication, influence and contact with those offices, as well as with the Office of the Clerk of the court, Probation Division, and with the press, are essential to present and prospective requirements of criminal law practice. Similarly, the subtle involvement of the press and other mass media in the court's organizational network is not readily discernible to the casual observer. Accused persons come and go in the court system schema, but the structure and its occupational incumbents remain to carry on their respective career, occupational and organizational enterprises. The individual stridencies, tensions, and conflicts a given accused person's case may present to all the participants are overcome, because the formal and informal relations of all the groups in the court setting require it. The probability of continued future relations and interaction must be preserved at all costs.

This is particularly true of the "lawyer regulars" *i.e.,* those defense lawyers, who by virtue of their continuous appearances in behalf of defendants, tend to represent the bulk of a criminal court's non-indigent case workload, and those lawyers who are not "regulars," who appear almost casually in behalf of an occasional client. Some of the "lawyer regulars" are highly visible as one moves about the major urban centers of the nation, their offices line the back streets of the courthouses, at times sharing space with bondsmen. Their po-

---

[3] For a concise statement of the constitutional and economic aspects of the right to legal assistance, see M. G. Paulsen, *Equal Justice for the Poor Man* (1964); for a brief traditional description of the legal profession see P. A. Freund, "The Legal Profession," *Daedalus* 689–700 (1963).

[4] I use the concept in the general sense that Erving Goffman employed it in his *Asylums: Essays on the Social Situation of Mental Patients and Other Inmates* (1961).

litical "visibility" in terms of local club house ties, reaching into the judge's chambers and prosecutor's office, are also deemed essential to successful practitioners. Previous research has indicated that the "lawyer regulars" make no effort to conceal their dependence upon police, bondsmen, jail personnel. Nor do they conceal the necessity for maintaining intimate relations with all levels of personnel in the court setting as a means of obtaining, maintaining, and building their practice, but also in the negotiation of pleas and sentences.[5]

The client, then, is a secondary figure in the court system as in certain other bureaucratic settings.[6] He becomes a means to other ends of the organization's incumbents. He may present doubts, contingencies, and pressures which challenge existing informal arrangements or disrupt them; but these tend to be resolved in favor of the continuance of the organization and its relations as before. There is a greater community of interest among all the principal organizational structures and their incumbents than exists elsewhere in other settings. The accused's lawyer has far greater professional, economic, intellectual and other ties to the various elements of the court system than

he does to his own client. In short, the court is a closed community.

This is more than just the case of the usual "secrets" of bureaucracy which are fanatically defended from an outside view. Even all elements of the press are zealously determined to report on that which will not offend the board of judges, the prosecutor, probation, legal-aid, or other officials, in return for privileges and courtesies granted in the past and to be granted in the future. Rather than any view of the matter in terms of some variation of a "conspiracy" hypothesis, the simple explanation is one of an ongoing system handling delicate tensions, managing the trauma produced by law enforcement and administration, and requiring almost pathological distrust of "outsiders" bordering on group paranoia.

The hostile attitude toward "outsiders" is in large measure engendered by a defensiveness itself produced by the inherent deficiencies of assembly line justice, so characteristic of our major criminal courts. Intolerably large caseloads of defendants which must be disposed of in an organizational context of limited resources and personnel, potentially subject the participants in the court community to harsh scrutiny from appellate courts, and other public and private sources of condemnation. As a consequence, an almost irreconcilable conflict is posed in terms of intense pressures to process large numbers of cases on the one hand, and the stringent ideological and legal requirements of "due process of law," on the other hand. A rather tenuous resolution of the dilemma has emerged in the shape of a large variety of bureaucratically ordained and controlled "work crimes," short cuts, deviations, and outright rule violations adopted as court practice in order to meet production norms. Fearfully anticipating criticism on ethical as well as legal grounds, all the significant participants in the court's social structure are bound into an organized system of complicity. This con-

[5] A. L. Wood, "Informal Relations in the Practice of Criminal Law," 62 *Am. J. Soc.* 48–55 (1956); J. E. Carlin, *Lawyers on Their Own* 105–109 (1962); R. Goldfarb, *Ransom—A Critique of the American Bail System* 114–15 (1965). Relatively recent data as to recruitment to the legal profession, and variables involved in the type of practice engaged in, will be found in J. Ladinsky, "Careers of Lawyers, Law Practice, and Legal Institutions," 28 *Am. Soc. Rev.* 47–54 (1963). See also S. Warkov & J. Zelan, *Lawyers in the Making* (1965).

[6] There is a real question to be raised as to whether in certain organizational settings, a complete reversal of the bureaucratic-ideal has not occurred. That is, it would seem, in some instances the organization appears to exist to serve the needs of its various occupational incumbents, rather than its clients. A. Etzioni, *Modern Organizations* 94–104 (1964).

sists of a work arrangement in which the patterned, covert, informal breaches, and evasions of "due process" are institutionalized, but are, nevertheless, denied to exist.

These institutionalized evasions will be found to occur to some degree, in all criminal courts. Their nature, scope and complexity are largely determined by the size of the court, and the character of the community in which it is located, *e.g.,* whether it is a large, urban institution, or a relatively small rural county court. In addition, idiosyncratic, local conditions may contribute to a unique flavor in the character and quality of the criminal law's administration in a particular community. However, in most instances a variety of stratagems are employed—some subtle, some crude, in effectively disposing of what are often too large caseloads. A wide variety of coercive devices are employed against an accused-client, couched in a depersonalized, instrumental, bureaucratic version of due process of law, and which are in reality a perfunctory obeisance to the ideology of due process. These include some very explicit pressures which are exerted in some measure by all court personnel, including judges, to plead guilty and avoid trial. In many instances the sanction of a potentially harsh sentence is utilized as the visible alternative to pleading guilty, in the case of recalcitrants. Probation and psychiatric reports are "tailored" to organizational needs, or are at least responsive to the court organization's requirements for the refurbishment of a defendant's social biography, consonant with his new status. A resourceful judge can, through his subtle domination of the proceedings, impose his will on the final outcome of a trial. Stenographers and clerks, in their function as record keepers, are on occasion pressed into service in support of a judicial need to "rewrite" the record of a courtroom event. Bail practices are usually employed for purposes other than simply assuring a defendant's presence on the date of a hearing in connection with his case. Too often, the discretionary power as to bail is part of the arsenal of weapons available to collapse the resistance of an accused person. The foregoing is a most cursory examination of some of the more prominent "short cuts" available to any court organization. There are numerous other procedural strategies constituting due process deviations, which tend to become the work style artifacts of a court's personnel. Thus, only court "regulars" who are "bound in" are really accepted; others are treated routinely and in almost a coldly correct manner.

The defense attorneys, therefore, whether of the legal-aid, public defender variety, or privately retained, although operating in terms of pressures specific to their respective role and organizational obligations, ultimately are concerned with strategies which tend to lead to a plea. It is the rational, impersonal elements involving economies of time, labor, expense and a superior commitment of the defense counsel to these rationalistic values of maximum production [7] of court organization that prevail, in his relationship with a client. The lawyer "regulars" are fre-

[7] Three relatively recent items reported in *The New York Times*, tend to underscore this point as it has manifested itself in one of the major criminal courts. In one instance the Bronx County Bar Association condemned "mass assembly-line justice," which "was rushing defendants into pleas of guilty and into convictions, in violation of their legal rights," *N.Y. Times,* March 10, 1965, p. 51. Another item, appearing somewhat later that year reports a judge criticizing his own court system (the New York Criminal Court), that "pressure to set statistical records in disposing of cases had hurt the administration of justice." *N.Y. Times,* Nov. 4, 1965, p. 49. A third, and most unusual recent public discussion in the press was a statement by a leading New York appellate judge decrying "instant justice" which is employed to reduce court calendar congestion "converting our courthouses into counting houses . . . , as in most big cities where the volume of business tends to overpower court facilities." *N.Y. Times,* Feb. 5, 1966, p. 58.

quently former staff members of the prosecutor's office and utilize the prestige, know-how and contacts of their former affiliation as part of their stock in trade. Close and continuing relations between the lawyer "regular" and his former colleagues in the prosecutor's office generally overshadow the relationship between the regular and his client. The continuing colleagueship of supposedly adversary counsel rests on real professional and organizational needs of a *quid pro quo*, which goes beyond the limits of an accommodation or *modus vivendi* one might ordinarily expect under the circumstances of an otherwise seemingly adversary relationship. Indeed, the adversary features which are manifest are for the most part muted and exist even in their attenuated form largely for external consumption. The principals, lawyer and assistant district attorney, rely upon one another's cooperation for their continued professional existence, and so the bargaining between them tends usually to be "reasonable" rather than fierce.

FEE COLLECTION AND FIXING

The real key to understanding the role of defense counsel in a criminal case is to be found in the area of the fixing of the fee to be charged and its collection. The problem of fixing and collecting the fee tends to influence to a significant degree the criminal court process itself, and not just the relationship of the lawyer and his client. In essence, a lawyer-client "confidence game" is played. A true confidence game is unlike the case of the emperor's new clothes wherein that monarch's nakedness was a result of inordinate gullibility and credulity. In a genuine confidence game, the perpetrator manipulates the basic dishonesty of his partner, the victim or mark, toward his own (the confidence operator's) ends. Thus, "the victim of a con scheme must have some larceny in his heart." [8]

Legal service lends itself particularly well to confidence games. Usually, a plumber will be able to demonstrate empirically that he has performed a service by clearing up the stuffed drain, repairing the leaky faucet or pipe—and therefore merits his fee. He has rendered, when summoned, a visible, tangible boon for his client in return for the requested fee. A physician, who has not performed some visible surgery or otherwise engaged in some readily discernible procedure in connection with a patient, may be deemed by the patient to have "done nothing" for him. As a consequence, medical practitioners may simply prescribe or administer by injection a placebo to overcome a patient's potential reluctance or dissatisfaction in paying a requested fee, "for nothing."

In the practice of law there is a special problem in this regard, no matter what the level of the practitioner or his place in the hierarchy of prestige. Much legal work is intangible either because it is simply a few words of advice, some preventive action, a telephone call, negotiation of some kind, a form filled out and filed, a hurried conference with another attorney or an official of a government agency, a letter or opinion written, or a countless variety of seemingly innocuous, and even prosaic procedures and actions. These are the basic activities, apart from any possible court appearance, of almost all lawyers, at all levels of practice. Much of the activity is not in the nature of the exercise of the traditional, precise professional skills of the attorney such as library research and oral argument in connection with appellate briefs, court motions, trial work, drafting of opinions, memoranda, contracts, and other complex documents

---

[8] R. L. Gasser, "The Confidence Game," 27 *Fed. Prob.* 47 (1963).

and agreements. Instead, much legal activity, whether it is at the lowest or highest "white shoe" law firm levels, is of the brokerage, agent, sales representative, lobbyist type of activity, in which the lawyer acts for someone else in pursuing the latter's interests and designs. The service is intangible.[9]

The large scale law firm may not speak as openly of their "contacts," their "fixing" abilities, as does the lower level lawyer. They trade instead upon a facade of thick carpeting, walnut panelling, genteel low pressure, and superficialities of traditional legal professionalism. There are occasions when even the large firm is on the defensive in connection with the fees they charge because the services rendered or results obtained do not appear to merit the fee asked.[10] Therefore, there is a recurrent problem in the legal profession in fixing the amount of fee, and in justifying the basis for the requested fee.

Although the fee at times amounts to what the traffic and the conscience of the lawyer will bear, one further observation must be made with regard to the size of the fee and its collection. The defendant in a criminal case and the material gain he may have acquired during the course of his illicit activities are soon parted. Not infrequently the ill gotten fruits of the various modes of larceny are sequestered by a defense lawyer in payment of his fee. Inexorably, the amount of the fee is a function of the dollar value of the crime committed, and is frequently set with meticulous precision at a sum which bears an uncanny relationship to that of the net proceeds of the particular offense involved. On occasion, defendants have been known to commit additional offenses while at liberty on bail, in order to secure the

requisite funds with which to meet their obligations for payment of legal fees. Defense lawyers condition even the most obtuse clients to recognize that there is a firm interconnection between fee payment and the zealous exercise of professional expertise, secret knowledge, and organizational "connections" in their behalf. Lawyers, therefore, seek to keep their clients in a proper state of tension, and to arouse in them the precise edge of anxiety which is calculated to encourage prompt fee payment. Consequently, the client attitude in the relationship between defense counsel and an accused is in many instances a precarious admixture of hostility, mistrust, dependence, and sycophancy. By keeping his client's anxieties aroused to the proper pitch, and establishing a seemingly causal relationship between a requested fee and the accused's ultimate extrication from his onerous difficulties, the lawyer will have established the necessary preliminary groundwork to assure a minimum of haggling over the fee and its eventual payment.

In varying degrees, as a consequence, all law practice involves a manipulation of the client and a stage management of the lawyer-client relationship so that at least an *appearance* of help and service will be forthcoming. This is accomplished in a variety of ways, often exercised in combination with each other. At the outset, the lawyer-professional employs with suitable variation a measure of sales-puff which may range from an air of unbounding self-confidence, adequacy, and dominion over events, to that of complete arrogance. This will be supplemented by the affection of a studied, faultless mode of personal attire. In the larger firms, the furnishings and office trappings will serve as the backdrop to help in impression management and client intimidation. In all firms, solo or large scale, an access to secret knowledge, and to the seats of power and influence is inferred, or presumed to

[9] C. W. Mills, *White Collar* 121–29 (1951); J. E. Carlin, *supra*, note 5.
[10] E. O. Smigel, *The Wall Street Lawyer* (New York: The Free Press of Glencoe, 1964), p. 309.

a varying degree as the basic vendible commodity of the practitioners.

The lack of visible end product offers a special complication in the course of the professional life of the criminal court lawyer with respect to his fee and in his relations with his client. The plain fact is that an accused in a criminal case always "loses" even when he has been exonerated by an acquittal, discharge, or dismissal of his case. The hostility of an accused which follows as a consequence of his arrest, incarceration, possible loss of job, expense and other traumas connected with his case is directed, by means of displacement, toward his lawyer. It is in this sense that it may be said that a criminal lawyer never really "wins" a case. The really satisfied client is rare, since in the very nature of the situation even an accused's vindication leaves him with some degree of dissatisfaction and hostility. It is this state of affairs that makes for a lawyer-client relationship in the criminal court which tends to be a somewhat exaggerated version of the usual lawyer-client confidence game.

At the outset, because there are great risks of nonpayment of the fee, due to the impecuniousness of his clients, and the fact that a man who is sentenced to jail may be a singularly unappreciative client, the criminal lawyer collects his fee *in advance*. Often, because the lawyer and the accused both have questionable designs of their own upon each other, the confidence game can be played. The criminal lawyer must serve three major functions, or stated another way, he must solve three problems. First, he must arrange for his fee; second, he must prepare and then, if necessary, "cool out" his client in case of defeat [11] (a highly likely contingency);

third, he must satisfy the court organization that he has performed adequately in the process of negotiating the plea, so as to preclude the possibility of any sort of embarrassing incident which may serve to invite "outside" scrutiny.

In assuring the attainment of one of his primary objectives, his fee, the criminal lawyer will very often enter into negotiations with the accused's kin, including collateral relatives. In many instances, the accused himself is unable to pay any sort of fee or anything more than a token fee. It then becomes important to involve as many of the accused's kin as possible in the situation. This is especially so if the attorney hopes to collect a significant part of a proposed substantial fee. It is not uncommon for several relatives to contribute toward the fee. The larger the group, the greater the possibility that the lawyer will collect a sizable fee by getting contributions from each.

A fee for a felony case which ultimately results in a plea, rather than a trial, may ordinarily range anywhere from $500 to $1,500. Should the case go to trial, the fee will be proportionately larger, depending upon the length of the trial. But the larger the fee the lawyer wishes to exact, the more impressive his performance must be, in terms of his stage managed image as a personage of great influence and power in the court organization. Court personnel are keenly aware of the extent to which a lawyer's stock in trade involves the precarious stage management of an image which goes beyond the usual professional flamboyance, and for this reason alone the lawyer is "bound in" to the authority system of the court's

---

[11] Talcott Parsons indicates that the social role and function of the lawyer can be therapeutic, helping his client psychologically in giving him necessary emotional support at critical times. The lawyer is also said to be acting as an agent of social control in the counseling of his client and

in the influencing of his course of conduct. See T. Parsons, *Essays in Sociological Theory*, 382 et seq. (1954); E. Goffman, *On Cooling the Mark Out: Some Aspects of Adaptation to Failure*, in *Human Behavior and Social Processes* 482–505 (A. Rose ed., 1962). Goffman's "cooling out" analysis is especially relevant in the lawyer-accused client relationship.

organizational discipline. Therefore, to some extent, court personnel will aid the lawyer in the creation and maintenance of that impression. There is a tacit commitment to the lawyer by the court organization, apart from formal etiquette, to aid him in this. Such augmentation of the lawyer's stage managed image as this affords, is the partial basis for the *quid pro quo* which exists between the lawyer and the court organization. It tends to serve as the continuing basis for the higher loyalty of the lawyer to the organization; his relationship with his client, in contrast, is transient, ephemeral and often superficial.

DEFENSE LAWYER AS DOUBLE AGENT

The lawyer has often been accused of stirring up unnecessary litigation, especially in the field of negligence. He is said to acquire a vested interest in a cause of action or claim which was initially his client's. The strong incentive of possible fee motivates the lawyer to promote litigation which would otherwise never have developed. However, the criminal lawyer develops a vested interest of an entirely different nature in his client's case: to limit its scope and duration rather than do battle. Only in this way can a case be "profitable." Thus, he enlists the aid of relatives not only to assure payment of his fee, but he will also rely on these persons to help him in his agent-mediator role of convincing the accused to plead guilty, and ultimately to help in "cooling out" the accused if necessary.

It is at this point that an accused-defendant may experience his first sense of "betrayal." While he had perhaps perceived the police and prosecutor to be adversaries, or possibly even the judge, the accused is wholly unprepared for his counsel's role performance as an agent-mediator. In the same vein, it is even less likely to occur to an accused that members of his own family or other kin may become agents, albeit at the behest and urging of other agents or mediators, acting on the principle that they are in reality helping an accused negotiate the best possible plea arrangement under the circumstances. Usually, it will be the lawyer who will activate next of kin in this role, his ostensible motive being to arrange for his fee. But soon latent and unstated motives will assert themselves, with entreaties by counsel to the accused's next of kin, to appeal to the accused to "help himself" by pleading. *Gemeinschaft* sentiments are to this extent exploited by a defense lawyer (or even at times by a district attorney) to achieve specific secular ends, that is, of concluding a particular matter with all possible dispatch.

The fee is often collected in stages, each installment usually payable prior to a necessary court appearance required during the course of an accused's career journey. At each stage, in his interviews and communications with the accused, or in addition, with members of his family, if they are helping with the fee payment, the lawyer employs an air of professional confidence and "inside-dopesterism" in order to assuage anxieties on all sides. He makes the necessary bland assurances, and in effect manipulates his client, who is usually willing to do and say the things, true or not, which will help his attorney extricate him. Since the dimensions of what he is essentially selling, organizational influence and expertise, are not technically and precisely measurable, the lawyer can make extravagant claims of influence and secret knowledge with impunity. Thus, lawyers frequently claim to have inside knowledge in connection with information in the hands of the D.A., police, probation officials or to have access to these functionaries. Factually, they often do, and need only to exaggerate the nature of their relationships with them to obtain the desired effective impression upon the client. But, as in the genuine confidence game, the victim who has participated is loath to do anything which will upset the lesser plea which his lawyer has "conned" him into accepting.[12]

In effect, in his role as double agent, the criminal lawyer performs an extremely vital and delicate mission for the court organization and the accused. Both principals are anxious to terminate the litigation with a minimum of expense and damage to each other. There is no other personage or role incumbent in the total court structure more strategically located, who by training and in terms of his own requirements, is more ideally suited to do so than the lawyer. In recognition of this, judges will cooperate with attorneys in many important ways. For example, they will adjourn the case of an accused in jail awaiting plea or sentence if the attorney requests such action. While explicitly this may be done for some innocuous and seemingly valid reason, the tacit purpose is that pressure is being applied by the attorney for the collection of his fee, which he knows will probably not be forthcoming if the case is concluded. Judges are aware of this tactic on the part of lawyers, who, by requesting an adjournment, keep an accused incarcerated awhile longer as a not too subtle method of dunning a client for payment. However, the judges will go along with this, on the ground that important ends are being served. Often, the only end served is to protect a lawyer's fee.

The judge will help an accused's lawyer in still another way. He will lend the official aura of his office and courtroom so that a lawyer can stage manage an impression of an "all out" performance for the accused in justification of his fee. The judge and other court personnel will serve as a backdrop for a scene charged with dramatic fire, in which the accused's lawyer makes a stirring appeal in his behalf. With a show of restrained passion, the lawyer will intone the virtues of the accused and recite the social deprivations which have reduced him to his present state. The speech varies somewhat, depending on whether the accused has been convicted after trial or has pleaded guilty. In the main, however, the incongruity, superficiality, and ritualistic character of the total performance is underscored by a visibly impassive, almost bored reaction on the part of the judge and other members of the court retinue.

Afterward, there is a hearty exchange of pleasantries between the lawyer and district attorney, wholly out of context in terms of the supposed adversary nature of the preceding events. The fiery passion in defense of his client is gone, and the lawyers for both sides resume their offstage relations, chatting amiably and perhaps including the judge in their restrained banter. No other aspect of their visible conduct so effectively serves to put even a casual observer on notice, that these individuals have claims upon each other. These seemingly innocuous actions are indicative of continuing organizational and informal relations, which, in their intricacy and depth, range far beyond any priorities or claims a particular defendant may have.[13]

---

[12] The question has never been raised as to whether "bargain justice," "copping a plea," or justice by negotiation is a constitutional process. Although it has become the most central aspect of the process of criminal law administration, it has received virtually no close scrutiny by the appellate courts. As a consequence, it is relatively free of legal control and supervision. But, apart from any questions of the legality of bargaining, in terms of the pressures and devices that are employed which tend to violate due process of law, there remain ethical and practical questions. The system of bargain-counter justice is like the proverbial iceberg, much of its danger is concealed in secret negotiations and its least alarming feature, the final plea, being the one presented to public view. See A. S. Trebach, *The Rationing of Justice* 74–94 (1964); Note "Guilty Plea Bargaining: Compromises by Prosecutors to Secure Guilty Pleas," 112 *U. Pa. L. Rev.* 865–95 (1964).

[13] For a conventional summary statement of some of the inevitable conflicting loyalties encountered in the practice of law, see E. E. Cheatham, *Cases and Materials on the Legal Profession* 70–79 (2d ed., 1955).

Criminal law practice is a unique form of private law practice since it really only appears to be private practice.[14] Actually it is bureaucratic practice, because of the legal practitioner's enmeshment in the authority, discipline, and perspectives of the court organization. Private practice, supposedly, in a professional sense, involves the maintenance of an organized, disciplined body of knowledge and learning; the individual practitioners are imbued with a spirit of autonomy and service, the earning of a livelihood being incidental. In the sense that the lawyer in the criminal court serves as a double agent, serving higher organizational rather than professional ends, he may be deemed to be engaged in bureaucratic rather than private practice. To some extent the lawyer-client "confidence game," in addition to its other functions, serves to conceal this fact.

THE CLIENT'S PERCEPTION

The "cop-out" ceremony, in which the court process culminates, is not only invaluable for redefining the accused's perspectives of himself, but also in reiterating publicly in a formally structured ritual the accused person's guilt for the benefit of significant "others" who are observing. The accused not only is made to assert publicly his guilt of a specific crime, but also a complete recital of its details. He is further made to indicate that he is entering his plea of guilt freely, willingly, and voluntarily, and that he is not doing so because of any promises or in consideration of any commitments that may have been made to him to anyone. This last is intended as a blanket statement to shield the participants from any possible charges of "coercion" or undue influence that may have been exerted in violation of due process requirements. Its function is to preclude any later review by an appellate court on these grounds, and also to obviate any second thoughts an accused may develop in connection with his plea.

However, for the accused, the conception of self as a guilty person is in large measure a temporary role adaptation. His career socialization as an accused, if it is successful, eventuates in his acceptance and redefinition of himself as a guilty person.[15] However, the transformation is

---

[14] Some lawyers at either end of the continuum of law practice appear to have grave doubts as to whether it is indeed a profession at all. J. E. Carlin, *op. cit., supra,* note 5, at 192; E. O. Smigel, *supra,* note 10, at 304–305. Increasingly, it is perceived as a business with widespread evasion of the Canons of Ethics, duplicity and chicanery being practiced in an effort to get and keep business. The poet, Carl Sandburg, epitomized this notion in the following vignette: "Have you a criminal lawyer in this burg?" "We think so but we haven't been able to prove it on him." C. Sandburg, *The People, Yes* 154 (1936).

Thus, while there is a considerable amount of dishonesty present in law practice involving fee splitting, thefts from clients, influence peddling, fixing, questionable use of favors and gifts to obtain business or influence others, this sort of activity is most often attributed to the "solo," private practice lawyer. See A. L. Wood, *Professional Ethics Among Criminal Lawyers,* Social Problems 70–83 (1959). However, to some degree, large scale "downtown" elite firms also engage in these dubious activities. The difference is that the latter firms enjoy a good deal of immunity from these harsh charges because of their institutional and organizational advantages, in terms of near monopoly over more desirable types of practice, as well as exerting great influence in the political, economic and professional realms of power.

[15] This does not mean that most of those who plead guilty are innocent of any crime. Indeed, in many instances those who have been able to negotiate a lesser plea, have done so willingly and even eagerly. The system of justice-by-negotiation, without trial, probably tends to better serve the interests and requirements of guilty persons, who are thereby presented with formal alternatives of "half a loaf," in terms of, at worst, possibilities of a lesser plea and a concomitant shorter sentence as compensation for their acquiescence and participation. Having observed the prescriptive etiquette in compliance with the defendant role expectancies in this setting, he is rewarded. An innocent person, on the other hand, is confronted with the same set of role prescriptions, structures and legal alternatives, and in any event, for him this mode of justice is often an ineluctable bind.

ephemeral, in that he will, in private, quickly reassert his innocence. Of importance is that he accept his defeat, publicly proclaim it, and find some measure of pacification in it.[16] Almost immediately after his plea, a defendant will generally be interviewed by a representative of the probation division in connection with a presentence report which is to be prepared. The very first question to be asked of him by the probation officer is: "Are you guilty of the crime to which you pleaded?" This is by way of double affirmation of the defendant's guilt. Should the defendant now begin to make bold assertions of his innocence, despite his plea of guilty, he will be asked to withdraw his plea and stand trial on the original charges. Such a threatened possibility is, in most instances, sufficient to cause an accused to let the plea stand and to request the probation officer to overlook his exclamations of innocence. The table that follows is a breakdown of the categorized responses of a random sample of male defendants in Metropolitan Court [17] during 1962, 1963,

and 1964 in connection with their statements during presentence probation interviews following their plea of guilty.

It would be well to observe at the outset, that of the 724 defendants who pleaded guilty before trial, only 43 (5.94 per cent) of the total group had confessed prior to their indictment. Thus, the ultimate judicial process was predicated upon evidence independent of any confession of the accused.[18]

As the data indicate, only a relatively small number (95) out of the total number of defendants actually will even admit their guilt, following the "cop-out" ceremony. However, even though they have affirmed their guilt, many of these defendants felt that they should have been able to negotiate a more favorable plea. The largest aggregate of defendants (373) were those who reasserted their "innocence" following their public profession of guilt during the "cop-out" ceremony. These defendants employed differential degrees of fervor, solemnity and credibility, ranging from really mild, wavering

[16] "Any communicative network between persons whereby the public identity of an actor is transformed into something looked on as lower in the local scheme of social types will be called a 'status degradation ceremony.'" H. Garfinkel, *Conditions of Successful Degradation Ceremonies,* 61 Am. J. Soc. 420–24 (1956). But contrary to the conception of the "cop out" as a "status degradation ceremony," is the fact that it is in reality a charade, during the course of which an accused must project an appropriate and acceptable amount of guilt, penitence and remorse. Having adequately feigned the role of the "guilty person," his hearers will engage in the fantasy that he is contrite, and thereby merits a lesser plea. It is one of the essential functions of the criminal lawyer that he coach and direct his accused-client in that role performance. Thus, what is actually involved is not a "degradation" process at all, but is, instead, a highly structured system of exchange cloaked in the rituals of legalism and public professions of guilt and repentance.

[17] The name is of course fictitious. However, the actual court which served as the universe from which the data were drawn, is one of the largest criminal courts in the United States, dealing with felonies only. Female defendants in the years

1950 through 1964 constituted from 7–10% of the totals for each year.

[18] My own data in this connection would appear to support Sobel's conclusion [Justice Nathan R. Sobel's analysis will be found in six articles which appeared in the *New York Law Journal,* beginning November 15, 1965, through November 21, 1965, titled "The Exclusionary Rules in the Law of Confessions: A Legal Perspective—A Practical Perspective"], and appears to be at variance with the prevalent view, which stresses the importance of confessions in law enforcement and prosecution. All the persons in my sample were originally charged with felonies ranging from homicide to forgery; in most instances the original felony charges were reduced to misdemeanors by way of a negotiated lesser plea. The vast range of crime categories which are available, facilitates the patterned court process of plea reduction to a lesser offense, which is also usually a socially less opprobrious crime. For an illustration of this feature of the bargaining process in a court utilizing a public defender office, see D. Sudnow, "Normal Crimes: Sociological Features of the Penal Code in a Public Defender Office," 12 *Social Problems* 255–76 (1965).

Table 1   Defendant Responses as to Guilt or Innocence after Pleading Guilty (N = 724; Years — 1962, 1963, 1964)

Nature of Response		N of Defendants
Innocent (Manipulated)	"The lawyer or judge, police or D.A. 'conned me' "	86
Innocent (Pragmatic)	"Wanted to get it over with" "You can't beat the system" "They have you over a barrel when you have a record"	147
Innocent (Advice of counsel)	"Followed my lawyer's advice"	92
Innocent (Defiant)	"Framed" — Betrayed by "Complainant," "Police," "Squealers," "Lawyer," "Friends," "Wife," "Girlfriend"	33
Innocent (Adverse social data)	Blames probation officer or psychiatrist for "Bad Report," in cases where there was pre-pleading investigation	15
Guilty	"But I should have gotten a better deal" Blames Lawyer, D.A., Police, Judge	74
Guilty	Won't say anything further	21
Fatalistic (Doesn't press his "Innocence," won't admit "Guilt")	"I did it for convenience" "My lawyer told me it was only thing I could do" "I did it because it was the best way out"	248
No Response		8
Total		724

assertions of innocence which were embroidered with a variety of stock explanations and rationalizations, to those of an adamant, "framed" nature. Thus, the "Innocent" group, for the most part, were largely concerned with underscoring for their probation interviewer their essential "goodness" and "worthiness," despite their formal plea of guilty. Assertion of his innocence at the post-plea stage, resurrects a more respectable and acceptable self concept for the accused defendant who has pleaded guilty. A recital of the structural exigencies which precipitated his plea of guilt, serves to embellish a newly proffered claim of innocence, which many defendants mistakenly feel will stand them in good stead at the time of sentence, or ultimately with probation or parole authorities.

Relatively few (33) maintained their innocence in terms of having been "framed" by some person or agent-mediator, although a larger number (86) indicated that they had been manipulated or "conned" by an agent-mediator to plead guilty, but as indicated, their assertions of innocence were relatively mild.

A rather substantial group (147) preferred to stress the pragmatic aspects of their plea of guilty. They would only perfunctorily assert their innocence and would in general refer to some adverse aspect of their situation which they believed tended to negatively affect their bargaining leverage, including in some instances a prior criminal record.

One group of defendants (92), while maintaining their innocence, simply employed some variation of a theme following "the advice of counsel" as a covering response, to explain their guilty plea in the light of their new affirmation of innocence.

The largest single group of defendants (248) were basically fatalistic. They often verbalized weak suggestions of their innocence in rather halting terms, wholly without conviction. By the same token, they would not admit guilt readily and were generally evasive as to guilt or innocence, preferring to stress aspects of their stoic submission in their decision to plead. This sizable group of defendants appeared to perceive the total court process as being caught up in a monstrous organizational apparatus, in which the defendant role expectancies were not clearly defined. Reluctant to offend anyone in authority, fearful that clear-cut statements on their part as to their guilt or innocence would be negatively construed, they adopted a stance of passivity, resignation and acceptance. Interestingly, they would in most instances invoke their lawyer as being the one who crystallized the available alternatives for them, and who was therefore the critical element in their decision-making process.

In order to determine which agent-mediator was most influential in altering the accused's perspectives as to his decision to plead or go to trial (regardless of the proposed basis of the plea), the same sample of defendants were asked to indicate the person who first suggested to them that they plead guilty. They were also asked to indicate which of the persons or officials who made such suggestion, was most influential in affecting their final decision to plead.

[The table below] indicates the break-down of the responses to the two questions.

It is popularly assumed that the police, through forced confessions, and the district attorney, employing still other pressures, are most instrumental in the inducement of an accused to plead guilty.[19] As Table [2] indicates, it is actually the defendant's own counsel who is most effective in this role. Further, this phenomenon tends to reinforce the extremely rational nature of criminal law administration, for an organization could not rely upon the sort of idiosyncratic measures employed by the police to induce confessions and maintain its efficiency, high production and overall rational-legal character. The defense counsel becomes the ideal agent-mediator since, as "officer of the court" and confidant of the accused and his kin, he lives astride both worlds and can serve the ends of the two as well as his own.[20]

While an accused's wife, for example, may be influential in making him more amenable to a plea, her agent-mediator role has, nevertheless, usually been sparked and initiated by defense counsel. Further, although a number of first suggestions of

[19] Failures, shortcomings and oppressive features of our system of criminal justice have been attributed to a variety of sources including "lawless" police, overzealous district attorneys, "hanging" juries, corruption and political connivance, incompetent judges, inadequacy or lack of counsel, and poverty or other social disabilities of the defendant. See A. Barth, *Law Enforcement versus the Law* (1963), for a journalist's account embodying this point of view; J. H. Skolnick, *Justice without Trial: Law Enforcement in Democratic Society* (1966), for a sociologist's study of the role of the police in criminal law administration. For a somewhat more detailed, albeit legalistic and somewhat technical discussion of American police procedures, see W. R. LaFave, *Arrest: The Decision to Take a Suspect into Custody* (1965).

[20] Aspects of the lawyer's ambivalences with regard to the expectancies of the various groups who have claims upon him, are discussed in H. J. O'Gorman, "The Ambivalence of Lawyers," paper presented at the Eastern Sociological Association meetings, April 10, 1965.

Table 2   Role of Agent-mediators in Defendant's Guilty Plea

Person or Official	First Suggested Plea of Guilty	Influenced the Accused Most in His Final Decision to Plead
Judge	4	26
District Attorney	67	116
Defense Counsel	407	411
Probation Officer	14	3
Psychiatrist	8	1
Wife	34	120
Friends and Kin	21	14
Police	14	4
Fellow Inmates	119	14
Others	28	5
No Response	8	10
Total	724	724

a plea came from an accused's fellow jail inmates, he tended to rely largely on his counsel as an ultimate source of influence in his final decision. The defense counsel, being a crucial figure in the total organizational scheme in constituting a new set of perspectives for the accused, the same sample of defendants were asked to indicate at which stage of their contact with counsel was the suggestion of a plea made. There are three basic kinds of defense counsel available in Metropolitan Court: Legal-aid, privately retained counsel, and counsel assigned by the court (but may eventually be privately retained by the accused).

The overwhelming majority of accused persons, regardless of type of counsel, related a specific incident which indicated an urging or suggestion, either during the course of the first or second contact, that they plead guilty to a lesser charge if this could be arranged. Of all the agent-mediators, it is the lawyer who is most effective in manipulating an accused's perspectives, notwithstanding pressures that may have been previously applied by police, district attorney, judge or any of the agent-mediators that may have been activated by them. Legal-aid and assigned counsel would apparently be more likely to sug-

gest a possible plea at the point of initial interview as response to pressures of time. In the case of the assigned counsel, the strong possibility that there is no fee involved, may be an added impetus to such a suggestion at the first contact.

In addition, there is some further evidence in Table [3] of the perfunctory, ministerial character of the system of Metropolitan Court and similar criminal courts. There is little real effort to individualize, and the lawyer's role as agent-mediator may be seen as unique in that he is in effect a double agent. Although, as "officer of the court" he mediates between the court organization and the defendant, his roles with respect to each are rent by conflicts of interest. Too often these must be resolved in favor of the organization which provides him with the means for his professional existence. Consequently, in order to reduce the strains and conflicts imposed in what is ultimately an overdemanding role obligation for him, the lawyer engages in the lawyer-client "confidence game" so as to structure more favorably an otherwise onerous role system.[21]

21 W. J. Goode, "A Theory of Role Strain," 25 *Am. Soc. Rev.* 483–96 (1960); J. D. Snoek, "Role Strain in Diversified Role Sets," 71 *Am. J. Soc.* 363–72 (1966).

Table 3 Stage at Which Counsel Suggested Accused to Plead (N = 724)

| Contact | Counsel Type | | | | | | | |
| | Privately Retained | | Legal-aid | | Assigned | | Total | |
	N	%	N	%	N	%	N	%
First	66	35	237	49	28	60	331	46
Second	83	44	142	29	8	17	233	32
Third	29	15	63	13	4	9	96	13
Fourth or More	12	6	31	7	5	11	48	7
No Response	0	0	14	3	2	4	16	2
Total	190	100	487	101*	47	101*	724	100

*Rounded percentage.

CONCLUSION

Recent decisions of the Supreme Court, in the area of criminal law administration and defendant's rights, fail to take into account three crucial aspects of social structure which may tend to render the more libertarian rules as nugatory. The decisions overlook (1) the nature of courts as formal organization; (2) the relationship that the lawyer-regular *actually* has with the court organization; and (3) the character of the lawyer-client relationship in the criminal court (the routine relationships, not those unusual ones that are described in "heroic" terms in novels, movies, and TV).

Courts, like many other modern large-scale organizations possess a monstrous appetite for the cooptation of entire professional groups as well as individuals.

Almost all those who come within the ambit of organizational authority, find that their definitions, perceptions and values have been refurbished, largely in terms favorable to the particular organization and its goals. As a result, recent Supreme Court decisions may have a long range effect which is radically different from that intended or anticipated. The more libertarian rules will tend to produce the rather ironic end result of augmenting the *existing* organizational arrangements, enriching court organizations with more personnel and elaborate structure, which in turn will maximize organizational goals of "efficiency" and production. Thus, many defendants will find that courts will possess an even more sophisticated apparatus for processing them toward a guilty plea!

THE SOCIETAL REACTION TO DEVIANCE: ASCRIPTIVE ELEMENTS IN THE PSYCHIATRIC SCREENING OF MENTAL PATIENTS IN A MIDWESTERN STATE

Thomas J. Scheff

The case for making the societal reaction to deviance a major independent variable in studies of deviant behavior has been succinctly stated by Kitsuse:

A sociological theory of deviance must focus specifically upon the interactions which not only define behaviors as deviant but also organize and activate the application of sanctions by individuals, groups, or agencies. For in modern society, the socially significant differentiation of deviants from the non-deviant population is increasingly contingent upon circumstances of situation, place, social and personal biography, and the bureaucratically organized activities of agencies of control.[1]

In the case of mental disorder, psychiatric diagnosis is one of the crucial steps which "organizes and activates" the societal reaction, since the state is legally empowered to segregate and isolate those persons whom psychiatrists find to be committable because of mental illness.

Recently, however, it has been argued that mental illness may be more usefully considered to be a social status than a disease, since the symptoms of mental illness are vaguely defined and widely distributed, and the definition of behavior as symptomatic of mental illness is usually

dependent upon social rather than medical contingencies.[2] Furthermore, the argument continues, the status of the mental patient is more often an ascribed status, with conditions for status entry external to the patient, than an achieved status with conditions for status entry dependent upon the patient's own behavior. According to this argument, the societal reaction is a fundamentally important variable in all stages of a deviant career.

The actual usefulness of a theory of mental disorder based on the societal reaction is largely an empirical question: to what extent is entry to the status of mental patient independent of the behavior or "condition" of the patient? The present paper will explore this question for one phase of the societal reaction: the legal screening of persons alleged to be mentally ill. This screening represents the official phase of the societal reaction, which occurs after the alleged deviance has been called to the attention of the community by a complainant. This report will make no reference to the initial deviance or other situation which resulted in the complaint, but will deal entirely with procedures used by the courts after the complaint has occurred.

The purpose of the description that follows is to determine the extent of uncertainty that exists concerning new patients' qualifications for involuntary confinement in a mental hospital, and the reactions of the courts to this type of uncertainty. The data presented here indicate that, in the face of uncertainty, there is a strong presumption of illness by

Reprinted from *Social Problems,* 11 (Spring 1964), pp. 401–13, by permission of the author and the Society for the Study of Social Problems.

This report is part of a larger study, made possible by a grant from The Advisory Mental Health Committee of Midwestern State. By prior agreement, the state in which the study was conducted is not identified in publications.

[1] John I. Kitsuse, "Societal Reaction to Deviant Behavior: Problems of Theory and Method," *Social Problems,* 9 (Winter, 1962), pp. 247–257.

[2] Edwin M. Lemert, *Social Pathology*, New York: McGraw-Hill, 1951; Erving Goffman, *Asylum*, Chicago: Aldine, 1962.

the court and the court psychiatrists.[3] In the discussion that follows the presentation of findings, some of the causes, consequences and implications of the presumption of illness are suggested.

The data upon which this report is based were drawn from psychiatrists' ratings of a sample of patients newly admitted to the public mental hospitals in a Midwestern state, official court records, interviews with court officials and psychiatrists, and our observations of psychiatric examinations in four courts. The psychiatrists' ratings of new patients will be considered first.

In order to obtain a rough measure of the incoming patient's qualifications for involuntary confinement, a survey of newly admitted patients was conducted with the cooperation of the hospital psychiatrists. All psychiatrists who made admission examinations in the three large mental hospitals in the state filled out a questionnaire for the first ten consecutive patients they examined in the month of June, 1962. A total of 223 questionnaires were returned by the 25 admission psychiatrists. Although these returns do not constitute a probability sample of all new patients admitted during the year, there were no obvious biases in the drawing of the sample. For this reason, this group of patients will be taken to be typical of the newly admitted patients in Midwestern State.

The two principal legal grounds for involuntary confinement in the United States are the police power of the state (the state's right to protect itself from dangerous persons) and *parens patriae* (the state's right to assist those persons who, because of their own incapacity, may not be able to assist themselves.) [4] As a measure of the first ground, the potential dangerousness of the patient, the questionnaire contained this item: "In your opinion, if this patient were released at the present time, is it likely he would harm himself or others?" The psychiatrists were given six options, ranging from Very Likely to Very Unlikely. Their responses were: Very Likely, 5%; Likely, 4%; Somewhat Likely, 14%; Somewhat Unlikely, 20%; Unlikely, 37%; Very Unlikely, 18%. (Three patients were not rated [1%].)

As a measure of the second ground, *parens patriae,* the questionnaire contained the item: "Based on your observations of the patient's behavior, his present degree of mental impairment is:

None . . . .
Mild . . . .
Severe . . . .
Minimal . . . .
Moderate . . . ."

The psychiatrists' responses were: None, 2%; Minimal, 12%; Mild, 25%; Moderate, 42%; Severe, 17%. (Three patients were not rated [1%].)

To be clearly qualified for involuntary confinement, a patient should be rated as likely to harm self or others (Very Likely, Likely, or Somewhat Likely) and/or as Severely Mentally Impaired. However, voluntary patients should be excluded from this analysis, since the court is not required to assess their qualifications for confinement. Excluding the 59 voluntary admissions (26% of the sample), leaves a sample of 164 involuntary confined patients. Of these patients, 10 were rated as meeting both qualifications for involuntary confinement, 21 were rated as being severely mentally impaired, but not dan-

[3] For a more general discussion of the presumption of illness in medicine, and some of its possible causes and consequences, see the author's "Decision Rules, Types of Error and Their Consequences in Medical Diagnosis," *Behavioral Science,* **8** (April, 1963), pp. 97–107.

[4] Hugh Allen Ross, "Commitment of the Mentally Ill: Problems of Law and Policy," *Michigan Law Review,* **57** (May, 1959), pp. 945–1018.

gerous, 28 were rated as dangerous but not severely mentally impaired, and 102 were rated as not dangerous nor as severely mentally impaired. (Three patients were not rated.)

According to these ratings, there is considerable uncertainty connected with the screening of newly admitted involuntary patients in the state, since a substantial majority (63%) of the patients did not clearly meet the statutory requirements for involuntary confinement. How does the agency responsible for assessing the qualifications for confinement, the court, react in the large numbers of cases involving uncertainty?

On the one hand, the legal rulings on this point by higher courts are quite clear. They have repeatedly held that there should be a presumption of sanity. The burden of proof of insanity is to be on the petitioners, there must be a preponderance of evidence, and the evidence should be of a "clear and unexceptionable" nature.[5]

On the other hand, existing studies suggest that there is a presumption of illness by mental health officials. In a discussion of the "discrediting" of patients by the hospital staff, based on observations at St. Elizabeth's Hospital, Washington, D.C., Goffman states:

[The patient's case record] is apparently not regularly used to record occasions when the patient showed capacity to cope honorably and effectively with difficult life situations. Nor is the case record typically used to provide a rough average or sampling of his past conduct. [Rather, it extracts] from his whole life course a list of those incidents that have or might have had "symptomatic" significance. . . . I think that most of the information gathered in case records is quite true, although it might seem also to be true that almost anyone's life course could yield up

enough denigrating facts to provide grounds for the record's justification of commitment.[6]

Mechanic makes a similar statement in his discussion of two large mental hospitals located in an urban area in California:

In the crowded state or county hospitals, which is the most typical situation, the psychiatrist does not have sufficient time to make a very complete psychiatric diagnosis, nor do his psychiatric tools provide him with the equipment for an expeditious screening of the patient . . .

In the two mental hospitals studied over a period of three months, the investigator never observed a case where the psychiatrist advised the patient that he did not need treatment. Rather, all persons who appeared at the hospital were absorbed into the patient population regardless of their ability to function adequately outside the hospital.[7]

A comment by Brown suggests that it is a fairly general understanding among mental health workers that state mental hospitals in the U.S. accept all comers.[8]

Kutner, describing commitment procedures in Chicago in 1962, also reports a strong presumption of illness by the staff of the Cook County Mental Health Clinic:

Certificates are signed as a matter of course by staff physicians after little or no examination . . . The so-called examinations are made on an assembly-line basis, often being completed in two or three minutes, and never taking more than ten minutes. Although psychiatrists agree that it is practically impossible to determine a person's sanity on the basis of such a short and hurried interview, the doctors recommend confinement in 77% of the cases. It appears in practice that the alleged-

---

5 This is the typical phrasing in cases in the *Dicennial Legal Digest*, found under the heading "Mental Illness."

6 Goffman, *op. cit.*, pp. 155, 159.

7 David Mechanic, "Some Factors in Identifying and Defining Mental Illness," *Mental Hygiene*, 46 (January, 1962), pp. 66–74.

8 Esther Lucile Brown, *Newer Dimensions of Patient Care*, Part I, New York: Russell Sage, 1961, p. 60. fn.

mentally-ill is presumed to be insane and bears the burden of proving his sanity in the few minutes allotted to him . . .[9]

These citations suggest that mental health officials handle uncertainty by presuming illness. To ascertain if the presumption of illness occurred in Midwestern State, intensive observations of screening procedures were conducted in the four courts with the largest volume of mental cases in the state. These courts were located in the two most populous cities in the state. Before giving the results of these observations, it is necessary to describe the steps in the legal procedures for hospitalization and commitment.

STEPS IN THE SCREENING OF PERSONS ALLEGED TO BE MENTALLY ILL

The process of screening can be visualized as containing five steps in Midwestern State:

1. The application for judicial inquiry, made by three citizens. This application is heard by deputy clerks in two of the courts (C and D), by a court reporter in the third court, and by a court commissioner in the fourth court.
2. The intake examination, conducted by a hospital psychiatrist.
3. The psychiatric examination, conducted by two psychiatrists appointed by the court.
4. The interview of the patient by the guardian *ad litem,* a lawyer appointed in three of the courts to represent the patient. (Court A did not use guardians *ad litem.*)
5. The judicial hearing, conducted by a judge.

These five steps take place roughly in the order listed, although in many cases (those cases designated as emergencies) step No. 2, the intake examination, may occur before step No. 1. Steps No. 1 and No. 2 usually take place on the same day

or the day after hospitalization. Steps No. 3, No. 4, and No. 5 usually take place within a week of hospitalization. (In courts C and D, however, the judicial hearing is held only once a month.)

This series of steps would seem to provide ample opportunity for the presumption of health, and a thorough assessment, therefore, of the patient's qualifications for involuntary confinement, since there are five separate points at which discharge could occur. According to our findings, however, these procedures usually do not serve the function of screening out persons who do not meet statutory requirements. At most of these decision points, in most of the courts, retention of the patient in the hospital was virtually automatic. A notable exception to this pattern was found in one of the three state hospitals; this hospital attempted to use step No. 2, the intake examination, as a screening point to discharge patients that the superintendent described as "illegitimate," i.e., patients who do not qualify for involuntary confinement.[10] In the other two hospitals, however, this examination was perfunctory and virtually never resulted in a finding of health and a recommendation of discharge. In a similar manner, the other steps were largely ceremonial in character. For example, in court B, we observed twenty-two judicial hearings, all of which were conducted perfunctorily and with lightning rapidity. (The mean time of these hearings was 1.6 minutes.) The judge asked each patient two or three routine questions. Whatever the patient answered, however, the judge always ended the hearings and retained the patient in the hospital.

9 Luis Kutner, "The Illusion of Due Process in Commitment Proceedings," *Northwestern University Law Review,* **57** (Sept. 1962), pp. 383–399.

10 Other exceptions occurred as follows: the deputy clerks in course C and D appeared to exercise some discretion in turning away applications they considered improper or incomplete, at step No. 1; the judge in Court D appeared also to perform some screening at step No. 5. For further description of these exceptions see "Rural-Urban Differences in the Judicial Screening of the Mentally Ill in a Midwestern State." (In press)

What appeared to be the key role in justifying these procedures was played by step No. 3, the examination by the court-appointed psychiatrists. In our informal discussions of screening with the judges and other court officials, these officials made it clear that although the statutes give the court the responsibility for the decision to confine or release persons alleged to be mentally ill, they would rarely if ever take the responsibility for releasing a mental patient without a medical recommendation to that effect. The question which is crucial, therefore, for the entire screening process is whether or not the court-appointed psychiatric examiners presume illness. The remainder of the paper will consider this question.

Our observations of 116 judicial hearings raised the question of the adequacy of the psychiatric examination. Eighty-six of the hearings failed to establish that the patients were "mentally ill" (according to the criteria stated by the judges in interviews).[11] Indeed, the behavior and responses of 48 of the patients at the hearings seemed completely unexceptionable. Yet the psychiatric examiners had not recommended the release of a single one of these patients. Examining the court records of 80 additional cases, there was still not a single recommendation for release.

Although the recommendation for treatment of 196 out of 196 consecutive cases strongly suggests that the psychiatric examiners were presuming illness, particularly when we observed 48 of these patients to be responding appropriately, it is conceivable that this is not the case. The observer for this study was not a psychiatrist (he was a first year graduate student in social work) and it is possible that he could have missed evidence of disorder which a psychiatrist might have seen. It

was therefore arranged for the observer to be present at a series of psychiatric examinations, in order to determine whether the examinations appeared to be merely formalities or whether, on the other hand, through careful examination and interrogation, the psychiatrists were able to establish illness even in patients whose appearance and responses were not obviously disordered. The observer was instructed to note the examiner's procedures, the criteria they appeared to use in arriving at their decision, and their reaction to uncertainty.

Each of the courts discussed here employs the services of a panel of physicians as medical examiners. The physicians are paid a flat fee of ten dollars per examination, and are usually assigned from three to five patients for each trip to the hospital. In court A, most of the examinations are performed by two psychiatrists, who went to the hospital once a week, seeing from five to ten patients a trip. In court B, C and D, a panel of local physicians was used. These courts seek to arrange the examinations so that one of the examiners is a psychiatrist, the other a general practitioner. Court B has a list of four such pairs, and appoints each pair for a month at a time. Courts C and D have a similar list, apparently with some of the same names as court B.

To obtain physicians who were representative of the panel used in these courts, we arranged to observe the examinations of the two psychiatrists employed by court A, and one of the four pairs of physicians used in court B, one a psychiatrist, the other a general practitioner. We observed 13 examinations in court A and 13 examinations in court B. The judges in courts C and D refused to give us the names of the physicians on their panels, and we were unable to observe examinations in these courts. (The judge in court D stated that he did not want these physicians harassed in their work, since it was difficult to obtain their services even under the best of

---

11 In interviews with the judges, the following criteria were named: Appropriateness of behavior and speech, understanding of the situation, and orientation.

circumstances.) In addition to observing the examinations by four psychiatrists, three other psychiatrists used by these courts were interviewed.

The medical examiners followed two lines of questioning. One line was to inquire about the circumstances which led to the patient's hospitalization, the other was to ask standard questions to test the patient's orientation and his capacity for abstract thinking by asking him the date, the President, Governor, proverbs, and problems requiring arithmetic calculation. These questions were often asked very rapidly, and the patient was usually allowed only a very brief time to answer.

It should be noted that the psychiatrists in these courts had access to the patient's record (which usually contained the Application for Judicial Inquiry and the hospital chart notes on the patient's behavior), and that several of the psychiatrists stated they almost always familiarized themselves with this record before making the examination. To the extent that they were familiar with the patient's circumstances from such outside information, it is possible that the psychiatrists were basing their diagnoses of illness less on the rapid and peremptory examination than on this other information. Although this was true to some extent, the importance of the record can easily be exaggerated, both because of the deficiencies in the typical record, and because of the way it is usually utilized by the examiners.

The deficiencies of the typical record were easily discerned in the approximately one hundred applications and hospital charts which the author read. Both the applications and charts were extremely brief and sometimes garbled. Moreover, in some of the cases where the author and interviewer were familiar with the circumstances involved in the hospitalization, it was not clear that the complainant's testimony was any more accurate than the version presented by the patient. Often the original complaint was so paraphrased

and condensed that the application seemed to have little meaning.

The attitude of the examiners toward the record was such that even in those cases where the record was ample, it often did not figure prominently in their decision. Disparaging remarks about the quality and usefulness of the record were made by several of the psychiatrists. One of the examiners was apologetic about his use of the record, giving us the impression that he thought that a good psychiatrist would not need to resort to any information outside his own personal examination of the patient. A casual attitude toward the record was openly displayed in 6 of the 26 examinations we observed. In these 6 examinations, the psychiatrist could not (or in 3 cases, did not bother to) locate the record and conducted the examination without it, with one psychiatrist making it a point of pride that he could easily diagnose most cases "blind."

In his observations of the examinations, the interviewer was instructed to rate how well the patient responded by noting his behavior during the interview, whether he answered the orientation and concept questions correctly, and whether he denied and explained the allegations which resulted in his hospitalization. If the patient's behavior during the interview obviously departed from conventional social standards (e.g., in one case the patient refused to speak), if he answered the orientation questions incorrectly, or if he did not deny and explain the petitioners' allegations, the case was rated as meeting the statutory requirements for hospitalization. Of the 26 examinations observed, eight were rated as Criteria Met.

If, on the other hand, the patient's behavior was appropriate, his answers correct, and he denied and explained the petitioners' allegations, the interviewer rated the case as not meeting the statutory criteria. Of the 26 cases, seven were rated as Criteria Not Met. Finally, if the examination was inconclusive, but the interviewer felt that more extensive investigation might have established that the criteria were met, he rated the cases as Criteria Possibly Met. Of the 26 examined, 11 were rated in this way. The interviewer's instructions were that whenever he was in doubt he should avoid using the rating Criteria Not Met.

Even giving the examiners the benefit of the doubt, the interviewer's ratings were that in a substantial majority of the cases he observed, the examination failed to establish that the statutory criteria were met. The relationship between the examiners' recommendations and the interviewer's ratings are shown in the following table.

terviews were hurried, with the questions of the examiners coming so rapidly that the examiner often interrupted the patient, or one examiner interrupted the other. All of the examiners seemed quite hurried. One psychiatrist, after stating in an interview (before we observed his examinations) that he usually took about thirty minutes, stated: "It's not remunerative. I'm taking a hell of a cut. I can't spend 45 minutes with a patient. I don't have the time, it doesn't pay." In the examinations that we observed, this physician actually spent 8, 10, 5, 8, 8, 7, 17, and 11 minutes with the patients, or an average of 9.2 minutes.

In these short time periods, it is virtu-

Table 1 Observer's Ratings and Examiners' Recommendations

Observer's Ratings:		Criteria Met	Criteria Possibly Met	Criteria Not Met	Total
Examiners' Recommendations	Commitment	7	9	2	18
	30-day observation	1	2	3	6
	Release	0	0	2	2
Total		8	11	7	26

The interviewer's ratings suggest that the examinations established that the statutory criteria were met in only eight cases, but the examiners recommended that the patient be retained in the hospital in 24 cases, leaving 16 cases which the interviewer rated as uncertain, and in which retention was recommended by the examiners. The observer also rated the patient's expressed desires regarding staying in the hospital, and the time taken by the examination. The ratings of the patient's desire concerning staying or leaving the hospital were: Leave, 14 cases; Indifferent, 1 case; Stay, 9 cases; and Not Ascertained, 2 cases. In only one of the 14 cases in which the patient wished to leave was the interviewer's rating Criteria Met.

The interviews ranged in length from five minutes to 17 minutes, with the mean time being 10.2 minutes. Most of the in-

ally impossible for the examiner to extend his investigation beyond the standard orientation questions, and a short discussion of the circumstances which brought the patient to the hospital. In those cases where the patient answered the orientation questions correctly, behaved appropriately, and explained his presence at the hospital satisfactorily, the examiners did not attempt to assess the reliability of the petitioner's complaints, or to probe further into the patient's answers. Given the fact that in most of these instances the examiners were faced with borderline cases, that they took little time in the examinations, and that they usually recommended commitment, we can only conclude that their decisions were based largely on a presumption of illness. Supplementary observations reported by the interviewer support this conclusion.

After each examination, the observer asked the examiner to explain the criteria he used in arriving at his decision. The observer also had access to the examiner's official report, so that he could compare what the examiner said about the case with the record of what actually occurred during the interview. This supplementary information supports the conclusion that the examiner's decisions are based on the presumption of illness, and sheds light on the manner in which these decisions are reached:

1. The "evidence" upon which the examiners based their decision to retain often seemed arbitrary.
2. In some cases, the decision to retain was made even when no evidence could be found.
3. Some of the psychiatrists' remarks suggest prejudgment of the cases.
4. Many of the examinations were characterized by carelessness and haste. The first question, concerning the arbitrariness of the psychiatric evidence, will now be considered.

In the weighing of the patient's responses during the interview, the physician appeared not to give the patient credit for the large number of correct answers he gave. In the typical interview, the examiner might ask the patient fifteen or twenty questions: the date, time, place, who, is President, Governor, etc., what is 11×10, 11×11, etc., explain "Don't put all your eggs in one basket," "A rolling stone gathers no moss," etc. The examiners appeared to feel that a wrong answer established lack of orientation, even when it was preceded by a series of correct answers. In other words, the examiners do not establish any standard score on the orientation questions, which would give an objective picture of the degree to which the patient answered the questions correctly, but seem at times to search until they find an incorrect answer.

For those questions which were an-swered incorrectly, it was not always clear whether the incorrect answers were due to the patient's "mental illness," or to the time pressure in the interview, the patient's lack of education, or other causes. Some of the questions used to establish orientation were sufficiently difficult that persons not mentally ill might have difficulty with them. Thus one of the examiners always asked, in a rapid-fire manner: "What year is it? What year was it seven years ago? Seventeen years before that?" etc. Only two of the five patients who were asked this series of questions were able to answer it correctly. However, it is a moot question whether a higher percentage of persons in a household survey would be able to do any better. To my knowledge, none of the orientation questions that are used have been checked in a normal population.

Finally, the interpretations of some of the evidence as showing mental illness seemed capricious. Thus one of the patients, when asked, "In what way are a banana, an orange, and an apple alike?" answered, "They are all something to eat." This answer was used by the examiner in explaining his recommendation to commit. The observer had noted that the patient's behavior and responses seemed appropriate and asked why the recommendation to commit had been made. The doctor stated that her behavior had been bizarre (possibly referring to her alleged promiscuity), her affect inappropriate ("When she talked about being pregnant, it was without feeling,") and with regard to the question above: "She wasn't able to say a banana and an orange were fruit. She couldn't take it one step further, she had to say it was something to eat." In other words, this psychiatrist was suggesting that the patient manifested concreteness in her thinking, which is held to be a symptom of mental illness. Yet in her other answers to classification questions, and to proverb interpretations, concreteness was not apparent, suggesting that the examiner's application of this test was arbitrary. In another case, the physician stated that he thought the patient was suspicious and distrustful, because he had asked about the possibility of being represented by counsel at the judicial hearing. The observer felt that these and other similar interpretations might possibly be correct, but that further investigation of the supposedly incorrect responses would be needed to establish that they were manifestations of disorientation.

In several cases where even this type of evidence was not available, the examiners still recommended retention in the hospital. Thus, one examiner, employed by court A stated that he had recommended 30-day observation for a patient whom he had thought *not* to be mentally ill, on the grounds that the patient, a young man, could not get along with his parents, and "might get into trouble." This examiner went on to say:

We always take the conservative side. [Commitment or observation] Suppose a patient should commit suicide. We always make the conservative decision. I had rather play it safe. There's no harm in doing it that way.

It appeared to the observer that "playing safe" meant that even in those cases where the examination established nothing, the psychiatrists did not consider recommending release. Thus in one case the examination had established that the patient had a very good memory, was oriented and spoke quietly and seriously. The observer recorded his discussion with the physician after the examination as follows:

When the doctor told me he was recommending commitment for this patient too (he had also recommended commitment in the two examinations held earlier that day) he laughed because he could see what my next question was going to be. He said, "I already recommended the release of two patients this month." This sounded like it was the maximum amount the way he said it.

Apparently this examiner felt that he had a very limited quota on the number of patients he could recommend for release (less than two percent of those examined).

The language used by these physicians tends to intimate that mental illness was found, even when reporting the opposite. Thus in one case the recommendation stated: "No gross evidence of delusions or hallucinations." This statement is misleading, since not only was there no gross evidence, there was not any evidence, not even the slightest suggestion of delusions or hallucinations, brought out by the interview.

These remarks suggest that the examiners prejudge the cases they examine. Several further comments indicate prejudgment. One physician stated that he thought that most crimes of violence were committed by patients released too early from mental hospitals. (This is an erroneous belief.)[12] He went on to say that he thought that all mental patients should be kept in the hospital at least three months, indicating prejudgment concerning his examinations. Another physician, after a very short interview (8 minutes), told the observer:

On the schizophrenics, I don't bother asking them more questions when I can see they're schizophrenic because I *know what they are going to say.* You could talk to them another half hour and not learn any more.

Another physician, finally, contrasted cases

[12] The rate of crimes of violence, or any crime, appears to be less among ex-mental patients than in the general population. Henry Brill and Benjamin Malzberg, "Statistical Report Based on the Arrest Record of 5354 Ex-patients Released from New York State Mental Hospitals During the Period 1946–48." Mimeo available from the authors; Louis H. Cohen and Henry Freeman, "How Dangerous to the Community Are State Hospital Patients?", *Connecticut State Medical Journal,* 9 (Sept., 1945), pp. 697–700; Donald W. Hastings, "Follow-up Results in Psychiatric Illness," *Amer. Journal of Psychiatry,* 118 (June 1962), pp. 1078–1086.

in which the patient's family or others initiated hospitalization ("petition cases," the great majority of cases) with those cases initiated by the court: "The petition cases are pretty *automatic*. If the patient's own family wants to get rid of him you know there is something wrong."

The lack of care which characterized the examinations is evident in the forms on which the examiners make their recommendations. On most of these forms, whole sections have been left unanswered. Others are answered in a preemptory and uninformative way. For example, in the section entitled Physical Examination, the question is asked: "Have you made a physical examination of the patient? State fully what is the present physical condition," a typical answer is "Yes. Fair." or, "Is apparently in good health." Since in none of the examinations we observed was the patient actually physically examined, these answers appear to be mere guesses. One of the examiners used regularly in court B, to the question "On what subject or in what way is derangement now manifested?" always wrote in "Is mentally ill." The omissions, and the almost flippant brevity of these forms, together with the arbitrariness, lack of evidence, and prejudicial character of the examinations, discussed above, all support the observer's conclusion that, except in very unusual cases, the psychiatric examiner's recommendation to retain the patient is virtually automatic.

Lest it be thought that these results are unique to a particularly backward Midwestern State, it should be pointed out that this state is noted for its progressive psychiatric practices. It will be recalled that a number of the psychiatrists employed by the court as examiners had finished their psychiatric residencies, which is not always the case in many other states. A still common practice in other states is to employ, as members of the "Lunacy Panel," partially retired physicians with no psychiatric training whatever. This was the case in Stockton, California, in 1959, where the author observed hundreds of hearings at which these physicians were present. It may be indicative of some of the larger issues underlying the question of civil commitment that, in these hearings, the physicians played very little part; the judge controlled the questioning of the relatives and patients, and the hearings were often a model of impartial and thorough investigation.

DISCUSSION

Ratings of the qualifications for involuntary confinement of patients newly admitted to the public mental hospital in a Midwestern state, together with observations of judicial hearings and psychiatric examinations by the observer connected with the present study, both suggest that the decision as to the mental condition of a majority of the patients is an uncertain one. The fact that the courts seldom release patients, and the perfunctory manner in which the legal and medical procedures are carried out, suggest that the judicial decision to retain patients in the hospital for treatment is routine and largely based on the presumption of illness. Three reasons for this presumption will be discussed: financial, ideological, and political.

Our discussions with the examiners indicated that one reason that they perform biased "examinations" is that their rate of pay is determined by the length of time spent with the patient. In recommending retention, the examiners are refraining from interrupting the hospitalization and commitment procedures already in progress, and thereby allowing someone else, usually the hospital, to make the effective decision to release or commit. In order to recommend release, however, they would have to build a case showing why these procedures should be interrupted. Building such a case would take much more time than is presently expended by the examiners, thereby reducing their rate of pay.

A more fundamental reason for the presumption of illness by the examiners, and perhaps the reason why this practice is allowed by the courts, is the interpretation of current psychiatric doctrine by the examiners and court officials. These officials make a number of assumptions, which are now thought to be of doubtful validity:

1. The condition of mentally ill persons deteriorates rapidly without psychiatric assistance.
2. Effective psychiatric treatments exist for most mental illnesses.
3. Unlike surgery, there are no risks involved in involuntary psychiatric treatment: it either helps or is neutral, it can't hurt.
4. Exposing a prospective mental patient to questioning, cross-examination, and other screening procedures exposes him to the unnecessary stigma of trial-like procedures, and may do further damage to his mental condition.
5. There is an element of danger to self or others in most mental illness. It is better to risk unnecessary hospitalization than the harm the patient might do himself or others.

Many psychiatrists and others now argue that none of these assumptions are necessarily correct.

1. The assumption that psychiatric disorders usually get worse without treatment rests on very little other than evidence of an anecdotal character. These is just as much evidence that most acute psychological and emotional upsets are self-terminating.[13]

[13] For a review of epidemiological studies of mental disorder see Richard J. Plunkett and John E. Gordon, *Epidemiology and Mental Illness.* New York: Basic Books, 1960. Most of these studies suggest that at any given point in time, psychiatrists find a substantial proportion of persons in normal populations to be "mentally ill." One interpretation of this finding is that much of the deviance detected in these studies is self-limiting.

2. It is still not clear, according to systematic studies evaluating psychotherapy, drugs, etc., that most psychiatric interventions are any more effective, on the average, than no treatment at all.[14]
3. There is very good evidence that involuntary hospitalization and social isolation may affect the patient's life: his job, his family affairs, etc. There is some evidence that too hasty exposure to psychiatric treatment may convince the patient that he is "sick," prolonging what may have been an otherwise transitory episode.[15]
4. This assumption is correct, as far as it goes. But it is misleading because it fails to consider what occurs when the patient who does not wish to be hospitalized is forcibly treated. Such patients often become extremely indignant and angry, particularly in the case, as often happens, when they are deceived into coming to the hospital on some pretext.
5. The element of danger is usually exaggerated both in amount and degree. In the psychiatric survey of new patients in state mental hospitals, danger to self or others was mentioned in about a fourth of the cases. Furthermore, in those cases where danger is mentioned, it is not always clear that the risks involved are greater than those encountered in ordinary social life. This issue has been discussed by Ross, an attorney:

A truck driver with a mild neurosis who is "accident prone" is probably a greater dan-

[14] For an assessment of the evidence regarding the effectiveness of electroshock, drugs, psychotherapy, and other psychiatric treatments, see H. J. Eysenck, *Handbook of Abnormal Psychology,* New York: Basic Books, 1961, Part III.

[15] For examples from military psychiatry, see Albert J. Glass, "Psychotherapy in the Combat Zone," in *Symposium on Stress,* Washington, D.C., Army Medical Service Graduate School, 1953, and B. L. Bushard, "The U.S. Army's Mental Hygiene Consultation Service," in *Symposium on Preventive and Social Psychiatry,* 15–17 (April 1957), Washington, D.C.: Walter Reed Army Institute of Research, pp. 431–43. For a discussion of essentially the same problem in the context of a civilian mental hospital, cf. Kai T. Erikson, "Patient Role and Social Uncertainty—A Dilemma of the Mentally Ill," *Psychiatry,* **20** (August 1957), pp. 263–275.

ger to society than most psychotics; yet, he will not be committed for treatment, even if he would be benefited. The community expects a certain amount of dangerous activity. I suspect that as a class, drinking drivers are a greater danger than the mentally ill, and yet the drivers are tolerated or punished with small fines rather than indeterminate imprisonment.[16]

From our observations of the medical examinations and other commitment procedures, we formed a very strong impression that the doctrines of danger to self or others, early treatment, and the avoidance of stigma were invoked partly because the officials believed them to be true, and partly because they provided convenient justification for a pre-existing policy of summary action, minimal investigation, avoidance of responsibility and, after the patient is in the hospital, indecisiveness and delay.

The policy of presuming illness is probably both cause and effect of political pressure on the court from the community. The judge, an elected official, runs the risk of being more heavily penalized for erroneously releasing than for erroneously retaining patients. Since the judge personally appoints the panel of psychiatrists to serve as examiners, he can easily transmit the community pressure to them, by failing to reappoint a psychiatrist whose examinations were inconveniently thorough.

Some of the implications of these findings for the sociology of deviant behavior will be briefly summarized. The discussion above, of the reasons that the psychiatrists tend to presume illness, suggests that the motivations of the key decision-makers in the screening process may be significant in determining the extent and direction of the societal reaction. In the case of psychiatric screening of persons alleged to be mentally ill, the social differentiation of the deviant from the non-deviant population appears to be materially affected by the financial, ideological, and political position of the psychiatrists, who are in this instance the key agents of social control.

Under these circumstances, the character of the societal reaction appears to undergo a marked change from the pattern of denial which occurs in the community. The official societal reaction appears to reserve the presumption of normality reported by the Cummings as a characteristic of informal societal reaction, and instead exaggerates both the amount and degree of deviance.[17] Thus, one extremely important contingency influencing the severity of the societal reaction may be whether or not the original deviance comes to official notice. This paper suggests that in the area of mental disorder, perhaps in contrast to other areas of deviant behavior, if the official societal reaction is invoked, for whatever reason, social differentiation of the deviant from the non-deviant population will usually occur.

CONCLUSION

This paper has described the screening of patients who were admitted to public mental hospitals in early June, 1962, in a Midwestern state. The data presented here suggest that the screening is usually perfunctory, and that in the crucial screening examination by the court-appointed psychiatrists, there is a presumption of illness. Since most court decisions appear to hinge on the recommendation of these psychiatrists, there appears to be a large element of status ascription in the official societal reaction to persons alleged to be mentally ill, as exemplified by the court's

16 Ross, *op. cit.*, p. 962.

17 Elaine Cumming and John Cumming, *Closed Ranks*, Cambridge, Mass.: Harvard University Press, 1957, 102; for further discussion of the bipolarization of the societal reaction into denial and labeling, see the author's "The Role of the Mentally Ill and the Dynamics of Mental Disorder: A Research Framework," *Sociometry*, **26** (December, 1963), pp. 436–453.

actions. This finding points to the importance of lay definitions of mental illness in the community, since the "diagnosis" of mental illness by laymen in the community initiates the official societal reaction, and to the necessity of analyzing social processes connected with the recognition and reaction to the deviant behavior that is called mental illness in our society.

SMALL CLAIMS COURT: REFORM REVISITED

Students of the Columbia Law School

Early twentieth century law reformers fought numerous inequities in the court system. They devoted particular attention to the related difficulties experienced by the poor litigant and the individual or institution with a valid but minor monetary claim.[1] No adequate forum existed to meet their special needs; meritorious claims had long been discouraged by the delay, cost, and procedural technicalities of the regular courts.[2] Legal aid societies, providing some measure of low-cost legal advice, were part of the answer, and their popularity spread widely.[3] However, a more fundamental answer, within the very structure of the court system, was also sought. As Dean Roscoe Pound said:

For ordinary causes our contentious system has great merit as a means of getting at the truth. But it is a *denial of justice* in small causes to drive litigants to employ lawyers and it is a shame to drive them to legal aid societies to get as charity what the state should give as a right.[4]

The phrase "denial of justice" in Dean Pound's statement rang true, and reformers sought effective legislation to meet the imperative in that phrase. The cost and vexation of suit was no longer to be a bar to settlement of bona fide disputes. No longer was the maxim "de minimis non curat lex" to be applied literally by the judicial system.[5] No one was to feel as Voltaire did: "Only twice in my life have I felt utterly ruined: once when I lost a lawsuit, and once when I won."[6] Justice was to be the goal, rather than "litigation for litigation's sake."[7]

I. THE SMALL CLAIMS COURT MOVEMENT

A. Initial Institutional Reform

As a result of reformist agitation, small claims courts were created, primarily in

Reprinted from *Columbia Journal of Law and Social Problems,* 5 (August, 1969), pp. 47–68, by permission of the publishers.

[1] *See generally* R. Smith, *Justice and the Poor* (3d ed. 1924); W. Willoughby, *Principles of Judicial Administration* 307 (1929); Maguire, "Poverty and Civil Litigation," 36 *Harv. L. Rev.* 361 (1923); Pound, "The Administration of Justice in the Modern City," 26 *Harv. L. Rev.* 302, 315 *et seq.* (1913); Comment, "Small Claims Courts," 34 *Colum. L. Rev.* 932 (1934).

[2] Maguire, *supra* note 1.

[3] *See generally* R. Smith & J. Bradway, *Growth of Legal-Aid Work in the United States* (U.S. Dept. of Labor Bull. No. 607, 1936); *Joint Committee for the Study of Legal Aid of the Association of the Bar of the City of New York and the Welfare Council Report* 55 (1928).

[4] Pound, "The Administration of Justice in the Modern City," 26 *Harv. L. Rev.* 302, 318 (1913) [emphasis added].

[5] Smith, *Justice and the Poor, supra* note 1, at 41.

[6] Cayton, "Small Claims and Conciliation Courts," 205 *Annals* 57 (1939).

[7] Harley, "Justice or Litigation," 6 *Va. L. Rev.* 143 (1919).

the period 1913–1940,[8] to provide forums where minor disputes were adjudicated at minimal cost by a judge using informal and summary procedure. The spread of small claims courts was widely acclaimed as one of the most far-reaching and effective of modern legal reforms; their rise was characterized as a "movement" and a "national phenomenon." [9]

Congress gave its consideration and endorsement to the "movement" when it created a Small Claims Court and Conciliatory Branch in the Municipal Court of the District of Columbia.[10] The District of Columbia Committee of the Senate unanimously reported:

The purpose of the bill is to improve the administration of justice in small civil cases and make the service of the municipal court more easily available to all of the people whether of large or small means; to simplify practice and procedure in the commencement, handling, and trial of such cases; to eliminate delay and reduce costs; to provide for install-

ment payment of judgments; and generally to promote the confidence of the public in the courts through the provision of a friendly forum for disputes, small in amount but important to the parties. It was emphasized before the committee that such cases frequently become tragic in their implications if not carefully and speedily determined.[11]

Three basic policy objectives emerged from the rhetoric of the original reformers and from legislative action on the problem: 1) Analyzing the importance of a claim from the litigant's viewpoint,[12] rather than with regard to such absolute determinants as dollar value or interest at the bar. 2) Avoiding alienation of large segments of the population from the court system.[13] 3) Securing the integrity of judicial institutions.[14]

Partially obscured by these objectives was recognition that, in addition to providing an avenue of judicial access for the poor, the small claims courts would serve a variety of interest groups who, while not necessarily poor, had legitimate claims of small value. Additionally, it was understood that such courts could help relieve congested dockets in the civil courts. Yet, at least initially, the charitable objectives for the small claims courts were of prime concern.

The flurry of excitement which greeted the small claims court movement soon subsided.[15] Since 1940 some additional

---

[8] Through the years nearly all jurisdictions have created small claims courts by statute. *See, e.g., Cal. Civ. Pro. Code* § 117 *et seq.* (West 1954); *D.C. Code* §§ 11–1301 *et seq.*, 13–101, 16–3901 *et seq.* (1967); *Ill. Ann. Stat.* ch. 110A, §§ 281 *et seq.* (Supp. 1968); *Mass. Ann. Laws* ch. 218, §§ 21 *et seq.* (Supp. 1969); *N.J. Rev. Stat. Ann.* §§ 2A:18–65 *et seq.* (1952); *Tex. Rev. Civ Stat.* art. 2460a, §§ 1 *et seq.* (1964); *N.Y. Uniform Dist. Ct. Act.* §§ 1801 *et seq.* (McKinney Supp. 1968); *Wis. State. Ann.* §§ 299.01 *et seq.* (Supp. 1969). The Municipal Courts of Chicago and Cleveland originally established small claims courts by rule of court. The Chicago court has been replaced by the statutory court created in *Ill. Ann. Stat.* ch. 110A, §§ 281 *et seq.* (Supp. 1968). Small claims courts are variously known as Conciliation Court, Wage Claims Court, Conciliation and Small Debtors' Court, and Small Debtors' Court. A few are small claims courts in name only, since the procedure and evidentiary requirements remain formal. *See, e.g., N.M. Stat. Ann.* §§ 16–5–1 *et seq.* (Supp. 1967); *N.C. Gen. Stat.* §§ 1–539.3 *et seq.*, §§ 7A–210 *et seq.* (Supp. 1967).

[9] Cayton, *supra* note 6, at 57, 59; R. Smith & J. Bradway, *supra* note 3, at 37.

[10] *Hearings on S. 1835 Before the District of Columbia Comm. of the Senate*, 75th Cong., 1st Sess. (1937).

[11] Cayton, *supra* note 6, at 60.

[12] Lummus, "Justice in Minor Courts Appraised by Expert," 22 *J. Am. Jud. Soc'y*, 38, 39 (1938).

[13] R. Smith & J. Bradway, *supra* note 3, at 45; Lummus, *supra* note 12, at 38, 39.

[14] *Id.*

[15] For an excellent bibliography of pre-1940 materials on small claims courts (when the bulk of writing on the subject was done), see Northrup, "Small Claims Courts and Conciliation Tribunals," 33 *L. Library J.* 39 (1940). *See also* Comment, *supra* note 1. For materials up to 1959, see *Institute of Judicial Administration, Small Claims Courts* (Rep. No. 2–U28, Jan. 26, 1954); *Institute of Judicial Administration, Small Claims Courts in the United States—1959 Supplement* (Rep. No. 7–U57, March 13, 1959).

states have established small claims courts, jurisdictions have been altered slightly, and some states have experimented with new procedures. In general, however, for more than 20 years, the small claims courts have become self-satisfied and static. Once successful, these courts are now under attack.

B. Reform Revisited

A major failing of the courts was condemned in a recent article [16] by Judge J. Skelly Wright of the U. S. Court of Appeals for the District of Columbia Circuit, a judge long interested in the legal rights of the poor. He deplores the manner in which business interests have been capturing the small claims court—except in those few jurisdictions where corporations and collection agencies have been expressly barred by statute.[17] The individual litigant increasingly finds himself on the receiving end of a set of institutions ". . . geared for, and used for the benefit of, the manufacturer-seller-financer complex. . ." [18]

The individual with a valid claim, particularly the ghetto resident, is unaware of the very existence of the small claims court. If he learns of its existence but appears without counsel, he may be subject to persuasion by opposing counsel or an aggressive business litigant. A pre-trial settlement, the terms of which are unfair to the individual litigant, may result.

The precise policy basis for small claims courts has been eroded—it is not clear whether small claims courts are designed for poor people, for small causes in terms of dollar amounts, for cases in which the procedure is not complete, or for combinations of these. This erosion is significant since the policy the courts are to effectuate

determines to some extent the procedures which will be followed.

Whether arbitration-conciliation is a desirable collateral effort is an additional important variable which has received contradictory answers. The quality of judges who serve is likewise a pressing problem, particularly because the small claims court expands the judge's traditional role. Yet another question concerns the proper degree of local flexibility to be retained in order to meet different individual and administrative needs. Finally, there is even disagreement concerning what a "small" claim is—jurisdictional amounts vary from $50 to $2000.

The small claims court must be re-examined in its modern context. Such a re-examination is best accomplished through study of small claims court procedures and analysis of the parameters of jurisdiction. Recommendations for change must be designed to curb existing abuses in small claims courts and to extend the possibility of benefits to a wider number of cases.

II. PROCEDURES IN SMALL CLAIMS COURT

The following procedures serve as the basic tools for small claims courts. Use of these features will vary somewhat from jurisdiction to jurisdiction, but most states employ nearly all of the methods within the following basic outline.

A. Pretrial Procedures and Jurisdictional Requisites

1. SIMPLIFIED AND UNIFORM STATEMENTS OF CLAIM. The language to be used in the statement of claim is usually set out in the statute,[19] and is designed to avoid technical or legal terminology. The state-

---

16 Wright, "The Courts Have Failed the Poor," *N.Y. Times*, March 9, 1969, § 6 (Magazine), at 26.
17 *Id.* at 102.
18 *Id.* at 104. The description is by an anonymous "commentator" quoted by Judge Wright.

19 *Cal. Civ. Pro. Code* § 117b (West Supp. 1968); *Fla. Stat. Ann.* § 42.19 (1961); *Okla. Stat. Ann.* tit. 39, § 653 (Supp. 1968); *Utah Code Ann.* § 78–6–2 (1953); *Wis. Stat. Ann.* § 299.05(6) (Supp. 1969); *Tex. Rev. Civ. Stat.* art. 2460a, § 4 (1964).

ment of claim must tell the defendant what the dispute concerns, how much money is involved, when the obligations arose, and when to appear in court.[20] Some statutes require a return answer to minimize delays due to surprise, avoid unnecessary appearance by the plaintiff if the defendant defaults, and clarify issues for the court; but return procedure is often rejected to speed trial.[21] The defendant, if he has no defense, may appear and seek the privilege of paying in installments.[22] Counterclaims and set-offs are permitted in the same informal manner as claims.[23]

Simplicity of claim statement and elimination of return answer can conceivably result in delays or injustices. For example, the defendant who is advised simply that he "owes Mr. X $130 for debts on goods purchased between May 13 and September 5" may not understand what particular merchandise is involved or what papers he must produce to establish a defense such as breach of warranty. Delay may occur if a continuance is needed to permit the defendant to prepare a defense; injustice may result if judgment is entered at the first hearing because there is no defense presented.

2. ASSISTANCE BY THE CLERK IN PREPARATION AND FILING OF PAPERS. To avoid the need for counsel and to eliminate unnecessary delay, plaintiffs are given the opportunity of using the services of a clerk to file claims and effect service. The claim may be stated orally to the clerk, but the plaintiff must execute a standard affidavit,[24] or sign [25] or verify [26] the statement prepared by the clerk. If empowered to do so, a competent clerk can settle many cases at this juncture through judicious questioning and rejection of cases which are not prima facie valid. If the claim is rejected by the clerk, a dissatisfied plaintiff may appeal the decision to the judge. Once the claim is prepared, the plaintiff is permitted to elect in what manner he wishes process to be served.

Where business interests are permitted to assert claims or lawyers are permitted to participate in small claims court proceedings, clerk services for these groups are not desirable, except perhaps to reject cases which are not prima facie valid. However, since business interests and other plaintiffs represented by lawyers rarely bring invalid claims, there is little justification for the expense of making clerks available to them.

3. SMALL FILING FEE AND WAIVER OF COSTS. A fee of $1.00 to $3.50 generally covers the filing, trial and judgment in the case.[27] These amounts represent an increase from previous levels, due in part to inflation, but the level remains rela-

---

[20] R. Smith & J. Bradway, *supra* note 3, at 41.

[21] *See, e.g., Ill. Ann. Stat.* ch. 110A, § 286 (Supp. 1968). *Contra, R.I. Gen. Laws Ann.* § 10–16–9 (Supp. 1968). *See also* Committee on Small Claims and Conciliation Procedure, *Report,* 10 A.B.A.J. 828, 829 (1924).

[22] *See. e.g., Fla. Stat. Ann.* § 42.14 (1961); *Ill. Ann. Stat.* ch. 110A, § 288 (Supp. 1968); *Me. Rev. Stat. Ann.* tit. 14, § 7455 (1964); *Minn. Stat. Ann.* § 491.04(2) (1958); *N.H. Rev. Stat. Ann.* § 503:7 (1955); *R.I. Gen. Laws Ann.* § 10–16–5 (1956).

[23] *See e.g., Cal. Civ. Pro. Code* § 117h (West 1954); *Fla. Stat. Ann.* § 42.13 (1961); *Okla. Stat. Ann.* tit. 39, § 659 (Supp. 1967); *R.I. Gen. Laws Ann.* § 10–16–9 (1956).

[24] *See, e.g., Cal. Civ. Pro. Code* § 117b (West Supp. 1968); *Okla. Stat. Ann.* tit. 39, § 652 (Supp. 1967); *Utah Code Ann.* § 78–6–2. (1953).

[25] *See, e.g., Fla. Stat. Ann.* § 42.10 (1961); *Wis. Stat. Ann.* § 299.05(2) (Supp. 1969).

[26] *See, e.g., Idaho Code Ann.* § 1–1507 (1948); *Wash. Rev. Code Ann.* § 12.40.070 (1962).

[27] *See, e.g., Cal. Civ. Pro. Code* 117p (West Supp. 1968) ($2.00 plus $1.50 for each copy of an affidavit sent to a defendant); *Fla. Stat. Ann.* § 42.11 (1961) ($3.50, but $10 if garnishment or attachment is issued); *Mass Ann. Laws* ch. 218, § 22 (1955) ($1.25); *N.H. Rev. Stat. Ann.* § 503.3 (1955) ($1.50 plus postage); *N.J. Rev. Stat. Ann.* § 2A:18–65 (1952) ($2.10 plus 40¢ for each extra defendant); *Utah Code Ann.* § 78–6–14 (1953) ($1.50 plus $1.00 per affidavit and mileage at 20¢ per mile one way charged for service); *Wash. Rev. Code Ann.* § 12.40.030 (1962) ($1.00). Some statutes set higher costs, e.g., *Vt. Stat. Ann.* tit. 12. § 5532 (Supp. 1967) ($5.00).

tively low. In some states the fee may be waived by the judge or clerk without need for plaintiffs to file degrading affidavits "in forma pauperis." [28] While some jurisdictions have eliminated fees, most feel at least a minimal one is desirable in order to discourage use of court mailing services by corporations and collection agencies which could at almost no cost to themselves continually bill and threaten debtors.[29] The aim is to set the fee at a level which slightly exceeds the usual costs to the business interests in preparing and sending a typical series of letters notifying customers that payment is overdue.[30]

It appears that the generally low fee for small claims courts would not deter groundless claims. Requiring the plaintiff to execute an affidavit of his good faith,[31] empowering the clerk to reject claims which are not prima facie valid, and imposing extra costs on frivolous claims [32] would seem to be better responses. Nevertheless, even these measures probably have little effect in discouraging invalid claims. Because the procedure is summary, small claims court personnel do not spend much time evaluating the indicia of groundless claims in detail.[33]

4. REGISTERED MAIL SERVICE. Registered mail service, a low-cost procedure supplementing the alternative marshal system, has met with a repeated and encouraging record of success.[34] A requirement of return-receipt to the clerk before the court will exercise jurisdiction insures that process has reached the defendant. Service by registered mail protects the defendant from the practice known as "sewer service" which developed in the civil court system. Under this practice, the plaintiff's process server makes no attempt to serve process effectively, and then swears in an affidavit that the process has been personally delivered to the defendant at the specified address.[35] A default judgment is then entered against the indigent defendant, who is often unaware of his rights and of the willingness of courts to open such default judgments, and the resulting judgment will stand. At a minimum, service of process through the mail curbs this type of abuse.

At various times some courts have adopted the practice of using the regular mails [36] to serve process because the return if undeliverable is faster than it would be using registered mail. Whether this method will be used in light of present problems in mail service is questionable.

5. SHORT NOTICE PERIOD. The usual

---

28 *See, e.g., Fla. Stat. Ann.* § 42.11 (1961); *N.Y.C. Civil Ct. Act* § 1803 (1963).

29 *See* 4 *Stan. L. Rev.* 237 (1952); Murphy, "District of Columbia Small Claims Court—The Forgotten Court," 34 *D.C. B.J.* 14 (Feb. 1967).

30 *Contra,* R. Smith & J. Bradway, *supra* note 3, at 40. *See also* Committee on Small Claims and Conciliation Procedure, *supra* note 21, at 829; Fernow, "Proposed Small Claims Branch of the City Court of Buffalo," 2 *Lincoln L. Rev.* 36, 38 (1929). But this aim can be achieved by forbidding suits by assignees (e.g., *Cal. Civ. Pro. Code* § 117f (West 1954); *Utah Code Ann.* § 78–6–6 (1953), or by limiting the number of claims a plaintiff can litigate without fees (*e.g.,* as was formerly done in Minnesota and New Hampshire). For an argument that litigation in small claims courts should be absolutely free, see Vance, "A Proposed Court of Conciliation," 1 *Minn. L. Rev.* 107, 116 (1917).

31 *See* note 24 *supra* and accompanying text.

32 *See, e.g., N.J. Rev. Stat. Ann.* § 2A:1870 (1952) (up to $10); *N.Y.C. Civil Ct. Act* § 1803 (1963).

33 Comment, *supra* note 1, at 945. Increased op-

erating expenses due to a slight excess of groundless claims may be partially defrayed by requiring the defeated litigant to pay the costs of the action to the state instead of to his adversary.

34 For a complete discussion of registered mail, telephone and word-of-mouth notification, see Comment, *supra* note 1, at 935 n. 24–31. Service of process by registered mail was upheld as constitutional in Wise v. Herzog, 114 F.2d 486 (D.C. Cir. 1940). In Washington, D.C., prior to 1940, in nearly 19,000 cases service proved 76% effective by mail, while the marshal system compiled only a 52% effective rate in 4,135 cases. *See also* Cayton, *supra* note 6, at 62.

35 For a full discussion of the problem of "sewer service," see "Abuse of Process: Sewer Service," 3 *Colum. J. L. & Soc. Prob.* 17 (1967).

36 Comment, *supra* note 1, at 935 n.26.

lengthy notice period is shortened to about five to 20 days from the date of filing.[37] Some jurisdictions have longer periods, and California distinguishes between in- and out-of-county defendants, giving the latter a longer notice period.[38] Originally, some statutes placed wage claim cases in a special short-notice category, recognizing that the wage earner might need his paycheck without delay, but this seemingly advisable practice has been dropped in the current statutes.

6. VOLUNTARY ARBITRATION AND CONCILIATION PROCEDURE. As an added feature, a few jurisdictions include either arbitration or conciliation proceedings to expedite dispute settlement.[39] The primary difference between the two is that arbitration is a binding judgment, while conciliation carries no force of final judgment and is totally dependent on both parties' consent for efficacy. Conciliation and arbitration proceedings are best staffed by experienced lawyers who have volunteered their services, and who perform their mediation functions on a regular but infrequent basis.[40]

The District of Columbia Municipal Court extends the benefits of conciliation and arbitration to disputes of any character and irrespective of the amounts involved.[41] Since the arbitration proceeding is separated from the small claims court, this type of case does not detract from the responsibilities of the small claims court itself.

In most states which utilize these procedures the judge is required to encourage the parties to conciliate or arbitrate before he will hear the case.[42] A judge can be almost coercive in his effort to speed procedure by getting the parties to arbitrate, and his explanation of alternatives is not always complete.[43] Again, there is no appeal from arbitration, and the judgment is final.[44]

7. VENUE. Recently it has become clear that venue restrictions present a problem for the effective operation of small claims courts.[45] For instance, a firm in one part of a state may dispatch salesmen throughout the state, selling shoddy merchandise on installment. If the buyer refuses to pay and the firm sues for non-payment, the buyer may have to travel long distances to defend since the contract was technically entered into at the home office of the firm. Limiting venue to the defendant's county may work hardship on the plaintiff. The best answer would be discretionary change

---

[37] *See, e.g., Fla. Stat. Ann.* § 42.10 (1961) (5 to 15 days); *Ill. Ann. Stat.* ch. 110A, § 283 (Supp. 1968) (14 to 30 days; *Ore. Rev. Stat.* § 46.470 (1968) (5 to 20 days); *Utah Code Ann.* § 78–6–4 (1953) (5 to 20 days); *Wis. Stat. Ann.* § 299.05(3) (Supp. 1967) (8 to 17 days).

[38] *Cal. Civ. Pro. Code* § 117d (West 1959) (10 to 30 days if defendant is in the county; 30 to 60 days if defendant is outside the county).

[39] *See, e.g., D.C. Code* § 11–1342 (1967); *Fla. Stat. Ann.* § 42.12 (1961); *Minn. Stat. Ann.* §§ 491 *et seq.* (Supp. 1967).

[40] Continued separation of identity between lawyers and judges is apparently necessary to retain integrity. Therefore, once qualified, New York City lawyers are asked to serve only one night per month. Interview with Daniel Gutman, Dean of the New York Institute of Judicial Administration, in New York City, Dec. 19, 1968.

[41] *D.C. Code* § 11–1342 (1967). *See also Minn. Stat. Ann.* §§ 491 *et seq.* (Supp. 1967). "Included among the cases submitted for arbitration was a variety of disputes, including a contest over the closed-shop issue between the local gas company and the union of its 12,000 employees. By this method a strike was avoided." Cayton, *supra* note 6, at 61.

[42] *See, e.g., N.Y.C. Civil Ct. Act* § 1804 (1963); *D.C. Code* § 11–1342 (1967); *Fla. Stat. Ann.* § 42.12(1) (1961). *See also* Comment, *supra* note 1, at 946 n.114, concerning the validity of making conciliation a condition precedent to docketing a small claims court case.

[43] Several visits to the Manhattan Small Claims Court on December 19–21, 1968, revealed a tendency to rush the whole process, thereby omitting explanations.

[44] By agreeing to arbitrate the parties have waived any right to appeal.

[45] Comment, "The California Small Claims Court," 52 *Calif. L. Rev.* 876, 889 (1964). [hereinafter cited as *Alameda Study*].

of venue.[46] The motion could be made by mail, with the judge deciding whether the facts warrant change of venue.[47]

B. Trial Procedures

1. WAIVER OF TECHNICALITIES AND EXPEDITING OF TRIAL ON THE RETURN DAY. Few dilatory motions and legal maneuvers are permitted in a small claims court proceeding. The aim is to secure settlement on the return day in an informal atmosphere, and in theory only illness and possibility of settlement are acceptable grounds for continuances.[48] In practice, it is observed that at least one continuance is easily obtained for a variety of uninvestigated reasons. The judge listens to the reasons and decides within his broad discretion.

2. SIMPLE, INFORMAL AND SPEEDY PROCEDURE. If either party refuses to attempt arbitration-conciliation or if the attempt fails, the case proceeds to trial. The trial is handled swiftly with the judge assuming a controlling role. The quality of judges and the nature of their service is a crucial determinant of whether small claims courts work. Problems exist in both the urban and rural environments. Where the court is a branch of a municipal or other civil court, the judges are usually rotated,[49] and the quality of judicial manpower is no worse than in the regular civil courts. However, in rural areas small claims courts are often merely an extension of the old justice of the peace system grafted onto a newer court structure, and the less able magistrate is attracted. With these judges come abuses and ineptness capable of destroying all the hoped-for gains.

The judge exercises liberal powers as he questions the parties. For example, a capable judge may notice a questionable link in a litigant's case and skillfully pursue it until the fallacy is exposed.[50] An inherent problem in such a situation is that over-identification with one party can result. It is difficult to be the representative of two interests as well as remaining arbiter.

Legislatures have empowered the small claims courts to modify rules of practice and evidence[51] as they see fit. A typical provision describes the proceeding as follows:

The parties and witnesses shall be sworn, the judge shall conduct the trial in such manner as to do substantial justice between the parties according to the rules of substantive law, and shall not be bound by the statutory provisions or rules of practice, procedure, pleading or evidence, except such provisions relating to privileged communications.[52]

In a well-run small claims court no lawyer will jump up to object if slight hearsay enters as the litigants tell their story. Indeed, counsel may be specifically excluded by statute. Histrionic appeals are fruitless since there is no jury. The subtleties of pleading and technicalities of trial procedure are laid aside and an attempt is made to approximate a just result, given the understanding that it is a summary proceeding. At its best, the small claims court lets the litigants participate and understand what happens to them. Given a capable judge and a good atmosphere, the

---

46 *Id.*

47 *Id.*

48 Cayton, *supra* note 6, at 62.

49 This is the procedure in New York City, and is the method usually followed in most urban areas. The justice of the peace system, which the small claims court was designed to replace, still is retained in some rural areas.

50 Kronheim, "Does the Small Claims Branch of Our Municipal Court Measure Up to the Standards of the Community," 18 *D.C. B.J.* 113, 115 (1951).

51 *See* 1 Wigmore, *Evidence* (2d ed. 1923) § 4(d), at 62: "In small cases generally . . . it would be a defiance of common sense and a nullification of the main purpose, to enforce the jury-trial rules of evidence; for the parties are expected to appear personally without professional counsel, and they cannot be expected to observe rules which they do not know."

52 Cayton, *supra* note 6, at 62.

result can be maximal and inspire respect.[53] At its worst, the court gives the litigant the impression that he is being rushed through a proceeding which he does not understand and that, if he is lucky, he will receive a very rough approximation of justice.

3. JURY TRIALS AND APPEALS. A small claims court system which made jury trials a common practice would necessarily fail in its objectives, due to the delays and the increased procedural and evidentiary requirements. Therefore, while guaranteeing the right to a jury trial in controversies above a certain amount,[54] most states encourage the litigant to choose a non-jury trial. In addition, they may specify that the plaintiff has waived his right to a jury trial by his choice of a particular forum.[55] The defendant may demand a jury trial in the small claims tribunal in some jurisdictions,[56] but in others [57] he may do so only by timely removal before hearing to the regular docket or by appeal after judgment.[58] Jury trials are discouraged in the District of Columbia court simply by requiring a fixed fee and written demand on short notice to obtain such a

trial.[59] Also, the defendant may be required to post cash or a bond as security for the payment of the judgment and costs.[60] The constitutionality of such measures has been upheld.[61] Further, use of jury requests as a dilatory tactic is discouraged by quick handling of the case after appeal or removal.[62]

Generally, the small claims tribunals are not courts of record,[63] and so appeal is *de novo* whether or not a jury is demanded.[64] Trial on the appeal level is carried out as if no small claims court proceeding had taken place. Thus, it has been held constitutional [65] to refuse defendant the right to transfer from the small claims court to a more "conventional" branch of the court system.[66] Where removal before hearing is permitted, it can be had only to obtain a jury trial, and the defendant must file an affidavit attesting to his good faith and listing his grounds of defense.[67] Accordingly, transfers are rare.[68]

---

[53] Interview with Daniel Gutman, *supra* note 40. *See also* Harley, *supra* note 7, at 144–45.

[54] For an extensive discussion of the constitutional guarantee of jury trial, see Comment, *supra* note 1, at 939 n.58.

[55] *See, e.g.,* N.Y.C. Civil Ct. Act § 1806 (1963); *Mass. Ann Laws* ch. 218, § 23 (1955); 12 *Vt. Stat. Ann.* § 5535 (1958); *Idaho Code Ann.* § 1–1511 (1948). *See also* Comment, "Courts: Jurisdiction of Small-Claims Courts," 11 *Calif. L. Rev.* 276, 279 (1923) ; Comment, *supra* note 1, at 939–40.

[56] *See, e.g.,* Ill. Ann. Stat. ch. 110A, § 285 (Supp. 1968); 12 *Vt. Stat. Ann.* § 5535 (1958) (prior to hearing) .

[57] *See, e.g.,* Fla. Stat. Ann. § 42.16 (1961) (by 5 days after service of notice); *Tex. Rev. Civ. Stat.* art. 2460a (11) (1964) (1 day before hearing, coupled with $3 fee) .

[58] *See, e.g.,* Idaho Code Ann. § 1–1511 (1948) (within 10 days of judgment, and if the defendant loses on appeal, he must pay $10 in attorney fees to the plaintiff); *Minn. Stat. Ann.* § 491.06 (1958) (within 10 days after judgment); *Utah Code Ann.* § 78–6–10 (1953) (within 5 days after judgment) .

[59] *See, e.g.,* N.Y.C. Civil Ct. Act § 1806 (1963) ($50); *Cal. Civ. Pro. Code* § 117j (West 1959) (adds $15 to be given to the plaintiff if the defendant loses the appeal); *Ill. Ann. Stat.* ch. 110A, § 285 (Supp. 1968) ($12.50 for a six-man jury, $25 for a 12-man jury); *Wis. Stat. Ann.* § 299.21(3) (Supp. 1967) ($24 for a 12-man jury, plus $4 suit tax fee, and $6 clerk's fee; $12 for a six-man jury) .

[60] *See, e.g.,* Cal. Civ. Pro. Code § 1171 (West 1959); *Mass. Ann. Laws* ch. 218, § 23 (1955) ($100); *Minn. Stat. Ann.* § 491.06(1) (1958).

[61] Capital Traction Co. v. Hof. 174 U.S. 1 (1899) . *But cf.* Flour City Fuel & Transfer Co. v. Young, 150 Minn. 452, 185 N.W. 934 (1921) .

[62] *See* N.Y.C. Civil Ct. Act § 1806 (1963) (may be a preferred case); *Mass. Ann. Laws* ch. 218, § 23 (1955) (case put at head of the docket of the appellate court).

[63] Prudential Ins. Co. v. Small Claims Court, 76 Cal. App. 2d 379, 73 P.2d 38 (1946) .

[64] *See* Comment, note 1, at 937 n.38, 941 n.71.

[65] Due process is assumed to be afforded by the summary procedure in McLaughlin v. Leverbaum, 248 Mass. 170, 142 N.E. 906 (1924) and in Flour City Fuel & Transfer Co. v. Young, 150 Minn. 452, 185 N.W. 934 (1921) .

[66] Comment, *supra* note 1, at 941 nn.69–71.

[67] *See, e.g.,* Mass. Ann. Laws ch. 218, § 23 (1955); *Minn. Stat. Ann.* § 491.06(2) (1958); *N.Y.C. Civil Ct. Act* § 1803 (1963).

[68] *See generally* Clerk, District of Columbia Small

4. NIGHT SESSIONS. Consistent with their objectives, some states have provided for night sessions to minimize the costs to litigants.[69] Therefore, the equivalent of at least one day's wages does not become the minimum floor below which, with added costs and counsel fees and the intangible nuisance factor, a dispute cannot be settled within the judicial framework.[70] Despite provisions for night sessions in some statutes, they are not mandatory, and therefore are often ignored except in the urban areas. Such provisions should be mandatory, with the caveat that they could be infrequent if the case load and needs of the litigants so warranted.

5. THE EXCLUSION OF LAWYERS. While some jurisdictions bar lawyers absolutely,[71] all actively discourage them.[72] As a source of delay, technicality, and even distortion of the process,[73] representation by counsel is unwelcome. Though possibly of value to handle a frightened party,[74] counsel finds his major functions assumed by the

judge who does fact-finding, questioning, and cross examining himself. Counsel is regarded as a luxury which the potential recovery in dollar amounts does not warrant. Further, the particular talents of a lawyer are not needed in small claims courts since the emphasis is on summary procedure.

The absence of lawyers certainly involves some sacrifice of accuracy and soundness of judgment. In some very simple cases, the sacrifice is minimal but in others, unless the judge is very capable, the loss may be substantial. Therefore, it is again clear that high quality of the court's judicial manpower is vital for effectiveness.

C. Judgments

1. INSTALLMENT PAYMENT OF JUDGMENTS. Settlement and voluntary disclosure of liability are encouraged by statutory provisions allowing installment payments.[75] The requirements for a showing of financial need sufficient to justify this procedure are minimal, and payments can be flexibly spaced in accordance with the defendant's own needs and earnings.[76] Such a provision is particularly desirable for the individual defendant. On the other hand, in the wage claim case, it is often imperative that a corporate defendant pay fully and immediately.[77]

Claims Court and Conciliation Branch, *Monthly Reports. See also* "Ninth Report of the Judicial Council of Massachusetts, 19 *Mass. L.Q.* 1, 95–96 (1933); Clark & O'Connell, "The Workings of the Hartford Small Claims Court," 3 *Conn. B.J.* 123, 128 (1929).

[69] *See, e.g., D.C. Code Ann.* § 11–1306 (1967). *See also* Vance, "A Proposed Court of Conciliation," 1 *Minn. L. Rev.* 107, 114 (1917).

[70] Often it would be at least two, due to ease with which a first continuance may be obtained.

[71] *See, e.g., Cal. Civ. Pro. Code* § 117(g) (West 1959); *Idaho Code Ann.* § 1–1508 (1948); *Ore. Rev. Stat.* § 46.500 (1968); *Wash. Rev. Code Ann.* § 12.40.080 (1951).

[72] Some of the discouragement is inherent since only very low fees are possible. Additional discouragement comes from the court itself, since the lawyer has a minimal role.

[73] For example, lawyers require continuances merely because of a conflict in schedules.

[74] *See* "Report of Committee on Small Claims and Conciliation Procedure," 10 *A.B.A.J.* 828, 830 (1924). Opposed to the view that attorneys should be excluded (see Vance, *supra* note 69, at 115) is the suggestion that they should be encouraged to attend the court and "freely imbibe the spirit of informal procedure." Harley, "The Small Claims

Branch of the Municipal Court of Chicago," 8 *Bull. Am. Jud. Soc'y* 25, 30 (1915). If attorneys are admitted some provision must be made for the assignment of counsel to poor parties. *Cf.* Maguire, *supra* note 1, at 388 *et seq.*

[75] *See, e.g., D.C. Code Ann.* §§ 16–3907, 16–3908 (1967); *Minn. Stat. Ann.* § 491.04 (1958); *N.J. Rev. Stat.* § 2A:18–66 (Supp. 1952).

[76] Cayton, *supra* note 6, at 63. For a discussion of the means employed to enable indigent debtors to discharge their obligations, *see* Nehemkis, "The Boston Poor Debtor Court—A Study in Collection Procedure," 42 *Yale L. J.* 561 (1933).

[77] *See* Comment, *supra* note 1, at 946 for an explanation of the various methods which might be utilized in wage claim cases.

2. GARNISHMENT AND ATTACHMENT. Some jurisdictions bar garnishment and attachment procedures completely [78] in the belief that they add unnecessary complexity. Other states handle the problem of the creditor more sympathetically by allowing garnishment to be implemented in a summary and simple fashion.[79] Simplified garnishment proceedings, however, are still not the complete answer. Judge J. Skelly Wright likens wage garnishment of the poor individual to a "debtors prison," labelling it iniquitous, ridiculous and self-defeating.[80] Once a garnishment order is obtained from the small claims court, the garnishee is sometimes fired by his employer to avoid the bother and bookkeeping which would result.[81] For this reason, Florida, Pennsylvania and Texas have eliminated wage garnishments. It is Judge Wright's opinion that this elimination can lead to job security, decreased welfare rolls and greater family stability.[82]

III. LIMITS ON JURISDICTION

A. Monetary

With rare exceptions, only money judgments may be obtained in small claims courts.[83] To keep pace with inflationary

trends and rising standards of living, which have been set upon a growing base of social security, insurance, Medicare, pensions and welfare benefits, ceilings have recently been increasing. Despite these increases, the limit in most jurisdictions has been set between $50 and $300.[84] A few states have limits ranging from $300 to $2000.

The breakdown of claims within a jurisdictional limit of $200 is indicated by the results of a study of the Alameda County, California, Small Claims Court.[85] Approximately 8.5 per cent of the cases were for under $10, 54.9 per cent were for $25-$100, 23.1 per cent were for $100-$175, 4.4 per cent were for $175-$199.99 and 9.1 per cent were exactly $200, indicating an effort by some plaintiffs to scale down their claims to get into the court.[86]

B. Type of Action

Actions are typically limited to tort and contract.[87] Libel and slander are often excluded,[88] and some jurisdictions also

---

[78] See, e.g., Cal. Civ. Pro. Code § 117(h) (a) (Supp. 1968); Idaho Code Ann. § 1–1509 (1948); Nev. Rev. Stat. § 73.020 (1967); Okla. Stat. Ann. tit. 39, § 660 (Supp. 1967); Utah Code Ann. § 78–6–8 (1953).

[79] See Minn. Stat. Ann. § 491.08 (Supp. 1967).

[80] Wright, supra note 16, at 106.

[81] Id.

[82] Id.

[83] See, e.g., Idaho Code Ann. § 1–1501 (1948); Nev. Rev. Stat. § 73.010 (1967); Utah Code Ann. § 78–6–1 (1953). Sometimes the phrase "for the recovery of money only" is used. This has been interpreted to include tort as well as contract claims despite the form of the affidavit which requires an allegation of indebtedness. Leuschen v. The Small Claims Court, 191 Cal. 133, 215 P. 391 (1923); see also Weir v. Mariott, 135 Ore. 214, 215–216, 293 P. 944, 945 (1930). Replevin suits are expressly provided for by statute. See, e.g., Wis. Stat. Ann. § 299.01(3) (Supp. 1967). Re-

cently, statutes have permitted suits for the collection of taxes: Cal. Civ. Pro. Code §117 (Supp. 1968) (if the legality is not contested); Ill. Ann. Stat. ch. 110A, § 281 (Supp. 1968).

[84] See, e.g., N.Y.C. Civil Ct. Act § 1801 (1963) ($300); Cal. Civ. Pro. Code § 117 (Supp. 1968); D.C. Code Ann. § 11–1341 (1967) ($150); Fla. Stat. Ann. § 42.03 (1961) ($250, but if the population in the county is over 400,000, the limit is $300); Ill. Ann. Stat. ch. 110A, § 281 (1968) ($500); Tex. Rev. Civ. Stat. Ann. art. 2460a, § 2 (1964) ($150, but if it is a wage claim case, $200) ; Utah Code Ann. § 78–5–1 (1953) ($100); Wash. Rev. Code § 12.40.010 (1951) ($50). A bona fide counterclaim above the jurisdictional limit will lead to removal. Some dropping of claim or counterclaim amount to the jurisdiction limit does occur. See Clerk, supra note 68; Alameda Study, supra note 45, at 884–898. See also Fowks, "Small Claims Courts: Simplified Pleadings and Procedure," 37. J. of Kan. B. Ass'n 167, 226–27 1968).

[85] Alameda Study, supra note 45.

[86] Id. at 884.

[87] See Ill. Ann. Stat. ch. 110A, § 281 (Supp. 1968).

[88] See, e.g., Alaska Stat. § 22.15.050 (1967); Mass. Ann. Laws ch. 218, § 21 (1955); Okla. Stat. Ann.

bar suits for malicious prosecution, false imprisonment, and assault and battery.[89] Such exclusions reflect the public policy of discouraging defamation suits.[90] This policy recognizes that some element of community judgment is involved and that such suits are therefore peculiarly amenable to jury determination, as well as the conviction that these actions involve a complexity of proof[91] which is beyond the ability of small claims procedure to handle. Some jurisdictions permit the judge to remove any case from the docket if it is of great complexity.[92]

Few studies have attempted to determine the relative percentages of types of claims in small claims courts. A Hartford, Connecticut, study,[93] compiled in 1929, and the Alameda, California, study[94] of 1964 are the most complete in terms of breakdown, and both indicate that "goods and services" claims predominate. But beyond the categories of loans (3.1 per cent and 4.1 per cent, respectively) and rent (7.0 per cent and 7.8 per cent, respec-

tively), the breakdowns are not closely comparable.[95]

C. Identity of Parties

There is no requirement or limitation concerning the identity of the defendant, but some jurisdictional statutes decline to accord plaintiff-status to corporations, partnerships, associations, insurers, or assignees.[96] Unless barred, business interests predominante in utilization of the small claims courts.

In the Alameda, California, small claims court study, it was discovered that business and government agencies were

[95] In the remainder of the 5,236 cases which made up the Hartford study, 60% were for goods furnished, 20% were for work and labor, 2.5% were for traffic negligence, 2% were for other negligence, and 3% were for miscellaneous claims. Out of the total of cases, 48% ended in judgment for the plaintiff and only 2.5% ended in judgment for the defendant. Thirty-one per cent were settled out of court and 14% were dismissed. There were 37.5% default judgments and only 46 cases were transferred to another court.

As a rough comparison, the Alameda study included the following categories in "goods and services": goods (29.5%), government services (14.2%), non-government services (9.3%), goods and services (6.2%), damages for non-performance or fault performance of services (2.3%), and breach of contract—other (2.6%), making a total of 64.1%. This total figure might be compared to the Hartford figures totaling over 80% for the combined categories of goods furnished (60%) and work and labor (20%). It would perhaps be inaccurate to compare the categories of property damage (12.7%) in the Alameda study to the combined categories of traffic negligence (2.5%) and other negligence (2%) in the Hartford study.

The Alameda study included several categories which had no comparison in the earlier Hartford study: refunds (3.4%), and personal property taxes (2.9%). The Alameda study showed that in 63.2% of the cases the judge took some action (tried case, dismissed, granted a continuance). In 80% of the cases action was taken within 40 days.

[96] *See, e.g., N.Y.C. Civil Ct. Act* § 1801 (1963); *Cal. Civ. Pro. Code* § 117(f) (Supp. 1968) (no assignees); *Okla. Stat. Ann.* tit. 39, § 657 (Supp. 1967) (no assignees); *Wis. Stat. Ann.* § 299.06(2)(a) (Supp. 1967).

---

tit. 39 § 651 (Supp. 1967); *Vt. Stat. Ann.* tit. 12, § 5531 (1958).

[89] The recent Alaska statute is most inclusive in its exclusions, ruling out imprisonment, criminal conversation, seduction under promise to marry, equity, malicious prosecution and cases where the state is the defendant. *Alaska Stat.* § 22.15.050 (1967). Two statutes, *D.C. Code Ann.* § 11–1341 (1967) and *N.H. Rev. Stat. Ann.* § 503:1 (1955), rule out real estate claims; Wisconsin forbids replevin actions, *Wis. Stat. Ann.* § 299.01(3) (Supp. 1967). Some statutes expressly provide for use of the court by municipalities to collect taxes, *e.g., Cal. Civ. Pro. Code* § 117 (Supp. 1968) (if the legality is not contested); *Ill. Ann. Stat.* ch. 110A, § 281 (Supp. 1968).

[90] *See* "Proceedings," 1921 *Conn. B. Ass'n* 58, 69.

[91] *See* Note, "Small Claims Courts in the United States," 20 *Colum. L. Rev.* 901, 904 (1920).

[92] *N.Y.C. Civil Ct. Act* § 1805 (1963); *Mass. Ann. Laws* ch. 218, § 24 (1955). *See also* "Ninth Report of the Judicial Council of Massachusetts," 19 *Mass. L.Q.* 1, 95–96 (1933).

[93] Clark & O'Connell, "The Workings of the Hartford Small Claims Court," 3 *Conn. B.J.* 123 (1929).

[94] *Alameda Study, supra* note 45.

plaintiffs in over 60 per cent of the cases.[97] Only 35 per cent of the plaintiffs were individuals. Significantly, 85 per cent of the defendants were individuals.[98] The study also revealed that group claims, where more than one claim is filed at a time, accounted for 59.3 per cent of all claims.[99] Tentative results from an unpublished study [100] conducted in Albany-Berkeley, California, a more rural area, indicates that few corporate plaintiffs and almost no group claims were experienced in the small claims court. It is in the urban area that business interests have tended to dominate the small claims court dockets.

There seems to be no doubt that professional people are beginning to use the small claims court apparatus more frequently,[101] but no study has yet attempted to determine how many individual plaintiffs are professionals. The Alameda County study indicates that in the more urban areas corporate plaintiffs, exclusive of the municipality itself, are primarily retailers, insurance companies and small businesses.[102]

IV. THE JURISDICTIONAL QUESTION

A. *Disparity as to Amount and Proper Parties*

The dual parameters of jurisdiction, amount and proper parties, serve to define the present problems in small claims courts. As noted, jurisdictional limits in monetary terms vary widely.[103] Just when a small claim gets too "big," and therefore requires procedural and evidentiary technicalities, thereby losing the stated advantages of small claim procedure, has eluded precise definition. Also, with respect to jurisdictional questions as to proper parties, the states have provided widely divergent criteria.[104]

Numerous interests clash in determining jurisdictional requisites. The result is often compromise, whether or not suited to the realities of dispute settlement or the rational exclusion of one type of party. A small claims court designed to serve the individual as plaintiff is different from one which permits corporations and collection agencies into court as plaintiffs to collect debts, often from the poor.[105] Placing these two contrasting types of cases on the same docket may be recreating inequities, such as exclusion of the poor from judicial redress. Yet, exclusion of one type of claim may not only be unfairly prejudicial to the group pursuing it, but also inimical to the interests of the judicial system and society. For example, if business interests are excluded their claims will congest the regular civil docket, or perhaps simply go unlitigated, being passed on to the consumer in the form of higher prices.

Consumers, small businessmen, judges, lawyers, collection agencies, insurance companies, credit agencies, legislators—all play a part in determining the parameters of small claims court jurisdiction. These groups have different lobbying powers and access to the legislatures. Some are better organized than others and can be "heard" more directly. The individual consumer of goods and services is in the

---

[97] This figure includes proprietorships, which numbered 16.8% of the total. *Alameda Study, supra* note 45, at 893.

[98] *Id.* at 884.

[99] Sixteen organizations accounted for nearly 45% of the claims, with the County of Alameda the largest user of the court (nearly 20%). Twenty per cent of the claimants were government agencies, and hospital claims accounted for nearly 75% of the government agency total. Corporations generally sued for goods or services or a combination of the two, while individuals sought recovery for property damage or rent in over 50% of the suits they brought. *Id.* at 887.

[100] *Id.* at 883.

[101] *Institute of Judicial Administration Report— 1959* Supplement, *supra* note 15, at 1.

[102] *Alameda Study, supra* note 45, at 897.

[103] *See* note 84 *supra* and accompanying text.

[104] *See* note 96 *supra* and accompanying text.

[105] Robinson, "A Small Claims Division for Chicago's New Circuit Court," 44 *Chi. B. Rec.* 421 (1963).

least desirable position, despite some recent advances in the nature of consumer councils, legislation to protect the purchaser, and distribution of literature which describes rights and obligations.

B. Complexity

Because jurisdiction is couched largely in monetary terms, it is deceptively attractive to evaluate jurisdiction by reference to dollar amounts. But this belies the nature of the underlying issue. Complexity of a case, not amount in controversy, is the true determinant of whether a claim is susceptible to the summary procedure of small claims courts. Dollar amounts are only a rough, indeed a very rough, approximation of complexity. In reality, they are quite arbitrary.

No correlation between jurisdictional amount and case complexity has been established. It is superficially said that : . . larger claims . . . are more complicated. Every lawyer knows that in contract and debt actions the size of the claim has little relation to the complexity of the issues or the difficulty of proof.[106]

Indeed, it has been stated that the average small claim is likely to be more complex than the average non-small claims case.[107] Nevertheless, it would seem that the intention in creating small claims courts was to eliminate cases under a specified dollar amount from the dockets of formal courts, irrespective of case complexity.[108]

It is clear that of the antitrust and securities regulation type, for example, involve extremely complex factual determinations and are out of the ambit of small claims courts. Long lists of expert witnesses, complicated pre-trial discovery hearings, extensive economic evaluations from lengthy data, and inclusion of numerous parties are not suited to small claims court determination. Thus a threshold of case complexity exists which will effectively preclude small claims court adjudication, but it is impossible to determine the specific line.

The usual contract or tort action for damages does not present especially difficult factual situations. However, some small contract claims will be less susceptible to easy proof than large ones,[109] since record-keeping is generally less accurate and complete, and since legal help is less frequently sought to draft instruments or to advise on policy. Also, in business dealing in large dollar volumes, irregular merchandising and inadequate record-keeping are less likely to occur due both to standardized techniques and to business pressures resulting from greater notoriety and therefore more accountability to the public.

C. Due Process and Hearsay

Another factor of importance in evaluating the jurisdictional problems is the changing body of evidentiary rules, and most particularly, the hearsay rule. The large number of exceptions to the hearsay rule has left doubt as to which is more important, the rule or its body of exceptions; but the admission of hearsay evidence is just one of a number of procedural points losing parties can be expected to raise in arguing that they have been deprived of due process in the small claims court. It is also an argument one can expect to hear from members of the bar critical of expanded small claims court jurisdiction.

Summary procedures, particularly if lawyers are excluded or prevented from playing a significant role, can be challenged in numerous ways. For instance, it is arguable that the parties' interests will not be adequately represented. Also, pertinent factors concerning character evi-

106 R. Smith, *supra* note 1, at 55.
107 *Alameda Study, supra* note 45, at 877.
108 *Id.*

109 *Id.*

dence may not be revealed. Reputation and prior crimes evidence if relevant will probably not be considered. Competency will probably not be adequately determined. Inferences and presumptions may not be forcefully developed and presented.

It is clear that there are countervailing considerations to the above challenges. As was pointed out,[110] jurisdictional expansion does not necessarily mean greater complexity, and in the relatively simple cases, due process problems are much less likely to occur. Most crucial is the role of the judge in handling the trial and perceiving what is relevant. In addition, in a number of jurisdictions, the judge may remove from the docket complex cases which are not suited to settlement in small claims court.[111]

Three other factors bear importantly on due process challenges. (1) The judge is not at liberty to apply his own personal standards in deciding cases. Substantive law must be correctly applied; erroneous interpretation of the law can be corrected on appeal.[112] (2) Many evidentiary rules are designed to prevent the jury from hearing unreliable or prejudicial evidence or from weighing evidence incorrectly. A competent judge need not be protected in the same manner as a jury. He knows the rules of evidence and will analyze testimony in light of these rules. For example, he can listen to hearsay and evaluate it for what it is worth, considering both the hearsay rule and the overall situation in the case. (3) Students of procedure recognize that evidence which is excluded for fear of unduly influencing the jury may be probative, and if there is no jury, this evidence can be properly considered.

D. Proper Plaintiffs

Closely related to a consideration of the monetary limits of small claims courts is the jurisdictional question of who is a proper plaintiff. The context in which small claims courts now function indicates that unless corporations, partnerships, and assignees are specifically excluded from the court as plaintiffs, they will tend to dominate the docket.[113] Unless lawyers are specifically excluded, they will appear in court to represent the business plaintiff, bringing in unwanted technicality and delay to the summary procedure and weighting the process against the individual defendant who is usually unrepresented by counsel.

Though counsel's role is limited in the small claims court, assuming that lawyers are permitted at all, there is an uneven balance between plaintiff and defendant where the former has counsel and the latter appears *pro se*. Default judgments and settlements abound in small claims courts,[114] and one reason may be that plaintiff's counsel convinces the *pro se* defendant of the futility of his defense before trial.[115] Concern about such unequal bargaining power has been the principal motivation leading some states to bar lawyers in small claims courts. A better solution, and one which will answer due process objections, would be to permit lawyers, with the state providing counsel for the indigent.

Despite extensive use of the court by business interests, contrary to the original philosophy underlying small claims courts, it is important to realize that the poor litigant continues to receive benefits in this court which would be unavailable to him elsewhere.[116] The individual defendant saves court costs and counsel fees, has the benefit of night sessions and relaxed procedural and evidentiary rules, and may pay a judgment entered against him in installments if he loses.

110 *See* notes 106–108 *supra* and accompanying text.
111 *See* note 92 *supra* and accompanying text.
112 *See* Kronheim, *supra* note 50, at 113.

113 *Alameda Study, supra* note 45, at 883.
114 *See* Clerk, *supra* note 68.
115 Robinson, *supra* note 105, at 423.
116 Note, "Small Claims Courts as Collection Agencies," 4 *Stan. L. Rev.* 237 (1952).

The extensive use of small claims courts by business interests is substantiated by data gathered in the Alameda County survey.[117] Judge Timothy Murphy has strongly criticized the preponderance of corporate plaintiffs in the District of Columbia Small Claims Court:

Does the court established in 1938 meet the needs of our poor? I submit not. The Court is not the court of the neighborhood litigant suing over small loans, minor property damage, or workingmen seeking wages. Quite the contrary, it is primarily the court of the skilled lawyer representing large debt collection agencies, credit stores, corporate defendants and insurance companies. Further, these lawyers and their organizations are almost without exception litigating against pro se parties (persons representing themselves).[118]

Some commentators do not object to use of small claims courts by business interests.

[C]ollection agencies and professional men employ the small claims courts facilities in increasing number. However, no serious objection has been raised to this tendency; in fact, two states . . . have deleted from their statutes a limitation on the number of claims which an individual may bring before the court during a particular week or month. This action would seem to encourage the use of small claims courts by repeating claimants as well as by the occasional litigant.[119]

However, despite the above statement, most states have either limited or withheld entirely from corporations, partnerships, assignees and collection agencies the right to sue in small claims court.[120] In a Model Small Claims Court Act the following language is proposed: "No action may be brought by any person, firm, partnership, association or corporation engaged, either primarily or secondarily, in the business of lending money at interest, nor by any collection agency or collection agent." [121] Perhaps the best solution to the problem of potential dominance of the small claims court by business interests is to create two sections—a business plaintiff section and an individual plaintiff section.[122]

V. PROPOSALS

The small claims court movement has experienced practical difficulties that its original proponents did not foresee. Yet these difficulties need not be debilitating. Rather, they argue for an expanded role of small claims courts in the future. Specifically, the following recommendations should be considered:

(1) Small claims court monetary jurisdiction should be extended to two or three times its present levels. A maximum of approximately $1000 in areas with a high cost of living is reasonable. Disparity in cost of living should be the primary basis for differences among other jurisdictions.

---

117 *See* note 97 *supra* and accompanying text. The Alameda County survey makes the following comments concerning its finding of extensive non-individual use of the small claims courts:

The original aim of the small claims court to provide an inexpensive, informal procedure for the plaintiff of limited means has no application to the large business group claimant. On the other hand, there may be valid contemporary reasons for permitting the use of small claims courts by business claimants. For example, it seems clear that the availability of small claims procedure tends to relieve the formal courts of the handling of petty claims. Also, there seems to be no self-evident reason why business plaintiffs should not be permitted to obtain justice in small disputes at a minimum expenditure of cost and time. The results of the study indicate the necessity for re-examining the purposes of the small claims court in the modern context.

Alameda Study, supra note 45, at 883.

118 Murphy, "District of Columbia Small Claims Court—The Forgotten Court," 34 *D.C.B.J.* 14 (Feb. 1967) .

119 *See Institute of Judicial Administration Small Claims Courts in the United States—1959,* Supplement 1–2 (Rep. No. 7–U57, March 13, 1959).

120 *See* note 96 *supra* and accompanying text.

121 Fowks, *supra* note 84, at 220–24.

122 Robinson, *supra* note 105, at 421–26.

Legislative review of jurisdictional monetary requisites should be scheduled every three years to adjust for inflation.

(2) Discretionary power to remove cases from the small claims docket should be vested with the judge in cases too complex to be handled by summary procedure. Power to remove should be explicitly granted by statute, and discretion should be exercised on motion made by the court, either party, or both parties. A removal should be without prejudice to either plaintiff or defendant. In the event that a case is removed from the docket, an indigent plaintiff or defendant should be informed of the various alternatives available by which he can continue to press or defend the claim, including legal aid services. This could be handled by the clerk, or appropriate printed material could be distributed. A lawyer should be provided for indigents when removal is ordered.

(3) Suits brought by corporations, partnerships, associations, and assignees should be heard separately from those brought by individuals,[123] either on different days or in a different branch of the same court. In such a business-plaintiff section of a small claims court, it is essential that an indigent defendant receive the benefit of counsel. As in the case of removal to a regular civil court, a lawyer should be provided at no cost. In the individual-plaintiff section of small claims court, if the judiciary is competent it is not so imperative that counsel be provided for indigents.

(4) Efforts to develop a more complete code of consumer protection should be pursued. While protecting the consumer, such legislation will directly and incidentally further the goals of the small claims court. The statute of limitations for suits brought involving credit should be extremely short—six months at most. Court costs for filing suits should be greater in the business-claimant branch, and high

enough to cover costs of operating the court. Court costs should be paid to the state or municipality, and not to the winning party. If the defendant loses, court costs should be lower than when the plaintiff loses.

(5) The court must remedy its public relations problems. The availability of small claims courts should be extensively advertised to individuals, particularly those at lower income levels, through consumer councils, neighborhood organizations, and other available means. Written material should accompany any claims to fully explain small claims court procedures and any options available to the party. It would be highly advisable to move the small claims courts into ghetto areas of our cities to make the facilities more accessible to the poor. If this is done, any venue problems should be handled by judicial discretion, with an eye to the relative cost and difficulty of travel for the ghetto resident.

(6) Arbitration, which few states are now utilizing, should be made available in both the business and individual branches of the small claims court. The judge should be required to attempt to get the parties to arbitrate before hearing the case. Arbitration should be available in any case, regardless of the type of litigant or amount in controversy. Printed material should be distributed to both plaintiff and defendant prior to trial to advise them of the arbitration possibilities.

Arbitrators should be lawyers who have at least ten years of experience, and who are approved by the Presiding Judge of the appellate branch of the state court system from a list of persons screened by the local bar association.[124] No compensation should be given, and arbitrators should serve only one night per month to preserve the separate identities of the bar and the bench.

---

123 *Id.*

124 Interview with Daniel Gutman, *supra* note 40.

VI. CONCLUSION

Chief Justice Hughes of the United States Supreme Court remarked:

The judicial quality does not reside in form or ceremony, still less in circumlocution and an avoidance of the pith of the matter. The judicial quality is found in the impartial hearing and reasoned determination upon ascertained facts, and it may be speedy, summary, and, as our clients would say, business-like without losing its character.[125]

[125] Kennedy, "The Poor Man's Court of Justice," 23 *J. Am. Jud. Soc'y.* 221, 224 (1941).

Judicial quality of this nature may be achieved in the small claims court. Advances in simplified procedure and trial, however, have not been extended to regular civil courts. Small claims court procedure, coupled with flexible arbitration machinery, offers promise for an administration of justice which conforms to the demands of contemporary society. It restores the judge to a pre-eminent role. It eliminates the discriminations inherent in a costly system of justice. And most importantly, if operated in accordance with its fundamental principles, it will approximate the average citizen's expectation of substantial justice.

THE INSTITUTIONALIZATION OF CONFLICT: JURY ACQUITTALS

Mortimer R. Kadish and Sanford H. Kadish

At least since the advent of legal realism in America and Europe it has become almost impossible to speak of the relationship between law and society without noting that law and society "interact," law "meets or ought to meet the needs of society," law must be understood as "serving a social function," society "influences" or "creates" law for its own purposes. Whatever such language means in detail, clearly the idea of a legal system standing apart from society, perhaps on pillars of natural law, and issuing pronouncements to society according to independently determined norms and principles of justice has

Reprinted from *Journal of Social Issues*, **27** (2, 1971), pp. 199–217, by permission of the authors and The Society for the Psychological Study of Social Issues.

been rejected. We would not, if we could, reverse jurisprudential direction. On the contrary, finding such "realistic" talk as right as it is vague, this essay is written to illustrate one way in which legal institutions, by virtue of their technical construction, may provide for the interaction of law and society. That way is through the distribution of legal powers, rights, duties, and privileges so that they conflict in their functioning and hence place a premium upon the development of a justification for undertaking departures from the rules of the system itself.

Our aim here is to explore and interpret that conflict as it might occur for the criminal jury in rendering a verdict of acquittal. We do not think that legal systems adjust to new circumstances, changing values, and emerging claims only through devising roles that confront those who enact them with conflict in rights, duties, powers, or privileges—that is to say, through the institutionalization of conflict. Nor do we believe it is necessarily the most important way; certainly, most people would think first of the explicit provisions incorporated into legal systems for judicial and statutory changes if they wished to show how the law adjusts to changing needs. Nevertheless, a case can be made that some legal systems at some points generate for their agents conflicts that introduce departures from the rules, and do so as modes of adjusting to change. We take the role of the criminal jury in the acquittal of defendants as a prototype case.

THE CRIMINAL JURY AND ITS DEVELOPMENT

In an earlier day juries were held accountable for their mistakes and misjudgments and their verdicts given effect only so long as they were considered right. The earliest mode of control over jurors was the attaint, which allowed a party against whom the verdict went to invoke a larger jury to find the facts anew. If the larger jury found contrary to the first, it could attaint its members—which meant loss of lands, fine, or imprisonment—and reverse its judgment. Though attaints, apparently seldom used in criminal cases, became obsolete in the fifteenth century, another means to control jury error took its place —the judges themselves assumed power to punish the juror for incorrect or corrupt verdicts. Indeed the practice was formalized in 1534 by a statute authorizing courts to punish jurors for giving "an untrue verdict against the King, . . . contrary to good and pregnant evidence ministered to them [*Statutes at Large: Henry VIII*, p. 326]." However, in criminal cases, though the jury could be punished for an erroneous acquittal, the prisoner could not be, for new trials could not be ordered as

they could in civil cases. This power was used from time to time (see Thayer, 1898, pp. 162–178) until the court of Common Pleas in 1670 (Bushell, 1670) repudiated the practice and discharged the jurors who had acquitted William Penn of unlawful assembly. Ordering a new trial was developed as a substitute device for controlling juries in civil cases. In criminal cases no comparable control evolved.

Since the end of the seventeenth century, then, the legal power of a jury in criminal cases has been substantial. They render a general verdict, i.e., they respond with a general finding of guilty or innocent of the crime charged, both finding the facts and applying the law. The varieties of special pleading developed in civil cases by which questions of law were separated from questions of fact were never extended to criminal proceedings. When criminal juries convict, a variety of checks and controls assure conformity with the law, including judicial power to set the verdict aside and grant a new trial. But where they acquit there are no such controls. The acquittal is a diktat, a "sovereign power [Devlin, 1956, p. 89]," for which stated reasons are neither expected nor permitted. The jurors may in no way be held accountable for their verdict, be made to explain it, or be questioned about it. The acquittal verdict is given final and conclusive legal effect, no matter how fully it may be demonstrated that it was contrary to law.

What did this development mean for the legal authority of the criminal jury to acquit? What *is* the legal role of the jury with respect to the rules of the criminal law? These questions underlay a classic debate in English and American law. From the end of the seventeenth century on, the books are filled with controversy over whether the jury in criminal cases had the right to determine the law as well as the facts, or if only the court could determine the law. The view that came to prevail was that the duty of the jury was to take the law strictly from the judge, notwithstanding the power to do otherwise. Behind this view stands the ideal of the rule of law, an ideal which, it is reasoned, is wholly incompatible with a jury's right to take law into its own hands (see, e.g., Justice Story in United States v. Battiste, 1835, pp. 243–244; Chief Justice Shaw in Commonwealth v. Porter, 1845, p. 280; Forsyth, 1852, p. 261). To recognize such freedom in a jury risks an intolerable uncertainty in the law as the law shifts from case to case depending upon the chance make-up of the jury. Moreover, to do so invites any group of twelve persons to abrogate a law duly enacted by the legislature on the basis of their own views of what the law should be. Protection against bad laws should not come through the nullification of democratically enacted legislation by any dozen jurors, but through the democratic processes for changing the law.

In recent days the rising moral repugnance to the Vietnam war and to the laws supporting it, such as the draft, has led lawyers to renew the old claims by arguing that jurors should be told they are free to disregard the court's instructions and that lawyers should be permitted to argue they should do so (United States v. Moylan, 1969; United States v. Sisson, 1968; Sax, 1968; Van Dyke, 1970). But the old tradition is apparently too long dead to be revived—the claims have been flatly rejected. A standard, representative instruction on the duty of the jury reads: "It is my duty to instruct you in the law that applies to this case and you must follow the law as I state it to you [California Jury Instructions, 1970, p. 2]."

The triumph of the restrictive view of the jury's competence in the formulations of the courts, however, has by no means cleared the air of the uncertainty and ambiguity concerning the jury role in acquittal. The setting and context in which the judge tells the jury what its duty is must also be considered if the conscientious juror is properly to understand what he is truly to do and not to do. And that setting and context tend in a number of respects to cloud the clarity of the judge's conventional instructions to the jury.

Power and Right

The criminal jury has evolved to where it exercises a sovereign power in criminal cases. The power to return a general verdict cannot be taken from it. It returns its verdict without stated reasons or justifications of any kind. If it finds the defendant not guilty, the acquittal must be given final and binding legal effect, no matter what may be thought or known about the jury's failure to follow the law. And the jury itself is fully insulated from any accountability for its action. In these circumstances Alexander Hamilton's argument (People v. Croswell, 1804) has to be fairly faced, given the contest and history of the criminal jury:

All the cases agree that the jury have the *power* to decide the law as well as the fact; and if the law gives them the power, it gives them the *right* also. Power and right are convertible terms, when the law authorizes the doing of an act which shall be final, and for the doing of which the agent is not responsible [p. 345].

He was not arguing that there should be no constraints upon the jury in the way it exercises its power. His point was that the legal right followed from the legal power (Goebel, 1964, pp. 828–829).

The Courts and the Jury

The force of this proposition is enhanced by the courts' statements and dealings with specific legal issues concerning the criminal jury. When a judge hears a criminal case without a jury and finds the defendant guilty of one charge and innocent of another in circumstances in which such a finding is illogical and inconsistent, the judgment of guilt is reversible, on the ground that there can be no confidence in the correctness of that judgment (see United States v. Maybury, 1959). But where a jury returns verdicts no less inconsistent and illogical, the guilty verdict is regarded as irreversible.

In civil cases tried before a jury the use of special interrogatories formulated by the court to assist the jury's arriving at a general verdict logically and according to the legal instructions is long accepted and quite common. So is the special verdict, in which the jury is instructed to return only a special written finding upon each issue of fact, leaving it for the court to enter judgment in accordance with the law as applied to the jury-found facts (see Rule 49 of the Federal Rules Civil Procedures, 1970). Both devices serve as controls on the jury, functioning to assure judgments in accordance with the law. At the common law there is authority for the use of such devices in criminal cases as well, although the jury can always decline and insist on returning a general verdict (see United States v. Ogull, 1957). However, these devices have been even more rarely used in this country than in England, and current authority finds their use violative of the right to trial by jury.

An instructive case is United States v. Spock (1969), in which the court reversed a conviction of conspiracy to counsel evasion of the draft. The trial court had put to the jury, in addition to the general issue of guilt or innocence, ten special questions calling for a yes or no answer. This was enough to require reversal of the conviction, even assuming the correctness of the questions proposed. The right to jury trial, the appellate court reasoned, would be meaningless if the jury were not free from judicial pressure. The prohibited directed verdict of guilty is the most direct of such pressures. But lesser and more indirect pressures, such as the requirement of a special verdict or the use of special interrogatories, are impermissible for the

same reason. The court reasoned that these procedures infringed on the jury power to follow or not follow the instructions of the court. The controlling principle, said the court, is that "the jury, as the conscience of the community, must be permitted to look at more than logic [United States v. Spock, 1969, p. 182]."

Also of substantial relevance in illuminating the jury's role is the basis on which the Supreme Court has held the right to trial by jury to be protected by the due process clause of the Fourteenth Amendment. Recently it recognized the jury's power to displace law by appeal to conscience as a characteristic so "fundamental to the American scheme of government" that a state violates due process of law in eliminating jury trial (Duncan v. Louisiana, 1968, p. 1444). In other words, the fundamental function of the jury is not only to guard against official departures from the rules of law, but, on proper occasions, to depart from unjust rules or their unjust application.

The Tradition of the Jury

The jury's obligations and freedoms are determined by tradition as well as law. In landmark cases, particularly involving criminal libel and sedition, the jury invoked its power to nullify what were widely regarded as unjust laws. These actions are commonly cited not as regrettable departures from the rule of law, but as historic and seminal acts, like Magna Carta and the Bill of Rights, by which men asserted their right to be free of unjust laws. Arguments in support of the fundamental value of the jury almost always rest on the nullifying function of criminal juries. For example, as Dean Pound (1910) noted:

Jury lawlessness is the great corrective of law in its actual administration. The will of the state at large imposed on a reluctant community, the will of a majority imposed on a vigorous and determined minority, find the same obstacle in the local jury that formerly confronted kings and ministers [p. 18].

Jury Behavior

There is ample evidence of the continuity of the tradition of jury nullification of unjust laws. The classic historical instances included the jury's refusal to convict in a number of famous cases of criminal libel until the law was changed to give juries the authority to acquit through general verdicts (e.g., Fox's Libel Act in *Statutes at Large, George III,* 1792, ch. 60), and the strategies of early English juries in avoiding capital punishment, such as finding against the evidence that only 39 shillings had been stolen when to find that more had been stolen meant a mandatory death sentence (Report of the Select Committee on Capital Punishment, 1930). More currently, we have witnessed the American jury's systematic nullification of the Prohibition laws during the 1920s—"the most intense example of jury revolt in recent history [Kalven & Zeisel, 1966, p. 291]." Recent cases have also been noted by Professors Kalven and Zeisel (1966). Their study of the American jury demonstrated the more subtle use of power by contemporary American juries. Of the 350,000 sample trials reported, about 19% were cases of jury acquittal and judge conviction. The authors determined that their category, "jury sentiments on the law," accounted for or contributed to 50% of all judge-jury disagreements. Of that 50%, twice as many disagreements were attributable to disagreements caused by a combination of facts and values than were attributable to values (jury sentiments on the law) alone. This revealed, they concluded, "the salient role played by jury sentiments on the law in causing disagreements [Kalven & Zeisel, 1966, p. 115]." It also revealed:

. . . that the jury does not often consciously and explicitly yield to sentiment in the teeth of the law. Rather it yields to sentiment in the apparent process of resolving doubts as to the evidence. The jury, therefore, is able to conduct its revolt from the law within the etiquette of resolving issues of fact [Kalven & Zeisel, 1966, p. 165].

The "revolt from the law," the authors noted, is presently a modest one reflecting a general acceptance of substantive criminal law. It manifests itself "as a moderate corrective against undue prosecutions for gambling, game and liquor violations and, to some extent, drunken driving [Kalven & Zeisel, 1966, p. 296]." It also demonstrated the jurors' rejection of particular rules of the criminal law which they feel inappropriate, such as the nice legal obstacles to the privilege of self-defense, and the legal irrelevancy of the contributory fault of the victim or the extent to which the defendant had already suffered (Kalven & Zeisel, 1966).

INTERPRETING THE JURY'S ROLE

If the juror is obliged to do as he is told in the court instructions and if he may, nevertheless, do as he thinks best—if in fact he is afforded every protection to do as he thinks best and his function as a juror is extolled because jurors sometimes do—how is the conscientious juror to understand his role? What is he to do in his jural role if following the court instructions would lead to a verdict he is convinced ought to go otherwise?

The question appears puzzling on the common and not implausible assumption that the law must speak univocally to its agents and that a proper understanding of what the law requires of an agent in any one respect will reveal a single, consistent directive fixing the agent's duty and, so far as the law extends, leaving nothing up to him. Therefore, in order to interpret the jury's role in acquittals, we shall comment on each of the two possible positions which, making the assumption of the single, consistent directive, hold that the duty of the juror to comply with court instructions is logically incompatible with his privilege to do as he thinks best, and that the legal system itself may have it one way or the other but not both. Then, we shall try to read the jury situation in acquittals on the hypothesis that the dilemma between duty and privilege is a false one for the legal system, and show how and in what sense.

Interpretation 1: The Jury's Role Is to Follow the Court's Instructions

According to this first way of understanding the evidence, official formulations fully state the proper role of the jury: The jury is strictly a fact-finding agency. It reaches its general verdict by applying facts found in accordance with the judge's legal instructions. Its own sentiments concerning the law, either generally or as applied to the case before it, are of no consequence. Of no consequence also is the jury's estimate of the force of any mitigating circumstances not comprehended in the law, or of its own conception of the nature of the law if it differs from the judge's. The vaunted sovereignty of the jury, therefore, is a matter of power, not of right. We often have the power to do things we have no right to do. The jury *can* reach a perverse verdict of acquittal and get away with it, but that does not imply the right to reach such a verdict. When juries reach verdicts that run counter to the expressed instructions of courts, they usurp a discretion not theirs to exercise. That jury nullification has sometimes produced good results does not show that nullification is within its legal role.

Such is one construal of the jury's role. The technique is to acknowledge an inconsistency between jury power and jury duty in cases of acquittal, assume that the inconsistency cannot be, and then explain away the class of evidence that points to jury privilege. Yet, except that one has

made an independent choice among competing values for the jury's doing as it was told, why may one not discover in the scrupulous protection of jury power the institutionalization of a sovereign right? There is nothing logically wrong with the finding of sovereignty. The question is how to construe the jury power to reach a perverse verdict of acquittal. Even in ordinary matters, when people are systematically protected not merely against incursions into their power to act as they think best, but also against any attempt to hold them accountable for an alleged misuse of that power, they begin to get the message that they have the right to act as they think best, whether or not they made the right decision. And if anyone calls them to account for a wrong decision, they do not simply accept the criticism as arguable—they are outraged. Why would the adherents of Interpretation 1 not apply similar reasoning to juries if it were not that for jury decisions they do not want it that way?

Interpretation 2: The Jury's Role Is to Follow the Law-in-Action

One use of Pound's famous distinction (1910) between law-in-action and the law-in-books is to make plausible the assumption of a single consistent directive defining the jury role in precisely the reverse sense of Interpretation 1. Instead of arguing that the role of the jury demands following the instructions of the judge, one holds that the instructions of the judge constitute only the formal law, and that the real law, the law-in-action, leaves it to the jury to follow the instructions of the judge only when so inclined. There is a real question what Pound and others who have adopted the distinction mean by the law-in-action. Sometimes they seem to mean that the law-in-action is, flatly, what people in authority do, their actual behavior independent of any formulable rule. In that sense, of course, the law-in-action lays down no requirement upon juries at all—whatever juries succeed in getting away with is the law-in-action. At other times the distinction serves to set off the actual norms of the political-legal community against the norms announced "in the books" and disregarded in practice. It is in this second sense that we propose that the Realist distinction shores up a rule of competence for the jury: "Do as you think best; take or leave the court's instructions." Any jury that thought itself bound to the court's instructions would then have misunderstood its own role. The inconsistency between duty and privilege has been overcome; the duty is merely formal; the privilege is real in the law.

But even if Interpretation 2 should rest on the law-in-action in this latter sense—i.e., on a determination of what the real, rather than the apparent, norms of the law may be—how does one determine what the real norm is? We propose that there is no direct inference from the law-in-action to the real norm of jury sovereignty postulated in Interpretation 2 without the addition of an independent preference for that condition. In the face of the history of the jury acquittal, Interpretation 2, like Interpretation 1, needs a normative principle to select one part of the evidence rather than the other as determinative.

The principle is necessary because for the law-in-action to be the *law* in action it must be possible for actual behavior to count as a transgression of the law even if the transgressor be an official. What actual behavior cannot violate can constitute no rule. Which class of behavior represents compliance with the actual norm, which a misguided attempt to follow merely fictitious ones—the behavior of deferring to the judge's instructions or the behavior of defying them? To ascribe to the jury a determinate role at all implies that the jury might deviate from the law-in-action. Why do the statistically far more numerous instances of compliance with court instructions carry so much less weight in determining the law-in-action than the far fewer instances of departure? Such questions are readily answerable only if one takes a preference for one sort of jury behavior over another to determine what the law-in-action actually is. Behavior that fulfills allegedly valuable functions will satisfy the law-in-action, while behavior grounded on formal obligations that fulfill no such functions becomes a misguided attempt to satisfy the law-in-books.

Moreover, even if the jury's role is indeed to follow the law-in-action and that law is determinable (by a proper judgment of value), there remains much that legal practitioners consider law, when they are not interpreting what law means, that is systematically ignored. Jurors are obliged to take an oath to decide the case according to the law and the evidence. The judge *does* instruct the jurors in the applicable law and direct them to arrive at verdicts accordingly. The lawyer for the defendant may not argue to jurors that the law is otherwise than as stated by the judge or that in any event they should disregard it. At the very least, the jury cannot be said to have the right to invoke its own sentiments on what the law should be in the sense that an official has that right when the law delegates an explicit discretionary authority.

In short, the logical source of the radical oversimplifications of both interpretations is the notion that the law has to speak to the jury in one consistent voice. It requires arguing that, in considering whether to acquit, the jury either has an obligation to follow the instructions of the court or has the power and a derivative right or privilege not to follow the instructions of the court. Either assumption leads covertly to introducing a normative principle, so that the notion of the single consistent directive can work.

Interpretation 3: The Jury Role as a Conflicted Role

We submit that logic does not prohibit interpreting the jury's role under the law in such a way that the role both requires conformity to the instructions of the court and extends a privilege to return a general verdict of acquittal contrary to those instructions. What prohibits such an interpretation is only the notion of the single, consistent directive which presumes that one and the same agency, one and the same voice, speaks to the jury. It is as though one were to imagine a judge saying, simultaneously, "Follow my instructions; it is your duty" and "Use your judgment." One could fairly conclude that such a judge did not know what he wanted; no guidance whatsoever could be conceived to come from him. And so it would be for the law as a whole if one conceived its directives and privileges to issue from the selfsame mouth, for the same subject and subject matter, in the same respect. Plainly, any single sovereign had better be consistent.

On the other hand, if one does not confuse a theory of the way legal judgments derive legitimacy with the structure of the law and its impact on persons enacting legally defined roles, the notion of a consistent directive of a single sovereign loses its apparent necessity. It is, after all, false that the judge says "Follow my instructions" and "Use your judgment." He says, "Follow my instructions." Other arrangements in the legal system convey a genuine privilege not to do so. If he listens, the juror hears many voices, some of them issuing from real bodies, others from traditions and ways of proceeding. Indeed the law may be conceived as the totality of all these voices. But whether so conceived or not, it remains true that a variety of claims and dispensations focus upon the man in the jury box. He is told what he ought to do—and yet he need not do it and is protected against any consequence

of not doing so. His role is conflicted in the sense that there is conflict in the authoritative rules governing his competence in his role. Judgment is thrust upon him, not merely of the guilt or innocence of the defendant, but of the merit of the judge's instructions for the particular case. He is told what the law is, authoritatively; he *is* obliged; and then he is told to reach his decision, he and he alone, immune from consequence, the verdict of acquittal safe from overturning. He has become the final *judge* whether or not to uphold his obligation.

How is that kind of role possible? How can the law distinguish a conflicted role such as the jury's from a role that is simply hung up, in the sense that the agents of that role have no way of deciding among the various voices that they hear? Such a distinction is possible for two reasons.

First, all roles are set up to perform certain jobs for certain ends and in certain prescribed ways, according to certain procedures and constraints. The jury has been set up to reach judgments of guilt or innocence for the ends of criminal justice, according to certain procedures and constraints including the instructions of the court. This creates the crucial problem of conflicted roles *and* the possibility of a solution. While the means to secure the role's end bind those who seek the end in the role, those means may from time to time prevent the role agent from achieving the role's ends, and that is the problem. But a solution is provided if the role has been set up, as has the jury role, to allow the role agent to consider the ends for which he accepts the constraints. So the conflicted role, in contrast to the hung up role, makes available to the agent a system of ends that enables him to "judge" the applicability of his obligations and ensures that he may act accordingly.

Secondly, a role agent's judgment of his obligations is made possible, and the transition from a hung up role to a conflicted one achieved, because an obligation is not necessarily denied when it is held as something less than absolute. Therefore, we may say that the judge's instructions are binding on the jury and, at the same time, that the criminal jury can be required to judge the obligation in its relevance to the particular case. Because the jury's role exacts from the conscientious juryman the distinction between departing from an instruction because he thinks it preferable (thereby ceasing to treat the instruction as obligatory) and departing from an instruction because he has "damn good reason" to do so, as determined by the role ends, the jury acquittal role retains the obligatory status of the instruction while permitting a departure from that instruction. For, in general, we recognize a constraint as obligatory upon us when we require not merely reason to defend our rule departures, but damn good reason.

It may be objected that we can rid ourselves of the notion of a conflicted role and save the acquittal jury for a single consistent directive simply by recognizing the actual rule that defines a juryman's role to be a conditional: "If you don't have good reason—'damn good reason'— then do what the judge tells you!" The current formulation of the judge's instructions to the jury is misleading. The proposed conditional expresses the meaning of the struggle between jury freedom and the judge's authority. We respond as follows:

The conditional formulation is spurious if it intends to restate the conditions of a conflicted role as a single, consistent directive that in itself generates no conflict but is either obeyed or disobeyed. Privileges can always be stated to qualify obligations, but the achievement does not diminish either the privilege or the obligation. Any juror reading the above conditional would know immediately that he faces no less an obligation because it was not universally overriding—precisely that,

he would understand, was the point of "damned good reason." Regardless of whether the receiver of the conditional message translated it into the language of privilege and obligation, the same consequences would prevail: The choice whether to obey the instructions of the judge would have been thrown back upon him; he would not escape a judgment on what obligations bind him in the instant case; and he would still need to find reasons of overriding weight.

Further, "damn good reason" in the above conditional requires jury action on some ultimate norm or norms of the legal system or of morality and is only poorly understood when assimilated with other, rather simpler conditions. "Do as the judge tells you unless the consequence is serious injustice" differs in important respects from "Assign applicants to windows according to their last names, unless the line exceeds ten persons." There exists no routine for saying what "serious injustice" means, as there does for determining the number of people on a line. That is why the juror in the conditional is told to consider whether a "serious injustice" may be done—because we cannot tell him precisely what it means. If there were such a routine, very likely it would be provided and his case would become rather like the clerk's in determining window assignments. Also, the two sorts of conditionals are unlike because there can be no question of being pulled between assigning people by last names and the results of counting persons, as there can be between the demand to obey the court's authoritative instruction and, at the same time, the legal or moral requirement to pursue the ultimate end of judgment, which is justice. Hence, it simply will not do to treat the introduction of an ultimate end into the deliberations as though one had introduced just another condition in a conditional directive for attaining some end, and thereby procured a directive that left the receiver of the law only the decision to comply or not.

In sum, then, the case for characterizing the role of the jury as conflicted turns on the following propositions. First, logical necessities do not prohibit such a role, nor does an easy reformulation make it disposable. Next, conflicted roles like that of the jury are functional; they perform distinct uses in the administration of justice. Lastly, this characterization of the jury's role accommodates the apparently divergent themes presented by the evidence. It does not require, as alternative interpretations do, that portions of the evidence be oversimplified or explained away.

So characterizing the role of the jury allows us to say the following. The duty of the jury is indeed to find the facts upon the basis of the evidence presented and to issue a general verdict by applying those facts to the propositions of law given by the judge. This is the rule, and it imposes an obligation to comply. But it is not therefore an absolute and unyielding obligation. Sometimes the jury's common sense perceptions, considerations of fairness to the defendant, or appraisal of the law (in contrast to the judge's statement of it) are so weighty that they justify departure from the requirement that the jury defer to the judge's instructions. Some roles, that is, permit departures from the very rules that bind their agents when the agents are satisfied that there is not merely reason, but extremely good reason for doing so. They are capable of recognizing conflicts between role ends and the obligatory means regulating their achievement, and of making provision for resolving the conflict.

LEGITIMATED INTERPOSITION AND THE INTERACTION OF LAW AND SOCIETY

We may use our analysis of the conflicted role of the jury to formulate a general conception for instances in which

the official's role provides the possibility of justifying, under the law, departures from binding rules. In contrast to discretion, which denotes an explicitly delegated legal power to act according to an agent's best judgment within defined limits, and also to usurpation, which denotes an exercise of power in outright defiance of the legal system, we propose the concept of *legitimated interposition* to cover instances comparable to that of the jury when it acquits. According to Justice White (in Williams v. Florida, 1970):

The essential feature of a jury obviously lies in the interposition between the accused and his accuser of the common-sense judgment of a group of laymen, and in the community participation and shared responsibility which results from that group's determination of guilt or innocence [p. 1906].

The concept of legitimated interposition generalizes this phenomenon. Actions are legitimated for a role agent insofar as the role justified his undertaking such an action. When a legal system presents an official with the freedom to depart from a legal rule that might work counter to the ends of his role in the legal system, we say it legitimates the official's departure from the rule. It legitimates the interposition, between the rule and his final action, of his own judgment that departure from the rule best serves the end.

For the most part, legal systems have been conceived to work independently of any set of principles for adjusting rules to the requirements of agents' roles. But we believe it false that the only possible relation of agents in a legal system is simply to hear and obey; therefore, we introduce *legitimated interposition* in order to discuss the properties of legal systems in relation to departures from rules.

The Conditions of Legitimated Interpositon

Generalizing from the instance of the acquitting jury, what characteristics of a working legal system support a reading of the official's role that justified his departure from a rule defining and limiting his competence?

First, legitimated interposition requires that the official receive an authority to effect legal consequences greater than that permitted by the rules defining his competence, and that in one way or another the system recognizes the exercise of this authority to produce those consequences with finality, either legally or practically. No effective legal recourse exists to test whether in exercising his authority the official complied with the rules. In addition, no other sanction is made available to call the official to account for his deviation from the rules of competence appropriate to his role. In short, a legal power is granted to effect legal consequences without recourse against either the action or the official.

Yet this is not and cannot be all if legitimation of a rule departure by an official is to have the force of a true justification. That an act and its agent are both unchallengeable may prove only the lamentable shortcomings of the system and confirm the truth of the famous dictum that all power tends to corrupt and absolute power tends to corrupt absolutely. If there is to be legitimation at all, the system must set up and make available to the agent who proposes to depart from a rule some set of ends that might truly justify the act of departure from a rule. Interposition must be shown to be the kind of act that on the whole has positive value for the legal system. For it is not the juryman's vote contrary to the judge's instructions as a consequence of a bribe that is legitimated; it is the juryman's vote as an essay, however mistaken, in the direction of justice, which is indeed an objective of the legal system. This condition, together with a power to effect legal consequences without recourse against the action or the official, establishes the presence of legitimated interposition.

But that this condition obtains is hardly self-evident. The relevant considerations are the extent to which a class of official deviation from rules is widely acknowledged, rationalized, and built upon, serves purposes consonant with those of the legal system, and has become a domesticated, integrally functioning instrument of the system. Yet when do the facts point that way? Involved in determining the presence of these circumstances is a reading of a complex and subtle interplay of rules, practices, and arrangements and of the underlying purposes achieved and missed. We have tried to show in the case of the jury what this might mean concretely.

The Possibility of a Justified Rule Departure

At this point we must meet a possible objection, one not ostensibly aimed against the notion of a conflicted role (like the jury role in acquittals), but against the coherence of the idea of a legally justified departure from a legal rule. At issue is the desirability of *post hoc* explanations of legal phenomena. To answer a question about how a system secures its results, one states the characteristics of the results. The statute under which the defendant was penalized, having turned out to be unconstitutional, was never the "law." The court instruction was never "obligatory" in the process of the jury's decision because the decision which deviated from the instruction was sustained in the ways we discussed earlier. The church never changes; the truth is merely recognized. This is the ordinary way of talking about legal matters.

The basic objection to such discourse is that it fails to describe how the agent confronts the rules in the process of deciding his action. It obscures the decision the agent must make in his actual situation. And for that reason it obscures the fact of what we may call "nonsystematic" change in accommodating conflict. To be sure, legal change occurs in the ordinary way of talking, but always "systematically," within established channels through the exercise of delegated authority. The system expands, the system contracts; but expansion or contraction occurs through means (like the introduction or repeal of statutes) that are part of the manifest content of the system.

But as the jury acquittal illustrated, systems change also when lines of development in a complex institution, each representing different values, come into conflict under the stress of particular circumstances. If systems are not complete historically, it is not only because the dialectic of conflict propels incessant changes. More important here, systems may be incomplete because, in consequence of the development of different lines of interest and value within the same institution, decision on which line shall be honored in particular cases must be thrown back upon individuals who receive only incomplete systematic guidance. So we speak of nonsystematic change through rule departures; and legitimated interposition constitutes a partial explanation of how, short of revolutionary abolition and institution of new legal systems, the legal system accommodates change.

There is another approach that would seem to deny us rule departures and hence cloud the accommodation to that conflict and incompleteness which characterize legal systems. One might say: You think you have found the legal system legitimating departures from its own rules when in fact you have found the legal system not legitimating *rule* departures but authorizing the deployment of different *principles* and *policies* to which different weights may be assigned.[1] The actual process of confronting conflicted

[1] Compare Dworkin's distinctions (1963, 1967) among rules, principles, and policies that might make such an objection possible. The points of agreement and disagreement of Professor Dworkin's analysis as such with the positions adopted here on rule departures we must leave to another occasion.

demands is absorbed into entities called principles or policies, with the consequence of enhancing the authority of the legal system.

Our response is that there are no principles or policies in themselves, but that directives of the legal system become rules, policies, or principles through the manner of their use. Their use does not follow from their nature, but their nature from their use. Generality, vagueness, and precision do not determine whether directives function as principles, policies or rules. The critical determinant, we propose, is the way such directives function in a context of directives. When they work in such a way that departures may be legitimated, then those directives tend to be adjudged principles and policies and not merely rules. Is "Keep off the grass" a policy or a rule? That will depend on whether that directive exists in a complex of directives such that sometimes the obligation to keep off the lawn cannot be maintained simultaneously in the instant case with other legally recognized obligations. Then, the fact accepted, it becomes a policy, to which we ascribe a certain weight.

The Institutionalization of Conflict and the Values of Conflict Systems

Conflicts are institutionalized through the organization of systems of behavior that permit the legitimation of rule departures. That is what it means for the conflict to be institutionalized. For if, given conflict situations, there is no legitimation of the departure from rules, then, while the conflict nonetheless occurs, the resolution is driven underground as an illegal act. But legitimated interposition preserves the act of rule departure from falling outside the system.

How far can that institutionalization go? How far does it go in any legal system? The answers to these questions we do not attempt here, although we submit that there are instances other than the jury in which the system of American law incorporates legitimated interposition and ways in which it legitimates rule departures by citizens as well as by officials. We do offer an observation that is of primary importance: However restricted or extended the legitimation of rule departures may be under the present legal system, the study of those legitimations—where and how they occur, how they are restricted, and how advantageously they might be extended or restricted—constitutes an aspect of jurisprudence of considerable practical and theoretical profit to the student of legal systems, an aspect of jurisprudence that we call "the jurisprudence of law-breaking."

An important consequence of the phenomenon of legitimation for the interaction of law and society—society as made up of autonomous individuals—is the installation of individuals as participants in the creation and administration of justice. A system that incorporates legitimated interposition generates for individuals, although always within limits, a place for the exercise of their judgment before the rules; and it extends such a place not simply in the sense of delegating specific discretion but with respect to the application and definition of those rules that define its discretion. In other words, such a system extends a discretion to deviate from the rules, a discretion which is not simply a violation (since it is legitimated), but not therefore a compliance. By the counterposition of duty to comply and privilege to depart, the legal system has generated freedom in a very fundamental respect: the freedom of men not simply subject to the law, but, always within limits, independent of the law and capable of using that law for the ultimate ends of the legal system. That consequence is itself a value, and brings in its train possibilities for adjustment to conditions that could not have been foreseen with

any clarity and hence could not have been planned for in detail.

The other side of the coin is that by the counterposition of duty and privilege a system also generates unpredictability, arbitrary action, and "justice" immune from planned social control. But what follows is not a need to decide between a system free of the possibility of legally justified rule departures or a system riddled with the possibility of such departures; what does follow is the challenge to create legal systems that under given historical conditions may attain the most salutary mix. For this last achievement there are no aphorisms.

REFERENCES

BUSHELL, *Howell's State Trials*, 1670, **6**, 999–1026.

California Jury Instructions. St. Paul, Minn.: West, 1970.

COMMONWEALTH v. PORTER. *Massachusetts Reports*, 1845, **51**, 263–287.

DEVLIN, P. A. *Trial by Jury.* London: Stevens, 1956.

DUNCAN v. STATE OF LOUISIANA. *Supreme Court Reporter*, 1968, **88**, 1444–1472.

DWORKIN, R. M. Judicial discretion. *Journal of Philosophy*, 1963, **60**, 624–641.

DWORKIN, R. M. The model of rules. *University of Chicago Law Review*, 1967, **35**, 14–46.

Federal Rules Civil Procedures. St. Paul: West, 1970.

FORSYTH, W. *History of Trial by Jury.* London: Parker and Sons, 1852.

GOEBEL, J., JR. (Ed.), *The Law Practice of Alexander Hamilton.* Vol. 1. New York: Columbia University Press, 1964.

KALVEN, H., JR., & ZEISEL, H. *The American Jury.* Boston: Little, Brown, 1966.

PEOPLE v. CROSWELL. *Johnson's Cases*, 1804, **3**, 336–413.

POUND, R. Law in books and law in action. *American Law Review*, 1910, **44**, 12–36.

Report of the Select Committee on Capital Punishment (House of Commons). London: Her Majesty's Stationery Office, 1930.

SAX, J. Conscience and anarchy: The prosecution of war resistors. *Yale Review*, 1968, **52**, 481–494.

Statutes at Large: George III, 1792, **37**, 627–628.

Statutes at Large: Henry VIII, 1534, **4**, 326–327.

THAYER, J. B. *A Preliminary Treatise on Evidence*

at the Common Law. Boston: Little, Brown, 1898.

UNITED STATES v. BATTISTE. *Sumner's United States Circuit Court Reports,* 1835, **2,** 240–251.

UNITED STATES v. MAYBURY. *Federal Reporter, Second Series,* 1959, **274,** 899–908.

UNITED STATES v. MOYLAN. *Federal Reporter, Second Series,* 1969, **417,** 1002–1009.

UNITED STATES v. OGULL. *Federal Supplement,* 1957, **149,** 272–279.

UNITED STATES v. SISSON. *Federal Supplement,* 1968, **294,** 520–524.

UNITED STATES v. SPOCK. *Federal Reporter, Second Series,* 1969, **416,** 165–194.

VAN DYKE, J. M. The jury as a political institution. *The Center Magazine,* 1970, **3** (2), 17–26.

WILLIAMS v. FLORIDA. *Supreme Court Reporter,* 1970, **90,** 1893–1914.

C: Post-Disposition Control Agencies: Correctional Organizations

The legal control of deviance continues beyond the police and courts through processing of deviants into one type or another of correctional organizations. They may be committed to a "total institution" (Goffman, 1961). Convicted criminal offenders are incarcerated in prisons, delinquents in institutions for juveniles, drug offenders in narcotics hospitals or treatment centers, and the mentally ill in mental hospitals. Many may be placed in community-based half-way houses or similar organizations for supervision and control midway between the supervision of a probation or parole agency and the more secure custody of a total institution.

The use of relatively long-term confinement in an institution as a formal means of societal control is recent in the history of the Anglo-Americal legal system. Until the latter part of the eighteenth century, the legal sanction applied after adjudication was likely to be harsh corporal or capital punishment. The utilitarian philosophy of the classical criminologist of the eighteenth century had been incorporated to the extent that the punishment was seen not just as retribution but as necessary to deter the offender and others from committing further crime. Punishment by incarceration in total institutions for a long period of time was virtually unknown. There were dismal places for the confinement of the insane and short-term jails and holding facilities to restrain those awaiting trial or to keep custody of the convicted until or while punishment was administered. But by the beginning of the nineteenth century, use of harsh physical punishment and the death penalty had declined and began to be replaced by confinement in prison.

Prisons as we know them today can be traced specifically to the construction of the New York State Prison at Auburn in 1819 and the Eastern Penitentiary in Pennsylvania in 1829. As the term "penitentiary" implies, another goal was added to punishment. The institutions were not meant to be just a place to hold people in order to punish them; confinement *itself* was the punishment, and the prison was a place for isolating inmates from the contamination of the evil influences of society in order that they could contemplate their errors, do penitence, and come out ready for a positive role in society. Silence was the rule (at Auburn, enforced silence with congregate labor and at Pennsylvania, complete isolation at all times). Hard work and discipline were introduced to teach habits of work and discipline and also as a way of exploiting the labor of the inmates in the effort to make the institutions self-supporting. Later the idea that something direct and specific beside enforced contemplation could be done while holding the prisoners to rehabilitate them led to the incorporation of educational and vocational training in newly built "reformatories" (the first at Elmira, New York in the 1870s). Probation and parole came into use and the goal of treatment and rehabilitation was added to the other purposes of the institutions. Mental hospitals, poor houses, and institutions for juveniles were also constructed in the nineteenth century for both custodial and reform purposes (Rothman, 1971; President's Commission, 1967; American Correctional Association, 1966).

Thus, by the end of the nineteenth century, all of the major purposes of correctional organizations recognized today had been formed. Such goals as revenge, restraint, deterrence, and punishment coalesce around the major goal of *custody-punishment;* and reformation, reintegration, rehabilitation can be grouped under the major goal of *treatment-rehabilitation.* The ultimate ideal aim of both, of course, is protection of society. While these goals have typically been attributed to prisons, they can also be attributed to juvenile institutions, mental hospitals, and other agencies of control. The treatment–rehabilitative goals have become intertwined with humanitarian concern with the welfare and dignity of inmates. Indeed, although the rhetoric continues to stress treatment, prison reform prompted by a treatment ideology has been primarily in the direction of more humanitarian control rather than the implementation of rehabilitative programs of proven effectiveness.

The treatment–rehabilitative goals were simply added to the longer standing custodial–punishment goals, and the two conflicting orientations exist side by side in correctional institutions today in an uneasy accommodation. The treatment purposes tend to be emphasized verbally by correctional administrators but the evidence is that they are rarely achieved (Levin, 1971; Bailey, 1966), and in the actual day-to-day operation custodial concerns are often given priority. However, some institutions are more treatment-oriented than other institutions, and the various adult and juvenile institutions can be arrayed along a custody–treatment continuum with the more open, treatment-oriented organizations at one end and the more closed, punitive organizations at the other. However, both goals continue to be pursued simultaneously in the same institution. Even the most treatment-oriented institution must maintain secure custody of inmates, and administrators of even the most custodial institution will feel they must do something in the way of recreational, training, educational, and other programs which are supposed to be rehabilitative. In the typical institution the two goals are reflected in two separate staff roles, the professional treatment staff on the one hand and the custodial staff on the other. Therefore, the custody-treatment conflict usually is acted out in the internal organizational conflict between treatment and custodial staff (Cressey, 1959; Weber, 1957; Zald, 1962). The movement toward more open institutions with liberalized visitation policies, reduction of censorship, involvement of community groups and volunteers, and work and education release programs, as well as the movement toward community-based half-way houses and similar facilities (Keller and Alper, 1970), as with earlier reform movements, may be justified on humanitarian and economic grounds; but there is little evidence to date that they are in fact effective rehabilitative procedures. Moreover, while there is clearly less concern with security in these programs, they only partially resolve the custody–treatment conflict, for the personnel in these programs are learning, as probation and parole officers learned long ago, that the very requirement for at least some supervision makes for a conflict in one's role as someone with punitive authority and his role as a "helping" person.

There is another conflict which arises from the newer emphasis on treatment in the control of deviance and one which is more ironic than the custody–treatment conflict. As noted above, the rehabilitation movement has been based on (often unrecognized) humanitarian interest in inmates as individuals. And there are some who claim that the rehabilitative ideal demands protection of individual rights:

> If the purpose of imprisonment is rehabilitation, however, then it is essential that the inmate not be deprived of his personal rights more than is absolutely necessary, since the primary goal of rehabilitation is to restore a sense of dignity and integrity. . . . [Smith and Pollack, 1972:240].

Nonetheless, the treatment philosophy which views incarceration as a means of exposing offenders to programs which are meant to rehabilitate and "help" them, not to punish them, has led to less of a concern for their due process rights. The "medical model" which sees deviance as an illness and the efforts to "cure" it as beneficial has not included much of a concern for the civil rights of the individual. While the legal model emphasizes protection of the individual even to the extent of risking letting the guilty go free, the medical model emphasizes treating the individual even to the extent of risking giving the treatment to someone who does not really need it (Scheff, 1966:114–15). The conflict is created by the fact that although this model is based on the assumption of voluntary, willing patients, it is applied in the legal control system where the "cure" is coerced on non-voluntary, unwilling clients (Kittrie, 1971:41). Protection of rights is crucial if the deviant is viewed as one who is to be convicted of wrong-doing and punished for it. It seems less important if the deviant is viewed as someone in need of cure and the state's intervention is viewed as a therapeutic device to help him. But if one is involuntarily incarcerated, whether it is called punishment or treatment, he in fact loses his freedom, and the requirement for protection of rights remains.

Thus, as Murphy suggests in the first article reprinted in this section (Murphy, 1969) the "medicalization of deviance" (Pitts, 1968), perhaps prompted by high humanitarian ideals, has in practice involved many unjust and inhumane aspects. This medical model has been applied primarily to the mentally ill, alcoholics, addicts, and juvenile delinquents (Kittrie, 1971:342; Platt, 1969), but also has been applied to and advocated for criminal deviance (Menninger, 1969). The medical model, when it involves coerced therapy, although sold as a service to society, becomes an agent of the state, and psychiatrists and other experts provide the definition of deviance and the appropriate response to it in what Szasz (1970) has characterized as the "therapeutic state." In the therapeutic state the psychiatrist is no longer just an expert witness on the question of *mens rea* in insanity pleas but also acts as a prognosticator and treater of socially deviant individuals, similar to the witch-hunters of old (Szasz, 1970:239). Moral and political decisions, then, are made under the guise of providing help for a "health" problem. Since the definitional boundaries of the therapeutic state are quite porous, one outcome has been an increase in the types of deviance seen as appropriate for the application of the medical model (Kittrie, 1971:383–84). This overweening application of the therapeutic approach has developed without attendant safeguards of individual rights, partially through the default of the courts and legislatures:

> Bowing to the desires and ostensible good-faith opinions of the experts, the law forsook its role as the censor of the exercise of state power and left the therapists to devise their means of bringing the therapeutic power to bear. . . . [C]onstitutional protections [have been withheld] from putative patients on the basis that the proceedings were noncriminal, and . . . the opinions of doctors, social workers, and others charged with the therapeutic mission [have been uncritically accepted]. By abridging the individual's rights to object and by neglecting to scrutinize the state's request to exercise therapeutic power, the courts have placed the therapist outside societal controls [Kittrie, 1971:371].

Reformers on behalf of prisoners' and other inmates' rights understandably, then, see the opposition as those who support the therapeutic philosophy and not those who support the old punitive philosophy. The increased politicization of prisoners, as recently evidenced in the demands of rioters at such places as Attica, are directed not only toward the more repressive practices of a custodial regime but also toward the failures and coercive aspects of the rehabilitative ideal. There has been an increased interest within the legal profession with rights of prisoners and other inmates incarcerated in total institutions (Turner, 1971). Similar concern is seen in recent higher court decisions and model acts drafted by the Center for the Study of Responsive Law (Wexler

1971:222–27). The rehabilitative philosophy is firmly enough entrenched in the legal control of deviance, however, and "for a long time to come, both the system of criminal justice and the therapeutic state are likely to coexist as dual modes of social control" (Kittrie, 1971:407).

The aspect of total institutions which has commanded the most attention from sociologists, however, has not been the unintended consequences of applying the rehabilitative ideal; rather it is the individual and collective responses which inmates make to incarceration. Goffman's (1961) term "self-mortification" aptly portrays the negative consequences which incarceration may have for the person's self esteem (see also Karmel, 1969). But at least since the work of Clemmer (1938), Hayner and Ash (1939), and others (Reimer, 1927; Weinberg, 1942), sociological research on correctional organizations has concentrated on the inmate code, roles, primary groups, antistaff orientation, leadership structure, and other aspects of the inmate system (Cloward et al., 1960; Cressey, 1961; Hazelrigg, 1969; Carter et al., 1972). The inmate culture is characterized by anticonventional criminalistic values and antistaff norms (Sykes and Messinger, 1960). It is found to some extent in all correctional institutions but seems to be strongest in its antistaff hostility in the more repressive and custodially oriented adult and juvenile institutions (Grusky, 1959; Berk, 1966; Street et al., 1966).

Clemmer (1938) coined the term "prisonization" to refer to socialization into the values and norms of the inmate culture as one becomes assimilated into inmate groups. Based on his observations, Clemmer proposed that the longer the inmate served time in the prison, the more he became prisonized. Wheeler's (1961) findings that prisonization increased with time served supported this proposition. However, Wheeler also found that when the inmate's stay in prison was divided into early, middle, and late phases, prisonization is most evident in the middle phase. Tittle and Tittle (1964) also found that adherence to the inmate code is related to length of stay. Wellford (1967) did not support Wheeler's findings on the relationship between time served and adoption of the inmate code, although he did support the finding that the degree of prisonization is highest in the middle phase of the inmate's institutional career. In Atchley and McCabe's (1968) research, however, prisonization was not related to either time served or phase of institutional career. There is some question as to whether or not assimilation into primary groups in prison facilitates prisonization (Wheeler, 1961; Cline and Wheeler, 1968; Wellford, 1973), but the research makes it fairly clear that the degree of prisonization is related to the type of inmate role [1] (Garabedian, 1963; Wellford, 1967; Thomas and Foster, 1972).

[1] The best known description of inmate roles is that provided by Schrag (1961a; 1961b), but others have also delineated similar roles in the prisoner society (Sykes, 1958; Hayner, 1961). Schrag depicts four basic inmate roles: Square John—a conventional, pro-social type who is positively oriented to the norms of the prison staff and administration; Right guy—an antisocial type who epitomizes the inmate culture in his loyalty to the inmate system and opposition to staff; Con politician—a pseudo-social type who is oriented to either staff or inmates according to which serves his interest in manipulating others to his benefit; Outlaw—basically an asocial type who is oriented to neither staff nor inmates and is apt to make trouble for both.

The question of prisonization relates to the broad question of what accounts for the type of adaptations inmates make and the nature of the inmate system. Efforts to answer this question fit into one or another of two theoretical models. One is a functional model which sees the inmate culture as an adaptation to the deprivation and degradation of imprisonment (Sykes, 1958; Sykes and Messinger, 1960; Cloward, 1960). The other model presents the genesis of the inmate culture as lying primarily outside of the institution; it reflects the criminal roles and values acquired by inmates on the outside and brought into the prison with them (Irwin and Cressey, 1962; Irwin, 1970; Wellford, 1967) and the other preprison characteristics of the inmates (Thomas, 1973). (For a discussion of both models, see Petersen and Thomas, 1973.)

It is this central question of whether inmate adaptations are the result of influences imported into the institution or the impact of the organizational environment once inside which Tittle (1969) addresses in the second article reprinted in this section. He concludes that "inmate organization is largely a response to institutional conditions" (Tittle, 1969:503). However, his finding of some differences between the inmate system of the females and the system of male prisoners indicates that inmate cultures are also influenced by sex role characteristics formed prior to imprisonment. Homosexual behavior in prison, which Tittle also examines, is a good example of how total institutions may induce certain forms of deviant behavior, and provides another case for examining the impact of in-prison and preprison variables on inmate behavior patterns (Sykes, 1958; Kirkham, 1971; Gagnon and Simon, 1972). Homosexual behavior is clearly a response to the heterosexual deprivation of a one-sex social system, and the amount of homosexual involvement is highest in the most custodially oriented institutions (Akers et al., 1974). At the same time, the nature and meaning of homosexual liaisons in prison differ between male and female inmates, reflecting differences in male and female roles in the larger society (Giallombardo, 1966; Ward and Kassebaum, 1965).

The functional and importation models, then, are not mutually exclusive. Preinstitutional experiences and the institutional environment interact to produce inmate adaptations. The existence of an inmate culture and social structure may be accounted for by the necessity of solving common problems faced by all inmates in adjusting to incarceration, but the content of the culture may be reflective of behavior patterns and values imported from the outside (Thomas, 1970).

REFERENCES

AKERS, RONALD L., NORMAN S. HAYNER, and WERNER GRUNINGER, 1974. "Homosexual and Drug Behavior in Prison: A Test of the Functional and Importation Models of the Inmate System," *Social Problems,* **21** (3):410–22.

AMERICAN CORRECTIONAL ASSOCIATION, 1966. "Development of Modern Correctional

Concepts and Standards," in Robert Carter, Daniel Glaser, and Leslie Wilkins, eds., *Correctional Institutions*. Philadelphia: J. B. Lippincott, 1972.

ATCHLEY, ROBERT C., and M. PATRICK MCCABE, 1968. "Socialization in Correctional Communities: A Replication," *American Sociological Review*, 33 (October): 774–85.

BAILEY, WALTER C., 1966. "Correctional Outcome: An Evaluation of 100 Reports," *Journal of Criminal Law, Criminology, and Police Science* (June):153–60.

BERK, BERNARD B., 1966. "Organization Goals and Inmate Organization," *American Journal of Sociology*, 71 (March):522–34.

CARTER, ROBERT, DANIEL GLASSER, and LESLIE WILKINS, eds., 1972. *Correctional Institutions*. Philadelphia: J. B. Lippincott.

CLEMMER, DONALD, 1938. *The Prison Community*. New York: Holt, Rinehart, and Winston.

CLINE, HUGH F. and STANTON WHEELER, 1968. "The Determinants of Normative Patterns in Correctional Institutions," in Nils Christie, ed., *Scandinavian Studies in Criminology*. Tavistock, Vol. 2.

CLOWARD, RICHARD, 1960. "Social Control in the Prison," in Richard Cloward *et al.*, eds., *Theoretical Studies in Social Organization of the Prison*. New York: Social Science Research Council.

CLOWARD, RICHARD, *et al.*, eds., 1960. *Theoretical Studies in Social Organization of the Prison*. New York: Social Science Research Council.

CRESSEY, DONALD R., 1959. "Contradictory Directives in Complex Organizations: The Case of the Prison," *Administrative Science Quarterly*, 4 (June):1–19.

CRESSEY, DONALD R., ed., 1961. *The Prison: Studies in Institutional Organization and Change*. New York: Holt, Rinehart, and Winston.

GAGNON, JOHN N. and WILLIAM SIMON, 1972. "The Social Meaning of Prison Homosexuality," in Robert M. Carter, Daniel Glaser, and Leslie T. Wilkins, eds., *Correctional Institutions*. Philadelphia: J. B. Lippincott.

GARABEDIAN, PETER G., 1963. "Social Roles and Processes of Socialization in the Prison Community," *Social Problems*, 11 (Fall):139–52.

GIALLOMBARDO, ROSE, 1966. *Society of Women*. New York: John Wiley and Sons.

GOFFMAN, IRVING, 1961. *Asylums*. New York: Doubleday-Anchor.

GRUSKY, OSCAR, 1959. "Organizational Goals and the Behavior of Informal Leaders," *American Journal of Sociology*, 65 (1959):59–67.

HAYNER, NORMAN S., 1961. "Characteristics of Five Offender Types," *American Sociological Review*, 26 (February):96–102.

HAYNER, NORMAN and ELLIS ASH, 1939. "The Prisoner Community as a Social Group," *American Sociological Review*, 4 (June):362–69.

HAZELRIGG, LAWRENCE, ed., 1969. *Prison within Society*. Garden City, N.Y.: Anchor Books.

IRWIN, JOHN, 1970. *The Felon*. Englewood Cliffs, N.J.: Prentice-Hall.

IRWIN, JOHN and DONALD R. CRESSEY, 1962. "Thieves, Convicts, and the Inmate Culture," *Social Problems*, 10 (Fall):142–55.

KARMEL, MADELINE, 1969. "Total Institution and Self-Mortification," *Journal of Health and Social Behavior*, 10 (June):134–41.

KELLER, OLIVER J. and BENEDICT S. ALPER, 1970. *Halfway Houses: Community-Centered Correction and Treatment*. Lexington: D. C. Heath.

KIRKHAM, GEORGE L., 1971. "Homosexuality in Prison," in James M. Henslin, ed., *Studies in the Sociology of Sex*. New York: Appleton-Century-Crofts.

KITTRIE, NICHOLAS N., 1971. *The Right To Be Different: Deviance and Enforced Therapy*. Baltimore: John Hopkins Press.

LEVIN, MARTIN A., 1971. "Policy Evaluation and Recidivism," *Law and Society Review*, 6 (August):17–46.

MENNINGER, KARL, 1968. *The Crime of Punishment*. New York: Viking Press.

MURPHY, JEFFRIE G., 1969. "Criminal Punishment and Psychiatric Fallacies," *Law and Society Review*, 4 (August):111–122.

PETERSEN, DAVID M. and CHARLES W. THOMAS, 1973. "Review of Relevant Research in Correctional Rehabilitation," in John G. Cull and Richard E. Hardy, eds., *Law Enforcement and Correctional Rehabilitation*. Springfield, Ill.: Charles C Thomas.

PITTS, JESSE R., 1968. "Social Control." *International Encyclopedia of the Social Sciences*. New York: Macmillan.

PLATT, ANTHONY, 1969. *The Child Savers*. Chicago: University of Chicago Press.

PRESIDENT'S COMMISSION ON LAW ENFORCEMENT AND ADMINISTRATION OF JUSTICE, 1967. *Task Force Report: Corrections*. Washington, D.C.: U.S. Government Printing Office.

REIMER, HANS, 1927. "Socialization in a Prison Community," *Proceedings of APA*, 151–55.

ROTHMAN, DAVID, 1971. *The Discovery of the Asylum*. Boston: Little, Brown.

SCHEFF, THOMAS J., 1966. *Being Mentally Ill*. Chicago: Aldine Publishing Co.

SCHRAG, CLARENCE, 1961a. "A preliminary Criminal Typology," *Pacific Sociological Review*, 4 (Spring):11–16; 1961b, "Some Foundations for a Theory of Corrections," Donald R. Cressey, ed., *The Prison*. New York: Holt, Rinehart and Winston.

SMITH, ALEXANDER B. and HARRIET POLLACK, 1972. *Crime and Justice in a Mass Society*. Waltham, Mass.: Xerox Publishing Co.

STREET, DAVID, ROBERT D. VINTER, and CHARLES PERROW, 1966. *Organization for Treatment*. New York: Free Press.

SYKES, GRESHAM, 1958. *The Society of Captives*. Princeton: Princeton University Press.

SYKES, GRESHAM and SHELDON L. MESSINGER, 1960. "The Inmate Social System," in Richard Cloward, *et al.*, eds., *Theoretical Studies in Social Organization of the Prison*. New York: Social Science Research Council.

SZASZ, THOMAS S., 1970. *The Manufacture of Madness*. New York: Harper and Row.

THOMAS, CHARLES W., 1970. "Toward a More Inclusive Model of the Inmate Contraculture," *Criminology*, 8 (November):251–62; 1973, "Prisonization or Resocialization? External Factors Associated with the Impact of Imprisonment," *Journal of Research in Crime and Delinquency*, 10 (January):13–21.

THOMAS, CHARLES W. and SAMUEL FOSTER, 1972. "Prisonization in the Inmate Contraculture." *Social Problems*, 20 (Fall):229–39.

TITTLE, CHARLES R., 1969. "Inmate Organization: Sex Differentiation and the Influence of Criminal Subcultures," *American Sociological Review*, 34 (August):492–505.

TITTLE, CHARLES R. and DROLLENE P. TITTLE, 1964. "Social Organization of Prisoners: An Empirical Test," *Social Forces*, 43:216–21.

TURNER, WILLIAM B., 1971. "Establishing the Rule of Law in Prisons: A Manual for Prisoners' Rights Litigation," *Stanford Law Review*, 23 (February):473–518.

WARD, DAVID A. and GENE G. KASSEBAUM, 1965. *Women's Prison: Sex and Social Structure*. Chicago: Aldine.

WEBER, GEORGE H., 1957. "Conflict between Professional and Non-Professional Personnel in Institutional Delinquency Treatment," *Journal of Criminal Law, Criminology, and Police Science*, 48 (June):26–43.

WEINBERG, S. KIRSON, 1942. "Aspects of Prison's Social Structure," *American Journal of Sociology*, 47 (March):717–26.

WELLFORD, CHARLES, 1967. "Factors Associated with Adoption of the Inmate Code: A Study of Normative Socialization," *Journal of Research in Crime and Delinquency*, 58 (2):197–203; 1973. "Contact and Commitment in a Correctional Community," *The British Journal of Criminology* (April):108–20.

WEXLER, DAVID B., *et al.*, 1971. "The Administration of Psychiatric Justice: Theory and Practice in Arizona," *Arizona Law Review*, 13:1–259.

WHEELER, STANTON, 1961. "Socialization in Correctional Communities," *American Sociological Review*, 26 (October):699–712.

ZALD, MAYER M., 1962. "Power Balance and Staff Conflict in Correctional Institutions," *Administrative Science Quarterly*, 7 (June):22–49.

CRIMINAL PUNISHMENT AND PSYCHIATRIC FALLACIES

Jeffrie G. Murphy

Experience should teach us to be most on our guard to protect liberty when the government's purposes are beneficent. Men born to freedom are naturally alert to repel invasions of their liberty by evil-minded rulers. The greatest dangers to liberty lurk in insidious encroachment by men of zeal, well meaning but without understanding.—Louis D. Brandeis

Nowhere is this general tendency expressed by Brandeis more prominent than in the area of criminal law. In spite of the reasoned warnings of some writers, we are greeted by a continuous stream of books and articles from psychiatrists and psychoanalysts (and their judicial followers) with one common theme: Criminal punishment is an unscientific survival of barbarism and must be replaced by a system of individual and social therapy.[1] To believe otherwise is to be unscientific and (if the distinction is recognized) immoral.

The most recent attempt to argue this position comes from the pen of Dr. Karl Menninger. In his Isaac Ray Award book, *The Crime of Punishment,* Dr. Menninger launches (in the name of scientific psychiatry) a radical attack on the institution of criminal punishment as it operates in the context of the Anglo-American legal system. He does not wish merely to change parts of the existing system (e.g., the insanity defense) but wants, as an ideal, the elimination of that system entirely. The idea is then to replace this system with a

Reprinted from the official publication of the Law and Society Association, *Law and Society Review,* 4 (August 1969), pp. 111–22, by permission of author and The Law and Society Association. Slightly revised by the author: 1972.

[1] Standard sources for such a view are Alexander and Staub (1956), and Abrahamsen (1960). This theme is also to be found throughout most of the books produced by winners of the Isaac Ray Award. The most detailed and persuasive case against this position has been made by Szasz (1963). See also Wertham (1955).

more "scientific" system of social control. With sentencing largely in the control of psychiatrists and other health workers, and increased use of preventive detention, the new system would not be subject to the inefficiencies in controlling crime that characterize our present judicial adversary system.

The juridical system seems to the doctor to be an unscientific jumble based on clumsy and often self-defeating precedents. Psychiatrists cannot understand why the legal profession continues to lend its support to such a system after the scientific discoveries of the past century have become common knowledge. That this knowledge is coolly ignored and flouted by the system is not so much an affront to the scientists as it is a denial of what was once mystery and is now common sense. . . .

Being against punishment is not a sentimental conviction. It is a logical conclusion drawn from scientific experience.

The criminal court should cease with the findings of guilt and innocence, and the "procedure thereafter should be guided by a professional treatment tribunal composed, say, of a psychiatrist, a psychologist, a sociologist or cultural anthropologist, an educator, and a judge with long experience in criminal trials and with special interest in the protection of the rights of those charged with crime."[2]

Why not a large number of *community safety centers* or crime prevention centers? Such a

[2] It is significant that the judge is listed last, and that it is not specified whether or not he is to have a decisive veto power with respect to a violation of the prisoner's rights. The judge must simply be "interested" in these rights. The quoted portion of the extract is from Glueck (1936).

center would be concerned far more with the prevention of crime than with the arrest and mop-up. Offenders or supposed offenders upon capture would be conveyed immediately to the proper center for identification and examination, and then, if indicated, transferred to a central court and/or diagnostic center. Later—if the judge so desires—a program for continuing correction and/or parole could be assigned, again to the officers of the local center. [pp. 91-92; 204; 139; 268] [3]

It is my view that Menninger's position is totally and systematically wrong—that its defense is fabricated solely upon confusions and fallacies (e.g., that moral conclusions can be drawn from scientific premises). And thus, in this brief essay, I should like to expose these confusions and fallacies. This task is important for three main reasons. First, though his book is in many ways erroneous, Dr. Menninger is a popular and widely influential practitioner in his field; and thus it is important to show that he is wrong and to point out the implications of his positions.[4] Second, if my reading constitutes a fair sample, his views are representative of what is a common position among psychiatrists, psychoanalysts, and social scientists in general. Third, and perhaps most important, his views are not merely incorrect, but are of a kind that is socially and politically dangerous.

[3] It is important to note that Menninger's recommendations range over supposed offenders. Nowhere does he suggest that the operations of these centers (including their detention powers) are to be restricted to those who have been convicted of some legal wrong.

[4] Menninger is often called in for expert testimony at legislative hearings on criminal law reform, for he is taken to be a chief spokesman for a liberal and humane jurisprudence. Such a reputation accounts, I gather, for his selection for a feature interview in the issue of "Psychology Today" devoted to law and psychology (February 1969). Views like Menninger's are surely in part behind the pressure for sexual psychopath laws and other laws for the preventive detention of those (e.g., drug addicts, homosexuals, and drunks) who are judged to present a "potential danger" to the community.

Enough by way of introduction. I should now like to pass to a consideration of the argument itself and the character of the confusions and fallacies it exhibits. These are of three main kinds: moral, legal, and (ironically) scientific.

VALUES, COMPETING VALUES, AND JUSTICE

When we speak of moral values we can mean either of two very different things. First, we can mean those moral beliefs which, as a matter of fact, people or groups of people have. The term "mores" is sometimes used for values in this sense. Second, we can mean those values which ought to be promoted—regardless of whether or not they are in fact promoted or believed valuable. This is the sphere, not of mores, but of ethics or morality proper. And quite clearly the two spheres are different. No one, for example, really believes that it was morally right for the Nazis to persecute the Jews (or that they ought to have done it) just because they believed it was right. One holding such a view would be committed to the proposition that the Nazis were subject to no moral criticism for what they did, and this is absurd. Being wrong about morality may, under some circumstances, excuse; but it can never justify. For example, we may absolve from moral blame the Jehovah's Witness who lets his child die for lack of a transfusion without thereby agreeing that the action performed was really right and ought to be recommended to others.

Now it should be fairly clear that it is only values in the first sense (mores) which can be regarded as discoverable by empirical science. Beliefs about values are not themselves values; they are facts. And thus, like all facts, they are open to the expert analysis of the behavioral scientists. But we must not be deceived into thinking that this expert authority about beliefs or mores extends to pronouncements about what really ought to be done. The scientist, like any other rational and informed man, may certainly be competent in moral discussion; but (and this is crucial) he is not *professionally* competent. Though his studies may give him access to facts relevant in moral argument, they do not give him special insight into moral conclusions. To put the point in another and perhaps even more obvious way: Scientists are professionally competent to tell us the most efficient means for the technical attainment of our goals; but they are not competent *qua* scientists to set those goals or to morally assess the means. Efficiency is not to be identified with morality.

These points are often forgotten when important decisions of social policy are being made. Menninger ignores them entirely:

> The very word *justice* irritates scientists. No surgeon expects to be asked if an operation for cancer is just or not. No doctor will be reproached on the grounds that the dose of penicillin he has prescribed is less or more than *justice* would stipulate. Behavioral scientists regard it as equally absurd to invoke the question of justice in deciding what to do with a woman who cannot resist her propensity to shoplift, or with a man who cannot repress an impulse to assault somebody. This sort of behavior has to be controlled; it has to be discouraged; it has to be *stopped*. This (to the scientist) is a matter of public safety and amicable coexistence, not of justice. . . .
>
> Being against punishment is not a sentimental conviction. It is a logical conclusion drawn from scientific experience. [pp. 17; 204]

It is almost impossible to believe that Menninger intends that we take these remarks seriously. How in the world is "being against" anything logically derivable from scientific premises? (I would love to see such an argument formalized.) And what moral are we supposed to draw from the remarks about the surgeon? It is, of course, true that no surgeon expects to be asked if an operation is just. But neither

does he expect to be asked if an operation is hexagonal, approaches middle C, or tastes good. Are we thus to conclude that hexagonality, middle C, and good taste are meaningless concepts?

Of course, Menninger's thesis may be restricted solely to moral values, and the argument may be that their inaccessibility to scientific procedures renders them meaningless. But there is not a single reason to hold such a view (to hold that "meaningful" means "scientifically useful"); and, in fact, I do not think that Menninger himself really holds such a view—even if he does espouse it in theory. To say that a concept is meaningless and to really believe this are two different things. For example: Does Menninger really believe that, if police broke into his home and detained him for months without trial because some psychiatrist thought he was dangerous, he would be talking nonsense if he described his treatment as unjust? I seriously doubt it.

What is really going on in the quoted passage is, I think, the following: Menninger has noted that science, as a social institution,[5] has incarnate in it certain mores. And it is Menninger's view that these mores ought to be elevated to a more influential place in our moral decisions than they now occupy. But this is itself a piece of moral advice—a judgment of value priority and not of fact—and so it is open to the same kinds of standards we use in evaluating any moral recommendation. No matter how much Menninger propagandizes for the scientific status of his recommendations, the fact remains that they are recommendations and not findings. Thus with respect to them he has no professional competence. We must, therefore, evaluate his proposals in the light of all those considerations which are relevant from the moral point of view.

What are these considerations? To avoid

---

[5] For an elaboration of the institutional character of science, and of psychiatry in particular, see the material by Szasz in Schoeck and Wiggins (1962).

starting a treatise in moral philosophy, I shall state rather dogmatically that there are two main kinds of considerations relevant to moral evaluation: considerations of utility; and considerations of justice. Utilitarian considerations are concerned with promoting the greatest amount of happiness and well-being in the world as possible. Considerations of justice function as checks on social utility, weighing against promoting happiness if in so doing some people must be treated unfairly in the process. These considerations compete and often have to be weighed against each other. But it is just this competitive nature of basic moral values that Menninger fails to appreciate. In effect, he opts for considerations of utility (e.g., health and public safety) to the exclusion of considerations of justice. And he does this with a vengeance:

Eliminating one offender who happens to get caught *weakens* public security by creating a false sense of diminished danger through a definite remedial measure. Actually, it does not remedy anything, and it bypasses completely the real and unsolved problem of how to *identify, detect, and detain potentially dangerous citizens.* [p. 108]

The argument here seems to be that since health is the predominant value in psychiatry, its social analogue (public safety) ought to be the predominant political value. What is being suggested is that we deprive people of their liberty as a kind of preventive medicine, and this is clearly to choose social utility over one of the mainstays of criminal justice: procedural due process.

Our system of criminal due process involves such guarantees as the following: (1) No man is to be deprived of his liberty for what he is or what he might do, but only because he has in fact violated some legal prohibition. This is the traditional requirement for an overt act. (2) A man is to be presumed innocent. This means that the state must prove its case beyond a reasonable doubt to a jury of the defendant's peers and that the defendant may exploit the adversary system to its full to make such proof impossible. (3) A man is to be responsible only for what he has done as an individual. He is not to be held guilty because others like him often commit crimes.[6] (4) a man is not to be forced to testify against himself, to help the state in its attempt to deprive him of his liberty.

Such guarantees would have no place in a purely therapeutic or preventive context, and Menninger quite correctly argues that the procedures they involve are not the best way to arrive at truth and thus that they interfere with the efficiency of securing public safety (pp. 53 ff.). But of course they do; *that is their very function!* They aim, not at the discovery of truth, but at the protection of the defendant in his otherwise unequal battle with the state. And our employment of these procedures tests the sincerity of our commitment to what is often claimed as the basic moral value in our system of criminal justice— namely, the belief that it is better to free some guilty persons than to convict some innocent ones.

We can begin to understand the tensions inherent in the criminal process only if we realize how the values of justice and due process compete with the utilitarian value of public safety.[7] If we were only interested in public safety, we would let

---

[6] It is often not noticed that provisions for preventive detention (especially if they rest on statistical evidence) tend to involve *collective* rather than individual criteria for guilt. It is judged that Jones is to be detained because he is a member of some class (e.g., vagrants) which manifests a high crime rate. This point is totally missed in the otherwise excellent article on preventive detection by Dershowitz in the "New York Review" (13 March 1969). For more on the issue of preventive detention, see my "Preventive Detention and Psychiatry" in *Dissent* (Sept.-Oct.), 1970.

[7] An important recent book, Packer (1968), illuminates the tension inherent in our system of criminal punishment by contrasting the "crime control model" with the "due process model."

the police coerce confessions, deny any excuses for wrongdoing, and even punish some innocent people to keep everyone else careful. One only has to call to mind Nazi Germany, Soviet Russia, and present-day South Africa and Greece for a picture of the logical outcome of a society which places order and public safety over all values of justice. (Almost unbelievably, from a man famous for his liberal and benevolent humanism, Menninger looks with wistful longing at the security provided by the legal systems of Greece and China!) [p. 277]

Being involuntarily deprived of our liberty (even by a benevolent Dr. Menninger who calls it therapy rather than punishment) is an evil most of us would like to avoid—particularly if we have done nothing wrong, but only appear to have "dangerous tendencies." Thus we should be quite stupid to take steps that would involve giving up the guarantees which help us avoid this evil. Menninger, of course, does not explicitly say that he is against due process (who would?); but if he is not against it, then his set of proposals involves a fundamental paradox. For if his proposed system is to retain all present guarantees to preserve fairly the freedom of each individual, why suppose that it will be any more efficient than present practices? To make it more efficient, some due process will necessarily have to be sacrificed.

THE SCIENTIFIC EXAMINATION OF DETERRENCE THEORY

It is absurd to characterize public safety as the *real* problem of criminal law (as though other issues, like due process, are illusions), but surely such safety is admittedly one of the important values that any system of criminal law must seek to promote. And so it is worth inquiring if it is even true that, as a matter of fact, our present system of criminal punishment fails to work in providing for our security. Here we are dealing with an empirical scientific issue, and one would think that Menninger would be on safe ground. But he is not. He tells us that we must replace punishment with therapy because the only possible defense for punishment is deterrence theory; and this theory is known to be false.[8] But he is quite wrong here. Deterrence theory is not known to be false, and Menninger fails to show that it is false. His whole case is one of ridicule supported by no evidence whatsoever. Here is all that he says to support his attack on deterrence theory:

["Brushes" with the law] are dreary, repetitious crises in the dismal, dreary life of one of the miserable ones. They are signals of distress, signals of failure, signals of crises which society sees primarily in terms of *its* annoyance, *its* irritation, *its* injury. They are the spasms and struggles and convulsions of a submarginal human being trying to make it in our complex society with inadequate equipment and inadequate preparations.

[We have described] a man who seemed to have spent his life going from one difficulty into another, into the jail and out of it, only to get back in again, like one caught in a revolving door. It ended in death. The grinding mills of the law did nothing for Crow; they cost Kansas City a lot of money, mostly wasted. It gave a score of people something to do, mostly useless. One might wonder what could have been done early in this chap's life to have protected his victims better. [pp. 19; 21-22]

It is almost impossible to know what Menninger expects us to conclude from these passages, for they appear to involve at least two gross confusions. First, as a psychiatrist, Menninger has perhaps seen a limited number of criminals who really

---

[8] Menninger dismisses entirely the arguments of those who have advocated a retributive theory of punishment. For example, he fails to consider the possible alteration in our concept of a human being (and how we *treat* human beings) if we cease to regard people as agents of dignity and responsibility who are capable of being blameworthy for what they do. To see that one can offer a retributive theory which is something more than disguised vengeance, consult Morris (1968).

are compulsive and thus are nondeterrable. And the existence of such people certainly points up a distinct failure within our system of criminal punishment. But they will indict the system *as a whole* only if they can be regarded as representative of criminality in general. But this is just the conclusion we may not draw on the basis of so limited a sample. What about the college student who smokes marijuana, or the Martin Luther King who engages in civil disobedience, or the university professor who omits some lecture fees on his tax return? These are all legally criminals, but are their actions "the spasms and struggles and convulsions of a submarginal human being?" Note what Menninger says:

"Ah," the reader will say, "perhaps what you say is true in those violent rape and murder cases, but take everyday bank robbing and check forging and stealing—you cannot tell me that these people are not out for the money!"

I would not deny that money is desired and obtained, but I would also say that the *taking* of money from the victim by these devices means something special, and something quite different from what you think it does. [p. 183]

Here we enter the world of apparent fantasy. The actions of our pot smoker, our civil disobedient, and our tax evader are all symbolic of something unconscious. But, even if this is true, just how is it relevant? It will presumably be relevant only if it is the case that these unconscious motives can be said to compel the agent in such a way that he is not responsible and thus not a proper object for punishment. But, having ridiculed the notions of fault and responsibility, and having modestly declared the inability of the psychiatrist in a courtroom ever to say with any certainty that an action of a particular man was compulsive (and thus nonresponsible) because of mental disorder (pp. 132 ff.), Menninger can hardly go forth and present a perfectly general theory of determinism for all human action.

A general theory of determinism, if it rests on no inductive basis of established particular cases, is a metaphysical theory and not a scientific conclusion. And if, as a metaphysical theory, it requires that we stop distinguishing the actions of a Martin Luther King from those of a Daniel M'Naghten, then it is a useless bit of stipulation.

The second confusion in Menninger's rejection of deterrence theory is related to the first. It is the failure to distinguish special from general deterrence.[9] He thus makes a quite misleading use of the facts of recidivism. Recidivism surely shows that criminal punishment does not deter many of the particular people who are caught up in the criminal process. But this fact is quite irrelevant to the claim that having a deterrence system has the general effect of keeping many members of society from ever engaging in criminal conduct and thus making themselves eligible for the process. It is not difficult to believe, for example, that one major reason why more of us do not smoke marijuana or submit fraudulent tax returns is that we are deterred by the criminal penalties. To scientifically refute deterrence theory, and thus provide a basis for replacing our entire system of punishment with something else, it would have to be shown that substantial numbers of those who do not now commit crimes would continue to be law-abiding if all criminal sanctions were abolished. But we have no evidence at all on this complex counterfactual. And, in the absence of any such evidence, it is irresponsible to ridicule and reject deterrence theory in the name of science.

LAW AND PSYCHIATRY

The psychiatrist, Menninger argues, should be removed from the courtroom entirely (p. 138). I have some sympathy with these sentiments, but not for the reasons Menninger offers. His suggestion (a not unfamiliar one) is that at most

9 For more on this distinction, see Packer (1968).

psychiatric testimony is relevant to establishing the *mens rea* of the offense—that is, the mental element which establishes the degree of personal responsibility or blameworthiness for what was done. But, with much invective and ridicule, Menninger says that we should drop inquiries into mens rea entirely. We should simply inquire if the offense was committed, regardless of the mental state with which it was committed. If we determine that the prisoner (patient?) did commit the offense, he should be turned over to a team of psychiatrists and other experts. They would then inquire into his mental state in order to determine how long to detain him for society's protection and his own rehabilitation (pp. 113 ff., 139).

Though this proposal has a plausible ring to it, it is in fact almost impossible to give it a coherent interpretation. How, for example, can one convict for the offense alone when a mens rea is typically a material (i.e., defining) element of the offense itself? Was the offense murder or manslaughter? The question cannot be answered without an inquiry into mens rea—i.e., did the actor have malice aforethought? The revisions and complexities that elimination of mens rea would introduce into our legal system are vast. If he is aware of such problems, Menninger totally ignores them.[10]

Suppose, however, we did eliminate mens rea at the trial and then had our fellow convicted for the offense of (say) "causally bringing about the death of an-

other human being." And now he is turned over to psychiatrists. The kinds of problems that might arise become obvious. Suppose he caused the death by nonculpable accident (that is, he did not even have what we would now call the mens rea of negligence). Further suppose that, upon examination, he was found to be "potentially dangerous." Should he be locked up for a period of enforced therapy (perhaps for life) even though he had committed no wrong at all? Or consider trivial offenders. Should a man who compulsively cashes bad checks be sent to a mental institution for an indeterminate period because he is hopeless? The questions are not medical or scientific. They are questions of *moral* and *political decision,* and we should be foolish to entrust our responsibility for them to a team of "experts." Criminal judges, whatever their weaknesses, are at least bound by the rules of our community. They may not, as may psychiatrists, act on their own personal conceptions of what is good for or dangerous to the community.

An actual example is illustrative here: The closest existing analogue to what Menninger advocates is to be found in the American juvenile courts. Here it has been traditional to suspend guarantees of due process because the state was presumably acting in the benevolent interest of the juvenile rather than a punishing agent. (It is really astounding how we can deceive ourselves merely by changing the name of what we do.) A reading of the opinion of Justice Fortas in the 1967 Gault case (where some due process is finally guaranteed to juveniles) should give us pause before we hand over any other area of human liberty to benevolent experts.[11] Menninger is right in his prem-

---

[10] Some psychiatrists try to meet this worry by advocating a *bifurcated trial* (something along the lines of the California practice). There is to be a guilt trial and a sanity trial. At the former, considerations of mens rea will be relevant and allowed. All questions of sanity, however, will be reserved for the second trial; and thus it is only at this second trial that psychiatric testimony will be allowed. This system, however, will fail for the following reason: If a man is insane, he might be incapable of having the mens rea required for the commission of the offense. It would thus deny him due process to exclude psychiatric testimony from the first trial. See People v. Wells.

[11] See also the horror stories of arbitrary mental commitment cited by Szasz (1963). Szasz has raised profound questions and deserves a serious answer. Menninger simply proposes to eliminate such abuses by training police and mental health workers with the proper *therapeutic attitudes* (pp. 260; 271). But this misses the point entirely; benevo-

ise that science and due process do not mix well. The moral to be drawn, however, is the following: Beware of psychiatrists bearing gifts.

Near the end of his argument, after dismissing the notions of blameworthiness and responsibility, Menninger suggests that instead of punishing people we might impose *penalties* on them:

If a burglar takes my property, I would like to have it returned or paid for by him if possible, and the state ought to be reimbursed for its costs, too. This could be forcibly required to come from the burglar. This would be equitable; it would be just, and it would not be "punitive." [p. 203]

Just how "punitive" this would be depends, I suppose, on just how rich the burglar is and on just what happens to him for nonpayment. But this is not the objection I want to pursue. What interests me is the suggestion that criminal law ought to move toward becoming a part of tort law—the law of damages for harms done not involving breach of contract. Does Menninger find damages attractive for any other reason than that they are not *called* "punishment"? After all, in tort law conditions of blameworthiness and responsibility are relevant. We do not normally make a man pay damages in the absence of any fault on his part. We rather, as the phrase goes, let the loss lie where it falls. If I am not negligent, then normally (though not always) I am not liable for damages. What if Menninger's burglar was a man who believed the property was his own, or who was sleepwalking, or caused damage in an epileptic

seizure, or took it to use for his self-defense? Judgments of liability for damages might well differ in all these areas. And so even this move toward tort will not allow us to avoid something like the criminal law's mens rea.

CONCLUSION

Dr. Menninger is a decent and generous man, and I do not mean to charge that he intentionally advocates injustice. He has simply fallen victim to the trap which often leads benevolent men to pursue an unjust course: the singleminded pursuit of one social goal to the exclusion of all others. In addressing himself to the limited goals of public safety and rehabilitation, he does highlight some terrible abuses (e.g., inhuman brutality) and inadequacies (e.g., the tendency of current prisons to breed crime) that exist within our present system of criminal punishment. What we do not get from him, however, is a persuasive case against the criminal process itself.

I would not pose as a man devoted to our system of criminal punishment. It contains much hypocrisy and moral pretension and is, at best, a necessary evil. However, in spite of its admitted shortcomings, the criminal process is at least an attempt to balance public safety against the often competing values of liberty and due process. In so far as it does not succeed in attaining such a balance, it would appear that some reforms short of throwing away the process entirely would be in order. Thus there seems to me to be a presumption in favor of a criminal process as a general response to anti-social conduct. By this I mean nothing more than that the burden of proof lies on the man who would replace such a process to provide careful arguments which are conceptually clear, empirically well-founded, and morally cogent. It is just this burden which Dr. Menninger has failed totally to bear.

---

lence is not justice, and therapeutic attitudes are not necessarily due process attitudes. Menninger might also recall Lord Acton's reminder about the corruptive nature of power. Or does he perhaps think that psychiatrists are immune from such corruption? Nice, benevolent people are perhaps preferable to mean, stubborn ones, but it does not follow from this that the former should be allowed to coerce and confuse the latter.

CASES

PEOPLE v. WELLS (1949) Cal.2d. 33: 330; P.2d.
202: 53.

In re GAULT (1967) U.S. 387: 1.

REFERENCES

ABRAHAMSEN, D., 1960. *The Psychology of Crime.*
New York: Columbia Univ. Press.

ALEXANDER, F. and H. STAUB, 1956. *The Criminal,
the Judge and the Public: A Psychological Analysis.* Glencoe: Free Press.

GLUECK, S., 1936. *Crime and Justice.* Boston: Little,
Brown.

MORRIS, H., 1968. "Persons and punishment,"
Monist, 52 (October): 475–501.

PACKER, H. L., 1968. *The Limits of the Criminal
Sanction.* Stanford: Stanford University Press.

SCHOECK, H. and J. W. WIGGINS (eds.), 1962. *Psychiatry and Responsibility.* Princeton: Van Nostrand.

SZASZ, T. S., 1963. *Law, Liberty, and Psychiatry.*
New York: Macmillan.

WERTHAM, F., 1955. "Psychoauthoritarianism and
the law," *Univ. of Chicago Law Rev.* 22 (Winter): 336–38.

INMATE ORGANIZATION: SEX DIFFERENTIATION AND THE INFLUENCE OF CRIMINAL SUBCULTURES

Charles R. Tittle *

Sociological literature on institutional adaptation suggests that male and female innate organizational structures differ markedly. The evidence suggests that male inmates tend to organize into an overall symbiotic structure characterized by a shared normative system epitomized in a prison code (Clemmer, 1940; Sykes, 1958; Wheeler, 1961; Sykes and Messinger, 1960; Garabedian, 1963; Schrag, 1954; Schrag, 1961), but that within that community considerable individualism and personal isolation prevail (Clemmer, 1940; Glaser, 1964; Morris and Morris, 1963). In contrast, female inmates are characterized neither by overall cohesion nor by individual isolation. Instead, they tend to organize into relatively enduring primary relationships, often involving dyadic homosexual attachments and extensive "family" relationships (Ward and Kassebaum, 1965; Giallombardo, 1966; Halleck and Hersko, 1962; Kosofsky and Ellis, 1958; Taylor, 1965; Harris, 1967).

Both male and female inmate organizations have been theoretically explained as responses to institutional environments. Deprivations of prison living are said to lead to adjustments which reduce the discomfort of incarceration. Hence, an integrated inmate organization is thought to serve as a mechanism for controlling the environment while permitting the maintenance of a sense of masculinity and self-dignity for male prisoners (Sykes, 1958; Sykes and Messinger, 1960; McCorkle and Korn, 1954). In like manner, the primary relationships, characteristic of female inmate populations, are said to serve dependency and social supportive needs generated through expectations attached to the female role in the larger society

Reprinted from *American Sociological Review,* 34 (August 1969), pp. 492-505, by permission of the author and The American Sociological Association.

* This research was supported by National Science Foundation Grant GS 1714. I wish to acknowledge the invaluable assistance of Drollene P. Tittle.

(Ward and Kassebaum, 1965; Giallombardo, 1966). In general, inmate organization in either of its two characteristic forms is thought to emerge as an institutional product with problem solving functions for the inmates, and maintenance of the inmate organization is thought to be achieved through a socialization process sometimes called "prisonization" (Clemmer, 1940; Wheeler, 1961).

However, the research evidence for this general theory is not compelling. Although descriptive accounts (Sykes, 1958; Morris and Morris, 1963); cohort studies (Wheeler, 1961; Glaser, 1964; Tittle and Tittle, 1964), and organizational comparisons (Wilson, 1968; Berk, 1966; Street, et al., 1966; Grusky, 1959) have tended to substantiate the argument for male inmates, the fundamental premise that inmate behavior is an institutional product continues to be challenged (Irwin and Cressey, 1962; Wellford, 1967; Cline, 1966). Some investigators have maintained that inmate organization is largely an extension of a criminal social organization imported into the institution. Although Roebuck (1963) convincingly criticized the Irwin and Cressey position, their dissent and some research evidence point out the need for a more stringent test of these ideas. Moreover, only limited data confirming the institutional product theory for female inmates have been reported (Ward and Kassebaum, 1965; Giallombardo, 1966; Harris, 1967).

Further, it is not clearly established that male and female inmate organizations differ in form. No actual comparisons of male and female inmate populations under similarly confining situations have been made from common data collected by identical methods. It may well be that the alleged male-female differences are attributable to differences in social backgrounds of typical male and female inmates, differences in the nature and extent of inmate-staff interaction between male and female institutions, or to differences in actual physical conditions of incarceration.

This paper reports data gathered in an institution where both males and females are confined under similar custodial conditions. Its purpose is (1) to determine whether structural characteristics of female inmate organization differ from the male under these similar conditions, and (2) to test the institutional product theory of inmate organization by examining cohort variations in inmate organizational characteristics of males and females, holding constant criminal subcultural involvement.

RESEARCH PROCEDURES

The data for this paper were gathered at a Federal hospital serving volunteer and imprisoned narcotic addicts of both sexes. Volunteers were admitted on their own request and were free to leave at anytime. Many of them, however, were under various kinds of official and informal pressure to complete a full course of treatment involving at least five months at the institution. As a result a large proportion of volunteer patients thought of themselves as prisoners (40% of 115 interviewed). Those inmates legally defined as prisoners were convicted violators of Federal laws judged by Bureau of Prisons to be in need of treatment for narcotic addiction. Included were inmates with sentences as high as ten years, although the bulk of the prisoners were sentenced from two to five years.

At the time of the study, the hospital was operated under custodial conditions similar to a minimum security prison. All patients were restricted in freedom of movement in the institution. Most doors and grilles were locked, and patients were required to obtain "passes" from the staff for most movement. Inmates were governed by numerous behavioral restrictions, and they were supervised by uniformed security personnel who controlled the patients through the issuance of demerit-type reports which could result in extra work duty, the loss of privileges, transfer to a Federal prison, or the loss of accumulated days of "good time" (or dismissal from the hospital in the case of the volunteer). The patients were required to work without pay, and they were regimented in terms of eating and sleeping schedules, but they experienced substantial freedom to shape their own life patterns in the institution. For instance, they were permitted to accept or reject therapy, had a choice of a variety of recreational activities, and, in their jobs, were often allowed considerable self-direction and discretion.

In light of the comparative freedom experienced by the inmates at this institution, it is important to consider whether this research provides data relevant to theories developed in ordinary prison contexts. Information concerning role definitions and deprivations experienced by the patients at this hospital suggest that such theories can be addressed meaningfully, although cautiously. For example, 61% of the respondents reported that they felt like an inmate in a prison rather than a patient in a hospital, while an additional 18% reported feeling "somewhat" like an inmate in a prison. Moreover, 54% of the subjects described life in the institution to be "difficult."

At the time the study was begun, the patient population included approximately 100 females and 500 males. Each sex was housed in a separate section of the institution, the female unit being locked off from the remainder of the hospital. Both sexes were assigned to jobs in common areas; they dined in the same area and attended jointly many activities. In all these situations, careful supervision was exercised to maintain segregation and minimize personal interaction. The men and women, however, were allowed to interact in therapy and rehabilitative activities, and occasionally heterosexual

recreational activities such as dances were allowed. In general, the two sexes existed under similar custodial conditions, although some differences were evident. The major difference was in extent of confinement. The women were not allowed to move about the hospital without an escort and were much less free to engage in recreational and other activities at their own discretion. They were also more frequently in contact with security personnel in their living units and daily activities than the men, although the nature of the interaction between female patients and security seemed to be less authoritarian than for males. Further, the location and nature of the female living unit created a greater likelihood of contact with clinical personnel.

Interviews were conducted with a representative sample of patients that included (1) all female prisoners present at the beginning of the study, with the exception of a few who refused to participate (N=44), (2) a 50% random-start, systematic selection of female volunteers present at the beginning of the study (N=20), (3) a 50% continuous sample of new female patients admitted during the first five-month period of the study who stayed at least two weeks (N=27), (4) a 25% random-start systematic selection of male prisoners and volunteers present at the beginning of the study (N=139), and (5) a 25% continuous sample of new male patients admitted during the first five-month period of the study who stayed at least two weeks (N=45). In addition a subsample of respondents was reinterviewed four months after the first encounter. This subsample included (1) all respondents who entered the hospital during the first five months of the study and who remained long enough, and (2) a one-tenth, random-start, systematic sample of the prisoner respondents already at the hospital at the beginning of the field research. These procedures yielded a sample of 47 female volunteers, 44 female prisoners, 68 male volunteers, and 116 male prisoners. Of these, 12 females and 24 males were interviewed twice.

Interviews, including both structural and open-ended questions, were conducted by the author and a female assistant. Potential respondents were assigned to each of the interviewers on a fortuitous basis without regard to sex or status. The interviewing phase of the study was preceded by a period of observation and "getting acquainted." During the initial observational period, the two researchers made the acquaintance of as many patients as possible, and took every opportunity to make their presence known in the hospital. In all situations they explained the nature and purpose of the study. Patient cooperation for pretesting the interview schedule was solicited and obtained. Throughout the five-month period of data gathering, the researchers attempted to become integrated into the hospital life; they were invited to parties and recreational events by patients and asked to "chaperone" mixed gatherings, and they became friends with many patients.

The actual 45 to 90-minute data-gathering interviews were conducted in a private office provided by the hospital. Each subject was notified of our desire to talk with him by receipt of a "pass." Each patient who wished to participate would present himself at a major control point in the building containing our assigned quarters. Being notified by telephone of his arrival, the interviewer would then meet the patient and escort him to the interview office. Female subjects were escorted from their living units to the interview offices by the interviewer. Once in the office, an explanation was made of the study and how the patient came to be selected. The patient was then given a second opportunity not to participate. The total response rate under this general procedure was 90% for males and 85% for females. In addition to formal interview data, information was gathered from field observa-

tion and from unstructured interviews with patients, not included in the sample, who expressed a desire to talk with us. Further data were abstracted from the hospital records. Some of the information is handled as individual-indicator measures while some items are combined to form scales of measurement for certain variables. The operational measures employed are reported below.

PRIMARY GROUP FORMATION. Three different single-item indicators were used to measure the extent of primary group affiliation. Each respondent was asked how many same sex patients he considered to be his good friends, whether these friends and he formed a group, and whether he thought of another patient as being a "best friend." Two categories of response were delineated for each of these items. With respect to number of good friends, those who reported having one to five good friends were considered to have primary group affiliations while those with no good friends or those with more than five good friends were considered not to have primary group affiliations. With respect to group formation and having a best friend, responses fell into "yes" and "no" categories.

EXTENT OF HOMOSEXUAL ACTIVITY. Each respondent was asked to report on his own involvement in homosexual activity as well as to estimate the number of patients of his sex who had engaged in homosexual activity while in the hospital. A mean of the estimates for each sex was calculated. In addition each respondent was asked to describe the nature of the homosexual liaisons he knew about.

SUBSCRIPTION TO AN INMATE CODE. This is taken as an indication of the extent of affiliation in an overall symbiotic inmate organization. It is measured by a Guttman type scale reflecting elements of an inmate code as specified by Sykes and Messinger (1960). The five elements are: noninterference with other inmate interests, non-intercourse with security personnel, loyalty to other inmates, maintenance of self-dignity, and manipulation of the official system. Responses to eight items reflecting these elements were tested for scalability by the Cornell technique. The initial eight items included one each reflecting non-interference with other inmate interests, admiration of those who maintain their self dignity, and extent of fraternization with security personnel; two reflecting manipulation of the official system; and three reflecting loyalty to other patients. Through successive reduction of items and categories of response, five dichotomous category items (one representing each element of the code) were derived to form a cumulative scale (cf. Tittle and Tittle, 1964; Wheeler, 1961; Wellford, 1967; Ward and Kassebaum, 1965).

The items and categories are: (1) Do you feel that a patient should ever report rule violations to security? If so, under what conditions? (yes, under unrestrictive conditions—all other degrees), (2) Do you ever engage in friendly conversation with security? How often? (very often-less), (3) Suppose the patients here agreed to go on a work strike to improve conditions, and the hospital authorities responded by giving each individual patient (in private) the choice of returning to work or of being sent to a prison (being dismissed from the hospital in case of volunteers), how do you think you would respond? (would certainly choose prison or dismissal-other), (4) Do you admire patients who "don't take anything off of anybody?" (no-maybe and yes), (5) When do you feel that breaking rules here is justified? (great commitment-less commitment). The final scale is characterized by a coefficient of reproducibility of .905 with an improvement of .189 over the minimal marginal reproducibility.[1] For this paper, high subscription to

an inmate code is defined as a scale score of three or more, while low subscription is defined as a scale score of less than three.

AWARENESS OF INFORMAL NORMATIVE SYSTEM. Each respondent was asked if he knew of any unwritten rules for getting along in the hospital that the (same sex) patients shared. If he reported such awareness, he was then asked to specify the nature of such rules. An additional indicator of awareness of an informal normative system is the response to the question, "Would a patient here run any risks if he were to report a rule violation to security?"

INMATE COHESION. A four-item Guttman type scale was used to measure the extent of cohesion among the patients. Responses to eight items thought to reflect aspects of inmate cohesion were tested for scalability. Through successive reduction of items and categories of response, the following dichotomous items were derived to form a cumulative scale: (1) How often do you go out of your way to help other patients? (very often-less), (2) Which is the best way for patients to get along here—everybody stick together or each patient do his best on his own? (stick together-other), (3) After you are released, will you associate with people you have known here as fellow patients? (yes and maybe-no), (4) How often do you personally share your possessions with other patients? (often or very often-less). The final scale is characterized by a coefficient of reproducibility of .918 and an improvement of .202 over the minimal marginal reproducibility. For this analysis, high cohesion is defined as a scale score of three or more, while low cohesion is defined as a scale score of less than three. No attempt was made to distinguish between primary group cohesion and cohe-

---

[1] Although this degree of reproducibility may occur frequently by chance with this number of items (Schooler, 1968), and the scalability applies only to the subset of retained items rather than the total universe, the scalogram technique is nevertheless appropriate for purposes of this research. The object was not to prove unidimensionality, but rather to employ an objective technique for ordering the subjects along a continuum from high to low with respect to these items.

sion with the inmate group as a whole, hence this measure probably incorporates aspects of both.

Inmate cohesion is also reflected in responses to two additional questions. Each subject was asked to describe the types of people with whom he shared his personal possessions and the types of people he went out of his way to help. A person is judged to have a high degree of cohesiveness with other inmates when he expressed a willingness to share or help others on a nonrestrictive basis; that is, he specified no restriction as to ability to reciprocate or necessity for close friendship or association.

CRIMINAL SUBCULTURAL ORIENTATION. Eight pieces of information judged to be indicative of criminal backgrounds and commitments were tested for scalability in the Guttman sense. Five of these items, in dichotomous form, were found to form a cumulative scale. The scalable items are: (1) Response to the question: How many addicts did you know on the outside? (fewer than 20—20 or more). (2) Response to the question: How many professional law violators did you know on the outside? (less than 100—100 or more). (3) Response to the question: When you violated the law on the outside, how often did you feel guilty? (most of the time or always-less), (4) Response to the question: On the outside, if a person wants to get ahead, which is more important—hard work or having the right connections? And (5) the total number of arrests recorded in the hospital records (none-some). The scale has a coefficient of reproducibility of .893 with an improvement of .158 over the minimal marginal reproducibility. When this variable is used as a control factor, high criminal orientation is taken as a scale score of three or more, and low criminal orientation is reflected in a scale score of less than three.

INSTITUTIONAL CAREER PHASE. The career phase is operationalized as a combination of length of time spent in the hospital and length of time remaining before the patient expects to leave the hospital. Early phase inmates are designated as those who have been at the institution less than four months and have more than two months remaining before expected release. Middle phase inmates are those who have been at the hospital more than four months and have more than two months remaining. Late phase inmates are designated as those who have been at the institution more than one month and have less than two months remaining before their expected release. A fourth category called "winders" is excluded from this analysis because it included those short-term volunteers who had been at the hospital only a short time (less than one month) and who expected to remain less than two months more.

INDIVIDUAL BACKGROUND VARIABLES. These include legal status, age, education, race, intelligence, psychiatric diagnosis, disorganization of social background, and length of time previously spent in jail or prison. Based on information recorded in the hospital records, legal status is categorized here simply as volunteer (including those with legal or other pressure to remain) and prisoners; age is categorized as young (21 or less), medium (22–29), and older (30 plus); education is categorized as high (12 years or more), medium (some high school), and low (less than high school); and race is treated as a two-category variable, white and nonwhite. Previous incarceration time (self-reported) is classified as high (more than six months), and low (less than six months).

Intelligence level is estimated from information contained in the clinical records. In some cases, actual scores on tests were available, and, in some others, only a judgment by a therapist as to the subject's intelligence level was recorded. In many cases both pieces of information were included. For this analysis, subjects with test scores above 105 or who were judged by a therapist to be "high average" or above in intelligence were categorized as the higher intelligence group, while the others were categorized as lower.

Psychiatric diagnosis was likewise extracted from the clinical records. The principal diagnosis specified in the clinical records is classified according to the scheme of the American Psychiatric Association. For purposes of use as a control variable, diagnoses are considered in two broad categories. The first includes character disorders and sociopathic disorders, while the second is composed of psychoneurotic and psychotic disorders.

Disorganization of social background is measured by a five-item (in dichotomous form) cumulative scale. The five items were derived by the Cornell technique from a beginning set of six multiple response items. The scale items are: (1) age at which the subject first used drugs (from hospital records), dichotomized as 17 or over and less than 17; (2) quality of the family unit (interpretation by the female investigator of judgments by clinical personnel recorded in the hospital records), categorized as poor and other; (3) age at first sexual intercourse (self-reported), classified as 14 or over and less than 14; (4) completion of the family unit (a judgment of the amount of time the family of the subject was intact during the childhood and adolescence period, based on materials in the hospital records), dichotomized as completed (both parents present all the time) and incomplete (one or both parents absent at least part of the time); and (5) whether the subject has ever used marijuana (from hospital records). The coefficient of reproducibility of this scale is .895 with an improvement of .172 over the minimal marginal reproducibility. As a test factor, this variable is considered in two categories. Highly disorganized backgrounds are taken as a score of three or above on the scale, while less disorganized backgrounds are indicated by a score of less than three on the scale.

INSTITUTIONAL VARIABLES. Four items reflecting differing experiences within the institution are employed in the analysis. An indicator of contact with meaningful others on the outside is taken as the amount of mail received (self-reported). Those receiving less than five letters per month were judged to have low contact, and those receiving five or more letters per month are classified as having high contact.

Contact with security personnel in the hospital is indicated by interview data in which the respondent reported how frequently in a typical day he came in contact with security personnel. The data are categorized as high contact (20 or more contacts per day), medium contact (5–19 times per day), and low contact (less than 5 per day). In addition, the nature of the contacts between patient and security personnel is estimated from an item in which the patient reported whether he thought the security personnel defined him as a patient or as a prisoner. Two categories are considered—those who thought the definition was clearly prisoner and those who thought they were treated as patients or were ambiguous about the definition.

A fourth institutional variable is the extent of contact with professional personnel reported by each patient. Those reporting less than one hour of contact per week are classified as low contact patients, those reporting one to two hours of contact per week are classified as medium contact patients, and those with greater frequency of contact are classified in the high contact category.

FORM OF ANALYSIS. Three types of analysis are employed. In comparing men with women on organizationally relevant variables, simple percentage differences in a contingency situation are examined. The statistical significance of these differences are measured by chi square. Techniques of elaboration are used to test for spurious relationships.

Cohort analysis is used to examine the pattern of variation with respect to inmate organizational variables. Cohorts (actually synthetic cohorts) are designated, as described above, in terms of institutional career phase. Because changes in the hospital program and structure were occurring at the time the data were being gathered, it was deemed advisable to confirm the results based on the cross sectional data with analysis of data on a small sample of subjects interviewed a second time after a brief experience in the institution (referred to as a partial panel).

RESULTS

The data seem to confirm the greater propensity of females to organize into small primary groups (Table 1). Thus a larger proportion of the females reported having 1–5 good friends (70% vs. 49%); more of the women thought of themselves and their friends as a group (55% vs. 48%); and the females more often reported having a "best friend" among their same sex peers (65% vs. 52%).

However, the notion that differences in inmate structures are reflected in the extent of homosexual activity does not appear to be substantiated in these data. The mean estimate of homosexual activity is almost equal for the men and women (23% vs. 24%). Moreover, the degree of self-involvement reported by the males and females is very similar. Fourteen percent of the women reported themselves to have been involved in homosexual activity, and an additional 5% gave answers indicating that they probably had been so involved while at the hospital. Among the men, 11% admitted present involvement, and an additional 8% indicated a high probability of involvement.

These findings suggest that the conclusion of greater homosexuality among the female inmates than among male inmates

Table 1   Male-Female Differences on Variables Relevant to the Form of Inmate Organization

Variables	Male (percent)	Female (percent)	Diff. (percent)
I. Primary Group Formation			
One-Five Good Friends	49	70	21**
Friends Form a Group	48	55	7
Has One Best Friend	52	65	13*
Extent of Homosexual Activity	23	24	1
II. Symbiotic Organization			
High Score on Scale of Adherence to Inmate Code	63	56	7
a. Non-fraternization with Security	48	21	27**
b. Non-acceptance of Ratting	69	56	13
c. Group Loyalty	42	34	8
d. Admiration of Autonomy	46	39	7
e. No Respect for Official Rules	20	17	3
Perception of Informal Norms	52	42	10
Perception of Risk in Ratting	55	48	7
High Score on Scale of Cohesion	40	21	19**
a. Belief in Cohesion	37	23	14*
b. Long Range Association	57	47	10
c. Has Covered for Non-associates	18	14	4
d. Frequent Sharing with Other Patients	80	77	3
e. Frequent Helping of Other Patients	48	46	2
Shares on a Non-restrictive Basis	34	31	3
Helps on a Non-restrictive Basis	41	36	5
(N)	(184)	(91)	

*p < .05
**p < .01

(Ward and Kassebaum, 1965) may not be valid when conditions of incarceration are similar. This interpretation may not be warranted, however, since other evidence suggests the influence of unique factors in this research context. The overall extent of homosexual activity among the women in this institution appears to be substantially less than that reported in other contexts, and the level of male homosexual activity is somewhat below that found in other places. These lower levels may be due to the fact that the period of incarceration for many of the subjects was comparatively short, but unstructured interview data suggest that the opportunity for heterosexual interaction in this institution is a more compelling explanation. If it is true that homosexuality in institutions is at least partly a sexual role fulfillment rather than simply a form of physical gratification, then heterosexual interaction would tend to reduce the need for homosexual involvement and thus lead to lower rates in this institution. Furthermore, since the number of males exceeds the number of females, the possibility for meaningful relationships with members of the opposite sex is greater for the women than for the men. Greater involvement (57% of the women exchange more than one letter per week with male patients while only 20% of the men communicate with the women to this extent) would therefore reduce to a greater extent their need for sexual role fulfillment through homosexuality than such need among the males. Hence, it may be the case that if no heterosexual interaction were allowed, the extent of homosexual activity among both sexes would be higher and the level of such activity among the women would exceed that among the men. Of course, this could also account for the fact that difference between the men and women in the extent of primary group affiliation generally is not greater than it is.

Although the men and women may not differ in the extent of homosexual activity,

the data do suggest that the nature and meaning of homosexuality for the two are quite different. Apparently, homosexual liaisons among the females tend to be more affective, take place in more stable unions, and be viewed more often in terms of a total relationship. For the men, on the other hand, homosexual activity seems to have as a primary focus of attention physical gratification, representing to a greater extent a commodity for economic exchange; and it is more likely to be a casual act. These differences are clearly revealed by the fact that 50% of the total sample of men reported that "homosexual favors are bought and sold," while among the females only 19% thought this to be the case. Responses to open-ended questions about the nature of homosexuality in the institution also illustrate this point. Twenty-one percent of all the female respondents described homosexual liaisons as involving affection and as occurring in stable, emotionally charged relationships. Only 4% of the men, however, characterized male homosexual activity in those terms. For the men, homosexual acts were usually described simply as sexual outlets with no real emotional meaning. The following comments illustrate typical interpretations of homosexuality among the men:

Well, everyone has to have sexual satisfaction. Making it with a man is such a drag, though, because it takes so much imagination. I buy the job for five or six packs of cigarettes. In only one case have I really felt any affection for a fag; usually it is simply physical.

Once a week I get physical release with a fag. I just go in and put my cigarettes down on the dresser, lay down on the bed, and take out my joint. This guy sucks me off and that's it.

Women, on the other hand, view homosexual activity in a rather different light and tend to interpret it as a vehicle for primary social relationships. Thus:

I am a different person because of my (homosexual) partner. When I first came here, I messed up all the time. I rebelled at every opportunity, broke the rules, cussed the aides, and even got drunk once. But then I met this friend who talked to me and persuaded me to change my ways. We eventually established a sexual thing. I had real love for her; we did everything for each other.

Yes, I gave my friend a lot of attention. It was not strictly sexual. They say I'm a stud, but I helped her know how to act here. I helped her make parole. We really cared for each other, and all the time she was here we had no one else.

In general, the evidence seems to indicate fairly clear distinctions between the men and women in terms of primary group affiliations, and if these distinctions are not reflected in the extent of homosexual activity, they do seem to be reflected in the character of homosexual liaisons. Moreover, the data also suggest that the women are less involved in an overall symbiotic inmate organization. This is evidenced in response to items indicating recognition of and conformity with a system-wide normative code, although the differences in some instances are slight (Table 1). Women score lower on the scale of subscription to an inmate code (56% vs. 63% score high), and they are less likely to endorse the specific terms reflecting belief in a prison normative system or to report behavior consistent with an overall symbiotic inmate structure.

Males report somewhat greater awareness of an informal normative system relevant to all inmates. Forty-two percent of the males felt that there were unwritten rules governing the conduct of patients in the hospital, while 34% of the women recognized such norms. Moreover, of the men who were aware of such rules, 80% first mentioned inmate behavioral standards reflective of symbiotic organization. These include such things as "mind your own business," "be loyal to other patients," "be

a man" (display autonomy), and "don't rat." Only 55% of the rule-conscious women gave these types of understandings first priority. The women were more likely than the men to describe rules having to do with individual characteristics such as personal hygiene or caring for borrowed items (21% vs. 8%). Differences are also revealed in the fact that the men, more often than the women, perceived that "snitching" would entail some risk regardless of the circumstances surrounding the act (55% vs. 48%).

Finally, the sexes appear to be distinguished by degree of group cohesion. A greater proportion of the men scored high on the scale of cohesion (40% vs. 21%), and this difference is shown in variations with respect to the individual components of the cohesion scale, although again some of the differences are slight (Table 1). Two additional indicators of cohesion also show some slight difference by sex. Thus, the males more often expressed a willingness to share with non-associates (34% vs. 31%), and they more often reported helping other patients on a non-restrictive basis (41% vs. 36%).

Overall, some differences are evident for all 20 variables considered here as relevant to the structure of inmate organization (Table 1). Although only six of these can be measured as statistically significant, the direction and nature of differences in all instances is consistent with the idea that males and females organize themselves in distinct kinds of inmate structures. If it is true that the men and women in this study did in fact experience a similar environment, and that they were similar in most other ways prior to the institutional experience, then these data could be interpreted as at least moderately supportive of the sex difference proposition. There are indications, however, that even though in the same institution, the sexes were treated somewhat differently in ways relevant to inmate organizational formation and that the men and women were differentiated in terms of preinstitutional social characteristics.

Fewer of the women in the sample than men were actually legally defined as prisoners (49% vs. 62%); the females were younger (48% vs. 34% under age 29) and were more intelligent (36% vs. 27%) rated high average or above). Moreover, the women were less often diagnosed as having some form of character disorder or sociopathic personality (56% vs. 70%), were characterized by less criminalistic background and orientations (19% vs. 31% scored in the two highest categories on the scale of criminal orientation), and had less incarceration experience (59% vs. 74% had previously spent more than six months incarcerated). In terms of situational factors, the females reported maintaining more extensive contact with significant others on the outside (63% vs. 49% received five or more letters per month), experienced more contact with security personnel (37% vs. 19% reported 20 or more contacts per day), and experienced more favorable contact (35% vs. 49% thought that the security personnel treated them like prisoners). Furthermore, the women reported more frequent contact with members of the professional staff (19% vs. 34% had about one hour or less per week of contact with clinical staff members).[2]

These variations in institutional and background characteristics suggest that the observed structural differences may not be due to differences in sex role behavioral patterns at all. In order to test the possibility of spurious relationships, the associations between crucial variables and sex were examined, holding constant the ten factors described above. For this elaboration, two alternative indicators of primary group formation, and two alternative measures of symbiotic organization were

chosen. Indicators of primary group formation include the report of whether the patient's friend formed a group, and whether the respondent reported having a best friend. These two items were selected because they seem to have the greatest face validity. The multi-item scales of inmate code subscription and inmate cohesion were employed as measures of symbiotic organization because the technique of item combination used tends to minimize the influence of idiosyncratic response inconsistencies.

With only slight variations, the basic associations between sex and inmate structural indicators remain substantially unchanged when legal status, age, intelligence, diagnosis, criminal orientation, incarceration experience, outside contact, frequency and quality of security contacts, and extent of contact with professional staff are controlled. The slight variations that are observed appear to be random, with no consistency for any given control factor across the various indicators of the dependent variables nor for various categories of any given control variable. For example, the association between sex and subscription to an inmate code does not hold at medium levels of criminal orientation, but it holds at high and low levels, and the association between sex and the other three indicators of inmate organizational characteristics holds for all levels of criminal orientation. Similarly, the original association between sex and primary group formation disappears for the young age category but holds for older ages, and the relationship between sex and the other three indicators is maintained for both the young and older age categories. Thus, for 35 of the 40 controlled relationships examined, the original association is undisturbed in all categories of the test factor. The inconsistent and apparently random nature of the five variations suggests a statistical artifact rather than spurious associations.

In light of this evidence, it seems reason-

[2] No differences were observed between men and women in education, race, or disorganization of social background.

able to conclude that real sex differences in the nature of inmate organization in the institution studied do exist, although the differences are not great. Presumably these structural variations are linked to sex-role factors brought to the institution from the larger society. It is not known whether the propensity to form primary groups is more evident for women than men on the outside. The data do suggest, however, that once in the institution, the females are more likely to be drawn into primary group affiliation. Table 2 shows

career. Table 2 shows the proportion of each sex which displays high subscription to an inmate code by career phase. Two observations are noteworthy. First, the patterns for men and women are similar. The by-now-familiar curvilinear pattern with the highest subscription in the middle stage cohort (Wheeler, 1961; Glaser, 1964; Wellford, 1967) holds for both. Second, at each stage the proportion of women with high subscription is seen to be less than the proportion for men.

These observations reinforce the con-

Table 2   Primary Group Formation and Inmate Code Subscription by Institutional Career Phase and Sex

	Early Phase		Middle Phase		Late Phase	
	%	N	%	N	%	N
In Primary Groups						
Female	39	23*	60	35	71	28
Male	47	40	51	83	50	48
High Subscription to Inmate Code						
Female	50	24	64	36	50	30
Male	55	44	66	86	58	48

*Figures represent base N for the category on which the percent is based. Differences between totals for the two main classifications are due to missing data for one of the variables.

variations by stage of the institutional career. In the early stages of the institutional experience, a larger proportion of the men report primary group affiliation than of the women (39% vs. 47%). Over time, however, the direction of the difference appears to shift. The proportion of middle-phase women in primary groups is 60%, but for comparable men it is 51%. For the late-phase inmates this difference becomes even greater (71% vs. 50%). Thus, over time the proportion of females affiliated in primary groups appears to increase steadily, whereas for the men it remains relatively constant at approximately 50%.

Differences in integration into the symbiotic structure are also evident by cohorts representing stages in the institutional

clusion that the prevailing form of organization differs between male and female inmates. But they also point up the fact that the two organizational forms are not mutually exclusive for either sex. There is ample evidence to suggest that women are predominantly affiliated in primary group structures, but the data also reveal a fairly strong symbiotic structure. Males, on the other hand, show considerable propensity to form primary groups and at the same time they maintain a somewhat stronger symbiotic system. Symbiotic structures for both sexes seem to be similar in that they are apparently strongest for those farthest removed from the outside society.

Cohort variations not only emphasize the nature of male-female differences in inmate organization, but they also tend

to confirm the notion that inmate organizational characteristics are situationally
generated through adaptations to an institutional environment. The institutional
product theory is further strengthened by
the fact that these cohort variations are
similar for those who have previously
served long prison terms and for those
who have spent little or no time incarcerated. Apparently these behavioral forms
are not simply imported, but are rather
adopted anew by most inmates with each
new incarceration (Wheeler, 1961).

Considerations of the respondents interviewed at four-month intervals provide
more confirmation. Twelve females and
24 males were included in the subsample
interviewed twice. Of these, five females
and eight males were new arrivals at the
hospital after the data gathering began.
Changes in primary group affiliation for
these new arrivals suggest the occurence
of a socialization or an adaptational process. Initially, three of the five new women
were affiliated in primary groups, but four
of the five were so affiliated at the end of
the first four months. The proportion of
new females scoring high on the inmate
code scale was 60% at both points in time.
For the new male arrivals, the change
with respect to inmate code adherence
was from 75% to 100% during their first
four months in the hospital and 50% to
62% for primary group affiliation.

These before-after data are especially
suggestive since the observed changes occurred despite modifications in the hospital program and staff structure which
were being made to moderate the quasi-
prison atmosphere of the institution at
the time these patients were experiencing
their first few months there. During the
study a slow process of reorganization was
just beginning to implement recently enacted Federal legislation which would
permit the hospital staff to exercise a
greater voice in determining the patients to be admitted and retained. Consequently, adjustments were being made

to ameliorate the custodial character of
the institution. Near the end of the study
period brown-uniformed security personnel were already slowly being transformed
into white-uniformed aides, and patients
were beginning to experience additional
freedoms. However, these adjustments
were apparently not yet successful in discouraging the prisonization processes. The
magnitude of the percentages reported
above, relative to figures for the sample
as a whole (Table 2), suggests that, if
anything, the process of assimilation into
the inmate culture was being accelerated.

The data examined so far tend to substantiate the institutional product theory
of inmate organization, but the possibility
still exists that these patterns actually
reflect behavioral characteristics brought
into the institution from a criminal subculture. The degree of association between
indicators of affiliation in inmate organization and scores on the scale of criminal subcultural orientation suggests that
this alternative interpretation has limited
utility. The magnitude of association
(Lambda) between primary group formation and criminal orientation is only .03
for females and .11 for males, while the
association (Gamma) between subscription
to an inmate code and criminal orientation is .28 for females and −.01 for males.
Furthermore, the basic patterns of variation in affiliational indicators by institutional career phase remain substantially
unchanged when the level of criminal
orientation is held constant (Table 3).

Only two variations are apparent. For
the men with low criminal orientation,
primary group affiliation is found to follow a curvilinear cohort pattern similar to
the pattern of subscription to an inmate
code, while for the men with strong criminal orientations there remains essentially
no cohort variation. Perhaps this indicates
that affiliation into primary groups facilitates integration into the symbiotic structure for those with little experience in the
criminal world. Second, it can be seen

Table 3   Primary Group Formation and Inmate Code Subscription by Institutional Career Phase and Sex, Controlling for Criminal Subcultural Orientation

| | Weak Criminal Orientation | | | | | | Strong Criminal Orientation | | | | | |
| | Early Phase | | Middle Phase | | Late Phase | | Early Phase | | Middle Phase | | Late Phase | |
	%	N	%	N	%	N	%	N	%	N	%	N
% in Primary Groups												
Female	30	10*	70	10	73	11	46	13	56	25	70	17
Male	40	15	62	24	55	11	52	25	46	59	49	37
% with High Subscription to Inmate Code												
Female	36	11	45	11	33	12	61	13	72	25	65	18
Male	47	15	68	25	64	11	59	29	66	61	57	37

*Figures represent base N for the category on which the percent is based. Differences between totals for the two main classifications are due to missing data for one of the variables.

that the proportion of women who strongly subscribe to an inmate code is considerably greater for those with high than for those with low criminal orientations. Moreover, the level of inmate code adherence for women who are high in criminal orientation is actually greater than for the men, at all stages of the institutional career. Hence, it would appear that criminal orientation does have some influence on secondary forms of inmate organization—on the patterns of primary group formation among men and on the extent of symbiotic affiliation among women. Yet the overall impact of criminal orientation in determining the form and strength of inmate organization seems to be minimal.

SUMMARY

Differences in inmate organizational structures by sex have been examined in an institution where men and women are incarcerated under similar conditions. The data indicate small but consistent differences between the sexes with respect to form of inmate organization. The females show greater propensity to affiliate in primary groups while the men display greater tendencies toward integration into an overall symbiotic organization. This is consistent with previous research, but the magnitude of the differences suggests that, in this context at least, the influence of sex-linked factors is much less pervasive than might have been expected. The two types of inmate structure were found to be somewhat parallel for both sexes rather than mutually exclusive. For both males and females in the institution studied, primary group organization and symbiotic organization appear to exist side by side with one form slightly predominating in each context.

Synthetic cohort variations and partial panel data tend to confirm the theory of inmate organization as an institutional product. Examination of cohort patterns, controlling for criminal orientation, suggests that imported criminal subcultural patterns have minimal influence. Changes in behavioral and affiliational patterns over a four-month period of initial hospital experience for a panel of new arrivals also support a socialization or adaptational explanation. In general, the data seem to justify the conclusion that inmate organization is largely a response to institutional conditions.

Cumulative knowledge of inmate social behavior requires that four additional steps be taken. First, the proposition that inmate organization emerges as a response to deprivations of institutional living must be tested directly by examination of variations in the experience of deprivations as these relate to affiliation patterns. Second, it is essential that the process by which characteristics of individual inmates interact with institutional environments to produce patterns of affiliation in the inmate society be explicated. Third, some assessment of the impact of inmate organization on the correctional endeavor is essential. It is widely assumed that integration into an inmate society has long-range consequences for post-institutional career patterns and for accomplishment of institutional goals of an internal nature. Yet, data are sketchy on both points. Finally, it is important that inmate behavior be conceptualized within a broader theoretical context so as to have more general sociological relevance. Perhaps inmate behavior represents a subclass of subordinate behavior in general, with organizational manifestations similar in a wide range of environments.

REFERENCES

BERK, BERNARD B., 1966. "Organizational Goals and Inmate Organization," *American Journal of Sociology,* **71** (March) :522–34.

CLEMMER, DONALD, 1940. *The Prison Community.* Boston: Christopher Publishing Company.

CLINE, HUGH F., 1966. "The Determinants of Normative Patterns in Correctional Institutions." Unpublished paper read at the annual meeting of the American Sociological Association.

GARABEDIAN, PETER G., 1963. "Social Roles and Processes of Socialization in the Prison Community," *Social Problems,* **11** (Fall) :139–52.

GIALLOMBARDO, ROSE, 1966. *Society of Women: A Study of a Women's Prison.* New York: John Wiley and Sons.

GLASER, DANIEL, 1964. *The Effectiveness of a Prison and Parole System.* Indianapolis: Bobbs-Merrill Company.

GRUSKY, OSCAR, 1959. "Organizational Goals and the Behavior of Informal Leaders," *American Journal of Sociology,* **55** (July):59–67.

HALLECK, SEYMOUR L. and MARVIN HERSKO, 1962. "Homosexual Behavior in a Correctional Institution for Adolescent Girls," *American Journal of Orthopsychiatry,* **32** (October) :911–17.

HARRIS, SARA, 1967. *Hellhole.* New York: E. P. Dutton and Company.

IRWIN, JOHN and DONALD R. CRESSEY, 1962. "Thieves, Convicts and the Inmate Culture," *Social Problems,* **10** (Fall) :142–55.

KOSOFSKY, SIDNEY and ALBERT ELLIS, 1958. "Illegal Communication among Institutionalized Female Delinquents," *Journal of Social Psychology,* **48** (August) :155–60.

McCORKLE, LLOYD W. and RICHARD KORN, 1954. "Resocialization within Walls," *The Annals,* **293** (May) :88–98.

MORRIS, TERENCE and PAULINE MORRIS, 1953. *Pentonville: A Sociological Study of an English Prison.* London: Routledge and Kegan Paul.

ROEBUCK, JULIAN, 1963. "A Critique of 'Thieves, Convicts and the Inmate Culture'," *Social Problems,* **11** (Fall) :193–200.

SCHOOLER, CARMI, 1968. "A Note of Extreme Caution on the Use of Guttman Scales," *American Journal of Sociology,* **74** (November):296–301.

SCHRAG, CLARENCE, 1954. "Leadership among Prison Inmates," *American Sociological Review,* **19** (February) :37–42; 1961, "Some Foundations for a Theory of Correction," in Donald R. Cressey, ed., *The Prison: Studies in Institutional Organization and Change.* New York: Holt, Rinehart and Winston.

STREET, DAVID, ROBERT D. VINTER, and CHARLES PERROW, 1966. *Organization for Treatment.* New York: The Free Press.

SYKES, GRESHAM M., 1958. *Society of Captives.* Princeton: Princeton University Press.

SYKES, GRESHAM M. and SHELDON L. MESSINGER, 1960. "The Inmate Social System," in *Theoretical Studies in Social Organization of the Prison.* Social Science Research Council Pamphlet No. 15 (March) :5–19.

TAYLOR, A. J. W., 1965. "The Significance of 'Darls' or 'Special Relationships' for Borstal Girls," *British Journal of Criminology,* **5** (October) :406–18.

TITTLE, CHARLES R. and DROLLENE P. TITTLE, 1964. "Social Organization of Prisoners: An Empirical Test," *Social Forces,* **43** (December) :216–21.

WARD, DAVID A. and GENE G. KASSENBAUM, 1965.

Women's Prison: Sex and Social Structure. Chicago: Aldine Publishing Company.

WELLFORD, CHARLES, 1967. "Factors Associated with Adoption of the Inmate Code: A Study of Normative Socialization," *Journal of Criminal Law, Criminology and Police Science,* **58** (June) :197–203.

WHEELER, STANTON, 1961. "Socialization in Correctional Communities," *American Sociological Review,* **26** (October) :697–712.

WILSON, THOMAS P., 1968. "Patterns of Management and Adaptations to Organizational Roles: A Study of Prison Inmates," *American Journal of Sociology,* **74** (September) :146–57.

part four

THE IMPACT OF LAW IN SOCIETY: LAW AS INDEPENDENT

It bears repeating that the central issue in the sociology of law is the inter-relationship between law and other institutions, norms, and behavior in society. In Part Two the question of what forces shape the law was examined. In this part we return to the issue to consider law as an independent force in society.

Perhaps the clearest way to conceptualize the issues in the study of the impact of law on society is to refer again to the concept of law as a form of social control presented in Part One. As with any control system the law sets up some normative standards (usually proscribing but also prescribing or requiring something) and provides sanctions to promote compliance with that standard. In politically organized society there is an organizational apparatus or system for the application of sanctions and the implementation and interpretation of the law. There are secondary norms (both legislative and judicial) which set standards for the proper operation of this system and provide procedures for enhancing compliance to them by the administrative, judicial, and enforcement actors in the system.

Therefore, whether the intent is to undergird extant customs or introduce changes in them, the formal and authoritative promulgation of a legal norm and the application of sanctions to its breach are meant to bring conformity by individuals, groups, and organizations to the norms in the criminal law and legal policy related to the family, educational, economic, class, racial, and other systems in society. But, again, as with any social control system, current application of external sanctions is combined with socialization resulting in internalization of values and norms (hence self-regulation) to produce conformity. As a number of sociologists and legal scholars have pointed out, compliance with legal norms depends for the most part on socialization within primary and other groups outside of the specifically legal institution into values which are congruent with the normative expectations of the law. Thus, when referring to the impact of law as such, the discussion often revolves around the instrumental function of the threat and application of external legal sanctions; that is, how much is compliance based on legal sanctions apart from whatever compliance is produced by prior socialization? However, the incorporation of a norm into law and attaching sanctions to non-conformity with it are also felt by some to have "educative" impacts on beliefs, values, attitudes, and opinions; that is, they propose that law itself can socialize or persuade compliance as well as coerce it. The basic question, then, is whether and under what conditions law influences *behavior* and *attitudes*.

Jones (1966) has argued that there has been an overemphasis on law as dependent to the neglect of research "tracing the consequences of decisional outcomes within legal process upon values and institutions in society" (Jones, 1966:332). If this were ever true, it no longer is. Although conceptual and methodological problems remain (Wasby, 1970a; Levine, 1970), research strategies have been specified for doing such aptly named "legal impact studies" (Lempert, 1966). A body of research is accumulating, and theoretical perspectives have been presented, which attempt to establish when and under what conditions law can "not only *codify* existing customs, morals, or mores but also . . . modify the behavior and values presently existing in a particular society" (Evan, 1962:168, italics in original).

In this part we examine some of that literature dealing with the question of the law's effect on behavior and attitudes. The aim is not to review systematically the evidence which supports or contradicts particular theoretical perspectives; rather the purpose is to review (1) some historical and contemporary instances of the impact of law on social change and (2) the literature on the extent to which compliance to law is obtained through its socializing influence or threat of sanctions.

LAW AS AN INSTRUMENT OF SOCIAL CHANGE

There are abundant historical illustrations in which the enactment and implementation of law have been used more or less deliberately to engineer broad social changes in society. These show that while dramatic social changes have been brought about by legal changes, the law often fails in its intended purposes and some of the changes it does make in social structure and culture are clearly unintended.

For instance, it is clear that in spite of the Marxist–Leninist belief that law is an epiphenomenon of bourgeois class society destined to disappear with the fulfillment of the Communist Revolution, the Soviet Union has attempted to make wholesale changes in society by manipulation of the laws, courts, and other aspects of the legal system (Dror, 1968). A case in point is given by Massell (1968) in which legal rules and institutions were pressed into service after the Russian Revolution to replace the traditional Islamic socio–cultural system (specifically the marriage–family system and sex-role structure) in the central Asian societies with the new Soviet order. The effort proved, after several years, to be ineffective and produced a number of unintended consequences. Thus, the "cultural revolution" was halted (as was the modern one in China), and the emphasis shifted to a slower social rebuilding. Similarly, Connor (1972) reports that the Stalinist purges of 1936–1938 which subjugated the arrest and court processes toward the uncovering of political enemies did result in getting rid of some "subversives," but the major effect was the unanticipated one of a self-perpetuating witch-hunt resembling the witch-hunts in Renaissance Europe (Currie, 1968). The volume of identified deviants became so great that the physical limits of the system to confine them were reached. Another case of failure, or at least limited success, of changes in law to effect the desired changes in social structure comes from the modernization efforts in nineteenth century Japan. In spite of political and legal changes meant to break up the old feudal system of village communities, especially a series of laws designed to wrest control of primary education from the local village, feudalistic structures survived at least until World War II and still persist to some extent today (Chiba, 1968). These illustrations are selective, however, and there is no denying that dramatic transformations of Soviet and Japanese (as well as Chinese) societies have been brought about—by terroristic, economic, military, and political means to be sure, but also partly through changes in the legal structures.

In the United States significant efforts have been made in legislation and court decisions both to impede and promote political, economic, and educational equality for minorities; to promote adherence to Constitutional requirements and rights; and to control "morality" related to alcohol, drugs, gambling, and prostitution. (See the discussion in Part Two of "crimes without victims.") A survey of these efforts, too, demonstrates both success and failure in provoking societal change through the law.

C. Vann Woodward (1966) supports his view that legal policies can change patterns of race relations by tracing the history of Jim Crow laws in the southern United States. It is his contention that while law sometimes merely registers what has already been sanctioned by custom, far from being simply the inevitable outgrowth of the deeply ingrained racial attitudes and practices of the South, the Jim Crow laws represented only one of several prevalent attitudes in the late nineteenth-century South. Once enacted, however, they gave legitimacy to that position and wrought changes in segregationist attitudes and behavior. There was noticeably more public support in deed and word for segregation of black and white after the passage of the laws than there was before that. The legislation "gave free rein and the majesty of the law to mass aggression that might otherwise have been curbed, blunted, or deflected."

> [Negroes'] presence on trains upon equal terms with white men was once regarded in some states as normal, acceptable, and unobjectionable . . . Later on the stateways apparently changed the folkways . . . for the partitions and Jim Crow cars became universal. And the new seating arrangement came to be seen as normal, unchangeable, and inevitable as the old ways" [Woodward, 1966:108].

However much the law simply reflected prevailing segregationist mores it is clear from Woodward's analysis that the structure of racial segregation in residences, schools, public accommodations, and in other areas of social interaction was very much a product of law. Even when not specifically required by law, the racist practices and attitudes were given aid and comfort by legislation and Supreme Court decisions.

At least since the landmark 1954 decision of the United States Supreme Court in *Brown vs. Board of Education of Topeka,* judicial decisions and both federal and state legislation have moved away from support for segregation and toward equal protection of rights regardless of race and integration. Apparently, the result has not been as dramatic as when law supported segregation. The law has had effect; actual practice and attitudes have moved in the direction required by law, but slowly, with much resistance, backtracking, and evasion.

Ten years after *Brown vs. Board of Education,* one-fourth of the school districts in the South had ended *de jure* segregation, and about one out of ten Negro pupils was going to school with white pupils (Knoll, 1967). Moreover, racist attitudes among whites began to decline with further legislated and court-ordered equality and integration. By the mid-1960s, the majority of white Americans favored integration and believed in the equal ability of black Americans. White endorsement of school integration in the North went from 40 percent in 1942 to 50 percent by 1956 to 60 percent by 1964. In the South, only 2 percent of the white population favored racially integrated education in 1942; by 1956 this had risen to 14 percent and by 1964 to 30 percent (Hyman and Sheatsley, 1970).

> If there ever had been a doubt—except as a false rationalization for real opposition—that a United States Supreme Court decision can change social behavior and social institutions, the implementation undertaken by the federal courts of the *Brown vs. Board of Education* decision of 1954, should have dispelled it quickly. Throughout the Southern and Border states, where until 1954 the schools were segregated by state law, desegregation is going on apace. The miracle is not only 15% of the Negro children by 1966 were attending desegregated schools, but that practically every school district, even in the deep southern states . . . had set up some facility for desegregation . . . [Rose, 1967:126].

Nevertheless, while segregation as an overt public policy of the states and localities has virtually disappeared, other segregation, which subsequent legislation such as the 1964 Civil Rights Act was intended to overcome, has been more resistant to change. Case studies of the efforts in eight communities to decrease racial imbalances and implement desegregation programs showed mixed results—three were successful, three unsuccessful, and two partially successful (Schwartz, 1967). Resistance to court-ordered bussing to achieve racial balance within a community's schools was quite apparent in the results of polls and the presidential primaries in 1972, and it remains to be seen whether racial balance can be legally forced. But the ability of the law to produce changes in segregation practices and attitudes must be separated from the ability of these changes to work toward the achievement of some more ultimate goal. Thus, whether or not integrated education can in fact do away with the inequalities in opportunities and performance documented in the Coleman report (Coleman et al., 1966) remains to be seen. The evidence is clear that the surest way to make the school performance of black children equal to that of whites is to have them in racially balanced schools (Rose, 1967:139), but that is not relevant to the question of whether or not the law can produce that racial balance in the first place. Likewise, federal law in the "war on poverty" has been successful in instituting educational, employment, and job training programs. The failure of these programs to make any real difference in employment indicates that the programs did not work (Rossi and Williams, 1972); it says nothing about the effectiveness of the law requiring that they be started in the first place.

On balance, then, the law has made some difference for behavior and attitudes in race relations. But the continuing pattern of *de facto* segregation, patterned evasion of legal policies, inequality of blacks, other minorities, and women, and white racism and the unanticipated growth of separatism and racist attitudes among some blacks in spite of forceful legislation and court decisions to the contrary argues that the impact of modern civil rights policies has not come near the almost total acceptability and compliance that the earlier segregation laws had.

Other judicial decisions have met with much the same mixed response as have the decisions related to desegregation and race relations. According to a study in one state, some five years after the decision there was virtually no compliance with the Supreme Court's rulings on prayers in public schools (Dolbeare and Hammond, 1971). But according to a national survey of elementary school teachers, three years after the decision there were significant reductions in prayers and bible readings in the classroom (Way, 1970). Of three juvenile courts studied (in three different large cities) up to about six months after the Supreme Court's *Gault* decision, only one adhered to any substantial degree to the *Gault* requirements that juveniles coming before the juvenile courts must be assured of their rights to counsel, confrontation of witnesses, and protection against self-incrimination. And that court had been essentially upholding these rights prior to *Gault* (Lefstein et al., 1969). On the other hand, improvements in compliance of police and court practices took place in all states following the *Mapp* decision on the exclusion of illegally seized evidence, and the greater changes occurred in those states which had not previously had such a rule (Nagel, 1965). Also, although there were no measures of behavioral compliance, the police in four cities in Wisconsin responded correctly to questions about the requirements regarding obtaining confessions set forth in the *Miranda* decision (Milner, 1970).

As this review of some Supreme Court decisions makes clear, compliance with decisions of the highest court in the nation is by no means certain. Wasby (1970b) suggests that the extent of compliance with the law as contained in judgments rendered by the Supreme Court depends on a number of variables, including, among others, the relative political and social power of those to whom the decision is addressed, beliefs of the population affected, the process by which decisions are communicated to the public, and features of the decision-making process of the court itself.

The well-known failure of prohibition of alcohol through constitutional amendment and legislation to produce a truly "dry" society or to keep most people from drinking comes most readily to mind as an example of the ineffectiveness of law to bring about social change in public "morals." It would appear that law is faced with a similar failure in the prohibition of several kinds of drugs, especially marihuana. In fact, the marihuana laws have been called the "new prohibition" to underscore the similarity to alcohol prohibition in the futility of legal control of consumption of these substances (Kaplan, 1971).

It is true that there has been in the last decade a dramatic increase in the use of marihuana and other drugs (resembling the "epidemic" of drug use following World War II) in spite of long-standing stringent laws against them. On the other hand, it should be noted that the legal prohibition of heroin and control of other opiates has not only effectively curtailed heroin use, but has also changed public attitudes toward addicts. The rate of opiate addiction in the United States prior to the first enactment and enforcement of federal and state laws was several times greater than it has been at any time since. Drug policy effectively shifted public sentiment from a tolerant attitude toward addiction to intolerance and a view of the addict as a depraved criminal. There also occurred a shift in the social characteristics of addicts following the enactment of legal control. Also, the later legal prohibition of marihuana played a significant role in developing the widespread belief in the dangers of marihuana (Lindesmith, 1967; Lindesmith and Gagnon, 1964; Duster, 1970).

The reduction in use of drugs was one purpose accomplished by law, at least at one time. The increase in drug use after World War II and again in the last decade indicates that the law has not continued to be effective in achieving its desired ends. The shifts in public opinion and social characteristics of users probably were not intended by those who enacted and enforced the laws. Other outcomes almost surely were not anticipated. For instance, the prohibition of certain goods and services for which there remains a relatively inelastic demand acts as a "crime tariff." This sets up monopoly conditions for organized criminal groups who enter the illicit market to supply the demand and artificially inflates the prices and profits which make them willing to run the risks (Packer, 1968). Some (e.g., addicts) for whom the commodity (e.g., drugs) becomes necessary at almost any price are induced to engage in a range of income-producing crimes to meet the prices artificially inflated by the crime tariff (O'Donnell, 1966). Also, the enforcement of laws forbidding these and other "crimes without victims" (Schur, 1965) interferes with the ability of the police, the courts, and correctional organizations to enforce the laws against property and violent crimes with victims (Morris and Hawkins, 1970). Finally, there is a whole body of literature which argues that the very fact of exercising control over individuals by publicly stigmatizing them with a criminal label (whether for victimless offenses or for crimes with victims) may simply stabilize deviant careers and promote further law violation (See Lemert, 1972; Becker, 1964; Schur, 1965). There is, however, a scarcity of research evidence supporting this view.

The point is that in addition to whatever change in the intended direction is made by law, there are apt to be other unforeseen and unwanted consequences. As Rose notes, attempts to solve social problems with law often "transform the social problems in some unanticipated way; in so doing they often create new social problems" (1968:35). When this occurs the law is still causing social changes: they just are not the ones intended.

This brief review of some of the intended and unintended consequences of law for social change has been primarily discursive; no attempt has been made to offer a coherent framework for summarizing the major variables determining when law will be an effective instrument of social change. The first article reprinted in this part by Zimring and Hawkins (1968) is presented as one notable effort to provide such a framework. Their view is that the effectiveness of social change through law depends upon variables in the custom to be changed, the social characteristics of the groups whose norms are challenged by the law, and variations in the enforcement of the law.

An earlier statement by Evan (1962) lays down seven conditions for law as an effective impetus for social change: (1) The law must emanate from an authoritative and prestigeful source; (2) the law must present its rationale in terms which are understandable and compatible with existing values; (3) the proponents of the change should make reference to other communities or countries with which the population identifies and where the law is already in effect; (4) the enforcement of the law must be aimed toward making the change in a relatively short time; (5) those enforcing the law must themselves be very much committed to the change intended by the law; (6) the implementation of the law should include positive as well as negative sanctions, and (7) the enforcement of the law should be reasonable not only in terms of the sanctions used but also in the protection of the rights of those who stand to lose by violation of the law (Evan, 1962:171–74).

DETERRENCE, COMPLIANCE, AND LEGAL SANCTIONS: COERCION AND PERSUASION TO VIRTUE

The foregoing has emphasized the capacity of legislation, law enforcement, and judicial decisions to support or induce social changes in the behavior and attitudes of both the general population and officials in the legal and political systems. We turn now to a more specific consideration of the bases on which behavioral and normative compliance with the law (whether or not it represents change) is secured.

The idea that the citizenry conforms to the law because of fear of the legal punishment which would follow violation is an old one, going back at least to the "Classical School" of criminology. The classical criminologists maintained that the proper function of penal sanctions was to deter crime both by directly punishing offenders and serving as threatening examples to potential offenders—"special" or specific deterrence of those actually punished and "general" deterrence of those who have not been directly punished. (Zimring, 1971:2) Men were assumed to be rational, calculating ahead of time the probable pain and pleasure to be derived from acts. Thus the law must provide actual or threatened punishment so that when taken into account in the rational calculus, it would offset the probable gain from violation and thereby prevent further violations. To do this the punishment provided must not only be just severe enough to overcome the potential reward of a specific crime ("let the punishment fit the crime"); it must also be applied swiftly, and surely—severity, celerity, and certainty of punishment (Vold, 1958). Although our criminal justice system is still very much predicated upon these classical assumptions, attention to whether or not legal punishment in fact operated severely, swiftly, and certainly enough to have the intended impact was rare until fairly recently. As a number of writers have pointed out, even most of the scholarly discussions tended to revolve around the humanitarian and moral implications of punishment (Ball, 1965; Toby, 1964).

Modern research on the question began with the study of the relationship between capital punishment and homicide rates. The usual finding was that the existence of the death penalty had no effect on the rate of homicide. (See the collection of studies dating back to about two decades ago in Bedau, 1964; Sellin, 1959.) [1] For some time this was taken as the basis for the general statement that punishment does not deter law violation. Subsequently, however, researchers have devised measures of severity and certainty of punishment (although so far not of celerity of punishment) and tested their deterrent impact on various types of offenses and offenders. The question then has become not "Does punishment in general deter crime in general?" but rather

---

[1] Thus, the declaration by the Supreme Court in *Furman vs. Georgia,* 1972, that capital punishment is unconstitutional, even if it is not bypassed by new state legislation and results in the total abolition of the death penalty in the United States, is not likely to make much difference in the homicide rate.

"What kinds and aspects of punishment have what effect on what kinds of offenses and actual or potential offenders?" (See Zimring, 1971, for the most general discussion.)

Gibbs (1968) measured the association between the official homicide rate (the FBI Uniform Crime Reports rate of "crimes known to the police") and the severity (a median length of prison terms for homicide) and certainty (proportion of known homicides resulting in prison sentence) of punishment. He found a fairly strong tendency for reduced homicide rates to accompany high certainty of punishment; to a lesser extent the homicide rate was also negatively related to severity of punishment. Tittle (1969) extended this type of analysis to all seven of the FBI Uniform Crime Reports "Major Index Crimes" (homicide, assault, rape, burglary, larceny, robbery, and auto theft). His findings on homicide agree with Gibbs', but he found that the rate of the other offenses was affected only by the certainty, not the severity, of imprisonment. This seemed to support the contention that the probability of being caught and punished has a greater impact on the rate of the major criminal offenses than does the severity of the punishment actually meted out. However, later research by Chiricos and Waldo (1970) raised doubts as to whether either the risk or severity of punishment has any demonstrable effect on crime rates. They traced the changes in crime rates following changes in certainty and severity of punishment for the same offenses studied by Tittle and discovered no consistent tendency for either more certain or more severe penalties to reduce crime.

Increases in the number of policemen, law enforcement budgets, the clearance rate (number of reported crimes "solved" by police arrests), and other features of law enforcement efforts can also be viewed as measures of the extent to which legal sanctions will in fact be applied to offenders. By these measures, increased control efforts do not have an appreciable impact on the rate of serious crimes (Wellford, 1972); the recorded rates of minor offenses, in fact, tend to go up with the deployment of more policemen (McDonald, 1969). Certain features of control policy do, however, seem to have an effect on some major crimes. For instance, enforced legislation restricting gun ownership among the population *does* lower the number of guns in private possession, a fact which in turn reduces homicides among white citizens (but not among black citizens) (Seitz, 1972). An armed police force also appears to make for more killing and wounding of citizens by the police and of police by citizens than does a similar, but unarmed, police force (Hawkins and Ward, 1970).

The deterrent effect of legal sanctions has also been investigated with regard to minor offenses and rule violations. Chambliss (1966) reported significant improvement in compliance with campus parking regulations after a police policy change which produced more certain and severe penalties for violations. Those who had complied with regulations or only infrequently violated them before the change continued to do so, and nearly all of those who had been frequent violators either began to comply completely with the parking rules or reduced their violations to infrequent intervals. A careful "quasi-experimental" analysis of driving behavior following a "crackdown on speeding" (step-up in stopping, issuing citations, and arresting) in Connecticut indicated that, although other factors accounted for much of the variation, the increased certainty of apprehension and sanction did decrease speeding on the highways (Campbell and Ross, 1968). Drivers stop at an intersection marked with a stop sign apparently more from fear of collision with other cars than from fear of legal penalties or respect for the law, for while they will always stop for cross traffic, only a few make a full stop in the absence of cross traffic (although most will make a "rolling stop") (Feest, 1968). Mechanical deterrence of the illegal use of slugs in parking meters (by installing a slug rejector device in the meters) is quite effective; threatening fines and imprisonment (by labeling the meters with warnings of the penalties attached to slug use) is not (Decker, 1972).

Ball and Friedman (1965) conclude that fines are effective deterrents to "profit-making" violations of legislation regulating economic behavior because they reduce the profit which the violation was meant to bring and they also conclude that criminal prosecution of businessmen and professionals is effective in controlling their "economic" crimes. The evidence that such legal sanctions are effective in controlling white-collar crime and adherence to economic regulations is not conclusive. Most of the landlords in Ball's (1960) study of rent control violations did comply with the rent regulations, and Schwartz and Orleans (1967) report that groups threatened with penalties increased compliance with tax laws on reporting income from interest compared with an unthreatened group (but complied less than the group to whom "conscience appeals" were made). However, Stigler (1966) concludes that while the enforcement of the Sherman Anti-Trust Act has reduced collusion in fixing prices, it has had only a marginal effect on monopolistic corporate concentration.

Others have also suggested that the more the behavior is economically rational, the more readily affected by law or deterred by criminal sanctions it is. For instance, Dror (1968), citing cases from Japan, Turkey, Soviet Union, and Israel, maintains that new laws can effectively change "instrumental" activities such as business activity but that "expressive" customs such as marriage and family institutions cannot be changed very much or very fast by law. Similarly, Chambliss (1967) argues that instrumental crimes committed by those with low commitment to a criminal way of life (e.g., the nonprofessional shoplifter, white-collar criminal) are the most deterrable while expressive crimes by those with high commitment to their way of life (e.g., most drug addicts, sex offenders) are the least deterrable by the threat of criminal sanctions.

The attention to the severity and certainty of penal sanctions does not mean that the researchers accept the assumption of the classical criminologists that men rationally calculate the coercive sanctions as pain weighted against the pleasure to be gained from an act (although some recent statements such as

Freeley's [1970] do accept this assumption). Rather as Zimring (1971:3) says, they "have recognized the plausibility of the notion that people might refrain from crime specifically to avoid unpleasantness, while discarding the image of the super-rational potential criminal that used to accompany the theory." Thus, while eschewing a completely rational model of man, much of the research on the deterrent effects of legal sanctions is based on the underlying assumption that the affected population has some perception of how severe the penalties are and what the risk of being punished is and that it behaves on the basis of that awareness, whether or not it is an accurate assessment of the real severity and probability of sanction.

Direct tests of the extent to which persons act in accordance with such perceptions, however, have been rare. Claster (1967) found no difference between a delinquent and non-delinquent sample of adolescents in perceptions of the general risk of apprehension for delinquent behavior; but the delinquents perceived less and the non-delinquents perceived more risk for themselves. Jensen (1969) also found a negative relationship between the belief that there is a high risk of law-breakers being caught and punished and self-reported delinquency. Jensen concluded, however, that this belief is a "misunderstanding" held mainly by younger adolescents, and faith in it declines with age. Indeed, a generalized belief in the benign efficacy of law and favorable attitude toward law as something to be obeyed seems to be characteristic of young adolescents in the United States, England, and Germany. Later more skeptical and more realistic views of the law develop (Adelson and Beal, 1970). It may be then that a firm belief that the chances of being caught and punished for wrongdoing is a somewhat childish view which loses its deterrent force with increasing age. The most systematic research into the question in an adult (but nonrepresentative) population is that by Waldo and Chiricos (1972), whose report is reprinted here as the second selection in this part. They find that certain perceptions of risk do not lose their deterrent effect. Reported involvement in either marihuana use or theft are not forestalled by perceptions of severe penalties, but the belief that one runs a high risk of apprehension and punishment does tend to keep him from using marihuana and, to a lesser extent, from stealing.

It is widely assumed in the literature, however, that for most people conformity to the law depends less upon the actual or perceived threat of negative legal sanctions and more upon prior socialization into the values incorporated into the law (Toby, 1964; Zimring and Hawkins, 1968; Tapp and Levine, 1970; Andenaes, 1971). People obey the law only in part, if at all, because they fear the penal sanctions; they obey primarily because they believe that what is called for by law is right or that the behavior prohibited by law is wrong anyway. From this point of view compliance is greatest when the informal norms are in consensus with the law, and the probable penalties attached to law violation play a predominant part in securing conformity only for those who are in opposition to or morally neutral toward the law.

There is some empirical support for these contentions. For instance,

Schwartz and Orleans (1967) found that an appeal to conscience produced even more compliance in income reporting than the threat of sanctions. Salem and Bowers (1970) report that deviant behavior among college students (alcohol use, stealing library books, cheating, etc.) tended to decrease as the severity of the sanctions imposed increased, but that conformity was greatest where the sanctions were congruent with an informal normative context which strongly disapproved of such behavior. Waldo and Chiricos (1972) report that the perception of risk of criminal penalties is important in deterring marihuana usage which, in the population studied, was not viewed as intrinsically bad. On the other hand, considerations of risk were less important in deterring theft which was viewed as wrong even if it were not outlawed; presumably, prior socialization would lead the individuals to refrain from stealing, aside from whatever chance there might be of being caught and punished.

Several writers contend, however, that even if those toward whom the law is directed are initially opposed or neutral to it, the law can change their attitudes so that they come to agree with the law as right. The evidence that law can have this "educative" effect is mixed. In the third article reprinted in this part, Colombotos (1969) presents persuasive evidence that legislation can directly induce a change of attitudes; there was a notable increase in the proportion of physicians favorably disposed toward the idea of Medicare after the enactment of the federal law. The research by Walker and Argyle (1964) and Berkowitz and Walker (1967), reported in the last article reprinted here, however, indicates that knowledge of peer agreement with a moral judgment is more likely to increase the amount of agreement with it than is the knowledge that it has been made a part of law.

But in so far as law does have a persuasive or socializing impact it may do so by first gaining behavioral compliance. As Sumner (1906:61) said, men can be made to perform *prescribed acts*, "ritual," without having the *prescribed thoughts*. This behavioral compliance may come from the general belief that the law ought to be obeyed even if one disagrees with it (Andenaes, 1971:20), or it may simply be coerced by the threat of punishment. But by whatever means, it is true that people often comply with the law in spite of their disagreement with it and the feeling that it is unfair (Ball, 1960). After a while, however, what *is* may become what *ought to be*. The application of sanctions may induce "a sense of moral obligation" or "moralistic attitude toward compliance" (Schwartz and Orleans, 1967) or in a number of other ways influence internalized concepts of right and wrong (Zimring, 1971:4–6). Eventually, the requirement that people behave in a certain way may change their attitudes so that they come to believe that it is the right and proper thing to do (Evan, 1962; Schur, 1968:135–37). Then the rightness or wrongness of the values supported by law may be passed along through the generations without regard to their legal status so that they become incorporated into the behavior patterns and attitudes of the population which comes to act and believe in accordance with the law or without awareness of what legal policy has to say on the matter. It may take some time, then, for the moral suasion of the law to achieve salience in the lives of individuals, but once that has occurred it is part of the general socialization process.

In summary, compliance with the law has been explained by reference to one or more of the following: (1) Law violation is deterred by the actual or perceived risk and severity of legal penalties; (2) those governed by the law in question comply with it because they agree with its normative content, that is, the conception of what is right or wrong embodied in it. This may come about in two ways: (a) Previous socialization in one's social groups leads one to adhere to the values even if they were not in the law; and (b) through the existing legitimacy accorded the law and the application of sanctions people come to believe in the rightness of the legal norm. (3) Compliance comes from the belief that the law should be obeyed, even if one disagrees with its content or is unconcerned about the penalties attached to a violation. Ultimately, compliance with law is produced by the cumulative effect of socialization (including that accomplished by the law) and legal sanctions. This point is succinctly made by Zimring and Hawkins (1971) in the first selection in this part:

> Thus, knowledge of the law prohibiting burglary is preceded in the socialization process by messages about the wrongness of stealing and home invasion. By the time a citizen reaches adulthood, he has monitored a consistent stream of messages about burglary—messages which, with the specific legal threat, form a network of restraining influences probably stronger than the sum of its separate components [Zimring and Hawkins, 1971:36].

REFERENCES

ADELSON, JOSEPH and LYNETTE BEAL, 1970. "Adolescent Perspectives on Law and Government," *Law and Society Review,* 4 (May):495–504.

ANDENAES, JOHANNES, 1971. "The Moral or Educative Influence of Criminal Law," *Journal of Social Issues,* 24 (2):17–31.

BALL, HARRY V., 1960. "Social Structure and Rent Control Violations," *American Journal of Sociology,* 65 (May):598–604.

BALL, HARRY V. and LAWRENCE FRIEDMAN, 1965. "The Uses of Criminal Sanctions in the Enforcement of Economic Legislation: A Sociological View," *Stanford Law Review,* 17 (January):197–223.

BALL, JOHN C., 1955. "The Deterrent Concept in Criminology and the Law," *Journal of Criminal Law, Criminology, and Police Science,* 46 (September–October):349–54.

BECKER, HOWARD S., ed., 1964. *The Other Side.* Glencoe: The Free Press.

BEDAU, HUGO A., ed., 1964. *The Death Penalty in America.* Garden City, N.Y.: Anchor Books.

BERKOWITZ, LEONARD and NIGEL WALKER, 1967. "Laws and Moral Judgements," *Sociometry,* 40 (December):419–22.

CAMPBELL, DONALD T. and H. LAURENCE ROSS, 1968. "The Connecticut Crackdown on Speeding: Time-series Data in Quasi-experimental Analysis," *Law and Society Review,* 3 (August):33–54.

CHAMBLISS, WILLIAM J., 1966. "The Deterrent Influence of Punishment," *Crime and Delinquency*, **12** (January):70–75; 1967, "Types of Deviance and the Effectiveness of Legal Sanctions," *Wisconsin Law Review* (Summer):703–19.

CHIBA, MASAJI, 1968. "Relations between the School District System and the Feudalistic Village Community in Nineteenth-Century Japan: A Study of the Effect of Law upon Society," *Law and Society Review*, **2** (February):229–40.

CHIRICOS, THEODORE G. and GORDON P. WALDO, 1970. "Punishment and Crime: An Examination of Some Empirical Evidence," *Social Problems*, **18** (Fall):200–17.

CLASTER, DANIEL S., 1967. "Comparison of Risk Perception between Delinquents and Non-Delinquents," *Journal of Criminal Law, Criminology, and Police Science*, **58** (March):80:86.

COLEMAN, JAMES S., ERNEST Q. CAMPBELL, C. F. HOBSON, *et al.*, 1966. *Equality of Educational Opportunity*. Washington, D.C.: U.S. Government Printing Office.

COLOMBOTOS, JOHN, 1969. "Physicians and Medicare: A Before-After Study of the Effects of Legislation on Attitudes," *American Sociological Review*, **34** (June):318–34.

CONNOR, WALTER D., 1972. "The Manufacture of Deviance: The Case of the Soviet Purge, 1936–1938," *American Sociological Review*, **37** (August):403–13.

CURRIE, ELLIOT P., 1968. "Crimes without Criminals: Witchcraft and Its Control in Renaissance Europe," *Law and Society Review*, **3** (August):7–32.

DECKER, JOHN F., 1972. "Curbside Deterrence? An Analysis of the Effect of a Slug-Rejector Device, Coin-View Window, and Warning Labels on Slug Usage in New York City Parking Meters," *Criminology*, **10** (August):127–42.

DOLBEARE, KENNETH M. and PHILLIP E. HAMMOND, 1971. *The School Prayer Decisions*. Chicago: University of Chicago Press.

DROR, YEHEZKEL, 1968. "Law and Social Change," in Rita James Simon, ed., *The Sociology of Law*, San Francisco: Chandler Publishing Co.

DUSTER, TROY, 1970. *The Legislation of Morality*. New York: Free Press.

EVAN, WILLIAM M., 1962. "Law as an Instrument of Social Change," *Estudies de Sociologia*, **2** (August):167–76.

FEEST, JOHANNES, 1968. "Compliance with Legal Regulations: Observation of Stop Sign Behavior," *Law and Society Review*, **2** (May):447–61.

FREELEY, MALCOLM, 1970. "Coercion and Compliance," *Law and Society Review*, **4** (May):505–19.

GIBBS, JACK P., 1968. "Crime, Punishment, and Deterrence," *Southwestern Social Science Quarterly*, **48** (March):515–30.

HAWKINS, GORDON and PAUL WARD, 1970. "Armed and Disarmed Police: Police Firearms Policy and Levels of Violence," *Journal of Research in Crime and Delinquency*, **7** (July):188–97.

HYMAN, HERBERT H. and PAUL B. SHEATSLEY, 1970 (originally 1964). "Attitudes toward Desegregation," in Richard D. Schwartz and Jerome H. Skolnick, eds., *Society and the Legal Order*, New York: Basic Books, 487–96.

JENSEN, GARY F., 1969. " 'Crime Doesn't Pay': Correlates of a Shared Misunderstanding," *Social Problems*, **17** (Fall):189–201.

JONES, ERNEST M., 1966. "Impact Research and Sociology of Law: Some Tentative Proposals," *Wisconsin Law Review* (Spring):331–39.

KAPLAN, JOHN, 1971. *Marihuana: The New Prohibition*. New York: Pocket Books.

KNOLL, ERWIN, 1967. "Ten Years of Deliberate Speed," in Harry Gold and Frank R. Scarpitti, eds., *Combating Social Problems*. New York: Holt, Rinehart and Winston.

LEFSTEIN, NORMAN, VAUGHAN STAPLETON, and LEE TEITELBAUM, 1969. "In Search of Juvenile Justice: *Gault* and Its Implementation." *Law and Society Review*, **3** (May):491–562.

LEMERT, EDWIN M., 1972. *Human Deviance, Social Problems, and Social Control.* Englewood Cliffs, N.J.: Prentice-Hall.

LEMPERT, RICHARD, 1966. "Strategies of Research Design in the Legal Study: The Control of Rival Hypotheses," *Law and Society Review,* 1 (November):111–32.

LEVINE, JAMES P., 1970. "Methodological Concerns in Studying Supreme Court Efficacy," *Law and Society Review,* 4 (May):583:607.

LINDESMITH, ALFRED, 1967. *The Addict and the Law.* New York: Vintage Books.

LINDESMITH, ALFRED and JOHN GAGNON, 1964. "Anomie and Drug Addiction," in Marshall B. Clinard, ed., *Anomie and Deviant Behavior.* New York: Free Press.

MASSELL, GREGORY J., 1968. "Law as an Instrument of Revolutionary Change in a Traditional Milieu: The Case of Soviet Central Asia," *Law and Society Review,* 2 (February):179–228.

McDONALD, LYNN, 1969. "Crime and Punishment in Canada: A Statistical Test of the Conventional Wisdom," *Canadian Review of Sociology and Anthropology,* 6 (November):212–36.

MILNER, NEAL, 1970. "Comparative Analysis of Patterns of Compliance with Supreme Court Decisions: Miranda and the Police in Four Communities," *Law and Society Review,* 5 (August):119–34.

MORRIS, NORVAL and GORDON HAWKINS, 1970. *The Honest Politician's Guide to Crime Control.* Chicago: University of Chicago Press.

NAGEL, STUART S., 1965. "Testing the Effects of Excluding Illegally Seized Evidence," *Wisconsin Law Review* (Spring):283–310.

O'DONNELL, JOHN A., 1966. "Narcotic Addiction and Crime," *Social Problems,* 15 (Summer):73–84.

PACKER, HERBERT L., 1968. *The Limits of the Criminal Sanction.* Stanford, California: Stanford University Press.

ROSE, ARNOLD M., 1967. "School Desegregation: A Sociologist's View," *Law and Society Review,* 2 (November):125–40; 1968. "Law and the Causation of Social Problems," *Social Problems,* 16 (Summer):33–43.

ROSSI, PETER H. and WALTER WILLIAMS, 1972. *Evaluating Social Programs: Theory, Practice, and Politics.* New York: Seminar Press.

SALEM, RICHARD G. and BOWERS, WILLIAM J., 1970. "Severity of Formal Sanctions as a Deterrent to Deviant Behavior," *Law and Society Review,* 5 (August):21–40.

SCHUR, EDWIN M., 1965. *Crimes Without Victims.* Englewood Cliffs, N.J.: Prentice-Hall; 1968. *Law and Society.* New York: Random House.

SCHWARTZ, RICHARD D., ed., 1967. "Affirmative Integration: Studies of Efforts to Overcome de facto Segregation in the Public Schools," *Law and Society Review, special issue* 2 (November).

SCHWARTZ, RICHARD D. and SONYA ORLEANS, 1967. "On Legal Sanctions," *University of Chicago Law Review,* 34 (Winter):274–300.

SEITZ, STEVEN T., 1972. "Firearms, Homicides, and Gun Control Effectiveness," *Law and Society Review,* 6 (May):595–613.

SELLIN, THORSTEN, 1959. *The Death Penalty.* Philadelphia: American Law Institute.

STIGLER, GEORGE, 1966. "Economic Effects of the Anti-Trust Laws," *Journal of Law and Economics,* 9:225–30.

SUMNER, WILLIAM GRAHAM, 1906. *Folkways.* Boston: Ginn and Co.

TAPP, JUNE L., Issue Editor, 1971. "Socialization, the Law, and Society." *The Journal of Social Issues* 27 (2).

TAPP, JUNE L. and FELICE J. LEVINE, 1970. "Persuasion to Virtue: A Preliminary Statement," *Law and Society Review,* 4 (May):565–82.

TITTLE, CHARLES, 1969. "Crime Rates and Legal Sanctions," *Social Problems,* 16 (Spring):409–22.

TOBY, JACKSON, 1964. "Is Punishment Necessary?" *Journal of Criminal Law, Criminology, and Police Science,* 55 (September):332–37.

VOLD, GEORGE, 1958. *Theoretical Criminology*. New York: Oxford University Press.

WALDO, GORDON P. and THEODORE G. CHIRICOS, 1972. "Perceived Penal Sanction and Self-Reported Criminality: A Neglected Approach to Deterrence Research," *Social Problems*, **19** (Spring):522–40.

WALKER, NIGEL and MICHAEL ARGYLE, 1964. "Does the Law Affect Moral Judgments," *British Journal of Criminology*, **4** (October):570–81.

WASBY, STEPHEN L., 1970a. "The Supreme Court's Impact: Some Problems of Conceptualization and Measurement," *Law and Society Review*, **5** (August):41–60; 1970b. *The Impact of the United States Supreme Court*. Homewood, Ill.: Dorsey.

WAY, FRANK H., 1970. "The Impact of Supreme Court Decisions on Religious Practices in Public Schools," in Richard D. Schwartz and Jerome H. Skolnick, eds., *Society and Legal Order*. New York: Basic Books.

WELLFORD, CHARLES, 1972. "Crime and the Police: A Multivariate Analysis." Unpublished manuscript.

WOODWARD, C. VANN, 1966. *The Strange Career of Jim Crow*, second revised ed. New York: Oxford University Press.

ZIMRING, FRANKLIN E., 1971. "Perspectives on Deterrence," NIMH Monograph Series on. Crime and Delinquency Issues. Washington, D.C.: U.S. Government Printing Office.

ZIMRING, FRANK and GORDON HAWKINS, 1968. "Deterrence and Marginal Groups," *Journal of Research in Crime and Delinquency*, **5** (July):100–115.

ZIMRING, FRANKLIN and GORDON HAWKINS, 1971. "The Legal Threat as an Instrument of Social Change," *Journal of Social Issues*, **27** (2):33–48.

THE LEGAL THREAT AS AN INSTRUMENT
OF SOCIAL CHANGE

Franklin Zimring and Gordon Hawkins

LAW AND BEHAVIOR

There exist two contrasting views on the relationship between legal precepts and public attitudes and behaviour. According to the one, law is determined by the sense of justice and moral sentiments of the population, and legislation can only achieve results by staying relatively close to prevailing social norms. According to the other view law and especially legislation is a vehicle through which programmed social evolution can be brought about [Aubert, 1969, p. 69].

At one extreme then is the view expressed in Dicey's lectures (1905) at Harvard Law School in 1896 and a few years later in Sumner's celebrated pioneer study (1906): Law is a dependent variable determined and shaped by current mores and the opinion of society. At the other extreme, the view is exemplified by Soviet jurists like Kechekyan (1956) who see the law as an instrument for social engineering. It is also true, as Aubert (1969) points out that some sociologists "try, in a limited way, to confront the two views and determine the conditions under which the law may change social relationships [p. 69]." Yet none of those who have addressed themselves to this problem appear to have made any systematic attempt to consider the factors which militate for and against the success of law to induce change in customary behavior. This is not to say that no attempt has been made to take account of the variables which determine the effectiveness of law as a means to socialize change. The truth is rather that such attention has been limited to the significance of particular variables in spe-

cific situations. Thus Aubert (1966) in his study of the Norwegian Housemaid Law of 1948 emphasizes the importance of the level of information and the process of communicating norms. Goreck (1966) has drawn attention to the way in which such conditions as the socio-economic structure of the Polish rural areas and social pressures of a customary and religious nature have prevented the realization of the legislative aim of the Polish divorce rules. Dror (1959) has commented on the failure of law to change family life and marriage habits in Turkey and Israel. Indeed on the basis of the Israeli and Turkish experience he formulates a "basic hypothesis" to the effect that "changes in law have more effect on emotionally neutral and instrumental areas of activity than on expressive and evaluative areas of activity [Dror, 1959, p. 801]. Yet while it is conceivable that such an hypothesis—though the distinction between "instrumental" and "expressive" activities is by no means clear—may have some validity, it can hardly be regarded as doing much more than focusing attention on one aspect of an extremely complex problem.

One other matter deserves comment by way of introduction. Aubert (1966) remarks on what he calls an "ambivalence" or "curious dualism" which ran through the legislative debates on the Housemaid Law:

It was claimed, on the one hand that the law is essentially a codification of custom and established practice, rendering effective enforcement inessential. On the other hand, there was a tendency to claim that the Housemaid Law is an important new piece of labour legislation with a clearly reformatory purpose attempting to change an unacceptable *status quo* [p. 110].

Reprinted from *Journal of Social Issues,* **27** (2, 1971), pp. 33–48, by permission of the authors and The Society for the Psychological Study of Social Issues.

329

We too have noticed an ambivalence or dualism, although of a rather different character, in discussions of the efficacy of legal attempts to control behavior. Thus in casual conversations we have noted a reluctance on the part of friends and colleagues to formulate objective principles about the extent to which the threat of punishment conveyed by law can change customary behavior. In particular, there seems to be a failure to recognize a distinction between issues relating to the *morality* or *expediency* of prohibiting particular types of behavior and issues relating to the *efficacy* of such prohibitions. Thus there is a tendency for the views expressed to vary as the subject changes from alcohol to marijuana to firearms to racial discrimination, and to vary according to the speaker's view of the rightness or wrongness of prohibiting the particular behavior under discussion. Commonly, the conclusion to such discussions is the comforting one that the law can succeed in doing right but will inevitably fail when authorities attempt to prohibit what should not be prohibited. Unfortunately, since there is a wide variation in moral views among our acquaintances, this general principle leads to contradictory conclusions about the efficacy of particular attempts to control behavior. In the preliminary note that follows, we attempt to discuss in objective terms the use of the legal threat of punishment to induce social change. Our emphasis is more on the narrow issue of the deterrent effect of threat of punishment than on the great variety of other mechanisms associated with compliance to legal commands. Yet we feel a discussion of the narrow topic will inform the general topic of law as an agent of social change.

THREAT AS A SOCIALIZING MECHANISM

By definition, the threat of sanctions cannot achieve a deterrent effect unless the presentation of that threat results in some individuals acting differently from the way they would in the absence of the legal threat. In this sense at least the legal threat can always be seen as an attempt to change patterns of behavior. Yet in our view it is important to distinguish between cases where the main thrust of the threat of punishment is aimed at preserving the status quo in social relations from isolated temptations to deviation, and the increasing number of cases in which the legal threat is used in the attempt to change social customs.[1] When the threat of punishment is aimed at preserving the status quo, the formal legal command is usually only one of many forces pushing socialized potential offenders toward conformity. Other social norms will usually exist to complement the behavioral command of the law. Thus knowledge of the law prohibiting burglary is preceded in the socialization process by messages about the wrongness of stealing and home invasion. By the time a citizen reaches adulthood, he has monitored a consistent stream of messages about burglary—messages which, with the specific legal threat, form a network of restraining influences probably stronger than the sum of its separate components. And for most people, when the legal threat is directed at reinforcing a long standing and important social norm, it is usually correct to view a demand for compliance as not requiring the learning of new patterns of behavior. In most cases the traditional habit of

[1] See Stjernquist (1963), at p. 158: "The above division into behavior-changing and behavior-stabilizing norms has proved to be practical in different social sciences. Means, in *The Structure of the American Economy* 1 (Washington: National Resources Committee, 1939), uses the terms 'administrative rules' and 'canalizing rules' respectively. . . . Homans, *The Human Group* (London, 1951), applies a similar division of norms but has a special terminology: 'norms apply to the maintenance of established behaviour, orders to future changes in behaviour.' Homans also points out that 'orders are always changing into law and custom.' "

imagining that threats are directed by the legal system at each individual in his separate capacity also seems justified.

When the law is used as an instrument of social change, it is more likely that the achievement of acceptable rates of compliance will require an active reorientation of the values and behaviors of the significant part of a threatened audience that has previously followed the outlawed custom. Under these circumstances it would not be surprising to find that the behavior which such threats seek to restrain will have acquired positive social meaning for members of a threatened audience far more often than in the case of traditional crimes. Further, there is reason to suppose that when law seeks to restrain customary behavior, those whose responses are most important in predicting rates of compliance will be, not individuals, but groups among whom the forbidden behavior has been customary (Massell, 1968; Stjernquist, 1963).

If these assertions are correct, it will be important to note, in any analysis seeking to predict and understand the operation of legal threats, whether the aim of the law is change or stability, because there are differences between the two types of situation that can lead to differences in threat effectiveness. But before elaborating somewhat on the use of threats to achieve social change, a few qualifications are in order.

Some of the conditions associated with the use of legal threats to promote social change occur in other situations where law and custom are not synchronized. In particular, the same kind of circumstances can obtain when the law has not changed but the social values and customs that traditionally supported a law have changed. A change in social conditions without change in legal rules creates much the same kind of disequilibrium between custom and rule that is created by altering the law, and it is this disequilibrium between custom and rule that makes it nec-

essary to consider separately legal threats aimed at social change. In fact, in the contest between an old rule and a new custom, the attempt to return social relations to a prior state can be seen as a subcategory of law as an instrument of social change, albeit a special subcategory, because the legitimacy of the old rule at least will have the support of a tradition of lip service in the community. For this reason there is a basis for viewing America's experiences with alcohol in the 1920s and marijuana in the 1960s as similar attempts to legislate social change. However, it is important to distinguish the cases because, among other reasons, we ordinarily expect the new-law-versus-old-custom contest to provoke more widespread resistance than the old-law-versus-new-custom; the tradition of lip service mentioned above is an inertial force of some consequence.

There are important similarities as well as differences between deterrent threats used to reinforce existing social conventions and those aimed at social change. It would be naive to suppose that the lessons learned about the operation of threats in other settings can have no relevance to the analysis of threats directed at changing customary behavior. The motive force of deterrence in each case is the fear of unpleasant consequences, and many of the same factors that are important in predicting the outcome of threats that reinforce traditional prohibitions will bear significantly on the ability of threats to achieve social change. The vocabulary of deterrence—stressing threat credibility, the severity of sanctions, and modes of communication—will thus be a necessary, if inadequate, tool for analyzing this special class of laws.

There are important differences among threats aimed at social change, and these differences can lead to substantial variations in threat effectiveness. If this is the case, it is a mistake to base general conclusions about the effectiveness of threats as instruments of change on single observations. To deny, for instance, that stateways can change folkways on the basis of "our experience with Prohibition" is to operate from an insufficient inductive basis, unless it can be demonstrated that all attempts to change social behavior through the use of legal threats are similar in all important respects. The essence of this note is that this is not the case. We hope to suggest some of the variations in situations that might explain why some attempts to change customary behavior through legal sanctions succeed while others fail dismally. Among the factors that appear to be most important are variations in the nature of the custom, variations in the social characteristics of the individuals and groups that have adhered to the custom before it was forbidden, and variations in the way in which the threat of punishment is carried out.

VARIATIONS IN THE NATURE OF THE CUSTOM

Differences in the nature of the custom that appear to influence the probability that a custom will be successfully suppressed include: (a) the utilitarian and moral significance of a custom to its adherents, (b) the extent to which a custom enjoys popular support, (c) the degree to which practice of the custom is visible to enforcement agencies, (d) the extent to which the custom is of such a nature that a general change may extinguish individual drives to follow it, and (e) the degree to which the change in custom meets current community needs.

The Significance of Customs

Of obvious importance in predicting the effect of threatening customary behavior is the degree of commitment to a particular custom on the part of members of a threatened audience. Public religious observance and burning high-sul-phur coal for home-heating are both social customs of some popularity in the United States, but the two customs are poles apart if the first is a central expression of deeply held religious convictions, while the second persists by reason of casual tradition and convenience. Behavior that is perceived of as satisfying important drives is more difficult to extinguish than behavior that satisfies less compelling drives, and this axiom provides us with one basis for ranking the differential significance of customary behavior. A second index for ranking the importance of customs is the extent to which adherents of a particular custom perceive that legitimate alternatives to the prohibited custom exist which can fulfill the drives associated with the customary behavior. Thus, while high-sulphur coal is associated with the admittedly important aim of keeping warm during winter, the availability of other heat sources makes this custom less important than it would be if those who ordinarily heat their houses with this type of coal can be persuaded that practicable heating alternatives exist. Clearly, some forms of customary behavior are more amenable to substitution than others. It would seem difficult, for instance, to persuade a group associated with a suppressed religion that belief in a nonforbidden dogma would yield the satisfaction they associate with their present faith.

When the law seeks to prohibit behavior that has been customary, it is also possible that the prohibited behavior will have acquired a *moral* significance for many of its adherents (as, for example, was the case for Mormons who practiced polygamy in the nineteenth century). The possibility of normative support for a custom introduces a problem that traditional criminal law prohibitions do not often encounter. The moral dimension of adherence to custom is an important element to consider when trying to predict the effect that threatening behavior might have, because the prohibition of conduct that is considered morally right or even morally imperative may give an entirely different character to the reactions of a threatened audience.

Variations in the importance of a custom play a significant role in the simple utilitarian calculus that has long been accepted as a major explanation of the deterrent effect of threats. The more important a custom, the more severe and more certain must be the punishment threatened, if the legal policy is to prove effective as a means of social change. Yet, while this simple formulation might accurately state the relationship between variations in the purely utilitarian value of customary behavior and the effect of legal prohibitions, the situation is somewhat more complex when we consider the ways in which variations in the moral significance attached to customary behavior affect the prospects for prohibition. To be sure, the greater the moral importance of a custom, the greater the unpleasantness of the penalty that must be attached to that custom to secure a change in behavior. But moral support for a prohibited custom can further inhibit the preventive effect of threats by rendering ineffective two usually powerful reasons for complying with legal threats—respect for law and lawabidingness, and the negative social connotations normally conveyed by punishment. Most groups in society believe in the legitimacy of law as a system of social control, which is one important explanation of why so many people obey so many laws. Yet the belief that violation of any law is wrong may be overwhelmed by a specific moral sense when individuals feel that a customary behavior is of greater moral importance than whatever force a general respect for law brings to bear on a particular situation. Thus a man who finds it difficult to commit a petty crime, such as illegal parking for minor pecuniary advantage, because of his feelings—not about

parking but about violations of the law—might feel different when the motives he has for law violation are altruistic. Those who continue to place a higher moral value on prohibited behavior may feel more like the doctor exceeding the speed limit to visit a patient than like the petty law violator mentioned above, and even if they continue to express respect for law in general terms, this respect will not be seen as a barrier to violation of the prohibition of the valued custom.

At the same time, the moral significance of a prohibited custom may act to make the consequences of conviction and punishment less worthy of avoidance than they would be otherwise. For the majority of people the most degrading aspect of punishment is the social message it conveys. Conviction and punishment for serious offenses carry social stigma, and the fear of stigma is a significant aspect of the unpleasantness that constitutes the deterrent stimulus. The moral value of customary behavior may result in the would-be offender rejecting the negative significance of punishment for himself if he is punished in a worthy cause. Indeed, he may invert the moral value of the ordinary symbols of degradation by viewing the discomfort and disrepute he suffers as signs of personal dedication. Moreover, if most of his peers share his moral views about a particular type of law violation, their perception of the negative value of punishment may also be inverted and the effects of severe punishment may include positive status for the person subjected to that punishment.

Extent of Popular Support for the Custom

The popularity of a prohibited custom is an important element in predicting the effects of attempting its abolition. At the outset, information about the number of people in society who have supported a now-prohibited custom should help define the sheer size of the social-control task that faces those attempting to enforce the new law. In addition, information about the number of individuals who adhere to the custom can also provide clues as to the types of person the legal threat must reach. The more widespread adherence to a custom has been, the more it will be the case that the legal threat is aimed at normally socialized individuals. The smaller the number of individuals adhering to a custom threatened by law, the more the legal system is on notice that potential violators of the legal prohibition may differ from the general population in ways that might make predicting their responses to threat a special problem.

The extent to which a forbidden custom has adherents in society is also important in predicting how difficult the new law will be to enforce. The more widespread the support for a forbidden custom, the greater the probability that judges, juries, and other administrative personnel will identify with the custom itself or the type of people who adhere to it, and this can undermine enforcement of the law against all offenders or against a class of offenders with which the rest of the community identifies.

One might question whether there are many occasions in which customs with a degree of public acceptance sufficient to generate forces that might inhibit enforcement are outlawed in democratic societies. Yet, while it is certainly the case that authoritarian and "occupation" regimes more commonly institute laws against popular customs, the democratic process can produce such attempts at social change when groups or even regions are in sharp disagreement over the moral propriety of a particular customary behavior. For this reason, any time that the power to declare law is more centralized than, or otherwise removed from, the responsibility of enforcing it, the law itself may not compel the sympathy of the enforcement agencies. Moreover, as long as the group adhering to a particular custom is not thought of as unambiguously deviant, the attempt to maintain customary behavior may attract the sympathies of members of the community who do not identify with the custom, but have no strong scruples against it.

The fact that it is more difficult successfully to prohibit customary behavior should not be interpreted as indicating that success in suppressing the customary behavior is unattainable in such situations. The point is limited to the prediction that suppression of popular custom will require substantial amounts of enforcement activity, which may be difficult to generate.

Visibility of the Custom

Since enforcement of law is a significant part of the basis for predicting whether or not the legal threat will achieve high rates of compliance, the extent to which customary behavior is visible and therefore easier to bring to the attention of an enforcing authority can play a significant role in determining whether an attempt at changing custom through law will succeed. Some customs may be visible because the public nature of the behavior is part of the defining characteristic of the custom. Such is the case with demonstrations, refusals to pledge allegiance to the flag, and certain types of communication. The customary behavior may also achieve a high degree of visibility, without involving large numbers of people, if the practice often comes to the attention of a person who is out of sympathy with the custom. This type of visibility will often occur when a behavior can realistically be thought of as having a victim, as, for example, in the case of face-to-face racial discrimination. The fact that a custom is highly visible is no guarantee that a prohibition will be effectively enforced. And substantial enforcement efforts are, of course, no guarantee that punishment on a mass scale will achieve social change. But it is certainly the case that visibility makes the task of enforcement easier if the will and ability to enforce the law exists, and it is clearly more probable that a law against social custom will succeed under conditions of widespread enforcement than under limited or nonexistent enforcement.

Will General Change Make the Custom Obsolete?

Sometimes the law can succeed in changing patterns of behavior because the change in law, if it reduces the gross rate of a custom or behavior, removes some of the reasons that individuals had previously supported the custom. To a certain extent this is true with all patterns of customary behavior, because a large part of the reason why any individual follows a particular custom will usually be that most of the people he knows follow that custom and expect him to do so as well. Any law that changes his expectation of other people's behavior and his notion of what other people expect from him will thus go part of the way toward restructuring the conditions that led to his initial compliance with the custom. In addition to this broad point about the interdependence of expectations, there are a number of other ways in which the abolition of a general expectation that other people will be adhering to a custom may undercut the incentive for an individual's doing so himself. Many people keep firearms in their homes, not because they think other people expect them to, but out of fear of guns in the hands of others. For this type of individual a change in law might provide a credible promise that others would not be armed and thus make it much easier for him to give up his gun. By the same token, the owner of a drugstore lunch counter in the South might be unwilling to desegregate his facility if it meant that his white customers would attribute the responsibility for this change to him, and if he faced the probability of losing his white clientele to other lunch counters that did not desegregate. Prohibition of the custom would, however, put him in the position where he could not be personally blamed for the change in policy, and his white patronage would be protected from raids by his competitors because of the generality of the change in practice. Under these circumstances, prohibiting the custom of discrimination might be an economic advantage to the individual entrepreneur by increasing the demand for his service, while a unilateral change in conduct might be to his economic disadvantage. Given this type of condition, change in custom can be more easily achieved if preceded by change in law.

Custom and Current Needs

It is more likely that the prohibition of customary behavior will attract enthusiastic enforcement and secure widespread compliance if there is a clear necessity which provides a socially acceptable reason for the change in custom. The best reasons yet devised for justifying change in legal relationships are external threat and internal emergency. It is thus much easier in times of war to explain to those affected why previously allowed behavior is being outlawed, e.g., featherbedding in the labor market, or the freedom to determine prices normally accorded to private producers. The drama of changing circumstance and needs can provide a basis for enthusiastic support among the general population for the enforcement of the new prohibition and give what is at least a powerful excuse for compliance to those who were following the old custom.

Because the reason for change is of some importance in predicting the consequences of a change in law, it should not be assumed that certain types of social change, adopted into law during periods of crisis, could be as successfully replicated in the absence of a similar crisis. This does not mean, however, that a change in custom facilitated through change in law may not often survive the crisis which initially gave rise to it. Though to some extent the end of a war or depression marks the end of the need for the change in custom, it cannot be seen as automatically heralding a return to the status quo. Intervening experience with the new way of doing things and the advantages of the change to some groups (perhaps at the expense of others) provide some reason for continuing the change beyond the duration of the conditions that accounted for its initial acceptance. Therefore the suggestion that many types of change in custom are not attainable in the absence of common crisis does not imply that the same changes are not maintainable in the absence of crisis. Indeed a history of emergency tax measures might suggest that some forms of change are very difficult to reverse.

SOCIAL CHARACTERISTICS OF THE THREATENED AUDIENCE

Different types of groups who have been used to adhering to customary behavior may come in conflict with a new law. Some groups are more cohesive than others, and cohesive group structure can militate for or against change in custom, depending upon whether group leadership chooses to urge compliance with or defiance of the new law. Perhaps the most important characteristic of groups adhering to custom, from the standpoint of predicting the reponse to prohibition, is the degree to which group members are integrated participants in the larger social system. The greater the degree of agreement among members of the group with the values of the larger society, the greater will be the pressure upon members of the group to comply with the command of the law. Similarly, incentive to comply with the new law will increase in proportion to the success that group members have experienced in participation in the

larger society. Wealth and status provide a powerful motive for support of the legal system and the larger social system it usually represents. Poverty and discrimination, particularly if born of differentiations directly related to group membership, provide fertile ground for rebellion against the prohibition of custom, as well as a basis for generalizing that rebellion into a rejection of the entire value matrix of the legal system.

One complication in the relationship between group identification with the larger society and susceptibility to threat is that high status provides an incentive for compliance only if the threat of punishment for violation is credible. Even values in accordance with the larger society's values will usually require some assurance that the new law will be enforced before they provide a motive for complying. And it is precisely the high status and well-integrated groups in society against whom laws prohibiting customs are most difficult to enforce. But if the will to enforce is sufficient, the incentives that enforcement gives to a successful group to comply with the prohibition of custom will be substantial.

VARIATIONS IN LAW ENFORCEMENT

Any discussion of the variables involved in explaining why some attempts to legislate social change succeed while others fail must deal with the character of law enforcement as both a dependent and independent variable. The level of law enforcement must be seen as a dependent variable because many of the factors we have been discussing, such as the popularity of a custom and the characteristics of groups who adhere to it, may influence the kind of enforcement that an attempt to legislate change will produce. Yet the kind and degree of enforcement will itself have a significant impact on the prospects for successful social change. And since many variations in law enforcement are not inevitably determined by situational factors of the type discussed above, the character of law enforcement deserves independent attention as a predictor of the effects of an attempt to change custom through law. The degree to which enforcement activities entail likelihood of detection, the extent of enforcement across class and group lines, and the severity of punishments meted out for offense—all are included among the significant variations in law enforcement that may condition rates of compliance.

Likelihood of Apprehension

The simplest statement one can make about the extent of enforcement is that the likelihood of achieving the aim of the law will increase as the perceived likelihood of apprehension for law violation increases. This axiom might deserve some qualification in the situation where a custom is viewed as morally imperative and conscientious objection occurs with a frequency that does not seem to be conditioned by the rate of apprehension or punishment. However, even in the case of a law that generates conscientious objection, increased probability of apprehension and punishment may still reduce the rate of deviation, if only because potential offenders with fewer scruples will respond to such increases.

Selective Enforcement

A second qualification of the general relationship between success in suppressing a custom and perceived likelihood of apprehension is that broader law enforcement means arresting greater numbers of high status people for violation. This increases the pressure on enforcement agencies to reduce and rechannel enforcement efforts and confronts the community with the full implications of what it means to punish deviation from the new law whenever it occurs. Under some circumstances,

then, broad law enforcement can lead to an earlier crisis test of the law and perhaps ultimately to its demise. But if broad and nonselective enforcement is somewhat unpredictable in consequence, this in no way implies that the prospects for effective change in custom are any brighter when selective enforcement, focusing on low status groups, becomes the order of the day. Aside from its manifest injustice, the principal danger of highly selective enforcement is that groups who are spared will disobey the law because no real risks accompany their violations, while the target groups for enforcement efforts will perceive the enforcement as being directed against the group, rather than against the behavior. If such conditions persist, neither high nor low status groups are apt to show much respect for the specific law, and rates of noncompliance in the groups for whom the threat of enforcement is quite small will probably continue to be substantial.

If it is not exclusively based on caste or class factors, selective enforcement can have a profound deterrent effect on those with relatively little chance of being caught, since it is these high status groups in society that "scare easier" when confronted with the threat of social disapproval. Thus while one small businessman will doubtless be more impressed if he hears of another businessman of similar station in life being sent to jail for not reporting some of his income, even the incomplete analogy of a racketeer being jailed for this type of offense can teach the small businessman that people can and do get caught for this type of practice. Unless he can persuade himself that enforcement is based exclusively on class factors, this knowledge can produce the kind of anxiety associated with extensive general deterrence.

There is little doubt that enforcement plays a key role in determining whether an attempt to abolish a custom will succeed. We could go further and suggest that, with respect to customary behaviors that are not very important to a threatened audience, the risk of apprehension and punishment is the most important criterion of whether the new law will succeed. The policy value of knowledge about enforcement is less than it might seem, however, for two reasons previously mentioned. First, so many factors relating to the nature of the custom and the type of people against whom the law must be enforced have an effect on the rate of enforcement of a law that it might be wise to think of the risk of apprehension as merely a shorthand expression for a complex of variables. Second, because so many factors affect the rate of detection and punishment, it is difficult to estimate the parameters of practical variability in the enforcement of a particular law. Thus if unalterable conditions make Γ the maximum achievable level of enforcement, it will be of little comfort to the law enforcer to tell him that a rate of detection of twice Γ rather than Γ will reduce the rate of crime by half. So the practical importance of enforcement may be far less than its predictive value.

Rate of Detection

One further question of importance is the degree of detection and punishment necessary to suppress customary behavior. If a custom is popular, the punishment for violating the new law prohibiting it must be severe enough to outweigh, for potential offenders, the advantages of continuing the custom even after the punishment is discounted by the chance of escaping detection. But the risks associated with escalating the level of punishment too far are substantial, because severe penalties may increase pressure on sympathetic jurors, judges, prosecutors, and police, thereby contributing to a breakdown in law enforcement and, ultimately, nullification of the law.

As to what rate of detection will suffice

to suppress customary behavior, we would make one comment. The specific rate required will vary from case to case, of course, but the minimum level of apprehension sufficient to abolish customs may be lower than one would expect. While some early authors speak of "certainty" of punishment, rather than some less absolute term, as the key to deterrence, it is not inconceivable that for some customs a detection rate of one per several hundred offenses could lead to the general abandonment of a custom, or at least to substantial repudiation. It must also be added that such a detection rate would be a tribute to efficient enforcement in light of the present rates of one in many thousands that obtain for many victimless crimes in the United States.

UNFINISHED BUSINESS

We conclude this note with the list of significant variables hopelessly incomplete. It may be as well therefore to indicate briefly some of the more important lacunae.

One important omission is the failure to speculate on what differences between cultures make it easier for some legal systems to engineer change than others. The possibilities for discussion here are manifold, but we leave them for another time and more qualified discussants.

We have also failed to mention variations in the conditions of government that would influence the prospects of social change through law. Rather, we have assumed a government that has achieved legitimacy; occupation forces and other nonlegitimate governing bodies will operate under a set of further handicaps—and possibly also with some advantages—which we have not discussed.

A third gap in coverage, this one perhaps more a deficiency of emphasis, is the absence of sustained speculation about how variations in social-change situations might affect the extent to which the law can succeed in prohibiting custom through its moral and educative effects. We have suggested that this is more difficult to achieve when the custom being prohibited has acquired positive moral value among its constituency, and we have hazarded a guess that selective enforcement based on caste or class and the lack of an adequate rationale for change might impede the moralizing potential of criminal law. But there are other, more basic, questions. Does the criminal law have the same moralizing and habit-building potential when it acts against the grain of custom? Under what circumstances will the prohibition of custom be counterproductive and act as a negative socialization force by turning parts of a threatened audience against the legal system in general because of the value the threatened individuals place on the prohibited custom? Our failure to treat these issues in detail is no indication that they lack importance but rather a tribute to their richness and complexity.

We have not discussed the many costs associated with regimes of threat and punishment. Thus, it does not follow from the fact that abolition of custom is possible that legal prohibitions will be worth their cost. Among the more interesting relevant questions is this: At what point will citizen loyalty snap under the pressure of coerced social change? Again, we must admit to being presently incapable of adequately discussing this question.

Finally, we have failed to examine, in detail, a single episode of attempted social change through legal threat in order to demonstrate the importance of some of the variables we have been discussing. We look forward to pursuing this path at some later date.

REFERENCES

AUBERT, V., 1966. Some social functions of legislation. *Acta Sociologica*, **10**, 98–110.

AUBERT, V., 1969. *Sociology of law*. Baltimore: Penguin Books.

DICEY, A. B., 1905. *Lectures on the relation between law and public opinion in England during the nineteenth century*. London: Macmillan.

DROR, Y., 1959. Law and social change. *Tulane Law Review*, **33**, 787–802.

GORECKI, J., 1966. Divorce in Poland: A socio-legal study. *Acta Sociologica*, **10**, 68–80.

KECHEKYAN, S. F., 1956. Social progress and law. *Transactions of the Third World Congress of Sociology*, **6**, 42–51.

MASSELL, G. J., 1967. Law as an instrument of revolutionary change in a traditional milieu: The case of Soviet Central Asia. *Law and Society Review*, **2**, 179–228.

STJERNQUIST, P., 1963. How are changes in social behavior developed by means of legislation? In *Legal essays: A tribute to Frede Castberg on the occasion of his 70th birthday, 4 July 1963*. Oslo: Universitets-forlaget.

SUMNER, W. G., 1906. *Folkways*. Boston: Ginn.

PERCEIVED PENAL SANCTION AND SELF-REPORTED CRIMINALITY: A NEGLECTED APPROACH TO DETERRENCE RESEARCH

Gordon P. Waldo and Theodore G. Chiricos

The entire system of American criminal justice—from the debate of legislators to the maximum custody prison—is based, in part, on the assumption that punishment of criminal offenders will deter future criminality. Despite its antiquity,[1] this assumption has received little more than speculative attention from legal philosophers, jurists, politicians, and the general public.[2] Only recently have social scientists put this assumption to empirical

Reprinted from *Social Problems,* **19** (Spring, 1972), pp. 522–540, by permission of the authors and The Society for the Study of Social Problems.

This research was supported, in part, by Ford Foundation grant number 67–586. The authors would like to express their appreciation to John Cardascia and Robert Camacho for their assistance in this project.

[1] Among the earliest to crystalize this issue was Jeremy Bentham, whose Principles of Penal Law was published in 1843.

[2] Even among social scientists, most of the input on this issue has been theoretical or moralistic in nature (Mead, 1918; Wood, 1938; Ball, 1955; Polier, 1956; Barnes and Teeters, 1959; Toby, 1964; Jeffery, 1965; Bittner and Platt, 1966; Zimring and Hawkins, 1968) and as noted by Chambliss (1966:70), ". . . the question of deterrence has frequently turned into a debate over the *morality* of *capital* punishment."

test, and to date, the evidence appears somewhat contradictory and inconclusive.

The earlier studies by Schuessler and Savitz questioned the deterrent effectiveness of *capital* punishment. Their research showed little difference in homicide rates when: (1) comparable abolitionist and retentionist states were examined (Schuessler, 1952) and (2) when rates were compared before and after well-publicized executions (Savitz, 1958). Sellin (1967:124) later showed that rates of homicide were relatively unaffected by the temporary abolition and eventual reinstatement of capital punishment in 11 states. He concluded that:

. . . there is no evidence that the abolition of the death penalty generally causes an increase in criminal homicides or that its reintroduction is followed by a decline. The explanation of changes in homicide rates must be sought elsewhere.

The study of crime rates for clues to questions about deterrence was extended by Gibbs (1968) to alternative measures of the severity and certainty of punishment,[3] and by Tittle (1969) to alternative criminal offenses.[4] The former (Gibbs, 1968: 523–527) found inverse relationships

[3] *Severity of punishment* was operationally defined by Gibbs as "the median number of months served on a homicide sentence by all persons in prison on December 31, 1960." This measurement was taken for each state in the United States, as was his index of the certainty of imprisonment:

$$\frac{\text{\# of State Prison Admissions for Homicide in 1960}}{\text{Mean \# of Homicides Known to Police for 1959–1960}}$$

[4] Tittle examined the following offenses: homicide assault; sex offenses; robbery; larceny; burglary and auto theft. His principal measure of severity was provided by the "mean length of time served for felony prisoners released from state prisons in 1960." Certainty of punishment for the several felonies was given by the following ratio:

$$\frac{\text{\# of State Prison Admissions for "X" Offense in 1960 \& 1963}}{\text{\# of "X" Crimes Known to the Police in 1959 \& 1962}}$$

between rates of homicide and the severity (phi $= -.25$) and certainty (phi $= -.48$) of punishment. This contradiction of earlier deterrence findings was reinforced by Tittle's (1969:409) study of seven criminal offenses, which revealed:

Strong and consistent negative associations . . . between certainty of punishment and crime rates, while a negative association is observed between severity of punishment and crime rates only for homicide.

However, Tittle's findings were called into question by Chiricos and Waldo (1970) who extended a similar mode of analysis to additional points in time and to measures of change in the levels of certainty, severity and criminality.[5] Their data showed little consistent support for the assumption that rates of crime are inversely related to the certainty and severity of punishment, and several methodological issues were raised which cast doubt upon the appropriateness of findings derived from this approach to deterrence research.[6]

The studies cited represent the major thrust of sociological research in the area of criminal deterrence and each has opera-tionalized the dependent variable—criminality—by some use of available, aggregate *rates* of crime. For several reasons, not the least of which is the inconsistency of conclusions among the studies, such an approach to questions of deterrence may never prove definitive. A major problem is the sensitivity of official crime rates to changes in the reporting of crime to the police and the recording of crime by the police. These difficulties are compounded by the fact that variation in the *official* level of crime may reflect variation in the age distribution of the population or in the concentration of that population in urban areas.[7]

In addition, official statistics limit the researcher to seven "crime index" offenses, inasmuch as "crimes known to the police" [8] are unavailable for additional specific crimes. If one wished to examine deterrence for other types of criminality— such as victimless crime or white collar crime—official statistics would be of little use. Indeed, the need for deterrence research to distinguish among types of crimes is underscored by Andenaes' (1966: 957) distinction between crimes that are *mala per se* and those that are *mala quia prohibita*:

---

[5] Certainty of punishment was calculated for three time periods, 1950, 1960, and 1963. The general format for certainty measures is given by the 1950 index:

$$\frac{\text{1950 Admissions to Prison for "X" Offense}}{\text{Mean of "X" Crimes Known to Police in 1949 \& 1950}}$$

Severity of punishment for 1960 and 1964 were given by the "median length of sentence served by state prisoners released in 1960 and 1964," respectively.

[6] In brief, this criticism suggests that Tittle's "strong and consistent" inverse relationships between certainty of punishment and crime rates, may be the product of correlated bias existing in his measures of certainty and criminality. That is, the numerator of Tittle's criminality index is almost identical to the denominator of his certainty index. Thus, any computed relationship between such variables would have to be inverse. Implementing successive samples of random digits in the terms of the certainty and criminality measures, it was found that Tittle's actual relationships were no greater than could be found using random data.

[7] See, for example, Crime and Its Impact: An Assessment (President's Commission, 1967:24–28), which summarizes the effects of these and other sociological factors upon the official rates of crime. For a discussion of problems in the under-reporting of crimes *to the police*, see the victimization survey conducted by the National Opinion Research Center (President's Commission, 1967:17–19). The impact of irregularities in the reporting of crime *by the police* is discussed in the same volume (President's Commission, 1967:22–24).

[8] One may consult any recent issue of Uniform Crime Reports, published annually by the Federal Bureau of Investigation, Washington, D.C., to confirm this limitation.

In the case of *mala per se,* the law supports the moral codes of society. If the threats of legal punishment were removed, moral feelings and the fear of public judgment would remain as powerful crime prevention forces, at least for a limited period. In the case of *mala quia prohibita,* the law stands alone; conformity is essentially a matter of effective legal sanctions.

A further limitation of the aggregate data approach is the researcher's inability to discern those social-psychological processes by which the presumed effects of punishment are realized.[9] For example, when correlating crime rates with the severity of statutory provisions for punishment, one knows nothing of how the penalties are perceived by potential offenders —if, indeed, they are perceived at all. Clearly, the deterrent effectiveness of punishment presumes that potential offenders *know* or *think* they know what the penalties are. Further, it must be assumed that offenders and non-offenders *act* on the basis of their knowledge. However, these assumptions received critical attention in a recent California survey (Assembly Committee on Criminal Procedure, 1968: 13–14):

While the Legislature has supposedly responded to public appeal and increased the penalties for crimes of violence to victims, this was not known by the public . . . people were in general unaware that the Legislature had taken any action at all when in fact the Legislature had increased the minimum penalties . . . When the public did answer these items, they tended to underestimate the amount of the penalty. . . .

Even assuming awareness of penal sanctions it remains impossible, using aggregate data (with states or other political categories as the unit of analysis), for the researcher to determine whether individual offenders are actually deterred by the threat of formal punishment or by the social embarrassment of detection. The functional relationship between formal and informal sanctions is well summarized by Andenaes (1966:961):

If the criminal can be sure that there will be no police action, he can generally rest assured that there will be no social reprobation. The legal machinery, therefore, is in itself the most effective means of mobilizing that kind of social control which emanates from community condemnation.

Finally, the approach to deterrence research through aggregate data precludes an examination of situational differences that could affect an individual's response to threats of punishment. For example, one cannot ask whether some people are deterred from some crimes in certain situations by a particular set of deterrents, or whether different persons, in different situations may be differentially affected by threats of penal sanction. Further, the possibility that the *same* individual would respond to different deterrents for different crimes in different situations, must be ignored when dealing with these data.[10]

In short, while official aggregate data have been useful in the study of deterrence, alternative modes of analysis must be tried if some of the remaining deterrence questions are to be answered. The research reported here provides one alternative approach to several deterrence questions that have not, as yet, been answered by traditional (i.e., based upon official aggregate statistics) deterrence research. In all, six related questions are being considered.

1. Is the admitted frequency of a specific criminal offense lowest for those who perceive the most severe penalties for that offense?

From deterrence theory, one would ex-

---

[9] See the discussion by Zimring (1971:56–61) concerning "Public Knowledge as a Threshold Requirement" in the study of deterrence.

[10] Zimring's (1971:33–96) entire discussion of the many factors related to the success or failure of deterrence threats, is supportive of this point.

pect those perceiving the harshest penalties for a specific offense to be the least likely to engage in that offense. However, the empirical evidence that does exist (Schuessler, 1952; Sellin, 1967; Gibbs, 1968; Tittle, 1969; Chiricos and Waldo, 1970) neither deals with the issue of perceptions, nor does it confirm deterrence theory. In short, prior research has shown that *official* rates of crime are generally insensitive to variations in penal severity. It remains to be seen whether self-reported crime is responsive to *perceptions* of severe punishment.

2. Is the admitted frequency of a specific criminal offense lowest among those who perceive the greatest likelihood of someone like themselves receiving the maximum penalty if convicted for that offense?

Harsh statutory penalties would seem to have little deterrent effectiveness if potential offenders perceive little chance that the courts will invoke them. Such a situation may, in fact, currently exist with regard to marijuana offenses. Grupp and Lucas (1969) have documented a widely held suspicion that court dispositions of marijuana cases have become less severe over time. Their study in California during the period from 1960 to 1967 indicates that while arrests for marijuana offenses have increased by 525 percent in those eight years, the percentage of convictions that resulted in a *prison sentence* dropped from 27 percent in 1960 to 11 percent in 1967. At the same time, the use of probation increased to the point that 46 percent of those convicted in 1967 were placed on probation, as opposed to 24 percent in 1960 (Grupp and Lucas, 1969:5-8).

3. Is the admitted frequency of a specific criminal offense lowest for those who perceive the greatest likelihood that law-violators will be caught by the police?

While the deterrence hypothesis would anticipate such an inverse relationship, existing empirical evidence is somewhat contradictory. With regard to a belief that "people who break the law are almost always caught and punished," Jensen (1969:194-196) found the greatest support from self-reported *non-delinquents*,[11] and the slightest support from youths reporting two or more delinquencies. On the other hand, Claster (1967:83–84) showed that "training school" delinquents[12] had a pronounced tendency to *overestimate* arrest rates for the general public, whereas "non-delinquents" had an almost equivalent tendency to *underestimate* those rates. Clearly, if one considers the perceptions of law-enforcement efficiency to precede delinquent activity, then Jensen's data support classical deterrence expectations, while Claster's does not.[13]

4. Is the admitted frequency of a specific criminal offense lowest for those who have had the greatest contact with others who have been arrested or convicted for that offense?

It is assumed that persons who have had the greatest contact with others who have been punished for a specific crime, will have the most proximate knowledge of the consequences of the criminal justice system. On that account, they should be more readily deterred from that crime

11 Jensen's (1969) "non-delinquents" are those who *admit* to no delinquent activities.

12 It must be remembered, when comparing Claster's (1967) "delinquent" with Jensen's (1967), that the former "delinquents" are those who had been admitted to training school—whereas Jensen used self-reporting techniques.

13 In actuality, however, one could argue that the experiences of the two samples of "delinquents" may have resulted in their perceptions of law enforcement. That is, training school "delinquents" might easily be expected to over-estimate arrest probabilities—simply because they have experienced the formal sanctions of the police. On the other hand, self-reported "delinquents," because they have not received such formal sanction, could be just as likely to under-estimate police efficiency. Should this be the case, then the logical time-order of deterrence relationships does not obtain.

than others having less contact with the "clients" of criminal justice. At an earlier time, public penitence was demanded from offenders and public executions were significant community events. Today, the process of formal community response and the affixing of criminal labels is still intended to be a public ritual with at least two objectives: (1) the exemplary transfer of the offender from the status of "law-abiding citizen," to the "temporary" role of criminal, and (2) the definition of acceptable behavioral boundaries for the remainder of the community.[14]

5. Is the admitted frequency of a specific criminal offense lowest for those who perceive the greatest likelihood of arrest for someone like themselves committing that offense?

While the prior questions deal with arrests of "others," this question considers perceptions of law enforcement for a specific offense and for "someone like" the respondent. For example, in accord with deterrence theory, the lowest frequency of admitted marijuana use was expected for those who perceive the greatest likelihood of somone like themselves being arrested *if* they used marijuana. This expectation receives some support from another aspect of Claster's (1967:83–84) work with training school delinquents. Even though his "official" delinquents over-estimated the chances of arrest for the general public, they perceived significantly lower probabilities of being arrested *themselves* for a hypothetical offense, than did a sample of "non-delinquents." Curiously, these "delinquents" who had been officially responded to by society were still willing to believe in their relative immunity from legal sanction. From a deterrence perspective, one could argue that this type of perception helps facilitate delinquency, rather than deter it.

[14] Excellent discussions of these consequences of labeling are provided by Erikson (1962) and Garfinkel (1956).

6. Are the foregoing deterrence relationships any stronger for crimes that are *mala prohibita* [e.g., marijuana use] than they are for crimes that are *mala in se* [e.g., larceny]?

This question recognizes the need for deterrence research to consider fundamental differences in *types* of crimes that may or may not be deterred by legal threats. Most empirical studies of deterrence have limited themselves either to homicide or to F.B.I. "crime index" offenses,[15] all of which are *mala in se*. The legal sanctions against these crimes have massive support in the mores and on that account, may be relatively unnecessary for deterrence.

On the other hand, many criminal activities such as gambling, marijuana use, under-age drinking, etc., are widely practiced and condoned among large segments of our society—despite the legal proscriptions. In the case of these crimes, which are *mala prohibita,* the mores may be sufficiently ambivalent to cause the law to "stand alone" as a deterrent (Andenaes, 1966:957). These distinctions have prompted Zimring (1971:44–45) to hypothesize that:

. . . where a threatened behavior is considered to be a serious breach of society's moral code [i.e., larceny] the major explanation for the higher rate of compliant behavior is the strongly socialized citizen's sense of right and wrong, rather than his special sensitivity to the negative aspects of threatened consequences. Where a threatened behavior is considered a less drastic breach of the moral code [i.e., marijuana use], a special sensitivity to the negative aspects of threatened consequences may play a noteworthy part in explaining the difference between these two groups.

[15] Exceptions to this concentration on crimes that are *mala in se* are, of course, provided by Chambliss' (1966) work with parking violations and Schwartz and Orleans' (1967) work with income tax evasion—both of which may be considered *mala prohibita.*

In short, this hypothesis suggests that "the effectiveness of deterrence varies in inverse proportion to the moral seriousness of the crime" (Morris, 1951:13). For the purposes of this study, we are assuming that stealing is a crime of greater moral seriousness than possession of marijuana. This assumption is supported by the fact that 98.2 percent of the study population *disagreed* with the statement that "stealing *shouldn't* be a crime," whereas only 25 percent disagreed with a similar assertion for marijuana possession. Thus, if Andenaes, Zimring, and Morris are correct, deterrence relationships should be stronger for marijuana offenses than they are for theft crimes.[16]

RESEARCH METHOD

An approach to the foregoing questions is sought through data collected in 321 interviews of undergraduates at The Florida State University.[17] The completed interviews represent 82.3 percent of an original sample of 390 students. From the latter group, which represents a three per-

cent random sample of the undergraduate population (stratified by school year), 44 were out of town on internships, or had dropped from school sometime after the registrar's lists were completed. An additional 25 interviews could not be completed after initial contact was made. Of these, only seven involved refusals on the part of potential respondents. Given the size of the sample and the low rate of incompleted interviews, it is felt that a representative sample of the undergraduate population was obtained.

The interviews were carried out between January and May, 1970, by five undergraduate research assistants who had participated in the construction, pretesting, and revision of the interview schedule. Respondents were assigned to the five interviewers in a random manner.

A short, self-reported crime inventory was included in the interview schedule. Comprising the inventory were questions relating to several dimensions of criminal activity: (1) how often has it been done; (2) at what age was it first done; (3) with how many other people was it first done; (4) how often has it been done in the past year; (5) with how many other people is it normally done? Several of these questions were used to distinguish self-reported users of marijuana from those who claim to have "never used," while similar distinctions were made between those who admit to stealing and those who have "never stolen." [18]

Perception of the severity of penalties for theft and marijuana offenses was indicated by responses to the following questions: What would you say is the maxi-

---

[16] An alternative perspective on "types of crime" and deterrence is offered by Chambliss (1969:368–370) who hypothesized that *instrumental* actions (i.e., theft) are subject to greater control through formal sanctions than *expressive* actions (i.e., marijuana use), inasmuch as the latter are engaged in as a part of a broader style of life to which the individual may be committed. Applying this perspective, we might expect deterrence relationships to be stronger for larceny offenses than for marijuana offenses.

[17] The limitations of a student sample are readily acknowledged; however, the researchers were not expecting to settle the issue of deterrence for all time. Quite the contrary, for they would argue that different kinds of people, in different kinds of situations are deterred from different kinds of crimes for entirely different reasons. This sample deals with a segment of our population that may be over-represented on one of the crimes we are studying—marijuana use, and, perhaps, under-represented on the second crime—theft. We simply want to know whether the perceptions of this particular sample are related to the performance of two specific criminal activities.

[18] Several possible methods of delimiting "levels" of admitted theft were attempted. A simple distinction between those admitting to grand larceny and those admitting to petit larceny was not feasible because only seven students admitted to the more serious offense. Simple frequency of petit larceny was rejected, inasmuch as most of the frequent larcenies were committed at an early age —and it was felt that larcenies committed in the past year would probably be more significant.

mum prison penalty in Florida for someone who:

(a) takes or steals something worth less than $100

(b) illegally possesses marijuana—first offense?

For purposes of contingency analysis, respondents were grouped into three categories for each of the crimes: (1) those *overestimating* the penalty; (2) those with *accurate* perceptions of the penalty; and (3) those *underestimating* the penalty.

Perceptions of the certainty of punishment were obtained from responses to several questions. Respondents were asked to estimate the percentage of people committing crimes who are caught by the police. This general question was followed by estimates pertaining to specific offenses and to persons "like the respondent." In this latter instance, students were asked how likely the police were to catch "someone like yourself" if you used marijuana or stole something worth less than $100. The responses were given in a Likert-type format ranging from "very likely" to "very unlikely." A third set of questions—also in Likert format—asked the respondent how likely it was for "someone like yourself" to receive the maximum prison sentence if you were convicted for one of the several offenses under consideration.

Finally, contact with previously punished offenders was determined by asking the respondent how many individuals he knew personally who had been arrested and/or convicted for theft and marijuana offenses.

FINDINGS

The relationships between self-reported criminal behavior and perceptions of the penal structure are analyzed in contingency tables with Gamma computed to indicate the strength of association. The data in Table 4 are not appropriate for the 2 × 3 format used in other tables, and

a Q-value rather than Gamma is reported.

Deterrence theory suggests that use of marijuana and admitted larceny should be most frequent among those who underestimate the penalties, and least frequent among those who overestimate the penalties for each offense. An inspection of Tables 1-A and 1-B reveals that the present data do not confirm this expectation. While marijuana use is least frequent among those who over-estimate the penalties, it is *most* frequent among those whose perceptions of the law are the *most accurate*. Further, admitted use of marijuana is less common for those *under-estimating* the penalties than for those whose estimates are accurate. At the same time, deterrence logic is contradicted by the fact that admitted theft (Table 1-B) is as prevalent among respondents who over-estimate penalties for petty larceny as it is among those who under-estimate. In addition, the most frequent theft activity is found among those who accurately perceive the penalty for petty larceny. The low Gamma values reinforce the conclusion that admitted criminality appears unrelated to perceptions of the severity of punishment. This interpretation applies to theft, which is *mala in se,* as well as to marijuana use, which is *mala prohibita.*

It is interesting to note that a larger proportion of the respondents underestimated penalties for marijuana possession (43.7 percent) than for petty larceny (19.3 percent). This greater tendency to underestimate marijuana penalties should, according to deterrence theory, eventuate in a greater frequency of marijuana as opposed to theft offenses. However, the opposite is true. Whereas a total of 33.3 percent of the respondents admit to some experience with marijuana, 58.6 percent have stolen something in their life. Thus, something other than a perception of severe penalties appears to be operating in the presumed deterrence of these students from marijuana and theft crimes.

The actual level of punishment avail-

Table 1-A   Admitted Marijuana Use by Perceived Severity of Florida Penalty for First Marijuana Possession*

Perceived Penalty	% Having Used Marijuana	% Never Using Marijuana	Total	(N)
Over-Estimated	27.0	73.0	100.0	(74)
Accurately-Estimated	37.3	62.7	100.0	(102)
Under-Estimated	33.6	66.4	100.0	(137)

Gamma = −.07

Table 1-B   Admitted Stealing by Perceived Severity of Florida Penalty for Petty Larceny*

Perceived Penalty	% Having Stolen	% Never Stealing	Total	(N)
Over-Estimated	54.9	45.1	100.0	(142)
Accurately-Estimated	61.7	38.3	100.0	(115)
Under-Estimated	54.8	45.2	100.0	(62)

Gamma = −.04

*Data for these items are obtained from responses to the questions, "Could you estimate the maximum prison penalty in Florida for illegal possession of marijuana — first offense?" "What would you say the maximum prison penalty in Florida is for someone who takes or steals something worth less than $100?"

able for any crime may be irrelevant as a deterrent if citizens understand or believe that courts are unwilling to impose harsh penalties. The strength of this belief was elicited for both offenses, with the exception that criminal behavior would be more frequent among those who believe that the courts would spare them the maximum allowable penalty. This expectation is borne out for marijuana offenders, but not for theft offenders.

Tables 2-A and 2-B give the frequency of marijuana use and admitted theft for groups of respondents with varying perceptions of the court's leniency. Among those respondents who are most optimistic about avoiding the maximum penalty upon conviction, marijuana use is more than twice as common (43.4 percent) as it is among those who consider the maximum penalty "likely" (19 percent). A moderately strong Gamma value (−.41) suggests that this optimism may be closely associated with the admitted use of marijuana. While admitted theft is more common among those who think the maximum

penalty is "unlikely" than it is among those who consider it "likely," it is *most* common among those who see the maximum penalty as a 50-50 probability. However, the percentage differences among the several groups are sufficiently small to generate a very small Gamma value (−.02) and a conclusion that the perceived likelihood of severe court disposition is apparently unrelated to admitted theft activity. The discrepancy between deterrence relationships involving marijuana and theft behavior is consistent with the expectation raised by Zimring (1971), who hypothesized stronger deterrence relationships for crimes that are *mala prohibita* (marijuana use) than for crimes that are *mala in se* (larceny).

As suggested by Jensen's (1969) findings cited earlier, a deterrent to crime may be provided by the perception that law-violators in general are caught by the police. This approach, dealing with certainty of punishment at the *general* level, assumes that punishment of "others" will deter "ego's" criminal behavior. Tables 3-A and

Table 2-A   Admitted Marijuana Use by Perceived Likelihood of
Receiving Maximum Penalty Upon Conviction for Marijuana Possession*

Perceived Likelihood of Maximum Penalty	% Having Used Marijuana	% Never Using Marijuana	Total	(N)
Likely	19.0	81.0	100.0	(79)
50/50	26.5	73.5	100.0	(83)
Unlikely	43.4	56.6	100.0	(159)

Gamma = −.41
p < .001

Table 2-B   Admitted Theft by Perceived Likelihood of Receiving
Maximum Penalty Upon Conviction for Petty Larceny*

Perceived Likelihood of Maximum Penalty	% Having Stolen	% Never Stealing	Total	(N)
Likely	44.4	55.6	100.0	(18)
50/50	63.1	36.9	100.0	(65)
Unlikely	56.7	43.3	100.0	(238)

Gamma = −.02

*Data for these items are obtained from responses to the questions, "If you were
convicted of possession of marijuana, how likely would you be to get the maximum
Florida penalty?" "If you were convicted of stealing something worth less than
$100, how likely would you be to get the maximum Florida penalty?"

Table 3-A   Admitted Marijuana Use by Perceived Probability of Arrest
for Law Violators*

% of Law Violators Arrested by Police	% Having Used Marijuana	% Never Using Marijuana	Total	(N)
50%+	25.0	75.0	100.0	(104)
21-49%	30.6	69.4	100.0	(108)
0-20%	43.5	56.5	100.0	(108)

Gamma = −.28
p < .01

Table 3-B   Admitted Theft by Belief in the Probability of Arrest for
Law Violators*

% of Law Violators Arrested by Police	% Having Stolen	% Never Stealing	Total	(N)
50%+	51.0	49.0	100.0	(104)
21-49%	60.2	39.8	100.0	(108)
0-20%	61.1	38.9	100.0	(108)

Gamma = −.14

*Data for these items are obtained from responses to the question, "What percent-
age of the people who commit crimes do you think ever get caught by the police?"

3-B show the frequency of admitted criminality for respondents with varying perceptions of the probability that law-violators will be caught by the police.

As expected from deterrence theory, the lowest frequency of marijuana use (25.0 percent) and larceny (51.0 percent) is found among those who perceive the greatest likelihood (50 percent+) that law-violators will be apprehended by the police. Conversely, those perceiving little chance (0–20 percent) for such apprehension are much more likely to have used marijuana (43.5 percent) or to have stolen something (61.1 percent). Given the middle-class character of the student sample [19] it is not surprising that potential *arrest* should, by itself, loom so important as a deterrent to crime. For "respectable" criminals, an arrest—with its attendant publicity—may be as socially and personally consequential as any subsequent court action. This point was considered by Cameron (1964), who noted that formal legal action was frequently not taken in the cases of apprehended middle-class shoplifters. Both police and storekeepers apparently felt that the situation of arrest, even without publicity, was a sufficient deterrent to future pilfering. In the case of our student sample, *arrest* for a drug offense carries a particularly harsh consequence. A recent and well publicized Florida statute [20] requires the summary suspension of any student arrested for drug offenses. Since reinstatement must await court disposition and since trial delays are excessive, and a loss of student status could result (for males) in a change of military draft status, an arrest for marijuana possession could have drastic consequences

for the accused student. Thus, arrest may carry as strong a sanction as a subsequent conviction—which frequently results in probation for first offenders.

For the punishment of "other" to have an impact upon one's own behavior, that punishment must, of course, be known. Thus, proponents of *general* deterrence would argue that knowledge of society's punishment of others will deter one from similar criminal endeavor. Presumably, then, the *less* contact one has had with punished "others" the *more likely* is he to commit the punished act. Tables 4-A and 4-B summarize data pertaining to respondent contacts with others who had been arrested or convicted for marijuana possession and petit larceny.[21]

Contrary to general deterrence expectations, use of marijuana is more than twice as great among respondents who had knowledge of someone arrested for possession (47.2 percent) than among those without such knowledge (21.8 percent). A computed Q-value (.53) that is statistically significant but in the "wrong" direction for the deterrence hypothesis, further indicates that general deterrence appears *not* to be working among marijuana offenders. Of course, we cannot tell from these data whether one's knowledge of another's arrest for marijuana possession preceded or followed his use of marijuana. However, one-half of the self-reported users of marijuana admit to having used it at least six times in the previous year. Thus, it is probable that for many of the marijuana users at least some criminal activity was preceded by knowledge of an arrested "other."

In this regard, it is interesting to note that 104 of the 105 admitted marijuana

---

[19] The median income of the respondents' fathers was $10,000, and 55 percent of the fathers had at least some college training.

[20] Legislation passed in 1969 called for automatic suspension of any student arrested for a drug offense. Subsequent legislation passed in 1970, and effective on October 1 of that year, gives university officials the authority to suspend such a student if they so desire.

[21] The question of how many "others" one knew who had been arrested or convicted of selling marijuana was deliberately not asked, so as to avoid the appearance of seeking information that was too sensitive. Too few students knew "others" who had been arrested or convicted of grand larceny to warrant the inclusion of this crime.

Table 4-A   Admitted Marijuana Use by Knowledge of Others Arrested
for Marijuana Possession*

Number Known	% Having Used Marijuana	% Never Using Marijuana	Total	(N)
1 or More	47.2	52.8	100.0	(142)
None	21.8	78.2	100.0	(179)

Q = .53
p < .001

Table 4-B   Admitted Theft by Knowledge of Others Arrested
for Petty Larceny*

Number Known	% Having Stolen	% Never Stealing	Total	(N)
1 or More	66.7	33.3	100.0	(105)
None	52.8	47.2	100.0	(214)

Q = .28
p < .01

*Data for these items are obtained from responses to the questions, "Altogether, how many people that you know personally have been arrested for illegal possession of marijuana?" "How many people that you know personally have ever been arrested for stealing something of little value (worth less than $100)?"

users indicate that their crime was initially committed *in the company* of at least one other person and 48 of those using for the first time were with three or more persons. Indeed, the social character of this offense [22] makes it more likely that one will have contact with similar offenders—some of whom may have been arrested and/or convicted. At the same time, a subculture of drug use probably countermands the deterrent effect of knowing punished offenders, by providing "definitions favorable to violation" of marijuana laws, as well as the opportunity and techniques for doing so.[23]

Knowledge of arrested offenders, while generally not as extensive for theft as for

[22] Among the earliest to describe the social character of marijuana use, and the processes of socialization into marijuana subcultures, was Becker (1963:41–58).
[23] For a discussion of the importance of "definitions favorable to violation of law," in the genesis of crime, see Sutherland and Cressey (1970: chapter 4). Cloward and Ohlin (1960) offer a cogent analysis of differential access to "illegitimate opportunity."

marijuana use, also appears positively related to admitted theft activity. As seen in Table 4-B, those respondents who know of at least one other person arrested for petty larceny, are more likely to have committed some larceny themselves (66.7 percent) than those who have no such knowledge (52.8 percent). Again, something other than general deterrence appears to be working inasmuch as the computed Q-value is statistically significant in the "wrong" direction. The fact that the positive relationship between knowledge of apprehended others and criminality is stronger for marijuana use than for theft, may be partially explained by the fact that larceny is not as "social" an offense as marijuana use. Approximately 42 percent of those admitting to some theft activity (77/184) indicate that their first petty larceny was committed alone. Thus, it may be somewhat more difficult for petty thieves to meet others who have been arrested for that offense.

The deterrent effectiveness of arrest is brought into sharper focus when percep-

Table 5-A   Admitted Marijuana Use by Perceived Likelihood of Arrest
for Marijuana Possession*

Perceived Likelihood of Arrest	% Having Used Marijuana	% Never Using Marijuana	Total	(N)
Likely	0.0	100.0	100.0	(28)
50/50	10.7	89.3	100.0	(28)
Unlikely	38.9	61.1	100.0	(265)

Gamma = −.84
p < .001

Table 5-B   Admitted Theft by Perceived Likelihood of Arrest
for Petty Larceny*

Perceived Likelihood of Arrest	% Having Stolen	% Never Stealing	Total	(N)
Likely	40.6	59.4	100.0	(32)
50/50	48.5	51.5	100.0	(68)
Unlikely	62.4	37.6	100.0	(221)

Gamma = −.31
p < .01

*Data for these items are obtained from responses to the questions, "If someone like yourself used marijuana occasionally in Tallahassee, how likely are the police to catch him (her)?" "If someone like yourself stole something worth less than $100 in Tallahassee, how likely are the police to catch him (her)?

tions of its likelihood for *specific* offenses, and for *oneself,* are considered. Tables 5-A and 5-B show the relative frequency of admitted criminality for respondents with varying perceptions of the likelihood that *they* would be arrested for the specific offenses of stealing or marijuana use. The data, though varying somewhat by crime, provide what appears to be consistent support for deterrence theory.

As expected, the use of marijuana and belief in the likelihood of arrest for marijuana possession, were inversely related (Gamma = −.84, p < .001). In fact, *none* of the respondents believing that their use of marijuana would *likely* lead to an arrest, have ever used marijuana! By contrast, 38.9 percent of those believing that such an arrest is *unlikely,* admit to some use of marijuana. The large Gamma value may be slightly misleading, however, since it is greatly enhanced by the one zero cell in the table. While intra-offense comparisons suggest that perceptions of arrest po-

tential may be serving as a deterrent, the fact is that hardly anyone, user or non-user, sees that potential as very great. Indeed, 75 percent of the non-users and almost all of the users think there is *less* than a 50-50 chance of being arrested for marijuana possession. Thus, it is not entirely clear just how strong a deterrent is offered by the threat of arrest for marijuana possession.

Also as expected, those who think their chances of arrest for petty larceny are lowest, are the most likely to have committed a theft (62.4 percent). Those who believe they are likely to be arrested should they ever steal something, admit to such theft much less frequently (40.6 percent). Although statistically significant (p < .01) the Gamma value for petty larceny (−.31) is appreciably smaller than the corresponding value for marijuana use. This difference in strength of relationship when marijuana and theft data are compared, offers further support for Andenaes'

(1966) and Zimring's (1971) contention that for crimes that are *mala prohibita* (marijuana use), the law may stand alone as a deterrent. Because laws have the support of the mores in the case of theft (*mala in se*), the relationship between deterrence and perceptions of the law may be more difficult to establish. For theft, deterrence may, indeed, be more the consequence of internalized morality than internalized legality.

SUMMARY AND DISCUSSION

In an effort to answer questions that have not been resolved by prior research, this paper has used a different approach to the empirical study of deterrence theory. Whereas most of the earlier studies were concerned with rates of crime for large geographic units, the present study used the admitted criminality of a specific sample of individuals as the dependent variable. It was expected that deterrence —if it existed—would likely vary with the perceptions of punishment held by potential and actual self-reported criminals, as well as with the types of crime presumably being deterred.

Interviews with 321 university students were used to determine relationships between admitted marijuana use and theft, and perceptions of the severity and certainty of punishment. From deterrence theory it was expected that admitted criminality would be *least frequent* among those who: (1) perceive the most severe penalties for larceny and marijuana use, (2) perceive the greatest chances of receiving the maximum penalties for those offenses upon conviction, (3) perceive the greatest probability that law-violators will be arrested, (4) have the greatest familiarity with others who have been arrested for larceny or marijuana possession, and (5) perceive the greatest probability of their own arrest in the event that they stole something or used marijuana.

The data for marijuana use and theft

indicate that *no relationship* exists between perceptions of severe punishment and admitted criminality. This finding runs counter to deterrence theory, but is in accord with several earlier studies of deterrence (Schuessler, 1952; Sellin, 1967; Gibbs, 1968; Tittle, 1969; Chiricos and Waldo, 1970). While these and the earlier findings cannot be held conclusive, they strongly question the assertion that crime may be deterred by increasing penalties.

If the viability of severe punishment as a deterrent to crime has been seriously questioned by empirical findings, the same cannot be said for certain punishment. The latter dimension of deterrence has emerged from recent empirical tests with a considerable amount of credibility (Chambliss, 1966; Gibbs, 1968; Tittle, 1969; Jensen, 1969). In the present study, perceived certainty of punishment appears to be related to admitted criminality. However, the strength of this relationship varies by crime and by the index of certainty employed. For each of the certainty indices, marijuana use seems more related than admitted theft activity to perceptions of the certainty of punishment.

Although the present data provide only moderate support for this aspect of deterrence theory, the strongest support is found in the perception that one's own criminality is likely to result in an arrest (Tables 5-A and 5-B). The next greatest support appears to come from the perception that one's own criminality is likely to eventuate in the maximum allowable penalty for a specific crime (Table 2-A). Both of these situations have a common focus on the individual and *his* chances of arrest and punishment for a *specific* crime. Thus, perceptions of the certainty of punishment appear most viable as a deterrent when they involve the potential criminal's estimate of his *own chances* for arrest and harsh penalties for a particular crime—independent of the chances for any "generalized other."

This latter point receives support from two sources. First, the weakest deterrent among the several certainty dimensions is the perception that lawbreakers *in general* are likely to be arrested or convicted. Only for marijuana use (Table 3-A) is the relationship between admitted criminality and this perception of punishment in general, statistically significant (p < .01). Second, personal knowledge of the punishment of "others" for marijuana use or theft is apparently ineffective in deterring these offenses. On the contrary, use of marijuana and admitted theft are *most likely* for those who know someone else who has been arrested for these offenses. Thus, little support is found for a basic premise of deterrence theory; i.e., the punishment of alter, if known to ego, will serve as a general deterrent, keeping ego from involvement in that criminal activity.

As noted above, marijuana use appears more likely than theft to be deterred by perceptions of the certainty of punishment. Such a finding is consistent with Andenaes' (1966) distinction between crimes that are *mala prohibita* and crimes that are *mala in se,* and with Zimring's (1971) hypothesis cited earlier. That is, one might expect the law to "stand alone" in the deterrence of marijuana use (*mala prohibita*) inasmuch as the law has little support in the mores of the university student subculture. In this regard, it is recalled that only 25 percent of the respondents disagreed with the assertion that "possession of marijuana should be legalized for adults," while 78.5 percent of all respondents agree that the "penalties for possession of marijuana are too harsh." Thus, it seems reasonable to conclude that the norms prevalent in student groups are not likely to deter marijuana use. Whatever deterrence is to occur must be the product of some other force, such as the law.

For the crime of theft, the law has a great deal of support in the mores. Be-

cause of this, it may be difficult to separate the deterrent effect of the *law* from other aspects of deterrence.[24] Again, 68 percent of the respondents *disagreed* with an assertion that "the penalties for stealing are too harsh" (even though most perceived the penalty to be *greater* than it actually is), and 98.2 percent *disagreed* with the statement that "stealing shouldn't be a crime."It is not, then, surprising to note that perceived certainty of punishment has little discernible deterrent impact upon the crime of theft. For most who are deterred, pressures from alternative sources—such as moral values that have long been internalized—are likely sufficient to inhibit the proscribed theft activity.

The important point to note is that the law, and more specifically, perceptions of the certainty of punishment, cannot be assumed to deter *all* criminal activities in the same way. The deterrence equation may be more or less complex, depending upon the type of crime and the degree of congruence between formal and informal reactions to that crime. Thus, an understanding of deterrence further presumes an understanding of the kinds of persons[25] involved, and the way in which

[24] The possibility that the threat of law will be less a deterrent for crimes that are strongly abhorred in the mores of the people, has been suggested, as well, by Zimring (1971:44–45) and by Morris (1951:13).

[25] When considering the variation in deterrence effectiveness for different "kinds of persons" it is interesting to note that "casual users" of marijuana are frequently the most likely to minimize the threat of legal reprisal (data analyzed, but not presented in this paper). It is entirely possible that this response represents an over-reaction to the sudden awareness that one can commit the crime without immediate response from the criminal justice system. That is, confidence of immunity may not lead to the use of marijuana, as much as it follows the experience of non-apprehension. "Regular users," who may participate more fully in a subculture of drug use, are much more likely to know others who have been arrested for possession of marijuana. It may well be this knowledge which gives the "regular user" a less optimistic outlook on the chances of apprehension, than that espoused by the "casual user."

their values reflect upon the illegal activity. Should these values be inconsistent with the formal dictates of law, then the latter will "stand alone" as a deterrent. How strongly the law stands as a deterrent may further depend upon how serious the conflict between the mores and the law.

Just how strong the marijuana law stands as a deterrent within the particular group studied is questionable—despite the fact that deterrence relationships *appeared* to be strongest for marijuana offenses. As noted above, more than three-fourths of the students sampled feel that marijuana laws are too harsh. In addition, all respondents were asked the following question:

If the penalties for the use of marijuana were reduced, would you consider using it, or using it more often?

Of the 215 students who claimed to have never used marijuana, only 26 percent affirmed that they would consider using the drug if the laws were made less harsh. For the remainder, it may not be unreasonable to assume that their perception of the law was *not* the principal reason for their non-use of marijuana. The impact of extra-legal factors may be even stronger for theft offenses than for marijuana use. Ninety-one percent of those who claim to have never stolen, assert that they would *not* consider stealing if the laws governing theft were reduced. This further confirms the possibility that the law itself is not deterring these activities to a significant degree.

It is difficult to foresee what would happen to the situation of deterrence if, in fact, laws were changed or eliminated. To some extent, the informal norms and mores of the people are prompted and supported by the formal laws [26]—even

though it may appear that the mores themselves are what deter or stimulate criminality. Should, for example, the laws against theft be eliminated, would the moral repulsion against stealing persist? At the same time, would the mores of the general public come to accept marijuana if the laws forbidding it were erased? [27] Answers to these and related questions are beyond the scope of this paper. However, the results of this study may justify the conclusion that the effects of law in deterring crime are probably not as great, and certainly less uniform than many have heretofore assumed.

REFERENCES

ANDENAES, JOHANNES, 1966. "The General Preventive Effects of Punishment," *University of Pennsylvania Law Review*, 114 (May):949–83.

Assembly Committee on Criminal Procedure, 1968. *Deterrent Effects of Criminal Sanctions.* (May) Assembly of the State of California.

BALL, JOHN C., 1955. "The Deterrence Concept in Criminology and Law," *Journal of Criminal*

[26] This point is supported in the findings of Schwartz and Orleans (1967) who note that: "the results of the study . . . suggest that the threat of sanction can deter people from violating the law, perhaps in important part by inducing a moralistic attitude towards compliance."

[27] The Florida Legislature has recently (May, 1971) reduced to a misdemeanor the penalty for possessing a small amount (less than five grams, or about four "joints") of marijuana. The official rationale for this change is that the prosecutors were unwilling to prosecute and the courts were unwilling to convict under the existing law which provided for a maximum of five years in prison. Clearly, the shift in penal sanction reflects a prior shift in community mores regarding the use of marijuana. As long as marijuana use was largely confined to black-slum communities, there was apparently little pressure upon the police to enforce marijuana laws. However, as the popularity of marijuana spread to respectable, white, middle-class colleges and high schools, the initial expectation was that stronger enforcement of the laws would make the problem go away. Yet with time, the increased enforcement of the law only served to crowd police stations with sons and daughters of judges, business leaders, and lawmakers. Indeed, it was not until the mores of white, middle-class and prosperous youth showed themselves to be persistent and growing in their acceptance of marijuana that the legislators were motivated to act. It will be interesting to observe whether this change in law, brought by a change in the mores of youth, will precipitate a wider acceptance of marijuana within the adult or youth communities of Florida.

Law, Criminology and Police Science, **46** (September-October) :347–54.

BARNES, HARRY E. and NEGLEY K. TEETERS, 1959. *New Horizons in Criminology.* Englewood Cliffs, N.J.: Prentice-Hall.

BECKER, HOWARD, 1963. *Outsiders: Studies in the Sociology of Deviance.* New York: Free Press.

BENTHAM, JEREMY, 1843. "Principles of Penal Law," in John Bowring, ed., *The Works of Jeremy Bentham.* Edinburgh: W. Tait.

BITTNER, EGON and ANTHONY PLATT, 1966. "The Meaning of Punishment," *Issues in Criminology,* **2** (Spring) :77–99.

CAMERON, MARY, 1964. *The Booster and The Snitch: Department Store Shoplifting.* New York: Free Press.

CHAMBLISS, WILLIAM J., 1966. "The Deterrent Influence of Punishment," *Crime and Delinquency,* **12** (January):70–75; 1969, *Crime and The Legal Process.* New York: McGraw Hill.

CHIRICOS, THEODORE G. and GORDON P. WALDO, 1970. "Punishment and Crime: An Examination of Empirical Evidence," *Social Problems,* **18** (Fall) :200–17.

CLASTER, DANIEL, 1967. "Comparison of Risk Perception between Delinquents and Non-Delinquents," *Journal of Criminal Law, Criminology and Police Science,* **58** (March) :80–86.

CLOWARD, RICHARD and LLOYD OHLIN, 1960. *Delinquency and Opportunity.* New York: Free Press.

ERIKSON, KAI T., 1962. "Notes on the Sociology of Deviance," *Social Problems,* **9** (Spring) : 307–14.

Federal Bureau of Investigation, 1969. *Crime in the United States: Uniform Crime Reports —1968.* Washington, D.C.:66–75.

GARFINKEL, HAROLD, 1956. "Conditions of Successful Degradation Ceremonies," *American Journal of Sociology,* **61** (March) :420–24.

GIBBS, JACK P., 1966. "Sanctions," *Social Problems,* **14** (Fall) :147–59; 1968, "Crime, Punishment, and Deterrence," *Southwestern Social Science Quarterly,* **48** (March):515–30.

GRUPP, STANLEY and WARREN LUCAS, 1969. "The 'Marijuana Muddle' as Reflected in California Arrest Statistics and Dispositions." Unpublished revision of a paper read at 1969 Annual Meeting of the American Sociological Association, September 4, 1969, San Francisco, California.

JEFFREY, C. RAY, 1965. "Criminal Behavior and Learning Theory," *Journal of Criminal Law, Criminology and Police Science,* **56** (September) :294–300.

JENSEN, GARY F., 1969. " 'Crime Doesn't Pay': Correlates of a Shared Misunderstanding," *Social Problems,* **17** (Fall) :189–201.

MEAD, GEORGE H., 1918. "The Psychology of Punitive Justice," *American Journal of Sociology,* **23** (March) :577–602.

MORRIS, NORVAL, 1951. *The Habitual Criminal.* Cambridge: Harvard University Press.

President's Commission on Law Enforcement and Administration of Justice, 1967. *Task Force Report: Crime and Its Impact—An Assessment.* Washington: U.S. Government Printing Office.

POLIER, JUSTINE W., 1956. "The Woodshed Is No Answer," *Federal Probation,* **20** (September) : 3–6.

SAVITZ, LEONARD D., 1958. "A Study in Capital Punishment," *Journal of Criminal Law, Criminology and Police Science,* **49** (November-December) :338–41.

SCHUESSLER, KARL, 1952. "The Deterrent Influence of the Death Penalty," *The Annals,* **284** (November) :54–62.

SCHWARTZ, RICHARD C. and SONYA ORLEANS, 1967. "On Legal Sanctions," *The University of Chicago Law Review,* **34:** 274–300.

SELLIN, THORSTEN, 1967. "Homicides in Retentionist and Abolitionist States," in Thorsten Sellin, ed., *Capital Punishment.* New York: Harper and Row, 135–38.

SUTHERLAND, EDWIN and DONALD R. CRESSEY, 1970. *Criminology,* 8th Edition. Philadelphia, J. B. Lippincott Company.

TITTLE, CHARLES R., 1969. "Crime Rates and Legal Sanctions," *Social Problems,* **16** (Spring) :409–23.

TOBY, JACKSON, 1964. "Is Punishment Necessary?" *Journal of Criminal Law, Criminology and Police Science,* **55** (September) :332–37.

WOOD, LEDGER, 1938. "Responsibility and Punishment," *Journal of Criminal Law, Criminology and Police Science,* **28** (January-February) : 630–40.

ZIMRING, FRANK, 1971. *Perspectives on Deterrence.* National Institute of Mental Health, Washington, D.C.

ZIMRING, FRANK and GORDON HAWKINS, 1968. "Deterrence and Marginal Groups," *Journal of Research in Crime and Delinquency,* **5** (July) : 100–14.

PHYSICIANS AND MEDICARE:
A BEFORE-AFTER STUDY OF THE EFFECTS
OF LEGISLATION ON ATTITUDES

John Colombotos

Seldom has a law been more bitterly opposed by any group than was Medicare by the medical profession (see Harris, 1966; Feingold, 1966; Rose, 1967:400–455). Just before Medicare was passed by Congress in 1965, there was even talk about a "boycott" of the program by physicians. This paper examines how individual physicians reacted, in their behavior and in their thinking, to Medicare after it became law.[1] The more general issue raised by this question is the role of law as an instrument of social change, an old sociological problem.

LAW AS AN INSTRUMENT OF SOCIAL CHANGE. One view, attributed to early sociologists such as Herbert Spencer and William Graham Sumner, is that law can never move ahead of the customs or mores of the people, that legislation which is not rooted in the folkways is doomed to failure. Social change must be slow, and change in public opinion must precede legislative action. In brief, "stateways cannot change folkways." This view was expressed by Senator Barry Goldwater in the 1964 Presidential campaign (*The New York Times,* Nov. 1, 1964:1): "I am unalterably opposed to . . . discrimination, but I also know that government can provide no lasting solution. . . . The ultimate solution lies in the hearts of men."

Others see law as a positive force in initiating social change (Allport, 1954: 471): "It is a well known psychological fact that most people accept the results of an election or legislation gladly enough after the furor has subsided. . . . They allow themselves to be re-educated by the new norm that prevails."[2]

These are oversimplified statements of the role of law as an instrument of social change and miss the complexity of the problem. The question must be specified: under what conditions do laws have what effects?

EFFECTS: BEHAVIOR VS. ATTITUDES. Sumner's negative position on law as an instrument of social change has been distorted, according to one reappraisal of his writings (Ball et al., 1962:532–540). Sumner (1906:68), in distinguishing between the effects of law on behavior and on attitudes, did not reject the power of law to influence men's behavior: "Men can always perform the prescribed act, although they cannot always think or feel prescribed thoughts or emotions."

Reprinted from *American Sociological Review,* **34** (June, 1969), pp. 318–32, by permission of the author and The American Sociological Association.

Supported by U. S. Public Health Service Research Grants 5 RO1 CH 00045 and CH 00249. This is a revised version of a paper read at the Annual Meeting of the American Sociological Association, San Francisco, California, August 31, 1967. The interviewing for the study was done by the National Opinion Research Center, University of Chicago.

[1] It is of course necessary to distinguish between the attitudes of individual physicians toward Medicare and official AMA policy. The AMA leadership is commonly regarded as more conservative than the rank-and-file; however, the opposition of the AMA to Medicare before its passage apparently was supported by the majority of its membership. In a national poll of private practitioners in 1961, less than 20% were in favor of the program "to provide hospital and nursing home care for the aged through the Social Security System" (Medical Tribune, May 15, 1961).

[2] Allport qualifies this remark elsewhere in his book. It is quoted here to state the issue in its sharpest form.

This is in agreement with the views of the majority of contemporary politically liberal social scientists, who see law primarily as a way of changing behavior, not attitudes. For example: "[Legal action] cannot coerce thoughts or instill subjective tolerance. . . . Law is intended only to control the outward expression of intolerance" (Allport, 1954:477). And according to MacIver (1954:viii), "No law should require men to change their attitudes. . . . In a democracy we do not punish a man because he is opposed to income taxes, or to free school education, or to vaccination, or to minimum wages, but the laws of a democracy insist that he obey the laws that make provisions for these things. . . ."

The distinction between the effects of law on attitudes and on behavior is supported by empirical studies showing a discrepancy between the two (see Deutscher, 1966:235–254). In race relations, for example, study after study has shown that in concrete situations—in hotel accommodations (LaPiere, 1934:230–237), restaurant service (Kutner et al., 1952:649–652), department store shopping (Saenger and Gilbert, 1950:57–76), hospital accommodations, and school desegregation (Clark, 1953:47–50)—expressions of prejudice are not necessarily accompanied by discriminatory behavior. There are undoubtedly instances of the opposite, that is, verbal expressions of tolerance accompanied by discriminatory behavior, but they are not as well documented. The flight of white, liberal, middle-class families from the cities to the suburbs may be such an instance (Scott and Scott, 1968:-46 ff.).

But to say that attitudes and behavior are not perfectly correlated is not to say they are unrelated, and there is evidence that change in behavior leads to change in attitudes. Studies of integrated army units, housing projects, and children's camps show that white people in these situations develop more favorable attitudes toward Negroes (Swanson et al., 1952:502; Deutsch and Collins, 1951; Yarrow, 1958). In an analysis of school desegregation, Hyman and Sheatsley (1964:6) describe the process thus: "There is obviously some parallel between public opinion and official action. . . . Close analysis of the current findings . . . leads us to the conclusion that in those parts of the South where some measure of school integration has taken place official action has preceded public sentiment, and *public sentiment has then attempted to accommodate itself to the new situation* [emphasis added]."

Other studies (Mussen, 1950:423–441; Campbell, 1958:335–340), however, have found that social contact has little effect in reducing prejudice.[3]

If indeed behavioral change does lead to attitudinal change, then law, by first changing behavior, may ultimately lead to changes in attitudes. As Allport says: "Outward action, psychology knows, has an eventual effect upon inner habits of thought and feeling. And for this reason we list legislative action as one of the major methods of reducing, not only public discrimination [behavior], but private prejudice [attitudes] as well" (1954:477). Berger, too, writes: "Law does not change attitudes directly, but by altering the situations in which attitudes and opinions are formed, law can indirectly reach the more private areas of life it cannot touch directly in a democratic society" (Berger, 1954:187). Clark (1953:72), among others, states the issue in more problematic terms: "Situationally determined changes in behavior [as in response to a law] *may or*

---

[3] In Campbell's study of a desegregating school system, the results were mixed. White students who claimed Negroes as personal friends were more likely to show a reduction of prejudice than those without Negro friends, but the time order of these factors is ambiguous: those who became less prejudiced may then have chosen Negro friends. Also, those who had many classes with Negroes were no more likely to become less prejudiced than those with few classes with Negroes.

may not be accompanied by compatible changes in attitudes or motivation of the individuals involved [emphasis added]."

Others, however, see law exerting a *direct* influence on attitudes, without necessarily changing behavior first. Law is conceived as a legitimizing and educational force, supporting one value or set of values against another. For example, according to Dicey (1914:465): "No facts play a more important part in the creation of opinion than laws themselves." And according to Bonfield (1965:111): "Past the change in attitude which may be caused by legally mandated and enforced nondiscriminatory conduct, *the mere existence of the law itself affects prejudice* [emphasis added]. People usually agree with the law internalize its values. This is because considerable moral and symbolic weight is added to a principle when it is embedded in legislation.

The results of the few studies done on the effects of law on behavior and attitudes are mixed. Cantril (1947:228) notes: "When an opinion is held by a slight majority or when opinion is not solidly structured, an accomplished fact tends to shift opinion in the direction of acceptance. Poll figures show that immediately after the repeal of the arms embargo, immediately after the passage of the conscription laws, and immediately after favorable Congressional action on lend-lease and on the repeal of the neutrality laws [just before the United States' entry into World War II] there was invariably a rise of around ten per cent in the number of people favorable to these actions." And Muir (1967) found that the Supreme Court decision banning religious exercises in the nation's schools had an over-all positive effect on the attitudes and behavior of 28 officials in one public school system, though there was some evidence of a backlash.

Other studies, however, show that laws and court decisions have negligible effects on relevant attitudes. Hyman and Sheats-

ley (1964:3) and Schwartz (1967:11–12, 28–41) interpret the increasing acceptance of integration between 1942 and 1964 as a complex of long-term trends that are not easily modified by specific, even highly dramatic events, such as the Supreme Court decision of 1954. The physicians' strike against the province's medical care plan in Saskatchewan, Canada, in 1962 (Badgely and Wolfe, 1967) is an extreme case of noncompliance with a program implemented by a law.[4]

CONDITIONS FOR EFFECTIVENESS OF LAW. Three commonly cited factors determining the effectiveness of law are: (1) the degree of compatibility of the law with existing values, (2) the enforceability of the law, (3) the clarity of public policy and the diligence of enforcement.[5]

1. To say that a law must be compatible

---

[4] In an experimental study, information that a behavior was illegal did not change the subjects' attitudes toward that behavior (Walker and Argyle, 1964:570–581). In a follow-up experiment, however, it was found that knowledge of the law and knowledge of peer consensus did change attitudes, and, furthermore, these effects depended on the authoritarianism of the subjects (Berkowitz and Walker, 1967:410–422).

[5] These conditions are discussed in the following: Berger, 1954:173–177; Clark, 1953:53–59; Allport, 1954:469–473; Roche and Gordon, 1955:10, 42, 44, 49; Rose, 1959:470–481; Evans, 1965:285–293; Bonfield, 1965:107–122; Mayhew, 1968:258–284. Problems of implementation, specifically, the work and effects of antidiscrimination enforcement agencies, are analyzed by Berger (1954) and Mayhew (1968).

Less commonly cited factors determining the effectiveness of law are, (1) The amount of opposition to the law and the distribution of this opposition. The stronger and the more concentrated the opposition in politically relevant units, along geographical or occupational lines, for example, the more effectively it can oppose the law (Roche and Gordon, 1955:341). (2) The quality of support. A law is more likely to be effective if supported than if it is opposed by community leaders (see Killian, 1958:65–70). (3) The tempo of change. It is argued that the less the transition time, the easier the adaptation to the change enacted by the law (see Clark, 1953: 43–47; Evans, 1965:290; Badgley and Wolfe, 1967: 45).

with some major existing values is not to say that it must be compatible with all values. In any society, especially in modern, industrial society, values themselves "are full of inconsistencies and strains, unliberated tendencies in many directions, responsive adjustments to new situations well conceived or ill conceived" (MacIver, 1948:279). A law, then, "maintains one set of values against another" (Pound, 1944:25). Thus desegregation and civil rights laws find support in the democratic creed and due process; Medicare finds support in the principle that adequate medical care is a right, rather than a privilege. This position appears to be in agreement with Sumner's principle of a "strain toward consistency." There is an important difference, however. Whereas Sumner posed the question of compatibility between a new law and existing mores as one of all or nothing, the current view emphasizes conflicts and strains among a system of mores and poses the question of compatibility as a matter of degree (Myrdal, 1944:1045–1057).

2. In order for a law to be enforceable, the behavior to be changed must be observable. It is more difficult to enforce a law against homosexual behavior, for example, than a law against racial discrimination in public transportation.

3. The authorities responsible must be fully committed to enforcing the new law. One reason for the failure of Prohibition was the failure, or disinclination, of law enforcement agents to implement the law. Civil rights legislation runs into the same problem where local authorities, especially in the deep South, look the other way.

THE MEDICARE LAW. Medicare, signed into law in July, 1965, is a major piece of social legislation. It is often compared in importance with the original Social Security Act of 1935.

Medicare, Title 18 of the Social Security Amendments Act of 1965 (Public Law 89–97), established a new program of health insurance for people 65 years old or over. It has two parts: hospital insurance (Part A), applying automatically to almost all people 65 or over, which covers inpatient hospital services, outpatient hospital diagnostic services, and posthospital care in the patient's home or in an extended care facility (such as a nursing home); and medical insurance (Part B), a voluntary plan elected by over 90% of those eligible for Part A, which covers physicians' services wherever they are furnished, home health services, and a number of other medical services. Part A is financed by the same method that finances retirement, disability, and death benefits under Social Security, i.e., special Social Security contributions by employees and their employers. Part B is financed by a monthly premium of $3.00, from each participant who elects to pay, matched by $3.00 from the general revenues of the Federal Government.[6]

For twenty years the American Medical Association fought bitterly and effectively against such a Federal program of health insurance under Social Security. Now, however, that the program has become law, the question is: How have individual physicians reacted, in their behavior and in their attitudes, to Medicare?

RESEARCH DESIGN

Our data come from standardized interviews in 1964 and early 1965, before Medicare was passed, with 1,205 physicians in private practice in New York State (about 80% of a probability sample), and from reinterviews with subsamples of these physicians at two different points in time after Medicare was passed. The interviews were conducted mainly by telephone. An experimental comparison of telephone and personal interviews with small, random

[6] Amendments to the Social Security Act in 1967 made some minor changes in the Medicare program and included an increase in the monthly premium.

subsamples of physicians showed that the responses obtained by the two methods were essentially similar.[7]

The purpose of the first wave of interviews was to study physicians' political attitudes, their attitudes toward issues in the organization of medical practice, and their career values, and to examine the relationship between background characteristics, such as their social origins and specialties, and their attitudes.[8] Among the questions in the first wave of interviews was: "What is your opinion about the bill that would provide for compulsory health insurance through Social Security to cover hospital costs for those over 65—Are you personally in favor of such a plan, or are you opposed to it?"

The bill referred to was passed, as noted above, in July, 1965, as Part A of Title 18. Part B of Title 18, the voluntary insurance plan that pays for physicians' bills and other services, and Title 19, which provides for Federal matching funds to states for medical care for the "medically indigent," were not covered in the first wave of interviews because they were not introduced in the bill until the spring of 1965. Title 19, as a matter of fact, received little publicity until after the bill was passed. Title 19 is commonly called *Medicaid;* Title 18, parts A and B, *Medicare.*

Thus, before the law was passed, measures were available of physicians' attitudes toward what was generally considered the major feature of the bill, hospital insurance for the elderly, and many related issues, providing a unique opportunity for a natural experiment of the effects of legislation on attitudes.

The 1,205 physicians were stratified on their initial attitude toward Title 18A (i.e., before it was passed) and on geographic area, religious background, and political ideology, all of which were highly correlated with their initial attitude toward Title 18A,[9] and randomly divided into two subsamples, one with 804 and the other with 401 physicians.

The first subsample of 804 physicians was contacted between the middle of May, 1966, and the end of June, 1966, nearly one year after Medicare was passed and just before it was to go into effect. The second subsample of 401 doctors was contacted between the end of January and April, 1967, a little over six months after the main provisions of the Medicare program had gone into effect. More than 80% of each of these subsamples—676 and 331, respectively—were successfully reinterviewed.

To summarize, 1,205 doctors were interviewed before Medicare was passed (call this Time 1). Of these, 676 were reinterviewed about ten months after the law was passed and just before its implementation (call this Time 2),[10] and another 331 were reinterviewed a little over six months

---

[7] Reported in "The Effects of Personal vs. Telephone Interviews on Socially Acceptable Responses," presented by the author at the annual meeting of the American Association for Public Opinion Research, Groton, Connecticut, May 14, 1965.

[8] Some of these data are reported in the following papers: Colombotos, 1968; Colombotos, 1969a; Colombotos, 1969b.

[9] Physicians in New York City were more pro-Medicare than physicians in upstate New York; Jewish physicians were more pro-Medicare than Protestant physicians, with Catholics in between; and those who were Democrats and took a liberal position on economic-welfare issues were more pro-Medicare than those who were Republicans and took a conservative position (see Colombotos, 1968:320–331).

[10] Actually, the 676 physicians interviewed at Time 2 include 100 who could not be reached by June 30 and were interviewed between July and October, after Medicare went into effect. Those interviewed after June 30 were a little better informed than those interviewed before June 30 about the services covered by the Medicare program, which is not surprising, but the patterns of change in the attitude toward Title 18A of the two groups were practically the same. The specific month within the Time 2 or Time 3 periods when respondents were interviewed also made no difference in the pattern of change in their attitude toward Title 18A.

after its implementation (call this Time 3).[11] Thus, differences in attitudes between Time 1 and Time 2 would reflect the effects of the Medicare law before actual experience with it; differences between Time 1 and Time 3 would reflect the combined effects of the Medicare law and short-term experience with the program. This design makes it possible to separate the effects on attitudes of the law itself from the effects of its implementation, that is, short-term experience with the program. The design is represented in Figure 1.

a "boycott," or "nonparticipation," when it was passed (*The New York Times,* June 22, 1965:1). Immediately after the law was passed, the president of the AMA predicted that "quite a few" physicians throughout the country would refuse to participate in the program (The New York Times, August 18, 1965:55). By the following March, however, it was reported that "threats of a boycott, if not dead, are at least moot" (The New York Times, March 28, 1966:1). When the AMA House of Delegates met in June, 1966, a month before Medicare was to go

Figure 1   Research Design

	Medicare Becomes Law (July 30, 1965)		Medicare Program is Implemented (July 1, 1966)
Time 1	*Time 2*		*Time 3*
January to April, 1964; November, 1964, to March, 1965	May to June, 1966		January to April, 1967
Interviews with 1,205 physicians in private practice	Reinterviews with 676 of a stratified subsample of 804 from 1,205 interviewed at Time 1 [330 of a control sample of 472 also interviewed]		Reinterviews with 331 of remaining stratified subsample of 401 from 1,205 interviewed at Time 1

THE FINDINGS

PHYSICIANS' BEHAVIOR. As the Medicare bill was going through its final stages in Congress in June, 1965, resolutions were introduced at the semiannual meeting of the AMA's House of Delegates calling for

11 The original plan of this phase of the study was to reinterview all 1,205 physicians just before Medicare went into effect and again three to four years after it had been in effect. It was decided, however, to set aside a third of this sample (401) to be reinterviewed six months after the law was implemented in order to test the *short-run* effects of implementation. The original sample of 1,205 was not reinterviewed both before and immediately after Medicare's implementation because of the financial cost and because, with the two interviews coming so close together, of a concern about a high refusal rate in the third interview. Reinterviews with all 1,007 (676 plus 331) physicians, interviewed both before and after Medicare, are planned for 1970.

into effect, there was little, if any, talk of a boycott.

There has been no boycott, that is, no concerted noncooperation on a large scale, to date.

Responses from the New York State private practitioners interviewed in this study are consistent with the evidence of nationwide compliance by physicians. In the fall of 1965, just a few months after the law was passed, the New York State Medical Society issued a statement that "now that 'Medicare' is an accomplished fact, [the Society] will cooperate in every way possible with the government. . . . As citizens and as physicians, the members of the State Society will obey, and assist in the implementation of the law of the land . . ." (New York State Journal of Medicine, 1965:2779).

The physicians interviewed were asked

Table 1   Responses of Physicians Indicating Compliance with Medicare at Time 2 and Time 3[a]

		Time 2	Time 3
Last fall the New York State Medical Society said it would cooperate with the government on Medicare — do you agree or disagree with this policy?[b]	Agree	90%	91%
	Disagree	8	8
	Don't know, no answer	2	1
		100%	100%
	Weighted totals	(10,214)	(4,954)
	Unweighted totals	(676)	(331)
(If the physician had been asked to serve on a utilization review committee under Title 18): Have you agreed to serve?	Yes	87%	94%
	No	10	6
	Not decided	4	0
		101%	100%
	Weighted totals	(1,810)	(1,441)
	Unweighted totals	(156)	(123)
(If the physician had not been asked to serve on a utilization review committee under Title 18): If you were asked, would you agree to be a member of such a committee?	Yes	66%	71%
	No	27	26
	Don't know	7	3
		100%	100%
	Weighted totals	(8,323)	(3,513)
	Unweighted totals	(516)	(208)
According to your present thinking, do you plan to accept patients who get benefits under Medicare, or not?[c]	Accept (have treated)	93%	93%
	Will not accept (have not treated)	4	6
	Don't know, no answer	4	1
		101%	100%
	Weighted totals	(8,941)	(4,345)
	Unweighted totals	(609)	(299)

[a]"Time 1" in these tables refers to interviews conducted before the passage of Medicare, from January to April, 1964, and from November, 1964, to March, 1965; "Time 2," to interviews done after the passage of Medicare but before its implementation, from May to June, 1966; "Time 3," to interviews done after the implementation of Medicare, from January to April, 1967.

   All percentages in these tables are based on the weighted figures, which estimate the total number of private practitioners in New York State. The weighted figures do not add up to the actual number of private practitioners in the State because of noninterviews. The sampling design was stratified on geographic area, size of city, and part-time participation in a health department. The unweighted totals represent the number of physicians in a given category actually interviewed.

[b]This is the Time 2 question. The Time 3 question was: "The New York State Medical Society has said it would cooperate with the government on both Titles 18 and 19. Regarding Title 18, do you agree or disagree with this policy?"

[c]This is the Time 2 question. The Time 3 question was: "Have you treated any patients who get benefits under Part B of Title 18, or not?" The figures for both questions exclude those physicians who indicated in a previous question that they had no patients 65 years of age or over.

   Of the 18 physicians with patients 65 or over who had not treated any of these patients under Title 18B at Time 3, only one had actually refused. The others reported that no elderly patients had come to them for treatment since Medicare.

if they agreed or disagreed with their Society's policy of cooperation. (Note that the answers to this question indicate physicians' *attitudes* toward cooperation with Medicare. They are not reports of actual cooperation.) Ninety percent agreed at

Time 2; 91% agreed at Time 3 (see Table 1).

   At Time 2, 87% of those who had been asked to serve on a hospital utilization review committee for Medicare patients had agreed to serve; and of those not asked,

66% said they would serve if asked. Slightly higher proportions indicated willingness to serve at Time 3. Furthermore, a physician's refusal to serve on such a committee does not necessarily indicate protest against Medicare. He may refuse for other reasons (see Footnote 12, below).

At Time 2, less than 5% said they would not accept patients who get benefits under Medicare. At Time 3, 6% of those who had any patients 65 or over had not treated any patients under Title 18B, but only one of the 331 physicians interviewed at that time had actually *refused* to treat any patients under Title 18B. That doctor explained he was in "semi-retirement" (he was 73 years old), and he wasn't "going to bother with this." The remainder of the 6% indicated that none of their elderly patients had come to them for treatment yet.

To sum up, despite what appeared to be threats of a boycott before Medicare was passed, practically all physicians complied after it became "the law of the land." [12]

12 Our measures of compliance, apart from being reports of own behavior rather than observations of actual behavior, are admittedly simple measures of a complex variable. Consider the following: (1) A physician may provide some services under Medicare, but refuse to provide other services; (2) He may provide services to some patients, but refuse to provide them to other patients; (3) He may cooperate at one point in time after the program goes into effect, and not cooperate at another; (4) He may sabotage the program by "over-complying," that is, by providing more services than are medically indicated. Also, the question of compliance is irrelevant for physicians without patients 65 or over, such as pediatricians.

As a matter of fact, when the specific behaviors required of physicians under Medicare are examined, it is difficult to conceive what form a physicians' boycott of Medicare could have taken. What is a physician asked to do under Medicare?

(1) He must certify that the diagnostic or therapeutic services for which payment is claimed are "medically necessary." Such certification can be entered on a form or order or prescription the physician ordinarily signs.

(2) Under Title 18, Part B, the physician can

PHYSICIANS' ATTITUDES. It is possible, of course, for physicians to comply with

choose between two methods of payment for his services: he can accept an assignment and bill a designated carrier (such as Blue Shield, or another private insurance company, depending on the geographic area), or he can bill the patient directly. If he takes an assignment, he agrees that the "reasonable charge" determined by the carrier will be his full charge and that his charge to the patient will be no more than 20% of that reasonable charge. If the physician refuses to take an assignment and bills the patient directly, the patient pays the physician, and then applies to the carrier for payment. Under this method, a physician is not restricted by the "reasonable charge" for a given service. The patient, however, will be reimbursed only 80% of the reasonable charge by the carrier. Although the Social Security Administration had hoped for wide use of the assignment method, the AMA's House of Delegates adopted a resolution at its 1966 meeting recommending the use of the direct billing method (The New York Times, June 30, 1966:1). Use of the direct billing method cannot be called "noncooperation," however, since the law provides for either method.

(3) In order to promote the most efficient use of facilities, each participating hospital and extended care facility is required to have a utilization review plan. A committee set up for such a purpose must include at least two physicians. Many hospitals already had such review procedures before Medicare went into effect. One way in which a physician can protest against Medicare is to refuse to serve on such a committee if asked. But refusal to serve does not necessarily mean a protest against Medicare, anymore than unwillingness to run for a local Board of Education is an indication of protest against the public school system.

To sum up, the direct and immediate effects of Medicare on a physician's day-to-day practice are minimal. For the vast majority of services under Medicare, the physician is not required to do anything more or differently in treating patients than he did before Medicare was passed. One form a boycott of Medicare could have taken would be for physicians to have refused to treat patients 65 or over, most of whom are eligible for benefits under both Part A and Part B of Medicare. This, apparently, few physicians chose to do. Furthermore, it would be difficult to interpret such acts as "non-cooperation," unless the physician himself said so. A physician's refusal to admit an elderly patient to the hospital, for example, could mean that, in his medical judgment, hospitalization was not necessary.

Table 2   Attitudes of Physicians toward Medicare (Title 18A) at
Time 1, Time 2, and Time 3*

	Time 1	Time 2	Time 3
Favor	38%	70%	81%
Strongly		38	45
Somewhat		31	33
Don't know, no answer		1	3
Oppose	54	26	19
Strongly		14	10
Somewhat		11	9
Don't know, no answer		1	*
Don't know, no answer	8	5	*
	100%	101%	100%
Weighted totals	(18,044)	(10,214)	(4,954)
Unweighted totals	(1,205)	(676)	(331)

aAt Time 1, the question was: "What is your opinion about the bill that would provide for compulsory health insurance through Social Security to cover hospital costs
for those over 65 — are you personally in favor of such a plan, or are you opposed
to it?" Respondents were not asked whether they were "strongly" or "somewhat"
in favor or opposed at Time 1.

    At Time 2, the questions were: "What is your opinion of Part A of Medicare —
the part that provides for compulsory health insurance through Social Security to
cover hospital costs for those over 65 — are you personally in favor of this plan, or
opposed to it?" "Would you say strongly (in favor) (opposed) or somewhat (in
favor) (opposed)?" At Time 3, the words "Part A of Title 18" were substituted for
the words "Part A of Medicare."

*Less than 0.5 percent.

Medicare without changing their minds about it. What effects has Medicare had on physicians' attitudes toward the program? In 1964 and early 1965, before Medicare was passed (Time 1), 38% of the private practitioners in New York State were "in favor" of "the bill that would provide for compulsory health insurance through Social Security to cover hospital costs for those over 65," the bill that became Title 18A. This is a sizeable number, but nevertheless, a minority.

At Time 2, ten months after the law was passed, even before it went into effect, the proportion "in favor" jumped to 70%. At Time 3, a little over six months after the program went into effect, the proportion "in favor" again jumped, to 81%. At both Time 2 and Time 3, more than half of those in favor felt "strongly," rather than only "somewhat" in favor (see Table 2).

Table 3 shows that of those opposed to Title 18A at Time 1, more than half (59%) had switched by Time 2; 70% had

switched by Time 3.[13] Very few switched from favoring it to opposing it.

Although the absolute percentage increase favoring Title 18A of Medicare is greater between Time 1 and Time 2 (from 38 to 70%), than between Time 2 and Time 3 (from 70 to 81%), it might be misleading, because of the operation of a "ceiling effect," to argue that the Medicare law itself had a stronger impact than experience of the physicians with the program implemented by the law.[14] What

[13] Physicians' attitudes toward Title 18B, highly correlated with their attitudes toward Title 18A, were also very favorable. Seventy-eight percent were "in favor" at Time 2 and 83% at Time 3.

[14] The effect of an experimental variable on a group is limited by the initial frequency giving a certain response before exposure to that variable. Since the percentage in favor of Medicare is higher at Time 2 than at Time 1, there is "less room" for an increase in the percentage in favor between Time 2 and Time 3 than between Time 1 and Time 2. The statistical effect of this "ceiling" may be "corrected" by dividing the actual percentage difference by the maximum possible

Table 3   Attitudes of Physicians toward Medicare (Title 18A) at Time 2 and Time 3 by Their Attitudes at Time 1

| | Time 1 attitude toward Medicare | |
	Favor	Oppose
Time 2 attitude toward Medicare		
Favor	90%	59%
Strongly	59	25
Somewhat	30	33
Don't know, no answer	1	1
Oppose	11	40
Strongly	5	22
Somewhat	6	16
Don't know, no answer	0	2
	101%	99%
Weighted totals	(3,757)	(5,098)
Unweighted totals	(193)	(411)
Time 3 attitude toward Medicare		
Favor	98%	70%
Strongly	84	19
Somewhat	10	48
Don't know, no answer	4	3
Oppose	2	30
Strongly	*	17
Somewhat	2	13
Don't know, no answer	0	*
	100%	100%
Weighted totals	(1,877)	(2,787)
Unweighted totals	(95)	(213)

*Less than 0.5 percent.

can be asserted, however, is that the law itself had a large effect on physicians' attitudes toward Medicare even before it was implemented.

increase. Hovland et al. (1949:285–289) call such a measure the "effectiveness index." Such an index for the Time 1-Time 2 change is .52[(70–38)/ (100–38)=.52]. For the Time 2-Time 3 change it is .37[(81–70)/(100–70)=.37]. The fact that the Time 1-Time 2 index is larger than the Time 2-Time 3 measure indicates that the larger increase in the percentage of those in favor of Medicare between Time 1 and Time 2 than between Time 2 and Time 3 cannot be explained away as being entirely due to a statistical ceiling effect.

There is another type of ceiling effect, this one due to *selection*. Those still opposed to Medicare at Time 2 are likely to include a higher propor-

THE EFFECTS OF IMPLEMENTATION ON ATTITUDES. Consistent with the increase in the level of physicians' support for Medi-

tion of "hard-core" opponents of Medicare than those opposed at Time 1. We found, however, that the Time 2 opponents of Medicare were no more conservative on other measures of political ideology at Time 1 than the Time 1 opponents.

The study design has a limitation, too. Since it provides for only one measure of the physicians' attitudes after the law was passed and before its implementation, it is not possible to assess the effect of time alone. It is possible that the change in attitude toward Medicare between Time 2 and Time 3 is a function of time alone and has nothing to do with the implementation of the program. As a matter of fact, the "transition probabilities" between Time 2 and Time 3 are the same as those between Time 1 and Time 2.

Table 4   Perceived Effects of Medicare (Title 18A) at Time 2 and at Time 3

		Time 2	*Time 3*
	Weighted totals	*(10,214)*	*(4,954)*
	Unweighted totals	*(676)*	*(331)*
In your opinion, how will Medicare (Title 18) affect the *quality* of care doctors give their elderly patients — in general, will doctors give *better* medical care, or *not as good* care, or won't Medicare (Title 18) make any difference?	Better	14	30
	Not as good	28	8
	No difference	54	60
	Don't know	5	2
		100%	100%
In your opinion, will there be a great deal of *unnecessary hospitalization* under Medicare (Title 18), or a fair amount, or very little, or none at all?	Great deal	32	12
	Fair amount	37	26
	Very little	18	38
	None at all	9	20
	Don't know	4	4
		100%	100%
Will there be a great deal of *unnecessary* utilization of *doctors' services* under Medicare (Title 18), or a fair amount, or very little, or none at all?	Great deal	39	8
	Fair amount	38	28
	Very little	15	39
	None at all	4	20
	Don't know	4	5
		100%	100%
In your opinion, will doctors *earn more* money under Medicare (Title 18) than before, or less money, or won't Medicare (Title 18) make any difference?	More	35	42
	Less	12	11
	No difference	41	38
	Don't know	12	9
		100%	100%
In your opinion, will the Federal government, under Medicare (Title 18), interfere with the individual doctor's professional freedom — Would you say a great deal, or a fair amount, or very little, or not at all?	Great deal	17	21
	Fair amount	37	26
	Very little	25	31
	Not at all	15	16
	Don't know	6	6
		100%	100%

care between Time 2 and Time 3 is the fact that they were less worried about the consequences of Medicare at Time 3 than at Time 2. Their earlier fears simply did not materialize.[15]

For example, the proportion who thought that the quality of care physicians give their elderly patients would be "not as good" under Medicare dropped from 28% at Time 2 to 8% at Time 3 (see Table 4). The proportion who thought there would be "a great deal" or "a fair

---

[15] Clark (1953:47–50) reports a similar pattern in cases of desegregation.

amount" of unnecessary hospitalization under Medicare dropped from 69% at Time 2 to 38% at Time 3 (27% thought there had actually been "a great deal" or "a fair amount" of unnecessary hospitalization up to Time 3). The proportion who thought there would be "a great deal" or "a fair amount" of unnecessary utilization of physicians' services under Medicare also dropped from 77% to 36% (25% thought there had actually been "a great deal" or "a fair amount" up to Time 3). It is only in the questions about government interference under Medicare and its effects on physicians' income that there were not significant changes, but only 12% at Time 2 and 11% at Time 3 thought that they would earn less money under Medicare than before, compared with more than a third who thought they would earn more money.[16]

ALTERNATIVE INTERPRETATIONS

Let us consider some alternative explanations of the large shifts in attitude toward Title 18A:

1. It could be argued that the changes described above could have taken place without the Medicare law and its implementation; that the shift in physicians' attitudes toward Medicare is part of a general, long-term liberal trend in their thinking. Obviously, there is not available a control group of physicians from whom the facts of the passage of the Medicare law and its implementation could be withheld. The argument that the changes in attitude toward Medicare are due to the law, however, is supported by the following observations:

a. The change in attitude toward Title 18A is a large change—from 38% in favor to 70 to 81% in a period of no longer than three years. It is not plausible to argue that this is due to a general ideological trend unrelated to the passage and implementation of Medicare.

b. The attitudes that do change are highly specific to Medicare. Physicians' responses to questions indicating their position on economic-welfare issues, political party preference, group practice, and colleague controls, all of which strongly related to their attitudes toward Title 18A at Time 1 (Colombotos, 1968), are relatively stable at Time 1, Time 2,

[16] There is no increase in the level of physicians' knowledge about the details of Medicare between Time 2 and 3—they are poorly informed at both times—and there is no association between their level of knowledge and the amount of experience with Medicare, on the one hand, and change in their attitude toward Medicare, on the other.

and Time 3 compared with their responses to the question on Medicare. If the change in attitudes toward Medicare was part of a more general trend in physicians' thinking and unrelated to the passage of Medicare, then one would expect changes in attitudes toward these other issues as well.

2. It could be argued that the increasingly favorable medical opinion about Medicare and the passage of the Medicare law were both the result or part of a third factor occurring immediately before Medicare was passed. Strong public support for Medicare, for example, could have influenced both medical and legislative opinion. Data in the present study from two independent samples of Manhattan doctors who were interviewed at two different times before Medicare was passed are inconsistent with such an argument. The first sample of 70 physicians was interviewed from January to April in 1964, about 18 months before Medicare was passed. The second sample of 61 physicians was interviewed from November, 1964, to March, 1965, scarcely six months before the law was passed. There was essentially no difference in the proportion in favor of Title 18A in the two samples— 53% in the first sample, 57% in the second.

3. It is possible that New York State physicians' acceptance of Medicare after the enactment of the law was influenced by their opposition to the State's Medicaid program. The New York State implementation of Medicaid was one of the most liberal in the country. The first version of the New York State program was signed into law on April 30, 1966. The program was amended and curtailed two months later after strong opposition in upstate New York and threatened boycotts by county medical societies.

At Time 2, just after the first version of Medicaid was passed by the state legislature, 42% of the doctors interviewed said they were in favor of the law. At Time 3, despite, or perhaps because of, the fact the program had been curtailed six months earlier, it was still only 42%.

On all other questions about Medicaid asked at Time 3, it was less well received than Medicare:

a. Forty-six percent thought that the government would interfere "a great deal" with the individual physicians' professional freedom under Medicaid, compared with 21% for Medicare.

b. Fifty-nine percent thought that the State Medical Society should cooperate with the Government on Medicaid, compared with 91% on Medicare.

c. Fifty-five percent said they planned to accept (or had already accepted) patients under Title 19, compared with all but one physician under Title 18B.

It could be argued that the opposition to Medicaid in New York State had a "contrast" effect on physicians" responses to Medicare; that Medicare looked better to physicians than it would have looked had Medicaid not been passed, and that this "contrast" inflated the size of the oppose-favor switchers on Medicare. For example, at the height of the furor over Medicaid in the state, one county medical society in an advertisement in *The New York Times* agreed to "cooperate" with the "Federal Medicare Law, which provides a sensible and reasonable plan of medical care for all people over 65 . . . ," but found it "impossible to cooperate with the implementation of this State law [Medicaid] . . . as it is presently proposed. . . ." (June 10, 1966:36). It called Medicaid "socialized medicine."

There is no evidence of such a contrast effect in our data. Rather, among those physicians who opposed Title 18A at Time 1, those who were in favor of Medicaid at Time 2 and Time 3 were much more likely to switch and favor Title 18A than those who opposed Medicaid.[17]

4. It could be argued that the physicians' attitudes toward Medicare expressed at Time 1, before its passage, were superficial and equivocal, and merely reflected official AMA policy, and that once the program became law, physicians felt freer to express their "real" attitudes toward Medicare. But this argument misses the point that law may "legitimate" opinion. The fact that the Medicare program was not law is as significant a part of the social situation at Time 1 as the fact that it had become law at Time 2 and Time 3. One could just as plausibly argue for the superficiality of attitudes expressed after the law, because of a "bandwagon effect," as for the superficiality of attitudes expressed before the law.

As a matter of fact, neither the attitudes toward Medicare at Time 1 nor at Time 2 and Time 3 appear superficial. The sub-question on intensity of feeling was not asked at Time 1. In the Time 1 measure, however, less than 8% were "don't knows." Also, attitude toward Medicare at Time 1 was strongly related to other political questions and issues in the organization of medical practice, as noted above (Colombotos, 1968), which argues against its being superficial. In the Time 2 and 3 measures, the number of "don't knows" was even smaller than at Time 1: at Time 2, it was 5%, and at Time 3, it was less than 0.5%. Also, of those in favor, more than half responded they felt "strongly" in favor, rather than only "somewhat" in favor.

5. Finally, a number of methodological problems in panel surveys may be involved:

a. REINTERVIEW EFFECT. It could be argued that the Time 1 interview generated an interest in Medicare, thus influencing physicians' responses in the Time 2 interview. We found no difference be-

---

17 Another test of the effects of Medicaid on attitude change toward Title 18A would be to examine the problem in a state where physicians' attitudes toward Title 18A were similar to those

in New York State, but where the Medicaid program did not arouse as much opposition as the one in New York State. Unfortunately, such data are not available.

tween the responses to selected questions, including the one on Medicare, obtained from the reinterviewed sample at Time 2 and from a control sample of 330 physicians not interviewed before.

b. CHANGE IN THE INTERVIEW INSTRUMENT, specifically in the sequence of the questions. The items preceding the question on Medicare in the Time 2 interview were different from those in the Time 1 interview. We found no difference between the responses obtained in two different versions of the interview at Time 2: one in which the repeat (retest) questions were mixed with new questions and one in which the repeat (retest) questions were asked first, followed by the new questions.

c. MORTALITY EFFECT. It could be argued that physicians in the panel not interviewed at Time 2 and Time 3 were less likely to be pro-Medicare than those who were interviewed. We found that physicians who could not be reinterviewed at Time 2 and Time 3 did not differ from those who were reinterviewed in their background characteristics or attitudes, including their attitude toward Medicare, expressed at Time 1.

SUMMARY AND CONCLUSIONS

Despite their opposition to Medicare before the law was passed in 1965, physicians are complying with the program. There may be individual instances of noncooperation, but they are rare, at least in New York State, and there has been no boycott in the sense of concerted noncompliance.

Consistent with their compliance with Medicare, a large number of physicians who were opposed to Medicare before it became law switched and accepted it after it became law. In New York State, the proportion in favor rose from 38% before the law was passed to 70% less than a year after it was passed, even before it was implemented, and once again to 81% six

months after the program went into effect.[18] The first increase, from 38 to 70%, argues that for law to influence attitudes it does not necessarily have to change relevant behavior first. We have in physicians' response to Medicare a case in which attitudes adapted to the law even before it went into effect.

The ready accommodation, both in deed and in mind, of these physicians to Medicare contrasts sharply with their continuing opposition to Medicaid and, to take a more extreme example, with physician strikes, such as the one in Saskatchewan, Canada, in 1962, against the province's medical care program.

What accounts for such differences in response to a law? The following differences between Medicare and the New York State Medicaid law illustrate some of the conditions listed above and suggest others that promote the effectiveness of a law:

1. THE CONTENT OF THE PROGRAM. The direct impact on physicians' practice of Medicaid in New York State is much greater than that of Medicare.

a. The number of people covered under Medicare in the state (those 65 or over) is less than two million. Estimates in May, 1966, of the number eligible under Medicaid ranged from 3.5 to 7 million. Furthermore, the number covered by Medicaid could be increased by liberalizing the definition of eligibility.

b. The clients of Medicare are the aged and the program is based on the insurance principle. The clients of Medicaid are the "medically indigent" and the program is

---

[18] The proportion of private practitioners in favor of Medicare was higher in New York State than in the country as a whole before Medicare was passed (see Footnote 1). No post-Medicare data from a national sample of physicians are available, however. Note also that our New York State study sample excludes physicians on full-time salary, who are more likely to be politically liberal and in favor of Medicare than private practitioners. (For data supporting the latter point, see Lipset and Schwartz, 1966:304).

based on the welfare principle. Physicians may be more sympathetic to a program serving the medical needs of the aged through insurance than to a program serving the "(medically) indigent," classified with "welfare cases."

c. Medicaid provides more services than Medicare, including drugs, dental bills, and other services not covered by Medicare.

d. New York State's Medicaid affects the physicians' practice more directly than Medicare. Medicaid attempts to control the quality and cost of medical care: the quality, by establishing criteria for determining who can render care, thus limiting the free choice of physicians; and the cost, by paying physicians fixed fees rather than "usual and customary" charges. Medicare has attempted neither. The direct effects of Medicare on physicians' practice, as a matter of fact, are minimal. Somers and Somers (1967:1) put it this way:

The 1965 enactment of Medicare was heralded as "revolutionary." But, in fact, it was neither a sudden nor radical departure from the march of events in the organization and financing of medical care and government's growing participation. No existing institutions were overturned or seriously threatened by the new legislation. On the contrary, Medicare responded to the needs of the providers of care as well as those of the consumers. It was primarily a financial underpinning of the existing health care industry—with all that implies in terms of strengths and weaknesses.

As a matter of fact, Medicare supports the stability of physicians' income under Title 18B, without controlling their fees. As noted above, more than a third of New York State physicians interviewed thought that under Medicare physicians would earn more money than before, and only about 10% thought they would earn less; the remainder thought it would not make any difference.

Both in terms of consistency with their ideology and in terms of their self-interest,

then, Medicare is more acceptable to New York State physicians than Medicaid.

2. DEGREE OF POPULAR SUPPORT. Medicare was passed with overwhelming popular support. Two-thirds of the public were in favor of Medicare, according to a nationwide Gallup poll in January, 1965, six months before it was passed. The percentage was probably higher in New York State. In contrast, there was little awareness about Medicaid before it was passed, and there was strong opposition, particularly in upstate New York, from industry, farm organizations, and in the press, after the first version of the New York Medicaid law was passed in April, 1966.

3. MEDICARE IS THE SAME THROUGHOUT THE COUNTRY, WHEREAS MEDICAID VARIES GREATLY FROM STATE TO STATE. It is possible that the opposition of New York physicians to their state's Medicaid program, the most liberal in the country, is reinforced by their feeling "worse off" than their colleagues in other states where the Medicaid programs are not as ambitious. A plausible hypothessis, setting aside regional and local differences in values that may or may not be congruent with a given law, is that a national law is more "legitimate" and more likely to be effectively complied with than a state or local law.[19]

Outside the area of medical care, public response in many parts of the country to statutes and judicial decisions requiring the desegregation of schools and other institutions contrasts sharply with physicians' response to Medicare. The issues of desegregation and civil rights will not be

[19] In terms of these conditions, the prospects of the plan that physicians struck against in Saskatchewan in 1962 were, in retrospect, not good: (1) the plan's impact on physicians' practice was much greater than Medicare's, providing for universal coverage for all residents in the province and a comprehensive range of services; (2) public opposition to the plan appeared to be stronger and better organized than the opposition to Medicare; and (3) it was a provincial, not a national plan.

taken up here in any detail, but some obvious differences between them and Medicare come to mind:

1. Despite the "American creed" and trends showing a reduction of prejudice and discrimination, at least up to 1964, "white racism" may be more firmly entrenched among large segments of the American public than the fear of government participation in health care among physicians.

2. The distributions of opposition to desegregation and to Medicare are different. Social supports to segregationists are more widely available than social supports to physicians opposed to Medicare. The general public strongly supported Medicare, and it was the medical profession that was out of step.

3. Desegregation, like Medicaid, runs into a hodgepodge of inconsistent and contradictory local, state, and Federal laws concerning different facilities and institutions—schools, transportation, recreation, housing, employment, marriage. Some of these laws actually *prescribe* segregation. Consider a hypothetical situation in which some states had laws that made it illegal to provide hospitalization and medical care under the terms ultimately provided by the Federal Medicare law! [20]

[20] The effects of law on behavior and attitudes are interpretable in terms of cognitive dissonance theory. According to this theory, the greater the dissonance between an individual's continued opposition to a program, behaviorally and attitudinally, and other elements in his cognitive structure, the greater is the probability of his complying and accepting the program. If we conceive as elements in an individual's cognitive structures the passage of a law and the specific conditions for its effectiveness, then it follows that the more of these conditions that apply, the greater the dissonance and the greater the probability of compliance and attitudinal acceptance.

That part of the theory that focuses on the effects of compliance on attitude change and the conditions under which dissonance between these two elements is aroused, however, is not particularly relevant to our case, since we found a large shift in attitudes toward Medicare even before physicians had an opportunity to comply (unless

Having established in this paper the fact that the passage and implementation of Medicare had a sharp effect in changing the attitudes of physicians toward the program, the next steps will be (1) to examine the *conditions* under which physicians make both short-term and long-term changes in their attitudes toward Medicare, (2) to examine the long-term effects of Medicare on physicians' attitudes toward the program and toward other related political and health care issues, and (3) to compare the long-term and short-term responses of physicians to Medicare and Medicaid. A fourth wave of interviews with our physician panel is being planned in 1970—five years after the passage of Medicare—to answer these questions.

1. The two major sets of conditions of individual change in attitudes toward Medicare we shall examine are attitude-structural and social-structural variables. The general assumption is that there is pressure toward both intrapersonal and interpersonal consistency. For example, among those opposed to Medicare before the law was passed, it is predicted that Democrats are more likely to change their attitudes toward Medicare than Republicans; that physicians in areas where support for Medicare was initially strong are more likely to change than those in areas where support was weak; and that physicians who perceive themselves as having different opinions from their colleagues are more likely to change than those who see themselves as being in agreement. Other variables such as physicians' knowledge about Medicare, their experience with it, and their perceptions of its effects on their practice will also be studied as conditions of change in their attitudes toward Medicare.

planning to comply is seen as equivalent to complying). The effects of compliance on attitude change in terms of dissonance theory is explicitly applied to desegregation in Brehm and Cohen (1962:269–285).

2. a. The short-term effects of the Medicare law and program on physicians' attitudes toward it were indeed dramatic. What will be the long-term effects—five years later? Will opposition to Medicare continue to wither away or will it stiffen?

b. We have found that the Medicare law had little short-term effect on physicians' attitudes toward other related political and health care issues. The stability of these attitudes, as a matter of fact, was offered to support the argument that the change in attitude toward Medicare was indeed an effect of the Medicare law and program rather than a part of a more general liberal trend in physicians' thinking. Katz observes that "it is puzzling that attitude change seems to have slight generalization effects, when the evidence indicates considerable generalization in the organization of a person's beliefs and values" (Katz, 1960:199). But our results, and Katz' observation, refer to the short-run. It is plausible to expect that a change in one part of an attitude structure will produce changes in other parts of the structure, but the generalization of change *may not take place immediately*. It may take some time for the structure to become reintegrated. Will physicians' acceptance of Medicare make them more liberal in the longer run in their thinking about political issues and about changes in the organization of medical practice, or will it make them more conservative and resistant to such changes, or will it simply have no effects?[21]

3. In contrast to the ready acceptance of Medicare, physicians continued to oppose Medicaid in New York State nearly a year after it was implemented. How will

[21] Note that "short-term" and "long-term" in attitude change research mean quite different things depending on the perspective of the investigator and the design used. In experimental studies, "short-term" effects are measured within minutes, hours, or at most, a few days after the introduction of the experimental variable; "long-term" effects usually mean no more than a few weeks later. In panel surveys, the time intervals are longer.

they feel four years later? What will be the conditions under which physicians make long-term changes in their attitudes toward Medicaid, and how will these conditions differ from those that distinguish changers and non-changers on Medicare? A comparison of the dynamics of the short-term and long-term responses of physicians to Medicare and Medicaid represents a modest test of the conditions under which laws influence behavior and attitudes.

REFERENCES

ALLPORT, GORDON W., 1954. *The Nature of Prejudice.* Cambridge, Mass.: Addison-Wesley Publishing Co.

BADGLEY, ROBIN F. and SAMUEL WOLFE, 1967. *Doctors' Strike, Medical Care and Conflict in Saskatchewan.* New York: Atherton Press.

BALL, HARRY V., GEORGE EATON SIMPSON and KIYOSHI IDEDA, 1962. "Law and Social Change: Sumner Reconsidered," *American Journal of Sociology,* **67** (March):532–40.

BERGER, MORROE, 1954. *Equality by Statute.* New York: Columbia University Press.

BERKOWITZ, LEONARD and NIGEL WALKER, 1967. "Laws and Moral Judgments," *Sociometry,* **30** (December):410–22.

BONFIELD, ARTHUR EARL, 1965. "The Role of Legislation in Eliminating Racial Discrimination," *Race,* **7** (October):108–9.

BREHM, JACK W. and ARTHUR R. COHEN, 1962. *Explorations in Cognitive Dissonance.* New York: John Wiley and Sons.

CAMPBELL, ERNEST Q., 1958. "Some Social Psychological Correlates of Direction in Attitude Change," *Social Forces,* **36** (May):335–40.

CANTRIL, HADLEY, 1947. *Gauging Public Opinion.* Princeton: Princeton University Press.

CLARK, KENNETH (issue ed.) , 1953. "Desegregation: An Appraisal of the Evidence," *The Journal of Social Issues,* **9**:47–50.

COLOMBOTOS, JOHN, 1968. "Physicians' Attitudes toward Medicare," *Medical Care,* **6** (July–August):320–31; 1969a, "Physicians' Attitudes toward a County Health Department," *American Journal of Public Health,* **59** (January):53–59; 1969b, "Social Origins and Ideology of Physicians: a Study of the Effects of Early Socialization," *Journal of Health and Social Behavior,* **10** (March):16–29.

DEUTSCH, MORTON and MARY E. COLLINS, 1951. *Interracial Housing: A Psychological Evaluation of a Social Experiment*. Minneapolis: University of Minnesota Press.

DEUTSCHER, IRWIN, 1966. "Words and Deeds," *Social Problems*, **13** (Winter):235–54.

DICEY, ALBERT VENN, 1914. *Law and Opinion in England during the Nineteenth Century*, second edition. London: Macmillan and Co., Ltd. [Printing used, 1963].

EVANS, WILLIAM M., 1965. "Law as an Instrument of Social Change," in A. W. GOULDNER and S. M. MILLER, eds., *Applied Sociology*. New York: The Free Press.

FEINGOLD, EUGENE, 1966. *Medicare: Police and Politics*. San Francisco, Cal.: Chandler Publishing Co.

HARRIS, RICHARD, 1966. *A Sacred Trust*. New York: The New American Library.

HOVLAND, CARL I., ARTHUR A. LUMSDAINE and FRED D. SHEFFIELD, 1949. *Experiments on Mass Communication, Vol. III, Studies in Social Psychology in World War II*. Princeton: Princeton University Press.

HYMAN, HERBERT H. and PAUL B. SHEATSLEY, 1964. "Attitudes toward Desegregation," *Scientific American*, **211** (July):6.

KATZ, DANIEL, 1960. "The Functional Aproach to the Study of Attitudes," *Public Opinion Quarterly*, **24** (Summer):163–204.

KILLIAN, LEWIS M., 1958. *The Negro in American Society*. Florida State University Studies, No. 28:65–70.

KUTNER, BERNARD, CAROL WILKINS and PENNEY B. YARROW, 1952. "Verbal Attitudes and Overt Behavior Involving Racial Prejudice," *Journal of Abnormal and Social Psychology*, **47**:649–652.

LAPIERE, RICHARD T., 1934. "Attitudes vs. Actions," *Social Forces*, **13** (March):230–37.

LIPSET, SEYMOUR MARTIN and MILDRED A. SCHWARTZ, 1966. "The Politics of Professionals," in Howard M. Vollmer and Donald L. Mills, eds., *Professionalization*. Englewood Cliffs, N.J.: Prentice-Hall.

MACIVER, ROBERT M., 1948. *The More Perfect Union*. New York: Macmillan; 1954, Forward. P. viii in Morroe Berger, *Equality by Statute*. New York: Columbia University Press.

MAYHEW, LEON H., 1968. *Law and Equal Opportunity*. Cambridge, Massachusetts: Harvard University Press.

MUIR, WILLIAM K., JR., 1967. *Prayer in the Public Schools: Law and Attitude Change*. Chicago: The University of Chicago Press.

MUSSEN, PAUL H., 1950. "Some Personality and Social Factors Related to Changes in Children's Attitudes toward Negroes," *Journal of Abnormal and Social Psychology*, **45** (July):423–41.

MYRDAL, GUNNAR, 1944. *An American Dilemma*. New York: Harper and Row.

New York State Journal of Medicine, 1965. *Editorial*. Vol. 65 (November 15):2779; "Opinions about Negro infantry platoons in white companies of seven divisions," 1952, in Guy E. Swanson, *et al.*, eds., *Readings in Social Psychology*. New York: Holt.

POUND, ROSCOE, 1944. *The Task of Law*. Lancaster, Pa.: Franklin and Marshall College.

ROCHE, JOHN P. and MILTON M. GORDON, 1955. "Can Morality be Legislated?" *New York Times Magazine* (May 22):10, 42, 44, 49. In Kimball Young and Raymond W. Mack, eds., *Principles of Sociology: A Reader in Theory and Research*. New York: American Book Co., 1966.

ROSE, ARNOLD M., 1959. "Sociological Factors in the Effectiveness of Projected Legislative Remedies," *Journal of Legal Education*, **11**:470–81; 1967. *The Power Structure: Political Processes in American Society*. New York: Oxford University Press. Chap. xii, pp. 400–455, "The Passage of Legislation: the Politics of Financing Medical Care for the Aging."

SAENGER, GERHART and EMILY GILBERT, 1950. "Customer Reactions to the Integration of Negro Sales Personnel," *International Journal of Opinion and Attitude Research*, **4** (Spring): 57–76.

SCHWARTZ, MILDRED A., 1967. *Trends in White Attitudes toward Negroes*. Chicago: National Opinion Research Center, University of Chicago.

SCOTT, JOHN FINLEY and LOIS HEYMAN SCOTT, 1968. "They Are Not So Much Anti-Negro as Pro-Middle Class." *New York Times Magazine* (March 24):46 ff.

SOMERS, HERMAN M. and ANNE R. SOMERS, 1967. *Medicare and the Hospitals: Issues and Prospects*. Washington, D.C.: The Brookings Institution.

SUMNER, WILLIAM GRAHAM, 1906. *Folkways*. New York: The New American Library [printing used, 1960].

SWANSON, GUY E., *et al.* (eds.), 1952. "Opinions about Negro Infantry Platoons in White Companies of Seven Divisions," *Readings in Social Psychology*. New York: Holt.

WALKER, NIGEL and MICHAEL ARGYLE, 1964. "Does the Law Affect Moral Judgments?" *British Journal of Criminology*, **5**:570–81.

YARROW, MARION RADKE, 1958. "Interpersonal Dynamics in a Desegregation Process," *Special Issue, Journal of Social Issues*, **14**.

YOUNG, KIMBALL and RAYMOND W. MACK, 1960. *Principles of Sociology: A Reader in Theory and Research*. New York: American Book Comany.

LAWS AND MORAL JUDGMENTS

Leonard Berkowitz and Nigel Walker

There is considerable controversy as to the degree to which criminal law should be employed in regulating private conduct. The Wolfenden Committee in England, for example, contending that private homosexual behavior between consenting adults should not be regarded as criminal, argued for severe restrictions on the scope of criminal law.[1] The Committee maintained law should intervene as little as possible in the private lives of citizens. A number of legal scholars as well as politicians have taken a quite different stand, however,[2] and American history is fairly full of attempts to control private behavior by means of criminal law. Here we need only remember the Puritan statutes regarding sex and the Prohibition Amendment.

Many of the points made by both sides in this controversy assume that legal control is at least partly affected by social influences. As an illustration, people advocating limitations on the scope of criminal law frequently argue that unenforceable laws can bring a good deal of the legal system into general disrepute. They may be right. This type of phenomenon could well have occurred in the Prohibi-

tion era. Those Americans who defied the laws against the sale of alcoholic beverages might have been, as a result, somewhat readier to break other laws as well. Even if an individual did not himself break the Prohibition laws, seeing that many other people did so could have led him to believe law violations generally were not so bad. Social influences may also operate when a criminal law is abolished. Consider the possible consequences of new laws making, say, homosexual behavior or suicide no longer a crime. In discussing such a matter, proponents of the use of criminal laws in regulating conduct have often resorted to a contention termed by Walker[3] the "declaratory argument." This position asserts that, whether a legal prohibition acts as a deterrent or not, to repeal it would give the impression that the conduct in question is no longer regarded by society as morally wrong. Thus, removing homosexual conduct and/or suicide from the purview of criminal law supposedly places an implicit stamp of social approval on these behaviors, or at least makes them less disapproved socially, and therefore heightens the likelihood that people will engage in homosexual actions and/or commit suicide. Criminal law is here regarded as providing a social definition of what is proper or improper conduct.

Walker and Argyle[4] carried out two investigations in England as a test of this declaratory argument. One of these (by Walker) was a survey of attitudes toward attempted suicide, a form of conduct which had recently ceased to be criminal in England. No significant differences were found between those people who knew the law had been changed and those

Reprinted from *Sociometry*, **30** (December, 1967), pp. 410–22, by permission of the authors and The American Sociological Association.

The research reported in this paper was conducted under grant GS–345 from the National Science Foundation to the senior author. We are grateful to Mrs. Valerie Patterson for her capable assistance in the data collection and analysis, to Professor M. Vernon of the University of Reading Psychology Department for making a class available to us, and to Professors Ronald Maudsley and Stewart Macaulay for their comments on a preliminary draft of this paper.

[1] Cf. N. Walker, *Crime and Punishment in Britain,* Edinburgh: University of Edinburgh Press, 1965, pp. 8–9.
[2] Walker, *ibid.* Chapter 1.

[3] Cf. N. Walker and M. Argyle, "Does the Law Affect Moral Judgments?" *British Journal of Criminology,* (1964), pp. 570–581.
[4] Walker and Argyle, *ibid.*

who did not have this knowledge. In the second study (by Walker and Argyle) an experiment was devised in which young men and women were informed that various actions were or were not criminal offences. This information did not influence the subject's judgments of the moral propriety of the actions. Their judgments were successfully influenced, however, when they were given the results of a fictitious survey of peers' opinions. All in all, Walker and Argyle interpreted their findings as casting doubt on the validity of the declaratory argument.

A second test of the declaratory argument by a somewhat differently designed experiment seemed advisable, nevertheless. Walker and Argyle had found small but by no means negligible minorities among their respondents who *said* their moral attitudes toward a noncriminal activity (heavy smoking) would become more censorious if Parliament passed a law making this form of behavior a criminal offense. A different research procedure conceivably might detect shifts in moral judgments arising from knowledge of the existence of a law. While we cannot trace the origins or operation of criminal law to any single set of processes,[5] experts agree, as was noted above, that legal control is affected by social influences. Among these are social consensus and the legitimation of authority, and these influences might conceivably affect the judged propriety of actions regulated by laws.

The greater the social consensus the more likely it is, of course, that people will act in conformity with the majority view.[6] This heightened conformity arises

in part because the consensus enhances the perceived validity of the shared opinion; attitudes and beliefs that are held by all or nearly all members of the individual's reference group are frequently regarded as being probably correct.[7] Laws may often be taken as implying a social consensus, and this implied consensus could influence attitudes toward the behavior that is the subject of the laws. Thus, unless the law is clearly violated with relatively great frequency, as happened in the case of Prohibition, the implied consensus associated with the legal definition of an action as "criminal" could result in a judgment of the action as "immoral."

But, in addition, many people also view laws as legitimate authority. Although, as Parsons suggested,[8] lawyers tend to take this legitimacy for granted,[9] theory and empirical research indicate that legitimate authority can wield considerable influence over both action and attitudes.[10] While some writers [11] emphasize coercive processes arising from other group members in accounting for conformity to legitimate authority, most theorists stress the part played by the in-

[5] Cf. R. Pound, *Interpretations of Legal History*, New York: Macmillan, 1923; W. M. Evan, *Law and Sociology*, New York: Free Press of Glencoe, 1962; M. P. Golding, *The Nature of Law: Readings in Legal Philosophy*, New York: Random House, 1966.

[6] V. L. Allen, "Situational Factors in Conformity," In L. Berkowitz, ed., *Advances in Experimental Social Psychology*, *Vol. 2*, New York: Academic Press, pp. 133–175.

[7] L. Festinger, H. B. Gerard, B. Hymovitch, H. H. Kelley and B. Raven, "The Influence Process in the Presence of Extreme Deviants," *Human Relations*, 5 (1952), pp. 327–346.

[8] T. Parsons, "The Law and Social Control," In W. M. Evan, ed., *Law and Sociology*, New York: Free Press of Glencoe, 1962, pp. 56–72.

[9] Legal tradition seems to favor a cost-benefit (or "decision-theory") analysis of reactions to the law, according to Professor Macaulay. A person weighs the benefit to him of the prohibited conduct against all the costs and the chances that he will have to pay these costs. Following this line of thought, conformity to the law could also be affected by the anticipated costs of frequent violations to the system of law and order.

[10] M. Weber, *The Theory of Social and Economic Organization*, New York: Oxford University Press, 1947; J. R. P. French, Jr. and B. Raven, "The Bases of Social Power," In D. Cartwright, ed., *Studies in Social Power*, Ann Arbor: University of Michigan, 1959, pp. 150–167; P. M. Blau, *Exchange and Power in Social Life*, New York: Wiley, 1964.

[11] For example, Blau, *ibid.*, Chapter 8.

dividual's internalized values. As an example, according to Parsons,[12] "the well integrated personality . . . has and feels obligations to respect legitimate authority. . . ." The felt obligation, Parsons maintained, is "disinterested," and the person adheres to the prescribed code of conduct because he thinks it is "right." Something like the following may therefore happen in the case of an individual for whom a newly passed law represents legitimate authority: First, he believes the law has the right to regulate his behavior. Then, to justify his conformity to the law and lessen any cognitive dissonance he may feel,[13] he may interpret the legally forbidden action as "wrong," or morally bad.[14] In the course of time, with several repetitions of this process, behaviors disapproved by legitimate authority may perhaps come to be seen as morally improper without the intermediate behavioral compliance. Finally, as yet another possibility, Frank [15] argued that authoritative laws are often desired because of an unresolved childish need for the certainty of a father's commands. A person seeking the elimination of disturbing uncertainty may then attribute the father's "rightness" to legitimate authority; it is as if he reasons, "I myself do not know, but if the law (my father) says the action is wrong, it must be bad."

All of these possible processes leave considerable room for individual differences. It is particularly likely that persons will differ in their reactions to legitimate authority, and the present paper will examine two sets of personality characteristics that may govern responses to legal controls. The first of these has to do with social responsibility tendencies. Somewhat akin to Parsons' previously cited suggestion regarding the obligations felt by "well-integrated personalities," Berkowitz and Lutterman (unpublished study) have described the high scorers on a Social Responsibility Scale (SRS) [16] as being people who have adopted many of the traditional values of their society and, consequently, often feel obligated to do the socially "right" thing. These people presumably (a) tend to participate actively in the life of their community rather than being alienated from their fellows, (b) have a good deal of trust in other people and even liking for them, and (c) possess the ego strength enabling them to postpone gratifications and adhere to their ideals. Berkowitz and Lutterman presented data consistent with this analysis. Also in accord with their description, Wrightsman [17] has reported that college students' conformity to the officially-imposed obligation to take part in psychology experiments is positively related to scores on the SRS. It could well be, then, that high scorers on the SRS will also be more inclined to judge legally prohibited behavior as "immoral." Being highly traditional and feeling obligated to act in a traditionally proper manner, they may generally view deviations from the approved code of conduct—as defined by criminal law—as morally wrong.

The California F Scale is conceivably also related to reactions to legitimate au-

---

[12] T. Parsons, *Essays in Sociological Theory*, Glencoe: Free Press, 1949, p. 206.

[13] Blau, *op. cit.*, also discusses the part cognitive dissonance may play in the legitimation of authority.

[14] For related observations cf. E. Aronson and J. M. Carlsmith, "The Effect of the Severity of Threat on the Devaluation of Forbidden Behavior," *Journal of Abnormal and Social Psychology*, 66 (1963), pp. 584–588; and J. L. Freeman, "Long-term Behavioral Effects of Cognitive Dissonance," *Journal of Experimental Social Psychology*, 1 (1965), pp. 145–155.

[15] J. Frank, *Law and the Modern Mind*, New York: Brentano, 1930.

[16] Cf. L. Berkowitz and Louise Daniels, "Affecting the Salience of the Social Responsibility Norm," *Journal of Abnormal and Social Psychology*, 68 (1964), pp. 275–281.

[17] L. S. Wrightsman, "Predicting College Students' Participation in Required Psychology Experiments," *American Psychologist* (1966), pp. 812–813.

thority as represented by the law. While the present authors are not aware of any explicit discussion of just this point, the usual conception of the authoritarian personality might suggest that high F persons would tend to be rigidly conformistic to laws. They therefore might also be likely to state that illegal actions are immoral. Other considerations, however, lead to just the opposite prediction. Srole [18] has argued that the high authoritarian is actually often greatly alienated from his society, and we have just suggested that this alienation may produce only weak felt obligations to adhere to criminal laws. Then too, the original investigators of the authoritarian personality have contended that this type of individual is actually only a "pseudoconservative." [19] He may voice the tenets of traditional conservatism but, nevertheless, supposedly possesses a violent readiness to abolish many of the institutions he says he cherishes. These violent tendencies could cause him to believe his society's criminal laws are not necessarily correct. All in all, the authoritarian may be even more ambivalent to the laws then he is said to be toward father-figures.

METHOD

SUBJECTS. The subjects in this study, carried out in England, are 41 students from Ruskin College of Oxford University and 46 students from Reading University. Only two of the Ruskin students but half of the Reading subjects are women. While there are more male than female subjects, the three experimental conditions have roughly the same ratio of men to women.

The Ruskin students participated in return for a ten pound grant to their class treasury, while the Reading students came from a psychology class. A preliminary inspection of the data indicated there were no systematic differences in scores on the dependent measure between the men and women or the Ruskin and Reading subjects, and these distinctions are ignored in the following analysis.

PROCEDURE. The experiment was carried out in one session at each university. As soon as the students were all seated a two-part questionnaire, was distributed. The cover page informed the subjects that the investigators were conducting "a survey of student opinions regarding different forms of conduct," and pointed out that there were no right or wrong answers since views differed on these issues. The subjects had to write down their age, sex and religious denomination, but not their names. A sample question was then provided and the subjects were given instructions as to how each question was to be answered. Each item was in the form of a statement, such as, "A person who uses public transport while he has been quarantined for scarlet fever is not doing anything morally wrong." A six-inch line having no demarcations was beneath each statement, with the ends of the line being marked either "strongly agree" or "strongly disagree." The subject was to place "a tick at the appropriate place on the rating scale" indicating how strongly he agreed or disagreed with the statement.

There were 47 such statements in Part One. Twenty were F scale items, of which 10 came from the list of "reversed" items established by Christie, Havel and Seidenber.[20] Three of the reversed F scale items are shown in Table 1B. There were also 16 SRS items taken from the 22 used by Berkowitz and Daniels,[21] and 3 of these

[18] L. Srole, "Social Integration and Certain Corollaries," *American Sociological Review*, 21 (1956), pp. 709–716.
[19] Else Frenkel-Brunswik, D. J. Levinson and R. N. Sanford, "The Authoritarian Personality," In H. Proshansky and B. Seidenberg, eds., *Basic Studies in Social Psychology*, New York: Holt, Rinehart & Winston, 1965, pp. 670–679.

[20] R. Christie, J. Havel and B. Seidenberg, "Is the F-Scale Irreversible?" *Journal of Abnormal and Social Psychology*, 56 (1958), pp. 143–159.
[21] Berkowitz and Daniels, *ibid.*

items are given in Table 1C. The remaining 11 dealt with matters of conduct. There were an equal number of positive and negative items in each personality scale.

Where Part One was the same for all students, three different conditions were established by having three different forms of Part Two: a control condition in which only repeated judgments were obtained, a condition in which peer influence was exerted, and a condition told of the existence of laws. Each of these three different forms dealt with the four statements listed in Table 1A.

following: "In order to stimulate you to think about some of the issues, we give you this information. A recent national survey of students similar to yourself obtained these findings. . . ." They were informed that "over 80 per cent of the students *strongly agreed*" with the statements listed as A1 and A2 of Table 1, and that "over 80 per cent of the students *strongly disagreed with*" the statements A3 and A4 from this table. Finally, in the condition of primary concern to us here (*Law* group), the introduction to Part Two read: "In order to stimulate you to think about some of the issues, we give

Table 1   Some of the Questionnaire Items

A. The Four Statements Used for the Moral Judgments

1. A man who is drunk in a public place is acting in an immoral manner even if he is not disorderly.
2. A person is *not* in the wrong morally if he allows someone else to borrow his car without checking this individual's license.
3. The person who borrows money for the purpose of betting is *not* doing anything morally wrong even if he does not inform the lender why he wants the money.
4. The individual who sees another person attempting to commit suicide and does not try to stop him is acting immorally himself.

B. Some of the Christie-Havel Seidenberg Modified F-Scale Items

4. Insults to our honour are not always important enough to bother with. (Disagree)
25. It would be a good thing if people spent more time thinking and talking about ideas just for the fun of it. (Disagree)
41. People should be willing to overlook failures in the manners and unpleasant habits of other people. (Disagree)

C. Some of the Social Responsibility Scale Items

7. It is always important to finish anything that you have started. (Agree)
27. It is no use worrying about current events or political matters; I can't do anything about them anyway. (Disagree)
39. I would never let a friend down when he expected something of me. (Agree)

The subjects receiving one form (*Test-Retest* group) read the following introduction: "You may want to alter your judgments after thinking about these issues a bit more. Here are several of the statements from Part One. Please indicate your present opinion about each statement by showing how strongly you now agree or disagree with it." The subjects getting a second version of Part Two (*Peer Opinion* condition) were told the

you this information. Various recently enacted statutes are relevant to some of the previous statements." They were told that as a result of these statutes the behaviors referred to in statements A1 and A2 were now "legally permissible," and that the actions described in statements A3 and A4 were now "illegal." Fictitious laws were cited for each.

The four statements were then again repeated in all three forms of Part Two, and the subjects were asked to indicate their *present* opinion about each statement by placing the tick at the appropriate place on the linear rating scales.

At the conclusion of the session the questionnaires were collected and the deceptions were explained. The experiment was discussed and all questions were answered.

Each item was scored by measuring the distance in quarter-inch units from one end of the linear scale. In obtaining the index of change in moral judgments for each of the four crucial statements, changes in the direction of the presumed influence were scored as positive, while changes in the opposite direction were taken as negative changes. The directions followed in the *Law* condition were employed in scoring the changes in the *Test-Retest* group.

RESULTS

Analyses of variance were performed on the changes in moral judgments employing a 3 x 2 factorial design composed of the three experimental conditions and the two levels of personality variable. In setting up this design the subjects within

each experimental condition were first dichotomized in terms of their scores on the given personality scale (either SRS or F scale), and then cases were randomly eliminated until proportional cell frequencies had been obtained. Nine subjects were discarded in the SRS analysis, 4 from the *Test-Retest* group, 3 from the *Law* condition, and 2 from the *Peer Opinion* condition. For the F-scale analysis 15 cases were eliminated, 8 from the *Test-Retest* conditions, 5 from the *Law* group, and 2 from the *Peer Opinion* condition. This procedure again resulted in roughly the same number of women in the three experimental groups.

Table 2 summarizes the findings of the analyses of variance, and shows that both designs led to the same significant effects: (1) there were significant differences in change scores among the three experimental conditions, and (2) the judgmental changes varied across the four items. This similarity in results, whether the subjects were classified in terms of the SRS or the F scale, does not stem from a strong association between the two personality scales; disregarding the experimental conditions, there was no relationship at all between the classification of a subject as

Table 2   Results of Analyses of Variance with Subjects Classified in Terms of SRS or F-Scale Scores

		SRS		F-Scale	
	df	MS	F-ratio	MS	F ratio
Conditions	2	135.30	4.36*	121.56	3.37*
Scale level	1	15.26	—	98.79	—
1 x 2	2	24.50	—	34.46	—
Ss w/in condition	72 (66)a	31.06	—	36.08	—
Items	3	191.83	7.78***	158.72	6.52**
1 x 5	6	44.94		49.50	—
2 x 5	3	10.33		2.51	—
1 x 2 x 5	6	21.29		16.42	—
Residual	216 (198)	24.67		24.35	—

aThe numbers in parentheses refer to the degrees of freedom in the F-Scale analysis when these are not the same as in the SRS analysis.

*p < .05.
**p < .01.
***p < .001.

Table 3   Mean Change in Judgments of Morality for Subjects Divided in Terms of SRS Scores

	Experimental Conditions		
	Test-Retest	*Law*	*Peer Opinion*
Total Group	(24) -2.62_a	(26) $+3.19_b$	(28) $+6.46_c$
High SRS	(12) -4.42_x	(13) $+4.54_{yz}$	(14) $+4.29_{yz}$
Low SRS	(12) -0.83_{xy}	(13) $+1.85_y$	(14) $+8.64_z$

Note: Cells having the same subscript are not significantly different, by Duncan Multiple Range Test, at the .05 level. Separate tests were made for the Total Group and SRS-level analyses. The number of cases in each cell is given in parentheses.

either high or low on the SRS and his high or low classification on the authoritarianism measure (chi-square=0.00).

Looking at the top line of Tables 3 and 4, which shows the results of Duncan Range tests of the condition means, we can see that there were reliable differences among all three groups. The subjects informed that laws existed regarding the four kinds of behavior tended to alter their judgments of the moral propriety of the actions in accord with the laws, and this change in the direction of the supposed laws was significantly greater than the change (generally in the opposite direction) occurring in the *Test-Retest* condition. The greatest shift in judgments, however, arose in the *Peer Opinion* condition. The subject's opinions evidently were more strongly influenced by knowledge of the consensus among their peers as to whether the given acts were good or bad than by knowledge of the existence of laws on these matters.

Even though the interaction of personality scale level and experimental conditions failed to achieve the customary level of significance, we examined this interaction for heuristic purposes and also because of the conservatism of the Duncan Multiple Range Tests. As shown in Table 3, high and low scorers on the SRS tended to react somewhat differently to the experimental conditions. The high "responsibles" generally were equally affected by knowledge of the law and knowledge of their peers' opinions, and altered their

judgments (in the direction of these influences) to a significantly greater extent than did the high scorers in the *Test-Retest* group. As we had expected, the low "responsibles" were somewhat less influenced by the law than were their high scoring counterparts, although this difference is not reliable, and they did not display a greater judgmental change than their similarly low scoring controls. The low "responsibles" in the *Peer Opinion* group, on the other hand, exhibited a reliably greater shift in response to the information about the opinion consensus among their fellow students than did the low scorers in the other groups. The strong traditionalistic responsibility tendencies tapped by the SRS evidently produce a moderate susceptibility to both conventional influences, laws and peer opinion, while a low level of these tendencies seems to lead only to a strong susceptibility to peer consensus.

This shift in moral judgments toward the peer opinions is especially characteristic of people with relatively strong authoritarian tendencies, as is indicated in Table 4. The condition means given in this table show that the *High F* subjects altered their moral judgments toward the peer opinions to a relatively great extent, but were not influenced to any significant degree by the knowledge of the laws. The low authoritarian subjects, on the other hand, tended to be somewhat more susceptible to information regarding the existence of laws. While these people were

Table 4   Mean Change in Judgments of Morality for Subjects Divided in Terms of F-Scale Scores

	Experimental Conditions		
	Test-Retest	Law	Peer Opinion
Total Group	(20) -3.40_a	(24) $+1.46_b$	(28) $+5.71_c$
High F	(10) -2.10_{xy}	(12) -0.25_{xy}	(14) $+10.21_z$
Low F	(10) -4.70_x	(12) $+3.17_{yz}$	(14) $+1.21_{xy}$

Note: Cells having the same subscript are not significantly different, at the .05 level, by Duncan Multiple Range Test. Separate tests were made for the Total Group and F-Scale-Level analyses. The number of cases in each cell is given in parentheses.

not significantly more affected by law information than by peer opinions, it was only the *Low F Law* condition that differed reliably from the *Low F* controls. All in all, strong authoritarianism seems to produce a sensitivity to peer opinions but not necessarily to the legitimate authority represented by laws.

We might well stop at this point to discuss a matter that could be troubling the discerning reader. Having carefully studied the procedure followed in the various experimental conditions, he will have noted that the *Law* and *Peer Opinion* treatments did not attempt to influence the subjects in the same direction for Items 1 and 4. (The changes were always scored in the same direction in the *Test-Retest* and *Law* conditions, however.) Conceivably, then, differences between the Law and Peer opinion groups could be due to these differences in influence direction; it might have been easier to produce a change in one direction than in

the other. What can be said about this possibility?

For one thing, the analyses of variance summarized in Table 2 did not yield any significant interaction of items by conditions, although in the case of the F scale analysis this interaction did approach significance ($F=2.03$, 6 and 222 df, $p<.10$). The condition means involved in this interaction were subjected to a Duncan Test in order to determine where the group differences might be. The results are presented in Table 5. We note here that the *Peer Opinion* group did not differ significantly from the *Law* condition as any of the four items, and was reliably different from the control condition only on Item 2 (Borrowing money for betting purposes without informing the lender)—an item in which the influence direction was the same for all three experimental conditions.

In addition, a separate analysis of variance was conducted using only the change

Table 5   Changes in Moral Judgments on Each Condition — F-Scale Analysis

	Items			
	1	2	3	4
Test-Retest (N = 20)	+1.25 bc	−2.75 a	+0.15 ab	−2.05 ab
Law (N = 24)	+0.54 ab	+0.33 ab	+1.29 bc	−0.71 ab
Peer Opinion (N = 28)	+0.89 ab	1.36 ab	+4.64 c	+1.54 bc

Cells having a subscript in common are not significantly different at the .05 level.

scores for Items 2 and 3, the items for which the change direction was the same in all three groups. The findings here paralleled the results obtained with the four-item analysis: Again, the only significant effects were for Experimental Condition ($F=3.55$, $p<.05$) and Items ($F=13.31$, $p<.001$). The Condition x Items interaction was again relatively large ($F=2.60$), but this time did not even approach significance.

All in all, inspection of Table 5 indicates the group results summarized in Tables 3 and 4 are primarily due to Items 3 and 4, and to Item 2 in the *Law* condition. These items differ considerably in content (borrowing a car, borrowing money, and preventing a person from committing suicide), and also vary in the direction of the influence attempt. They do not seem to have anything in common. What is clear is that the experimental treatments produced greater alterations in moral judgments in the case of Item 3, dealing with borrowing money for betting purposes, than on any of the other issues. All laws apparently do not produce the same modification in the judged propriety of the actions they seek to regulate, whether these laws are supported by an opinion consensus or legitimate authority.

DISCUSSION

The implications of this experiment can be summarized fairly briefly. If a number of different forms of conduct and criminal laws are sampled and if a sufficiently broad range of people are studied, relatively sensitive measures should show that knowledge of the existence of laws has modified judgments of the moral propriety of the actions regulated by these laws. There appears to be a comparatively small but nevertheless significant tendency for some people to alter their views of the morality of some actions in accord with laws specifying that these actions are legal or illegal. Knowledge of the existence of these laws, however, does not have as much effect in changing the moral judgments as knowledge of a consensus of opinions among one's peers.[22]

This distinction between laws per se and peer opinion, while conceptually important, cannot be made in many instances in the "real" world. As we indicated earlier, the extent to which criminal laws are successful in regulating conduct frequently depends upon the magnitude of the social consensus regarding the behavior with which it deals. The passage of fair housing laws may mean there is widespread agreement that racial discrimination is now more likely to be viewed as immoral. But the apparent consensus can also prove to be illusory. A person may see that a given law is frequently violated, and, as probably happened in the case of the Prohibition Amendment, the law then ceases to influence his moral

---

[22] Professor Macaulay (personal communication) has suggested that the apparent shifts in moral judgments due to knowledge of the law, or for that matter peer opinions, might be produced by the two somewhat different processes. On one hand, the individual might have started out by believing a certain action was morally proper or improper, and then experienced an alteration in this belief. Other persons, however, could initially have believed that the particular form of conduct was morally neutral. This suggestion essentially holds that the influence source could have placed the behavior on a dimension of moral propriety-impropriety, where initially the conduct was regarded as being irrelevant to this dimension, in addition to moving the statement's position along such a dimension. Whatever the exact process that might be involved, the present writers prefer to regard any shift in scale response as a change in moral judgment, in part for convenience and in part because this shift is presumptive evidence of some form of alteration in belief. For that matter, as Professor Macaulay has hypothesized, there might be very different reactions to knowledge that a certain form of conduct is now illegal and to knowledge that a given type of action no longer is illegal. The form of conduct that is regulated probably also influences the individual's response to knowledge of the law and/or peer opinion.

judgments.[23] Sometimes only one violation is enough to break this implied consensus, particularly if it is carried out by someone high in social status.[24]

Other considerations, nevertheless, suggest that the distinction between law effects and social consensus should be maintained. As an example, our findings indicate that the moral judgments of highly authoritarian people, as assessed by the California F scale, are quite susceptible to peer influence, but are not significantly affected by knowledge of the law. Authoritarians tend to be strongly conformistic,[25] perhaps because of an extreme concern with social approval, but they do not necessarily accept the views of legitimate authority, at least as represented by the law. Laws can be for them just another source of frustration. They will obey the law if they must, if deviation from the law is punished or brings disapproval, but probably not because they truly believe the law is "right." According to our results, it is primarily those persons who are deeply involved in their society, who are traditional and conventional and socially responsible, who are most likely to adopt the judgments implied by the law.

[23] Frequent violations of a law might also influence a person's decision-making in cost-benefit terms. Seeing that many other people transgress without apparent penalty, the individual might decide that the benefits obtained from breaking a certain law far outweigh the costs considering the low probability of being caught.

[24] M. M. Lefkowitz, R. R. Blake and Jane S. Mouton, "Status Factors in Pedestrian Violation of Traffic Signals," *Journal of Abnormal and Social Psychology,* 51 (1955), pp. 704–706.

[25] I. D. Steiner and H. H. Johnson, "Authoritarianism and Conformity," *Sociometry,* 26 (1963), pp. 21–34.